DISCARD

Encyclopedia of
POPULATION

EDITORIAL BOARD

Encyclopedia of
POPULATION

EDITED BY

Paul Demeny

Geoffrey McNicoll

VOLUME

2

I-W
APPENDIX
INDEX

MACMILLAN
REFERENCE
USA™

THOMSON

GALE

New York • Detroit • San Diego • San Francisco • Cleveland • New Haven, Conn. • Waterville, Maine • London • Munich

THOMSON

GALE

Encyclopedia of Population

Paul Demeny

Geoffrey McNicoll

Editors in Chief

LIBRARY OF CONGRESS CATALOGING-IN-PUBLICATION DATA

Encyclopedia of population / edited by Paul Demeny, Geoffrey McNicoll.
    p. cm.
       Includes bibliographical references and index.
       ISBN 0-02-865677-6 (hardcover (set))—ISBN 0-02-865678-4 (v. 1)—
       ISBN 0-02-865679-2 (v. 2)
       1. Population—Encyclopedias. I. Demeny, Paul George, 1932- II.
       McNicoll, Geoffrey.
    HB871.E538 2003
    304.6'03—dc21
    2003002712

I

IMMIGRATION, BENEFITS AND COSTS OF

There was a resurgence of immigration in the United States and in many other countries in the last third of the twentieth century. By the year 2002, about 175 million persons—or roughly 3 percent of the world's population—resided in a country different from where they were born. Nearly 6 percent of the population in Austria, 17 percent in Canada, 11 percent in France, 17 percent in Switzerland, and 10 percent in the United States was foreign-born. One central concern has motivated economic research on international migration: what is the economic impact of international migration on the *host country*?

The Skills of Immigrants

The skill composition of the immigrant population, and how the skills of immigrants compare to those of natives, determines many of the economic consequences of immigration on the host country. Unskilled immigrants will typically compete for jobs with unskilled natives; skilled immigrants will compete with skilled natives. A host country benefits from immigration because it can import workers with scarce qualifications and abilities. Immigrants, though, make different demands than the native-born on the many programs that make up the welfare state, which tend to redistribute resources from high-income workers to persons with less economic potential.

Many studies have attempted to document trends in the skill endowment of the immigrant population in host countries, and to examine how that skill endowment adapts to economic and social conditions through the process of assimilation. The ear-liest studies used cross-section data sets to trace the age-earnings profiles of immigrants and native-born workers in the United States. A cross-section survey allows the comparison of the current earnings of newly-arrived immigrants (measured at the time of the survey) with the current earnings of immigrants who migrated years ago. Typically, these cross-section studies found that the earnings of newly-arrived immigrants were substantially lower than the earnings of immigrants who had been in the host country for one or two decades. Researchers interpreted the cross-section data to mean that newly-arrived immigrants lack many of the skills valued by host-country employers, such as language and educational credentials. As immigrants learn about the host country, their human capital grows relative to that of the native-born, and economic assimilation occurs in the sense that immigrant earnings "catch up" to the earnings of natives.

This "assimilationist" interpretation draws inferences about how the earnings of immigrant workers evolve over time from a single snapshot of the population. Suppose, however, that today's immigrants arrive with less skills than those who arrived twenty years ago. Because of these intrinsic differences in skills across immigrant cohorts, one cannot use the current labor market experiences of those who arrived 20 or 30 years ago to forecast the future earnings of newly arrived immigrants. If there are skill differentials among immigrant cohorts at the time they entered the host country, a cross-section survey yields an incorrect picture of the assimilation process.

Many studies, using either longitudinal data or repeated cross-sections, have calculated the rate of economic assimilation and measured the importance of cohort effects in host countries. In the United States, the immigrant waves that entered the country in the 1980s and 1990s were relatively less skilled than the waves that entered in the 1960s and 1970s. Immigrants in the United States do experience some economic assimilation, but the rate of assimilation is unlikely to be sufficiently high to permit recent cohorts to catch up to their native-born counterparts.

Labor Market Effects

Economic theory predicts that the entry of immigrants into a particular labor market will lower the wage of competing workers (workers who have the same types of skills as immigrants), and increase the wage of complementary workers (workers whose skills are more in demand because of immigration's effect on labor market conditions).

In many host countries, immigrants cluster in a limited number of geographic areas. In 1990, in the United States, 42 percent of immigrants lived in just five metropolitan areas—New York, Miami, Chicago, and Los Angeles and nearby Anaheim—but only 13 percent of the native-born U.S. population lived in those localities. Many empirical studies exploit this clustering to identify the labor market impact of immigration by comparing labor market conditions in "immigrant cities" with conditions in markets untouched by immigration. These studies typically correlate some measures of economic outcomes for native workers with a measure of immigrant presence in the locality, and usually report a correlation that is near zero. This evidence is then interpreted as indicating that immigration has little impact on the labor market opportunities of the native-born.

The short-run perspective of this type of research can be misleading. Over time, native workers and employers will likely respond to the entry of immigrants. Native-owned firms see that cities flooded by immigrants tend to pay lower wages, and often relocate to those cities. The flow of jobs to areas of high immigrant presence helps cushion immigration's adverse effect on the wage of competing workers in those localities. Similarly, workers living in areas not directly affected by immigration will choose not to move to the cities penetrated by immigrants, and some native-born workers living in the immigrant cities will seek better opportunities elsewhere.

Such effects on the internal migration of native-born workers and jobs within the host country spread out the impact of immigration across the entire host country. A comparison of the employment opportunities of native workers in different localities might show little or no difference because, in the end, immigration affected *every* city, not just the ones that actually received immigrants.

Because local labor market conditions may not provide valuable information about the economic impact of immigration, a number of studies have attempted to measure the impact at the national level. The factor proportions approach compares the host country's actual supplies of workers in particular skill groups to those it would have had in the absence of immigration, and then uses outside information on how wages respond to changes in labor supply to simulate the wage consequences of immigration. During the 1980s and 1990s, when the immigrant flow to the United States was relatively less skilled, the factor proportions approach finds that immigration had an adverse impact on the relative wage of native-born workers who are high school dropouts at the lower end of the skill distribution.

Fiscal Impacts

Income differences across countries are the dominant influence on a person's migration decision. The most important of these are wage differences that arise in the labor market, but the safety net provided by the welfare state may also have an influence. Welfare programs can generate two distinct types of "magnet" effects, with potential implications for public expenditures: welfare programs may attract persons who otherwise would not have emigrated, and might discourage immigrants who are not successful in the host country's labor market from returning to their home countries. Despite the prominence given to these magnet effects in the immigration policy debate, there is little empirical evidence that either supports or refutes the existence of them.

Most of the existing studies have focused instead on documenting the extent of welfare use by immigrant households. In the United States, there has been a rapid rise in immigrant welfare use. In 1970, immigrants were slightly less likely to receive cash benefits than native-born people. However, by 1998, over 10 percent of immigrant households received cash benefits, as compared to 7 percent of native households.

Some studies have also examined the magnitude of the income transfer to the immigrant population that occurs through the welfare state. An influential 1997 study conducted by the U.S. National Academy of Sciences attempted to calculate the fiscal impact for two major immigrant-receiving states, California and New Jersey. The study included an item-by-item accounting of expenditures incurred and taxes collected, and calculated how immigration affected each of these entries. Immigration increased the annual state and local taxes of the typical native household by $1,200 in California and by $200 in New Jersey. Much of the short-run fiscal impact of immigration is in the form of expenditures in public schooling. Immigrant families tend to have more children than native families, and the schooling provided to immigrant children—such as bilingual education—is often more expensive than the schooling provided to natives.

Economic Benefits

The native-born benefit from immigration in many ways. Immigrants buy goods and services, and native-owned firms and native-born workers profit by providing these to new consumers. Immigration may also increase the productivity of some native workers. Less-skilled immigrants, for example, can perform many of the service tasks in a modern industrialized economy, freeing up time for native-born workers to engage in activities where they are more productive. Immigration can also lower the price of many goods and services, benefiting consumers in the host country.

It is difficult to calculate these measurable benefits from immigration unless one has a model of the host country's economy detailing how the various sectors are linked. Such a model could simulate how the economy changes when the labor market is expanded by large numbers of immigrant workers, and would record the ripple effects of immigration on other sectors of the economy.

A number of studies use the "textbook model" of a free-market economy—in which wage and employment levels are set by the interplay between the supply of workers and the demand for workers—to examine the economic benefits from immigration. This model isolates two main effects of immigration. First, because immigrants increase the number of workers, there is additional competition in the labor market and the wage of native workers falls. Second, at the same time, native-owned firms gain because they can now hire workers at lower wages, and many

native consumers gain because the lower labor costs eventually lead to cheaper goods and services. It turns out, however, that the gains accruing to the persons who use or consume immigrant services exceed the losses suffered by native-born workers, and hence society as a whole is better off. The difference between what the winners win and what the losers lose is called the "immigration surplus," and reflects the gain in national income accruing to the native-born as a result of immigration.

Applied to the United States, however, this model suggests that the net benefit from immigration is quite small. If a 10 percent increase in labor supply lowers the wage by 3 percent, the immigration surplus is on the order of 0.1 percent of gross domestic product (GDP)—about $10 billion in 2002. Moreover, this small average net gain disguises the fact that there may be substantial wealth transfers from native-born workers to the capitalists who employ the immigrants.

Effects on Source Countries

Although much of the existing research focuses on how immigrants alter economic opportunities in the host country, they also alter economic opportunities in the source countries. Emigration might drain certain types of workers from particular countries. (The highly-skilled component of such migration is popularly labeled the "brain drain".) Against this, immigrants transfer substantial funds from the host to the source countries. Despite the sizable impact that international migration might have on the global distribution of wealth, the economic effects on the source countries have not been studied systematically.

See also: *Cost of Children; Immigration Policies; Migration Models.*

BIBLIOGRAPHY

Altonji, Joseph G., and David Card. 1991. "The Effects of Immigration on the Labor Market Outcomes of Less-Skilled Natives." In *Immigration, Trade, and the Labor Market*, ed. John M. Abowd and Richard B. Freeman. Chicago: University of Chicago Press.

Borjas, George J. 1985. "Assimilation, Changes in Cohort Quality, and the Earnings of Immigrants." *Journal of Labor Economics* 3: 463–489.

————. 1995. "The Economic Benefits from Immigration." *Journal of Economic Perspectives* 9: 3–22.

Borjas, George J., Richard B. Freeman, and Lawrence F. Katz. 1997. "How Much Do Immigration and Trade Affect Labor Market Outcomes?" *Brookings Papers on Economic Activity* pp. 1–67.

Card, David. 1990. "The Impact of the Mariel Boatlift on the Miami Labor Market." *Industrial and Labor Relations Review* 43: 245–257.

Chiswick, Barry R. "The Effect of Americanization on the Earnings of Foreign-Born Men." *Journal of Political Economy* 86: 897–921.

Smith, James P., and Barry Edmonston, eds. 1997. *The New Americans: Economic, Demographic, and Fiscal Effects of Immigration.* Washington, D.C.: National Academy Press.

GEORGE J. BORJAS

IMMIGRATION, UNAUTHORIZED

Unauthorized migration is the international movement of people through irregular or extralegal channels. At their destinations such people are often termed "illegal" or "undocumented" immigrants. States have the sovereign right to regulate entry into their territories, but the sheer volume and tenacity of unauthorized migrants speak to the tenuousness of any state's ability to exert complete control over cross-border movements. In exercising their prerogative, states attempt to identify foreigners' residence either as legal, according to their particular immigration laws, or illegal. Migration is deemed unauthorized if: (1) the migrants in question avoided inspection by crossing borders clandestinely or if they traveled with fraudulent documents (e.g., falsified visas or counterfeit passports); (2) if migrants have overstayed the time limit of a legally obtained non-immigrant temporary visa; or (3) if they have violated explicit visa conditions, e.g., obtaining employment while holding a student visa. In most of the world arrival as a non-immigrant (tourist, student, temporary laborer, etc.) and staying beyond the legally sanctioned period is the most common source of unauthorized immigration. In the United States,

however, the majority of undocumented migrants have entered without inspection over land borders with Mexico and Canada.

The International Organization for Migration (IOM) (2000, p. 46) estimates that smugglers, paid by migrants to arrange transportation to the country of destination, assist more than 50 percent of unauthorized migrants. In addition, a substantial number of women and children, estimated to number between 700,000 and 2 million per year globally, are "trafficked"—that is, kidnapped, coerced, or deceived into migrating, then sold or indentured in the country of destination.

If discovered by immigration authorities, unauthorized migrants are generally required to depart voluntarily or become subject to involuntary deportation to the country of most recent citizenship or to the country through which they entered (the transit country). In the United States there is a process of "expedited exclusion" to combat the high incidence of repeat unauthorized entry: first-time unauthorized offenders are barred from reentry for five years; second-time or subsequent offenders are disqualified for twenty years. Unauthorized migrants apprehended within the country are often detained in custody until a decision on their immigration status is reached.

Unauthorized migration is a volatile political, social, and economic issue in many destination countries. Supporters of tighter controls on migration often portray the unauthorized international movement of people as a strain on receiving countries' social service budgets as well as a threat to the job security and wages of the domestic labor force. Country-specific studies on such economic effects, however, have been inconclusive. Even so, the late 1990s saw a decline in the number of countries offering social services, including health care, to unauthorized migrants.

Unauthorized Labor Migration

Due to the surreptitious character of unauthorized migration, unauthorized migrants are more likely than legal migrants to be employed in low-skilled, low-paid positions that require no documentation, credentials, or licenses. For example, in the United States a major portion of the undocumented migrant population is employed in industries such as meatpacking, construction, housekeeping, childcare, and agricultural work.

As demand for low-skilled labor rises in developed countries, employers have a growing economic incentive to encourage extralegal immigration for employment in sectors where domestic labor is scarce or is unwilling to work at prevailing wage levels. This has become a contentious issue. In countries with strong labor rights traditions, the perception that undocumented migrants drive down wages has mobilized unions and union supporters against government leniency. Whether, for the economy as a whole, unauthorized migrants' economic contribution outweighs the costs of the social services they receive remains unsettled.

Measurement

In all regions of the world statistics on unauthorized migration are apt to be incomplete and unreliable. Methods of assessing the size of the unauthorized population vary by country and there are often variant estimates for a single country. The most common measurement procedure is to compare census data with information on visas issued. In the United States, the census-reported foreign-born population is classified either as legal immigrant or temporary non-immigrant based on such a comparison. The census foreign-born numbers in excess of the official visa-based count are the residual foreign-born population. A portion of this residual population is assumed to be refugees and asylum seekers awaiting adjustment to permanent or protected status; the remainder is considered to be unauthorized. The accuracy of such estimates is dependent on the degree of completeness with which the census enumerates the foreign born population. Countries also rely on records of the numbers of apprehensions and deportations of illegal migrants kept by law enforcement to estimate the flow of undocumented migration.

Numbers and Trends

During the 1990s the volume of unauthorized international migrant flows increased greatly (For instance, it has been estimated that net illegal immigration to the United States in the late 1990s was half a million per year) Unauthorized migration still shows a surplus of males (just over 50%), but much less so than in the past. With large numbers of women in developed countries working outside of the home, opportunities for employment in domestic work and childcare have attracted women from developing countries, swelling both legal and unauthorized migrant numbers. Most unauthorized migrants are young, between 18 and 35 years of age. Most are from developing countries, although the IOM reports that visa overstayers from developed countries comprise a significant portion of illegal migrants in several countries, e.g., Australia and New Zealand (IOM, 2001). Selected estimates, by country, on the number of unauthorized migrants are shown in Table 1.

In each world region particular countries have become "magnets" for illegal movements of people.

Africa. Post-Apartheid South Africa emerged as a prime destination for migrants seeking work in the mining and agriculture sectors—not only from other parts of Southern Africa, but continent-wide. Because South Africa has retained restrictive immigration policies from the Apartheid period, most African migrants enter the country informally. In 1997, according to the IOM (2001, p. 136), over 3.5 million unauthorized migrant workers and about 750,000 visa overstayers were resident in South Africa. Unauthorized migrants are granted no protection under South African law, are targets of widespread violence fueled by high unemployment rates, and remain subject to immediate expulsion on apprehension.

Asia. Unauthorized migration has centered on Japan, South Korea, and Malaysia. Since 1990, these countries have imposed strict controls, backed by heavy fines, on employment of undocumented labor. In Malaysia, where most undocumented migrants are Indonesians, employed in factories, on plantations, and as domestic workers, sanctions are imposed on both workers and their employers— enforced more strongly during periods of economic downturn.

Western Europe. An IOM report indicates that in the late 1990s it is believed that over 500,000 migrants from Asia, Eastern Europe, Africa, and the Middle East were being smuggled into the European Union annually (IOM, 2001). The stock of undocumented migrants in Europe was estimated at 3 million. Historically, a large majority of migrants from both developing and developed countries seeking to work or settle in Europe chose the United Kingdom, Germany, France, Belgium, the Netherlands, and Switzerland as their final destination. In the early 1990s these countries adopted strict immigration laws; in consequence, migration flows shifted to the south—with Turkey favored as a transit route to the

TABLE 1

Unauthorized Migrants in Selected Countries: Estimated Numbers and Proportions of the Total Population, around 2000		
Country (Year)	Estimated Unauthorized Migrants (thousands)	Unauthorized Migrants as Proportion of Total Population (percent)
Australia (2000)	60	0.3
Greece (1999)	264	2.5
Israel (2000)	150	3.3
Italy (1998)	300	0.5
Japan (2000)	500	0.4
Malaysia (2000)	450	2.0
South Africa (2000)	4,000	9.2
United States (2000)	8,000	2.8

SOURCES: IOM (2001); Population Reference Bureau <www.popnet.org>

EU, and Italy, Spain, and Portugal favored as destinations.

Historically, Greece, Spain, Portugal, and Italy were countries of mass emigration; they were unprepared to manage a massive influx of migrants. The increasing visibility of immigrants in these Southern European countries spurred public debate regarding how to deal with uncontrolled, unauthorized migration. Italy's 1990 Martelli Law and a 1998 presidential decree in Greece (see Amnesty below) were attempts to regulate immigration, including illegal immigration, at the national level. Both laws granted undocumented migrants, who had obtained formal sector jobs, the right to legal employment and residence. This shift in migration priorities created tensions within the EU, since the northern member states have systems in place that make it far more difficult for a non-EU citizen to stay illegally.

North America. In 2000 there were estimated to be about 8 million unauthorized migrants in the United States. The overwhelming volume of undocumented migration in the Western Hemisphere is directed to the United States, with Mexico the most frequent sender (according to the Census Bureau, 54% of undocumented migrants in the United States in 1999 were from Mexico).

Amnesty

In some countries unauthorized migrants who were long residents and employed have been allowed to obtain legal status. Under the Immigration Reform and Control Act of 1986 (IRCA), the United States granted legal permanent resident status to 2.7 million undocumented qualified migrants who had entered the United States prior to 1982 (prior to 1986 for agricultural workers). Greece implemented a similar program in 1998, issuing a presidential decree that allowed illegal workers who had entered the country prior to 1998 to become legal residents. And South Africa, between 1996 and 2000, regularized the status of over 350,000 long-standing undocumented contract workers, undocumented Southern African Development Community (SADC) citizens residing in South Africa, and Mozambican refugees.

See also: *Asylum, Right of; Immigration Policies; Labor Migration, International.*

BIBLIOGRAPHY

Athukorala, Prema-chandra, Chris Manning, and Piyasiri Wickramasekara. 2000. *Growth, Employment and Migration in Southeast Asia.* Cheltenham, Eng.: Edward Elgar Publishing.

Chiswick, Barry R. 1988. *Illegal Aliens: Their Employment and Employers.* Kalamazoo, MI: W.E. Upjohn Institute for Employment Research.

Crush, Jonathan, ed. 2001. South African Migration Project (SAMP). *Immigration, Xenophobia and Human Rights in South Africa.* Cape Town, South Africa: Idasa Publishing.

Fix, Michael, and Ron Haskins. 2002. "Welfare Benefits for Non-citizens." Welfare Reform Brief, No. 15. Washington, D.C.: The Brookings Institution.

Haines, David W., and Karen E. Rosenblum, eds. 1999. *Illegal Immigration in America: A Reference Handbook.* Westport, CT: Greenwood Press.

International Organization for Migration (IOM). 2001. *World Migration Report 2000.* New York: IOM and United Nations.

Meissner, Doris M., Robert D. Hormats, Antonio Garrigues Walker, and Shijuro Ogata. 1993. *International Migration Challenges in a New Era: A Report to the Trilateral Commission.* New York: The Trilateral Commission.

Stalker, Peter. 2001. *The No-Nonsense Guide to International Migration.* London: Verso Books.

INTERNET RESOURCE.

United Nations. *Convention Against Transnational Organized Crime.* [Protocols on smuggling of migrants and on trafficking in persons], <http://www.odccp.org/palermo/convmain.html>.

ADRIA N. ARMBRISTER

IMMIGRATION POLICIES

Less is known about the sources and consequences of immigration policies than about the dynamics of migration flows and the behavior of migrants. Political science, the discipline best suited to explore the role of the state in stimulating, regulating, and preventing migration, long declined to take up this challenge but is making progress elucidating one of the most contentious political issues of our time.

States in the developed world are much alike in facing largely similar migration challenges and opportunities, but have had different migration histories. The majority of the world's 120 million or so voluntary and involuntary international migrants (a stock figure derived from data by country on the numbers of foreign-born residents around 1990) are in the developing world (about 66 million of the 120 million), but many seek to enter countries with more advanced political liberties, better political stability, robust economies, and generous welfare programs. These countries have aging populations that may threaten their economic and financial viability and are integrated into highly competitive regional and global economic networks. Important domestic interest groups, which have emerged in these countries, support the recruitment of the highly skilled. Furthermore, these interest groups tolerate unskilled, often illegal, migrants as a necessary feature of modern capitalism because they fill jobs disdained by natives. Liberal democratic governments, however, are loath to concede control of their borders and are accountable to electorates that consistently express unhappiness with immigration, especially from ethnically or culturally distant areas. Immigration policymaking entails managing these conflicting attitudes and deciding whether to cater to economic imperatives or to cultural and political preferences.

National Immigration Regimes

There are three types of national immigration regimes in the developed world. The United States, Canada, and Australia are the most important traditional countries of immigration. Founded by European settlers, they have long experience with immigration and allow acquisition of citizenship through naturalization or birth within their territory. The United States received about 850,000 legal immigrants per annum in the middle to late 1990s. Australia and Canada admit more immigrants in proportion to their size, however, and the foreign born make up a substantially larger share of their total populations (in 2000, 23% and 17% respectively, compared to 10% for the United States). Annual admissions in all three countries are allocated among family, economic, and refugee/humanitarian categories. The family category dominates U.S. flows; both Australia and Canada admit more skilled migrants, selected through a points system that favors individuals assessed as likely to contribute to economic growth. The United States distributes visas through a range of preference categories, only one of which is tied to skills. All three countries ceased to discriminate on the basis of national origin by the early 1970s. This last policy has produced a major shift to Third World source countries and is gradually changing the ethnic composition of their populations. Canadian and Australian policy does not consider nationality while the United States limits the number of visas granted to immigrants from any single country in a given year. Even so, because many illegal immigrants benefit from amnesty, regularization, and family reunion, Mexicans receive a disproportionate share of U.S. permanent residence visas. With the inclusion of illegal residents, the Mexican-born population in the United States was estimated to be about 8 million in 2000.

The refugee system in these countries, based on the 1951 Geneva Convention and premised on selective acceptance of stateless persons from overseas, is being altered by the sheer number of onshore asylum claimants and the court-driven expansion of the basis for asylum claims. Canada has one of the most expansive refugee systems in the world. Australia's relative geographic isolation has not prevented sizable influxes of asylum seekers and that country's efforts to deter ships bearing potential claimants and its strict policy of mandatory detention of unauthorized arrivals has drawn international opprobrium. While legal migration ordinarily provokes little controversy, illegal migration and on-shore asylum seeking are highly contentious issues. In the United States, legislation in 1986 granted amnesty to nearly 3 million undocumented migrants and imposed employer sanctions against hiring persons without legal status. In 1996 substantial new resources were concentrated at the border with Mexico to deter unauthorized entry. Nevertheless, by 2001 the illegal population had grown to an estimated 7 to 8 million. The estimates for Canada (20,000 to 200,000 overall) and Australia (about 6,000 entering per year) are much lower both absolutely and proportionately.

European countries that recruited temporary labor (guest workers) or received substantial colonial migration during the post–World War II economic expansion have a second type of immigration regime. Migrants came primarily from Southern and Eastern Europe, North Africa, Turkey, South Asia, and the West Indies—countries of close proximity or with colonial ties to host countries. They were the first significant influx of non-Europeans into Europe in modern times. Germany developed the prototypical guest worker program, but most other Northern and Western European countries also recruited temporary labor. Colonial migration was especially important in Britain, France, and the Netherlands and differed from guest worker programs in that many colonial migrants possessed or easily obtained citizenship and enjoyed preferential treatment with respect to admissions and residence.

Little thought was given to the difficulties of enforcing temporary contracts, but when the global slowdown prompted a Europe-wide recruitment halt during the period 1973–1974, only a small percentage of the immigrant workforce returned home. Employers were reluctant to lose experienced workers, and welfare institutions and courts dispensed entitlements largely without regard to citizenship. In the first fifteen years after the recruitment halt, migration declined very little since workers sent for their families, producing a secondary migration that liberal governments were unable to stem. By the 1980s most of the countries in Europe had substantial foreign-born populations and numerous second-generation "immigrant residents" who often did not or could not obtain citizenship. Discontent over the failure of governments to control foreign entries and concern about the difficulties of integrating these new populations put immigration on the political agenda in the 1980s and helped spawn right-wing political movements that became particularly strong in France, the Netherlands, Denmark, Italy, and Austria. With the admission of new primary immigrants effectively ended and the family reunion process largely complete, by the 1990s the only legal route into Europe for most prospective migrants was via political asylum. Asylum claims in the European Union (EU) member states rose dramatically, briefly peaking in 1992 at about 600,000, but then rising again in 1997. Germany received the bulk of the applications, over 438,000 in 1992 alone, according to the Continuous Reporting System on Migration of the Organisation for Economic Co-operation and Development (SOPEMI) (acronym is derived from the French name of the Organization) in 2000, but subsequently revised its liberal asylum provisions. Refugee-processing systems were overwhelmed by numbers and costs, and long backlogs developed. Most applicants were eventually rejected, but the majority of these stayed in the host countries anyway.

The final category of immigration regimes is found in Southern and Eastern European countries that have recently become states that are more likely to receive than to send immigrants, in particular Spain, Portugal, Italy, and Greece. Gateways for illegal migrants seeking entry into the EU, these countries are evolving immigration programs and bureaucracies in reaction to a rapidly escalating situation. Over a million illegal migrants may have been living in Greece in 2001, with Spain, Italy, and Portugal having smaller but substantial numbers as well.

By 2000 there were approximately 18.5 million foreigners in the EU, or about 7 percent of the total population. Children of migrants make the foreign-origin population much larger. Some 12 million Muslims live in Western Europe, most of recent immigrant origin. After long ignoring settlement issues, states began to grapple with political incorporation. The traditional immigration countries embraced formal (Australia and Canada) or informal (United States) multiculturalism with a degree of enthusiasm; the European countries, however, have had more difficulty. Even access to citizenship has been problematic. Nevertheless, an authoritative review shows that there is almost complete convergence among European states "on extending a citizenship entitlement to second-generation migrants. . .[and]. . .a more limited, but nonetheless clear, convergence in northern Europe on an inclusive definition of nationality law for first-generation immigrants" (Hansen and Weil, p. 19).

Explaining Immigration Policy

Immigration scholars are in sharp disagreement over both empirical and analytical issues. Is immigration policy pervasively restrictive or surprisingly open? Are policies converging or diverging? Have states lost control of their borders or is control capacity greater than ever? Does the scale of illegal migration reflect ineluctable pressures or absence of political will? Has immigration been a boon to the host societies, giving them new vitality, or has it created dangerous ethnic and religious tensions? Does migration pose security threats? Do anti-immigrant parties and popular prejudice endanger the rights of minorities and threaten to erode liberal constitutions? There are few commonly accepted evaluative standards, thus, researchers analyzing the same data can, and do, draw contradictory conclusions. Often, research is unacceptably shaped by the subjective values of the researcher.

The prevailing opinion of experts in this area is that immigration policy in Europe is predominantly restrictive in intent, as represented by the image of "Fortress Europe." Many researchers also describe the policies of the traditional immigration countries as prejudiced, exploitative, and hypocritical, despite the great number of admissions. Ironically, scholars who criticize restrictive policies often also argue that national states have lost control of their borders. Most specialists resist linking migration to security threats or crime, considering that argument to be politically inspired rhetoric. (The conclusions of Weiner and Guiraudon and Joppke are notable exceptions to this prevalent approach.)

Some scholars are undertaking systematic research to uncover the causes of empirical outcomes. A promising line of inquiry proceeds from the observation of a gap between the intentions and outcomes of immigration policies as noted by Wayne Cornelius, Philip Martin, and James Hollifield in 1994. Several theoretical models have been employed to address this and related questions, not one of which has yet emerged as the most persuasive.

Globalization theory, as it bears on migration, takes two forms. One perspective, focusing on the economic transformation of the world economy, holds that intensifying patterns of trade in goods, services, and capital create pressures that make mobility of labor inevitable. Traditional notions of national sovereignty and secure borders are, in this view, obsolete as states are driven by their economic

goals to accommodate mass migration. Another school of thought, focusing on the growth of transnational human rights norms, argues that the traditional idea of citizenship has been transcended by more general concepts of personal rights. Embodied in treaties, endorsed by courts, and espoused by international organizations and other transnational actors, these rights are granted to long-term residents (denizens) as well as citizens and create an international norm that liberal states cannot ignore. An alternative view, described by Randall Hansen in 2002 as "embedded realism," is that the nation state is alive and well but its sovereignty is, as Christian Joppke described it in 1999, "self-limited." Subscribers to this theory stress the importance of domestic political forces. Hollifield (2000) contends that there is a "rights-based discourse" in which national courts are critical participants that legitimize migrant claims and constrain policy options. Other analyses focus on the groups that have direct interests in policy outcomes and the incentives to organize and agitate around immigration issues. The distribution of costs and benefits of immigration, in this view, gives organizational advantages to its proponents, typically producing client politics, in which well-organized interest groups negotiate policy with the authorities with minimal public participation. In 1999 Jeannette Money derived various hypotheses linking the territorial distribution of the costs and benefits of immigration to the decision of political parties to take up immigration issues. Historical institutionalists have demonstrated that contemporary migration policy decisions are path dependent, that is "a decision limits the range of available options at subsequent points and, in so doing, encourages continuity in the form of a retention of the original choice." (Hansen, p. 270) Finally, many scholars approach immigration politics from cultural perspectives. No book has had a greater impact on the field than Rogers Brubaker's *Citizenship and Nationhood in France and Germany* (1992), which explores how deeply-rooted national traditions of citizenship and nationhood yield divergent immigration and citizenship frameworks that are resistant to change.

There is a substantial body of research on anti-immigrant parties, movements, and opinion, but less on the larger question of how party systems have shaped and been transformed by immigration. There are a great number of studies analyzing the reasons why people choose to vote for extreme-right parties. Support for these parties comes predominantly from voters in the declining sectors of economies that are in the process of transforming from manufacturing to knowledge-based industries. Mainstream parties have alternated between ignoring anti-immigrant sentiment and catering to it to outflank parties on the right. Generally, discontent over immigration has harmed the electoral prospects of parties of the left more than those of the center or right. The failure of governing parties to handle immigration in a way that satisfies democratic majorities has arguably contributed to the decline of support for democratic institutions.

Toward Regional Immigration Regimes?

There is a trend toward development of multilateral immigration and asylum policies. Nowhere is this more evident than in the EU where, since 1986, the development of immigration and asylum policies has been closely tied to the effort to create a single market. Free movement for the purposes of work and relocation has been achieved for citizens of the member states, although that same freedom is denied to third-country nationals living in the EU. Border controls have largely been eliminated inside the EU, but this has required strict controls at external frontiers and necessitated an unusual degree of cooperation. In 1997 the EU adopted a convention on a common asylum policy, but harmonization in this and other areas has been difficult to achieve. The 1997 Treaty of Amsterdam contained important advances toward the "communitarization" of immigration and asylum policies by moving them into the Community "pillar." A key challenge facing migration scholars at the beginning of the twenty-first century is explaining when and why regional immigration regimes emerge, and how they differ from regimes regulating trade and finance.

Students of the politics of immigration policy have made considerable headway in understanding this complex subject, but exciting empirical, theoretical, and normative issues remain unresolved. Progress is most likely possible only if these separate aspects of the problem are kept analytically distinct.

See also: *Asylum, Right of; International Migration; Labor Migration, International; Population Policy.*

BIBLIOGRAPHY

Baldwin Edwards, Martin, and Martin A. Schain, eds. 1994. *The Politics of Immigration in Western Europe.* Newbury Park, Eng.: Frank Cass.

Betz, Hans-Georg. 1994. *Radical Right-Wing Populism in Western Europe.* New York: St. Martin's Press.

Brochmann, Grete and Tomas Hammar, eds. 1999. *Mechanisms of Control: A Comparative Analysis of European Regulation Policies.* Oxford: Berg.

Brubaker, Rogers. 1992. *Citizenship and Nationhood in France and Germany.* Cambridge, MA: Harvard University Press.

Cornelius, Wayne, Philip L. Martin, and James F. Hollifield, eds. 1994. *Controlling Immigration: A Global Perspective.* Stanford, CA: Stanford University Press.

Freeman, Gary P. 1995. "Modes of Immigration Politics in Liberal Democratic States." *International Migration Review* 112: 881–902.

Geddes, Andrew. 2000. *Immigration and European Integration: Towards Fortress Europe?* Manchester: Manchester University Press.

Guiraudon, Virginie, and Christian Joppke, 2001. "Controlling a New Migration World." In Virginie Guiraudon and Christian Joppke, eds. *Controlling a New Migration World.* London: Routledge.

Hammar, Tomas, ed. 1985. *European Immigration Policy: A Comparative Study.* Cambridge, Eng.: Cambridge University Press.

Hansen, Randall. 2002. "Globalization, Embedded Realism, and Path Dependence." *Comparative Political Studies* 35(3): 259–283.

Hansen, Randall, and Patrick Weil, eds. 2001. *Towards a European Nationality: Citizenship, Immigration and Nationality Law in the EU.* Houndsmills, Basingstoke, Eng.: Palgrave Macmillan.

Hollifield, James F. 2000. "The Politics of International Migration: How Can We Bring the State Back In?" In *Migration Theory: Talking Across Disciplines.* ed. Caroline B. Brettell and James F. Hollifield. New York: Routledge.

Joppke, Christian. 1999. *Immigration and the Nation State: The United States, Germany, and Great Britain.* Oxford: Oxford University Press.

Money, Jeannette. 1999. *Fences and Neighbors: The Geography of Immigration Control.* Ithaca, NY: Cornell University Press.

Sassen, Saskia. 1996. *Losing Control? Sovereignty in an Age of Globalization.* New York: Columbia University Press.

SOPEMI (Continuous Reporting System on Migration). 1999 and 2000. *Trends in International Migration.* Paris: OECD.

Soysal, Yasemin. 1994. *Limits of Citizenship: Migrants and Postnational Membership in Europe.* Chicago: University of Chicago Press.

Tichenor, Daniel. 2002. *Dividing Lines: The Politics of Immigration in America.* Princeton, NJ: Princeton University Press.

Weiner, Myron, ed. 1993. *International Migration and Security.* Boulder, CO: Westview Press.

Zolberg, Aristide. 1999. "Matters of State: Theorizing Immigration Policy." In *Becoming American, America Becoming.* ed. Douglas Massey. New York: Russell Sage.

GARY P. FREEMAN

IMMIGRATION TRENDS IN MAJOR DESTINATION COUNTRIES

International migrants are defined as persons who reside for an extended length of time or indefinitely—possibly permanently—in a foreign country. Tourists, persons who commute daily or weekly to jobs in neighboring countries, and persons employed for a short period outside their country of origin are not considered international migrants.

The minimum stay necessary for a person to be considered an international migrant differs from country to country. Official migration statistics in Germany include foreign citizens who have resided in that country for at least three months. In contrast, in Switzerland only persons who have stayed in the country for a minimum of twelve months are considered migrants. Students and temporary workers can reside for many years in the United States without being officially registered as immigrants. Unlike European censuses, U.S. censuses include data on undocumented persons who have not been granted legal residence. Inadequacies in official statistical data in many developing countries make it impossible to specify the exact number of international migrants worldwide. But commonly cited estimates for the end of the twentieth century are between 120 and 175 million people.

Historical Survey

Migration has taken place throughout history but did not become a mass phenomenon until the industrial revolution. A prerequisite to this development was the emergence of demand for industrial labor. A second prerequisite was the development of widely available and relatively inexpensive means of transportation, particularly railroads and steamships. Improved public transportation allowed large numbers of people to become mobile. This led to considerable intra-European migration and later to the recruitment of migrant workers from abroad to the metropolises and industrial centers of France, Germany, and the United Kingdom. Starting as early as the 1840s, France was the first European country to recruit foreign workers; other Western European countries did not follow its example until the mid-twentieth century.

Starting in the European age of discovery and conquest, Europe became a continent of emigration. Between 1600 and 1950, approximately 70 million people left that continent for destinations overseas. In particular, they aimed to reach North and South America, Algeria, southern Africa, Palestine, Australia, and New Zealand. Most of these emigrants were political and religious dissidents, adventurers, and above all the poor and persons without property. As early as the nineteenth century Europeans began to outnumber the indigenous people in many settlement countries.

In some respects this movement prefigured modern labor migration. It included not only migration from Europe to North and South America but also the recruitment of laborers from India and China as plantation workers in British and Dutch possessions in the Caribbean and Southeast Asia. In the late nineteenth and early twentieth centuries, Chinese laborers were recruited to work on railroad construction and as lumberjacks in the western United States and Canada. Earlier, the slave trade had brought approximately 9.5 million people—mostly residents of sub-Saharan Africa—to North and South America between the seventeenth and nineteenth centuries.

Immigrants in the Twentieth Century

Twentieth-century immigrants to the major settlement countries can be broadly categorized as refugees and expellees, migrants from former colonies, economic migrants, and "ethnically privileged" migrants.

Refugees and Expellees. In the twentieth century in Europe alone, approximately 45 million persons migrated internationally as refugees or through forced deportations. The causes of their relocation included, for example, the Russian Revolution of 1917 (1.5 million refugees), the Turkish-Greek war of 1922 (2 million forced migrants), the policies of Nazi Germany (6 million deported persons and 8.5 million forced laborers), and the new political order that followed World War II (12 million forced German migrants and 2.5 million forced Polish and Ukrainian migrants).

During the Cold War migrants from communist-ruled countries were granted asylum as political refugees in the West, although economic reasons were the primary motive for many of those migrants. Since the 1990s the proportion of asylum seekers granted permanent residence in Western Europe, the United States, and Australia has fallen markedly. Most of the world's refugees (estimated at some 15 million in 2001) are in developing countries, usually in geographic vicinity to their countries of origin.

Postcolonial migrants. Beginning in the 1950s and as a result of decolonization, many colonial settlers, government employees, and soldiers returned to the United Kingdom, France, the Netherlands, Belgium, and, in 1974–1975, Portugal. The 1990s witnessed the return migration of an estimated 5 million ethnic Russians from Central Asia, the Caucasus, and the Baltic region to Russia. Ultimately, this movement too was a result of a decolonization process.

Also since the 1950s, indigenous peoples from former colonial territories in southern and southeastern Asia, Africa, and the Caribbean have migrated to the European countries that had colonized them in search of better living conditions and to escape political and ethnic conflict. This type of migration was fostered by the demand for low-cost labor in Europe.

The European metropolitan powers originally facilitated this migration by recognizing the inhabitants of former colonies as their own citizens or as preferred immigrants. The result was a substantial movement of Irish, Indians, Pakistanis, Bangladeshis, and West Indians to the United Kingdom; Vietnamese and northern and western Africans to France; and Moluccans and Surinamis to the Netherlands.

Economic migrants. In the United States the active recruitment of workers that had begun with Chinese laborers continued with the recruitment of other temporary labor migrants, predominantly from Mexico. Between 1942 and 1964 Mexican workers were recruited through so-called Bracero programs. In contrast to regular migrants, these temporary workers were not seen as candidates for permanent U.S. residency. After 1964 large numbers of undocumented migrants arrived in the United States, mostly from Mexico and South America. Many of them became legal residents between 1986 and 1989. However, the 2000 U.S. census revealed that there were some 8 million undocumented migrants, mostly labor migrants, living in the United States. As legal immigrants to the United States and Canada have immediate access to the labor markets of these countries, regular migration to North America is also largely driven by economic motives.

In Europe, France and Switzerland have the longest history of recruiting foreign workers; in the case of France this practice dates back to the nineteenth century. In the mid-1950s other West European countries started recruiting foreign workers to do low-skilled jobs. Those labor migrants came from Italy, Spain, Portugal, and Greece and later from North Africa, Turkey, and the former Yugoslavia. Bilateral treaties between origin and destination countries provided a formal regulatory framework for those flows. Employment of migrant workers in Western Europe reached a high in the early 1970s.

After the first international oil crisis in 1973, state recruitment of workers was halted and quotas were placed on immigration from former colonial territories to Western Europe. Family unification and network migration to Western Europe resulted in continued inflows of persons from countries that previously had supplied migrant labor.

The internationalization of the European labor market in the second half of the twentieth century brought over 30 million people to Western Europe and brought persons residing in Western Europe's peripheries—such as Ireland, Portugal, and southern Italy—to its industrial centers and metropolises.

TABLE 1

Foreign-Born Population in the United States, Canada, and Australia, 1950–2000

		1950	1960	1970	1980	1990	2000
United States	Foreign-born (millions)	10.4	9.7	9.6	14.0	19.8	29.3
	Percent of total population	6.9	5.4	4.7	6.2	7.9	10.4
		1951	**1961**	**1971**	**1981**	**1991**	**1996**
Canada	Foreign-born (millions)	2.1	2.8	3 3		4.3	5.0
	Percent of total population	14.7	15.6	18.0		16.1	17.4
		1954	**1966**	**1976**	**1986**	**1996**	**2000 (est.)**
Australia	Foreign-born (millions)	1.3	2.1	2.7	3.3	43	4.3
	Percent of total population	14.3	18.4	20.1	21.1	22.8	23.3

SOURCE: U.S., Canadian and Australian censuses.

Only in Finland and Greece about one in two migrant workers stayed in Western Europe; the others eventually returned home.

In addition to legal migrant workers Western Europe received a growing number of illegal and undocumented labor migrants. Estimates from around 2000 suggest that there are more than 2 million undocumented migrants in Western and southern Europe. Many of these migrants stay for only a few months, while others manage to establish themselves. In addition, new types of international seasonal work and cross-border commuter labor have evolved, originating in a variety of source countries. The main source areas are Poland, Romania, North Africa, the Middle East, and southern Asia.

Outside Europe and North America labor migration currently occurs from southern and southeastern Asia to the Persian Gulf states and to South Africa from its bordering countries. In southeastern Asia, Malaysia and Singapore attract regional labor migrants. Brazil and Argentina receive regional labor migration from poorer Andean countries.

Ethnically privileged migrants. Several states have special migration programs for persons with the same ethnic or religious origins as the majority population. An example of a country with this migration policy is Israel. All persons who are of Jewish descent or are members of the Jewish faith are allowed to immigrate to Israel (from 1948 to 2001 there were 3 million ethnic and religious immigrants). Since 1950 Germany has granted members of the German ethnic minority in central and eastern Europe the right to immigrate to Germany and ob-

tain German citizenship (from 1950 to 2001 there were 4 million ethnic migrants). In the 1990s Russia allowed the immigration of citizens from the successor states of the former Soviet Union (from 1990 to 2000 there were 5 million migrants); most of those migrants were ethnic Russians.

Foreign-Born and Foreign Citizens in Major Destination Countries

The most popular geographic destination of migrants is North America, followed by Western Europe, Australia, and the Persian Gulf States.

In the United States, Canada, and Australia, national censuses include statistics on the immigrant population (Table 1). The United States was home to 10 million immigrants in 1950—6.9 percent of the total population—after a long period of restrictive migration policies. By 1970 the proportion of the foreign-born had dropped to 4.7 percent. In subsequent years it increased steadily, reaching 10 percent, or 29 million immigrants, in 2000.

In Canada the share of the immigrant population hardly changed during the second half of the twentieth century, staying at around 17 percent; the absolute numbers increased significantly. In 1950 Canada had 2.1 million immigrants; in 1980, 3.3 million; and in 1996, 5 million. At the beginning of the twenty-first century a total of 34 million foreign-born people lived in North America.

In 2000 the foreign-born population in Australia was 4.3 million, amounting to 23.3 percent of the total population.

In Europe official statistics contain information only about foreign citizens with legal residency and

TABLE 2

Foreign Citizen Populations in 18 Western European Countries, 1950–2001 (in Thousands and as Percentage of Total Population)

	1950		1970–1971		1982		1990		1999–2001	
	Total	%	Total	%	Total	%	Total	%	Total	%
Austria	323	4.7	212	2.8	303	4.0	482	6.2	730	9.1
Belgium	368	4.3	696	7.2	886	9.0	903	9.0	853	8.3
Denmark	*	*	*	*	102	2.0	161	3.1	259	4.9
Finland	11	0.3	6	0.1	13	0.3	26	0.5	88	1.7
France	1,765	4.2	2,621	5.1	3,660	6.7	3,607	6.3	3,263	5.6
Germany**	568	1.1	2,976	4.9	4,667	7.6	5,338	8.4	7,297	8.9
Greece*	31	0.4	15	0.2	60	0.6	173	1.7	166	1.6
Ireland	*	*	137	4.6	232	6.6	81	2.3	127	3.3
Italy	47	0.1	122	0.2	312	0.6	469	0.8	1,271	2.2
Liechtenstein	3	21.4	7	33.3	9	34.1	11	38.1	11	34.3
Luxembourg	29	9.8	63	18.5	96	26.3	109	28.2	153	35.6
Netherlands	104	1.0	255	1.9	547	3.8	692	4.6	652	4.1
Norway	16	0.5	76	2.0	91	2.2	143	3.4	179	4.0
Portugal	21	0.2	32	0.4	64	0.6	108	1.1	191	1.9
Spain	93	0.3	148	0.4	183	0.5	279	0.7	801	2.0
Sweden	124	1.8	411	5.1	406	4.9	484	5.6	487	5.5
Switzerland***	285	6.1	1,080	17.4	926	14.4	1,127	16.7	1,459	20.1
United Kingdom	*	*	2,000	3.6	2,137	3.8	1,904	3.3	2,298	3.9
Western Europe, Total	3,788	1.7	10,857	3.3	14,694	4.2	16,096	4.5	20,416	5.2

*Reliable data are not available.
**Before 1990 data are for West Germany.
***Excluding seasonal labor migrants and employees of international organizations.

SOURCE: Council of Europe (2001); OECD/SOPEMI (2001).

do not include information on all persons who were born abroad (i.e., migrants). In most Western European countries the number of foreign citizens increased from the 1950s to the 1970s and increased again in the 1990s. This was due only in part to an actual increase in the number of new immigrants. For example, Western European countries that naturalize immigrants rapidly are home to fewer legal foreign residents than are countries with lower naturalization rates. Many European countries do not grant citizenship to native-born children with noncitizen parents. This increases the official number of foreigners living in those countries.

In 1950 fifteen European Union countries were home to 3.8 million foreign citizens (Table 2). By 1970–1971 that number had risen to almost 11 million. At the beginning of the twenty-first century, approximately 20 million foreign citizens lived in those European countries. Additionally, 8 million people—either citizens of European countries returning from stays abroad or former immigrants who had become naturalized —were living in Western Europe.

France was home to the largest foreign citizen population in 1950. In 1970 Germany hosted the largest number of foreign citizens in Europe, followed by France, the United Kingdom, and Switzerland. Foreign citizens residing in Europe were predominantly labor migrants.

At the turn of the twenty-first century, Germany was still home to the greatest number of foreign citizens, with 7.3 million people (8.9% of the total population), followed by France with 3.3 million people (5.6%), the United Kingdom with 2.3 million people (3.9%), and Switzerland with 1.5 million people (20.1%).

Other important countries of destination in 2000–2001 were Italy with 1.3 million people (2.2%), Belgium with 0.9 million people (8.3%), Spain with 0.8 million people (2.0%), Austria with 0.7 million people (9.1%), and the Netherlands with 0.7 million people (4.1%).

As a proportion of the total population, foreign citizens were most strongly represented in 1950 and in 2000–2001 in the small countries of Liechtenstein

(34.3% in 2000) and Luxembourg (35.6% in 2000). Among larger Western European countries, Switzerland had the highest percent of foreign nationals (20.1% in 2001). All other Western European countries had a foreign citizen population that was under 10 percent of the total population in 2000. Thus, among the 390 million people living in those eighteen European states, only a little over 5 percent were not citizens of the countries in which they resided; one-third of these persons came from other countries of Western Europe. If one includes the number of naturalized citizens living in Western Europe, 7 percent of the persons residing in Western Europe at the beginning of the twenty-first century were immigrants.

See also: *International Migration; Labor Migration, International; Trans-Atlantic Migration.*

BIBLIOGRAPHY

Castles, Steven, and Mark Miller. 1998. *The Age of Migration: International Population Movements in the Modern World,* 2nd edition. New York: Guilford Press.

Cohen, Robin, ed. 1995. *The Cambridge Survey of World Migration.* New York: Cambridge University Press.

Council of Europe. *Recent Demographic Developments in Europe.* Strasbourg, annual.

International Organization for Migration. 2000. *World Migration Report 2000.* Geneva: United Nations.

OECD/SOPEMI. *International Migration Trends.* Paris, annual.

Straubhaar, Thomas. 2002. "Migration im 21. Jahrhundert." *Beiträge zur Ordnungstheorie und Ordnungspolitik.* Vol. 167. Tübingen, Germany: Mohr Siebeck Verlag.

United Nations High Commissioner for Refugees. 2000. *The State of the World's Refugees: Fifty Years of Humanitarian Action.* Geneva: UNHCR, New York: Oxford University Press.

Zolberg, Aristide R., and Peter M. Benda, eds. 2001. *Global Migrants, Global Refugees: Problems and Solutions.* New York and Oxford: Berghahn Books.

INTERNET RESOURCES.

International Organization for Migration. 2003. <http://www.iom.ch>.

Migration Policy Institute. 2003. <http://www. migrationinformation.org>.

United Nations High Commissioner for Refugees. 2003. <http://www.unhcr.ch>.

RAINER MÜNZ

INDIGENOUS PEOPLES

In the year 2000 the United Nations established a Permanent Forum on Indigenous Issues as a subsidiary organ of the Economic and Social Council. Much deliberation preceded this initiative, not least because precise demarcation of the world's indigenous populations has been elusive. In the early twenty-first century there is no single and unambiguous definition of indigenous peoples; even indigenous groups may disagree about their composition. Attempts at definition tend to follow three guiding principles.

Indigenous peoples include descendants of the original inhabitants of a country

- Who have become encapsulated in their lands by a numerically and politically dominant invasive society
- Who retain a cultural difference from that society
- Who self-identify as indigenous

In describing the demographic features of indigenous peoples, the third criterion is crucial. For these peoples to exist at all in a statistical sense requires both administrative mechanisms to ascribe and record indigenous status *and* a willingness—or insistence—on the part of indigenous people to be counted as such rather than as a minority population with some distinctive characteristics (such as language, religion, or ethnicity) that differentiates it within a broader society. The degree to which these prerequisites combine to enable the compilation of demographic data varies greatly both historically and between nations. The statistical basis for a consistent global description of indigenous demography is thus tenuous at best.

Population Size

Although estimates of population size are available for most indigenous groups, the availability and quality of data on births and deaths is more sporadic. The most complete census and administrative data sources are available in North America and Australasia. With varying degrees of coverage and changing interpretations of race and ethnicity, indigenous people have been recorded in national censuses since 1870 and 1871 in the United States and Canada, since 1881 in New Zealand, and since 1901 in Australia.

In Latin America, most countries have indigenous inhabitants, but only half have a census and/or household survey program that includes information about the indigenous population. The situation in northern Europe and Russia is equally mixed: The formal acquisition of demographic data about the indigenous Saami of northern Scandinavia is still under development, but decades of Soviet administration among minority indigenous peoples of the Russian Federation has yielded basic demographic information since 1926. For countries in Africa and Asia, demographic data are also intermittent. So-called ethnic minorities have been identified in the Chinese census since 1953, and postwar censuses in India have identified separate "Scheduled Tribes" populations. Japan has arguably the longest time-series data in Asia, with regular counts of the Ainu since the early nineteenth century.

Many national governments and statistical agencies deny the existence of indigenous peoples within their borders, partly because it is difficult to establish antecedence and partly because of unresolved political tensions in defining the social basis of the nation-state. Accordingly, demographic knowledge of the indigenous San peoples of southern Africa and similar populations elsewhere emerges only from dedicated field studies.

Estimates of the number of indigenous people worldwide toward the end of the twentieth century converged on the 300 million mark, or approximately 5 percent of the world population. This number is distributed across almost half the world's countries and can be further disaggregated into some 5,300 distinct political/legal/cultural groupings described variously as "tribal," "Fourth World," or "first" nations.

Most indigenous peoples (207 million) live in Asia—overwhelmingly in China (108 million) and India (68 million)—with an estimated 50 million in Africa and 40 million in Latin America. The New World countries of Australasia and North America, which have yielded the most comprehensive and accurate data on indigenous populations, account for only a small estimated share of the global total—4.4 million, or 1.5 per cent, in 2000. Within this total the estimated size of the indigenous population in the United States (American Indian, Eskimo, and Aleut) was 2.4 million.

Indigenous Demographic Transition

The shared characteristics that define indigenous peoples are manifest in "enclave demographies" that are clearly distinct from mainstream or national demographic profiles. These characteristics derive from common historical experiences of severe population decline as a consequence of colonization by nonindigenes, followed by a period of stabilization and in some cases recuperation. In Australasia and North America rapid growth in recent decades has coincided with a shift from exclusion to inclusion of indigenous peoples in the provisions of modern states. In broad terms these phases describe an "indigenous" demographic transition along the lines of the classical model, although a significant revision is represented by the recognition of an initial, or pre-transition, phase of depopulation during the period of first contact with nonindigenes. At the beginning of the twenty-first century indigenous populations could be found in each of the phases of transition. The prospect of an indigenous mobility transition has also been studied.

Consideration of the size of indigenous populations before their encapsulation by invading groups requires a temporal cutoff point. One convenient device is to distinguish populations colonized in relatively recent times after contact with European and other intercontinental migrants from those which have been subjugated for millennia by intracontinental migrations. For the former group such a "precontact" population has been estimated at 17 million for North America, lowland South America, and Oceania in the mid-eighteenth century.

By the early twentieth century the main impact of nonindigenous settlement in those regions had been to reduce autochthonous numbers to barely 1.3 million. Casting the net wider to incorporate Russia, southern Asia, island southeast Asia, and central and southern Africa, the decline in the population of indigenous peoples could have amounted to as much as 50 million between 1780 and 1930. The causes of this population loss are well understood and include disease, frontier violence, and the loss of land by what were predominantly hunter-gatherer populations.

Demographic Transition in Australia and Canada

The existence of relatively robust time-series data for indigenous populations in Australia and Canada since the mid-nineteenth century provides an opportunity to explore the course of indigenous demographic transition. Similar overviews are available for the Maori of Aotearoa in New Zealand and for Native Americans. It is clear that indigenous populations in these New World countries have undergone a series of systematic fluctuations in fertility and mortality levels that have been uneven over space and time but ultimately comprehensive and uniform in effect. These fluctuations have been conceived of as separate but overlapping transitions from the pre-European contact period of stable growth with high mortality and fertility through a phase of postcontact population decline to a stationary state, followed by a period of high growth and finally a regime of lower natural growth based on reduced mortality and fertility.

In light of the evidence for human habitation in present-day Australia and Canada for tens of thousands of years, it is reasonable to assume that the indigenous population levels first encountered by European settlers were the product of a long-term balance between birth rates and death rates. Most analysts suggest that this stationary state was due to sustained high birth rates and death rates.

In Australia controversy surrounds the exact estimation of population size at the time of the first sustained contact with Europeans in 1788, with 300,000 as the likely minimum figure and 1 million as an upper bound. In either case a drastic decline in numbers accompanied the process of European occupation as a result of reduced fertility and rising mortality. This decline was rapid until about 1890, after which the population was probably stationary until the 1930s at roughly 20 percent of its original estimated minimum size. In Canada the precontact Indian population has been estimated at a roughly similar size (250,000). This was reduced to around 120,000 by 1900 as a consequence of introduced diseases and hostilities between native populations and invading settlers (Norris 1990).

In both Australia and Canada the first sign of further transition appeared with a rise in the birth rate to over 40 per 1,000 in the post–World War II years, falling back to around 35 per 1,000 by the 1970s and 1980s. This was accompanied in the 1960s and 1970s by a sudden and substantial drop in the death rate, which leveled off at 16 per 1,000 among indigenous Australians and 10 per 1,000 among Canadian Indians. In each case this heralded a period of rapid population increase with annual growth rates of up to 2.5 percent by the 1970s.

The current phase of transition is to a regime of lower natural increase based on reductions in both fertility and mortality. By 2000 the rate of natural increase among indigenous Australians and Canadians had fallen to 2 percent per year, although this was still four times the level of their respective national rates.

Trends in Mortality

The crude death rate for indigenous people in Australia remained high until the mid-1960s but declined sharply between 1965 and 1978, falling from 19 to 13 per 1,000. The primary cause was a precipitous reduction in the infant mortality rate (IMR) from around 100 per 1,000 births in the mid-1960s to 26 by 1981. This was a direct consequence of greatly enhanced access to the health infrastructure, especially community-based prenatal and hospital-based postnatal care. Further improvement in infant survival since the 1980s has been less impressive, with indigenous IMRs remaining around three times the Australian average. A similar decline was recorded over the same period in Canada, with the indigenous IMR falling from 42 to 15 between 1971 and 1981.

Improvement in life expectancy has been far less dramatic. In Australia the first reliable national estimates in 1981 revealed life expectancies for indigenous people of around 56 years for males and 64 years for females, some 20 years below those of the general population. This situation had not altered by 2000. In Canada the equivalent gap in life expectancy in the 1990s was eight years despite a steady improvement in indigenous mortality since the 1950s. In both countries the overall level of indigenous mortality reflects persistently higher indigenous death rates at all ages but especially in middle adulthood between 30 and 50 years of age. This lack of improvement relative to the life expectancy of the general population despite lowered infant mortality is a unique demographic phenomenon and reflects the influence of lifestyle factors as a primary cause of death among marginalized populations.

Trends in Fertility

Total fertility rates (TFRs) among indigenous women in Australia peaked in the decade 1956–1966, remained high until 1971, and then fell sharply throughout the 1970s, effectively halving the TFR from around 5.9 in the period 1966–1971 to around 3.3 in the period 1976–1981. Results from the 1996 census indicated further lowering of the TFR to 2.7, representing a drop of around 50 percent since 1971. The overall expectation is for steady progress toward replacement fertility in the early decades of the twenty-first century.

In explaining this decline in Australia, the focus has been on the effect of increased participation by indigenous people, particularly women, in mainstream institutional structures, which has altered the costs and benefits of having children. Three factors—age at leaving school, labor force status, and income—are regarded as particularly instrumental. In Canada fertility has also been lowered by delayed marriage and childbirth.

Nondemographic Factors in Population Growth

Despite reduced natural growth, recent census counts of indigenous populations in Australia and Canada reveal an apparent population explosion. Between 1971 and 1996 the census count of the indigenous Australian population increased by 200 percent, substantially above the underlying rate of natural increase. A similar discrepancy was observed in Canada. This "error of closure" reflects the contributions of a greater propensity of individuals to self-identify as indigenous, an expanded potential pool of a self-identified population as a result of out-marriage, and legislative change, notably the reinstatement and registration provisions of the 1985 Indian Act (Bill C-31) in Canada, which relaxed the rules governing entitlement to Indian status.

The current high indigenous population growth rates reflect the interplay of political, administrative, and cultural processes. In the past these processes effectively excluded or devalued indigenous representation in official statistics. In the contemporary period efforts increasingly are being made to encourage and facilitate self-identification. This means that populations that are portrayed as discrete and homogeneous for statistical and administrative purposes are in reality becoming less discrete, less homogeneous, and more difficult to quantify unambiguously. Despite this process, demographic divergence from national profiles remains a hallmark of indigenous populations.

See also: *Caste; Hunter-Gatherers; Nomads; Prehistoric Populations.*

BIBLIOGRAPHY

Bodley, John H. 1990. *Victims of Progress,* 3rd edition. Mountain View, CA: Mayfield.

Goehring, Brian. 1993. *Indigenous Peoples of the World: An Introduction to Their Past, Present and Future.* Saskatoon, Saskatchewan: Purich Publishing.

Gonzalez, Mary L. 1994. "How Many Indigenous People?" In *Indigenous People and Poverty in Latin America: An Empirical Analysis,* ed. George Psachanopoulos and Harry A. Patrinos. Washington D.C.: World Bank Regional and Sectoral Studies.

Gray, Alan. 1990. "Aboriginal Fertility: Trends and Prospects." *Journal of the Australian Population Association* 7(1): 57–77.

Hitchcock, Robert K., and Tara M. Twedt. 1995. "Physical and Cultural Genocide of Various Indigenous peoples." In *Genocide in the Twentieth Century: Critical Essays and Eyewitness Accounts,* ed. Samuel Totten, William S. Parsons, and Israel W. Charny. New York: Garland Publishing.

Kunitz, Stephen J. 1994. *Disease and Social Diversity: The European Impact on the Health of Non-Europeans.* New York: Oxford University Press.

Norris, Mary J. 1990. "The Demography of Aboriginal People in Canada." In *Ethnic Demography: Canadian Immigrant Racial and Cultural Variations,* ed. S. Shiva, Frank Trovato, and Leo Driedger. Ottawa, Ontario: Carelton University Press.

Passel, Jeffery S. 1996. "The Growing American Indian Population, 1969–1990: Beyond Demography." In *Changing Numbers, Changing Needs:*

American Indian Demography and Public Health, ed. Gary D. Sandefur, Ronald R. Rindfuss, and Barney Cohen. Washington D.C.: National Academy Press.

Pennington, Renee. 1991. *Te Iwi Maori: A New Zealand Population Past, Present, and Projected.* Auckland, New Zealand: Auckland University Press.

———. 2001. "Hunter-Gatherer Demography." In *Hunter-Gatherers: An Interdisciplinary Perspective,* ed. Catherine Painter-Brick, Robert H. Layton, and Peter Rowley-Conwy. Cambridge, Eng.: Cambridge University Press.

Smith, Leonard R. 1980. *The Aboriginal Population of Australia.* Canberra: Australian National University Press.

Snipp, Matthew C. 1997. "Some Observations about Racial Boundaries and the Experiences of American Indians." *Ethnic and Racial Studies* 20(4): 667–689.

Taylor, John. 1997. "The Contemporary Demography of Indigenous Australians." *Journal of the Australian Population Association* 14(1): 77–114.

Taylor, John, and Martin Bell. 1996. "Indigenous Peoples and Population Mobility: The View from Australia." *International Journal of Population Geography* 2(2): 153–169.

Thornton, Russell. 1987. *American Indian Holocaust and Survival: A Population History Since 1492.* Norman: University of Oklahoma Press.

JOHN TAYLOR

INDUCED ABORTION

HISTORY	Etienne van de Walle
PREVALENCE	Stanley K. Henshaw
LEGAL ASPECTS	Laura Katzive
	Stanley Henshaw

HISTORY

Women throughout the world have probably attempted to procure abortion—premature artificial termination of pregnancy—from before recorded history. The earliest recorded version of the Hippocratic Oath (c. 500 B.C.E.) includes the physician's pledge: "I shall not give women a [fetus]-destroying pessary." This constitutes a testimony both to medical attitudes and practices in antiquity, and to the technology of the time.

Attitudes

Plato and Aristotle accepted the practice of abortion for eugenic reasons. Roman and Jewish law considered that the fetus had no independent existence and was part of the woman's body, subject to the authority of her husband. Legal conflicts originated when the termination of pregnancy was the result of violence inflicted by a third party, or was carried out by a woman against her husband's wishes. Opposition to abortion, together with opposition to infanticide, crystallized under the influence of Christianity. The Church fathers associated abortion first with magical procedures, and second with fornication and adultery, as the epitome of sexual sin. The fetus was thought to become formed or alive only after a delay, such as 40 days; a corollary of this belief was that penalties for abortion increased with the duration of gestation. Christian beliefs from the fourth century on identified this stage—40 days after conception, called "quickening"—with animation, the time when the fetus was endowed with an immortal soul; a similar belief prevailed in Islam. The distinction between abortion before and after quickening survived for a long time in canon law and civil jurisprudence (including common law in England and the United States), although it was abandoned by the Catholic Church in modern times.

Physicians of antiquity generally admitted the legitimacy of therapeutic abortion when the woman was immature or ill-formed, where pregnancy or delivery would endanger her life. Soranus, the Greek gynecologist of the second century C.E., gave recipes for abortion under these conditions, although he preferred the use of contraception for the same purpose. Soranus's position influenced the western medical tradition through Rome, Byzantium, and the translations of Arabic medical texts in the Middle Ages, and justified the publication of *Materia Medica* featuring abortive herbs and their continued availability to physicians. Although some Christian theologians accepted abortions for therapeutic reasons, most were opposed to the practice. Civil codes condemned abortion with great severity, but it remained a rare event until the nineteenth century, reserved for desperate women. Its practice spread with the need for better methods of birth control, even against the increasing opposition of physicians. During the second half of the twentieth century, early-term abortion (with various definitions of what qualifies as such) was legalized in many countries of the world. However, the moral acceptability of abortion remains controversial. Powerful movements of public opinion support the right of the fetus to life; others, equally influential, support a woman's freedom to choose the outcome of her pregnancy.

Techniques

Methods of abortion in the past either were ineffective or endangered the life of the mother. Vaginal suppositories appear to have been the most commonly used medical technique in the ancient world, because of the intuitive appeal of this route of access to the uterus; they were still mentioned in medical texts of the eighteenth century. Reference to abortive drugs in classical writings or Church pronouncements may refer either to suppositories or oral poisons, or even to spells and magic. The most frequently mentioned alternative technique consisted of violent movements, massage or blows, although milder methods like bleeding or cold baths were also cited. The use of sharp objects is rare before the seventeenth century, although various obstetrical instruments that could have been used for abortion have been described or even unearthed by archeologists. Soranus cautioned against the use of "something sharp-edged to separate the embryo." Dioscorides's second-century C.E. *Materia Medica* mentioned a number of drugs that would kill a fetus. In addition he listed more than one hundred substances that hastened delivery, expelled a dead fetus, or stimulated the menses. The latter were not abortifacients, but were supposed to act on the uterus. Learned as well as popular medicine and folklore in Europe through the medieval and modern periods attributed abortive properties to many herbal substances, including rue, artemisia, pennyroyal, ergot of rye, tansy, and saffron. A tea or potion made from savin, a species of juniper, was the most widely reputed abortifacient. These substances are implicated in many court proceedings, although it was the attempt (often unsuccessful) to procure an abortion, rather than the actual abortion, that was prosecuted. (Abortion was featured much less often in the courts than infanticide.) Similar substances are reputed as abortifacients in all world cultures, but their effectiveness has never been reliably ascertained. It seems their reputation was greatly inflated, although their popular use in the nineteenth and twentieth centuries, and their deplorable reputation among physicians, suggest that attempts at abortion through oral means were sometimes successful.

Other techniques, such as injections and the use of sharp instruments to kill the fetus, became increasingly common from the seventeenth century in Europe. In the early nineteenth century, most professional abortionists who were prosecuted on the basis of existing penal codes appeared to belong to the medical professions and to use uterine sounds and curettes. By the end of the century, some relatively proficient abortionists operated underground. The numerical importance of abortion during the fertility transition is a matter of controversy.

Throughout most of history, abortion must have been a dangerous and rare procedure, probably practiced almost exclusively outside of marriage, and with little impact on fertility. With the development of antisepsis the procedure of dilatation and curettage could be performed with relative safety by skilled medical personnel. The introduction of methods of early abortion during the second half of the twentieth century—by vacuum aspiration, as well as chemical procedures such as the administration of prostaglandins—coincided with the widespread legalization of abortion, and the blurring of the boundaries between contraception (particularly its post-coital forms) and abortion.

See also: *Birth Control, History of; Infanticide.*

BIBLIOGRAPHY

Brodie, Janet Farell. 1994. *Contraception and Abortion in 19th-Century America.* Ithaca, NY: Cornell University Press.

McLaren, Angus. 1984. *Reproductive Rituals: The Perception of Fertility in England from the Sixteenth to the Nineteenth Century.* London: Methuen.

Noonan, John, ed. 1970. *The Morality of Abortion: Legal and Historical Perspectives.* Cambridge, MA: Harvard University Press.

Potts, Malcolm, Peter Diggory, and John Peel. 1977. *Abortion.* Cambridge, Eng.: Cambridge University Press.

Van de Walle, Etienne. 1999. "Towards a Demographic History of Abortion." *Population. An English Selection* 11: 115–132.

ETIENNE VAN DE WALLE

PREVALENCE

The term "abortion" as used in this article refers to the induced termination of a pregnancy with intent other than to produce a live birth. An abortion may be induced legally or illegally, according to the laws of each country. It is to be distinguished from spontaneous abortion, including stillbirth, which is a natural outcome for a small proportion of pregnancies.

Sources of Data

The most accurate sources of information on the incidence of induced abortion are official statistics in countries where abortion is legal. In most of these countries, abortions are required to be reported to health authorities. However, the completeness and accuracy of reporting and the quantity and quality of the resulting tabulations vary widely among and even within countries. Reporting is probably most complete where a procedure for authorization is prescribed by statute and where abortions are required to be performed in hospitals or other facilities subject to official licensure.

In countries where no statistics are kept because abortion is illegal or there is no reporting system, a number of methods have been used to estimate the incidence of abortion. Household surveys yield minimum estimates because underreporting of abortions is common, even where the procedure is legal. These estimates may nevertheless be useful where abortion is widely practiced and accepted. Several studies have estimated abortion rates from the number of women treated in hospitals for abortion complications. These estimates rely on assumptions about the proportion of treated complications that result from induced rather than spontaneous abortions, the proportion of women needing treatment who seek hospital care, and the proportion of induced abortions that cause complications requiring treatment. A third approach is to survey the providers of abortions; this is rarely possible in countries where abortion is illegal. A fourth approach is to infer the abortion rate from the difference between the fertility rate and natural fertility, taking

TABLE 1

Estimated Number of Abortions by Legal Status, Abortion Rate Per 1,000 Women Aged 15–44, and Percentage of Pregnancies Ending in Abortion, by Region and Subregion, 1995

| | Number of abortions (millions) | | | | % of |
	Total	Legal	Illegal	Rate	pregnancies*
Total	45.5	25.6	19.9	35	26
Developed regions	10.0	9.1	0.9	39	42
Developing regions	35.5	16.5	19.0	34	23
Africa	5.0	**	5.0	33	15
Eastern Africa	1.9	**	1.9	41	16
Middle Africa	0.6	**	0.6	35	14
Northern Africa	0.6	**	0.6	17	12
Southern Africa	0.2	**	0.2	19	12
Western Africa	1.6	**	1.6	37	15
Asia	26.8	16.9	9.9	33	25
Eastern Asia	12.5	12.5	**	36	34
South-central Asia	8.4	1.9	6.5	28	18
South-eastern Asia	4.7	1.9	2.8	40	28
Western Asia	1.2	0.7	0.5	32	20
Europe	7.7	6.8	0.9	48	48
Eastern Europe	6.2	5.4	0.8	90	65
Northern Europe	0.4	0.3	**	18	23
Southern Europe	0.8	0.7	0.1	24	34
Western Europe	0.4	0.4	**	11	17
Latin America	4.2	0.2	4.0	37	27
Caribbean	0.4	0.2	0.2	50	35
Central America	0.9	**	0.9	30	21
South America	3.0	**	3.0	39	30
Northern America	1.5	1.5	**	22	26
Oceania	0.1	0.1	**	21	20

*Abortions divided by abortions plus births
**Fewer than 50,000
Note: Developed regions are Europe, Northern America, Australia, New Zealand, and Japan; all others are considered developing. Regions are as defined by the United Nations.

SOURCE: Henshaw et al. (1999).

into account the reduction in fertility caused by contraceptive use, women not in unions, and rates of infecundity. This method, however, is extremely sensitive to the assumed rate of natural fertility and to small errors in calculating the impact of the other factors.

Incidence

With appropriate caution regarding the high margin of error, it has been estimated that 46 million abortions were performed worldwide in 1995—about 26 million legal abortions and 20 million that were illegal (see Table 1). (The true numbers could be several million higher or lower.) This estimate implies an average annual rate of 35 abortions per 1,000 women aged 15 to 44. Cumulated, the estimate would mean that women, on average, have close to one abortion

TABLE 2

Abortion Rate per 1,000 Women Aged 15–44, and Percentage of Pregnancies Ending in Abortion, in Selected Developed and Developing Countries

Country and Year	Rate	% of pregnancies[a]
Developed countries		
Netherlands, 1996[b]	6.5	10.6
Germany, 1996	7.6	14.1
Finland, 1996	10.0	14.7
Canada, 1995	15.5	22.0
England & Wales, 1996[b]	15.6	20.5
Denmark, 1995	16.1	20.3
Sweden, 1996	18.7	25.2
Czech Republic, 1996	20.7	34.0
Australia, 1995–1996	22.2	26.4
United States, 1996	22.9	25.9
Hungary, 1996	34.7	42.1
Belarus, 1996	67.5	61.9
Russian Federation, 1995[c]	68.4	62.6
Romania, 1996[c]	78.0	63.0
Developing countries, legal abortion		
Tunisia, 1996	8.6	7.8
Puerto Rico, 1991–1992	22.7	23.0
China, 1995[c]	26.1	27.4
Khazakstan, 1996	43.9	41.3
Cuba, 1996[d]	77.7	58.6
Vietnam, 1996[c]	83.3	43.7
Developing countries, illegal abortions (estimated)		
Egypt, 1996	23.0	15.7
Philippines, 1994	25.0	16.0
Mexico, 1990	25.1	17.1
Nigeria, 1996	25.4	12.0
Bangladesh, 1995[d]	28.0	18.0
Brazil, 1991	40.8	29.8

[a]Abortions divided by abortions plus births six months later (so that time of conception of pregnancies ending in abortion and birth would correspond)
[b]Residents only
[c]Reporting incomplete
[d]Includes menstrual regulation

SOURCE: Henshaw et al. (1999).

during their lifetimes. About 26 percent of all pregnancies, excluding miscarriages and stillbirths, were ended by induced abortion.

The abortion rates in developed and developing regions are broadly similar, despite the prevalence of restrictive laws in most developing countries. China, India, and Vietnam account for almost all of the legal abortions in the developing regions. Most abortions in other parts of Asia and also in Africa and Latin America are illegal.

Eastern Europe, including the Russian Federation, is the subregion with the highest abortion rate. In these countries, the lack of access to contraceptive methods and ready availability of abortion services

under Communism resulted in heavy reliance on abortion to limit fertility. Western Europe, where abortion is legal and readily available, has the lowest rate. The percentage of pregnancies ending in abortion is lowest in Africa, a consequence of the region's high birth rates.

Abortion rates vary widely among countries, as indicated in Table 2. Among low-fertility countries, the level of abortion appears to be determined primarily by the availability, accessibility, and acceptability of contraceptive services. During the 1990s, the lowest recorded rate—less than 7 abortions per 1,000 women aged 15 to 44—was in the Netherlands, despite a low fertility rate and abortion services that are readily available without charge. Only 11 percent of pregnancies nationwide were ended by abortion, with only 3 to 4 percent among the Dutch-born population. The highest abortion rate ever recorded for a country was 252 per 1,000 women in Romania in 1964 and 1965.

Abortion rates are generally higher in developing countries, because of less established contraceptive use, less accessible contraceptive services, and the limited range of contraceptive methods available. The example of Tunisia, however, demonstrates that the use of modern contraceptives can keep the rate low even where abortion services are available and free. Vietnam, on the other hand, had one of the highest abortion rates in the 1990s as a consequence of a rapid drop in desired family size and limited access to modern contraceptive methods. Including abortions performed in the private sector and not counted officially, the abortion rate in Vietnam was estimated to be 111 per 1,000 women in 1996. Estimates of abortion rates in several countries where abortion is illegal are in the range of 23 to 41 per 1,000 women, and the percentage of pregnancies ended by abortion ranges from 12 to 30.

Trends

During the 1990s, abortion rates fell slowly in several Western European countries and the United States, and they fell rapidly in most of the formerly-Communist countries as contraceptive supplies and services became more available. In many developing areas, the demand for both abortion and contraception increased as desired fertility fell, marriage was delayed, and sexual activity before marriage became more common.

In developed countries, non-surgical abortion by means of mifepristone (RU-486) together with a prostaglandin became increasingly common but did not appear to affect overall abortion rates. In developing countries where abortion is illegal, misoprostol, a prostaglandin used to prevent stomach ulcers among long-term users of pain medications, is increasingly used to induce abortion, although it is not always effective. Its effect on abortion rates is unknown, but in Brazil and other countries it has reduced the number of serious complications of illegal and unsafe abortions.

See also: *Contraceptive Prevalence; Fertility, Proximate Determinants of; Spontaneous Abortion.*

BIBLIOGRAPHY

Henshaw, Stanley K., Susheela Singh, and Taylor Haas. 1999. "The Incidence of Abortion Worldwide." *International Family Planning Perspectives* 25(Supplement): S30–S38.

Henshaw, Stanley K., Taylor Ann Haas, Kathleen Berentsen, and Erin Carbone, eds. 2001. *Readings on Induced Abortion, Volume 2: A World Review 2000.* New York: The Alan Guttmacher Institute.

Koonin, Lisa M., Lilo T. Strauss, Camaryn E. Chrisman, and Wilda Y. Parker. 2000. "Abortion Surveillance—United States, 1997." *Morbidity and Mortality Weekly Report, CDC Surveillance Summaries* 49(SS–11): 1–43.

World Health Organization Division of Reproductive Health. 1998. *Unsafe Abortion: Global and Regional Estimates of Incidence of and Mortality Due to Unsafe Abortion, with a Listing of Available Country Data (WHO/RHT/MSM/97.16).* Geneva: World Health Organization.

STANLEY K. HENSHAW

LEGAL ASPECTS

Around the world, the widely varying legal status of abortion reflects a range of social priorities and values, including women's health, views on religion or morality, and reproductive rights. While over 60 percent of the world's population lives in countries where abortion is a woman's choice or available on broad grounds, in many countries it is a crime and the procedure is permitted by law only under limited circumstances.

In any given country, abortion may be treated in multiple legal codes, statutes, and regulations. Where abortion is or has historically been criminalized, it is usually included in the country's penal code. Numerous other sources of law, including judicial opinions and health codes, may elaborate upon and sometimes moderate criminal laws, delineating the circumstances in which abortion may be legally performed. Abortion's legal status may also be affected by "general principles" of law, which are widely recognized legal norms used to interpret legislation. Many countries that ostensibly prohibit the procedure under all circumstances may permit life-saving abortions under the general principle of necessity, which justifies actions taken reasonably to save one's life or the life of another.

Abortion laws within one country also may vary according to jurisdiction. Several countries, including Australia, Canada, Mexico, and the United States, have legal systems at the provincial or state level as well as the national level, creating variations in abortion regulation among jurisdictions. While constitutional guarantees in Canada and the United States provide protection for women's right to choose abortion, its legality varies by state in Australia and Mexico, where no such guarantees have been recognized.

Categories of Abortion Laws

The world's abortion laws can be classified into five broad categories, reflecting varying degrees of restrictiveness. They are described below, in order from the most to the least restrictive.

1. Abortion is prohibited entirely or permitted only to save a woman's life. This category, the most restrictive, applies to 73 countries with about one-quarter of the world's population. These countries, primarily in Africa, Asia, and Latin America, include Brazil, Chile, Colombia, Ireland, Iran, Indonesia, Kenya, the Philippines, Senegal, Syria, and Uganda. In some countries in this category, including El Salvador and Guatemala, criminal prohibitions of abortion are supported by constitutional provisions protecting life from the moment of conception.

2. Abortion is permitted only when a woman's life or physical health is in jeopardy. Laws in this only slightly less restrictive category

apply in 33 countries, affecting nearly 10 percent of the world's population. Argentina, Bolivia, Peru, Morocco, Saudi Arabia, Pakistan, Thailand, Poland, Burkina Faso, and Zimbabwe are among the countries in this category. While some of the laws in this category may be interpreted to permit abortion on mental health grounds, none does so expressly.

3. Abortion is explicitly permitted on the grounds of mental as well as physical health. Laws in this category are in effect in 19 countries with just over 2.5 percent of the world's population. These include Israel, Malaysia, Portugal, Spain, Ghana, Namibia, and New Zealand. The term ''mental health'' is potentially open to broad interpretation; it can, for example, address the psychological distress associated with pregnancy resulting from rape or incest in situations where abortion on these grounds is not explicitly recognized in the law.

4. Abortion is permitted on socioeconomic grounds. These laws are in force in 14 countries accounting for nearly 21 percent of the world's population, including Great Britain (not Northern Ireland), India, Japan, and Zambia. They typically permit consideration of a woman's economic resources, her age, her marital status, and the number of children she has. Such laws tend to be interpreted liberally and, in their implementation, may differ very little from laws in category 5.

5. Abortion is permitted without restriction as to reason during a prescribed period of the pregnancy. In most countries, this period corresponds to the first 12 or 14 weeks of the pregnancy. Among the 52 nations in this category, representing about 41 percent of the world's population, are most industrialized countries, including the United States, Canada, China, Vietnam, France, Germany, Italy, the Russian Federation, and South Africa. Countries that require a woman to affirm that she is in a state of ''distress'' or ''crisis'' in order to terminate a pregnancy—like Belgium, France, and Hungary—have been included in this least restrictive category, because it is the woman herself who ultimately decides whether she qualifies for an abortion.

Additional Grounds and Requirements

Countries that fall into any of the five categories described above may permit abortion on other grounds, such as in cases of rape, incest, and fetal impairment. Likewise, a country may place additional legal restrictions on abortion. These may include requirements that women obtain permission for abortion from spouses or parents, conditions on the type of providers who may perform abortions and the facilities in which they may be provided, mandatory counseling and waiting periods, constraints on abortion advertising, and restrictions on public funding for abortion. Where son preference is widespread, some countries have adopted legal measures to prevent the practice of sex-selective abortion. India has prohibited prenatal sex determination for the purpose of sex-selective abortion and, more recently, China and Nepal have adopted similar provisions while also prohibiting sex-selective abortion itself.

Even where abortion laws are highly restrictive, criminal prosecutions of abortion providers and patients may be rare or inconsistent. Similarly, laws providing for legal abortion do not guarantee access to the service for all women who qualify under the law.

Trends over Time

Abortion laws are not static. A global trend toward liberalization began during the latter half of the twentieth century and has continued into the twenty-first century, albeit with some signs of a restrictive counter-trend in Latin America and Central Europe. Some countries, such as Malaysia and Ghana, have made incremental steps toward liberalization, maintaining abortion's criminal status while recognizing therapeutic and/or juridical grounds for abortion. Other countries, such as Nepal and Cambodia, have rejected longstanding criminal bans on abortion in favor of laws that are among the world's least restrictive.

In societies that have traditionally placed a high value on fertility, abortion is often illegal and the prohibition is supported by strong social norms. Women in these societies who seek to limit their family size because of changing economic and social conditions often turn to illegal abortions performed by poorly trained practitioners. The need to protect women's health from unsafe abortion providers has historically been the main impetus for liberalizing abortion laws. Other motivations for reducing abortion restrictions have included bringing the law into conformity with practice, responding to demographic considerations, and, most recently, recognizing women's reproductive rights.

The world is likely to see further liberalization of abortion laws in the years to come, as reform movements develop momentum in countries around the world. In national and international forums, governments have shown increasing recognition of the costs of restrictive abortion laws, which are borne not only by the women immediately affected, but also by their families, communities, and societies.

See also: *Feminist Perspectives on Population Issues; Reproductive Rights.*

BIBLIOGRAPHY

Rahman, Anika, Laura Katzive, and Stanley Henshaw. "A Global Review of Laws on Induced Abortion, 1985–1997." *International Family Planning Perspectives* 24(2): 56–64.

INTERNET RESOURCES.

United Nations Department for Economic and Social Development. 1999. *Abortion Policies: A Global Review.* <http://www.un.org/esa/population/publications/abortion/abortion.htm>.

United Nations Population Fund and Harvard Law School. 2002. *Annual Review of Population Law.* <http://www.law.harvard.edu/programs/annual_review/annual_review.htm>.

Laura Katzive
Stanley K. Henshaw

INFANT AND CHILD MORTALITY

During the twentieth century almost all countries experienced decreases in child mortality rates. How-

ever, the timing and pace of the decline varied substantially. Sustained reductions in child mortality began in the nineteenth century in Europe, North America, and Japan and continued gradually throughout the twentieth century. Major declines in other parts of the world generally began only after World War II. Mortality reductions in Asia, Latin America, and Africa were usually much more rapid than they had been in countries that began mortality declines earlier. By 1999 there were great variations in child mortality among countries. For example, although fewer than 0.5 percent of children died before the fifth birthday in Iceland, more than 33 percent died by age five in Niger.

Since the 1960s the decline in child mortality sometimes has appeared to have stagnated. One such period was 1975–1985, when many poor countries experienced severe debt crises and other problems, such as economic recovery from the oil crisis of 1973–1974. Recent evidence suggests that child mortality has continued to decline in most countries since 1980. However, during the 1990s the HIV/AIDS epidemic halted or reversed declines in child mortality in some eastern and southern African countries. For example, in Zimbabwe in the period 1990–1994 there were 80 deaths under age five per 1,000 live births. By 1999 that rate had increased to 118 deaths per 1,000 live births.

Measuring Infant and Child Mortality

Mortality rates often are calculated separately for the neonatal period (from birth to age 28 days) and the postneonatal period (from 1 to 11months of age). Infant mortality rates, which measure the probability of death in the first year of life, are the sum of neonatal and postneonatal mortality rates. The under-5 mortality rate (U5MR) refers to deaths from birth up to a child's fifth birthday. Each rate is calculated as the number of deaths in the specific age group per 1,000 live births. For example, a U5MR of 150 indicates that there are 150 deaths before the fifth birthday for every 1,000 live births, or that 15 percent of children die before age five. Estimates of infant and child mortality rates for every country are produced regularly by the United Nations Population Division.

Causes of Death and Morbidity

Causes of death vary substantially by age during the first five years of life. Deaths in the neonatal period are likely to be caused by "endogenous" conditions such as congenital malformations, chromosomal abnormalities, and complications of delivery, as well as by low birthweight. Deaths during the postneonatal period and between ages one and four years are likely to be caused by "exogenous," or external, factors such as infectious disease, accidents, and injury. As mortality rates decline, both postneonatal mortality rates and rates for one- to four-year-olds decline more rapidly than does neonatal mortality. The reason for this is that improved living standards, better health care, and public health programs have greater effects on exogenous causes of death than on endogenous causes.

As mortality rates decline, deaths under age five typically become more concentrated in the neonatal period until the infant mortality rate reaches about 20 deaths per 1,000 live births. With further reductions in infant mortality below this level this pattern generally reverses and child deaths become less clustered in the neonatal period as better prenatal, delivery, and postnatal care reduce mortality in the first month of life.

The leading causes of death for young children vary considerably, depending on the overall level of mortality. In countries with higher mortality rates infectious and parasitic diseases, especially acute respiratory infections (ARIs) and diarrheal disease, are the most important causes of death after the first month of life. In 1995 more than 50 percent of deaths among children under age five in poorer countries were due to ARIs, diarrhea, measles, or malaria. In low-mortality countries such as the United States the primary causes of death under age five are generally accidents, injuries, and perinatal conditions. In 1999 the leading causes of death in the United States were (1) in the neonatal period, congenital malformations and chromosomal abnormalities and complications of delivery, low birthweight, and a short gestation, (2) in the postneonatal period, sudden infant death syndrome (SIDS), congenital malformations and chromosomal abnormalities, accidents, and circulatory diseases, and (3) for one- to four-year-olds, accidents, congenital malformations and chromosomal abnormalities, cancers, homicide, and heart disease. In the year 2000 the cause-of-death structure in poor countries, in which infectious diseases are still a major cause of death, was very similar to that in the United States around 1900, when the U5MR was almost 200 deaths per 1,000 live births.

Reasons for Child Mortality Decline and Differential Child Mortality

The dramatic decline in mortality rates at all ages during the last 200 years in most human populations can be attributed to four broad causes: (1) increases in household income and associated improvements in nutrition, housing quality, and standards of living, (2) investments in public works (e.g., sanitation systems, garbage disposal, water quality, roads) and public health interventions (e.g., quarantines, mosquito eradication, vaccination), (3) changes in beliefs about disease causation and concomitant behavioral changes (e.g., hygiene, better treatment of illness), and (4) improvements in medical technology (e.g., pharmaceuticals, medical practices, vaccine development).

These factors all significantly reduced infant and child mortality and morbidity. Better living standards improved the diet of mothers and young children and reduced children's exposure to infectious organisms. Public works and public health programs further reduced exposure to infections and disease vectors (e.g., mosquitoes and other carriers), and vaccinations increased children's resistance to infection. Changes in beliefs about disease causation have substantially changed the way families and medical personnel care for infants and young children. For example, widespread knowledge that germs (e.g., bacteria and viruses) cause infectious diseases has led to improved hygiene particularly in food preparation for children, which has substantially reduced the prevalence of childhood diarrheal infections in low-mortality countries. Advances in medical technology have greatly improved the prevention and treatment of childhood illnesses, although this effect occurred mostly after World War II.

Extensive research has shown that socioeconomic status, particularly family income and maternal education, affects children's risk of illness and death. Poor, uneducated parents have more difficulty preventing their children from becoming ill and treating or seeking treatment for illness when it occurs. It has been suggested that socioeconomic status affects child health through five proximate determinants:

1. Maternal fertility patterns;
2. Environmental contamination;
3. Nutrient deficiency;
4. Personal illness control; and
5. Injury.

Certain maternal fertility patterns, including having children at very young (under 15 years) or very old (over 40 years) maternal ages, high parity (having had a large number of previous births), and having a child after a short time interval since the last birth (less than 24 months), appear to reduce children's survival chances, particularly when mothers are malnourished and high-quality prenatal and maternity care are not readily available.

Because infectious diseases are a major cause of child illness and death in high-mortality countries, environmental contamination in the household puts children at higher risk. Environmental contamination includes inadequate hand washing before food preparation and the feeding of children; contaminated water, clothing, and air; allowing children to put dirty objects in their mouths; and exposure to vectors of disease such as mosquitoes. Nutrient deficiency is important because malnutrition makes children more vulnerable to disease. Common types of malnutrition in poor children include inadequate caloric intake, protein-calorie malnutrition (inadequate caloric and protein intake), and micronutrient deficiencies (e.g., anemia and inadequate vitamin A intake). Breastfeeding provides an essential source of sanitary and complete nutrition for infants, particularly those who live in poverty. Personal illness control includes taking advantage of preventive measures such as immunizations, prenatal care, and malaria prophylaxis and treating illnesses promptly either through effective home remedies (such as oral rehydration therapy for the treatment of diarrhea) or by seeking help from medical personnel.

Sex Differences

In almost all populations mortality rates at all ages are lower for females than they are for males. Almost universally, girls have lower neonatal, postneonatal, and U5MR mortality rates than do boys. Research suggests that the differences are due to female genetic and biological advantages over males (Perls and Fretts 1998). Nonetheless, because the sex ratio at birth is generally about 105 male babies to 100 female babies, the number of boys in a population generally slightly exceeds the number of girls throughout childhood.

In a few cases, such as northern India, Pakistan, and Bangladesh, girls experience higher child mortality than do boys. Higher female child mortality also was observed historically in some European populations. This unusual pattern generally results from poorer care, less food, and less health care for girls than for boys. In these populations families coping with poverty may decide to invest their limited resources more heavily in sons, who are more likely to remain with the parents throughout their lives, than in daughters, who traditionally marry into other families at an early age.

The Role of Policy

Public policies have had both indirect and direct effects on child mortality and morbidity. Those with indirect effects include: (1) economic development policies that improved living standards and diet; (2) compulsory education, particularly for girls, which has changed the role of children in families and has led to higher levels of educational attainment for mothers; and (3) investments in transportation, communications, and public works projects, which have reduced the costs of transporting food, increased mobility and the diffusion of ideas and information, and provided clean water and sanitation.

International, national, local, and international agencies have attempted to improve child health directly through a wide array of programs and policies. For example, in the late 1800s and early 1900s New York and other American cities introduced milk stations where pasteurized milk was made available for children and eventually mandated commercial milk pasteurization. They also licensed midwives, implemented compulsory vaccination for schoolchildren, removed tuberculosis patients from their households, and provided widespread health education, including the promotion of breastfeeding.

Since World War II international agencies and national governments have coordinated efforts to improve children's health in African, Asian, and Latin American countries. These efforts have included improving access to health care, especially in rural areas; immunization campaigns; nutritional supplementation programs; and insecticide spraying to kill mosquitoes. In the 1980s international agencies and donors funded a series of child survival programs in low-income countries. Those programs were based on a set of "selected primary health care" measures that would have a substantial effect on child health but would not depend on the existing health care system in poor countries. Those efforts included child immunization programs, the distribution of oral rehydration packets, growth monitoring for children to detect malnutrition, and education programs to encourage breastfeeding. Some national programs also include nutritional supplementation for pregnant and breastfeeding women, malaria prophylaxis for pregnant women and children, and the distribution of "safe motherhood" kits.

An evaluation of these programs suggests that although immunization programs were often quite effective, some important causes of childhood illness and death, such as ARIs and diarrhea, cannot be reduced by selective primary health programs alone. Since the late 1990s the World Health Organization has been promoting a more comprehensive approach to improving child health in poor countries. Known as the Integrated Management of Childhood Illnesses (IMCI), this program includes three major elements: (1) improving the case management skills of health-care personnel, (2) improving overall health systems, and (3) improving family and community health practice. By June 2001 IMCI had been implemented in most Asian, Middle Eastern, and Latin American countries and in the countries of the former Soviet Union. Many African countries were also beginning implementation.

See also: *Causes of Death; Health Transition; Maternal Mortality; Mortality Decline; Mortality Differentials, by Sex.*

BIBLIOGRAPHY

Ahmad, Omar B., Alan D. Lopez, and Mie Inoue. 2000. "The Decline in Child Mortality: A Reappraisal." *Bulletin of the World Health Organization* 78(10): 1,175–1,191.

Ewbank, Douglas C., and James N. Gribble, eds. 1993. *Effects of Health Programs on Child Mortality in Sub-Saharan Africa.* Washington, D.C.: National Academy Press.

Mosley, W. Henry, and Lincoln C. Chen. 1984. "An Analytic Framework for the Study of Child Survival in Developing Countries." *Child Survival: Strategies for Research. Population and Development Review* 10(supplement): 25–48.

Pebley, Anne R. 1993. "Goals of the World Summit for Children and Their Implications for Health Policy in the 1990s." In *The Epidemiological Transition: Policy and Planning Implications for Developing Countries,* ed. James N. Gribble and Samuel H. Preston. Washington, D.C.: National Academy Press

Preston, Samuel H., and Michael R. Haines. 1991. *Fatal Years: Child Mortality in Late Nineteenth-Century America.* Princeton, NJ: Princeton University Press.

World Health Organization, Department of Child and Adolescent Health and Development (WHO/CAH). 1999. *IMCI Information.* Geneva: WHO publication WHO/CHS/CAH/98.1A Revision 1.

INTERNET RESOURCES.

Anderson, Robert N. 2001. "Leading Causes of Death for 1999." *National Vital Statistics Report* 49(3): 1–88. United States National Center for Health Statistics. <http://www.cdc.gov/nchs/data/nvsr/nvsr49/nvsr49_11.pdf>.

Hill, Kenneth, and Rohini Pande. 1997. "The Recent Evolution of Child Mortality in the Developing World." Arlington, VA: BASICS, Current Issues in Child Survival Series. <http://www.basics.org>.

Perls, Thomas T., and Ruth C. Fretts. 1998. "Why Women Live Longer Than Men." *Scientific American* June. <http://www.sciam.com/1998/0698womens/0698perls.html>.

United Nations, Population Division. 2001. *World Population Prospects: The 2000 Revision.* New York: United Nations. <http://www.un.org/esa/population/publications/publications.htm>.

ANNE R. PEBLEY

INFANTICIDE

Although the term is sometimes used to denote the willful killing of children of any age, infanticide usually refers to the newborn; infanticide occurs mostly soon after birth. There are broadly speaking two kinds of infanticide. The first is practiced as a method of family formation; the second occurs mostly outside of marriage, to avoid the shame of illegitimate births.

Infanticide as Tool of Family Formation

In Greek and Roman antiquity, the decision to kill a child was a prerogative of the family head. Evidence about its practice is largely anecdotal, often in the form of narratives about famous men who were abandoned at birth and saved from death, such as Oedipus or Romulus and Remus, the mythical founders of Rome. Typical grounds for killing a child, such as physical impairment or the unwanted sex of the child, could only be recognized after delivery. Infanticide by exposure was practiced in Sparta for eugenic reasons, and was approved for similar reasons by Aristotle. It is speculated that female infanticide was practiced widely in antiquity, although statistical evidence in the form of imbalance of the sex ratio is ambiguous. Historian John Boswell, in his study published in 1988, hypothesized that child abandonment in antiquity was a benign form of population control, allowing people who did not welcome the arrival of a child to entrust it to "the kindness of strangers" desirous of adopting it. The inference is questionable, since most children could not survive without access to human milk, and the availability of a nurse at the time a child was found could not be taken for granted, even though mythical stories often involve the intervention of animals such as goats or she-wolves.

Christian and Jewish influences were largely responsible for the condemnation of deliberately caused infant death in the West, but infanticide was widely practiced in ancient Asian societies, and its importance is attested by historical studies on Tokugawa Japan and imperial China, and by testimonies on nineteenth-century India. Female infanticide dominated, particularly among the poor, and was justified by the fact that daughters would contribute little to their family of origin, while sons were responsible for the care of parents in old age and for performing familial rites. Neglect, harsh treatment, and preferential male feeding led to the higher mortality of girl babies, and might be considered a form of infanticide.

Infanticide to Conceal a Birth

The second type of infanticide, practiced by unmarried mothers right after delivery in order to avoid shame, prevailed in Western countries and is still encountered in the early twenty-first century. In the past, concealing a pregnancy and killing or abandoning the infant was the most readily available method of "birth control" for unmarried women. However, its effect on population numbers must have been small. In most countries of Europe, legal codes dating back to the Middle Ages prescribed punishment by death for women convicted of infanticide, but in practice the penalty was typically less severe. In the sixteenth and seventeenth centuries, the authorities of several countries passed legislation designed to regulate the unruly poor and impose strict norms of morality. In England, for example, a serious attempt was made to control extramarital relations and deter bastardy as a way of avoiding a potential burden on local finances. In Germany, unmarried mothers were mostly seduced maidservants, who were banished from the community.

Concealing the pregnancy and the birth was a desperate reaction. Royal edicts in France and England created a presumption of infanticide, punishable by death, when an unreported extra-marital pregnancy resulted in miscarriage or death of the infant. By the eighteenth century the severity of the penalty seemed to deter juries from convicting a woman whose child had died. In most countries, there was a relaxation of attitudes, and systems aiming at the protection of infants rather than at the punishment of mothers were set in place.

Foundling Hospitals

The first foundling hospitals were created in Italy as early as the thirteenth century. Some were eventually created in France too, and "tours" (revolving doors where a child could be abandoned without any questions asked) were installed in churches and hospitals. It is sometimes assumed that the extraordinarily high mortality rate of children in foundling hospitals amounted to the institutionalization of infanticide, but it is a more plausible explanation that the institutions failed in their mission because of the technical difficulty of keeping children alive without reliable access to a supply of maternal breast milk. Abandonments grew in numbers together with the institutions designed to cope with the practice. Paris in the late eighteenth century, with a population of half a million, admitted more than 7,000 foundlings a year, but at least a third of those came from out of town. By the beginning of the nineteenth century, many large Western cities had institutions for foundlings recording sizable populations (there were between three and four thousand foundlings per year in New York in the 1870s) and a mortality well over 50 percent of admissions was common.

The Italian system in the early nineteenth century was characterized by a multiplicity of "tours" even in rural churches, and foundling homes with very high mortality. Unmarried mothers would nurse children other than their own before they were reintegrated in their communities, where the birth would have been kept secret. Men rarely assumed responsibility for their illegitimate offspring. In English-speaking countries, however, the responsibility for the care of illegitimate children was to the extent possible shifted to the mother and father of the child.

Demographic Effects

The demographic impact of infanticide was probably small. Some writers have suggested that it constituted an important check on population growth, but this is based on assumptions rather than recorded facts, in an area that is notoriously difficult to investigate and document. Actual condemnations for infanticide remained infrequent in all periods, and were mainly restricted to extra-marital relations. The controversy concerning the quantitative importance of infanticide hinges on the frequency of the practice among married couples. There it took the form of neglect, making it difficult to distinguish from high mortality from poverty and natural causes. The church and civil authorities expressed concern about overlaying (the accidental smothering of infants sleeping with their parents) and other accidental deaths, but it may well be that they were implicitly accusing poor parents of responsibility for deaths that in the twenty-first century would be blamed on unidentified causes, such as the sudden infant death syndrome. There is little evidence of differential female mortality in this context.

See also: *Birth Control, History of; Induced Abortion: History; Sex Selection.*

BIBLIOGRAPHY

Boswell, John. 1988. *The Kindness of Strangers: The Abandonment of Children in Western Europe from Late Antiquity to the Renaissance.* New York: Pantheon Books.

Fuchs, Rachel G. 1984. *Abandoned Children: Foundlings and Child Welfare in Nineteenth-Century France.* Albany: State University of New York Press.

Hoffer, Peter C. and N.E.H. Hull. 1981. *Murdering Mothers: Infanticide in England and New England 1558–1803.* New York: New York University Press.

Kertzer, David I. 1993. *Sacrificed for Honor. Italian Infant Abandonment and the Politics of Reproductive Control.*. Boston: Beacon Press.

Rublack, Ulinka. 1999. *The Crimes of Women in Early Modern Germany.* Oxford: Clarendon Press.

Etienne van de Walle

INFERTILITY

Infertility—the biologically-based inability to conceive, also referred to in the literature as infecundity—is of enormous concern to those immediately affected. In affluent societies it is the focus of intensive remedial efforts by physicians and medical researchers. In the developing world, it has been relatively neglected: attention to fertility issues has been overwhelmingly directed to the problem of limiting the number of births. This imbalance only began to change with the shift in family planning programs toward an emphasis on reproductive health, as signaled in the *Programme of Action* of the 1994 United Nations International Conference on Population and Development. Reproductive health care, according to this statement, includes safe delivery, prevention and appropriate treatment of infertility, abortion, and treatment of reproductive health conditions. Each of the conditions included within reproductive health care affects infertility.

Definitions and Measurement

The clinical definition of infertility is the absence of conception after 12 months of regular, unprotected intercourse. The World Health Organization (WHO) definition is the same except that it specifies a period of 24 months. (The discrepancy occurs because in clinical practice it is important to initiate treatment as early as possible, while in research it is important to reduce the number of fertile women falsely classified as infertile.)

Demographers define infertility as the inability of a sexually-active woman who is not using contraceptive methods to have a live birth. Demographers have shifted the endpoint from conceptions to live births because it is difficult to collect complete data about conceptions in population-based studies. The fertility surveys that are typically used in demographic analyses of infertility usually contain complete birth histories but no information about abortions and stillbirths. Because it is difficult to assess exposure from such data, demographic estimates of infertility need to be based on relatively long periods of exposure to childbearing. Based on simulation studies, demographers recommend using seven years of exposure to measure childlessness and five years to measure subsequent infertility (that is, to be considered infertile, a non-contracepting, sexually-active woman who has a child must not have another birth within five years, counting from the month after the last birth). The proportion of women subsequently infertile at five-year age intervals provides a measure of the age pattern of infertility in the population.

Infertility is measured from information about the woman, and infertility of the woman cannot be distinguished from infertility of the couple. The cause of infertility may be the infertility of the woman's sexual partner(s).

Infertility may be divided into primary infertility, which denotes infertility of women who have never conceived, and secondary infertility, which denotes infertility of women who have conceived at least once. According to the demographic definitions, primary infertility is approximated by childlessness and secondary infertility by the proportion subsequently infertile measured for women with children.

Infertility in Societies with Little Contraception

On average, less than 3 percent of all couples are biologically unable to have children: primary infertility is relatively rare in most populations. In terms of country averages, the proportion of currently married women ages 25 to 49, in first union, married over five years that are childless ranges from 1.7 to 2.5 percent in Asia, from 0.9 to 2.8 in Latin America, from 2.2 to 2.8 in North Africa, and from 0.9 to 2.3 in sub-Saharan Africa.

Secondary infertility varies over a wider range. Most estimates of its level refer to sub-Saharan Africa, where some countries have particularly high prevalence. For instance, among women aged 20 to 44, secondary infertility is estimated at 25 percent in Central African Republic and 21 percent in Mozambique; in contrast, the level is 5 percent in Togo. The

African data indicate that secondary infertility is consistently as high or higher in urban areas in comparison to the corresponding rural areas. Furthermore, women married more than once, women in polygamous unions, and women who initiated sexual relations in their early teenage years tend to have higher infertility, suggesting that sexual practices and sexually transmitted diseases (STDs) are main causes of infertility in the region. Further evidence on the role of STDs comes from a 1979–1984 WHO multi-center study of infertile couples, which recorded a two- to three-fold higher level of bilateral tubal occlusion or other tubal damage in sub-Saharan Africa than in Asia, the Eastern Mediterranean, and Latin America. This finding suggests a higher incidence of infertility in sub-Saharan Africa caused by infections from STDs, such as chlamydia and gonorrhea, and complications following delivery and abortion (induced abortion is illegal in most of Africa). Hence, in sub-Saharan Africa the causes of secondary infertility are often *acquired*: they result from infectious factors that can be prevented. Primary infertility is modest relative to secondary infertility, probably because sub-Saharan women start childbearing early and they have one or more children before they become infertile.

Infertility in Societies with Widespread Contraceptive Use and Later-Age Childbearing

It is not possible to provide accurate country-level estimates of infertility in populations with widespread contraception, because in these societies fertile women have the number of children they want, and subsequently they use contraception to prevent further unwanted births. As a result, samples of non-contraceptors contain disproportionate numbers of women with lower fecundability and women who have postponed childbearing to older ages. Estimates of the prevalence of infertility in contracepting populations should therefore be treated with caution. In the United States, the 1995 National Survey of Family Growth found that about 10 percent of women reported fertility problems (defined as at least 36 months preceding the survey without a pregnancy), a slight increase over the 1970s and 1980s. The higher proportion of older women trying to have a child in 1995 may explain this trend in infertility.

American women seeking infertility services are a select group that is more likely to be married, to have a high income, and to have private health insurance. Most of these women receive low-technology interventions. With use of modern technologies, it would be possible to provide genetically related offspring to 80 percent of infertile couples, and pregnancy to a further 10 to 15 percent using donated gametes. However, worldwide only a small fraction of infertile couples can afford such treatment.

See also: *Childlessness; Fecundity; Reproductive Technologies.*

BIBLIOGRAPHY

Arnold, Fred, and Ann K. Blanc. 1990. *Fertility Levels and Trends.* Columbia, MD: Demographic and Health Surveys, Institute for Resource Development/Macro Systems, Inc.

Bentley, Gillian R., and C. G. Nicholas Mascie-Taylor, eds. 2000. *Infertility in the Modern World: Present and Future Prospects.* Cambridge, Eng.: Cambridge University Press.

Cates, Willard, Robert T. Rolfs, and Sevgi O. Aral 1990. "Sexually Transmitted Diseases, Pelvic Inflammatory Disease, and Infertility: An Epidemiologic Update." *Epidemiologic Review* 12: 199–220.

Cates, Willard, Tim M. M. Farley, and P. J. Rowe. 1985. "Worldwide Patterns of Infertility: Is Africa Different?" *Lancet* II: 596–598.

International Conference on Population and Development. 1995. "Programme of Action of the 1994 International Conference on Population and Development." *Population and Development Review* 21: 187–215 and 437–463.

Larsen, Ulla. 2000. "Primary and Secondary Infertility in Sub-Saharan Africa." *International Journal of Epidemiology* 29: 285–291.

Larsen, Ulla, and Jane Menken. 1989. "Measuring Sterility from Incomplete Birth Histories." *Demography* 26: 185–201.

Stephen, Elizabeth H., and Anjani Chandra. 2000. "Use of Infertility Services in the United States: 1995." *Family Planning Perspectives* 32(3): 132–137.

ULLA LARSEN

INFLUENZA

Influenza (flu) is an important cause of morbidity and mortality. Flu is caused by infection with the influenza virus, a member of the Orthomyxoviridae family. Infection leads to illness, typically lasting a week, characterized by fever, sore throat, cough, headache, runny nose, and fatigue. Mild cases of flu can result in the common cold. In the medically more severe cases of flu, and in all fatal cases, a secondary pneumonia arises as a complication.

Flu is spread from person to person through sneezing and coughing. Influenza is zoonotic, that is, it has an animal origin, with avian and porcine strains able to jump species. The flu genome consists of eight single strands of RNA, which means that new strains can arise whenever an individual is infected with two existing strains. To be effective, flu vaccines, formulated on the basis of surveillance of early cases, must be given every year because of these constantly-changing strains.

Influenza is an epidemic disease in several respects. There is great year-to-year variability in morbidity, mortality, and incidence, and more intense periods are labeled as epidemics. New strains spread in epidemic style across regions, documented in a rich body of work by medical geographers, using both historical and modern data. There are occasional pandemics—severe outbreaks, global in scope; twentieth century pandemics occurred in 1918, 1946–1947, 1957, and 1968.

Age Profiles of Mortality

Figure 1 shows the age profile of death rates (per 100,000 population) for influenza and pneumonia (combined) for males and females in the United States in the years 1900, 1918, 1939, and 1998. Since fatal cases of influenza involve pneumonia, it is customary for statistical bureaus to merge influenza and pneumonia in published vital statistics. The patterns in the figure illustrate notable aspects of influenza demography and yield insight into mortality patterns more generally. To permit comparisons, all four panels in the figure are drawn to the same scale, with a horizontal rule across each panel at a mortality level of 100 per 100,000.

The influenza mortality rates exemplify three major mortality age patterns, named after letters of the alphabet: U, W, and J. In 1900, the pattern is U-shaped (sometimes called V-shaped), with peak

FIGURE 1

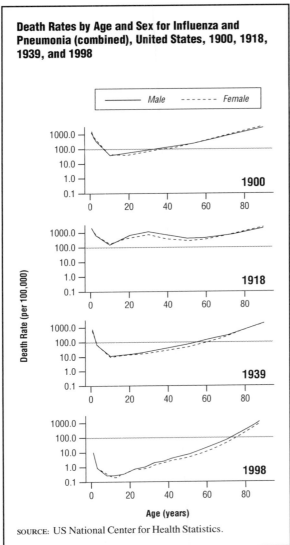

Death Rates by Age and Sex for Influenza and Pneumonia (combined), United States, 1900, 1918, 1939, and 1998

SOURCE: US National Center for Health Statistics.

mortality at the upper and lower ranges of the age distribution. Though influenza occurs at all ages, mortality is concentrated among the youngest and oldest. A similar pattern is seen in 1939, except that the base of the U (but not the top prongs) has descended to a lower level and remains below the 100 per 100,000 line until a much later age. The 1939 panel represents the end of the pre-antibiotic era. Flu, being a viral disease, is not treatable with antibiotics, but secondary pneumonias often involve or are exacerbated by bacterial coinfection, which can be treated with antibiotics.

The mortality pattern in 1918 is completely atypical, even for a pandemic. Due to that year's epidemic of hypervirulent influenza, the pattern is W-shaped, with a peak at middle age in addition to peaks at infancy and old age. Such a pattern is unusual among biological causes of death: tuberculosis is perhaps the closest parallel. The entire mortality curve in 1918 lies above the 100 per 100,000 line, reflecting the severity of the epidemic. The male excess death rate, in absolute terms, was also exceptionally high in 1918, particularly at the middle-age peak of the W-pattern. The leading explanation for the decline in death rates above age 35, which gives rise to the W shape, is that at least one flu strain that was circulating in the late nineteenth century was similar to the 1918 strain, and had imparted partial immunity to those who, by 1918, were above age 35; in demographic terms, it is a cohort-effect explanation.

Since 1950, influenza death rates in developed countries have declined more at young ages than among the elderly, transforming the U shape into a J shape, as seen in the 1998 data.

The 1918 Epidemic

The 1918 influenza epidemic was an important event not only in the history of influenza, but also in world demographic history. Usual estimates are 20 to 40 million deaths worldwide, with great uncertainty because much of the world did not have vital registration in 1918. By the measure of its death toll and its global reach, it was the biggest epidemic of any disease in the twentieth century. In the United States, the estimate is 550,000 deaths (0.5% of the population), with about one-fourth of the population having had recognizable cases of flu. The 1918 epidemic is sometimes called the "Spanish flu." It is not thought to have had a Spanish origin, but since Spain, as a neutral power, did not censor newspapers during World War I, early accounts of the flu came from Spain. There is debate about whether the epidemic began in the United States and then spread to Europe and the rest of the world, or vice versa. Late twentieth and early twenty-first century studies, using modern laboratory techniques and preserved tissue samples, have focused on deciphering the molecular basis for the virulence of the 1918 strain, so far without conclusive results.

There is a hypothesis, based on data from the United States, that the 1918 influenza epidemic had a selective effect. Specifically, the suggestion is that many of those who died of flu in 1918 already had chronic illness (most notably, tuberculosis, highly prevalent at the time). The supporting evidence is that after 1918, death rates, especially from tuberculosis, dropped relative to their pre-1918 trend. The logic is that if the 1918 victims had already been sicker than average, then the post-1918 population would be healthier and therefore death rates should decline. It is rare to see such selection effects in the population at large, but the magnitude of the 1918 epidemic was large enough to be exploited as a natural experiment (i.e., a natural event which mimics an actual experiment in certain respects).

As noted, there has been little reduction in influenza and pneumonia death rates above age 80, in contrast to younger ages, which have seen dramatic declines. With the worldwide population aging, influenza is certain to remain an important cause of death for many years to come. Moreover, the possibility of another pandemic of hypervirulent influenza, comparable to that of 1918, cannot be ruled out.

See also: *Diseases, Infectious; Epidemics.*

BIBLIOGRAPHY

Crosby, Alfred W. 1989. *America's Forgotten Pandemic: The Influenza of 1918.* Cambridge, Eng.: Cambridge University Press.

Kilbourne, Edwin D. 1987. *Influenza.* New York: Plenum.

Kolata, Gina. 1999. *Flu: The Story of the Great Influenza Pandemic of 1918 and the Search for the Virus That Caused It.* New York: Farrar, Straus and Giroux.

Noymer, Andrew, and Michel Garenne. 2000. "The 1918 Influenza Epidemic's Effects on Sex Differentials in Mortality in the United States." *Population and Development Review* 26(3): 565–581.

Pyle, Gerald F. 1986. *The Diffusion of Influenza: Patterns and Paradigms.* Totowa, NJ: Rowman & Littlefield.

ANDREW NOYMER

INTERGENERATIONAL TRANSFERS

An intergenerational transfer is the transmission of something from a member of one generation to a member of another. Unlike an exchange, loan, or purchase, there is no expectation that the recipient will repay the giver either directly or indirectly. Often, this refers to a transfer across generations of kin, for example from a grandparent to a grandchild. However, generation is a loosely-defined concept, and it can simply mean a different age group; a public sector intergenerational transfer could be said to occur between a 25-year-old taxpayer and a 17-year-old student in a public high school.

Although transfers do not involve a quid pro quo between the giver and the receiver, they may instead involve an understanding or at least an expectation that the recipient will make a similar transfer to someone in a symmetric position. For example, children may receive transfers from their parents with an implicit understanding that they will in turn make similar transfers to their own children when they are adults. Alternatively, adult children may support their elderly parents with the implicit understanding that their children will support them in their old age.

Intra-family intergenerational transfers are important in all societies. Examples are child-rearing costs borne by parents; costs of higher education borne by parents; end-of-life bequests to children or grandchildren; economic support of elderly parents by their children; time spent by adult children caring for or managing the care of their elderly parents. But significant intergenerational transfers can also be mediated through the public sector. Examples are tax receipts used to provide public education, state-run pension schemes, and other publicly financed payments or in-kind services to particular groups. In the United States, Social Security, Medicare, Medicaid, and various programs providing child benefits, welfare payments, and unemployment insurance exemplify such arrangements. Still other intergenerational transfers are imposed indirectly by the public sector, such as when governments incur debt today for consumption-type expenditures (rather than capital items)—debt which must be repaid or serviced by future generations.

Why Study Intergenerational Transfers?

While intergenerational transfers are pervasive in all societies, with the rise of the modern welfare state, there has been an increase in public sector transfers and a decrease in private transfers. Study of these transfers is important for many reasons, as they affect individuals, families, and whole populations.

Transfers have a major influence on the interpersonal distribution of income, because a high proportion of total household income is reallocated from the earner to some other person, either through public or private channels. Beyond the distribution of income, transfers are important in the study of families. A major component of the costs of rearing children is borne by parents. Although the level of such transfers is subject, within certain limits, to parents' discretion, they constitute a crucial element in parental fertility decisions. If parents intend to leave a bequest for each child, the level of these intended bequests is also a part of the cost of child rearing. Decisions about the level of private costs, or the size of the transfer to children, also determine the human capital of the next generation. The greater share of elder care is also provided by relatives, rather than by alternative institutional arrangements.

A further reason to study transfers is that the patterns of intergenerational transfers, both public and private, are a major determinant of the financial consequences of changing population age distributions, and specifically of population aging.

Private transfers can add to, substitute for, or be crowded out by public transfers. To design policy, and to understand the impact of existing age-based or need-based policies, it is essential to understand and quantify these processes of substitution and crowding out. In particular, the interaction between public and private transfers depends in part on the motives for private transfers—for example whether they are motivated by altruism (in which case there should be a high degree of substitution and crowding out, because altruists care about the well-being of another person rather than about the transfer itself) or by exchange (in which case there should be very little crowding out, because there is an obligation to repay).

Patterns of intergenerational transfers in traditional societies may play a key role in shaping fertility decisions and trigger the onset of secular trends (as is argued, for example, in John Caldwell's theory of the demographic transition). Patterns of transfers in preindustrial societies also may play an important role in evolutionary processes affecting fertility and mortality. Theorists suggest, for example, that the elderly contribute to the reproductive fitness of their children and grandchildren, which may explain why humans have such long post-reproductive survival.

Theorists like Laurence Kotlikoff and Lawrence Summers argue that the desire to make familial intergenerational transfers, particularly bequests, may be the dominant motive for saving, investment, and capital formation in industrial countries—more so than the life cycle saving motive.

Public Sector Transfers

Development of the modern theory of intergenerational transfers began with a seminal paper by Paul Samuelson published in 1958. Samuelson showed that in a world without durable goods, in which workers wished to provide for consumption in old age, the competitive market for borrowing and lending would lead to a negative interest rate with high consumption when young, and very little consumption when old. Life-cycle utility would be correspondingly low. However, if the population enacted a binding social compact according to which workers would transfer income to the old, without any expectation of being repaid by *them*, but with the assurance that they would be similarly treated when they were old, then consumption could be more evenly distributed across the life cycle, and life-cycle utility would be higher. In place of the negative rate of interest provided by the market outcome, people would earn through the transfer system an implicit rate of return equal to the population growth rate (plus, in a more realistic context, the rate of productivity growth). Thus intergenerational transfers supported by a social compact could make everyone in every generation better off.

Systems of this sort are called pay-as-you-go, or PAYGO, because the obligations created are not backed up by assets accumulated in a fund; rather, future payments of benefits come from future contributions by future workers. Such a system is politically easy to start—at least when the age distribution of the population is such that the size of the working-age population is much larger than that of the old-age population (hence modest per-capita contributions by the former can provide generous per-capita benefits for the latter)—because all current and future generations apparently gain. These systems are very painful to end, however, because if the compact is terminated the last generations of workers end up making transfers to the elderly but receive nothing in their own old age. At any time during its operation, such a transfer system has an implicit debt that is owed to those who have already paid in, thus acquiring an entitlement for later support.

Traditional familial support systems for the elderly are PAYGO transfers, but are sustained by individual values and social norms instead of a formal social compact (although private transfers can sometimes be reinforced by law, as is the case in Singapore). Public pension systems in much of the industrial world, including the U.S. Social Security system, are operated on a pay-as-you-go basis. The transition from a family support system to a public system is relatively painless, since the implicit debt to be repaid is just transferred from one system to the other.

Slow population growth and rising life expectancy make both familial and public pension systems much less attractive compared to such systems in a situation when population is growing rapidly and expectation of life in old age is short. Nonetheless, despite growing dissatisfaction with such arrangements generated by the emergence of demographic conditions marked by slow population growth and longer life expectancies, and the appeal of potentially higher rates of return available from other kinds of investments, the systems cannot be shut down or converted to privately-funded systems without repaying the implicit debt. For families, such a shift would mean that one generation would have to support both its aging parents and save for its own retirement. For current public sector programs, the existing implicit debts are typically huge—often one, two, or three times the size of the country's annual gross domestic product—and often larger than the existing explicit government debt. Nonetheless, a number of countries, mostly in Latin America and most notably Chile, have made or initiated the transition to a funded system.

In the late 1980s Gary S. Becker and Kevin M. Murphy developed an influential theoretical construct that would link the provision of public education and public pensions, so as to bring about an efficient level of investment in education when parents' altruism is insufficient to ensure such a level, and institutions that would enforce repayment of intergenerational familial loans do not exist. The introduction of a modified public pension system would compel the children who received the education to repay their parents through their contributions to the system, and no generation would get a windfall gain or suffer a loss.

Family Intergenerational Transfers

Transfers to and from children and the demographic aspects of such transfers are discussed in a substantial literature. Caldwell argued that "in all primitive and nearly all traditional societies the net flow [of wealth] is from child to parent" (1976), and that this net flow motivated high fertility. At some point, labeled the "great divide," the direction of flow reverses as children become costly rather than assets in modern industrial settings. At that point, in narrowly economic terms it would be rational to have no children; positive fertility results from the psychic utility children represent for parents. Caldwell's wealth flows theory has been criticized by behavioral ecologists, who argue that species have evolved to maximize reproductive fitness by transferring resources from parent to child, and that parents would not use children merely as a means to supply family labor or to support them in old age. Arguing in this vein, Hillard Kaplan reported in 1994 that in a hunter-gatherer group in the Amazon Basin, even the oldest members of the population make transfers to their children and grandchildren, and the more of these they have, the greater the transfers they make. Thus transfers are downward rather than upward, counter to Caldwell's claim. Ronald Lee also found that in agricultural and pre-agricultural societies, the net direction of total transfers is strongly downward across age, from older to younger. In modern industrial societies, however, new institutional arrangements reverse the direction of net intergenerational flow of resources, in part reflecting the generosity of public pension and health-care transfers to the elderly, and in part a result of population aging which greatly increases the proportion of elderly in the population. Even in modern industrial societies, however, *private* net flows within the family are downwards.

At the micro-level, there is extensive theoretical and empirical work on transfers to children, since transfers are equivalent to investments in child quality—a crucial element in fertility theory. There is also an extensive literature on the motivations for familial intergenerational transfers (see, for example,

Cox, 1987). A debated issue is whether apparent altruistic intrafamilial transfers actually involve an implicit quid pro quo, and, therefore, are best interpreted as exchanges. Empirical findings shedding light on the answer are mixed.

See also: *Age Structure and Dependency; Caldwell, John C.; Evolutionary Demography.*

BIBLIOGRAPHY

Becker, Gary S., and Kevin M. Murphy 1988. "The Family and the State." *Journal of Law and Economics,* April: 1–18.

Caldwell, John C. 1976. "Toward a Restatement of Demographic Transition Theory." *Population and Development Review* 2: 321–366.

Cox, Donald. 1987. "Motives for Private Income Transfers." *Journal of Political Economy* 93: 508–546.

Kaplan, Hillard. 1994. "Evolutionary and Wealth Flows Theories of Fertility: Empirical Tests and New Models." *Population and Development Review* 20: 753–791.

Kotlikoff, Laurence J., and Lawrence H. Summers. 1981. "The Role of Intergenerational Transfers in Aggregate Capital Accumulation." *Journal of Political Economy* 89: 706–732.

Lee, Ronald. 2000. "A Cross-Cultural Perspective on Intergenerational Transfers and the Economic Life Cycle." In *Sharing the Wealth: Demographic Change and Economic Transfers between Generations,* ed. Andrew Mason and Georges Tapinos. Oxford: Oxford University Press.

Samuelson, Paul A. 1958. "An Exact Consumption-Loan Model of Interest With or Without the Social Contrivance of Money." *Journal of Political Economy* 66: 467–482.

RONALD LEE

INTERNAL MIGRATION

Internal migration is defined as a change in permanent residence, typically of a year or more in duration, within the boundaries of a country.

Long-Distance Migration and Residential Mobility

A distinction is made between long-distance migration and short-distance migration in which the latter is referred to by the more specialized term *residential mobility.* Long-distance moves typically are operationalized as movement across broader areas, such as metropolitan areas or states and in some cases counties. They reflect movement across labor markets and often are associated with changes in economic conditions in those larger areas. Residential mobility typically occurs within the same labor market and is associated more frequently with neighborhood and housing considerations. The distinction is important because the two types of internal migration occur at different frequencies, are associated with different kinds of explanations, and often display different selectivities with respect to individual social and economic attributes (Speare, Goldstein, and Frey 1975; Long 1988).

Data Sources

In the United States and in most developed countries the basic sources for measuring both kinds of migration derive from nationwide censuses, population registers, and large surveys. In several European countries with population register traditions (e.g., the Netherlands and the Scandinavian countries) annual migration measures for localities can be traced back for many decades.

In the United States the decennial census provides the most comprehensive source of migration data based on the five-year fixed-interval migration question ("Where did you live five years ago?") that has been included in censuses since 1960 and also was included in the 1940 census. This question allows the calculation of a variety of migration measures, such as mobility-incidence rates, and measures of in-migration, out-migration, net migration, and migration streams for places, counties, metropolitan areas, and states (Shryock 1964). These measures can be cross-classified by an array of social and economic attributes available from the census and can be used to ascertain selective migration patterns.

These census data are limited by the restricted reference period of five years before each decennial census. For example, the 2000 Census permits the assessment of migration over the 1995–2000 interval but not over the 1990–1995 interval. Another U.S. Census item relevant to measuring internal migration over longer historical periods is the question on the respondent's state of birth. This question has appeared in every decennial census since 1850 and can be used to assess long-term and current internal moves across states as well as "return migration" when cross-classified by current residence and residence five years before the census (Long 1988).

The U.S. Census Bureau's *Current Population Survey* is another important source of migration data. It contains a fixed-interval one-year migration item and is used to assess time-series patterns of migration frequency and selectivity with respect to social and economic differentials. Time-series estimates of internal migration at the county and state level also are produced by the U.S. Census Bureau. Beyond these government sources, several national panel surveys conducted by universities and research organizations have been used to infer migration patterns for specific groups. In addition, administrative records collected for other purposes (e.g., Internal Revenue Service data) can be employed to examine migration patterns.

Reasons for Moving: The U.S. Case

The long-distance/short-distance migration dichotomy is reflected clearly in the frequency of movement in the United States Because long-distance, inter–labor market migration occurs only a few times during the life course (e.g., the move to college, the first job, retirement), the annual rate of interstate migration is relatively low (3.3 percent in the period 1999–2000) in comparison to the annual rate of movement within counties (9%). Overall, about 16 percent of the U.S. population moves in a given year, and only about one in five of those moves is across state lines.

The preponderance of local moves is a response to household and family changes as well as changing needs in regard to neighborhoods and homes. Among within-county moves in 1999–2000, 64 percent were for housing-related reasons and 26.5 percent were for family-related reasons. Only 6 percent of those moves were motivated by work and job-transfer considerations. In contrast, 47 percent of moves between counties undertaken by persons with postcollege training are related to work (see Figure 1) (Schacter 2001). Climate and natural amenities are becoming increasingly important in motivating long-distance moves, especially among the retired population (Gober 1993).

By far the strongest selectivity differential associated with both long-distance migration and residential mobility is a person's age. The incidence of making each kind of move is highest for persons in their early to middle twenties and then declines precipitously during the thirties and forties, with a sometimes small upturn in the early retirement years. Among persons age 20 to 24 in the United States about one-third make a move of some kind in any given year (see Figure 2) This is twice the overall migration rate for all ages combined and reflects important life-cycle transitions such as moving to a college or to a new job (among long-distance migrants), marriage, and moving out of the parental home (among local movers).

Most other selectivity differentials are more specific to either long-distance or short-distance movers. Among long-distance movers there is strong educational selectivity in movement. College graduates, who are likely to be in a national labor market, show higher rates of movement than do those with lesser educational attainment. Among local movers there is a large difference between homeowners and renters: Homeowners tend to form long-term economic bonds to a particular location.

The recent influx of foreign-born populations to the United States has had both direct and indirect effects on internal migration. Locally, foreign-born residents tend to make several additional internal moves after they initially settle. Indirectly, the influx of foreign-born populations in selected "port of entry" metropolitan areas has tended to precipitate out-migration among established native-born residents (Frey 2003).

Explanations for Migration

Explanations for migration can be divided into two essential classes: those which explain individual decision making and those which explain aggregate migration patterns across geographic regions. Individual decision-making models of long-distance migration tend to be formulated around economists' cost-benefit model. This model assumes a rational decision-making process that weighs the economic and noneconomic costs and benefits of making a move. It has to be modified for particular population groups such as retirees and the college-bound population and for individuals in particular statuses, such as single-earner husband–wife families. These mobility models of decision making make a distinc-

FIGURE 1

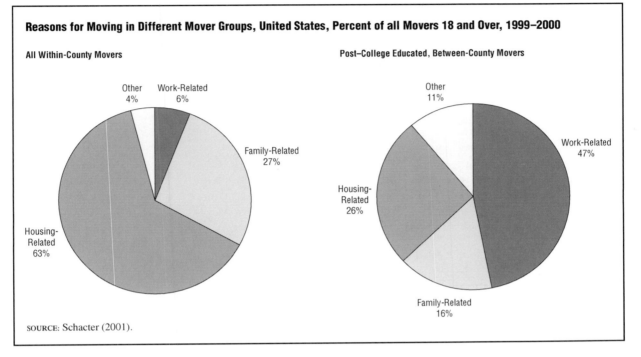

Reasons for Moving in Different Mover Groups, United States, Percent of all Movers 18 and Over, 1999–2000

All Within-County Movers

Other 4%
Work-Related 6%
Family-Related 27%
Housing-Related 63%

Post–College Educated, Between-County Movers

Other 11%
Work-Related 47%
Housing-Related 26%
Family-Related 16%

SOURCE: Schacter (2001).

tion between "the decision to move" and "the choice of destination" in which the former decision implies some kind of disruption in family status or housing need (Speare, Goldstein, and Frey 1975).

Aggregate models of long-distance migration can be used to explain net migration levels for specific areas, migration streams across pairs, and matrices of areas. The latter models tend to have a strong geographic base related to the classic "gravity model," in which migration is directly related to the number of opportunities at a destination but inversely related to the distance between the origin and the destination (Speare, Goldstein, and Frey 1975). This model has been modified to take into account various economic and noneconomic opportunities. Aggregate models that explain net migration as a dependent variable take both cross-sectional and time-series forms (Greenwood 1981).

Consequences of Internal Migration

The consequences of internal migration have been addressed from a variety of disciplinary perspectives. The demographic consequences of internal migration processes for spatial population change are treated in a formal demographic model developed by Andrei Rogers (Rogers 1995). Rogers and his associates at the International Institute for Applied

Systems Analysis also have developed techniques, including model age–migration schedules, for making population projections of subnational areas that take explicit account of internal migration streams.

See also: *Migration Models; Resettlement; Temporary Migration; Thomas, Dorothy Swaine; Urbanization.*

BIBLIOGRAPHY

DeJong, Gordon, and Robert W. Gardner, eds. 1981. *Migration Decision Making: Multidisciplinary Approaches to Microlevel Studies in Developed and Developing Countries.* New York: Pergamon Press.

Frey, William H. 2003. *Who Moves Where: A 2000 Census Survey.* Washington, D.C.: Population Reference Bureau.

Gober, Patricia. 1993. "Americans on the Move." *Population Bulletin* 48(3). Washington, D.C.: Population Reference Bureau.

Greenwood, Michael J. 1981. *Migration and Economic Growth in the United States.* New York: Academic Press.

Long, Larry. 1988. *Migration and Residential Mobility in the United States.* New York: Russell Sage Foundation.

FIGURE 2

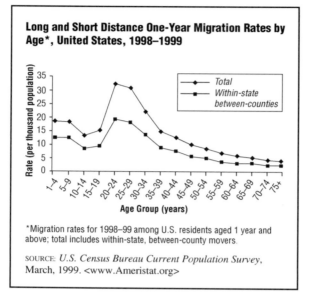

Long and Short Distance One-Year Migration Rates by Age*, United States, 1998–1999

*Migration rates for 1998–99 among U.S. residents aged 1 year and above; total includes within-state, between-county movers.

SOURCE: *U.S. Census Bureau Current Population Survey,* March, 1999. <www.Ameristat.org>

Rogers, Andrei. 1995. *Multiregional Demography: Principles, Methods, and Extensions.* New York: Wiley.

Schacter, Jason. 2001. "Why People Move: Exploring the March 2000 Current Population Survey." *Current Population Reports* P23–204. Washington, D.C.: U.S. Census Bureau (May).

Shryock, Henry S. 1964. *Population Mobility within the United States.* Chicago: Community and Family Studies Center, University of Chicago.

Speare, Alden, Jr., Sidney Goldstein, and William H. Frey. 1975. *Residential Mobility, Migration and Metropolitan Change.* Cambridge, MA: Ballinger.

WILLIAM H. FREY

INTERNATIONAL MIGRATION

The history of international migration over the last five centuries can be divided into four periods.

The Four Periods of Migration

During the mercantile period, from 1500 to 1800, the dominant flows were out of Europe and stemmed from processes of colonization and economic growth under mercantile capitalism. Over the course of 300 years, Europeans came to inhabit large portions of the Americas and some portions of Africa and Asia in numbers that were modest but sufficient to establish dominion.

During that period European emigrants fell into three classes: a relatively large number of agrarian settlers, a smaller number of administrators and artisans, and an even smaller number of plantation entrepreneurs. Although the number of Europeans involved in plantation agriculture was low, this sector had a profound impact on the size and composition of populations in the Americas, since the most important source of plantation labor was African slaves, some 10 million of whom were forcibly exported to the New World before the closing of the slave trade in the early 1800s.

The industrial period began early in the nineteenth century with the economic development of Europe and the spread of industrialism to former colonies in the New World. From 1800 to 1929, 48 million people left Europe in search of new lives in the Americas and the area now known as Oceania. (Many of them eventually returned; thus, net migration was appreciably smaller.) Among those emigrants 85 percent went to five destinations—the United States, Canada, Argentina, Australia, and New Zealand—with the United States receiving 60 percent. Key sending countries were Great Britain, Italy, Norway, Portugal, Spain, and Sweden, all of which exported a significant share of their population increase during the period of industrialization.

Mass emigration from Europe was brought to a halt in 1914 by the outbreak of World War I and definitively ended by the economic crash of 1929. The years 1930–1960 were a period of limited international migration. The Great Depression stopped virtually all such population movement during the 1930s, and in the 1940s international migration was checked by World War II. What mobility there was largely involved displaced persons and was mostly unrelated to the rhythms of economic growth and development. This pattern persisted well into the 1950s.

The period of postindustrial migration began around 1960 and constituted a sharp break with the past. Rather than being dominated by outflows from Europe to a handful of former colonies, international migration became a truly global phenomenon as the number of migrants expanded and the sources of supply shifted from Europe to the developing countries. Before 1930, 85 percent of all international migrants originated in Europe. Since 1960, 85 percent have come from Latin America, the Caribbean, Asia, and Africa. The variety of destination countries has grown to encompass all developed countries, including all the countries of the European Union, the oil-exporting countries of the Persian Gulf, Canada, the United States, Australia, Japan, and the Asian "tigers" of Singapore, South Korea, Hong Kong, and Malaysia. By 2000 a total of around 175 million persons were living outside their countries of birth, 45 percent in developed countries and 55 percent in developing countries.

Data Collection

The study of international migration is complicated by serious data problems. The definition of an "immigrant" varies from country to country and is bound up in legal codes, politics, and sometimes xenophobia. The collection of data on international entries and exits is sporadic and incomplete and is the responsibility of different agencies in different countries. Although data on numbers and characteristics of the foreign-born, or of "foreigners" in some other sense, are generally available from national statistical offices, standards of enumeration and definitions of who is included vary across countries.

Estimates of net international migration flows for major sending and receiving countries for which reasonably good quality data exist—the English-speaking traditional immigration countries and countries in Western Europe—are presented in Table 1 for periods somewhat different from those referred to above.

The United Nations Population Division has developed a set of standards for the classification of international migrants and publishes a regular series of reports on trends and patterns based on its reworking of national statistical data. According to these data, at the turn of the twenty-first century roughly a third of all international migrants were in Asia, a quarter were in North America and another quarter were in Europe, 13 percent were in Latin America and the Caribbean, and 4 percent were in Oceania. International migrants amounted to around 2.4 percent of the global population. The highest rates of out-migration were in Latin America, the Caribbean, the Pacific Islands, Southeast Asia, and South Central Asia. The highest rates of in-

TABLE 1

Net Migration: Western Europe, and Western Offshoots, 1870–1998
(Thousands)

	1870–1913	1914–1949	1950–1973	1974–1998
France	890	236	3,630	1,026
Germany	−2,598	−304[a]	7,070	5,911
Italy	−4,459	−1,771	−2,139	1,617
United Kingdom	−6,415	−1,405[b]	-605	737
Other[c]	−1,414	54	1,425	1,607
Total Western Europe	−13,996	−3,662	9,381	10,898
Australia	885	673	2,033	2,151
New Zealand	290	138	247	87
Canada	861	207	2,126	2,680
United States	15,820	6,221	8,257	16,721
Total Western offshoots	17,856	7,239	12,663	21,639

Note: (a) 1922–1939; (b) excludes 1939–1945; (c) includes Belgium, Netherlands, Norway, Sweden, and Switzerland. Minus sign indicates outflow.

SOURCE: Maddison (2001).

migration were in Australia–New Zealand, North America, Western Europe, and Western Asia (principally the Persian Gulf states). As a percentage of all residents, foreigners constitute 18 percent of the population in Oceania, 10 percent in North America, 4 percent in Europe, 3 percent in Africa, 2 percent in Latin America, and 1 percent in Asia.

Categories of International Migration

International migrants fall into four basic categories, depending on whether they leave voluntarily or involuntarily and whether they are well or poorly endowed with human capital. Involuntary migrants who lack skills and education are classified as refugees. Their out-migration is prompted directly or indirectly by persecution, threat of violence, or extreme deprivation and typically is directed toward a neighboring state. Involuntary migrants with significant human capital generally travel to nonadjacent states as asylum seekers; their departure is motivated by a fear of violence or persecution. Because of their education and in some cases their financial resources, they are better placed to gain entry to liberal, developed nations and to pursue claims for asylum. Voluntary migrants who lack human capital generally are classified as labor migrants. Their movement is motivated by economic aspirations, and so the flow is from less to more developed nations. Skilled immigrants carry significant amounts of human capital, and their migration decisions reflect the desire to maximize returns to their investments in skills, training, and education.

Just as markets for financial capital have globalized in recent years, so have markets for human capital. Although flows of human capital are predominantly from less to more developed countries, there is also significant mobility of skilled workers among the developed countries and among developing countries, as well as from developed to developing regions.

Only about 10 percent of the world's international migrants are refugees. Most refugee movement occurs among developing countries. Refugee migration tends to be localized and generally stems from civil conflicts within nations or the disintegration of a state. Although Africa contains only 13 percent of the world's people, it has a third of its refugees, mainly in sub-Saharan countries with weak and divided state structures inherited from colonial regimes. Another 36 percent of all refugees reside in Asia, mainly in the Middle East, Pakistan, and Southeast Asia. Finally, 25 percent are in Europe, principally in the former Yugoslavia and Soviet Union. Precise information on refugees is difficult to obtain; what little exists is tabulated by the United Nations High Commissioner for Refugees. There is little theoretical basis for predicting future trends.

Of the remaining international migrants, nearly 90 percent are workers (and their families) who left their countries of origin for economic reasons. They are predominantly unskilled.

Theories of International Migration

Theoretical work has sought to explain the movement of economic migrants in terms of (1) the structural forces that promote emigration, (2) the structural forces in destination countries that attract migrants, (3) the motivations, goals, and aspirations of those who respond to macrostructural forces by becoming international migrants, (4) the social and economic structures that connect areas of out- and in-migration, and (5) the responses of specific states to the resulting flows of people.

The frameworks that different analysts have drawn on are neoclassical economics, the new economics of labor migration, segmented labor market theory, world systems theory, social capital theory, and the theory of cumulative causation. World systems theory gives an account of the structural forces that promote out-migration from developing countries. Together, world systems theory, segmented labor market theory, and neoclassical economics explain why developed countries attract immigrants. Social capital theory and world systems theory explain how structural links emerge to connect areas of origin and areas of destination. Neoclassical economics and the new economics of labor migration deal with the motivations of the people who become international migrants in response to these forces. The theory of cumulative causation describes how international migration promotes changes in personal motivations and socioeconomic structures to give immigration a self-perpetuating, dynamic character. Finally, recent contributions to political economy offer a basic framework for understanding the role of state policy in determining the size and composition of international flows.

A Synthesis of Theoretical Approaches

Integrating the various theories in light of the empirical evidence yields the following synthetic account. Contemporary international migration originates in the social, economic, political, and cultural transformations that accompany the penetration of markets into nonmarket or premarket societies (as hypothesized under world systems theory). In the context of a globalizing economy, the entry of markets and capital-intensive production methods into peripheral areas disrupts existing social and economic arrangements and brings about the displacement of people from their customary livelihoods, creating a mobile population of workers who actively search for new ways of earning income, managing risk, and acquiring capital.

One means by which these people seek to assure their economic well-being is by selling their labor. Because wages are higher in urban than in rural areas, much of this process of labor commodification is expressed in the form of rural–urban migration. Such movement occurs even when the probability of obtaining an urban job is low, because when multiplied by high urban wages, the low employment probabilities yield expected incomes above those in rural areas. Wages are even higher, of course, in developed countries overseas, and the larger size of these wage differentials inevitably prompts some people to seek work abroad, often in geographically distant countries.

International wage differentials are not the only factor motivating people to migrate, however. Many households struggling to cope with the jarring transformations of economic development and market creation use international migration as a means of managing risk and overcoming barriers to capital and credit (considerations treated in the so-called new economics of labor migration).

In developing countries, markets (or government substitutes) for insurance, capital, credit, and old age security are poorly developed or nonexistent. Households turn to international migration to compensate for these market failures. By sending members abroad to work, households diversify their labor portfolios to control the risks stemming from unemployment, crop failure, and price uncertainty. Work abroad may also permit households more successfully to accumulate cash for large consumer purchases or productive investments or to build up savings for retirement. Whereas the rational actor posited by neoclassical economics takes advantage of a geographic disequilibrium in labor markets to move abroad permanently to achieve higher lifetime earnings, the rational actor assumed by the new economics of labor migration seeks to cope with market failure by moving abroad temporarily and repatriating earnings in the form of regular remittances or lump-sum transfers.

Whereas the early phases of economic development promote emigration, postindustrial transformations in high-income countries create a bifurcation of labor markets. Jobs in the primary labor market provide steady work and high pay for native workers, but those in the secondary labor market offer low pay, little stability, and few opportunities, thus repelling native residents and generating a structural demand for immigrant workers (treated by segmented labor market theory). This process of labor market bifurcation is most evident in global cities, where a concentration of managerial, administrative, and technical expertise leads to a concentration of wealth and a strong ancillary demand for low-wage services (as described in world systems theory). Unable to attract native workers for such service jobs, employers turn to immigrants and initiate immigrant flows directly through formal recruitment (segmented labor market theory).

Although instrumental in initiating immigration, recruitment becomes less important over time because the processes of economic globalization that create mobile populations in developing regions also generate a demand for their services in global cities and create links of transportation, communication, politics, and culture that make the international movement of people increasingly cheap and easy (world systems theory). Immigration also is promoted by foreign policies and military actions taken by core nations to maintain international security, protect foreign investments, and guarantee access to raw materials; these entanglements create links and obligations that generate ancillary flows of refugees and military dependents.

Once an immigration stream begins, it displays a strong tendency to continue through the growth and elaboration of migrant networks (social capital theory). The concentration of immigrants in certain destination areas creates a "family and friends" effect, which channels later cohorts of immigrants to the same places and facilitates their arrival and initial settlement. If enough migrants arrive under the right conditions, an enclave economy may form that further augments the specialized demand for immigrant workers (segmented labor market theory).

The spread of migratory behavior within sending communities sets off ancillary structural changes, shifting distributions of income and land and modifying local cultures in ways that promote additional international movement. Over time the process of network expansion tends to become self-perpetuating because each act of migration causes social and economic changes that promote additional international movement (theory of cumulative causation). Receiving countries may implement restrictive policies to counter rising tides of immigrants, but those measures create a lucrative niche into which enterprising agents, contractors, and other middlemen move to create migrant-supporting institutions, providing migrants with another infrastructure capable of supporting and sustaining international movement (social capital theory).

During the initial phases of emigration from any sending country the effects of capital penetration, market failure, social network expansion, and cumulative causation dominate in determining the international flows, but as the level of out-migration reaches high levels and the costs and risks of international movement drop, movement is determined increasingly by international wage differentials (neoclassical economics) and labor demand (segmented labor market theory). As economic growth occurs in sending regions, international wage gaps gradually diminish and well-functioning markets for capital, credit, and insurance come into existence, progressively lowering the incentives for emigration. If these trends continue, a country ultimately becomes integrated into the international economy as a developed, capitalist country, at which point it undergoes a migration transition. Massive net out-migration tails off, and the country itself is seen as an immigration destination; it becomes both a sender and a receiver of migrants.

These theoretical considerations go far toward explaining the initiation and perpetuation of international migration. The considerable regional variation in actual migration patterns stems from the fact that all national governments intervene in these flows to influence their size and composition. Sending countries, despite frequently voiced worries about the loss of human capital ("brain drain"), on balance have a strong interest in encouraging international migration as a means of acquiring capital, securing foreign exchange, relieving unemployment, and building skills. At the same time, however, migrant-receiving countries may be increasingly selective in their migrant intake or pursue more restrictive immigration policies.

Immigration and State Capacity

Globalization and technological change have combined to increase income inequality and unemployment in the world and have served to increase both the absolute and relative numbers of people seeking to enter the developed countries as immigrants. This process gives rise to more restrictive policies in the developed world. However, the ability of states to regulate and control the volume and composition of immigration is constrained by a variety of factors. Globalization itself limits the power of nation-states to control transnational movements of labor as well as those of capital, goods, and information. Similarly, the emergence of an international regime protecting human rights constrains the ability of governments and political leaders to respond to the racial and ethnic concerns of voters or to impose harshly restrictive measures on immigrants or their dependents. These constraints are particularly salient in nations with well-established constitutional protections for individual rights and strong, independent judiciaries.

Ultimately, the ability of immigrant-receiving states to impose restrictive immigration policies successfully depends on five main factors: the size of the potential flow, the degree of centralized power and relative efficiency of the national bureaucracy, the extent to which individual rights are constitutionally protected, the relative strength and independence of the judiciary, and the existence and strength of a historical tradition of immigration. The interplay of these factors determines a state's efficacy in restricting immigration.

Efficacy can be seen as a point on a continuum. At one extreme are countries, such as the Gulf states, which counter a moderate demand for entry with powerful centralized bureaucracies, few constitutional protections for individual rights, weak and dependent judiciaries, and no historical traditions of immigration. At the other extreme are countries such as the United States, which face a strong demand for entry with relatively weak and decentralized bureaucracies, strong constitutional protections for individual rights (including those of foreigners), a strong and independent judiciary, and a long historical tradition of immigration.

It is unclear how successful countries can expect to be in controlling immigration over the next century. Scattered evidence suggests that undocumented immigration is not unknown even in the Gulf states and is growing throughout Europe and Asia. In the United States both legal and illegal immigration continue to expand, and there is little evidence that the restrictive measures imposed so far have had much of an effect. U.S. policies have been more successful as symbolic political gestures, signaling to anxious citizens and workers that their concerns are being addressed while marginalizing immigrants socially and geographically to make them less visible. What remains to be seen is whether the majority of countries, situated at points on the continuum somewhere between the United States and the Gulf countries, will be able to regulate and control immigration over the next century.

See also: *Immigration, Unauthorized; Immigration Policies; Immigration Trends; Labor Migration, International.*

BIBLIOGRAPHY

Bongaarts, John, and Rodolfo A. Bulatao, eds. 2000. *Beyond Six Billion: Forecasting the World's Popu-*

lation. Washington, D.C.: National Academy Press.

Maddison, Angus. 2001. *The World Economy: A Millennial Perspective.* Paris: OECD.

Massey, Douglas S. 1999. "International Migration at the Dawn of the Twenty-First Century: The Role of the State." *Population and Development Review* 25: 303–323.

Massey, Douglas S., Joaquin Arango, Graeme Hugo, Ali Kouaouci, Adela Pellegrino, and J. Edward Taylor. 1998. *Worlds in Motion: Understanding International Migration at the End of the Millennium.* Oxford: Oxford University Press.

Massey, Douglas S., Jorge Durand, and Nolan J. Malone. 2002. *Beyond Smoke and Mirrors: Immigration Policy and Global Economic Integration.* New York: Russell Sage Foundation.

Zlotnick, Hania. 1998. "International Migration 1965–96: An Overview." *Population and Development Review* 24: 429–468.

Douglas S. Massey

J

JOURNALS, POPULATION

Just as other scholars and scientists do, demographers attempt to establish their status in the profession and communicate their ideas and findings to colleagues by publishing in the best journals. They also prefer to be cited in those journals because scoring high in citations is helpful in acquiring research funding, negotiating contracts, obtaining invitations to high-profile conferences, and winning prizes. The field of play is limited, and so the distribution of citations is very unequal and reportedly resembles that of income. Relatively few demographers become famous; some do not leave a trace, and most never achieve more than a modest citation index.

How Demographic Knowledge Travels

In demography, and in population studies in general, it is evident where aspiring and ambitious authors should submit their manuscripts. In a study about the way demographic knowledge travels, Hendrik van Dalen and Kène Henkens show that specialized demographic journals rarely communicate with one another. Those journals play a very modest role in the construction of demographic knowledge. In fact, a majority of the articles published in second-tier journals remain uncited five years after their publication.

Among the 330 population serials that exist worldwide, only 17 have been selected by the Social Science Citation Index (SSCI) as being important for the development of the discipline. Most demographic knowledge is created in the major general journals: *Population Studies, Population and Development Review,* and *Demography.* The first of these journals is published in Britain, the other two are U.S.-based.

(The last named is the journal of the Population Association of America [PAA]). From these three journals information trickles down to other regions and to the specialized journals. Language barriers are a serious problem. Except among English speakers, writing in one's native language is not helpful in gaining a world reputation. Roughly 50 percent of all articles published in the period 1990–1992 in the 17 journals analyzed by the SSCI were written by authors with a U.S. connection.

Increased Specialization

Increased specialization has been one of the dominant characteristics of demographic research since World War II. The remarkable increase in the number and range of population journals is an illustration of that phenomenon. The International Union for the Scientific Study of Population (IUSSP), which was established in 1928, has been particularly helpful in the dissemination of demographic knowledge by distributing four demographic journals to its members.

Three of those journals have existed for more than half a century: *Population* (1946, Paris), *Population Studies* (1947, London), and *Genus* (1934, Rome). All three journals cater in principle to the whole field of population studies and to all regions of the world. Migration is a topic that has never been favored by the editors of *Population Studies,* but in terms of continuity in quality, style, geographic scope, and technical standard of the published papers, that journal has an enviable reputation. The international impact of *Population* is bound to increase now that the publisher (INED—France's National Institute of Demographic Research) has decided to start publishing all papers simultaneously in English and French. Its coverage of the francophone region, the Balkans, the Baltic region, and Eastern Europe is without parallel. A valuable standard feature in *Population* is the yearly overview of recent demographic trends in developed countries. Although edited in Italy, *Genus* uses English as the preferred medium for its wide-ranging contributions to the discipline.

The IUSSP also greatly aided in the distribution of the reference journal *Population Index* (Princeton), which originally (1934—1936) was the bibliographical journal of the PAA. Unfortunately, its publication ended in 1999. Although its existing database can still be consulted electronically and most demographic journals publish book reviews and lists of the publications they receive, it will surely prove to be a great disadvantage for the discipline that an authoritative bibliographical source abstracting the contents of books, edited volumes, and a great variety of serials and working papers is no longer available. However, the creation of a central site for working papers provides some compensation.

The *Population Bulletin of the United Nations* and the *Population Bulletin* published by the Population Reference Bureau (1945) are equally longstanding and broad in orientation. Later additions to the range of journals demographers consult regularly, have on their shelves, or follow through abstracts in *Population Index* or a similar bibliographic source, most notably POPLINE, have tended to be more specialized. *The International Migration Review* (1966) and *International Migration* (1962) address a specialized audience. *International Family Planning Perspectives* (1974) and *Studies in Family Planning* (1969) also reflect a clear focus in their titles; they provide vital information for scholars concerned with population change, gender, and reproductive health in developing countries. The title of *Population and Development Review* (1975) suggests a similarly restricted orientation, but this journal has become one of the most prestigious in the field. It is eminently readable, regularly publishes topical supplements, and contributes to keeping alive the intellectual history of the discipline through its *Archives* department.

Readers with an interest in the biological aspects of the discipline can read the *Journal of Biosocial Science* (1968) and *Social Biology* (1953); for economic demographers the journals of *Family Welfare* (1954) and *Population Economics* (1987) are of prime importance. Other comparatively recent additions also are highly specialized: *Mathematical Population Studies* (1989), *Population and Environment* (1978), *Population Research and Policy Review* (1981), and *Health Transition Review* (1990) are good examples. Historical demographers; demographers concentrating on marriage, cohabitation, and the family; and those who combine studies of the family and history have their own means of communicating. Some of these publications have a long tradition (*Journal of Marriage and the Family*, 1938); others are more recent and reflect the further specialization noted above (*Journal of Family History*, 1975; *Journal of Family Issues*, 1979; *Perspectives on Sexual and Reproductive Health* (formerly *Family Planning Perspectives*), 1969.)

To cover areas where demography touches upon public health, gerontology, epidemiology, sociology, anthropology, psychology, policymaking or politics, human resources, the labor force, refugees, ethnic relations, urbanization, or prognoses, other relevant journals exist. The *Journal of Ethnic and Migration Studies* (1971), the *Revue Européenne des Migration Internationales* (1984), and the *International Journal of Population Geography* (1994) publish studies on international migration.

National and Regional Journals

Many countries have their own population journals or attempt to disseminate their findings internationally through a yearbook. The *Polish Population Review* (1991); the Hungarian *Demográfia* (1958); the Czech *Demografie* (1959); the German *Zeitschrift für Bevölkerungswissenschaft* (1975); the *Yearbook of Population Research* in Finland (1963); the Dutch-language *Bevolking en Gezin* (1971) and the English-language yearbook on the Low Countries associated with it, *Population Trends* (1975), which deals primarily with the United Kingdom; *Demography India* (1971); the Japanese-language journal *Jinko Mondai Kenkyu* (1944); the Mexican journal *Estudios Demográficos y Urbanos* (1985); and the *New Zealand Population Review* (1974) are good examples. These periodicals are required reading for regional specialists and frequently provide table headings and summaries in English.

A few of the national journals are attempting to acquire international stature. Recently retitled, the Australian Population Association's *Journal of Population Research* (1983), for example, has acquired a broad international mandate. Regional journals that are broadly focused substantively but maintain a distinct geographic focus include the *European Journal of Population* (1984), which still accepts papers in both English and French, is rather limited in size, but has improved in quality and scope; *Notas de Población* (1972) published in Chile by Celade; the *Asian-Pacific Population Journal* (1985); and the periodical *African Population Studies* (1985).

The Internet

The tables of contents of many demographic periodicals can be accessed directly on the Internet. Alternatively, they can be reviewed through the *Revue des Revues Démographiques:* Subscribers to these journals frequently are able to consult the articles in that manner. Electronic publishing probably is the direction in which several journals will go. Indeed, the online journal *Demographic Research* published by the new Max Planck Institute for Demographic Research established in Germany is available only on the Internet. In a laudable attempt to reduce the frequently long publication times of traditional journals it conducts review procedures entirely by email. Its focus to date has been slanted toward mortality and morbidity, but that is surely a temporary situation. If it also does well in citation analysis, it could set a new trend.

See also: *Bibliographic and Online Resources; Demography, History of; Population Organizations.*

BIBLIOGRAPHY

Van Dalen, Hendrik P., and Kène Henkens. 1999. "How Influential Are Demographic Journals?" *Population and Development Review* 25(2): 229–253.

———. 2001. "What Makes a Scientific Article Influential? The Case of Demographers." *Scientometrics* 50(3): 455–482.

Van Raan, Anthony F. J. 2001. "Two-Step Competition Process Leads to Power-Law Income Distributions. Application to Scientific Publication and Citation Distributions." *Physica A* 298: 530–536.

INTERNET RESOURCES.

JSTOR—The Scholarly Journal Archive. <http://www.jstor.org>.

Revue des Revues Démographiques. <http://www.cicred.ined.fr>.

University of Wisconsin–Madison Center for Demography and Ecology. <http://www.ssc.wisc.edu/cde/library/papers.htm>.

DIRK J. VAN DE KAA

K

KEYFITZ, NATHAN

(1913–)

Nathan Keyfitz was born and educated in Montreal, Canada. In 1936, two years after receiving a Bachelor of Science degree in mathematics from McGill University, he joined the Dominion Bureau of Statistics, now Statistics Canada, as a clerk, reaching the post of senior research statistician in 1950. He also found time to seek a Ph.D. in sociology from the University of Chicago (1952). In 1959, Keyfitz's career veered toward academia—a professorship at the University of Toronto. In 1963, he was appointed professor of sociology at the University of Chicago where, at age fifty, his exceptionally productive career as a researcher in demography began. Subsequently, he held successive appointments as professor of demography at the University of California, Berkeley, and as professor of sociology at Harvard University (from 1972 to 1981). After his retirement from Harvard, he taught at Ohio State University. Subsequently, for ten years (until 1993) Keyfitz led the population program at the International Institute for Applied Systems Analysis (IIASA) in Laxenburg, Austria.

At various times, Keyfitz also consulted, taught, or conducted research in many countries, but foremost in Indonesia—where his research and consulting activities began in the 1950s and continued intermittently over four decades. Keyfitz was president of the Population Association of America in 1970–71, and he received the Association's Mindel C. Sheps award in 1976. He is a member of the Royal Society of Canada, the American Academy of Arts and Sciences, and the U.S. National Academy of Sciences.

Keyfitz is best known for his work in mathematical demography, a branch of demography that his books largely defined for generations of students. In the early 1960s, he began to gather the literature on the application of mathematics to population, dispersed in the journals of many disciplines, and set out the findings in a uniform notation. Keyfitz gave his formulas meaning and interest by applying them to real data, making early use of the mainframe computers that were just then appearing. This work yielded his book, *Introduction to the Mathematics of Population* (1968), and a systematic compilation of country-level demographic estimates produced by his models, *World Population Growth* (1968, co-authored with Wilhelm Flieger). Somewhat dissatisfied with the rather abstract character of his initial effort, Keyfitz went on to write another book, *Applied Mathematical Demography* (1977), in which he examined "a great number of questions that could be dealt with mathematically and that involved techniques needed by demographers" (Van der Tak 1991, p. 287).

Keyfitz's influence on the field of demography and population studies is not limited to mathematical demography. Once immersed in demographic research, he broadened his research interests to substantive issues raised by population dynamics. His book *Population Change and Social Policy* (1982) collects a number of his articles and essays on topics ranging from the environmental effects of population growth to the socioeconomic implications of population aging.

See also: *Demography, History of; Renewal Theory and Stable Population Model.*

BIBLIOGRAPHY

SELECTED WORKS BY NATHAN KEYFITZ.

Keyfitz, Nathan. 1968. *Introduction to the Mathematics of Population*. Reading, MA: Addison-Wesley.

———. 1977. *Applied Mathematical Demography*, New York: Springer-Verlag.

———. 1982. *Population Change and Social Policy*. Cambridge, MA: Abt Books.

Keyfitz, Nathan, and Wilhelm Flieger. 1990. *World Population Growth and Aging: Demographic Trends in the Late Twentieth Century* (1968). Chicago: University of Chicago Press.

SELECTED WORKS ABOUT NATHAN KEYFITZ.

Van der Tak, Jean. 1991. "24. Nathan Keyfitz." In *PAA Oral History Project*, Vol. 1: *Demographic Destinies: Interviews with Presidents and Secretary-Treasurers of the Population Association of America*. Available from the author through the Population Association of America, Washington, D.C.

INTERNET RESOURCE.

Keyfitz, Nathan. 1996. "My Itinerary as Demographer and Sociologist." <http://people.ne.mediaone.net/keyfitz/itinerar.htm>.

JACQUES LEDENT

KEYNES, JOHN MAYNARD

(1883–1946)

British economist John Maynard Keynes was a civil servant in the India Office from 1906 to 1908, and a lecturer in economics at Cambridge University from 1908 to 1913. He was the editor of the *Economic Journal* from 1912 to 1945.

He joined Britain's Treasury in 1915 and was its principal representative at the Versailles Peace Conference in 1919. Believing the Versailles proposals on borders and reparations to be destructive and counter-productive, he resigned in 1919, setting out his objections in *The Economic Consequences of the Peace* (1919).

Keynes was closely associated with the Liberal Party; his influential and brilliantly written works attacked laissez-faire economics and the return to the gold standard, proposing a radically new approach to economic management. He returned to the Treasury in 1940, and in 1944 played a leading part in the Bretton Woods Conference that set up the International Monetary Fund and the International Bank for Reconstruction and Development (better known as the World Bank).

Keynes wrote extensively and influentially, producing, among others, the *Treatise on Money* (1930) and the controversial *General Theory of Employment, Interest and Money* (1936), arguably the most influential work on economics since Adam Smith's *Wealth of Nations*. The *General Theory* showed how aggregate demand, and therefore unemployment, was determined, and that economic systems at equilibrium had no necessary tendency toward full employment, not even with the most depressed wages. Because individual consumer spending could not create sufficient demand, unemployment must be cured by state demand management funded by a budget deficit.

Keynes devoted no major work specifically to population issues, but population concerns recur in his work. A neomalthusian view is prominent in the *Economic Consequences of the Peace*. There he noted that before World War I, Europe's dense population had enjoyed a high standard of living without self-sufficiency in agriculture or raw materials, relying instead on manufactured exports. He feared that such large populations could no longer be sustained following the destruction of industry and in the absence of opportunities for mass emigration.

Keynes was thus initially concerned with what he called the "Malthusian devil O of Overpopulation." This, chained up when productivity was rising, would be released when the temporarily advantageous conditions ended. Keynes campaigned against the then current pronatalist opinion, fearing that population growth would tend to reduce the standard of living, although he also feared adverse eugenic consequences if the more prudent nations, and classes, reduced their fertility before others. These views were summarized in a 1912 lecture, *Population*, not published until 2000 (in Toye's *Keynes on Population*).

In the late 1920s, Keynes changed his mind, rejecting his earlier economic pessimism and some of his Malthusian views on the perils of overpopulation. Instead he became more concerned with inadequate demand. In his 1933 biographical essay on T. R. Malthus he gave much more prominence to Malthus the economist (worried, like Keynes, about underconsumption) than to Malthus the demographer (worried about overpopulation). His Galton Lecture of 1937 was perhaps his most balanced view of population issues. In it, Keynes points to the risk that population decline—in the 1930s, for the first time in centuries, a real possibility—might unchain the other "Malthusian devil U of Underemployed resources" through excessive savings and underconsumption.

In a stationary population, he argued that the two Malthusian devils could only be kept in balance by increased consumption, more equal incomes, and low interest rates. He ended up promoting family allowances, which he had earlier condemned, while recognizing that overpopulation could exist elsewhere. Keynes was probably the most prominent economist of the twentieth century, but his inconstant efforts on population, little supported by data or technical understanding, did not show him at his best.

See also: *Population Decline; Population Thought, Contemporary.*

BIBLIOGRAPHY

SELECTED WORKS BY JOHN MAYNARD KEYNES.

Keynes, John Maynard. 1919. *The Economic Consequences of the Peace.* London: Macmillan.

———. 1930. "Economic Possibilities for Our Grandchildren." In his *Essays in Persuasion.* New York: W. W. Norton, 1991.

———. 1930. *A Treatise on Money.* 2 vols. London: Macmillan.

———. 1933. "Robert Malthus," in his *Essays in Biography.* London: Macmillan.

———. 1936. *The General Theory of Employment, Interest and Money.* London: Macmillan.

———. 1937. "Some Economic Consequences of a Declining Population." *The Eugenics Review* 29: 13–17.

SELECTED WORKS ABOUT JOHN MAYNARD KEYNES.

Blaug, Mark. 1990. *John Maynard Keynes.* London: Macmillan with the Institute of Economic Affairs.

Blaug, Mark., ed. 1991. *John Maynard Keynes.* 2 vols. Aldershot, Eng.: Edward Elgar.

Hutchison, T. W. 1977. *Keynes versus the 'Keynesians'. . .? An Essay in the Thinking of J. M. Keynes and the Accuracy of Its Interpretation by His Followers.* London: Institute of Economic Affairs.

Keynes, Milo. 1975. *Essays on John Maynard Keynes.* Cambridge, Eng.: Cambridge University Press.

Petersen, William. 1955. "J. Maynard Keynes' Theories on Population." *Population Studies* 8: 228–246

Skidelsky, Robert. 1983–1992. *John Maynard Keynes: A Biography.* 3 vols. London: Macmillan.

Toye, John. 2000. *Keynes on Population.* Oxford: Oxford University Press.

DAVID COLEMAN

KING, GREGORY

(1648–1712)

Gregory King was one of the earliest and most accomplished exponents of political arithmetic. He is described by Richard Stone (1997, p. xxii) as "the first great economic statistician" and the "ablest follower" of John Graunt (1620–1674). Born in Lichfield, England, at age fifteen King became clerk to a leading official of the College of Arms, the body concerned with the assignment of coats of arms and with investitures and similar ceremonies. In other employment he acquired skills as a mapmaker and surveyor, a better source of income. Over subsequent years he advanced to a senior level in the profession of heraldry, eventually being appointed to the positions known as Rouge Dragon and Lancaster Herald. An often-published engraving shows him in the extravagant costume of Rouge Dragon Pursuivant.

King is known mostly for statistical investigations of the population and economy of England in his day, the innovative accounting schemes he devised for those studies, and his early specification of a demand curve. Little of this work was published in his lifetime, and all of it was in the nature of an engrossing hobby, an unpaid sideline to his many other activities.

His major work, dating from 1696 but first printed only in 1802, was *Natural and Political Observations and Conclusions upon the State and Condition of England*. The *Observations* along with King's notebooks contain an astonishing array of statistical information, sought out and systematically presented—in historian Peter Laslett's words, "the first conscious and deliberate attack on social opacity which was ever made" (1985, p. 353). The statistics on population structure include classifications of population by occupation, sex, marital status, age group, and other characteristics. A facsimile of the 1696 manuscript and together with one of the notebooks was published in 1973 in the *Pioneers of Demography* series edited by Laslett. Another, apparently earlier, version of the manuscript exists with the variant title *Observations and Conclusions, Natural and Political, Upon the State and Condition of England*.

King's estimate of the population of England and Wales in 1695—5.5 million—compares with the Wrigley–Schofield figure of 4.95 million. His estimate of the average age of the population was 27.5 years. He also produced estimates of continental and world population at the end of the seventeenth century, based on assumed densities by latitude; these accord moderately well with modern historical estimates, although that may reflect the similarity of informed guesses in the absence of much new information.

See also: *Demography, History of; Graunt, John; Petty, William; Population Thought, History of.*

BIBLIOGRAPHY

SELECTED WORKS BY GREGORY KING.

King, Gregory. [c. 1695] 1973. *Notebook.* Unpublished manuscript. Facsimile in *The Earliest Classics: John Graunt and Gregory King,* ed. Peter Laslett. Farnborough, Eng.: Gregg International.

———. [1696] 1973. *Natural and Political Observations and Conclusions upon the State and Condition of England.* Unpublished manuscript. Facsimile in *The Earliest Classics: John Graunt and Gregory King,* ed. Peter Laslett. Farnborough, Eng.: Gregg International. First printed as an appendix in George Chalmers, *An Estimate of the Comparative Strength of Great Britain* (London, 1802).

SELECTED WORKS ABOUT GREGORY KING.

Glass, David V. 1965. "Two Papers on Gregory King." In *Population in History,* ed. David V. Glass and D. E. C. Eversley. London: Arnold.

Holmes, Geoffrey. 1977. "Gregory King and the Social Structure of Pre-industrial England." *Transactions of the Royal Historical Society* 27: 41–68.

Laslett, Peter. 1985. "Gregory King, Robert Malthus and the Origins of English Social Realism." *Population Studies* 39: 351–362.

———. 1992. "Natural and Political Observations on the Population of the Late Seventeenth Century England: Reflections on the Work of Gregory King and John Graunt." In *Surveying the People: The Interpretation and Use of Document Sources for the Study of Population in the Later Seventeenth Century,* ed. Kevin Schurer and Tom Arkell. Oxford, Eng.: Leopard's Head.

Stone, Richard. 1997. *Some British Empiricists in the Social Sciences, 1650–1900.* Cambridge, Eng.: Cambridge University Press.

GEOFFREY McNICOLL

KŐRÖSY, JÓZSEF

(1844–1906)

The nineteenth century witnessed the emergence of statistics and demography as independent and influential fields of scientific study within the social sciences at large. The increasingly rich materials produced by the census and by vital statistics provided the raw materials for analytic work, but these statistical operations, which by late in the century were routine and taken for granted by their consumers in most countries of Europe, had to be energetically promoted by imaginative statistical entrepreneurs who realized the potentially high payoff of statistics put to good use. Talent for statistical entrepreneurship and for incisive analysis were often combined in the same person. In Hungary this is exemplified by four statisticians—local variants of *eminent Victorians*—Elek Fényes (1807–1876), Károly Keleti (1833–1892), Gusztáv Thirring (1861–1941) and Kőrösy. The latter's work is distinguished by his wide ranging international engagements, both as organizer of cooperation among statisticians (he was one of the founders of the International Statistical Institute in 1885) and as a developer and promoter of analytic methods. Kőrösy was director of the Bureau of Statistics in Pest (1870–1906), and, after the unification of Pest and Buda, of the Budapest Bureau of Statistics. He was also a professor at the University of Budapest (1883–1906).

Kőrösy is the author of some 200 monographs and journal articles in Hungarian, French, German, and English. Many of these assess the changing demographic situation of Hungary and include highly innovative analyses of mortality conditions, and of behavior with respect to fertility and nuptiality and interaction between these variables, notably the effect of age at marriage on marital fertility and child survival. A collection of his demographic studies (he preferred the term "demology") appeared in 1889 in Hungarian and in 1892 in German. Difficulties in providing proper international comparisons for the structures and trends he described in these studies led him to advocate standardization of data collection methods, adoption of a uniform basic statistical nomenclature, and adoption of minimum standards of statistical coverage and publication. Especially high among his objectives was the international adoption of a plan that he worked out for a world census (1891 and 1898). He pursued the objective through successive international statistical congresses. Some of these proposals were adopted, notably those having to do with uniform procedures in collecting and tabulating census data (1899) and on statistical treatment of data regarding marital fertility (1905). His analyses of mortality were chiefly aimed at clarifying the reasons for the spread of various contagious diseases and their relationship to various societal and natural phenomena (such as housing conditions) and assessing the efficiency of specific medical treatments, such as the introduction of smallpox vaccination. Kőrösy's solutions for the problem of eliminating the effect of age distribution differences on vital rates through standardization were influential in affecting similar work in different fields and in various country population analyses.

See also: *Demography, History of.*

BIBLIOGRAPHY

SELECTED WORKS BY JÓZSEF KŐRÖSY.

Kőrösy, József. 1874. *Az emberi élettartam és halandóság kiszámításáról* [About the Calculation of Life Expectancy and Mortality]. Budapest: Eggenberger.

———. 1881. *Projet d'un recensement du monde.* Paris: Guillaumin.

———. 1889. *Demologiai Tanulmányok* [Studies in Demology]. Budapest: Magyar Tudományos Akadémia.

———. 1889. *Kritik der Vaccinations-Statistik.* Berlin: Puttkammer-Mahlbrecht.

———. 1890. *Neue Beiträge zur Frage des Impfschutzes.* Berlin: Puttkammer-Buchdruck.

———. 1894. *Über den Zusammenhang zwischen Armuth u. infectiösen Krankheiten.* Leipzig: Veit.

———. 1894. "Mass und Gesetze der ehelichen Fruchtbarkeit." Vienna: *Wiener Medicinische Wochenschrift.*

———. 1896. "An Estimate of the Degree of Legitimate Natality." *Philosophical Transactions B.* Vol. 186, pp. 781–875. London: Royal Society of London.

———. 1897. *Die seculäre Weltzählung.* Berlin.

———. 1891, 1899, 1900. "Le recensement séculaire du monde. Etude de statistique internationale." *Bulletin de l' Institut International de Statistique,* Vol. 2. 220–251, Vol. 11(1): 220–250, Vol. 12(1): 78–79.

PÁL PÉTER TÓTH

KUCZYNSKI, R. R.

(1876–1947)

Robert René Kuczynski was a German statistician and demographer who left Nazi Germany in 1933 and settled in London, becoming a British subject in 1946. Kuczynski had joined the Berlin Statistical Office under Richard Boeckh in 1898 and became the director of the Statistical Office of Elberfeld (1904–1905) and subsequently the director of that office in Berlin-Schoeneberg (1906–1921). Between 1900 and 1902 he worked at the Census Office in Washington, D.C., and in the late 1920s he worked at the Brookings Institution in Washington.

In England, Kuczynski worked at the London School of Economics, initially as a research fellow, and in 1938 he became a reader in demography, the first academic appointment in demography at a British university. He retired from that post in 1941 and became a demographic adviser to the Colonial Office in 1944. He was a founding member of the Population Investigation Committee in 1936, as he had been (through its German section) of the International Union for the Scientific Investigation of Population Problems in 1928, and a member of the statistics committee of the Royal Commission on Population from its inception in 1944 through 1947.

An important strand in Kuczynski's work was technical and methodological. Although Kuczynski did not devise the net reproduction rate (the demographic measure indicating the number of daughters who will replace each woman, given the prevailing patterns of childbearing and mortality by age)—he attributed this measure to Boeckh, 1886—he was its major explicator and popularizer. Moreover, he was the originator of the concept of the total fertility rate (1907), which indicates the number of children per woman implied by current age-specific birth rates, assuming no mortality, and the related gross reproduction rate, which is confined to daughters only. All these measures are still widely used.

Kuczynski also conceived of what might be termed birth-order-specific total fertility rates, indicating the births of a particular order per woman implied by current age- and order-specific birth rates, assuming no mortality. Kuczynski's thinking, and calculations, stimulated discussion of the likelihood and implications of below-replacement birth rates in the Western world during the 1920s, 1930s, and 1940s.

Kuczynski was interested in application, not just technique. His published work included reviews of past population movements as well as the contemporary situation. He also wrote about the historical development of thinking about population.

See also: *Projections and Forecasts, Population.*

BIBLIOGRAPHY

SELECTED WORKS BY R. R. KUCZYNSKI.

Kuczynski, Robert R. 1928. *The Balance of Births and Deaths*, Vol. 1. New York: Macmillan.

———. 1935. *The Measurement of Population Growth: Methods and Results.* London: Sidgwick & Jackson.

———. 1937. *Colonial Population.* London: Oxford University Press.

———. 1939. *Living-Space and Population Problems.* Oxford: Clarendon Press.

———. 1948–1953. *Demographic Survey of the British Colonial Empire.* London: Oxford University Press.

SELECTED WORKS ABOUT R. R. KUCZYNSKI.

Anonymous. 1948. "Memoir: R. R. Kuczynski, 1876–1947." *Population Studies* 1: 471–472.

Anonymous. 1948. "A Bibliography of the Demographic Studies of Dr R. R. Kuczynski." *Population Studies* 2: 125–126.

Hogben, Lancelot, ed. 1938. *Political Arithmetic.* London: George Allen and Unwin.

C. M. LANGFORD

KUZNETS, SIMON

(1901–1985)

Simon Kuznets was an economist, statistician, demographer, and economic historian. Born in Pinsk, Russia (now Belarus), he was educated in Kharkov (now Kharkiv, Ukraine), and headed a section of the bureau of labor statistics there under the Soviet government before emigrating to the United States at the age of 21. After receiving a Ph.D. from Columbia University in 1926, he joined the research staff of the National Bureau of Economic Research (NBER), where he conducted his seminal work on the estimation of national income. Both at Columbia and the NBER, he was strongly influenced by his mentor, economist Wesley C. Mitchell. From the 1950s on, the primary base for Kuznets's research was the Committee on Economic Growth of the Social Science Research Council, where he spearheaded an international program on the comparative study of economic growth. Kuznets held faculty appointments at the University of Pennsylvania (1930–1954), Johns Hopkins University (1954–1960), and Harvard University (1960–1971). He was president of the American Economic Association (1954), the American Statistical Association (1949), and was the third recipient of the Nobel prize in economics (1971) for his work on the comparative study of economic growth.

Kuznets's best-known contributions to population fall under three main heads: (1) measurement of population change; (2) analysis of interrelations between long swings in population growth and economic activity (Kuznets cycles); and (3) analysis of the long-term effect of population growth on economic growth.

Kuznets contributed to the development of new demographic data for the United States. His NBER Occasional Paper (written with Ernest Rubin) gives estimates of net immigration by decade, 1870–1940, and of the foreign-born white population by sex, annually, 1870–1939. In 1951, Kuznets and demographer and sociologist Dorothy S. Thomas initiated a study of population redistribution and economic growth. Under their joint direction, this work developed benchmark estimates of state internal migration (by Everett S. Lee), labor force (by Ann R. Miller and Carol Brainerd), and state income and manufacturing activity (by Richard A. Easterlin).

This work demonstrated conclusively that between 1870 and 1950 both international and internal migration in the United States fluctuated markedly over roughly twenty-year periods. Kuznets had earlier identified similar long swings in economic time series. In a major paper published in 1958, he brought together these two strands of work, pointing out a possible causal mechanism in which a swing in the growth rate of consumer goods output induced a corresponding movement in migration and this, in turn, caused a swing in population-sensitive capital formation. An outgrowth of this research on what came to be called Kuznets cycles was an NBER study of long swings in population and economic growth.

Demographers typically stress the adverse effects of population growth on economic growth. Kuznets adopted a more questioning stance. Based on evidence for 63 developed and developing countries from the early 1950s to 1964, he concluded that there was little empirical association between growth rates of population and output per capita, especially within the developing country bloc. Kuznets saw the basic obstacles to economic growth as arising from delays in adjusting social and political institutions, and viewed population growth, though an impediment, as of secondary importance. He was even more skeptical of the adverse effect of population growth for developed countries, and argued that more rapid population growth might promote economic development through a positive impact on the state of knowledge, the crucial factor underlying modern economic growth. This, along with Kuznets's empirical results, stimulated Julian Simon's assault on the premise of mainstream demography that population growth inevitably hinders economic development.

Most comparisons of the economic well-being of rich and poor use the distribution of income among families or households. But rich and poor families differ in size and age composition, and a meaningful comparison of economic welfare needs to allow for such differences. Beyond this, there is the question of how differences in mortality and fertility among income classes affect and are affected by the size distribution of income. These issues became the primary focus of Kuznets's research following his retirement from Harvard in 1971. This strand of Kuznets's work in demography has yet to be fully followed up.

In the discipline of economics where theory reigns supreme, Kuznets, though himself an original and creative thinker, was notable for his insistence on careful measurement and a respect for facts. In this regard he was, at heart, a demographer.

See also: *Cycles, Population; Development, Population and; Easterlin, Richard A.; Simon, Julian L.; Thomas, Dorothy Swaine.*

BIBLIOGRAPHY

SELECTED WORKS BY SIMON KUZNETS.

Kuznets, Simon. 1965. *Economic Growth and Structure: Selected Essays.* New York: Norton.

———. 1973. *Population, Capital, and Growth: Selected Essays.* New York: Norton.

———. 1979. *Growth, Population, and Income Distribution: Selected Essays.* New York: Norton.

———. 1980. "Recent Population Trends in Less Developed Countries and Implications for Internal Income Inequality." In *Population and Economic Change in Developing Countries: A Conference Report, Universities—National Bureau Committee for Economic Research, no. 30,* ed. Richard A. Easterlin. Chicago: University of Chicago Press.

———. 1989. *Economic Development, the Family, and Income Distribution: Selected Essays.* New York: Cambridge University Press.

Kuznets, Simon, and Dorthy S. Thomas, eds. 1957–1964. *Memoirs of the American Philosophical Society.* Vol. 45, 51, and 61: *Population Redistribution and Economic Growth: United States, 1870–1950.* Philadelphia: American Philosophical Society.

SELECTED WORKS ABOUT SIMON KUZNETS.

Bergson, Abram. 1986. "Simon Kuznets: 30 April 1901–8 July 1985." *American Philosophical Society Yearbook.* 134–138.

Easterlin, Richard A. 1987. "Simon Kuznets." In *The New Palgrave: A Dictionary of Economics,* ed. John Eatwell, Murray Milgate, and Peter Newman. New York: The Stockton Press.

INTERNET RESOURCE.

Fogel, Robert W. 2000. "Simon S. Kuznets: April 30, 1901–July 9, 1985," National Bureau of Economic Research Working Paper 7787. *Biographical Memoirs.* Washington, D.C.: National Academy of Sciences. <http://www.nber.org/papers/w7787>.

RICHARD A. EASTERLIN

L

LABOR FORCE

The labor force, as it is conventionally defined, is a measure of the economically active population: those persons who during a specified reference period and within a specific age range of the population are participating in the market economy by supplying labor for the production of goods and services. This concept, which was formalized in the United States during the 1930s as a way to capture the extent of joblessness during the Depression more objectively, is most relevant for modern market economies but is applied with some variations in developed and developing countries.

Definitions and Measurement

The labor force (LF), or the economically active population, can be defined as the sum of the employed population (E) and the unemployed population (U): LF = E + U.

Typically, the employed are defined for a specific age range and reference period as those who are in paid employment or self-employed, either currently at a job or with a job but not at work (e.g., on vacation or sick leave). The unemployed, also defined for the same reference period and population group, are those who are not currently in paid employment or self-employed but are available for work and actively seeking employment (or on layoff waiting to be recalled). Those neither employed nor unemployed are considered economically "inactive." Together the economically active and inactive populations constitute the total population (P) in the relevant age range. Thus the labor force participation rate (LFPR) is defined as LF/P: the ratio of the labor force (LF) to the total population (P). This measure captures the proportion of the population that is economically active at a specific point in time.

In most cases the population reference group for calculating LF, E, U, or LFPR is the working-age population, typically persons age 16 to 64. In most countries labor force statistics are based on sample surveys administered at a specific point in time to capture the primary activity status of individuals in the reference age group.

Conceptual Issues and Their Consequences

As a measure of economic activity the concept of the labor force distinguishes between economic and noneconomic uses of time and between those who are active and those who are inactive. In terms of the first distinction the emphasis on paid employment and on narrowly defined self-employment may exclude unpaid family workers who contribute to a family-owned business or farm. This distinction is more relevant at lower levels of economic development in which the agricultural sector dominates and family enterprises are more common even in the nonagricultural sector.

Because employment typically refers to any work during the reference period, no distinction is made between part-time and full-time employment, and the concept does not identify those who desire to work more hours than they actually work and are therefore "involuntarily" underemployed. In addition, most definitions of the labor force do not capture the so-called underground economy consisting of those engaged in illegal activities, and the so-called informal sector in many low-income countries may not be reflected in the recorded economic activity rates of those countries. Persons counted among the economically inactive population, P – LF, the segment that is not included in the labor force concept, are not necessarily idle. In many cases they are involved in productive activities such as child rearing, home production, volunteer efforts, acquisition of human capital through formal education, and other activities that are outside the market economy and therefore do not involve remuneration in the form of wages, a salary, or profit. In some cases time use surveys are available to gauge the allocation of time to these otherwise unmeasured activities.

The second distinction—between those actively seeking work and those not in the labor force—is largely a matter of definition. The U.S. concept of unemployment, as implemented in the government's monthly labor force survey, requires that an individual be engaged in an active job search (e.g., contacting employers in the reference period) to be classified as unemployed. Individuals who may want to work but have given up actively looking for employment, often labeled "discouraged workers," are excluded from the labor force concept. The existence of discouraged workers underlines the fact that over time the labor force is dynamic: Individuals enter the labor force by actively seeking work or obtaining a job, they remain in the labor force as employed, self-employed, or unemployed, or they leave the labor force through voluntary or involuntary departure from a job or by ceasing to look for work.

The ambiguities associated with what is defined as work or searching for work, as well as measurement errors introduced during the data collection process, mean that labor force data collected in different settings at a specific point in time are not necessarily comparable, and those data may not be comparable over time within a particular setting. Historical data in the United States before 1940 are based on the "gainful worker" concept that counted as employed only those who reported a usual occupation whether or not they were actually working. This approach tended to understate the participation rates of women, and so the measured rise in the economic activity rate of women over time (discussed below) may be overstated. Similarly, differences across countries in social, cultural, and legal norms may determine whether certain activities performed by women are counted as "economic activity" (e.g., unpaid family workers), often making female labor force measures across countries difficult to compare.

Levels and Trends

The economically active population varies across economies at a specific point in time and for the same economy over time, and the demographic composition of the labor force varies as well. In general, the process of economic development is associated with an overall rise in the measured economic activity rate as subsistence agriculture gives way to surplus agricultural production that is sold in the market and as the process of industrialization results in a pool of wage laborers. In the early stages of development a substantial proportion of the labor force is employed in the agricultural (primary) sector of the economy, in contrast to more advanced industrial economies, in which a greater proportion of the labor force is employed in the manufacturing (secondary) and services (tertiary) sectors.

Thus, the process of economic growth is associated with a shift from the primary to the secondary and eventually to the tertiary sector. In the United States, for example, the share of the labor force employed in agriculture declined steadily from 38 percent in 1900 to less than 3 percent in 2000. Since the 1970s, the proportion in manufacturing has declined, signaling the advent of the postindustrial age, and the services sector has made up the difference. In contrast, typically 40 percent or more of employment in countries classified as low-income by the World Bank is in the agricultural sector.

Female labor force patterns. With economic development, the labor force patterns can vary for different demographic groups. The economic activity rate for adult women, particularly married women, is hypothesized to follow a U-shaped pattern over the course of economic development. At low levels of development, in which certain forms of agriculture with a high demand for female labor dominate, most women participate in the labor force to a great extent, often as unpaid workers on the family farm or in small family enterprises. As incomes rise, their participation rates in the market economy decline as women increase their participation in home production, partly as a result of an income effect and often because social norms or other barriers prevent their employment in the growing manufacturing sector. With further development, women's participation in the market economy may increase as education levels and wages rise and the services sector provides more opportunities for female employment. The rise in women's labor force participation may be accompanied by other economic, social, and political transformations, such as the increased availability of market substitutes for home-produced goods, changes in family formation and the level and timing of fertility, and shifts in the power dynamics between men and women.

Tracing the upward-sloping portion of the U-shaped curve, the steep rise in the female labor force—the so-called feminization of the labor force—was one of the most significant labor force trends in the developed world in the twentieth century. In the United States, for example, about one in five women of labor force age was classified as being in the labor force in 1900; by 2000 that figure had tripled. The growth in the female participation rate accelerated during World War II and in the following decades, with a more rapid rise in the participation rate for married women than in that for single women, among whom participation rates were relatively high even in earlier times. The overall long-term growth of the female labor force has been replicated in many other developed countries, although the time path during the twentieth century differed among countries such as the United States, Great Britain, and France.

In the last decades of the twentieth century the most remarkable feature of the U.S. labor force was the increasing rates of participation among women with young children. About 70 percent of married women with one child or more participated in the labor force in 2000 compared with 40 percent in 1970, and the rate increased even faster (from 30% to 63%) for married women with children under age six. Whereas in the 1940s participation rates for women tailed off after ages 20 to 24, the life-cycle pattern for women in 2000 more closely resembled the life-cycle pattern for men, with a broad peak in the labor force participation rate at ages 25 to 44. Events, such as marriage and childbearing, that in the past would have led women to withdraw from the paid labor force, are less likely to elicit that response today.

Male labor force patterns. In high-income countries, at the same time that women have increased their rates of labor force participation, the reverse has taken place among men, largely as a result of later entry into the labor force caused by longer periods of education and earlier departure from the labor force as a result of a falling age of retirement. Again, taking the United States as an illustra-

tion, 87 percent of men of labor force age were classified as being in the labor force in 1900; by the year 2000 that percentage had fallen to 75. Among men over age 65 the reduction was from 68 percent to less than 20 percent. Similar patterns are observed in most other industrialized countries.

Over the course of the twentieth century the process and motivations for retirement changed as the secular rise in incomes and the increase in post-retirement income available through public and private pension plans allowed men to leave the labor force voluntarily to enjoy a period of leisure while living independently. This stands in contrast to earlier eras, when poor health typically might have been the primary cause for leaving the labor force and men who retired had to depend on family members for income support. In addition to rising incomes, these changes were made possible by advances in technology that reduced the price of recreation and the public provision of recreational goods and services.

The employment of children. The process of economic development also is associated with reduced rates of labor market activity for children as changes in technology and improvements in adult labor markets, along with the increased availability of (and necessity for) schooling, reduce the demand for child labor. In the United States, for example, the minimum age for being counted in the labor force was age 10 in 1900, age 14 by 1940, and age 16 by 1970. Rather than focusing on child labor per se, the debate in the United States centers on the costs and benefits for youth of participating in paid employment before reaching adulthood, and most U.S. states have some form of compulsory schooling laws and laws restricting the labor market activity of youth.

The employment of children is an issue of international concern because child labor, even at very young ages, is considerably more prevalent in many low-income countries. Although the International Labour Organization (ILO) defines age 15 as the minimum acceptable age for being economically active for most types of work, the ILO estimates that in 1995 some 120 million children age 5 to 14 were participating in full-time paid employment and another 130 million children worked part-time (ILO 1996). Despite such statistics, there is little agreement on either theoretical or policy grounds for specific courses of action in response to this situation, such as the use of international labor standards, trade sanctions, and outright bans on child labor.

See also: *Census; Occupation and Industry.*

BIBLIOGRAPHY

Basu, Kaushik. 1999. "Child Labor: Cause, Consequence, and Cure, with Remarks on International Labor Standards." *Journal of Economic Literature* 37: 1,083–1,119.

Behrman, Jere R. 1999. "Labor Markets in Developing Countries." In *Handbook of Labor Economics,* Vol. 3, ed. Orley Ashenfelter and David Card. Amsterdam: Elsevier.

Costa, Dora L. 1998. *The Evolution of Retirement: An American Economic History, 1880–1990.* Chicago: University of Chicago Press.

———. 2000. "From Mill Town to Board Room: The Rise of Women's Paid Labor." National Bureau of Economic Research Working Paper No. 7608. Cambridge, MA.

Goldin, Claudia. 1995. "The U-Shaped Female Labor Force Function in Economic Development and Economic History." In *Investment in Women's Human Capital and Economic Development,* ed. T. Paul Schultz. Chicago: University of Chicago Press.

Gruber, Jonathan, and David A. Wise, eds. 1999. *Social Security and Retirement around the World.* Chicago: University of Chicago Press.

International Labour Organization. 1996. *Economically Active Populations: Estimates and Projections, 1950–2010.* Geneva: International Labour Organization.

Killingsworth, Mark R., and James J. Heckman. 1986. "Female Labor Supply: A Survey." In *Handbook of Labor Economics,* Vol. 1, ed. Orley Ashenfelter and Richard Layard. Amsterdam: Elsevier.

Lazear, Edward P. 1986. "Retirement from the Labor Force." In *Handbook of Labor Economics,* Vol. 1, ed. Orley Ashenfelter and Richard Layard. Amsterdam: Elsevier.

Pencavel, John. 1986. "Labor Supply of Men: A Survey." In *Handbook of Labor Economics,* Vol. 1, ed. Orley Ashenfelter and Richard Layard. Amsterdam: Elsevier.

Ruhm, Christopher. 1997. "Is High School Employment Consumption or Investment?" *Journal of Labor Economics* 15(4): 735–776.

U.S. Census Bureau. 2001. *Statistical Abstract of the United States: 2001.* Washington, D.C.: U.S. Government Printing Office.

Lynn A. Karoly

LABOR MIGRATION, INTERNATIONAL

Migration for work is one of the major international migration streams. Although successful entry tends to generate international migration streams of dependents not seeking employment, and has other long-term demographic consequences, understanding such repercussions requires prior understanding of international labor migration per se.

Labor migration—as compared with admission of refugees and asylum seekers, and family reunification, which creates or reconstitutes families after one migrates—matches most directly the interests of immigrants with those of the receiving country. Indeed, the main form of international migration has been the "labor-" or work/skills-based one. It has been the dominant form of immigration to the United States in all but the most recent phase; it is the foundation and principal multiplier of the post–World War II migration to northern and western Europe; and it is the almost exclusive variant of the migration flows to the Gulf States since the 1970s, as well as to East Asian and certain South and Southeast Asian states since the 1980s.

Given the large differences in wages and opportunities between potential sending and receiving countries, labor migration streams are likely to remain very large. In the contemporary world, international migration tends to be strictly controlled by the receiving countries. Accordingly, permanent employment-based (also referred to here as "immigrant") visas issued on the ground that an employer seeks the recipient's skills are rather limited. The United States, Canada, Australia, New Zealand, and, in some ways, South Africa—the so-called traditional countries of immigration—have a history of offering permanent employment and skill-based visas as a major part of their immigration programs. The first four of these countries, as of the late 1990s, have accounted for roughly 300,000 such admissions annually—including both principals *and* their families. Few other states offer permanent immigration status up-front on the basis of skills, education, and/or fit with labor market needs.

On the other hand, *temporary* admissions of foreigners (also referred to here as "migrants") who either enter explicitly in order to work or gain a derivative right to do so have been growing rapidly. This is the primary means for gaining entry into most advanced industrial states; increasingly, it is also the means through which ever-larger proportions of permanent immigrants initially enter these states—particularly the United States but also key member-states of the European Union (EU) and Canada.

Most visas in this admission stream, whether permanent or temporary, are awarded to persons with education and skills. Admissions may also be based on a person's relevant experience for particular jobs, even in the absence of formal skills.

Most states follow a few more or less similar routes of selection and admission. They have mechanisms for admitting foreign workers for certain types of employment, both permanently and temporarily, and employ similar screening mechanisms for these admissions.

Skilled Migration: Converging Practices in Drawing on the Global Labor Pool

One component of the employment- or skill-based system of labor migration is temporary admission. This is gaining in popularity across states, with often-similar procedures being adopted. This increasing convergence is in large part the result of the reality of multilateral arrangements, such as those relating to trade-in-services, that are anchored on the principle of "national treatment" or reciprocity, as well as of demands among economic partners to codify reciprocal access for each other's nationals in the areas of business, trade, investment, or cultural exchanges. Many of these arrangements also include either explicit employment components (such as visas for about 70 professional occupations under the North American Free Trade Agreement) or allow employment that is "incidental" to the visa's primary purpose (such as when a student is allowed to work part-time during the school year and full-time when school is not in session, or when a cultural exchange visitor is allowed to teach or give lectures for a fee).

There is, however, another and more consequential reason for such convergence in practices. Competitive pressures in a globalized economy put a premium on cutting-edge technical skills and talent—wherever these may be found. With low trade barriers and with technology, like capital, recognizing neither borders nor nationality, individual initiative and talent may have become the most valuable global resource. As a result, the developed world's immigration systems are well on the way to guaranteeing access to those who have the desired attributes and are willing to put them to work for a firm—wherever that firm may be located.

Not all advanced industrial democracies draw on the global talent pool with the same intensity. It is clear, however, that the high-end immigration door is opening wider and by historical standards remarkably quickly. The EU member states, led by Germany and the United Kingdom, the latter an experienced user of highly skilled foreign nationals, are leading the way in selecting qualified workers from abroad.

This opening is likely to refuel two "old" political discourses. The first one focuses on the failure of the recipient country to adapt its own training and education systems to the requirements of the so-called new economy adequately enough to meet the needs of employers from within its own labor pool. The second discourse dwells on the effect (and propriety) of deeper and more systematic "helpings" by advanced industrial societies from the human capital pool of the developing world. With most EU member states, Japan, other advanced economies, and, increasingly, many advanced developing states poised to permit entry to highly qualified labor, the "brain drain" issue is likely to gain increasing political (and analytical) relevance in the years ahead.

Screening Foreigners Entering for Work Purposes

A state or its corporate citizens choose the foreign workers to be admitted in three principal ways. The first, emphasizing the protection of domestic workers, uses rigorous labor market tests. The second seeks to identify and rectify labor market shortages and skill/locational mismatches. The third stresses the long-term economic interests of the receiving society. In reality, of course, a combination of selection criteria is typically employed.

Most European systems emphasize domestic (and in the EU case, EU-wide) worker protection schemes—although an effort is underway to move away from that model. The United States places its primary focus on rectifying labor market shortages and mismatches—with an increasingly pronounced tendency toward simplifying the labor market tests it requires. Canada, Australia, and New Zealand have increasingly focused on long-term economic interests (what may be called, at least in their permanent systems, the "skills accretion" formula); they eschew most labor market tests.

The principal agent in each selection scheme varies accordingly. In most EU member states, the prospective employer plays an important role but is typically constrained by government predispositions to micromanage the process and deny the employer's petition. In the United States, the principal agent is almost always the prospective employer, both for the permanent and the temporary employment-based systems. In Canada and Australia, the principal agent for the permanent system is the government, with the prospective employer playing a minor role in the process. Employers, however, play a larger and increasingly independent part in the fast-expanding temporary worker admissions system.

Domestic Worker Protection Schemes

Domestic worker protection schemes differ in whether the controls are pre- or post-entry. The former is the dominant variant throughout the world; the latter is a U.S. innovation dating from 1989.

Pre-entry controls. One way to select foreign workers is to test each admission application against the availability of the eligible pool of workers for a particular job opening at a particular place and time. Under this system, the petitioner (typically the prospective employer) must demonstrate to the government's satisfaction that no domestic or other eligible workers are available for the job in question and that the employment of the foreign national will not depress the wages of such workers in similar jobs. Both requirements have proved extremely vexing both on administrative and methodological grounds.

Because of the cost and complexity of the process, an emerging consensus questions the value and efficacy of case-by-case assessments. Moreover, the

approach arguably focuses on the wrong goal. It views foreign workers as offering case-by-case relief for specific job vacancies, whereas in the twenty-first century's competitive environment firms often choose workers (domestic or foreign) because small differences in the quality and specificity of skills can lead to substantial differences in performance. This argues for selecting foreign workers on the basis of their mix of skills, experience, education, and other characteristics that maximize the probability both of immediate *and* long-term labor market and economic success.

Post-entry controls: attestations. Post-entry control systems expend most regulatory and enforcement energy on the terms and conditions of the foreign worker's employment. Unlike the pre-entry test, the post-entry one is entirely a U.S. innovation. In its various forms, the attestation mechanism is the principal example of this type of control.

An attestation—a legally binding set of employer declarations about the terms and conditions under which a foreign worker will be engaged—reduces up-front barriers to the entry of needed foreign workers but still seeks to protect domestic worker interests through subsequent auditing and enforcement of the terms of the attestation. (The terms are designed to protect domestic workers from employer reliance on foreign workers to affect a union dispute, reduce wages, or make working conditions worse.)

Attestations have a number of positive features. If well conceived and implemented, attestations give employers access to needed foreign workers without harming the interests of domestic workers. They give potentially affected parties an opportunity to challenge the matters to which an employer attests. They are responsive to changing labor market conditions. They require minimal hands-on engagement by the government in an area where both data and procedures are weakest. And they can be an inducement to cooperative labor-management relations in recruitment.

Attestations, as practiced in the early twenty-first century, however, also have a number of shortcomings. Some of these are similar to the problems with the pre-entry control process. For example, the government is typically ill-equipped to determine the appropriate wage for any particular foreign worker. Furthermore, some of the documentation requirements of an attestation appear to be quite burdensome for employers and require release of what they consider proprietary information on wages. Attestations could potentially become pawns in labor–management disputes, subject to frivolous challenge by worker representatives. And the system is open to abuse by unscrupulous employers.

The Points Test

If the two main selection methods identified above are flawed—the first mostly in concept, the second in execution—what might be an alternative? Some states rely systematically on a points test for selecting large pluralities of their permanent "labor" immigrants. (New Zealand's proportion stands at three-fifths of total immigration.) Only those foreign workers whose specified personal and quantifiable attributes add up to a pre-agreed "pass mark" are allowed to immigrate permanently. (Among the characteristics currently receiving the highest point totals are education, age [comparative youthfulness], language and communication skills, and experience in a professional field.) Variants of the points system are practiced in Canada, Australia, and New Zealand. Germany has shown interest in the system.

A points system has several advantages over other selection mechanisms, at least when it is relied upon selectively and in conjunction with mechanisms that allow firms to choose directly some of the foreign workers they need. It inspires confidence as a policy instrument that applies universal, and ostensibly "hard" (i.e., quantitative and objective), selection criteria to economic-stream immigrants. Hence, it is less susceptible to the criticisms associated with the case-by-case system's "gamesmanship" between employers and bureaucrats. It can reassure key segments of the receiving society that the selection criteria for economic-stream immigrants conform to the state's economic interests. (This makes immigration politically more defensible than the alternatives discussed earlier.) And the criteria included can be altered or reweighted, or the pass mark adjusted, to respond quickly to shifting economic priorities.

A points-like system can thus shift the focus of permanent economic-stream immigration from an almost exclusive emphasis on case-by-case determination of specific job vacancies to one that takes into greater account broad economic interests. Properly conceived and implemented, and accompanied by opportunities for firms to select key workers on their own, a points-like system asks the government to do what it can be fairly good at (i.e., gauging the broad direction and needs of the economy over an intermediate- to long-range time horizon) rather than forcing it to do what it is least good at (i.e., case-by-case job matching).

Other Labor Migration Schemes

This article's focus so far has been on the formal, and individualized, selection schemes practiced most diligently by advanced industrial societies. However, the largest share of labor migration occurs through the following routes: (a) outside of formal controls; (b) through seasonal and otherwise short-term work contracts; (c) through a variety of training and similar schemes; (d) through trans-border work schemes; and (e) finally, through contracts that involve large numbers of workers, most typically tied to a particular construction or other major project.

The first form includes not only illegal migration, but also forms of migration that in many ways both predate and bypass attempts at formal regulation. Much intra-Africa migration, for instance, fits that latter characterization, as is much of the seasonal migration discussed immediately below. Both forms together amount to a total of several million persons per year.

Formal seasonal, other short-term, and industry-specific labor migration is also significant in numbers yet its size is difficult to estimate. Suffice it to say that few nationals of advanced industrial societies pick their own fruits and vegetables, tend to their agricultural holdings, staff seasonal or tourist related activities, or perform domestic and other forms of menial, difficult, and poorly-compensated work. These jobs have become the domain of foreign workers throughout the developed and, increasingly, the developing world. The workers who staff these jobs number in the low millions—probably between 2 and 3 million—and they hold a variety of legal statuses (the dominant one being an illegal status).

Training and similar schemes are notable in such countries as Japan, Germany, the U.S., and other countries that rely on them rather systematically. The numbers involved are in the lower hundreds of thousands. Such schemes are typically thinly disguised efforts to circumvent a government's prohibition of particular forms of entry, most typically directed against the importation of low-skilled workers. In most of these instances, government agencies effectively collude with employers to admit such prescribed persons.

Trans-border work schemes are typically found in neighboring countries. In their most formal expression, such schemes explicitly or implicitly allow limited employment and take the form of bilateral arrangements that often predate the strict regulation of migration. The U.S. "border-crosser" scheme has its roots in practices that go back to the early twentieth century; several hundred thousand people have a right to participate in that scheme but not all do. Germany developed similar arrangements in the 1990s with neighbors to its East, as have some other European states, more recently Italy and Greece. The total number of these additional schemes, however, generates tens of thousands of work visas.

The final form of labor migration, contract labor schemes, saw their heyday in the 1970s and 1980s. At that time, hundreds of thousands of Middle Easterners (particularly Palestinians and Egyptians), as well as East-, Southeast-, and South-Asians found contract employment in often massive projects located mostly in the Gulf states. The number of such workers in that region has fluctuated but generally numbered in the neighborhood of 2 to 3 million in the 1970s and 1980s, but has shrunk to nearly half that much in the 1990s—with South Asians having replaced most other nationalities.

See also: *Immigration, Benefits and Costs of; Immigration, Unauthorized; International Migration.*

BIBLIOGRAPHY

Bertrand, Gilles, Anna Michalski, and Lucio R. Pench. 1999. "Scenarios Europe 2010: Five Possible Futures for Europe." Working Paper. Brussels: European Commission, Forward Studies Unit.

Bilsborrow, R. E., et al. 1997. *International Migration Statistics: Guidelines for Improving Data Collection Systems.* Geneva: International Labor Office.

Brown, Michael E., and Sumit Ganguly, eds. 1997. *Government Policies and Ethnic Relations in Asia and the Pacific.* Cambridge, MA: MIT Press.

Commission for Labor Cooperation and North American Agreement on Labor Cooperation. 1997. *North American Labor Markets: A Comparative Profile.* Lanham, MD: Bernan Press.

International Labor Office. 1999. "Meeting the Challenge of Global Labor Mobility." Issues Paper. Geneva: International Labor Office.

Massey, Douglas S., et al. 1998. *Worlds in Motion: Understanding International Migration at the End of the Millennium.* New York: Oxford University Press.

McDonald, David A., ed. 2000. *On Borders: Perspectives on Cross-Border Migration in Southern Africa.* New York: St. Martin's Press.

Newland, Kathleen, and Demetrios G. Papademetriou. 1998/1999. "Managing International Migration: Tracking the Emergence of a New International Regime." *UCLA Journal of International Law and Foreign Affairs* 3(Fall/Winter 1998–99): 637–657.

Papademetriou, Demetrios G., and Stephen Yale-Loehr. 1996. *Balancing Interests: Rethinking U.S. Selection of Skilled Immigrants.* Washington, D.C.: International Migration Policy Program, Carnegie Endowment for International Peace.

Salt, John. 1998. *Current Trends in International Migration in Europe.* Council of Europe.

SOPEMI. Various years. *Trends in International Migration Annual Report.* Paris: Organization for Economic Cooperation and Development.

Stalker, Peter. 2000. *Workers Without Fronteirs: The Impact of Globalization on International Migration.* Boulder, CO: Lynne Rienner.

United Nations Department of Economic and Social Affairs. 1998. *World Population Monitoring 1997,* ST/ESA/SER.A/169. New York: United Nations.

———. 2003. *International Migration Report 2002.* New York: United Nations.

DEMETRIOS G. PAPADEMETRIOU

LANDRY, ADOLPHE

(1874–1956)

Adolphe Landry was a French man of letters, economist, demographer, and statesman. He was educated in the Ecole Normale Superieure, but as a young man he was attracted by socialist ideas and abandoned plans for a literary career in preference for studies in the social sciences. Soon he was writing and publishing papers on a wide range of economic, historical, legal, and sociological subjects. In 1907, Landry was appointed to a chair at the Ecole Pratique des Hautes Etudes. In 1910, he was elected to Parliament as a deputy from his native Corsica, and during his long political career he occupied several ministerial posts.

Landry's special interest in population was first signaled by two articles that appeared in 1909. One was on the population ideas of the eighteenth-century French economist and intellectual leader of the Physiocrats, François Quesnay; Landry's later writings also were inspired by the study of the history of economic thought. The other article presented his first formulation of demographic evolution as a sequence consisting of three stages—a primitive regime, characterized by high (uncontrolled) fertility and high mortality; an intermediate regime, such as in eighteenth- and nineteenth-century France and Britain, in which the higher standards of living that had been attained began to be protected by restriction of fertility (primarily through later marriage); and finally the contemporary regime, in which control of fertility becomes a generalized practice through contraception and abortion.

The most important contribution made by Landry to population theory was a full development of these ideas in the book *La révolution démographique* that appeared in 1934 (preceded by an eponymous article published in 1933, which later also appeared in English). "La révolution démographique"—the Demographic Revolution—denotes essentially the same process that, under the influence of the English-language literature and parallel theoretical development of the concept in the United States by demographers such as Warren Thompson, Frank Notestein, and Kingsley Davis, is primarily known as the demographic transition. Stylized presentations of the demographic transition routinely pictured the process as leading from a high-level equilibrium of birth and death rates to a low-level one: a path from a quasi-stationary state to a stationary state, with a period of more or less rapid and sustained population growth in between. In contrast, Landry's more flamboyant label signaled that he perceived the dynamics as one leading to long-term population disequilibrium. He expected birth rates to fall below death rates, first in the West and eventually spreading to the rest of the globe.

Landry was deeply concerned with what he saw as the predictable consequences of impending depopulation in France (the country farthest along toward that prospect): decadence resembling that of Venice or even extinction of civilization, exemplified by Greece and the Roman Empire. His concern was manifested in some four decades of political activism aimed at halting or reversing the process. From 1912 on, Landry took a leading role in the *Alliance nationale contre la dépopulation* and, in the interwar years, initiated a variety of legislative measures intended to improve the economic status of families with children so as to stimulate fertility. These efforts culminated in the *Code de la famille,* adopted by Parliament barely a month before the outbreak of World War II. Landry was also influential in the design of postwar French social policy, shaping social legislation with a strong pronatalist orientation; he attributed the resurgence of the birth rate in France to the effects of these policies.

Landry's 1945 book, *Traité de démographie,* written in collaboration with younger French demographers, was a then-unparalleled and up-to-date single-volume summation of the methods of demographic analysis, but it also presented a substantive description of population processes and population issues. Continuing his prominent prewar role in international scientific activities in the field of population, in 1947 Landry was elected to serve as the first president of the reconstituted International Union for the Scientific Study of Population.

See also: *Demographic Transition; Population Thought, Contemporary; Sauvy, Alfred.*

BIBLIOGRAPHY

SELECTED WORKS BY ADOLPHE LANDRY.

Landry, Adolphe. 1909. "Les idées de Quesnay sur la population." *Revue d'histoire des doctrines économiques et sociales* 2.

———. 1909. "Les trois théories de la population." *Revue Scientia.*

———. 1929. "Le maximum et l'optimum de la population." *Revue Scientia* April.

———. 1934. *La révolution démographique.* Paris: Sirey.

———. 1936. "Quelques aperçus concernant la dé-population dans l'Antiquité gréco-romaine." *Revue Historique* January–February.

———. 1941. *La démographie française.* Paris: Press-es universitaires de France.

———. 1987. "Demographic Revolution." *Population and Development Review,* 13(4): 731–740; originally published in 1933 as "La révolution démographique." In *Economic Essays in Honour of Gustav Cassel.* London: George Allen and Unwin.

Landry, Adolphe, H. Bunle, P. Depoid, M. Huber, and A. Sauvy. 1945. *Traité de démographie.* Paris: Payot.

SELECTED WORKS ABOUT ADOLPHE LANDRY.

Demartini, A. M. 1990. "Un destin bourgeois: Adol-phe Landry et sa famille." *Ethnologie française* 20(1): 12–24.

Sauvy, Alfred. 1956. "Adolphe Landry." *Population* 11(4): 609–620.

JEAN-CLAUDE CHESNAIS

LAND USE

Humans use the foundation of land for dwellings, the crops of land for eating, the grass of land for grazing, and the timber of land for building. Land brings with it the minerals and fuel beneath, and it receives humanity's waste. People fight over land. Although environmental ethics strengthen human support for natural animals and plants in their competition for habitat, human dominion over the land still leaves for nature only what humanity spares from its own uses. Logically, land cover differs from land use, but it is useful to think of the covers of urban settlement, crop, grass, and forest as four classes or possibilities of land use.

A simple equation connects land use to population times average food requirement divided by food yield per unit area. The German geographer and geologist Albrecht Penck (1858–1945) wrote this equation in a journal of geopolitics in 1924. Earlier the English economist T. R. Malthus (1766–1834) phrased humanity's dependence on food from land in dynamic terms when he wrote that the slow *addition* of food from land would limit humankind's exponential *multiplication*.

Location

Before considering global land use in simple equations, the factor of location must be considered. In 1826 the Mecklenburg landowner and economist Johann von Thünen (1783–1850) published *Isolated State,* a work that introduced location into a model of a conceptually isolated land area surrounding a city. Accessibility was added to the well-known factors of soil and climate that determined land use. Von Thünen assumed, of course, that farmers would maximize their incomes by considering yield, price, and production expense. To these, however, he added the distance to market multiplied by transportation and produce-deterioration rates. The transport cost to the central city of his isolated state creates concentric zones. In the inner zone, gardening prevails but falls off in a short distance because fruit and vegetables deteriorate, and deterioration is part of transport cost. The low value of critical but bulky wood and hay restricts their production to the next zone. A dried crop containing many calories is worth many dollars per ton and does not deteriorate. Hence such crops as grain or onions grow in the third zone. Because cattle go to market on their own legs, the pastoral zone lies farthest from the city.

Beyond raising yields and cutting expenses, farmers soften von Thünen's law in other ways. Trains, trucks, and airplanes cheapen transport, while refrigeration slows deterioration, lowering the obstacle of distance. Nevertheless, as famine in isolated regions can still demonstrate, that the obstacle persists.

Urban Habitat

Location in the city itself imparts a value to developed or urban use that trumps other uses. An ancient city pressed upon local resources and demanded inventions in farming and transport not required by roaming hunters and fishers. A city could finance and build canals, roads, and irrigation, which scattered people could not. Urban use persists, as a ruin like a Roman road attests, whereas crops, grass, and trees can replace one another. Because urban use trumps and outlasts others, it is fortunate, as Ester Boserup argued, that paving and companions elicit

FIGURE 1

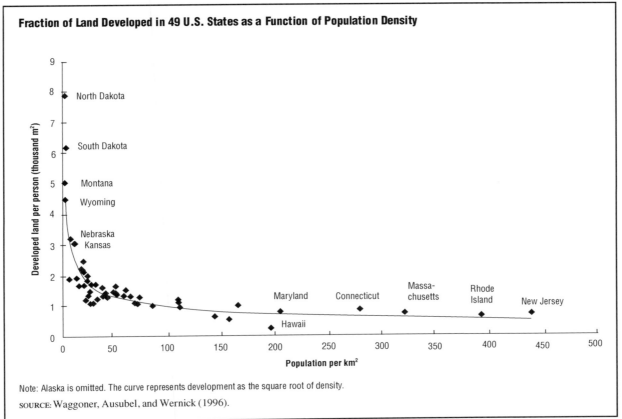

Fraction of Land Developed in 49 U.S. States as a Function of Population Density

Note: Alaska is omitted. The curve represents development as the square root of density.

SOURCE: Waggoner, Ausubel, and Wernick (1996).

more cleverness and invention than wilderness and solitude.

The intensity of urban use is indicated by the area in hectares developed or urbanized per thousand population. Assuming that the area of large cities is fully urbanized, one can calculate the area per thousand persons as less than 4 hectares in Mumbai (Bombay), India, and in Hong Kong in the 1990s. Focusing on smaller areas lowers the estimate of urban use: In 1995 the average use of land per thousand persons in New York City's five boroughs was 11 hectares; on the island of Manhattan, it was only 5 hectares. Twenty-four U.S. counties, including New York in the East and San Francisco in the West, as well as counties in Michigan and Minnesota in the North and Louisiana and Florida in the South, used fewer than 100 hectares per thousand inhabitants—that is, they had population densities of more than 1,000 persons per square kilometer.

Urban use encompasses more than dwellings. In the United States, for example, it includes industrial, commercial, and institutional land; construction and waste disposal sites; railroad yards, airports, and urban transport ways; cemeteries and golf courses; and water structures. The development of land in 49 U.S. states (omitting Alaska) demonstrates that urban use does not increase in proportion to population (see Figure 1). Thus rich as well as poor congregate and use little urban land, making city dwellers, despite their generally higher incomes, the most sparing of land.

At the same time that people congregate on one scale, however, they diffuse on another. Thus in the United States from 1920 to 1990, while the urban proportion grew, the number of persons per occupied housing unit declined from an average 4.3 to 2.7. Persistently willing to travel an hour a day in their journey to work while transport speeds increase, people spread from central cities over ever-larger metropolitan regions, building suburbs. During the 1990s, the population of metropolitan areas of 2 to 5 million people outgrew that of both more and less populous areas. From 1950 to 1990 urban land expanded at 2.8 percent per year versus total population growth of 1.2 percent, but in 1990 urban use still occupied less than 4 percent of all U.S. land. These trends are echoed in another developed nation, the Netherlands. And some slowing of the growth of urban land use can be seen in both countries.

Cropland

Of the calories and protein supporting people worldwide, 84 percent of the calories and 75 percent of the protein are from crops. Because many animals, bred for human consumption, eat crops, the dominance of crops exceeds even these high percentages. Nevertheless, such a simple proportionality as Penck envisioned between cropland and population must be modified. Dimensions prove that the forces on the right side of the following equation must be identical to the expanse of cropland:

$$Cropland = Population \times Income \times Appetite \times Yield$$

where cropland is area in hectares, income is gross domestic product (GDP) per person, appetite is food production divided by GDP, and finally what is termed yield is cropland in hectares divided by food production. This identity implies an independence of the forces. Nevertheless, per capita food consumption rises as income increases, but not in proportion to the rise of income, causing the force of appetite (food per GDP) to fall.

Since 1960, the annual growth of the first force, global population, has slowed from above 2 percent to appreciably below 2 percent. Growth of income also slowed from more than 3 percent to below 2 percent per year. As income rose, the appetite ratio fell. The final force, cropland over food production, fell rather steadily at 2 percent per year. The net of these forces is the rate of expansion of cropland. From 1961 to 1997 cropland expansion averaged about 0.33 percent per year. The decline of the appetite and yield ratios moderated the impact on cropland area that Penck's simple equation would have predicted. The negative income elasticity of the appetite ratio tempered the effect of rising income and, in combination with farmers' improving yields, spared natural habitat from crop use. While benefiting nature, this sparing also benefited humankind, because the area of prime land suitable to be converted to crops is limited.

Grassland

The Food and Agriculture Organization (FAO) reports a category of land use called "permanent pastures," which it defines as land used permanently (five years or more) for herbaceous forage crops, either cultivated or growing wild, but apologizes that the dividing line between this category and "forests and woodland" is rather indefinite. In 1993 permanent pasture comprised 26 percent of global land, slightly more than twice the total area of cropland, slightly less than that of forests and woodlands, and slightly more than the land unaccounted for by FAO.

Demand for the protein in the meat and milk of grazing animals might seem to connect pasture to population. The change in human and animal populations, animal protein production, and the land used for pasture, however, proves that the connection is not a simple proportionality. From 1961 to 1998 humans increased at an average rate of 1.8 percent per year, but cattle increased at only 1 percent per year. The FAO-estimated 0.9 percent rise of protein added to the 1.8 percent increase of people means protein production rose fully 2.7 percent per year, outpacing cattle populations.

Equally surprising, pasture, which might have been thought to expand enough to support the extra protein production, expanded at a rate of only 0.2 percent per year. In an identity connecting population and other factors to pasture, the ratio of protein in the food supply to pasture area had to fall 2.5 percent per year. Although more animals eating feed rather than grazing lay behind some of this finding, the principal explanation must be more productive pastures and animals plus less animal product lost before it reached the table.

Forestland

Humans harvest trees for lumber for construction, pulp for paper, and wood for fuel. They clear forests for crops and pastures. Thus the expectation that rising population will shrink forests comes easily. But, contrary to that expectation, whereas forests shrank in some places, especially Africa, they expanded in Europe and the United States. French forests, for example, began expanding in the nineteenth century despite a French population that kept growing, although relatively slowly. Geographers have labeled the change from a negative to a positive connection between population and forests (from growing population and shrinking forests to expanding forests despite growing population), the forest transition. The annual 0.2 percent shrinkage of the world forest during the 1990s was made up of disparate trends, such as a 0.8 percent shrinkage in Africa but a 0.1 to 0.2 percent expansion in Europe and the United States.

Forests can be converted to farming. Whereas global forests were shrinking by 9 million hectares per year during the 1990s, pasture was expanding only about by 2 million hectares per year and cropland by less than 1 million hectare. Thus a balance of some 6 million hectares must have gone to the residual area—neither forest, cropland, nor permanent pasture—that comprises about a third of global land. Decreasing the encroachment of crops and pasture on forest further, agricultural uses can be subtracted from the residual area, and—with soil improvement and irrigation—even on formerly barren land. Expanding agricultural use by 1 hectare need not shrink forest area by 1 hectare.

Worldwide, foresters annually harvest about 0.4 percent of the 386 billion cubic meter volume of wood standing, calling the harvest "industrial roundwood." Much fuelwood fails to appear in such statistics. Because trees grow, harvesting is not a permanent subtraction from the forest. In the timberland of the United States in 1991, for example, forests grew by 2 cubic meters per hectare, exceeding the harvest by a third. Substitutes such as coal for fuelwood, concrete for poles, electronic documents for paper, and chipboard for planks, plus more efficient mills, steadily lessened the role of timber products in the U.S. economy.

High-yielding trees can spare natural habitat. Plantation trees can grow up to 20 cubic meters per hectare per year, producing the same harvest from 1 hectare as 10 hectares of the average U.S. forest. South Africa has only 4 percent of African land and 1 to 2 percent of its forest cover, but it has 19 percent of all African plantations and in 1994 cut fully 26 percent of industrial roundwood harvested on the continent. The forest area of South Africa scarcely changed from 1990 to 2000, whereas the forest of the entire continent of Africa shrank 0.8 percent annually. Intensive management can lessen the extent of logging use on natural lands.

The Residuum

After subtracting agricultural and forest land from the global supply, a residuum remains. Urban uses, mines, and oil wells occupy a few percent of it, but people leave much dry, infertile, or cold land unused. With effort, irrigation, and fertilizer, people can put some of this residuum to use.

Conclusion

Land use means land use by people. Therefore, population is the first determinant of land use, followed by the income of the population, which multiplies capability per person. Generally, however, the consumption of food and other products of land (from space for foundations to wood for fuel) does not rise in proportion to income, meaning consumption grows more slowly than population multiplied by income. Substitutes such as electronic messages for paper messages and gas fuel for wood fuel are one reason. Other technological developments such as skyscrapers and high-yield grain or trees add further leverage to modify a simple projection of land use in step with population.

See also: *Carrying Capacity; Deforestation; Density and Distribution of Population; Remote Sensing; Sustainable Development; Water and Population.*

BIBLIOGRAPHY

Alexandratos, Nikos, ed. 1995. *World Agriculture: Towards 2010. A FAO Study.* New York: Wiley.

Ausubel, Jesse H., and Cesare Marchetti. 2001. "The Evolution of Transport." *Industrial Physicist* 7(2): 20–24.

Boserup, Ester. 1981. *Population and Technological Change.* Chicago: University of Chicago Press.

Cohen, Joel E. 1995. *How Many People Can the Earth Support?* New York: Norton.

Cronon, William. 1991. *Nature's Metropolis: Chicago and the Great West.* New York: Norton.

U.S. Department of Agriculture. 1997. *Agricultural Resources and Environmental Indicators, 1996–97.* Washington, D.C.: U.S. Department of Agriculture.

Van Diepen, A. 1995. "Population, Land Use, and Housing Trends in the Netherlands, since 1950." Laxenburg, Austria: International Institute for Applied Systems Analysis.

Waggoner, Paul E., and Jesse H. Ausubel. 2001. "How Much Will Feeding More and Wealthier People Encroach on Forests?" *Population and Development Review* 27: 239–257.

Waggoner, Paul E., Jesse H. Ausubel, and Iddo K. Wernick. 1996. "Lightening the Tread of Population on the Land: American Examples." *Population and Development Review* 22: 531–545.

Young, Anthony. 1998. *Land Resources Now and for the Future.* Cambridge, Eng.: Cambridge University Press.

INTERNET RESOURCES.

Demographia. 2001. "Largest International Urban Areas: Ranked by Density." <http://www.demographia.com/db-intluadens-rank.htm>.

Food and Agriculture Organization. 2002. "FAOSTAT." <http://apps.fao.org/>.

PAUL E. WAGGONER

LANGUAGES AND SPEECH COMMUNITIES

Languages cannot be counted precisely. Each language forms an integral part of a continuum of human communication. This global continuum, which is as old as speech itself, underlies the often neglected unity of humankind. Communities seemingly separated by language are bound together by bilingual voices on one or both sides of their divide, and words, sounds, and even grammatical rules are exchanged regularly among languages that are in contact with one another.

With the worldwide spread of electronic communication, the interfaces among individual languages will become even more fluid. Multilingualism will increase. The gulf between speech and writing will narrow, as each becomes a potential electronic product of the other. More and more small speech communities will enjoy worldwide mobility through migration and through worldwide usage of telecommunication.

The growth of electronic communication inevitably favors the domination of intercommunal and international relations among a restricted number of languages dominated by English. However, electronic communication also assists in maintaining the use of more localized languages and dialects as markers of communal identity, especially when their speakers are physically separated.

Distribution of Languages by Numbers of Speakers

Populations cannot be enumerated precisely in regard to individual languages except in the case of languages spoken within small circumscribed communities. One cannot define when learners become adequate speakers: Estimates of the global population of speakers of English thus may range from less than 1 billion to almost 2 billion, depending on the definition of proficiency. However, it is possible to make useful estimates of the relative importance of languages worldwide or within specific populations.

At the beginning of the twenty-first century 27 modern "arterial languages" are accessible to 1 percent or more of humankind (i.e., each language to a population of 60 million or more) (See Table 1). Two thirds of those languages fall within a band of between 1.0 and 2.5 percent of the world's total population, ranging from Tagalog, Korean, Vietnamese, Thai with Lao, Tamil, Telugu, Italian, Persian with Tajik, Panjabi, Marathi, Wu, Cantonese, and Swahili (between 60 million and 90 million speakers each) to Javanese, Turkish with Azerbaijani, Japanese, French, and German (between 100 million and 135 million speakers each).

The remaining nine arterial languages are the giants of modern spoken and written communication, with each one being accessible to more than 3 percent of humankind. Seven of these languages are closely related to and draw an important part of their heritage from five major classical written languages (listed with the names of the modern languages in parentheses): Classical Chinese (Mandarin and its close relatives), Sanskrit (Hindi with Urdu and Bengali, along with their close relatives), Classical Arabic (Modern Arabic in its western and eastern forms), Latin (Spanish and Portuguese and their close relatives), and Church Slavonic (Russian and its close relatives).

The phrase "close relatives" conceals the basic problem of what a language is. The name "Chinese" covers a unified writing system but a great variety of spoken forms that are used largely within the same nation-state. Speakers of Spanish and Portuguese have relatively easy access to other Latin-derived ar-

TABLE 1

Major Languages of the World

Language Group	Language	Population (millions)	Main Countries or Regions
Afro-Asiatic	Arabic	250	Middle East, North Africa
Austronesian	Malay, Indonesian	200	Indonesia, Malaysia
	Javanese	100	Indonesia
	Tagalog	60	Philippines
Other Eurasian	Turkish, Azerbaijani	100	Turkey, Azerbaijan, Turkmenistan
	Japanese	130	Japan
	Korean	75	South Korea, North Korea
	Vietnamese	75	Vietnam
	Thai, Lao	90	Thailand, Laos
	Tamil	90	India, Sri Lanka
	Telugu	70	India
Indo-European	Spanish	500	Spain, Latin America
	Portuguese	200	Brazil, Portugal, Mozambique, Angola
	French	135	France, Belgium, Switzerland, Canada, Central and West Africa
	Italian	70	Italy, Switzerland
	English	1000	(countries in all continents)
	German, Dutch	135	Germany, Austria, Switzerland
	Russian, Belarussian	320	Russia, Belarus
	Persian, Tajik	60	Iran, Afghanistan, Tajikistan
	Hindi, Urdu	900	India, Pakistan
	Panjabi	85	India, Pakistan
	Bengali	250	India, Bangladesh
	Marathi	80	India
Sino-Tibetan	Chinese (Mandarin)	1000	China, Taiwan, Singapore
	Wu (Hakka, etc.)	85	China
	Cantonese	70	China
Transafrican	Swahili	90	Kenya, Tanzania, Uganda

Note: The table lists the 27 languages that reach 1 percent or more (> 60 million) of the world population as either first or second languages.

SOURCE: Adapted from the Linguasphere Register of the World's Languages and Speech Communities (Dalby, 1999–2000). See <www.linguasphere.net>.

terial languages such as French and Italian, and vice versa, although all four of those languages developed as the languages of separate and rival nation-states. The relationship between Russian and the other Slavonic languages is somewhat similar.

Two arterial languages remain: Malay, including its modern derivative Indonesian, and English. Both owe their wide extension to maritime trade and conquest: Malay-Indonesian as a regional language now accessible to over 200 million people and English as a broadly spoken language accessible to a global population of 1 billion or more.

Is English the "most spoken language"? The answer still depends on the time of day. When the sun is over the eastern Pacific, Chinese is the world's most spoken language and Hindi with its close relatives is in the second position. When the sun is over the Atlantic and much of Asia sleeps, English is the most spoken language in the world, with Spanish in a strong second place.

Ebb and Flow of Languages

All spoken and recorded languages form part of a global continuum or "linguasphere," a shared framework for establishing personal and interpersonal thoughts, communications, and identities. The piecemeal approach to the study of individual languages belongs to the twentieth century, together with the spurious comparison of dying languages with dying species of animals and plants. The end of hunting and gathering as a viable lifestyle brought the inevitable end of a large number of minute speech communities. The heritage of those groups should be documented carefully if it is not already too late to do that. However, the natural diversity of humankind will always require and support linguistic diversity. Its extent would be better documented if population census data routinely included information on levels of multilingualism.

Future Trends

Every community that wants to preserve and promote its language should be encouraged to do so. Every child has the right to an education in her or his own language but arguably has also the right to learn a language that provides access to knowledge in all cultural and economic fields. The success or failure of globalization in all its meanings, including globalized respect for diversity and equality of opportunity, will depend on the global development of the world's languages as a shared human resource. This development will clearly benefit from the transnational use of English in the service of a multilingual and multicultural world, rather than as the vector of a dominating monolingual culture.

The most important linguistic development during the twenty-first century will be the increasing electronic empowerment of the spoken word, which is already superseding writing as the principal means of long-distance communication and also may challenge the printed word as the principal vehicle of permanent recording. English is likely to solidify its present position as the dominant vehicle for international communication, but most languages will survive within their own communities, which in several instances will be numerically larger than the population of native English speakers, as languages of cultural and localized identity.

See also: *Ethnic and National Groups; Literacy.*

BIBLIOGRAPHY

Crystal, David. 1998. *English as a Global Language.* Cambridge, Eng.: Cambridge University Press.

Dalby, Andrew. 1999. *Dictionary of Languages.* London: Bloomsbury.

Dixon, Robert M.W. 1997. *The Rise and Fall of Languages.* Cambridge, Eng.: Cambridge University Press.

Grimes, Barbara F. 2000. *Ethnologue: Languages of the World,* 14th edition, 2 vols. Dallas: Summer Institute of Linguistics.

INTERNET RESOURCE.

Dalby, David. 1999–2000. *Linguasphere Register of the World's Languages and Speech Communities.* <http://www.linguasphere.org>.

DAVID DALBY

LASLETT, PETER

(1915–2001)

British historian and historical demographer Peter Laslett was a fellow of Trinity College Cambridge, and in 1964 he became co-founder and co-director (with E. A. Wrigley) of the Cambridge Group for the History of Population and Social Structure. Laslett was a leading historian of political thought in his early career, but from his late 40s he began to establish his reputation as a pioneering historian of the family and as a historical demographer.

The two careers were linked, since Laslett had edited Sir Robert Filmer's *Patriarcha and Other Political Works* (1949) at an early stage, and in doing so had accepted the portrayal therein of the seventeenth-century English household as structured around a dominant patriarch and enclosing a large number of kin. Laslett's later work, starting with his most famous book, *The World We Have Lost* (1965), and using listings of inhabitants that pre-dated the first official census of England and Wales (1801) by two centuries, showed that social reality bore little relation to political theory. These sources showed that pre-industrial English households on average contained four persons, who were most likely married couples with their children. Few villagers were married under age twenty; resident unmarried servants, primarily aged 15 to 30, were surprisingly prevalent; and village populations turned over rapidly from year to year as people migrated across parish boundaries.

Laslett promoted the comparative history of household structure and formation processes. In collaboration with John Hajnal of the London School of Economics, he seeded the idea of a northwest European household formation system that was founded upon late and neo-local marriage, and the circulation of adolescents away from their natal hearth as servants and apprentices for long periods after the onset of sexual maturity. These were features that pre-dated the Industrial Revolution, yet in much of the extant secondary literature were supposed to have emerged only after the shift from an agrarian economy to one in which industry and urban living predominated. Laslett, while keen to promote comparative analysis of co-resident domestic groups, was also suspicious of contrasts drawn between measures of household composition that took little account of stochastic variation. With anthropologist E. A. Hammel and mathematical demographer K. Wachter, he promoted the use of probabilistic microsimulation for the study of household structure, illustrating that many attempts to show stem-family systems in western Europe foundered on the author's failure to think probabilistically.

Laslett also pioneered work on the history of illegitimacy and, in comparative analysis, showed that illegitimacy in England was most common from the sixteenth to the early-twentieth century when marriage was early for women, and least common when it was late—though a contrary relationship held in many continental European countries.

In retirement, Laslett began to research the history of aging and the elderly, long before these subjects were fashionable. He showed that the household formation system in pre-industrial England had not created a context within which the elderly were revered, but one in which they had usually depended upon support from a wider community that extended out beyond the kin group and not infrequently entailed poor relief. Work of this kind, like so much that he published after 1965, made it necessary for social scientists to abandon many of the older certainties regarding the notion of "modernization" and its impact upon demographic processes and family forms.

See also: *Family: History; Family Reconstitution; Henry, Louis; Historical Demography; Household Composition.*

BIBLIOGRAPHY

SELECTED WORKS BY PETER LASLETT.

Laslett, Peter. 1965. *The World We Have Lost.* London: Methuen.

———. 1977. *Family Life and Illicit Love in Earlier Generations.* Cambridge, Eng.: Cambridge University Press.

———. 1996. *A Fresh Map of Life: The Emergence of the Third Age,* 2nd edition. London: Macmillan Press.

Laslett, Peter, ed. 1972. *Household and Family in Past Time.* Cambridge, Eng.: Cambridge University Press.

Laslett, Peter, and James Fishkin, eds. 1992. *Justice Between Age Groups and Generations.* New Haven, CT: Yale University Press.

Laslett, Peter, E. A. Hammel, and K. Wachter. 1978. *Statistical Studies of Historical Social Structure.* London and New York: Academic Press.

Laslett, Peter, Karla Osterveen, and Richard Smith, eds. 1980. *Bastardy and Its Comparative History.* London: Edward Arnold.

Laslett, Peter, and Richard Wall, eds. 1983. *Family Forms in Historic Europe.* Cambridge, Eng.: Cambridge University Press.

SELECTED WORKS ABOUT PETER LASLETT.

Bonfield, Lloyd, Richard Smith, and Keith Wrightson, eds. 1986. *The World We Have Gained: Histories of Population and Social Structure.* Oxford, Eng.: Basil Blackwell.

RICHARD M. SMITH

LEBENSRAUM

The term *Lebensraum*, meaning "living space," originated with the German geographer and ethnographer Friedrich Ratzel (1844–1904). He wrote on Darwinism and did research in the Americas before lecturing at Munich University, then at the University of Leipzig, and writing on the physical and cultural relations between populations and their environments. The Swedish political scientist Rudolf Kjellén (1864–1922), who coined the term "geopolitics," adopted Ratzel's concept, arguing in his major work that states are organisms that grow and decay. These ideas were avidly adopted by Nazi Germany, giving Lebensraum the sinister overtones it often carries today.

Nevertheless, all living things do need space, at some bare minimum, for their physical structure and the necessities of life: water, food, waste disposal, and so on. This requirement is manifested in the territorial behavior of the lower animals, including the forceful rejection of intruders when instinctive mechanisms (e.g., threat displays) fail to repel them. In human populations analogous behaviors may therefore be inherent, predating agriculture and even language. Wherever possible, most human population groups, however, seek to claim appreciably more living space than this bare minimum.

The Book of Genesis (12:1–9) describes a Lebensraum deficit facing Abraham and his kin, leading to conflict among their herdsmen. The ancient Greek philosopher Plato, in *The Republic,* depicts the expanding territorial needs of neighboring populations as resulting in war. In the chapter on American Indian population controls in his *Essay on the Principle of Population,* the English economist T. R. Malthus (1766–1834) wrote: "American nations are well acquainted with the rights of each community to its own dominions . . . they guard this national property with a jealous attention . . . [and] live in a perpetual state of hostility" (Malthus, p. 33).

Most societies have clear demarcations of their territory and resources. Contentious historical, political, and ethical questions often arise about definitions of and entitlements to living space. These can concern sovereignty, legitimacy, territorial boundaries, identity, belongingness, citizenship, nationality, race, ethnicity, language, religion, culture, and the need to control migration, settlement, and resource exploitation. Rival claims on the same Lebensraum are an intractable source of conflict, as in the cases of Palestine/Israel and Kosovo.

The amounts and kinds of Lebensraum needed for an acceptable quality of life vary with economic, cultural, and individual characteristics. Hunter-gatherers need a lot of space, 1 to 3 square kilometers (0.4 to 1.2 square miles) each, as do nomadic groups, which serially exhaust grazing or other resources along their traditional routes. The American folk hero, Davy Crockett, is said to have moved on when he could see smoke from a neighbor's chimney. Most contemporary humans seem reasonably content to live in dense urban areas (though they value privacy and are inclined to maximize their personal space by renting or buying as much of it as funds allow). But people are also appreciative of urban "lungs," open spaces, parks, greenbelts, and conservation and wilderness areas. At the level of the nation-state, a national security rationale is sometimes invoked to support territorial claims, seeking advantage in nondependence on other countries for essential resources such as food and raw materials. In an open-trading world, however, territorial possession as demarcated by national boundaries is at best weakly correlated with living standards.

The demand for Lebensraum may be fostered by purposeful population competition, often involving competitive breeding. The Malthus quotation, above, continued: "The very act of increasing in one tribe must be an act of aggression on its neighbours; as a larger . . . territory will be needed." Alleging overcrowding and lack of natural resources, Nazi Germany demanded the right to take extra Lebensraum by force, while simultaneously pursuing strongly pronatalist and eugenic policies domestically. Population competition is a sensitive topic of political discourse and is rarely examined even in the academic world. A few substantial treatments, however, have appeared, including works by Milica Z. Bookman, Jack Parsons, and Michael S. Teitelbaum and Jay Winter.

The spread of environmental ethics has led to pressure to protect the Lebensraum of both domestic and wild animals—and even plants—from undue human competition. A significant majority finds "battery" farming of livestock (the mass-rearing of pigs and chickens, for example, in large numbers under cover, in artificial light, and in small pens that prevent virtually all natural movement) to be deeply repugnant. Some people in affluent countries feel guilty about consuming too big a share of the world's space and resources and wish to share these with large numbers of immigrants. Countries feeling well-endowed with Lebensraum often adopt policies to occupy it more fully, either in the name of progress or for reasons of national security.

Ratzel's interests have become subsumed under a variety of disciplines: geography, geopolitics, international relations, ecology, ethology, and demography. Concepts related to Lebensraum, but lacking its historical associations, include overpopulation, physical and cultural carrying capacity, population pressure, ecological footprint, and demographic entrapment.

See also: *Carrying Capacity; Geopolitics; Land Use; National Security and Population.*

BIBLIOGRAPHY

Allan, William. 1965. *The African Husbandman.* London: Oliver and Boyd.

Bookman, Milica Z. 1997. *The Demographic Struggle for Power: The Political Economy of Demographic Engineering in the Modern World.* London and Portland, OR: Frank Cass.

Hitler, Adolf. 1939. *Mein Kampf* (1925), trans. James Murphy. London: Hurst and Blackett.

Kjellén, Johan Rudolf. 1916. *Staten som lifsform.* 3 vols. Stockholm: Hugo Gaber.

Malthus, T. R. [1798] 1958. *Essay on the Principle of Population* London: Dent.

Parsons, Jack. 1971. *Population versus Liberty.* London: Pemberton.

———. 2002. *Population Competition for Security or Attack: A Study of the Perilous Pursuit of Power through Weight of Numbers* [CD-ROM]. Llantrisant, Wales: Population Policy Press.

Ratzel, Friedrich. 1882. *Anthropogeographie.* 2 vols. Stuttgart: J. Engelhorn.

———. 1885–1888. *Völkerkunde.* 3 vols. Leipzig: Bibliographisches Institut.

Sack, Robert David. 1986. *Human Territoriality: Its Theory and History.* Cambridge, Eng.: Cambridge University Press.

Teitelbaum, Michael S., and Jay Winter. 1998. *A Question of Numbers: High Migration, Low Fertility, and the Politics of National Identity.* New York: Hill and Wang.

Wackernagel, Mathis, and William E. Rees. 1996. *Our Ecological Footprint.* Gabriola Island, BC, Canada: New Society Publishers.

JACK PARSONS

LEIBENSTEIN, HARVEY

(1922–1994)

Harvey Leibenstein was an American economist and economic demographer. Born in Yanishpol, Russia (now Ukraine), educated in Canada and the United States (Ph.D. from Princeton University, 1951), he served on the faculties of the University of California, Berkeley (1951–1967) and Harvard University (1967–1992). A disabling automobile accident in 1987 forced his retirement. Leibenstein's early work focused on demographic determinants in economic development; later his attention turned to extra-rational calculations in human decision-making.

Influenced by Frank Notestein (an empiricist) and Oskar Morgenstern (by contrast a theorist), Leibenstein's 1954 book, *A Theory of Economic-Demographic Development,* an outgrowth of his dissertation, explains in the then-emerging algebraic abstraction how economic development worked to destabilize Malthusian population equilibria. Besides a conventional presentation (economic statics), he developed the topic according to several types of dynamics—as found in Samuelson's *Foundations of Economic Analysis* (1947). These involved interactions at critical time-points among such variables as the composition of the initial population, varying injections of new capital, and fortuitous changes in personal income (consumption)—involving different socioeconomic sectors.

Leibenstein's second book, *Economic Backwardness and Economic Growth* (1963), introduces his "critical minimum effort thesis" and further details the breakdown of Malthusian equilibria in developing nations. Again the language is often algebraic, but there are important data insertions: Leibenstein pioneered using nutritional inputs as a cause and a consequence of economic growth—indeed, Leibenstein increasingly employed the term growth to refer to higher average incomes rather than capital inputs.

As his career developed, Leibenstein's skepticism about using rational maximization as the explanation of economic behavior grew (he had Herbert Simon, the theorist of bounded rationality, as a quondam colleague). This skepticism, appearing in a 1974 article, "An Interpretation of the economic theory of fertility: Promising path or blind alley?," took issue with Gary Becker's view that couples would (or even could) actually calculate their preference functions before deciding to conceive an additional child.

Instead, Leibenstein turned to insights found in behavioral psychology and worked throughout his remaining career to develop a 'micro-micro' system in which individual workers operated within the framework of three, successively smaller, output levels: what they could produce, what was required to hold their jobs, and what they would have preferred. He used the term "X-efficiency" to describe the increment of the highest over the lowest. Of course, the critical area involves not only the attitudes of single workers but also how groups of workers, each capable of making his or her own choices and reacting to the difference between the three identified levels of output, will influence the stint. Leibenstein handled this set of interactions as illustrative of the well-known Prisoners' Dilemma problem.

Although X-efficiency underlay the reasoning in *Beyond Economic Man* (1976), the idea, after being ridiculed by the economist George J. Stigler in a 1976 article (to which Leibenstein replied in kind: "X-Inefficiency Xists: Reply to an Xorcist"), was further elaborated and fortified in *General X-Efficiency Theory and Economic Development* (1978), and in *Inflation, Income Distribution, and X-Efficiency* (1980). It culminated with *Inside the Firm* (1987).

See also: *Economic-Demographic Models; Microeconomics of Demographic Behavior.*

BIBLIOGRAPHY

SELECTED WORKS BY HARVEY LEIBENSTEIN.

Leibenstein, Harvey. 1954. *A Theory of Economic-Demographic Development.* Princeton, NJ: Princeton University Press.

———. 1963. *Economic Backwardness and Economic Growth: Studies in the Theory of Economic Development.* New York: John Wiley.

———. 1974. "An Interpretation of the Economic Theory of Fertility: Promising Path or Blind Alley?" *Journal of Economic Literature* 12: 457–479.

———. 1976. *Beyond Economic Man.* Cambridge, MA: Harvard University Press.

———. 1978. *General X-Efficiency Theory and Economic Development.* New York: Oxford University Press.

———. 1978. "X-Inefficiency Xists: Reply to an Xorcist." *American Economic Review* 68: 203–211.

———. 1979. "A Branch of Economics is Missing: Micro-Micro Theory." *Journal of Economic Literature* 17: 477–502.

———. 1981. "Economic Decision Theory and Human Fertility Behavior: A Speculative Essay." *Population and Development Review* 7: 381–400.

———. 1987. *Inside the Firm.* Cambridge, MA: Harvard University Press.

SELECTED WORKS ABOUT HARVEY LEIBENSTEIN.

Stigler, George J. 1976. "The Xistence of X-Efficiency." *American Economic Review* 66: 213–16.

MARK PERLMAN

LEXIS DIAGRAM

Lexis diagrams play a valuable role in demographic analysis by providing a highly effective visual language for conveying information about the sets of persons and events that are the basis of all population statistics. The diagrams complement verbal descriptions of these sets, which are often clumsy and hard to grasp. The diagrams are named after the German statistician and actuary Wilhelm Lexis (1837–1914).

There are four principles of Lexis diagram representation. *First,* a demographic event may be represented by a point on a coordinate plane whose coordinates are the time at which the event occurred and the age of the person to whom the event occurred. *Second,* each two dimensional set in the coordinate plane represents the set of events whose representing points fall within its boundaries. *Third,* a person may be represented by the straight line, called a "life line," connecting the points representing this person's birth and death. *Fourth,* each line in the coordinate plane represents the set of persons whose life lines intersect this line.

Figure 1 illustrates each of these principles. Line A is the life line of a person who was born at time *t* and died, at exact age 3, at time *t+3*. Lines B and C both represent persons who died during year *t+1* at 1 completed year of age (i.e., at an exact age ≥1 and <2). Square *abcd* represents the set of all such deaths, which divide into two parts: deaths of persons who were age 1 in completed years at the beginning of year *t+1*, represented by triangle *acd,* and

FIGURE 1

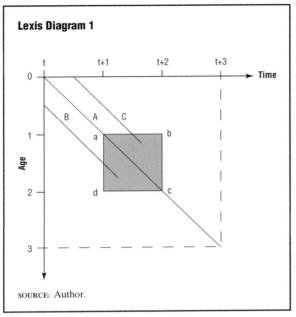

Lexis Diagram 1

SOURCE: Author.

FIGURE 2

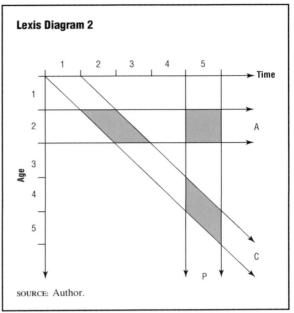

Lexis Diagram 2

SOURCE: Author.

deaths of persons who reached exact age 1 during that year, represented by triangle *abc*. The set of persons who reached exact age 1 (celebrated their first birthday) during year *t*+1 is represented by line *ab*. The set of persons who were age 1 in completed years at the beginning of year *t*+1 is represented by line *ad*.

The drawing and interpretation of Lexis diagrams is facilitated by two general methods. The "method of extremes" consists of identifying extreme cases, drawing lines or plotting points representing these cases, and connecting these points or lines to obtain the desired representation. Referring to Figure 1, for example, consider the set of persons who reach exact age 1 during year *t*+1. The extreme cases here are reaching exact age 1 at time *t*+1 and reaching exact age 1 at time *t*+2, corresponding to points *a* and *b*, respectively. The line *ab* connecting these points is the desired representation.

The "method of intersections," which applies only to sets of events, consists of identifying an age group, time period, and/or birth cohort, drawing the representations of the groups so identified, and taking the intersection of these representations. Three examples of practical importance are illustrated in Figure 2, in which age groups and time periods of equal length have been marked off.

Deaths occurring during the 5th time period to persons in the 2nd age group are represented by the

square, which is the intersection of the horizontal strip *A* corresponding to the age group and the vertical strip *P* corresponding to the time period. Numbers of deaths in such sets are the numerators of age-specific death rates.

Deaths of persons in the cohort born in the 1st period that occur when these persons are in the 2nd age group are represented by the parallelogram with sides parallel to the time axis, which is the intersection of the horizontal strip *A* representing the age group and the diagonal strip *C* representing the cohort. Numbers of deaths in such sets are the numerators of life table probabilities of death.

Deaths of persons in the cohort born during the 1st period that occur during the 5th period are represented by the parallelogram with sides parallel to the age axis, which is the intersection of the diagonal cohort strip *C* and the vertical time period strip *P*. Numbers of deaths in such sets figure in population projection calculations.

The age axis in the Lexis diagram may be replaced by an axis representing time elapsed since any event, such as marriage, divorce, or first birth, providing for description of a wider variety of sets of persons and events. The time axis most often represents calendar time, but diagrams for sample survey data may express time as months or years prior to interview. As the metric of age is elapsed time, units of time and age are represented by the same distance on the two axes. It follows that life lines form a 45-degree angle to the axes.

Lexis diagram representations apply to events of all kinds, including births regarded as events occurring to the mother, marriages, and divorces. The diagrams themselves do not indicate what kind of event is represented, however. This information must be supplied by context. The point representing any event occurring to a person necessarily lies on the life line representing this person. This obvious but important fact serves to identify persons experiencing particular events as members of various groups, for example, as members of a particular birth cohort.

Life lines may be generalized to represent a person's membership in a particular population by removing from the line those points corresponding to periods when the person was not a member of the population. These generalized life lines may be used, for example, to represent persons in populations that experience migration.

Different orientations of the Lexis diagram axes may be used for different purposes. The orientation shown above is most generally useful because it corresponds to the way tables of births and deaths are arranged, with rows for events occurring at older ages placed below rows for events occurring at younger ages.

See also: *Demography, History of.*

BIBLIOGRAPHY

Lexis, Wilhelm. 1880. "La représentation graphique de la mortalité au moyen des points mortuaires," *Annales de démographie internationale* Tome IV: 297–324.

INTERNET RESOURCE.

Vandeschrick, Christophe. 2001. "The Lexis diagram, a misnomer," *Demographic Research* Volume 4, Article 3 <http://www.demographic-research.org>

GRIFFITH FEENEY

LIFE COURSE ANALYSIS

The life course approach is an interdisciplinary program of study, under development since the mid-1970s, which has been increasingly influential in demographic research. It is concerned with explaining how and when events such as leaving the parental home, starting or dissolving a union, having a child, migration, job entry and exit, and retirement are experienced. Life course analysis entails the collection of life course data together with the (statistical) analysis of the *timing* of events (when do they happen?), their *sequencing* (in which order do they happen?), and their *quantum* (how many events happen?). The focus of this article is on quantitative methods, although qualitative life course analysis has also been influential and is sometimes integrated with quantitative research.

In their 1998 review of methods of life course research, Janet Giele and Glen Elder identify the chief elements that shape individual lives and that are crucial for the analysis of life courses. These are: individual development; history and culture (location in time and place); and social relations (linked lives). Parallel and potentially interdependent trajectories of individual lives are the main units of analysis, with the trajectories marked by events. These elements have natural counterparts at the macro level: individual development lies behind the use of age as the primary time axis; location in time and the idea of linked lives suggest using a cohort approach to the study of social change; history and culture emphasize the importance of period and location.

Collection of Life Course Data

Quantitative life course data may be collected in surveys, using either question lists or so-called event history calendars. Retrospective collection of the timing of events has become a standard feature of most demographic surveys. Life course data can also be obtained from panel surveys or other follow-up surveys and from civil registration data.

In surveys, the timing of events is usually asked within a roster of questions for each trajectory separately and following a particular order. For instance, the timing of events concerned with the relationships within the family of origin would be asked before the timing of events on union formation and dissolution. The quantum of events is collected in the same context, while the sequencing of events is derived indirectly from the information on timing. This way of collecting life course data has been widely advocated and used in life course research. In the 1990s it was implemented in surveys such as the Demographic and Health Surveys.

Studies employing event history calendars start by collecting data on the timing of so-called landmark events through a question list. Information on the timing of other events, and on the state the individual occupied in each time unit over the reference period, is then collected by use of a graphical display of the trajectory of primary interest (either on paper or on a computer screen). The complexity of the calendar depends on the length of the reference period and on the time unit used—typically one month. Event history calendars are extensively applied in panel surveys such as the U.S. Panel Study of Income Dynamics.

Robert F. Belli, William L. Shay, and Frank P. Stafford compared the two types of data collection in 2001; their results indicate that event history calendars generally yield more accurate reports, although sometimes with increased overreporting of events.

Statistical Analysis of Life Courses

Two approaches have been followed in the statistical analysis of life course data. Event history analysis focuses on time-to-event as the key dependent variable. Sequence analysis focuses on life courses or segments of the life course as a conceptual unit.

Event history analysis. This statistical method has found major application in demography since the 1980s. Applied to individual life course data, the approach uses life table nonparametric techniques to compare the timing of life course events across space (including international comparisons) and time (mostly using the cohort as the preferred time dimension). This is the individual-level equivalent of period and cohort analysis in traditional demography.

The regression models of event history analysis contribute to the explanation of life course dynamics by linking the time-to-event variable with explanatory variables (covariates). Covariates can be external to a trajectory (as is the case for macro-level variables, comprising period effects), or internal to a trajectory (as is the case for other trajectories of the life course that are potentially influencing the time-to-event). External covariates can be of three kinds:

those that are fixed during a life course or from a particular point of time (birth cohort, age-at-marriage when studying time-to-divorce); covariates whose temporal dynamics cannot be influenced by the events in the trajectory of interest (age of an individual in the case of time-to-divorce); and those located at an aggregate level of social dynamics (time period, regional economic indicators, policy indicators). Multilevel event history models, developed in the 1990s, allow accurate treatment of the case of individuals aggregated into household or regional clusters, therefore taking into account the "time and place" dimensions of life courses.

Internal covariates usually refer to other trajectories of the life course of the same individual or of linked individuals, and their use allows researchers to study complex interdependencies between trajectories. Event history analysis may take into account unobserved factors underlying these interdependencies, such as value orientations or attitudes. The relevance of time-constant unobserved factors for the analysis of parallel and potentially interdependent trajectories has been debated in the literature. The so-called causal approach of Hans-Peter Blossfeld and Götz Rohwer assumes that all factors that are relevant to the simultaneous analysis of several trajectories are observed and included in the past history of the trajectories. Other modeling approaches allow for the effects of time-constant unobserved factors. The most general applied approach is the multilevel and multiprocess modeling of life courses developed by Lee A. Lillard and Constantijn W.A. Panis.

Sequence analysis. Older life course concepts like that of the family life cycle were holistic and made more or less explicit reference to biological structures. The recent life course literature has been more analytic. Nevertheless, by focusing on specific events researchers may achieve a unitary, holistic perspective on trajectories of the life course. The most-used analytical technique for the holistic analysis of life courses is known as sequence analysis, introduced into the social sciences during the 1990s by Andrew Abbott.

In sequence analysis, each life course or trajectory in the life course is represented as a string of characters (states). This representation is analogous to the one used to code DNA molecules in the biological sciences. Indeed, one method used to analyze sequence-type data, optimal matching analysis

(OMA), was originally created for the alignment of DNA sequences. The goal of OMA is to compute a matrix of dissimilarities between pairs of sequences, starting from a definition of distance between states, and of "costs" of inserting and deleting states in a sequence. The dissimilarity matrix can be used as the input for statistical techniques based on dissimilarity, such as cluster analysis or multidimensional scaling. The method has been applied to the sociology of occupations. A demographic application—to the analysis of the transition to adulthood—is discussed in Francesco C. Billari's 2001 article.

Alternative approaches to the analysis of life courses as a conceptual unit have also been explored, although they have not surfaced extensively in the literature as of the early twenty-first century. These include the use of correspondence analysis and data-mining techniques.

See also: *Cohort Analysis; Event History Analysis; Family Demography; Family Life Cycle.*

BIBLIOGRAPHY

Abbott, Andrew, and Angela Tsay. 2000. "Sequence Analysis and Optimal Matching Methods in Sociology." *Sociological Methods and Research* 29: 3–33.

Belli, Robert F., William L. Shay, and Frank P. Stafford. 2001. "Event History Calendars and Question List Surveys: A Direct Comparison of Interviewing Methods." *Public Opinion Quarterly* 65: 45–74.

Billari, Francesco C. 2001. "The Analysis of Early Life Courses: Complex Descriptions of the Transition to Adulthood." *Journal of Population Research* 18: 119–142.

Blossfeld, Hans-Peter, and Götz Rohwer. 2002. *Techniques of Event History Modeling.* Mahwah, NJ: Erlbaum.

Dykstra, Pearl A., and Leo J. G. van Wissen. 1999. "Introduction: The Life Course Approach as an Interdisciplinary Framework for Population Studies." In *Population Issues: An Interdisciplinary Focus,* ed. Leo J. G. van Wissen and Pearl A. Dykstra. New York: Kluwer Academic/Plenum Publishers.

Freedman, Deborah, Arland Thornton, Donald Camburn, Duane Alwin, and Linda Young-DeMarco. 1988. "The Life History Calendar: A Technique for Collecting Retrospective Data." *Sociological Methodology* 18: 37–68.

Giele, Janet Z., and Glen H. Elder Jr., eds. 1998. *Methods of Life Course Research: Qualitative and Quantitative Approaches.* Thousand Oaks, CA: Sage.

Lillard, Lee A., and Constantijn W. A. Panis. 2000. *AML Multilevel Multiprocess Statistical Software, Release 1.0.* Los Angeles: EconWare.

Mayer, Karl Ulrich, and Nancy B. Tuma, eds. 1990. *Event History Analysis in Life Course Research.* Madison: University of Wisconsin Press.

Wu, Lawrence L. 2000. "Some Comments on Sequence Analysis and Optimal Matching Methods in Sociology: Review and Prospect." *Sociological Methods and Research* 29: 41–64.

Francesco C. Billari

LIFE SPAN

Life span, a characteristic of life history that is the product of evolution, refers to the duration of an organism's entire life course. Application of the concept is straightforward at both the individual and cohort levels. At the individual level, it is the period between birth and death; at the cohort level (including both real and synthetic cohorts), it is the average length of life or life expectancy at birth. Life span applied to a population or a species, however, requires a modifier to avoid ambiguity. Maximum observed life span is the highest verified age at death, possibly limited to a particular population or time period. The overall highest verified age for a species is also called its record life span. The theoretical highest attainable age is known as maximum potential life span, maximum theoretical life span, or species-specific life span. Depending on context, maximum life span can refer to either the observed or the potential maximum.

Maximum observed life spans (i.e., longevity records) are not synonymous with theoretical maximums for at least two reasons. First, maximum longevity is not an appropriate general concept because an animal dies before the age of infinity not because it cannot pass some boundary age but because the probability of its riding out the ever-present risk of death for that long is infinitesimally small. In other words, there is no identifiable age for each species to which some select individuals can survive but none can live beyond. Second, the number of individuals observed heavily influences the record age of a species. That is, the longevity records for species in which the life spans of large numbers of individuals have been observed will be significantly greater than the corresponding figure for a species that has the same longevity but is represented by a few dozen individuals. For the vast majority of longevity records by species, the population at risk, and therefore the denominator, is unknown.

Conceptual Aspects of Life Span

The life span concept is relevant only to species in which an individual exits—to entities circumscribed by distinct birth and death processes. Thus the concept does not apply to bacteria, which reproduce by binary fission, to plant species that reproduce by cloning, or to modular organisms with iterated growth such as coral or honeybee colonies. When a single reproductive event occurs at the end of the life course that results in the death of the individual, then life span is linked deterministically to the species' natural history. This occurs with the seed set of annual plants (e.g., grasses), in drone (male) honeybees as a consequence of the physical damage caused by mating, in many mayfly species when a female's abdomen ruptures to release her eggs after she drops into a lake or stream, and in anadromous (river-spawning) salmon that die shortly after spawning. Life span can be considered indeterminate for species (including humans) that are capable of repeated (iteroparous) reproduction. That life span is indeterminate in many species is consistent with what is known about the lack of cutoff points in biology—all evidence suggests that species do not have an internal clock for terminating life.

Changes that occur in organisms that enter resting states such as dormancy, hibernation, and estivation (a state of resting that occurs in summer) reduce mortality rates and thus increase longevity. This also occurs when individuals are subjected to caloric restriction or when their reproductive efforts are reduced. A species' life course may consist of many phases such as infant, juvenile, and pre- and postreproductive periods; therefore, a change in overall life span will correspond to a commensurate change in the duration of one or more of these stages. When environmental conditions are greatly improved, such as for animals kept in zoos or laboratories or under the conditions experienced by contemporary humans, mortality rates usually decrease and thus longevity increases. Whereas earlier stages, such as the prereproductive period, are evolved life history traits, the added segment(s) arising at the end of the life course are byproducts of selection for robustness or durability at earlier stages and are thus not evolved traits. Rather, these additional life segments are due to "ecological release" and are referred to as "post-Darwinian" age classes.

Life span can be thought of as the sum total of the duration of each phase of the life course, either potential or realized. Thus implicit in life span extension (shortening) is an increase (decrease) in one or more of the phases of the life course. Because it is not possible to change one segment of the life course without affecting all other segments, life span extension (and shortening) will affect either directly or indirectly the timing and rhythm of all life events, from maturation and parental care to reproduction and grandparenting.

Life Span as an Adaptation

In evolutionary biology an adaptation is a characteristic of organisms whose properties are the result of selection in a particular functional context. Different bird beaks are adaptations for exploiting different niches that have had to be balanced with other traits such as body size and flight propensity. In the same way, the longevity of an animal is an adaptation that has had to be balanced with other traits, particularly with reproduction. The variations in the relationship between reproduction and longevity can only make sense when placed within the context of such factors as duration of the infantile period, number of young, and the species' ecological niche—the organism's overall life history strategy. Indeed, the longevity potential of a species is not an arbitrary or random outcome of evolutionary forces but rather an adaptive one that must fit into the broader life history of the species. In as much as life spans differ by 5,000-fold in insects (2 days for mayflies to 30 years for termite queens), by 50-fold in mammals (2 years for mice to 122 years for humans), and by 15-fold in birds (4 years for songbirds to 60 years for the albatross), it is clear that life span is a life history adaptation that is part of the grand life history design for each species.

A Life Span Classification Scheme

The literature on aging and longevity contains descriptions of only a small number of life span correlates, including the well-known relationship between longevity and both body mass and relative brain size and the observation that animals that possess armor (e.g., beetles, turtles) or capability of flight (e.g., birds, bats) are often long-lived. But major inconsistencies exist within even this small set of correlates. For example, there are several exceptions to the relationship of extended longevity and large body size (e.g., bats are generally small but most bat species are long-lived), and this positive relationship may be either absent or reversed within certain orders—including a negative correlation within the Pinnipeds (seals and walruses) and no correlation within the Chiroptera (bats). Likewise, the observation that flight ability and extended longevity are correlated does not provide any insight into why within-group differences in life span (e.g., among birds) exist, nor does it account for the variation in longevity in insects where adults of the majority of species can fly.

A classification system for the life span determinants of species with extended longevity that applies to a wide range of invertebrate and vertebrate species consists of the following two categories: (1) environmentally selected life spans and (2) socially selected life spans (see Table 1). The first category includes animals whose life histories evolved under conditions in which food is scarce and where resource availability is uncertain or environmental conditions are predictably adverse part of the time. Some of the longest-lived small and medium-sized mammals (e.g., rodents, foxes, small equines, ungulates) live in deserts where rainfall and, thus reproduction, is episodic and unpredictable. Examples include gerbils, rock hyrax, and feral asses. The extended longevity of animals in this category evolved through natural selection. The second category, socially selected life spans, includes species that exhibit extensive parental investment, extensive parental care, and eusociality (the social strategy characteristic of ants, bees, wasps, and termites, featuring overlapping generations, cooperative care of young, and a reproductive division of labor). It includes all of the social primates including humans. The extended longevity of animals in this category results from natural, sexual, and kin selection.

This classification system places the relationship between life span and two conventional correlates, relative brain size and flight capability, in the context of life history. That is, brain size is related to the size of the social group and the degree of sociality, which is, in turn, linked to extended life span. And intensive parental care is linked to flight capability in birds and bats, which, in turn, is also linked to extended life span. For example, most bird species are monogamous, with both sexes helping in the rearing (e.g., one protecting the nest while the other collects food). The reproductive strategy of the majority of bat species is to produce only a single altricial (naked and helpless), relatively large offspring at a time—flight preempts the possibility of the female foraging for food while gestating multiple young. Thus bat parental investment in a single offspring is substantial.

Life Span Patterns: Humans as Primates

Estimates based on regressions of longevity against brain and body mass for anthropoid primate subfamilies or limited to extant (currently living) apes indicate a major increase in longevity between *Homo habilis* (52 to 56 years) and *H. erectus* (60 to 63 years), occurring roughly 1.7 to 2 million years ago (see Table 2). The predicted life span for small-bodied *H. sapiens* is 66 to 72 years. From a catarrhine (Old World monkeys and apes) comparison group, when contemporary human data are excluded from the predictive equation, a life span of 91 years for humans is predicted. For early hominids, to live as long as predicted was probably extremely rare; the important point is that the basic Old World primate design resulted in an organism with the potential to survive long beyond a contemporary mother's ability to give birth. This suggests that postmenopausal survival is not an artifact of modern lifestyle but may have originated between 1 and 2 million years ago, coincident with the radiation of hominids out of Africa.

The general regression equation expresses the relationship of longevity to body and brain mass when 20 Old World anthropoid primate genera are the comparison group. Ninety-one years is the predicted longevity for a 50-kilogram (110-pound) primate with a brain mass of 1,250 grams (44 ounces; conservative values for humans) when a case-deletion regression method is employed (that is, the prediction is generated from the equation excluding the species in question) and 72 when humans are included within the predictive equation. When six genera of apes are used as the comparison group, the regression equation is:

$$\log_{10} LS = 1.104 + 0.072\ (\log_{10} Mass)\ + 0.193\ (\log_{10} Brain)$$

yielding a predicted human longevity of 82.3 years. Thus, a typical Old World primate with the body size and brain size of *Homo sapiens* can be expected to live between 72 and 91 years with good nutrition and protection from predation.

The contemporary maximum human life span of over 120 years based on the highest recorded age at death consists of two segments: (1) the Darwinian or "evolved" segment of 72 to 90 years; and (2) the post-Darwinian segment, which is the artifactual component that emerged because of the improved living conditions of modern society. Therefore the arguments that the maximum human life span has not changed in 100,000 years can be considered substantially correct when the "evolved" maximum life span is considered. It is clear, however, that this is not correct when the nonevolved segment of the human life span is considered: There is evidence from Swedish death records that the record age in humans (the maximum observed life span) has been increasing for well over a century.

Life Span Extension in Humans Is Self-Reinforcing

Improved health and increased longevity in societies may set in motion a self-perpetuating system of longevity extension. Increased survival from birth to sexual maturity reduces the number of children desired by parents. Because of the reduced drain of childbearing and rearing, parents with fewer children remain healthier longer and raise healthier children with higher survival rates, which, in turn, fosters yet further reductions in fertility. Greater longevity of parents also increases the likelihood that they can contribute as grandparents to the fitness of both their children and grandchildren. This self-reinforcing cycle, a positive feedback relationship, may be one reason why the average human life span has been continuing to increase.

The decline in mortality rates during the early stages of industrialization in countries such as the United States was probably one of the forces behind

TABLE 1

The Two General Categories of Factors That Favor the Evolution of Extended Life Span and Examples of Species within Each

Category	Examples
Environmentally selected	Tortoises, sea turtles, deep-water tube worms, tuatara; birds, beetles, *Heliconius;* butterflies, tree-hole mosquitoes
Socially selected	Elephants, killer whales, dolphins, most primates (including humans), naked mole rats, microbats (brown bat, vampire), parrots, hornbills, albatross, termite, ant and bee queens, tsetse flies

SOURCE: Modified from Carey and Judge (2001).

the expansion of educational effort and the growing mobility of people across space and between occupations. Whereas previous conditions of high mortality and crippling morbidity (disease) effectively reduced the prospective rewards to investment in education during the preindustrial period, expectancy for a prolonged working life span must have made people more ready to accept the risks and costs of seeking their fortunes in distant places and in new occupations. The positive feedback of gains in longevity on future gains involves a complex interaction among the various stages of the life cycle, with long-term societal implications in terms of the investment in human capital, intergenerational relations, and the synergism between technological and physiological improvements. In other words, long-term investment in science and education provides the tools for extending longevity, which, in turn, makes more attractive further long-term investments in individual education. Thus humans gain progressively greater control over their environment, their health, and their overall quality of life.

The positive correlation between health and income per capita is well known in international development studies, usually interpreted with income as the determining factor. But the correlation is partly explained by a causal link running the other way—from health to income. In other words, productivity, education, investment in physical capital, and the "demographic dividend" (advantageous changes in birth and death rates) are all self-reinforcing—these factors contribute to health, and better health (and greater longevity) contributes to their improvement.

TABLE 2

Estimates of Longevity for Fossil Hominids

Hominid Species	Life Span (years)	Incremental Change
Australopithicus afarensus	46.6	
		8.4
Homo habilis	55.0	
		7.0
H. erectus	62.0	
		10.9
H. sapiens (pre-historical)	72.9	
		49.1
H. sapiens (contemporary)	122.0	

Note: Estimates based on hominoid body size range from 42–44 years for *Australopithecus* to 50 years for *Homo erectus*. Incorporation of brain mass increased estimates for *Homo habilis* from 43 years to 52–56 years and for *Homo erectus* from 50 years to 60–63 years.

SOURCE: Carey and Judge (2001).

See also: *Aging and Longevity, Biology of; Evolutionary Demography.*

BIBLIOGRAPHY

Carey, James R., and D. S. Judge. 2001. "Life Span Extension in Humans Is Self-Reinforcing: A General Theory of Longevity." *Population and Development Review* 27: 411–436.

Goldwasser, L. 2001. "The Biodemography of Life Span: Resources, Allocation, and Metabolism." *Trends in Ecology and Evolution* 16: 536–538.

Judge, D. S., and J. R. Carey. 2000. "Post-reproductive Life Predicted by Primate Patterns." *Journal of Gerontology: Biological Sciences* 55A: B201–B209.

Wilmoth, J. R., L. J. Deegan, H. Lundstrom, and S. Horiuchi. 2000. "Increase of Maximum Life-Span in Sweden, 1861–1999." *Science* 289: 2366–2368.

JAMES R. CAREY

LIFE TABLES

The life table is a device that describes a cohort's or a population's mortality experience. The life table, sometimes called table of mortality (*table de mortalité* in French, and similarly labeled in most languages other than English) is one of the oldest and probably the single most valuable tool in demography. It has many applications that range well beyond mortality analysis. It is called a table, because in its classical presentation it is made of a number of numerical columns representing various indicators of mortality, but the information it contains can be also conveyed in graphical form.

The concept of a life table comes from a cohort perspective. If one could follow a birth cohort of 100,000 individuals through time in a closed population (a population without in- and outmigration), the number of survivors at various ages would correspond to the "number left alive at age x," in the life table its l_x column. The difference between survivors at two consecutive ages, x and $x+n$, would correspond to the number of deaths between x and $x+n$, in the life table denoted by $_nd_x$. The ratio of $_nd_x$ to l_x produces another column of the life table, the probability of dying between age x and $x+n$, denoted by $_nq_x$. Thus, data on cohort survival can be readily converted into a life table.

In its classical form, the life table includes the following columns:

x = exact age

l_x = number still alive at age x

$_nd_x$ = number dying between ages x and $x+n$ = $l_x - l_{x+n}$

$_nq_x$ = probability of dying between ages x and $x+n$, conditional on survival to age x = $_nd_x / l_x$

$_np_x$ = probability of surviving from age x to age $x+n$, conditional on survival to age x = l_{x+n} / l_x

$_na_x$ = average number of person-years lived in the interval between age x and $x+n$ by those dying in the interval

$_nL_x$ = number of person-years lived between ages x and $x+n$ = $nl_x + _na_x \cdot _nd_x$

$_nm_x$ = death rate between ages x and $x+n$ = $_nd_x / _nL_x$

T_x = person-years lived above age x (sum of $_nL_x$ for ages x and higher)

$\mathring{e}_x$ = expectation of life at age x = T_x / l_x

Traditionally, a life table where $n = 1$ is called an "unabridged" or a "single-year" life table, and the left subscript can be omitted. A common alternative is to use 5-year age groups starting with age 5, and to present information for the age group 0–4 (that is, below exact age 5) in two groups: age 0 (i.e., less than age 1) and ages 1–4. In this case, the life table is called "abridged." It formerly was common practice to end a life table with an open-ended age interval starting at age 85. With the large proportions of survivors to age 85 in many low-mortality populations, though, the preferred practice is to present more detailed information above age 85, carrying it up to age 100 and concluding with an open-ended interval above that age. Because of the distinctive mortality differences between the sexes, life tables are commonly also presented separately for males and for females.

Although the life table is in principle a cohort concept, it is not commonly used in this fashion. The reason for this is both practical and substantive. Exhaustive cohort mortality data are rarely available, because that would require systematic death registration for a period spanning 100 years or more. In other words, it would be necessary to wait for a cohort to be extinct or near extinct to be able to construct a full cohort life table and obtain an accurate estimate of its life expectancy at birth. Accuracy would be compromised if the population was not closed—that is, if it were depleted not only by death but also outmigration—and if death registration included deaths of immigrants. A further and more substantive drawback of cohort life tables is that they refer to a period stretching over a century, during which mortality conditions are likely to have changed. For descriptive and policy purposes, typically less heterogenous and more timely information is necessary.

The limitations of cohort life tables have led demographers to design period life tables, based on the concept of "synthetic" cohorts. A synthetic cohort is a hypothetical cohort of persons subject through their life to the age-specific mortality rates of one specific period. This contrasts with a real cohort where each age-specific rate pertains to a different year. The theoretical construct of synthetic cohorts allows one to construct period life tables and compute life-cycle indexes (such as the life expectancy at birth) on the basis of observations relating to, and hence reflecting the mortality conditions for, a well-defined and relatively short time period. In practice, the period chosen is most often a single calendar year, or a two-year period bracketing a census count, or a quinquennium.

Life Table Construction

The construction of a period life table is not as straightforward as for a cohort, because many of the life table functions, including survivors at various ages, are not directly observable. One related life table function that can be estimated from actual data is $_nM_x$, the set of age-specific death rates in the population. This is commonly calculated as $_nD_x / _nN_x$, where $_nD_x$ is the number of deaths between age x and $x+n$ observed in a population during a specific period, and $_nN_x$ is the population aged x to $x+n$ at the middle of that period. The basic step in constructing a period life table is to estimate death probabilities, $_nq_x$, for the synthetic cohort, from $_nM_x$, the age-specific death rates observed in a population for a particular period.

Strictly speaking, $_nM_x$ is not exactly equivalent to $_nm_x$, the mortality rate observed in the corresponding synthetic cohort. This is because in a cohort (real or synthetic), $_nm_x$ results from $_nd_x$ and $_nL_x$, both of which are entirely produced by mortality conditions. That is, in a cohort, the number of survivors at various ages (and thus the corresponding person-years lived) is fully a product of underlying mortality conditions. Similarly, the number of deaths in the age-interval is also the product of mortality conditions applied to the number of survivors. Thus $_nm_x$ is an unbiased mortality measure. By contrast, $_nM_x$ is the product of specific mortality conditions applied to the population in the corresponding age-group, $_nN_x$. Unlike $_nL_x$, $_nN_x$ is not entirely produced by the mortality conditions to which the synthetic cohort is subject. It is also affected by the age distribution of the actual population within that age group, which is itself the product of past fluctuations in the number of births, past variations in mortality, and past migration. Thus $_nM_x$ and $_nm_x$ can differ. For most purposes, however, the difference is not large enough to produce significant differences in life table indexes such as life expectancy at birth. In life table construction, it is common to assume that $_nM_x = _nm_x$; there are, however, more involved methods of construction that do not require this simplifying assumption.

The second operation in constructing a period life table involves converting the set of $_nm_x$ to $_nq_x$. This is done by using the following exact equation, derived from the equation for $_nL_x$ specified earlier:

$$_nq_x = \frac{n \, _nm_x}{1 + (n - {_na_x}) \, _nm_x}.$$

This equation relates an age-specific mortality rate in a cohort (real or synthetic) to the corresponding probability of dying in the age interval x to $x+n$. After this operation, one can readily calculate the number of survivors at various ages in the synthetic cohort and the remaining columns of the life table.

This equation shows, however, that $_nm_x$ is not the only input for the $_nm_x$ to $_nq_x$ conversion. The conversion also involves $_na_x$, the average number of person-years lived between x and $x+n$ by persons dying during the age interval. These values are usually not readily available in a population. When dealing with an unabridged life table, it is not consequential to make the assumption that life table deaths occur on average at the middle of the single-year interval ($_1a_x = 0.5$).

When dealing with five-year age groups, there are a number of methods for estimating $_na_x$ in a population. One method involves graduation techniques that yield reliable results but that are not easy to implement. Another strategy consists of borrowing $_na_x$ from another population with comparable mortality levels and patterns and for which $_na_x$ values have been accurately estimated. The assumption that $_na_x = n/2$ is also used sometimes in abridged life tables. For the first two age groups (for ages 0 and 1–4), however, this assumption is seriously inadequate because mortality risks decrease rapidly within this age range, and thus deaths are more concentrated toward the beginning of the age interval rather than equally distributed. At these ages, it is possible to use estimation equations based on empirical populations at various mortality levels. These equations permit the estimation of $_1a_0$ and $_4a_1$ from the recorded level of $_1m_0$. Similar adjustments may be necessary in very old age groups, in which the reverse phenomenon occurs: deaths are more concentrated toward the upper end of the age interval.

With $_nN_x$, $_nD_x$, and $_na_x$ in hand, all life table columns can be derived. It is also necessary to choose an arbitrary value for l_0, called the *radix* of the life table, to which the columns l_x, $_nd_x$, $_nL_x$, and T_x are proportional. It is common to choose 100,000 as the value for l_0. At the other end of the life table, for an open-ended age interval starting at age x^*, it is usually assumed that $_\infty L_{x^*} = l_{x^*} / {_\infty M_{x^*}}$.

An abridged period life table for the female population of Austria in 1992 is presented in Table 1. In its first two columns, this table also shows the empirical data—population numbers by age, derived from census statistics and numbers of deaths by age, derived from vital statistics—from which the life table was calculated.

The functions of the life table describe the level and age-pattern of mortality of a population. The $_nq_x$ and $_nm_x$ columns are two related ways of showing how the risk of mortality varies by age, conditional on survival to age x. The $_nd_x$ column, if divided by l_0, can be viewed as the probability for a newborn to die in a particular age group. The l_x column, divided again by l_0, corresponds to the probability of surviving from birth to age x. More generally, l_y / l_x (with $y > x$) corresponds to the probability of surviving from age x to age y, conditional on survival to age x, and $1 - l_y / l_x$ is the probability that a person who survived to age x will die between age x and y. Furthermore, $(l_x - l_y) / l_0$ is the probability that a newborn will die between ages x and y, and $(T_x - T_y) / l_0$ is the number of years that a newborn can expect to live between ages x and y. Figure 1 shows l_x, $_1q_x$, and $_1d_x$ functions for the female population of Sweden. These data, presented for four different years during the twentieth century, illustrate how the age-pattern of life table functions varies as a country experiences mortality decline.

Perhaps the most widely-reported life table measure is $\mathring{e}_0$, the life expectancy at birth. In a period life table, it corresponds to the average number of years that a newborn cohort would live if subjected through the life course to the age-specific mortality rates of the particular period to which the life table pertains. By extension, this number can be said to represent the length of life an average individual can expect at birth under the given mortality conditions. In a life table pertaining to an actual cohort that is now extinct, $\mathring{e}_0$ corresponds to the observed mean age at death for that particular cohort. Life expectancy, as was indicated above, is also calculated for ages other than zero. For age x, $\mathring{e}_x$ can be interpreted as the number of years that an individual can expect to live above age x, conditional on survival to age x.

Life Table Applications

The life table has many applications beyond the measurement of mortality. One of these applications

TABLE 1

Abridged Life Table, Austria 1992, Females

Exact age x	Mid-year population in age interval x to $x+n$ $_nN_x$	Deaths between ages x and $x+n$ during the year $_nD_x$	Death rate between ages x and $x+n$ $_nm_x$	Average person-years lived in the interval by those dying in the interval $_na_x$	Probability of dying between ages x and $x+n$ $_nq_x$	Probability of surviving from age x to $x+n$ $_np_x$	Number surviving at age x l_x	Number dying between ages x and $x+n$ $_nd_x$	Person-years lived between ages x and $x+n$ $_nL_x$	Person-years lived above age x T_x	Expectation of life at age x $\overset{\circ}{e}_x$
0	47,925	419	0.008743	0.068	0.008672	0.991328	100,000	867	99,192	7,288,901	72.889
1	189,127	70	0.000370	1.626	0.001479	0.998521	99,133	147	396,183	7,189,709	72.526
5	234,793	36	0.000153	2.500	0.000766	0.999234	98,986	76	494,741	6,793,526	68.631
10	238,790	46	0.000193	3.143	0.000963	0.999037	98,910	95	494,375	6,298,785	63.682
15	254,996	249	0.000976	2.724	0.004872	0.995128	98,815	481	492,980	5,804,410	58.740
20	326,831	420	0.001285	2.520	0.006405	0.993595	98,334	630	490,106	5,311,431	54.014
25	355,086	403	0.001135	2.481	0.005659	0.994341	97,704	553	487,127	4,821,324	49.346
30	324,222	441	0.001360	2.601	0.006779	0.993221	97,151	659	484,175	4,334,198	44.613
35	269,963	508	0.001882	2.701	0.009368	0.990632	96,492	904	480,384	3,850,023	39.900
40	261,971	769	0.002935	2.663	0.014577	0.985423	95,588	1,393	474,686	3,369,639	35.252
45	238,011	1,154	0.004849	2.698	0.023975	0.976025	94,195	2,258	465,777	2,894,953	30.734
50	261,612	1,866	0.007133	2.676	0.035082	0.964918	91,937	3,225	452,188	2,429,176	26.422
55	181,385	2,043	0.011263	2.645	0.054861	0.945139	88,711	4,867	432,096	1,976,988	22.286
60	187,962	3,496	0.018600	2.624	0.089062	0.910938	83,845	7,467	401,480	1,544,893	18.426
65	153,832	4,366	0.028382	2.619	0.132925	0.867075	76,377	10,152	357,713	1,143,412	14.971
70	105,169	4,337	0.041238	2.593	0.187573	0.812427	66,225	12,422	301,224	785,699	11.864
75	73,694	5,279	0.071634	2.518	0.304102	0.695898	53,803	16,362	228,404	484,475	9.005
80	57,512	6,460	0.112324	2.423	0.435548	0.564452	37,441	16,307	145,182	256,070	6.839
85	32,248	6,146	0.190585	5.247	1.000000	0.000000	21,134	21,134	110,889	110,889	5.247

SOURCE: United Nations (1994).

FIGURE 1

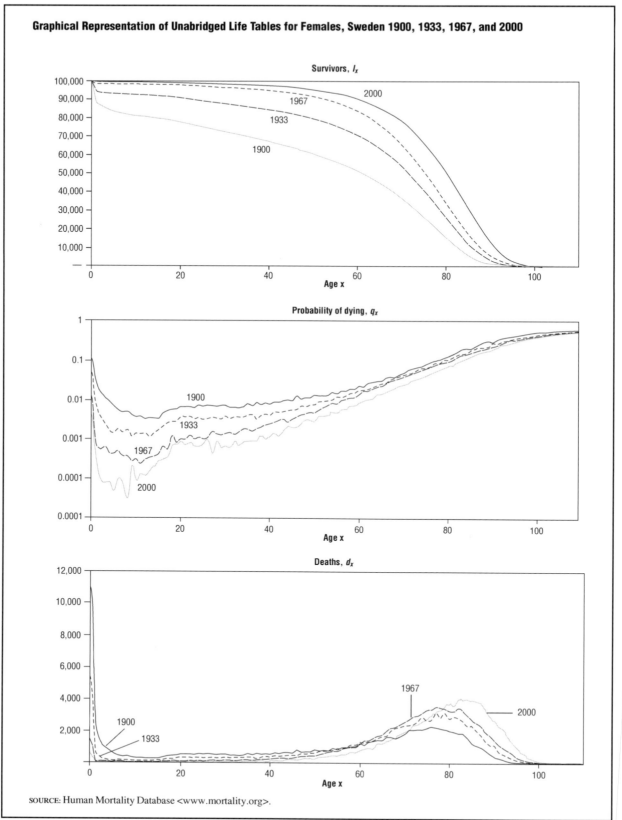

Graphical Representation of Unabridged Life Tables for Females, Sweden 1900, 1933, 1967, and 2000

SOURCE: Human Mortality Database <www.mortality.org>.

concerns the relationship between the mortality level of a population and its age structure. In particular, a life table can be conceived as a stationary population, which is a population closed to migration, where the annual number of births (B) and mortality conditions (embodied in the life table) are constant over time. If these conditions apply, the population will have an age distribution, $_nN_x$, that is proportional by a factor B/l_0 to the $_nL_x$ column of the life table, and a total population size, $P = B\,\mathring{e}_0$. The annual number of deaths in this population will equal the annual number of births, and the crude death and birth rates will have the value of $1/\mathring{e}_0$. In this population all demographic parameters, including total population size, are constant over time. The growth rate of this population is zero—hence the designation "stationary."

It follows that if a population can be assumed to be stationary, population parameters can be directly translated into life table parameters. For example, in a stationary population, $\mathring{e}_0 = P / B$, and $_nL_x = {_nN_x} \cdot l_0 / B$. Also, in a stationary population, the observed distribution of deaths, $_nD_x$ is proportional to the distribution of deaths in the life table, $_nd_x$. Thus, the observed mean age at death equals $\mathring{e}_0$, which is not the case in non-stationary populations. These equalities are useful for estimating mortality or other single-decrement processes in any population or sub-population that can be assumed to be stationary.

The life table can also be used to project a population in the future. If a particular life table can be assumed to represent mortality conditions of a specific population between time t and $t+5$, and if there is no migration between t and $t+5$, the population aged x to $x+5$ at time t, $_5N_x(t)$ can be projected to time $t+5$ using the $_5L_x$ column of the life table and the following equation:

$$_5N_{x+5}\,(t + 5) = {_5N_x(t)}\,\frac{_5L_{x+5}}{_5L_x}$$

This equation rests on the assumption that the population is stationary between age x and $x+5$, an assumption that is not very problematic for this purpose. The births that occurred between t and $t+5$ can also be projected to time $t+5$ to calculate the population under age 5 at time $t+5$ using the following equation:

$$_5N_0\,(t + 5) = B[t, t + 5]\,\frac{_5L_0}{5\,l_0}$$

Naturally, an important component of population projections involves making assumptions about the future course of mortality and the construction of corresponding life tables. The above equations describe the mechanical use of life tables for projection purposes, once life tables for future time periods have been estimated.

Mortality Models

Comparison of life tables in various populations has led demographers to observe regularities of age-patterns of mortality. In particular, across populations and time periods, age-specific mortality risks tend to follow a U-shape curve, with higher mortality risks at younger and older ages, with the lowest risks in the neighborhood of age 10 (see Figure 1). Another observation is that mortality rates are highly intercorrelated within a population. When mortality rates are higher at particular ages, they also tend to be higher at other ages. Although with a given level of mortality—as indexed, for example, by the value of the expectation of life at birth—somewhat different age-specific mortality rates may be associated in different populations, this variability is within relatively narrow bounds.

These observations have led demographers to search for parsimonious representations of mortality patterns, or mortality "models." The purpose of mortality models is the representation of complex age/level variations in life table columns with a small number of parameters. Mortality models can permit the estimation of mortality indicators in settings where the data ideally required for life table construction (an accurate census count of the population and accurate death registration for years fairly close to the time of the census, or corresponding statistics derived from an accurate population register) are absent. In such situations it may be still possible to estimate a limited number of population parameters, which, along with a model, can be useful for estimating a full life table.

Mathematical mortality models are the oldest parsimonious representations of mortality patterns. The purpose of such models is to present a functional form relating mortality risks to age, with a small number of parameters adjusting for varying levels and patterns across populations. Mathematical mortality models have not been very successful because the shape of the mortality curve is too complex to be easily summarized in a functional form. An important contribution of mathematical representations of mortality, however, is the Gompertz "law" of mortality, according to which the logarithm of the death rate is a linear function of age. The Gompertz equation is frequently used to represent or estimate mortality rates past middle adult ages, although it tends to overestimate mortality rates at older ages.

The most widely-used mortality models are model life tables. In their classical form, model life tables are a set of life tables indexed along two dimensions, *family* and *level*. A family is a group of model life tables with similar age patterns of mortality, often based on the experience of populations that are geographically close. Within a family, tables are indexed by level, from low to high life expectancy at birth. These model life tables are estimated by grouping high-quality empirical life tables with similar age patterns of mortality, and by observing how age-specific mortality rates typically vary as the overall mortality level changes. Regression equations are then used to construct model life tables for various families and mortality levels.

The most commonly used sets of model life tables were developed by A. J. Coale and P. Demeny and by the United Nations. Coale and Demeny model life tables are mostly based on the experience of European populations during the first half of the twentieth century, whereas United Nations tables are based on the experience of developing countries during the second half the twentieth century.

Model life tables are convenient to use, because within a family, a unique life table can be selected on the basis of only one life table indicator. The use of model life tables thus can flexibly accommodate various data configurations of the populations under study. However, the choice of the family of life tables appropriate for application to actual populations is not always straightforward, and the full range of age variations in actual mortality experience may not be fully represented in the currently available model life tables.

Another category of mortality models is the relational model, to which the *logit* model developed by William Brass belongs. Brass (1971) observed that any two life tables can be related to each other in a linear way after performing a "logit" transformation of q(x), the probability of dying before age x. The

logit system is thus a system in which a "standard" life table can be adjusted for varying levels and age-patterns of mortality across populations after solving for the two linear parameters relating empirical life table values to the standard. The Brass logit system is often used to smooth an empirical life table or to complete a life table with missing values.

Multiple-Decrements

Although life tables were originally developed to study mortality, the same logic can be used to study many other processes. The only requirement is that the process must be a single-decrement process, which means that there is only one mode of exiting a defined state of interest with no possible return to that state. When studying mortality, the state of interest is being alive, and the only way to leave that state, with no return permitted, is through death. The same logic can be applied, for example, to first marriages, in which case the state of interest is being never married and the event of interest is first marriage. Other single-decrement processes include first migration from place of birth, marital survival, or entry to the labor force.

In reality, single-decrement processes are rare. For a real cohort, mortality is in fact the only true single-decrement process. Other states such as "being never married" can be left not only by marriage, but also by death. Mortality always operates in addition to other processes, and thus multiple-decrement processes are far more common than single-decrement processes. Nonetheless, single-decrement life table logic can be applied to multiple decrements if the different sources of exits can be merged into one combined source of decrement, or if sources of decrements other than the one of interest can be ignored because they are very infrequent during the age-range under study. Also, if information is available only for individuals who did not experience other sources of decrement, the process of interest can be studied as a single-decrement process. For example, data on first marriages reported by individuals aged 85 can be used to reconstruct a life table in the single state where first marriage is the only source of decrement. Such strategy will provide an unbiased single-decrement life table if survivors had the same risks of experiencing a first marriage as those who did not survive (independence of probabilities).

In a multiple-decrement environment, it is sometimes useful to present information on the various modes of exits. Such analysis is commonly performed in a multiple-decrement life table, which is a life table where several sources of decrement affect the number of people still alive, and where each source of decrement is specified in various columns. For example, in a cause-specific life table, there are as many $_nd_x^i$ columns as there are causes of death i. The sum of $_nd_x^i$ in an age group is equal to $_nd_x$, the number of deaths from all causes in the corresponding single-decrement life table.

There are also methods that permit construction of a single-decrement life table in the absence of, or net of, other sources of decrement. Such life tables are sometimes called "associated single-decrement life tables" or "cause-deleted life tables." This approach involves information on a population subject to various sources of decrement, but it models the process of interest by reconstructing a hypothetical cohort where that process would be the only possible source of attrition. For example, if various causes of death are taken to be different modes of exiting the cohort, an associated single-decrement life table would permit estimation of the survival of a cohort in the absence of a particular cause (or group of causes).

Life table analysis is a powerful tool that has regained interest in the social sciences with recent developments in statistical techniques. If data on cohort survival is available at the individual level and includes covariates, it is possible to use a set of techniques termed "survival analysis" or "event-history analysis." The main purpose of these techniques is to estimate the influence of individual-level characteristics on the age-specific risk of attrition, the so-called "hazard rate." Because of their roots in classical life-table analysis, some of these procedures have been termed "life tables with covariates."

As noted earlier, the underlying assumption of single- and multiple-decrement life tables is that once the event of interest is experienced, individuals can never return to their original state. In reality, there are many processes where individuals can experience reverse flows. For example, if the state of interest is being "currently married," there are return flows as individuals who experience divorce or widowhood remarry and become "currently married" again.

Such processes can be analyzed through increment-decrement life tables, sometimes called multistate life tables. In an increment-decrement life table, there are as many l_x columns as there are states (excluding "being dead"), and these l_x columns can increase or decrease depending on the observed rates of transition from one state to the other. Among other uses, increment-decrement life tables allow estimation of the expected number of years in a particular state. For example, they can permit the estimation of the number of years that a newborn can expect to live in the "currently married" state, which could not be done using classical, single-decrement life tables.

Historical Note

The concept of life tables was first created in 1662 by John Graunt (1620–1674) in his *Natural and political observations made upon the bills of mortality* (1662). Further developments were made by the Huygens brothers and Gottfried Leibniz (1646–1716). The first systematic construction of a life table is credited to the astronomer Edmund Halley (1656–1742) in 1693. During the seventeenth century, life table construction was significantly improved due to the work of Willem Kersseboom (1691–1771), Nicolaas Struyck (1686–1769), and Antoine Deparcieux (1703–1768). However, these scientists lacked the two necessary data sources for the construction of a period life table—deaths and population by age. Therefore, early life tables were accurate only if the population under study was a closed cohort or a stationary population, and thus they had limited applicability. Taking advantage of the exhaustive Swedish data, Pehr Wargentin (1717–1783) constructed the first scientifically correct period life table in 1766.

Before the seventeenth century, death was believed to be either a magical or sacred phenomenon that could not and should not be quantified. The invention of life tables was thus an important scientific breakthrough, not only because of the technical aspects of life table construction, but also because of the concept of mortality as a measurable phenomenon following observable regularities.

See also: *Actuarial Analysis; Brass, William; Demography, History of; Event-History Analysis; Farr, William; Gompertz, Benjamin; Graunt, John; Mortality, Age Patterns of; Multistate Demography; Renewal Theory and Stable Population Model; Stochastic Population Theory.*

BIBLIOGRAPHY

Brass, William. 1971. "On the Scale of Mortality." In *Biological Aspects of Demography,* ed. W. Brass. London: Taylor and Francis Ltd.

Coale, Ansley J., and Paul Demeny. 1983. *Regional Model Life Tables and Stable Populations.* New York: Academic Press. (First edition 1965, Princeton: Princeton University Press.)

Dupâquier, Jacques. 1996. *L'invention de la table de mortalité: de Graunt à Wargentin: 1662–1766.* Paris: P.U.F.

Keyfitz, Nathan. 1985. *Applied Mathematical Demography,* 2nd edition. New York: Wiley.

Keyfitz, Nathan, and Wilhelm Flieger. 1990. *World Population Growth and Aging: Demographic Trends in the Late Twentieth Century.* Chicago and London: University of Chicago Press.

Pressat, Roland. 1972. *Demographic Analysis: Methods, Results, Applications.* Chicago: Aldine-Atherton.

Preston, Samuel H., Patrick Heuveline, and Michel Guillot. 2001. *Demography: Measuring and Modeling Population Processes.* London: Blackwell Publishers.

Schoen, Robert. 1988. *Modeling Multigroup Populations.* New York: Plenum Press.

United Nations. 1982. *Model Life Tables for Developing Countries.* New York: United Nations Population Studies, no. 77.

Michel Guillot

LIMITS TO GROWTH

For demographers, limits to growth is an old subject, at least as it relates to population growth, harking back to political economist T. R. Malthus (1766–1834) or even earlier writers. Since the 1972 publication of the Club of Rome study *Limits to Growth* the term has come to refer to both population and economic growth—that is, growth in population and growth in per capita resource use, the product of which gives the growth rate of total resource use. This total resource use is a flow from nature's sources (mines, wells, forests, fisheries, grasslands), through the transformations of production and consumption within the economy, and back as wastes to nature's sinks (atmosphere, oceans, a neighbor's back yard). Just as an animal lives from its metabolic flow, beginning with food from the environment, and ending with the return of wastes to its environment, so the economy lives from its metabolic flow, or "throughput." The throughput, like the metabolic flow, is entropic and irreversible. That is not to say that most waste materials are not recycled by biogeochemical processes powered by the sun. It is only to point out that such recycling is external to the animal or economy—whose life therefore depends on these natural services provided by its environment.

Two Kinds of Dissipative Structures

In physical terms human bodies are dissipative structures, which is to say that their natural tendency is to decay, die, and fall apart. The same is true for artifacts that we accumulate as wealth. A car, a house, or a shirt is a dissipative structure that requires a throughput to be maintained and replaced. A population of inanimate objects (e.g., shirts) inevitably wears out and depreciates over time, requiring new production to make up for the loss, as well as maintenance expenditures (replacing buttons) to slow down the rate of depreciation to a minimum. For demographers it is easy to think in terms of two populations of dissipative structures, one consisting of human bodies, the other of artifacts—basically extensions of human bodies. Each population, if it is to remain in a steady state, has both short-term maintenance requirements and long term reproduction requirements, each supplied by the entropic throughput from and back to nature. If these two steady-state populations are so large that the throughput necessary to maintain them requires inputs from nature's sources and outputs to nature's sinks at rates beyond nature's replenishing and absorptive capacities, then the throughput flow becomes ecologically unsustainable, and so do the two populations.

Definition of Limits to Growth

The limits to growth, in twenty-first century usage, refers to the limits of the ecosystem to absorb wastes and replenish raw materials in order to sustain the economy (the two populations of dissipative structures). The economy is a subsystem of the larger ecosystem, and the latter is finite, non-growing, and, in terms of materials, closed. Although the ecosystem is open with respect to solar energy, that solar flow is also nongrowing. Therefore in a biophysical sense there are clearly limits to growth of the subsystem. The difficulty in perceiving this is that these limits are not experienced as a rigid barrier, like an unyielding brick wall hit by a car. Instead, they are like the limits imposed by a budget that allows borrowing against the future or deferral of maintenance and replacement costs. Although limits to growth are ultimately physical and biological in their origin, society feels their effects economically long before they experience any absolute physical crash. The challenge for policy making is to express these limits in economic terms, and institutionalize them in decision making. Society needs to know not only what scale of economy and throughput will terminally disrupt the ecosystem, but also when the extra ecosystem disruptions required by a growing throughput begin to cost more in terms of sacrificed ecosystem services than they benefit others in terms of extra production. In other words, one must think in terms of the optimum *scale* of the economic subsystem (the two populations) relative to the total ecosystem. Beyond this optimal point further growth becomes in an ultimate sense uneconomic.

Harmful Effects of Economic Growth

The term "uneconomic growth" will not be found in the index of any textbook in macroeconomics. All growth (typically as measured by Gross Domestic Product [GDP]) is considered economic growth. Yet the concept of the optimum is central to economics, and nothing could be clearer than that growth beyond the optimum must be uneconomic—in the strict sense that it increases costs by more than benefits, thus making society collectively poorer, not richer. Politically it would be extremely inconvenient to discover that society has exceeded the optimal scale and that growth was now uneconomic. How could one fight poverty without growth? Society might have to redistribute existing wealth. How can one trust the demographic transition to automatically limit births as incomes increase, if growth no longer makes society richer? Society might have to purposefully limit births. How can society clean up the environment without growth to make people richer so that one can afford the costs of cleaning up? Society might have to pay those costs out of a lower income. The radical nature of these responses suggests that a world without growth has become politi-

cally unthinkable. Is it any wonder that there is a relentless intellectual effort devoted to debunking the notion of limits to growth or minimizing its relevance?

It is true of course that GDP growth can be made less material-intensive. (The analogous adjustment of making people less material-intensive—smaller—in order to allow for a larger population might meet more resistance.) But the scope for this substitution is itself limited, and appeal to it only serves to highlight the extent to which growth is the dominant value around which modern societies are organized. The reasoning in support of the ultimate reality of limits is unaffected.

The Future of Economic Growth

In the early twenty-first century it seems that society is witnessing the conflict between a physical impossibility (continual growth) and a political impossibility (limiting growth). But in the long run the physically impossible is more binding than the merely politically impossible. The hope is that growth will not prove politically impossible to limit, once society accepts that growth can be uneconomic. But society may have to suffer a bit before that becomes clear.

See also: *Carrying Capacity; Ecological Perspectives on Population; Sustainable Development; World Population Growth.*

BIBLIOGRAPHY

Daly, Herman E. 1996. *Beyond Growth: The Economics of Sustainable Development.* Boston: Beacon Press.

Meadows, Daniela H. 1992. *Beyond the Limits: Confronting Global Collapse, Envisioning a Sustainable Future.* Post Mills, VT: Chelsea Green.

Meadows, Daniela H., et al. [1972] 1992. *The Limits to Growth* (1972). New York: Universe Books.

HERMAN E. DALY

LITERACY

Literacy can be defined as the ability to read simple passages of printed text and sign one's name. The expansion of literacy is both a marker of and a contributory factor to economic development. It also may play a role in the mortality and fertility declines of the demographic transition.

Collection of Literacy Data

In developing countries literacy data are collected routinely in national censuses for the population above a specified age. For historical studies the data problems are much greater. One of the few sources that can be mined for historical Europe are parish records from the mid-sixteenth century to the mid-nineteenth century.

After the mid-eighteenth century in England marriage registration required that a couple and their witnesses sign (or mark) the parish register. Because people were taught to read before learning to write, the ability to sign one's name can be used as an indicator of literacy. In a society in which nearly all people married, information on historical levels of and trends in literacy therefore can be drawn from marriage records.

Findings from the Past

These snapshots from earlier periods made it clear that the acquisition of functional literacy was a dramatically stratified cultural resource. Men were more than twice as likely as women to be able to sign their names; the higher up the social scale one moved, the more likely it was that one could sign; the more urbanized one was, the less likely one was to identify oneself with a mark; and so on.

In the middle of the eighteenth century essentially one in two English men could sign his name and thus presumably could read. In economic terms those people who were active in a capitalist economy were likely to be readers who were able to keep ledgers and write letters to partners, customers, and others. In social and cultural terms those with leisure time were able to enjoy the burgeoning output of the presses; novels and newspapers were significantly new developments at that time. In demographic terms, however, it is not clear whether one can determine the characteristics that distinguished the literate from the illiterate. Readers (and signers) were not more "modern" than their illiterate families, neighbors, and friends; all belonged to a demographic culture marked by Malthusian prudential marriage and a fertility regime that was not so much "natural" as it was culturally constructed. There was

TABLE 1

Illiterate Population (Age 15 Years and Over) and Proportion Illiterate, by Sex, in Major World Regions, 1995

Region	Illiterate population (millions)	Illiteracy rates (percent)		
		Men	Women	Both sexes
Sub-Saharan Africa	140.5	33.4	52.7	43.2
Arab States	65.5	31.6	55.8	43.4
Latin America and Caribbean	42.9	12.3	14.5	13.4
Eastern Asia/Oceania	209.9	9.4	23.7	17.4
Southern Asia	415.5	37.1	63.4	49.8

SOURCE: UNESCO (1998); University of Pennsylvania/Graduate School of Education (1999).

little difference in fertility profiles between the literate and the illiterate.

During the classical Industrial Revolution (1770–1850) it seems that living in one of the northern English towns was no more likely to lead to the acquisition of literacy than it was to improve one's children's life expectancy. Early industrial society neither privileged literacy nor promoted it. Although functional literacy remained fairly constant, there was a significant demographic change: Marriages took place earlier in both town and country, illegitimacy rates skyrocketed, marital fertility became more duration-sensitive (higher levels in the first years of marriage, which might only reflect bridal pregnancy, but also higher levels in the later years), and mortality levels dropped in the countryside but rose dramatically in the inner cities.

The truly significant shift in popular functional literacy came about in the second half of the nineteenth century and coincided with the onset of the demographic transition and the fertility decline. In part this was a reflection of the declining value of children's labor; in part it was a reflection of the incursions of state-sponsored schools, which became compulsory only in the 1870s and were plagued with truancy for another generation; and in part it was a reflection of the reconfiguration of popular culture in the age of the Penny Post, the postcard, the penny newspaper, the train schedule, and a series of changes that made the acquisition and maintenance of literacy more relevant to the entire population. One could function as an illiterate in the pre-1850 oral culture, but this became less true afterward.

Even if most people never were required to sign their names on any occasion other than the marriage ceremony, illiteracy became a cultural disadvantage that discriminated against nonreaders.

The Contemporary Situation

Illiteracy remains a problem in much of the world. The statistics assembled by the United Nations Educational, Scientific, and Cultural Organization (UNESCO) and published in that organization's *World Education Report* estimated that worldwide in 1995 there were 885 million illiterates among the population 15 years old and over, 64 percent of whom were women. The corresponding rate of adult illiteracy was given as 22.6 percent (16.4 percent for men and 28.8 percent for women). The illiteracy data for developing countries as of 1995, grouped into UNESCO's five regions, are given in Table 1.

The connection between "modernizing" literacy and the demographic transition cannot be determined. Micro-level research that would analyze the demographic implications of literacy directly remains to be done.

See also: *Education; Historical Demography.*

BIBLIOGRAPHY

Goody, Jack. 1986. *The Logic of Writing and the Organization of Society.* Cambridge, Eng.: Cambridge University Press.

———. 2000. *The Power of the Written Tradition.* Washington, D.C.: Smithsonian Institution Press.

Goody, Jack, ed. 1968. *Literacy in Traditional Societies.* Cambridge, Eng.: Cambridge University Press.

Laqueur, Thomas. 1976. "The Cultural Origins of Popular Literacy in England 1500–1850." *Oxford Review of Education* 2: 255–275.

Levine, David. 1979. "Education and Family Life in Early Industrial England." *Journal of Family History* 4: 368–380.

———. 1980. "Illiteracy and Family Life during the First Industrial Revolution." *Journal of Social History* 14: 25–44.

———. 1984. "Parson Malthus, Professor Huzel, and the Pelican Inn Protocol: A Comment." *Historical Methods Newsletter* 17: 21–24.

Sanderson, Michael. 1974. "Literacy and Social Mobility in the Industrial Revolution in England." *Past and Present* 56: 75–104.

Schofield, R. S. 1973. "Dimensions of Illiteracy." *Explorations in Economic History,* 2nd series. 10: 437–454.

Spufford, Margaret. 1979. "First Steps in Literacy: The Reading and Writing Experiences of the Humblest Seventeenth-Century Spiritual Autobiographers." *Social History* 4: 407–435.

United Nations Educational, Scientific, and Cultural Organization. 1998. *World Development Report 1998: Teachers and Teaching in a Changing World.* Paris: UNESCO.

Vincent, David. 1981. *Bread, Knowledge and Freedom: A Study of Nineteenth-Century Autobiography.* London: Methuen.

———. 1989. *Literacy and Popular Culture. England, 1750–1914.* New York: Cambridge University Press, 1989.

———. 2000. *The Rise of Mass Literacy: Reading and Writing in Modern Europe.* Cambridge, Eng.: Polity Press.

INTERNET RESOURCE.

University of Pennsylvania/Graduate School of Education. 1999. International Literacy Explorer. <http://www.literacyonline.org/explorer/regsworld.html>.

DAVID LEVINE

LITERATURE, POPULATION IN

"Adam and Eve," wrote George Bernard Shaw in his ambitious play *Back to Methuselah*, "were hung up on two frightful possibilities. One was the extinction of mankind by their accidental death. The other was the prospect of living forever. They could bear neither. Consequently, they had to invent natural birth and natural death, which are, after all, only modes of perpetuating life without putting on any single creature the terrible burden of immortality." Thus not only the human race, but the science of demography was born.

Yet in demographic terms, for over a century Westerners have seemed unable to decide what they fear most. The precipitous drop in European fertility rates has produced anxiety about numerical dwindling, latterly echoed even in the United States. Yet the six-fold increase in worldwide population since the early 1800s has prompted a contrary fear of crushing biological overload. Given the emotive nature of these opposing horrors—*We are about to disappear! vs. We are being overrun!*—it is less surprising that population issues have filtered into the Western literary canon than that their direct treatment in mainstream literature is so rare.

Predictably, what Anton Kuijsten termed "demografiction" divides between the twin terrors of population decline and population excess. Less obvious is a third category: fear of population professionals.

Fear of Population Decline

When fertility fell earlier in France than in the rest of Europe, alarm spread that low birth rates would doom the French to obscurity. Horrified by Malthusianism, so at odds with the perceived French predicament, in 1899 Emile Zola published the pronatalist novel *Fécondité* in order to demonstrate that capitalism promotes poverty, while "fruitfulness" is the moral and economic strength of the working class.

Mathieu and Marianne Froment begin poor but happy, and heedlessly beget some dozen children, to the despair of their more prosperous betters, who promote Malthusian woe. By the time this gothic tale is through, the effete capitalists have paid for their venal shortsightedness with murder, suicide, and madness, their lines truncated when single sons fall prey to depravity or consumption. By contrast, Mathieu and Marianne's 158 progeny of three generations gather for their seventieth wedding anniversary on their thriving farm.

Zola's arguments retain remarkable resonance in the early twenty-first century. "Had not every civilization, every progress, been due to the impulse of numbers?," Mathieu asks, presaging Julian Simon. Warnings about "that terrible swarming of Asiatic barbarians" bound to "sweep down on our Europe, ravage it, and people it afresh" anticipate Pat Buchanan. And Mathieu's declaration that population equilibrium will only arrive "when the earth, being entirely inhabited, cleared, and utilized, shall at last

have accomplished its destiny" would hearten Wall Street globalists as much as it would sicken wilderness advocates.

Fécondité's present-day foil, *Headbirths, or The Germans Are Dying Out* by Günter Grass is a short, droll novel whose protagonists constitute the fecund Froments' demographic antithesis. The childless Harm and Dörte Peters take a sociologically edifying holiday tour of Asia while debating the torturous "Yes-to-baby No-to-baby" question. Counterintuitively for the field, economics barely enter in; instead the Peterses agonize about Third World poverty and nuclear radiation. Yet amidst the liberal pieties, the couple airs concerns that ring more true. Would this very holiday be possible with an infant? Encumberment could put their "sacred right to self-realization in danger." Finally, Dörte warms to a child, but Harm has gone off the idea, and on return they put pregnancy on hold pending the outcome of the German election.

The Peters's very method of decision making has predetermined its outcome. Harm shouts, "If I make a child, I want to do it consciously. Do you hear? Not the Hindu way!" But conscious reasoning will always come up with an excuse to forestall the inconvenience of Yes-to-baby, while the unthinking "Hindu way" will continue to people the planet.

Harm and Dörte embody the teleological revolution of the West's second demographic transition, whereby meaning has come to dwell inordinately in the present at the expense of the future. Yet P. D. James's *The Children of Men* hauntingly illustrates that the present's sense of fulfillment—not to mention its economy—is contingent on progenitors. The human race having become universally infertile post-1995, James's world of 2021 is a grim, senescent place, as the last, spoilt generation runs rampant and the burdensome elderly organize mass suicides to avoid being the last to turn out the light. Even more conceptually clever is Amin Maalouf's kindred novel, *The First Century After Beatrice*, whose instruction to the patriarchal Third World might run: Be careful what you wish for. A pill marketed as guaranteeing the birth of sons does just what it says; in Maalouf's future Third World there are plenty of people—for the time being—but hardly any girls.

Prospective human extinction has inspired a raft of commercial fiction. As a rule, thrillers like Michael Crichton's *The Andromeda Strain* are satisfied with sacrificing a handful of cautionary unfortunates before catastrophe is averted, while science fiction gleefully smites millions of walk-ons with no guarantee of a happy ending.

The nature of the catastrophe often expresses the prevailing angst of the era. E. M. Forster's story "The Machine Stops" reflects anxieties about automation: A machine that tends to every human need creates a race of biological incompetents, like domesticated pets; when the machine breaks down and no one understands how it works, the species is finished. Subsequent science-fiction authors have also demonized dependence on technologies, extrapolating social disaster when metal, electricity, or plastic cease to function. Novels like John Christopher's *No Blade of Grass* and J. G. Ballard's *The Burning World* convey concerns about food and water supply, others like Christopher's *The Long Winter* about global temperature shift. But fictional apocalypse comes in a festival of more inventive guises: volcanic gas, planetary collision, infectious insanity, and extraterrestrial wasps. Arthur C. Clarke, however, designs extinction with a more cheerful slant. When a computer prints out "The Nine Billion Names of God" in his eponymous short story, the stars wink out quietly one by one; in *Childhood's End*, the last generation of men watches helplessly as its children evolve into incomprehensibly superior beings.

Otherwise, most doomsday novels feature war or disease. During the Cold War, of course, the most common threat to the human race in bookstores was bellicosity. The specter of nuclear holocaust gave rise not only to death-ray shoot-outs in outer space, but to realistic accounts like Neville Shute's mournful *On the Beach* (humanity's last remnants in Australia await an approaching cloud of nuclear fall-out), as well as to witty satires like Kurt Vonnegut's *Cat's Cradle* (all water crystallizes into "ice-nine").

With fears of the Bomb receding and AIDS in ascendance, plague novels have become more the vogue. In a seminal work of this subgenre, George R. Stewart's *Earth Abides*, a young man in California recovers from a snakebite to find most of the human race dead from a new virus. As the handful of immune survivors form an ad hoc community, depopulation has some kid-in-a-candy-store appeal; houses, groceries, and liquor are free and abundant. But as Stewart tracks three post-plague generations, he vividly demonstrates that numbers maintain advanced civilization. Reduce the race to the size of a small town, and how many residents will remember

how to make plastic? The last Americans plunder canned goods (with little respect for sell-by dates), and literacy atrophies; electrical and water systems break down. At length, the community reverts to its hunter-gatherer forebears.

As demonstrated by T. C. Boyle's *After the Plague* of 2001, whose title story also deploys Stewart's premise, the emergence of HIV, the threat of biological weapons, and the multiplication of disease vectors via globalization make epidemiology more than physics the black art of the age. At least on paper, expect more plague.

Fear of Population Excess

In the literature of population decline, peril makes people seem precious. The same cannot be said of the literature of population excess, in which two may be company but 30 billion is a crowd.

In *Back to Methuselah,* George Bernard Shaw commends an ideal lifespan of at least 300 years, lest "mere human mushrooms . . . decay and die when they are just beginning to have a glimmer of the wisdom." Yet Kurt Vonnegut's playful story "Tomorrow and Tomorrow and Tomorrow" extrapolates what life might be like if "anti-gerasone" keeps folks alive for as long as they care to stick around. In a world of 12 billion, families of several generations live on top of one another, and the irritable 172-year-old Gramps tyrannizes his relatives with threats of disinheritance should he ever kick his own bucket. Taxed to penury to finance pensions, the youthful 112-year-old protagonist wails to his wife, "I don't think we're ever going to get a room to ourselves or an egg or anything."

With average Western lifespans climbing, its elderly cohorts swelling, and genetic research into the arrest of aging making headway, Vonnegut's premise becomes less fanciful. Likewise Simone de Beauvoir's novel, *All Men Are Mortal,* in which a fourteenth-century Italian takes a drug to induce immortality, only to discover that by the twentieth century his existence is boring, lusterless, and oppressive. While medical science still cannot offer eternal life, de Beauvoir's thesis—that brevity is one key to life's sweetness—suggests that great efforts lavished on longevity might be misspent.

Mainstream treatments of population excess are few. True, for those who argue that many poor countries are already too populous, the novels and travel books of V. S. Naipaul might qualify, and it is indeed sobering to come across in *The Overcrowded Barracoon* of 1972, "To be one of 439 million Indians is terrifying," when a slight three decades later Indians number over one billion. But for the most part authors define an "overpopulated" world as one more crowded than their own. Thus put off to the future, the issue has been primarily the purview of genre writers.

One exception is Colin Macpherson's *The Tide Turners,* set in his present of six billion people and credibly deploying available technology. Determined to give the earth a "rest" from human depredation, a group of young Australian eco-idealists design a virus that will leave humans sterile. Their aim is to disseminate the virus worldwide and shrink population to two billion over 40 years, though there's one unaddressed fly in the ointment: Total success would leave the species not reduced but extinct. Little matter, since the plot is foiled by a murderous cabal of anti-environmental capitalists.

As literature, *The Tide Turners* is pretty crude; the characters often speak like Sierra Club pamphlets. Moreover, the amateur virologists are portrayed as perfectly noble; proclaims the project's founder to his flock, "You're all heroes." Yet given that these do-gooders plan to expose the entire species to a contagious foreign virus after testing it for a few months on 150 subjects, *The Tide Turners* might better belong in the third category posited here.

Perhaps the most prestigious modern writer to take on population excess is Anthony Burgess, whose amusing social satire *The Wanting Seed* exemplifies how overdoing "fruitfulness" leads to biological perversity and moral inversion. In his antinatalist Britain of the near future, homosexuality confers prestige ("It's sapiens to be homo"); parenthood, shame. While in George Orwell's *1984* sham wars create social cohesion, here they are staged as a means of population control. When iron state control breaks down, wholesale cannibalism ensues.

Though aspiring to realism, George Turner's *The Sea and Summer* is set in mid-twenty-first century Australia—where, along with California, a disproportionate number of dystopic novels take place. (Perhaps a paradisiacal reputation helps set the stage for paradise lost.) Here multiple catastrophes intersect—global-warming floods, monetary collapse, food shortage, and mass unemployment—each exacerbated by population growth. In Turner's strict class structure, the middle-class "Sweet" live in constant terror of slipping to the "Swill," the dirty, teeming ruck living in tower blocks on meager state handouts.

Turner's book and Harry Harrison's entertaining *Make Room, Make Room*—set in a New York City of 35 million, and the basis of 1973's cannibalistic cult film *Soylent Green*—are two better representatives of a whole class of population pulp novels that took off in the 1960s, powered by Ehrlich-style alarmism. Overabundance in these books reliably cheapens humanity into chaff; in fact, cannibalism is a running theme. In swarming dystopias, civil liberties erode, and small, protected elites often control the seething horde through fascistic or mechanistic means. Drab, mass-produced garments portray a loss of individuality, as the one is lost in a sea of the many. Quality of life plummets: The food runs to tasteless seaweed pellets. Drink may be available, but only rotgut; writers seem especially distressed by the prospect of no longer being able to get a decent bottle of wine. Living space is at a premium, domestic architecture dismal, often vast banks of the bleak Bauhaus high-rises typical of 1960s public housing.

Yet by and large these high-density nightmares are uncomplicated by race, which lends them a certain innocence. The same cannot be said of Jean Raspail's *The Camp of the Saints,* a novel both prescient and appalling.

It is the year 2000, and Raspail's population projection of seven billion worldwide turned out to be close. Resentful and wretched, 800,000 residents of Calcutta swarm onto a fleet of ships and steer the convoy toward the coast of France. As the rutting, reeking, hate-driven throng approaches, liberal, multicultural France prepares to greet her "visitors" with open arms. Meantime, resident immigrants, despising their menial jobs, constitute a waiting fifth column. By the time the ships run ashore—and the first landing party is a tide of bloated corpses thrown overboard—similar sea-jackings have occurred elsewhere, and the full-scale invasion of the First World by the Third has begun.

Certainly *The Camp of the Saints* is racist. While Turner personalizes the "Swill," Raspail's stinking "river of sperm" floating toward France is dehumanized, its mascot at the prow a speechless deformed dwarf. Yet it's a tough call whether Raspail is more disgusted by "the sweating, starving mass, stewing in urine and noxious gases" or by his own countrymen, who are too paralyzed with self-contempt to defend their borders: "Cowardice toward the weak is cowardice at its most subtle, and indeed, its most deadly." And to give the novel its due, it is written with tremendous verbal energy and passion.

Raspail gives bilious voice to an emotion whose statement is increasingly taboo in the West, but that can grow even more virulent when suppressed: the fierce resentment felt by majority populations when that status seems threatened. And the Third World migration pressures that Raspail foresaw have been brought to bear on the early twenty-first century, as squalid human trafficking proliferates and hundreds of asylum seekers nightly storm the Channel Tunnel at Calais, often bringing rail service to a halt. In their even-handed work, *Fear of Population Decline*, even Michael Teitelbaum and Jay M. Winter concede, "It seems doubtful . . . whether large-scale immigration can ever serve as a politically viable response to declining population." If *The Camp of the Saints* contains a lesson, it is that nativist concerns about immigration need fair airing, for such primitive anxiety is too potent to be consigned solely to the far right.

Fear of Population Professionals

All of these works radically diverge on which human aggregate constitutes the intolerable, and which the ideal. Not only Raspail but also John Brunner (*Stand on Zanzibar*) presents a millennial total of seven billion as horrific; Vonnegut cites an alarming 12 billion. Zola counter-claims that the earth could readily support "ten times" his own time's population of 1.5 billion, while Olaf Stapledon's blissful, stable utopia in *Last and First Men* contains only 100 million people. Yet demographers no more agree on optimal and catastrophic numbers than do the amateurs—which has helped to foster a whole literature demonizing not a population problem itself, but the folks who think they know how to fix it.

One such specimen is this writer's *Game Control,* whose irascible protagonist Calvin Piper has been fired as head of USAID's population division for his unacceptable promotion of higher infant mortality in the Third World. But his retirement in Nairobi is hardly idle: Calvin is researching a pathogen that would neatly decimate a third of the world's population overnight. Despite its outlandish premise, *Game Control* is closer to social satire than science fiction, and focuses as firmly on demographers

as on their subject. Luminaries in the field like Julian Simon, John Bongaarts, Ben Wattenberg, and Garrett Hardin all make textual appearances, and Calvin's shy, worthy girlfriend Eleanor Merritt works for the Pathfinder Fund.

Calvin's fomenting about the dire consequences of inaction is sometimes convincing, but his motivation is suspect. He's resentful about having been fired. Though not strictly a bigot—dismisses Eleanor, "Calvin's not a racist. He hates everybody"—he is certainly a misanthrope. (In fact, Calvin finally comes to recognize the illogic of going to so much trouble to save a race he detests.) When, having uncovered his ludicrous scheme, Eleanor sets out to prove that AIDS alone will "cure" population growth, Calvin refuses to believe that the disease is up to the job. His attachment is not to humanity's salvation, but to his pet project, and most of all: to being right.

Zola also peopled *Fécondité* with glib demographic know-it-alls, and in Thomas Love Peacock's *Melincourt*, Malthus himself (as Mr. Fax) gives fatuous advice: "The world is overstocked with featherless bipeds. . . . It is better that the world should have a small number of peaceable inhabitants . . . than the disproportionate mass of fools, slaves, coxcombs, thieves, rascals, liars, and cutthroats with which it is at present encumbered." Peacock leaves little doubt that Malthus is an ass.

For Peacock, Malthusianism is class-driven: "It seems . . . peculiarly hard that all the blessings of life should be confined to the rich. If you banish the smiles of love from the cottage of poverty, what remains to cheer its dreariness?" Thus, the wealthy get all the land, the fine food, the wines, and the status, and now they want a monopoly on sex as well.

An array of commercial fiction, too, engenders a healthy suspicion of population snake oil. The plague in Chelsea Quinn Yarbro's *The Time of the Fourth Horseman* is caused by population control gone wrong. In the medical thriller *Benefits,* by Zoe Fairbairns, a contraceptive in the water supply gives rise to dreadful mutations, while both Turner's *The Sea and Summer* and Blanche d'Alpuget's *White Eye* put a more nefarious slant than *The Tide Turners* on a sterilization virus.

More serious writers have raised the alarm about social control of reproduction, notably Aldous Huxley in his *Brave New World* of fascistic eugenics.

Like Burgess, Huxley turns "family values" ingeniously on their head: with raising test-tube children the business of the state, promiscuity is lauded; love, monogamy, and childbirth are obscene. The principles of Henry Ford—from whose birthday all dates are marked, à la "the year of our Ford 600"—are applied to churn out identical editions of people, bred to be contented with their place. Margaret Atwood's *The Handmaid's Tale* has a gloomier texture, and there's no missing the feminist message: After environmental degradation has rendered much of the population sterile, fertile women are forced into sexual slavery to bear children for wealthy barren couples. Huxley is more fun.

The gentlest poke at the population pro would be R. K. Narayan's charming *The Painter of Signs*. During Indira Gandhi's aggressive vasectomy drive, a young artisan is smitten with a zealous family planning worker, who breaks his heart. Then, no woman who views children as "defeat for her cause" and is "obsessed with the sexual activities of others" could possibly have made a good wife.

Demography, Life, and Literature

Demography is a lightning rod for literary reservations about humanity itself, which can appear repulsive in sufficient quantity, or even seem to deserve its fate when having brought extinction upon itself. Alternatively, "demografiction" can animate the humanitarian truism that biologically people all sink or swim together. This collective existential ambivalence helps to express the dichotomy that other people are at once resource and rival: individuals need social cooperation to survive, yet the fiercest competition for that survival comes from our own kind. Because beneath the field's dry statistical surface there teems an irresistible Pandora's box of paranoia, nationalism, racism, rivalrous ambition, misanthropy, and apocalyptic dread, demography is sure to tempt more fiction-writing dabblers to prize open the lid.

See also: *Population Thought, History of.*

BIBLIOGRAPHY

FEAR OF POPULATION DECLINE.

Ballard, J. G. 1964. *The Burning World (An Earth Without Water)*. New York: Berkley Medallion.

Boyle, T. Coraghessan. 2001. *After the Plague*. New York: Viking Press.

Christopher, John. 1956. *No Blade of Grass*. New York: Simon and Schuster.

———. 1962. *The Long Winter*. New York: Simon and Schuster.

Clarke, Arthur C. 1953. *Childhood's End*. New York: Ballantine Publishing Group.

———. 1967. *The Nine Billion Names of God: The Best Short Stories of Arthur C. Clarke*. New York: Harcourt, Brace, and World, Inc.

Crichton, Michael. 1969. *The Andromeda Strain*. New York: Alfred A. Knopf.

Forster, E. M. 1911. *The Machine Stops and Other Stories*. Cambridge, Eng.: Provost and Scholars of King's College.

Grass, Günter. 1982. *Headbirths, or The Germans are Dying Out*, trans. Ralph Manheim. New York: Harcourt Brace Jovanovich.

James, P. D. 1994. *The Children of Men*. New York: Warner Books.

Maalouf, Anton. 1994. *The First Century After Beatrice*. London: Abacus.

Shaw, George Bernard. 1921. *Back to Methuselah*. London: Constable and Co.

Shute, Neville. 1957. *On the Beach*. New York: Morrow.

Stewart, George R. 1949. *Earth Abides*. New York: Ballantine Books.

Vonnegut, Kurt. 1963. *Cat's Cradle*. New York: Delacorte Press.

Zola, Emile. 1899. *Fécondité*, trans. E. Vizetelly. 1900. London: Chatto and Windus.

FEAR OF POPULATION EXCESS.

Ballard, J. G. 1967. "Billenium." In *Cities of Wonder*, ed. Damon Knight. New York: McFadden-Bartell.

Blish, James, and Norman L. Knight. 1967. *A Torrent of Faces*. New York: Doubleday.

Brunner, John. 1968. *Stand on Zanzibar*. New York: Doubleday.

Burgess, Anthony. 1962. *The Wanting Seed*. New York: Norton.

de Beauvoir, Simone. 1955. *All Men Are Mortal*. Cleveland, OH: World Publishing Co.

Ehrlich, Max. 1971. *The Edict.* New York: Double-day.

Goldberg, Marshall, and Kenneth Lay. 1980. *Disposable People.* New York: Tower.

Harrison, Harry. 1967. *Make Room, Make Room.* New York: Berkley Medallion.

Macpherson, Colin. 1999. *The Tide Turners.* Queensland, Australia: Mopoke Publishing.

Moorcock, Michael. 1975. *The Distant Suns.* New York: Unicorn. Anthologized in *Sailing to Utopia.* 1996. New York: Orion Publishing Group.

Naipaul, V. S. 1972. *The Overcrowded Barracoon.* London: André Deutsch.

Oliver, Chad. 1985. *Shadows in the Sun.* New York: Crown.

Pendleton, Don. 1970. *Population Doomsday.* New York: Pinnacle Books.

Raspail, Jean. 1975. *The Camp of the Saints,* trans. Norman Shapiro. New York: Charles Scribner's Sons.

Turner, George. 1987. *The Sea and Summer.* London: Faber and Faber.

Vonnegut, Kurt. 1968. "Tomorrow and Tomorrow and Tomorrow." In *Welcome to the Monkeyhouse.* New York: Delacorte Press.

FEAR OF POPULATION PROFESSIONALS.

Atwood, Margaret. 1986. *The Handmaid's Tale.* Boston: Houghton Mifflin.

d'Alpuget, Blanche. 1986. *White Eye.* New York: Simon and Schuster.

Fairbairns, Zoe. 1979. *Benefits.* New York: Virago.

Huxley, Aldous. 1932. *Brave New World.* London: Chatto and Windus.

Narayan, R. K. 1976. *The Painter of Signs.* London: William Heinemann.

Peacock, Thomas Love. [1817] 1948. *Melincourt.* In *The Novels of Thomas Love Peacock.* London: Rupert Hart-Davis.

Shriver, Lionel. 1994. *Game Control.* London: Faber and Faber.

Stapledon, Olaf. 1968. *Last and First Men.* New York: Dover Publications.

Yarbro, Chelsea Quinn. 1976. *The Time of the Fourth Horseman.* New York: Doubleday.

OTHER REFERENCES.

Kuijsten, Anton. 1999. "Demografiction." In *The Joy of Demography and Other Disciplines: Essays in Honour of Dirk van de Kaa,* ed. Anton Kuijsten, Henk de Gans, and Henk de Feijter. Amsterdam: Nethurd Publications, Amsterdam.

Teitelbaum, Michael S., and Jay M. Winter. 1985. *Fear of Population Decline.* San Diego: Academic Press.

LIONEL SHRIVER

LONGITUDINAL DEMOGRAPHIC SURVEYS

Longitudinal surveys are surveys that involve repeated data collection from individuals over time. They are of two types: specific-purpose surveys and panel surveys. Specific-purpose surveys collect information on a topic-specific basis at successive times from comparable populations but *not* the same individuals. These kinds of surveys may generically be termed *longitudinal surveys,* and have historically represented the dominant form of longitudinal data collection. They are most appropriate for comparing, for example, changes in demographic, socioeconomic, social-psychological, or health behaviors or attitudes in populations or subgroups of populations over time. *Panel surveys* involve the repeated interviewing, over time, of the *same* individuals. Surveys of this type permit examination of transitions in individual behaviors, attributes, or attitudes over time, and of linkages over time at the individual level. Analytically, these two forms of data collection can often complement each other, and they each have distinctive strengths and weaknesses. The surveys discussed in this article—selected longitudinal surveys with substantial demographic content undertaken in the United States—are of both types.

In addition to the brief appended bibliography, on-line addresses are provided that give access to more detailed accounts of the surveys described.

Health- and Fertility-Related Surveys

National Health Interview Survey (NHIS). The NHIS, the main longitudinal health data collection activity in the United States, is a continuing cross-sectional (non-panel) national survey of the civilian, non institutional population. The survey, entailing personal interviews, is conducted by the Bureau of the Census for the National Institutes of Health. Information is collected annually from about 40,000 households and over 100,000 individuals on basic demographics, illnesses, injuries, impairments, chronic conditions, activity limitations, utilization of health services, and other health topics. The survey has been conducted annually since 1957, although it has undergone several major changes. Since 1995, black and Hispanic households have been over-sampled. That is, they are over-represented in the survey compared to their actual representation in the population, in order to ensure sufficient numbers for statistically reliable group comparisons. A core questionnaire is completed each year including information of the type noted above; periodically, modules on selected topics such as disease prevention or cancer are added. The core questionnaire includes a basic family questionnaire, an adult questionnaire, a child questionnaire (information is collected from an adult), and a child immunization questionnaire.

The National Survey of Family Growth (NSFG). The NSFG collects detailed information about family relationships and fertility-related experiences from a representative national sample of adults of childbearing age. Five rounds were held from 1973 to 1995, covering only female respondents. Beginning with the sixth round in (2002), the sample (some 19,000 respondents) includes males. The sampling frame is the same as for the NHIS. Public user files for past rounds of the survey are available.

The National Health and Nutrition Examination Survey (NHANES). In contrast with the NHIS survey, NHANES focuses more directly on the collection of health measurement statistics. This survey has gone through several cycles. From 1960 through 1970, three National Health Examination Surveys (the name that it was known by prior to 1999) were conducted, covering (sequentially) chronic adult diseases, early and later childhood growth and development. Beginning in 1970, a new emphasis on health and nutrition was introduced, and increasing attention was given to over-sampling of minority groups in the population. Since 1999, NHANES has been an annual survey in which about 5,000 respondents are interviewed in each round. It entails detailed household interviews, physical examinations, and health and dietary interviews. Its data can be linked to related surveys such as the NHIS.

National Longitudinal Study of Adolescent Health (Add Health). Add Health is a panel survey of the health-related behaviors of adolescents who were in grades 7 through 12 as of the first survey wave (1994–1995). It is a fully representative national survey that focuses on adolescent sexuality, its social, psychological, and physiological correlates, and to some degree its determinants. Its premise is that families, friends, schools, and communities can encourage healthy or unhealthy behaviors among adolescents. In wave one, data were collected directly from about 90,000 youths in randomly selected schools in 80 U.S. communities. Three follow-up waves focused on a sub-sample of 20,000, who were interviewed at home—the last of them in 2001 to 2002, when the respondents were 18 to 25 years of age. Additional follow-up surveys are planned. Supplementary data collection from parents, school personnel, and siblings was also conducted. The sample includes a substantial number of minority youth. Public-use Add Health data are distributed by the Sociometrics Corporation on its web site.

Employment- and Income-Focused Surveys

The Current Population Survey (CPS). The CPS is a nationwide survey of about 50,000 to 60,000 civilian non-institutional households conducted monthly for the U.S. Bureau of Labor Statistics (BLS) by the Bureau of the Census. Dating from the 1940s, the CPS provides a continuous profile of the changing American population and is the primary source of information on the employment characteristics of the population. In addition to the core monthly employment and unemployment data, this survey also collects extensive demographic, social, and economic data. Recent CPS outputs of general interest include an annual demographic supplement that includes statistics on work experience over the year, income, migration, and household composition, and periodical supplements on race and ethnicity (in 1995 and 2000), marital history (1995), fertility (2000), and school enrollment (annually in October). Special topics vary from year to year, depending on current issues of interest to government agencies. While the CPS is usually thought of as a continuing cross-sectional survey, it also has some short-term panel qualities. Households selected for inclusion remain in the survey for four months, are skipped for eight months, and then return for an additional four months; hence, a relatively large sample is available for short-term panel analyses.

The Panel Study of Income Dynamics (PSID).

The PSID, begun in 1968, is essentially a longitudinal survey of a representative national sample of United States population, and the households in which they reside. The study is conducted by the Survey Research Center at the University of Michigan. It emphasizes the dynamic aspects of economic and demographic behavior, but its content includes explanatory and outcome measures drawn from several disciplines. PSID has sought to maintain continuity over time in the collection of basic data items, especially on the source and amount of income, family structure and demographic behavior, labor market activity, housing, and geographic mobility. Occasional survey supplements have covered such topics as wealth accumulation, neighborhood characteristics, health care, and child development.

The sampling methodology for the PSID is complex. For example, adults who form their own families become respondent units in subsequent rounds. Largely as a result of this, the sample size grew from 4,800 families in 1968 to over 7,000 by 2001. Since 1997, the survey has been conducted biennially.

The child development study, begun in 1997, involves a sub-sample of about 3,500 children, providing detailed information on care-giving, within-family time use of children, and selected measures of children's cognitive, emotional, and behavioral development—all of which can be readily linked with the main PSID data file. PSID data are available to public users on the Internet.

The National Longitudinal Surveys (NLS).

NLS is a generic term that encompasses a set of longitudinal panel surveys that have been conducted since 1966. Data were still being collected regarding four cohorts in 2002: (1) women who were 14 to 24 when first interviewed in 1968 or 30 to 44 in 1967—about 5,300 women; (2) men and women 14 to 21 in 1978—about 8,000 persons; (3) younger and older children of the NLSY79 female respondents —about 8,000 subjects; and (4) men and women ages 12 to 16 when first interviewed in 1997—about 8,000 subjects. Other than the child data collected in the NLSY97 survey, all these surveys focused on labor market dynamics. Their data also cover a wide range of complementary behavioral and attitudinal data on education, training, and family and household structure, enabling researchers to explore linkages between dimensions of employment and other factors. The 1979 survey's child data included in-depth information on psychometrics and other dimensions of child development. Information and data for these surveys are available from the Center for Human Resource Research at Ohio State University on its website.

Survey of Income and Program Participation (SIPP).

SIPP is a continuing series of national panel surveys undertaken by the Bureau of the Census, designed to collect data on income, labor force, participation in government transfer programs, and general demographic conditions. Sample sizes range from 14,000 to 36,000 households. The survey is built around a core of labor force, program participation, and income questions. At its outset in 1984, SIPP was intended to measure the effectiveness of transfer programs; over time, it has evolved to become more of an omnibus survey that meets a wide range of research objectives. Topical modules have included personal histories, childcare and support, and school enrollment. Public use data for selected waves of the survey are available, and additional information may be found on the Internet.

An add-on to SIPP is the Survey of Program Dynamics (SPD), conducted from 1997 through 2002 with a sample of 18,000 households. The SPD survey includes an extensive set of questions regarding the children of the interviewed adult—questions on schooling, health, and child-focused activities—and a self-report from adolescent children about a wide range of their activities and behaviors.

Education Surveys

NLS–72/HS&B/NELS:88.

Three longitudinal studies of youth, essentially covering the years since 1972, are panel surveys that follow a series of high school cohorts over time. These surveys are: (1) The High School Class of 1972 (NLS–72), a national sample of about 19,000 high school students followed from when they were seniors through 1986; (2) The High School and Beyond survey (HS&B), a sample from the class of 1980 initially comprising about 30,000 sophomores (followed to 1992) and 12,000 seniors (followed to 1986); and (3) The National Education Longitudinal Survey, 1988 (NELS:88) that followed about 18,500 8th graders from 1988 to 2000. These surveys collected detailed information about school progression and transitions to the work force, and a variety of demographic and family information.

Early Childhood Longitudinal Study (ECLS). The aim of these two panel surveys is to provide data on child development from infancy to the beginning of adolescence. The *kindergarten* component follows a nationally representative sample of about 22,000 children who attended kindergarten from 1998 to 1999 through the fifth grade; the *birth cohort* component follows 13,500 children born in 2001 from nine months of age through first grade. Both surveys examine the effects of family, school, community, and individual characteristics on a child's development. The samples include significant minority representation.

Aging Surveys/Family Processes Surveys

The Longitudinal Study of Aging. This panel survey was initiated in 1984 as a supplement on aging (SOA) to the NHIS. It included about 7,500 persons aged 70 and over, and reinterviews were conducted with most respondents in 1986, 1988, and 1990. The primary objective was to obtain data to (1) describe the continuum of movement from functional independence through dependence, including institutionalization and death; and (2) provide morbidity and mortality statistics by various demographic characteristics. These individual interview data have been linked with various other data files from the NHIS, and other forms of available records. The data are available on CD ROM.

Health and Retirement Study (HRS)/Study of Assets and Health Dynamics Among the Oldest Old (AHEAD). The HRS, a panel survey, was initiated by the National Institute on Aging in 1990. The first data collection wave in 1992 included over 12,600 persons in 7,600 households who were members of the 1931 to 1941 birth cohort. The sample includes an over-representation of minority respondents. The core sample has been reinterviewed at two-year intervals. The interviews cover health, retirement behavior and plans, family structure, income and employment, and related topics. The data can be linked with several administrative data sets including social security earnings data and the national death index.

Beginning in 1993, a parallel survey of 7,447 respondents (and spouses) aged 70 and over, the AHEAD study, was initiated. Additional birth cohorts have been added to this data set since its inception, and in 1998 the AHEAD and HRS samples were merged. The data are collected by the Survey Research Center at the University of Michigan.

National Survey of Families and Households (NSFH). This panel survey represents a first attempt to comprehensively interview a large nationally representative sample of the population about behaviors, attributes, and attitudes regarding a full range of family-linked activities for a wide variety of family types. Personal interview waves were conducted in 1987 to 1988, 1992 to 1993, and 2001 to 2002. The first wave includes 13,007 respondents in 9,637 households, with an over-representation of minority household units, single-parent families, families with step-children, cohabiting couples, and recently married persons, as well as selected *focal children* in the household. The second wave followed up on a large proportion of the original respondents, current and past spouses, partners and other core family members. The third wave consists of telephone interviews with a subset of the second wave respondents. The large sample size for family units undergoing transitions, in conjunction with the depth of behavioral and attitudinal detail, permit comprehensive examination of family processes and transitions.

See also: *Census; Databases, Demographic; Demographic Surveys, History and Methodology of.*

BIBLIOGRAPHY

Bureau of Labor Statistics, U.S. Department of Labor. 2002. *The National Longitudinal Surveys Handbook.* Columbus: Center for Human Resource Research, Ohio State University.

Carley, M. L., K. L. Muller, E. A. McKean, and E. L. Lang. 1997. *National Survey of Family Growth: Cycle V, 1995: A User's Guide to the Machine-Readable Files and Documentation.* (Data Set N8–O5). Los Altos, CA: Sociometrics Corporation, Data Archive on Adolescent Pregnancy and Pregnancy Prevention.

Curtain, T. R., S. J. Ingels, S. Wu, and R. Heuer. 2002. *National Education Longitudinal Study of 1988, Base Year to Fourth Follow-Up Data File User's Manua* (NCES 2002–323). U.S. Department of Education. Washington, D.C.: National Center for Education Statistics. Retrieved from

National Education Longitudinal Study: 1988–2000 Data Files and Electronic Codebook System—Base Year through Fourth Follow Up ECB/CD-ROM, Public Use.

Hill, Martha S. 1992. *The Panel Study of Income Dynamics: A User's Guide.* Newbury Park, CA: Sage Publications.

Kelley, M. S., and J. L. Peterson. 1997. *The National Longitudinal Study of Adolescent Health (Add Health), Waves I and II, 1994-1996: A User's Guide to the Machine-Readable Files and Documentation* (Data Sets 48–50, 98, A1–A3). Los Altos, CA: Sociometrics Corporation, American Family Data Archive.

U.S. Department of Education, National Center for Education Statistics. 2000. *National Education Longitudinal Study: 1988–2000 Data Files and Electronic Codebook System—Base Year through Fourth Follow-Up ECB/CD-ROM, Public Use.* [NCES 2002–322 CD-ROM]. Washington, D.C.: U.S. Department of Education, National Center for Education Statistics.

Westat. 2001. *Survey of Income and Program Participation Users' Guide Third Edition.* Washington, D.C.: Mathematica Policy Research.

Zill, Nicholas, and Margaret Daly, eds. 1993. *Researching the Family: A Guide to Survey and Statistical Data on U.S. Families.* Washington, D.C.: Child Trends.

INTERNET RESOURCES.

Child Development Supplement to the Panel Study of Income Dynamics. Sponsor: National Institute of Child Health and Human Development. <http://www.isr.umich.edu/src/child-development/home.html/>.

Current Population Survey. Bureau of Labor Statistics and Bureau of the Census. <http://www.bls.census.gov/cps//>.

Early Childhood Longitudinal Study. National Center for Educational Statistics. <http://www.nces.ed.gov/ecls/>.

Health and Retirement Study: A Longitudinal Study of Health, Retirement, and Aging Sponsored by the National Institute of Aging. Institute for Social Research, University of Michigan. <http://www.umich.edu/~hrswww>.

High School and Beyond: Overview. National Center for Education Statistics. <http://nces.ed.gov/surveys/hsb//>.

National Center for Health Statistics: Monitoring the Nations Health. Centers for Disease Control and Prevention (CDC). <http://www.cdc.gov/nchs/nhis.htm/>.

National Center for Health Statistics: Monitoring the Nations Health. Centers for Disease Control and Prevention (CDC). <http://www.cdc.gov/nchs/about/major/nsfg/nsfgback.htm/>.

National Center for Health Statistics: Monitoring the Nations Health. Centers for Disease Control and Prevention (CDC). <http://www.cdc.gov/nchs/nhanes.htm/>.

National Education Longitudinal Study of 1988: NELS 88 Overview. National Center for Education Statistics. <http://nces.ed.gov/surveys/nels88//>.

National Longitudinal Survey of the High School Class of 1972: Overview. National Center for Education Statistics. <http://nces.ed.gov/surveys/nls72//>.

National Survey of Families and Households. NICHD and NIA. <http://www.ssc.wisc.edu/nsfh/>.

Ohio State University Center for Human Resource Research. Ohio State University. <http://www.chrr.ohio-state.edu//>.

Overview of the Panel Study of Income Dynamics. National Science Foundation. <http://www.isr.umich.edu/src/psid/overview.html/>.

Research Design, Facts at a Glance. AddHealth. <http://www.cpc.unc.edu/addhealth/facts.html/>.

Research Practice Feedback. Sociometrics Corporation. <http://www.socio.com/>.

United States Census Bureau. <http://www.sipp.census.gov/sipp/>.

FRANK MOTT
THOMAS GRYN

LÖSCH, AUGUST

(1906–1945)

German economist and pioneer of locational analysis, August Lösch grew up in Heidenheim, Württemberg, Germany. He studied economics in Freiburg with Walter Eucken, and in Bonn, and later at Harvard, with Joseph Schumpeter. From 1940 to 1945 he served as a research director at the Kiel Institute for Global Economics. Some of Lösch's early research was concerned with the interaction of demographic and economic change, in particular, the effect of population on the business cycle. The work for which he is best known, however, is *The Economics of Location* (1940, American edition 1954), which applies general equilibrium theory to a spatially distributed economy.

Lösch used modern theoretical and statistical approaches to explore the impact of population change on economic cycles. Initially he believed that falling birth rates were disadvantageous to economic growth, as did most of his contemporaries. But his empirical investigations seemed to prove the contrary: population growth resulted in high costs to the national economy, while reduced population growth rates would potentially save capital for further investments. He buttressed his arguments by elaborate empirical investigations of demographic and economic growth in nineteenth-century Germany. One conclusion he reached, again contrary to general judgement, was that population change was more a cause than a consequence of business cycles. He propounded his findings in numerous articles, and in a 1936 lecture in Chicago, published the following year in the *Quarterly Journal of Economics*, where he also attacked the views of Raymond Pearl (1879–1940) and Corrado Gini (1884–1965) on population growth.

In his analyses Lösch started with as few assumptions as possible, establishing in theoretical terms in the manner of the classic pioneer of locational modelling, Johann Heinrich von Thünen (1783–1850), how characteristics of production and trade would give rise to spatial patterns of settlement. He concluded that this pattern must exhibit a hexagonal and hierarchical structure, which turned out to coincide with observed patterns. The study became one of the starting points of the field of Regional Science in the 1960s. Lösch's work on locational systems can be seen as a formal counterpart to that of the geographer Walter Christaller (1893–1969).

Historians have investigated how various aspects of Nazi policy were influenced by scientific knowledge, including findings from demography and economics. Lösch's work is sometimes mentioned in this context: his theoretical concepts were used in planning the intended settlement structure in Eastern Europe. But Lösch himself was strongly opposed to Nazi policies, even refusing to embark on a university career because he believed German universities had been corrupted by the regime. Unfortunately he did not live to participate in their restoration.

See also: *Central Place Theory.*

BIBLIOGRAPHY

SELECTED WORKS BY AUGUST LÖSCH.

Lösch, August. 1932. *Was ist vom Geburtenrückgang zu halten?* Dissertation, Bonn University.

———. 1937. "Population Cycles as a Cause of Business Cycles." *Quarterly Journal of Economics* 51: 649–662.

———. 1940. *Die räumliche Ordnung der Wirtschaft.* Jena: G. Fischer. English translation (of the 2nd rev. ed.): *The Economics of Location.* New Haven: Yale University Press, 1954.

SELECTED WORKS ABOUT AUGUST LÖSCH.

Christaller, Walter. 1933. *Die zentralen Orte in Süddeutschland.* Jena: Gustav Fischer. (Partial English translation: 1966. *Central Places in Southern Germany.* Prentice Hall).

———. 1941. "Raumtheorie und Raumordnung." *Archiv für Wirtschaftsplanung.* Vol. I. 116–3.

Felderer, Bernhard. 1990. "A Theory Explaining Lösch-Cycles," In *Infrastructure and the Space-Economy – in Honour of Rolf Funck,* ed. Karin Peschel. Berlin: Springer.

Funck, Rolf, and J. B. Parr, eds. 1978. *The Analysis of Regional Structure: Essays in Honour of August Lösch.* London: Pion. (Karlsruhe Papers in Regional Science, Vol. 2.)

Funck, Rolf H., and Antoni Kuklinski, eds. 1986. *Space-Structure-Economy: A Tribute to August Lösch.* Karlsruhe: von Loeper. (Karlsruhe Papers in Economic Policy Research, Vol. 3.)

Mackensen, Rainer. 1990."August Lösch as a Population Analyst," In *Infrastructure and the Space-Economy—in Honour of Rolf Funck,* ed. Karin Peschel. Berlin: Springer.

Preston, R. E. 1985. "Christaller's Neglected Contribution to the Study of the Evolution of Central Places," *Progress in Human Geography* 9: 177–193.

Stolper, Wolfgang F. 1954. "August Lösch in memoriam," Preface to the American edition of *The Economics of Location.* New Haven: Yale University Press.

Valavanis, Stefan. 1955. "Lösch on Location." *American Economic Review* 45: 637–644.

RAINER MACKENSEN

LOTKA, ALFRED J.

(1880–1949)

Alfred James Lotka was born in Galicia, in a city that was then part of the Austrian empire known as Lemberg, and which is now known as L'viv in Ukraine. Lotka's parents, Jacques and Marie (Doebely) Lotka, were U.S. citizens. He grew up in France and studied chemistry, physics and mathematics at Birmingham University in England, the University of Leipzig in Germany, and Cornell University in the United States, earning a D.Sc. from Birmingham in 1912. In 1902, he moved to the United States, where he spent most of the rest of his life. After working as an industrial chemist and at various other jobs, he held a temporary research appointment from 1922 to 1924 in American biometrician and eugenist Raymond Pearl's group at Johns Hopkins University. Lotka worked for the Metropolitian Life Insurance Company in New York City from 1924 until his retirement in 1948. Two months before his 55th birthday he married Romola Beattie; they had no children. He was president of the Population Association of America (1938–1939) and of the American Statistical Association (1943).

Lotka's concept of population embraced molecules, equipment, rotifers, Drosophila, humans, interacting species, interacting genotypes, and publications. He developed a powerful mathematical armamentarium for analyzing populations. He remains the population scientist nonpareil, whose five books and more than 100 papers not only shaped demography, the core population-science discipline, but also advanced ecology, evolutionary biology, epidemiology, economics, operations research, and chemistry among other subjects. Although the clarity and charm of his writings make them highly accessible to the reader, their range and profundity demand careful study. Most of the mathematical theory of population developed subsequently by other scientists is still best described as footnotes to Lotka's work.

While at Johns Hopkins University, Lotka completed his multifaceted book, *Elements of Physical Biology* (1925). Lotka's use of systems of differential equations, his emphasis on comparative statics and his focus on maximal principles and the stability of equilibria led to penetrating insights and opened new analytical perspectives.

A second book, *Théorie Analytique des Associations Biologiques,* was published in two parts (1934 and 1939). The second part focuses on demographic analysis with special application to humans. It lays out the three basic equations of Lotka's theory of stable populations:

$$b = 1 / \int_0^\omega e^{-ra} p(a) da,$$

$$c(a) = b e^{-ra} p(a),$$

and

$$1 = \int_0^\omega e^{-ra} p(a) m(a) da,$$

as well as the general renewal equation:

$$B(t) = \int_0^\omega B(t-a) p(a) m(a) da,$$

where the population is closed to migration and consists of "a large number of essentially similar units" (e.g., human females) and where a is age, b is the birth rate, r is the population growth rate, $c(a)$

is the proportion of the population at age a, $p(a)$ is the probability of survival from birth to age a, $m(a)$ is the maternity rate or rate of reproduction at age a, and $B(t)$ is the number of births at time t, and ω is an upper limit on age. These equations have been of fundamental importance to demographic theory and application. Lotka's research on the renewal equation began in 1908 at Cornell University in collaboration with Professor F. R. Sharpe.

Lotka devoted much thought to cyclical processes, from simple predator-prey interactions to global physico-chemical-biological systems. His research on the former led to the Lotka-Volterra equations used in ecology; his thinking about the latter anticipates current concerns about environmental stability.

The range of Lotka's interests is suggested by his study of the number of authors with n publications in lengthy bibliographies, such as Chemical Abstracts. He found that the probability of n is approximately $6/(\pi n)^2$, which implies that three-fifths of the authors listed contribute one article, 15 percent contribute two articles, and only a one-quarter contribute more than two.

See also: *Biology, Population; Demography, History of; Renewal Theory and the Stable Population Model.*

BIBLIOGRAPHY

SELECTED WORKS BY ALFRED LOTKA.

Lotka, Alfred J. [1906] 1977. "Relation Between Birth Rates and Death Rates." In *Mathematical Demography: Selected Papers,* ed. D. Smith and Nathan Keyfitz. Berlin: Springer-Verlag.

———. [1922] 1977. "The Stability of the Normal Age Distribution." In *Mathematical Demography: Selected Papers,* ed. D. Smith and Nathan Keyfitz. Berlin: Springer-Verlag.

———. 1925. *Elements of Physical Biology.* Baltimore: Williams & Wilkins. Reprinted as *Elements of Mathematical Biology* (1956). New York: Dover Publications.

———. 1926. "The Frequency Distribution of Scientific Productivity." *Journal of the Washington Academy of Sciences* 16: 317–323.

———. 1934, 1939. *Théorie Analytique des Associations Biologiques.* Paris: Hermann et Cie.

———. 1998. *Analytical Theory of Biological Populations,* (Théorie Analytique des Associations Biologiques) trans. David P. Smith and Helene Rossert (New York: Plenum Press.).

Sharpe, F. R., and Alfred J. Lotka. [1911] 1977. "A Problem in Age-Distribution." In *Mathematical Demography: Selected Papers,* ed. D. Smith and Nathan Keyfitz. Berlin: Springer-Verlag.

SELECTED WORKS ABOUT ALFRED LOTKA.

Arthur, W. Brian, and James W. Vaupel. 1984. "Some General Relationships in Population Dynamics." *Population Index* 50(2): 214–226.

Samuelson, Paul A. 1977. "Resolving a Historical Confusion in Population Analysis." In *Mathematical Demography: Selected Papers,* ed. David Smith and Nathan Keyfitz. Berlin: Springer-Verlag.

Simon, Herbert A. 1959. "Review of Elements of Mathematical Biology by Alfred J. Lotka." *Econometrica* 27(3): 493–495.

JAMES W. VAUPEL

M

MALTHUS, THOMAS ROBERT

(1766–1834)

Thomas Robert Malthus was a demographer, political economist, and Christian moral scientist. He was educated privately up to the age of 16 and then sent to a dissenting academy prior to entry into Cambridge, where, from 1784 to 1788, he undertook the course of studies designed to prepare him as a clergyman in the Church of England. These studies centered on theology, history, and mathematics, including Newtonian mechanics. Malthus first became a curate near the family home in Surrey, later adding a living in Lincolnshire. He retained these livings when he was appointed to a professorship at the East India College, Haileybury, in 1805, the post he held for the rest of his life.

It was during his initial period as a rural clergyman that Malthus composed his first published work: *An Essay on the Principle of Population as it affects the Future Improvement of Society, with Remarks on the Speculations of Mr. Godwin, M. Condorcet, and other Writers*, published in 1798. This anonymous work was originally intended to cast doubt on the doctrine of human perfectibility. By invoking a well-established principle, that population always expands in response to improvements in the supply of subsistence goods, Malthus showed that any attempt to create an ideal society in which altruism and common property rights prevailed would be undermined by its inability to cope with the resulting population pressure. In a context dominated by the hopes aroused by the French Revolution, this amounted to an assertion of the greater power of bioeconomic factors over human agency.

Malthus gave mathematical form to the principle by contrasting a maximum potential rate of population increase, the geometric ratio, with a posited arithmetic rate of increase in subsistence. But this deductive framework had an empirical foundation. Malthus employed Benjamin Franklin's figures for the increase in American population, under conditions in which subsistence posed no limits, to demonstrate that doubling was possible within 25 years. By contrast with his opponents he believed that his conclusions were the result of following a Newtonian procedure of arguing from observed effects to possible causes, rather than by speculating about the possible effects of known causes.

At this stage, Malthus had not yet reached the level of analysis that would later lead him to be called the founding father of modern demography. Indeed, his estimates of the rate of increase in the British population, like those of most of his contemporaries, were wide of the mark. He believed that it was doubling every 200 years, when it became clear, after the first census evidence collected from 1801 onwards, that it was doing so every 55 years. Thus, although Malthus was an acute observer of rural poverty, he was not, initially at least, reacting to the rapid population increase researchers now know to have been taking place. The special quality of his findings can be found in his contention that population pressure on living standards was "imminent and immediate." His opponents had maintained that while agriculture was in its present underdeveloped state there was no population problem. Although population pressure might threaten living standards at some distant point in the future, it would then be possible to remedy this by improvements in technology and recourse to birth control. Malthus, by contrast, held that the living standards of those who lived by labor had always been, and would remain, under pressure; that positive checks affecting mortality rates were still in operation in most parts of the world; and that preventive checks affecting marriage habits and birth rates were currently in operation in Western Europe and North America.

It followed from the immediacy of the population principle that attention needed to be focused on the way in which these checks operated to maintain the balance between population and available subsistence. In the polemical first edition of his *Essay*, Malthus treated all forms of check as varieties of "misery and vice." In the second much larger and more thoroughly empirical version published in 1803, commonly called the *Second Essay*, he introduced the idea of a virtuous check—moral restraint. This entailed postponement of marriage together with strict sexual continence during the waiting period. The second essay bore a new subtitle that signaled Malthus's endorsement of more positive solutions, partly via encouragements to individual prudence, partly via changes in social and political institutions. It became *An Essay on the Principle of Population; or a View of Its Past and Present Effects on Human Happiness; with an Inquiry into our Prospects respecting the Future Removal or Mitigation of the Evils which It Occasions.*

As a Christian moralist, Malthus thought it was his task to propose checks and institutional reforms that would reduce the harmful effect of population pressure on morals and happiness, even where this involved choosing the lesser of two evils. Since Malthus regarded birth control within marriage as a vicious practice, he cannot be described as a neo-Malthusian, the position adopted by many of his secular-minded followers. Prudishness plays no part here: he was opposed to birth control on the grounds that such "unnatural" expedients ran contrary to God's beneficent design in placing humankind under the right degree of pressure to ensure its development. It follows that use of the term "Malthusian devil" (as some have characterized what they consider the pessimistic aspects of Malthus's theories) is peculiarly inappropriate as a description of Malthus's own way of thinking. There had to be a reason why a beneficent Providence had endowed humanity with the sexual passion. It was to provide a spur to advance civilization by finding those means of living with its consequences that were consonant with human kind's long-term happiness. It also fol-

lows that Malthus was not an anti-populationist (that is, he did not oppose an increase in population or advocate a decrease) but rather, was a theorist of optimal population growth, inquiring into that relationship between the various physical and moral variables that would produce the best result. For this reason it is not entirely anachronistic to describe him as an early theorist of sustainable development.

Although Malthus was accused of propounding a form of bioeconomic determinism that ignored cultural variables, his mature procedure belies this charge. Once possessed of a fundamental natural law, inquiry could be centered on the surrounding circumstances—social, economic, and cultural—that determined how the law operated in any given setting. By appealing to the evidence provided by historians of the ancient world, and anthropological findings based on travel literature, as well as the new census material and other inquiries into the condition of the poor, Malthus established himself as a demographer in the modern vein: someone committed not merely to an examination of the relationship between births, deaths, and marriages, but to the cultural factors brought to light by other evidence on modes of life.

Studies of the response of population to wages and prices entailed lags that could generate cycles or fluctuations, during which there would be periods of maladjustment and market disequilibrium. Malthus was more impressed by these "irregular movements" than his friend and rival economist, David Ricardo: hence many of the disagreements over the causes of economic growth and the reasons for postwar depression that feature in their correspondence and in Malthus's attempt to provide an alternative to Ricardian economics in his *Principles of Political Economy* of 1820. This also explains J. M. Keynes's interest in Malthus in the 1920s and 1930s when he was formulating his own attack on economic orthodoxy.

Historical demographers have added greatly to our understanding by stressing the agrarian or essentially pre-industrial nature of Malthus's analysis of population problems. His arithmetic ratio became the basis for the law of diminishing returns, a proposition that dominated political economy up to John Stuart Mill, and has made a reappearance in the works of ecologists concerned with the global limits to growth. Malthus was one of the first to recognize the significance of what became known as the Western European marriage system of delayed marriage and hence lower birth rates. He also came to recognize one of the main features of the demographic transition. Higher incomes might lead not to more children, but to more goods and leisure. Comforts and luxuries could bring with them a desire to protect high and rising standards of living.

See also: *Condorcet, Marquis de; Demography, History of; Population Thought, History of.*

BIBLIOGRAPHY

SELECTED WORKS BY THOMAS ROBERT MALTHUS.

Malthus, Thomas Robert. [1803] 1989. *An Essay on the Principle of Population* (with the variora of 1806, 1807, 1817, 1826), ed. Patricia James. Cambridge, Eng.: Cambridge University Press.

———. [1820] 1989. *Principles of Political Economy,* ed. John Pullen. Cambridge, Eng.: Cambridge University Press.

SELECTED WORKS ABOUT THOMAS ROBERT MALTHUS.

Coleman, David, and Roger Schofield, eds. 1986. *The State of Population Theory; Forward from Malthus.* Oxford: Blackwell.

James, Patricia. 1979. *Population Malthus; His Life and Times.* London: Routledge and Kegan Paul.

Petersen, William. 1999. *Malthus: Founder of Modern Demography.* New Brunswick, NJ: Transaction Publishers. (Originally published by Harvard University Press, 1979.)

Winch, Donald. 1987. *Malthus.* Oxford: Oxford University Press.

Wrigley, E. A., and David Souden, eds. 1986. *The Works of Thomas Robert Malthus* (8 volumes). London: William Pickering.

DONALD WINCH

MARRIAGE

Marriage is a legal contract between two individuals to form a sexual, productive, and reproductive union. Through the marriage, this union is recognized by family, society, religious institutions, and the legal system. Marriage defines the relationship of the two individuals to each other, to any children they might have, to their extended families, and to society generally. It also defines the relationship of others, including social institutions, toward the married couple. Fundamental features of marriage include: a legally-binding, long-term contract; sexual exclusivity; coresidence; shared resources; and joint production. Spouses acquire rights and responsibilities with marriage, enforceable through both the legal system and through social expectations and social pressure.

Legal Aspects of Marriage

Marriage differs from other less formal relationships primarily in its legal status. Marriage is a legally-binding contract. Historically, both secular and religious law generally viewed marriage vows as binding and permanent. The contract could be broken only if one spouse violated the most basic obligations to the other and could be judged "at fault" in the breakdown of the marriage. Social changes lead, however, to shifts in the legal underpinning of marriage and, in turn, the legal treatment of marriage shapes the institution.

Changes in family law in many high-income countries appear to have made marriage less stable, as exemplified in the U.S. experience. Beginning in the mid-1960s, state governments in the United States substantially liberalized and simplified their divorce laws. One important feature of these changes was a shift from divorce based on fault or mutual consent to unilateral divorce, which required the willingness of only one spouse to end the marriage. Most states also adopted some form of "no-fault" divorce, which eliminated the need for one spouse to demonstrate a violation of the marriage contract by the other. The shift to unilateral or no-fault divorce laws in the United States was accompanied by a surge in divorce rates. The scholar Leora Friedberg has found that at least some of the increase in divorce rates resulted directly from the shift in the legal environment in which couples marry and decide to divorce or remain married. The link between divorce rates and laws that permit unilateral divorce has led several states to develop alternative, more binding, marriage contracts, such as "covenant marriage."

Fundamental Features of the Institution

According to Linda J. Waite and Maggie Gallagher, permanence, joint production, coresidence, and the social recognition of a sexual and childrearing union are the most important characteristics of the institution of marriage. These features lead to some of the other defining characteristics of marriage. Because two adults make a legally-binding promise to live and work together for their joint well-being, and to do so, ideally, for the rest of their lives, married couples tend to *specialize*, dividing between them the labor required to maintain the family. The coresidence and resource sharing of married couples have substantial economies of scale; at any standard of living, it costs much less for people to live together than it would if they lived separately. Both these economies of scale and the specialization of spouses increase the economic well-being of family members living together.

The institution of marriage assumes the sharing of economic and social resources and *co-insurance*. Spouses act as a small insurance pool against life's uncertainties, reducing their need to act individually to protect themselves against unexpected events. Marriage also connects spouses and family members to a larger network of help, support, and obligation through their extended family, friends, and others. The insurance function of marriage increases the economic well-being of family members. The support function of marriage improves married people's emotional well-being.

The institution of marriage also builds on and fosters trust. Since spouses share social and economic resources, and expect to do so over the long term, both partners gain when the family unit gains. This reduces the need for family members to monitor the behavior of other members, increasing efficiency.

Benefits of Marriage

The specialization, economies of scale, and insurance functions of marriage typically yield a substantial increase in the economic well-being of family members. Joseph Lupton and James P. Smith noted in their 2003 article that married people generally produce more and accumulate more assets than unmarried people. Married people also tend to have better physical and emotional health than single people. This is at least in part because they are married: the social support provided by a spouse, combined with the economic resources produced by the

marriage, facilitates both the production and maintenance of health.

In most societies, sexual relationships largely take place within marriage. Edward O. Laumann, John H. Gagnon, Robert T. Michael, and Stuart Michaels provide an analysis of data from the United States that indicates that almost all married men and women are sexually active, and almost all have only one sex partner—their spouse. Unmarried men and women have much lower levels of sexual activity than the married, in part because a substantial minority have no sex partner (survey data indicate that just under a quarter of unmarried men and a third of unmarried women who were not cohabiting had no sex partner in the year preceding the survey). Men and women who are cohabiting are at least as sexually active as those who are married, but are less likely to be sexually exclusive.

One central function of marriage is the bearing and raising of children. The institution of marriage directs the resources of the spouses and their extended families toward the couple's children, increasing child well-being.

Age at Marriage

In the United States and much of Europe age at marriage generally declined in the first half of the twentieth century, but then rose strongly, reaching levels not seen earlier in the century. Jason Fields and Lynne Casper noted in their 2001 study that between 1970 and 2000 the median age of first marriage for women in the United States increased by almost five years, from 20.8 to 25.1, and for men the median age increased by almost four years, from 23.2 to 26.8. In this same time period, the proportion of women who had never been married increased from 36 percent to 73 percent among those 20 to 24 years old and from 6 percent to 22 percent among those 30 to 34 years old. Similar increases occurred for men.

The delay in first marriage was especially striking for African Americans, as highlighted in a 2000 study by Catherine A. Fitch and Stephen Ruggles. Among African Americans, the median age at first marriage in 2000 was 28.6 for men and 27.3 for women, a rise of six and seven years, respectively, since the 1960s. Among those African Americans 30 to 34 years old in 2000, 44 percent of women and 46 percent of men had never married.

Trends in age at marriage in Europe have been broadly similar, although marriage patterns differ substantially by country. Sweden, Denmark and Iceland show the highest average ages at marriage for women (around age 29); the Eastern European countries of Bulgaria, the Czech Republic, Hungary, and Poland show the lowest (around age 22). Since societies with relatively high age at marriage also tend to be those in which many people never marry, this diversity suggests that marriage is a more salient component of family in some European countries than others.

Marriage typically takes place at younger ages in the developing countries of Africa, Asia, and Latin America. The average mean age at marriage in these regions is 25 for men and 21 for women, compared to almost 28 for men and 25 for women in the developed countries. Everywhere men tend to marry at older ages than women, but the gap in average age at marriage between spouses varies both within and between regions. According to United Nations data, this gap tends to be largest where women marry relatively early.

Union Formation

Declines in marriage are closely linked to increases in cohabitation, although it is difficult to untangle the nature of the association. In the United States cohabitation has become an increasingly common step in the courtship process. R. Kelly Raley noted that while only 7 percent of the women born in the late 1940s cohabited before age 25, 55 percent of those born in the late 1960s had cohabited by that age. Most couples begin their intimate life together by cohabiting rather than by marrying: the form of union has changed, but unions remain the norm. But even considering marriage and cohabitation together, in the early-twenty-first century young adults are less likely to be in a union than those of earlier cohorts. Among women born in the late 1960s, about a third had not formed a union by age 25, compared to a quarter of those born in the early 1950s.

Kathleen Kiernan has documented rising cohabitation in Europe, but with large variation among countries. It is strikingly common in Denmark, Sweden, and Finland; France too shows fairly high levels, with about 30 percent of the women ages 25 to 29 in cohabiting unions. A group of countries that includes the Netherlands, Belgium, Great Britain, Germany, and Austria shows moderate levels of cohabitation—from 8 to 16 percent of women from

25 to 29 involved in this type of union. In the Southern European countries and Ireland cohabitation remains rare: less than 3 percent of women ages 25 to 29 cohabit with a partner.

In many European countries, the majority of women are in cohabitational or marital unions by their mid- to late twenties. In the Nordic countries and France, about a third of women ages 25 to 29 are cohabiting, a third are married, and a third are single. However, over 60 percent of women in Italy, 50 percent in Spain, and over 30 percent in Portugal and Greece are neither cohabiting nor married at these ages.

Proportion Married

A consequence of the trends discussed above is that a larger proportion of adults is unmarried in the early twenty-first century compared to the past. In the United States in 1970, unmarried people made up 28 percent of the adult population. In 2000, that proportion was 46 percent. (The shift away from marriage has been even more pronounced among African Americans.) In Europe, marriage is most common in Greece and Portugal, where over 60 percent of women ages 25 to 29 are married, and least common in the Nordic countries, Italy, and Spain, where a third or less are married.

Nevertheless, the vast majority of adults still marry at some time in their lives. In the United States, the proportion of people ever married by age 50 is more than 95 percent for both men and women. Relatively high proportions of men and women have not married by their late 40s in the Nordic countries and in Caribbean countries such as Jamaica and Barbados, with a long history of visiting relationships that include sexual relationships but not cohabitation. In Sweden, for example, 76 percent of men and 84 percent of women in their late forties had ever married, whereas in Jamaica, only 52 percent of men and 54 percent of women had ever married by these ages.

Marital Disruption and Union Dissolution

A substantial proportion of all marriages end in divorce or separation due to marital discord. The divorce rate, which reflects the number of divorces in a year relative to the number of married people, rose continuously for more than a century in the United States and many other industrialized countries, then leveled off at a fairly high rate in about 1980. In the

United States, around half of all marriages end in divorce. According to Waite and Lillard and scholars Teresa Castro Martin and Larry L. Bumpass, the marriages most at risk are those with no children, those with children from a previous union or older children, those begun at a young age, and those between partners with relatively low levels of education.

Although high divorce rates make marriages seem unstable, other types of unions are much more likely to dissolve. Cohabitational unions show quite high chances of disruption, with a quarter ending in separation within three to four years compared to only five percent of marriages, according to one 1995 study by Zheng Wu and T.R. Balakrishnan. Many cohabitations become marriages, but these show lower stability than marriages not preceded by cohabitation.

Alternative Family Structures

The married, two-parent family has been the most common family form in the United States and other industrialized countries for some centuries. But even when this form was most prevalent, many people lived in other types of families, typically because of the death of one member of the couple before all the children were grown. With high mortality, frequently one partner in a marriage would die relatively early, so remarriage and stepfamilies were common as were single-parent families. The rise of cohabitation and non-marital childbearing have meant that unmarried-couple families and never-married-mother families have become common alternative family forms.

One alternative family form consists of two adults of the same sex, sometimes raising children. In the United States, about 2.4 percent of men and 1.3 percent of women identify themselves as homosexual or bisexual and have same-gender partners. According to one estimate by Dan Black, Gary Gates, Seth Sanders, and Lowell Taylor, in 1990 about 1 percent of adult men lived with a male partner and about the same percentage of adult women lived with a female partner, though these may be underestimates since some of those living in a gay or lesbian union do not identify as such in surveys. Legal and social recognition of these unions as "marriages" is generally not available in the United States, although France has enacted national registered partnerships, Denmark extended child custody rights to same-sex

couples, and in 2000 the Netherlands became the first country to grant same-sex couples full and equal rights to marriage.

See also: *Cohabitation; Divorce; Family: Future; Family Policy; Fertility, Proximate Determinants of; Partner Choice; Sexuality, Human.*

BIBLIOGRAPHY

Black, Dan, Gary Gates, Seth Sanders, and Lowell Taylor. 2000. "Demographics of the Gay and Lesbian Population in the United States: Evidence from Available Systematic Data Sources." *Demography* 37: 139–154.

Fields, Jason, and Lynne Casper. 2001. "America's Families and Living Arrangements: March 2000." *U.S. Census Bureau Current Population Reports,* 20–537.

Fitch, Catherine A., and Steven Ruggles. 2000. "Historical Trends in Marriage Formation: the United States 1850–1990." In *Ties that Bind: Perspectives on Marriage and Cohabitation,* ed. L. Waite, C. Bachrach, M. Hindin, E. Thomson, and A. Thornton. New York: Aldine de Gruyter.

Friedberg, Leora. 1998. "Did Unilateral Divorce Raise Divorce Rates? Evidence from Panel Data." *American Economic Review* 88: 608–627.

Kiernan, Kathleen. 2000. "European Perspectives on Union Formation." In *Ties that Bind: Perspectives on Marriage and Cohabitation,* ed. L. Waite, C. Bachrach, M. Hindin, E. Thomson, and A. Thornton. New York: Aldine de Gruyter.

Laumann, Edward O., John H. Gagnon, Robert T. Michael, and Stuart Michaels. 1994. *The Social Organization of Sexuality.* Chicago: University of Chicago.

Lupton, Joseph, and James P. Smith. 2003. "Marriage, Assets, and Savings." In *Marriage and the Economy,* ed. S. Grossbard-Shechtman. Cambridge, Eng.: Cambridge University Press.

Martin, Teresa Castro, and Larry L. Bumpass. 1989. "Recent Trends in Marital Disruption." *Demography* 32: 509–520.

Raley, R. Kelly. 2000. "Recent Trends in Marriage and Cohabitation." In *Ties that Bind: Perspectives on Marriage and Cohabitation,* ed. L. Waite, C. Bachrach, M. Hindin, E. Thomson, and A. Thornton. New York: Aldine de Gruyter.

United Nations. 2000. *Wall Chart on Marriage Patterns 2000*. New York: United Nations Department of Economic and Social Affairs, Population Division.

Waite, Linda J., and Lee A. Lillard. 1991. "Children and Marital Disruption." *American Journal of Sociology* 96: 930–953.

Waite, Linda J., and Maggie Gallagher. 2000. *The Case for Marriage: Why Married People are Happier, Healthier, and Better Off Financially*. New York: Doubleday.

Wu, Zheng, and T.R. Balakrishnan. 1995. "Dissolution of Premarital Cohabitation in Canada." *Demography* 32(4): 521–532.

LINDA J. WAITE

MARX, KARL

(1818–1883)

Karl Marx was born in Trier, Germany. He studied law in Bonn and Berlin and received his doctorate in 1841 at the University of Jena. Marx then devoted himself to the fields of classical philosophy and political economics. He earned his living as editor of the *Rheinische Zeitung* and as the author of various books and articles in which he analyzed the origins of industrial capitalism and its effects on the living conditions of the working classes. His scholarly studies were soon combined also with political activism, both often in collaboration with his life-long friend and supporter Frederic [Friedrich] Engels. Their most famous joint writing (albeit thought to be primarily Marx's), the *Communist Manifesto,* appeared in 1848, offering a summary of the Marxian theory of history as well as a political program statement. The first section of the *Manifesto* contains a compelling description of what today is called globalization—as a consequence of expanding capitalist markets. It also displays the literary verve characteristic of many of Marx's writings:

The bourgeoisie has subjected the country to the rule of the towns. It has created enormous cities, has greatly increased the urban population as compared with the rural, and has thus rescued a considerable part of the population from the idiocy of rural life. . . . The bourgeoisie keeps more and more doing away with the scattered state of the population, of the means of production, and of property. It has agglomerated population, centralized means of production, and has concentrated property in a few hands. The necessary consequence of this was political centralization. Independent, or but loosely connected provinces, with separate interests, laws, governments and systems of taxation, became lumped together in one nation, with one government, one code of laws, one national class-interest, one frontier and one customs-tariff. The bourgeoisie, during its rule of scarce one hundred years, has created more massive and more colossal productive forces than have all preceding generations together. Subjection of Nature's forces to man, machinery. . . whole populations conjured out of the ground — what earlier century had even a presentiment that such productive forces slumbered in the lap of social labour?

Marx moved to London in 1849 working on his magnum opus, *Das Kapital,* the first volume of which appeared in 1867 and was soon translated into many languages, serving as an ideological rallying point for political action. The main passages in that work that specifically address population questions are in Chapter XXV, Section 3. They set out the thesis that capitalism generates and is dependent upon a constantly renewed surplus population—an industrial reserve army that leads to unemployment and immiseration—and present a critique of Malthusian population theory.

The labouring population. . .produces, along with the accumulation of capital produced by it, the means by which itself is made relatively superfluous, is turned into a relative surplus-population; and it does this to an always increasing extent. This is a law of population peculiar to the capitalist mode of production; and in fact every special historic mode of production has its own special laws of population, historically valid within its limits alone.

The attack on Malthus is developed more elaborately in Section F of the *Foundations [Grundrisse] of the Critique of Political Economy,* a compilation of Marx's 1857–1859 notebooks, published more than half a century after his death. Marx recognizes Malthus's work as significant in two respects: "(1) because he gives brutal expression to the brutal viewpoint of capital; (2) because he *asserted* the fact of overpopulation in all forms of society." But he vehemently rejects the Malthusian theoretical construct, in terms spiked with unrelenting invective: "clerical fanaticism," "motley compilations from historians and travellers' descriptions," "a conception [that] is altogether false and childish."

Marx's own interpretation of the population law of capitalism, a topic to which he returned in passages of his *Critique of the Gotha Program* (1875), fueled much theoretical discourse. Among Marx's critics were Paul Mombert (1876–1938) and Georg Adler (1863–1908); they pointed out flaws in his use and interpretation of statistical surveys. Above all, they accused Marx of failing to take sufficiently into account changes in population dynamics and wages. And where capitalism flourished, history itself refuted the notion of the immiseration thesis, along with conception of the mechanisms, including population dynamics, that were supposedly leading to that state.

See also: *Communism, Population Aspects of; Social Reproduction.*

BIBLIOGRAPHY

SELECTED WORKS BY KARL MARX.

Marx, Karl. 1993 [1857–1858]. *Grundrisse: Foundations of the Critique of Political Economy.* Penguin Classics.

———. 1992 [1867]. *Capital: A Critique of Political Economy.* Penguin Classics.

———. 1933 [1875]. *Critique of the Gotha Program.* New York: International Publishers.

SELECTED WORKS ABOUT KARL MARX.

Adler, Georg. 1968. *Die Grundlagen der Karl Marxschen Kritik der bestehenden Volkswirtschaft. Kritische und ökonomisch-literarische Studien.* Hildesheim: Olms.

McLellan, David, ed. 2000. *Karl Marx: Selected Writings.* New York: Oxford University Press.

Meek, Ronald L. 1971 [1953]. *Marx and Engels on the Population Bomb.* Berkeley, CA: Ramparts Press.

Mombert, Paul. 1929. *Bevölkerungslehre. Grundrisse zum Studium der Nationalökonomie.* ed. Karl Diehl und Paul Mombert. Bd. 15, Jena: Fischer.

Petersen, William. 1988. "Marxisms and the Population Question: Theory and Practice." In *Population and Resources in Western Intellectual Traditions,* ed. M. S. Teitelbaum and J. Winter. Supplement to Vol. 14 of *Population and Development Review,* pp. 77–101.

Tucker, Robert C., ed. 1978. *The Marx-Engels Reader,* 2nd edition. New York: W. W. Norton & Co.

JOCHEN FLEISCHHACKER

MASCULINITY RATIO

See *Sex Ratio*

MASS MEDIA AND DEMOGRAPHIC BEHAVIOR

In the decades following World War II, radio and television broadcasting expanded rapidly throughout the developing world, and by the end of the century a substantial proportion of the world's population had routine access to them and to the information and entertainment they purvey. Plausibly, the spread of broadcast media, and mass media in general, in a society has some influence on both values and behaviors. This article is concerned with possible media influences in the areas of health and fertility.

According to International Telecommunication Union figures, among the population of low and middle income countries, in the year 2000 there were 265 radios and 185 television sets per 1,000 population. Television sets were more widely distributed in the countries of Europe and Central Asia (448 per 1,000), Latin America and the Caribbean (269 per 1,000), and East Asia and the Pacific (252 per 1,000) than in the countries of the Middle East and North Africa (172 per 1,000), South Asia (75 per 1.000), and Sub-Saharan Africa (59 per 1,000).

Intended and Unintended Effects

In thinking about the ways that the mass media may have influenced fertility and health, it is useful to distinguish between intended and unintended effects. Television, radio, and print media have frequently been mobilized to promote family planning, immunization, and a number of other services and behaviors ranging from safe sex to quitting smoking. These efforts have included both short-term and long-term information, education, and communication (IEC) campaigns, social marketing, as well as entertainment-cum-education programs that have used the appeal of entertainment in an attempt to show individuals how they can live safer, healthier, and happier lives. However, there is also reason to believe that the reception of regular commercial or public programming may have an unintended influence on ideas, values, and behaviors. The unintended effects of television viewing on fertility might include an influence on consumption aspirations as well as on norms and values regarding family life, sexuality and reproduction, and on the efficacy of modern medicine. The eventual influence is likely to be the result of continued, repetitive exposure over a long period of time.

Researchers, from both the communications field and the demography field, face difficult conceptual and methodological issues in identifying media effects. With respect to the general, unintended effects of mass media on demographic behavior, there is the familiar gap between empirical association and causal interpretation. Television ownership is highly correlated with many relevant indicators such as income, electrification, and other types of infrastructure. Those that choose to purchase televisions may have views that are different from those who do not. At higher levels of aggregation, there is the perennial question regarding content: Do the values and ideas conveyed on television lead or lag those of the audience?

In the case of commercial television programming in developing countries, the values conveyed in program content are likely to differ appreciably from the values of the audience. In some countries, much of the programming is imported. In others, it is locally produced but is tailored to relatively affluent metropolitan viewers—the target audience for advertisers—whose values may differ greatly from those of other, numerically more significant segments of the audience.

Evaluation of educational or motivational campaigns and of other programming intended to influence demographic behavior also presents substantial challenges. While they might be expected to be more effective, larger, longer, and more complex interventions are more difficult to evaluate than more limited IEC efforts for which it may be possible to establish a control group. A second difficulty is that recall of specific messages may well be affected by the salience of the message to the respondent, thus introducing a selection effect to recall in retrospective surveys.

The Evidence

With regard to the general, unintended effects of mass media on demographic behavior, strong empirical associations have been found in census and survey data between exposure to broadcast media and demographic variables such as the total fertility rate or level of contraceptive practice. Such associations have been demonstrated at various levels—across individuals, municipalities, and countries, after adjusting for the effects of possible confounding variables. Interpretations of such correlations have usually been cautious, even when based on longitudinal data. The threats to inference do not all run in the same direction, however, and it is possible that such associations may either under- or overestimate the true underlying influence.

A second source of evidence on unintended effects comes from qualitative studies of audiences, and their reception of radio and television programming. Several such studies in Brazil suggest, at the very least, that audiences engage with narratives about nontraditional roles for women, strains in intergenerational relations, and sensitive topics related to sexuality, infidelity, and abortion. In this context, such ideas provoked further discussion, comparison with local customs and values, and application to viewer's lives.

The interpretation of the evidence from evaluation studies on intended effects is controversial, with the advocates of purposeful communication claiming substantial influences, and others arguing that such effects are often overstated. In a 2001 review, Robert Hornik and Emile McAnany, both specialists in development communication, concluded that evaluation studies have shown that campaigns and entertainment–education programs have been effective in increasing the demand for services at family planning and health clinics, but only rarely have they shown much influence on population-level behavior. Moreover, when data are available over a longer period, it is observed that the program effects do not always outlast the programs. The second kind of evidence regarding intended effects comes from the association found in surveys between self-reports of exposure to messages and contraceptive practice and reproductive intentions. Although such correlations are often very strong, their interpretation must allow for the type of selection bias noted above.

It appears probable that there are both intended and unintended media effects on health and reproductive behavior, but their magnitude is uncertain. The relationship merits further study. As the role of values, ideas, and information in affecting demographic change is given more prominence, scholars are likely to pay increasing attention to the various and burgeoning means by which they are spread.

See also: *Culture and Population; Diffusion in Population Theory; Family Planning Programs; Fertility Transition, Socioeconomic Determinants of; Values and Demographic Behavior.*

BIBLIOGRAPHY

Hamburger, Esther Imperio. 1999. *Politics and Intimacy in Brazilian Telenovelas.* Ph.D. diss., University of Chicago. Ann Arbor, MI: University Microfilms.

Hornik, Robert, and Emile McAnany. 2001. "Mass Media and Fertility Change." In *Diffusion Processes and Fertility Transition: Selected Perspectives,* ed. John B. Casterline. Washington, D.C.: National Academy Press.

Kingcaid, D. L., A. P. Merritt, L. Nickerson, S. Buffington de Castro, M. P. de Castro, and B. M. de Castro. 1996. "Impact of a Mass Media Vasectomy Promotion Campaign in Brazil." *International Family Planning Perspectives* 22: 169–175.

La Pastina, Antonio Carmino. 1999. *The Telenovela Way of Knowledge: An Ethnographic Reception Study among Rural Viewers in Brazil.* Ann Arbor, MI: University Microfilms.

Rogers, E. M., P. W. Vaughan, R. M. A. Swahele, N. Rao, P. Svenkerud, and S. Sood. 1999. "Effects of an Entertainment–Education Radio Soap-opera on Family Planning Behavior in Tanzania." *Studies in Family Planning* 27: 193–211.

Singhal, Arvind, and Everett M. Rogers. 1999. *Entertainment–Education: A Communication Strategy for Social Change.* Mahwah, NJ: Erlbaum.

Westoff, Charles F., and A. Bankole. 1997. *Mass Media and Reproductive Behavior in Africa.* Analytical Reports No. 2. Calverton, MD: Macro International.

Westoff, Charles F., and German Rodriguez. 1995. "The Mass Media and Family Planning in Kenya." *International Family Planning Perspectives* 21: 26–31, 36.

JOSEPH E. POTTER

MATERNAL MORTALITY

Among women of reproductive age in developing countries, complications of pregnancy and childbirth are the major cause of death and disability. According to World Health Organization (WHO) estimates, for each year in the 1990s there were about 515,000 deaths world-wide from pregnancy-related causes, the vast majority (99%) occurring in Africa, Asia, and Latin America. Of all the health indicators monitored by the United Nations, the biggest disparity between developed and developing countries is in maternal mortality. The World Bank reports that an estimated 28 million years of healthy life are lost each year in developing countries due to maternal health conditions.

Even though there is agreement on the leading causes of maternal deaths and the magnitude of the problem, there is considerable disagreement and uncertainty about how to define, measure, and reduce maternal mortality.

Definitions and Levels

WHO defines a maternal death as "the death of a woman while pregnant or within 42 days of termination of pregnancy, irrespective of the duration or site of the pregnancy, from any cause related to or aggravated by the pregnancy or its management, but not from accidental or incidental causes" (WHO, 1992). Maternal deaths are divided into direct and indirect obstetric deaths, with direct obstetric deaths accounting for approximately three-fourths of all maternal deaths. The main causes of direct obstetric deaths are hemorrhage, unsafe abortion, eclampsia, infection, and obstructed labor. Indirect obstetric deaths are those related to conditions that are either pre-existing or exacerbated by pregnancy, such as malaria, anemia, hepatitis, and increasingly, HIV/AIDS. A potential source of definitional confusion is that in 2001, the U.S. Centers for Disease Control and Prevention (CDC) defined the term "pregnancy-related death" as "one that occurs during pregnancy or within 1 year of its end and is a result of complications of the pregnancy or a condition that was aggravated by the pregnancy." This is equivalent to the WHO definition of maternal death, except that the time frame is 365 days, rather than 42 days.

Statistics constructed from data on maternal deaths include: the maternal mortality ratio (maternal deaths per 100,000 live births); the maternal mortality rate (maternal deaths per 100,000 women of reproductive age, per year), and the lifetime risk (the probability that a woman will die of maternal causes). The maternal mortality ratio is sometimes erroneously called the maternal mortality "rate," creating confusion.

Lifetime risk is often used to illustrate the disparities between the developed and developing worlds. It takes into account both the risk of death that a woman faces each time she becomes pregnant and the total number of pregnancies she would expect to have over the course of her life. Calculated for a population or a cohort of women, lifetime risk thus depends on both the maternal mortality ratio and the total fertility rate, both of which are higher in developing countries. In many countries the lifetime risk of dying of pregnancy-related causes is staggeringly high. For example, WHO estimates lifetime risk as 1 in 13 women in West Africa, compared to 1 in 3,900 in Northern Europe. Other regional maternal mortality statistics are shown in Table 1.

Data on maternal mortality are difficult and expensive to gather, requiring nearly complete registration of deaths or demographic surveys with large sample sizes as well as accurate reporting of cause of death. For most developing countries only estimates are available.

An alternative to gauging the level of maternal mortality is to measure the availability, utilization, and quality of life-saving obstetric services (known as emergency obstetric care, or EmOC). UNICEF

TABLE 1

Estimates of Maternal Mortality by Region, 1995

Region	Maternal Mortality Ratio (maternal deaths per 100,000 live births)	Number of Maternal Deaths	Lifetime Risk of Maternal Death
Africa	1000	273,000	1 : 16
Asia*	280	217,000	1 : 110
Latin America and the Caribbean	190	22,000	1 : 160
Oceania*	260	560	1 : 260
Europe	28	2,200	1 : 2000
Northern America	11	490	1 : 3500
World Total	400	515,000	1 : 75

*Japan and Australia/New Zealand have been excluded from the regional averages and totals

SOURCE: WHO (2001).

and Columbia University have developed indicators of these service dimensions. They rely on the records kept by health facilities and existing estimates of population size by birth rates, and so can be built into existing record-keeping systems. Known as the UN Process Indicators, they were jointly issued by UNICEF, WHO and UNFPA in 1997. Their use has highlighted the large deficits in the availability and functioning of obstetric care services.

Historical Background

Maternal deaths used to be very common in Europe and the United States. As recently as the early-twentieth century, maternal mortality rates and ratios were as high in the United States as they are in areas of the developing world of the twenty-first century. Even though there were improvements in living conditions in the late 1800s and early 1900s, maternal mortality did not decline. The historian Irvine Loudon notes that it was not until the mid-1930s that a steep and steady decline in maternal mortality rates began. In 1915 the maternal mortality ratio in the United States was 608 maternal deaths per 100,000 live births; in 1933 it was 619, but by 1950 it had fallen to 83. The same pattern prevailed in other western countries. The great decline in maternal deaths in the West was not primarily due to gradual socioeconomic development (e.g., nutrition, education) but to the introduction of effective means of coping with obstetric complications: antibiotics for infection, blood transfusions for hemorrhage, and safer surgical techniques.

Strategies for Reducing Maternal Deaths

In the developing world, the major approaches to reducing maternal mortality are through nutritional programs, programs aimed at predicting or preventing serious obstetric complications, and programs aimed at ensuring treatment for complications.

Nutritional interventions. Serious anemia probably increases a woman's risk of dying of obstetric complications although the existing studies are flawed. Longstanding programs have sought to reduce anemia by giving women iron and folic acid supplements during pregnancy. However, serious anemia is generally due to a combination of factors, including not only iron deficiency, but malaria, intestinal parasites, and other ailments. Therefore, it is unlikely that iron folate supplementation alone will reduce maternal deaths.

More recently, vitamin A supplementation has been proposed as a way to reduce maternal deaths. The supporting evidence for this was a study in Nepal, which found a lower incidence of pregnancy-related deaths (from all causes up to 12 weeks after delivery) among women who received vitamin A. However, the meaning of this study is unclear since the greatest difference in relative risk of death was not in infections (which would support a biological explanation) but in accidents.

Predicting and preventing complications. Programs aimed at predicting and preventing serious obstetric complications include the training of traditional birth attendants (TBAs) and antenatal care. Despite the intuitive appeal of such programs, their potential effectiveness is much less than is generally thought. This is partly the result of the biological nature of the major complications: while some of them may be detected early (e.g., a substantial proportion of serious pre-eclampsia cases, and some cases of malposition of the fetus), they still require medical treatment to prevent harmful or even fatal progression.

Despite the great effort put into it, there are insurmountable obstacles to making this "risk approach" effective. While high-risk groups (e.g., very young women or those with a bad obstetric history) can be identified, the individual women who will develop complications cannot be. Moreover, most maternal deaths will take place in the low-risk group, simply because it is so much larger than the high-risk group. Thus, focusing on high-risk groups takes attention away from most of the women who will die.

Ensuring treatment for complications. Even though most life-threatening obstetric complications cannot be predicted or prevented, they can be effectively treated. Consequently, ensuring access to adequate emergency obstetric care is the central requirement for reducing maternal deaths. Other effective initiatives for reducing maternal mortality include increasing the use of contraception (since it reduces the number of pregnant women, and thus the number of women at risk of maternal death) and improving access to safe abortion procedures. Complications of unsafe abortion are the only major cause of obstetric deaths that is almost completely preventable, as experience in developed and developing countries has shown.

In recent years those concerned about high maternal mortality rates have had high hopes for programs aimed at increasing skilled attendance at delivery in developing countries, but there remain substantial questions about the potential of this initiative. If skilled attendance is interpreted as increasing women's access to treatment of complications, then it may well help reduce maternal deaths. If it only means training peripheral health workers to attend normal deliveries, with no feasible medical backup, then it is unlikely to make a difference in current high rates of maternal death.

Improving access to emergency obstetric care does not necessarily require building new hospitals or training new cadres of workers. Much can be achieved by improving the functioning and utilization of existing facilities and personnel. To a significant extent, this is a problem of policies, priorities, and management, not of resources. For example, there are countries where there are not enough obstetricians or anesthesiologists to post them in rural hospitals, and yet general physicians, nurses, and midwives are not permitted or trained to give lifesaving care to women with complications of pregnancy or delivery, or to administer simple forms of anesthesia.

Once adequate emergency obstetric care is provided in district hospitals and health centers, there emerge numerous opportunities to improve the utilization and quality of services with the help of nongovernmental organizations, community groups, and professional organizations. But without accessible services, no amount of community education or mobilization can save the lives of women with hemorrhage, eclampsia, or obstructed labor.

See also: *Causes of Death; Induced Abortion: History, Prevalence, Legal Aspects; Infant and Child Mortality; Mortality Differentials, by Sex; Reproductive Health.*

BIBLIOGRAPHY

Bailey, Patricia. E., and Paxton, Anne. 2002. "Using UN Process Indicators to Assess Needs in Emergency Obstetric Services." *International Journal of Obstetrics and Gynecology* 76: 299–305.

Goodburn, Elizabeth, Mushtaque Chowdhury, Rukhsana Gazi, Tom Marshall, and Wendy Graham. 2000. "Training Traditional Birth Attendants in Clean Delivery Does Not Prevent Postpartum Infection." *Health Policy and Planning* 15(4): 394–399.

Graham, Wendy J., Jacqueline S. Bell, and Colin H. Bullough. 2001. "Can Skilled Attendance at Delivery Reduce Maternal Mortality in Developing Countries?" *Studies in Health Services Organisation and Policy* 17: 97–130.

Loudon, Irvine. 1992. *Death in Childbirth, An International Study of Maternal Care and Maternal Mortality 1800–1950.* Oxford, Eng.: Clarendon Press.

Maine, Deborah. 1991. *Safe Motherhood Programs: Options and Issues.* New York: Columbia University, Center for Population and Family Health.

Maine, Deborah, Tessa M. Wardlaw, Victoria M. Ward, James McCarthy, Amanda Birnbaum, Murat Z. Akalin, and Jennifer E. Brown. 1997. *Guidelines for Monitoring the Availability and Use of Obstetric Services.* New York: UNICEF/WHO/UNFPA.

Rooks, J., and Beverly Winikoff. 1994. *A Reassessment of the Concept of Reproductive Risk in Maternal Care and Family Planning Services.* New York: Population Council.

Rush, David. 2000. "Nutrition and Maternal Mortality in the Developing World." *American Journal of Clinical Nutrition* 72(1) Supplement: 212S–240S.

Smith, Jason B., Nii A. Coleman, Judith A. Fortney, Joseph De-Graft Johnson, Daniel W. Blumhagen, and Thomas W. Grey. 2000. "The Impact of Traditional Birth Attendant Training on Delivery Complications in Ghana." *Health Policy and Planning* 15(3): 326–331.

Stephenson, Patricia, et al. 1992. "Commentary: The Public Health Consequences of Restricted Induced Abortion—Lessons from Romania." *American Journal of Public Health* 82(10): 1,328–1,331.

West, Keith P., et al. 1999. "Double Blind, Cluster Randomised Trial of Low Dose Supplementation with Vitamin A or Beta-carotene on Mortality Related to Pregnancy in Nepal." *British Medical Journal* 318: 570–575.

World Bank. 1993. *World Development Report 1993: Investing in Health.* Oxford and New York: World Bank.

World Health Organization. 1992. *International Classification of Diseases, 10th Revision.* Geneva: World Health Organization.

———. 2001. *Maternal Mortality in 1995: Estimates Developed by WHO, UNICEF, UNFPA.* Geneva: World Health Organization.

INTERNET RESOURCES.

Centers for Disease Control and Prevention (CDC). 2002. "Fact Sheet: Pregnancy-Related Deaths in the United States, 1987–1990." <http://www.cdc.gov/nccdphp/drh/mh_prgdeath.htm>.

United Nations. 2002. "The State of the World Population 2001. Monitoring ICPD Goals: Selected Indicators." <http://www.unfpa.org/swp/2001/english/indicators/indicators1.html>.

DEBORAH MAINE
KATRINA STAMAS

MATHEMATICAL DEMOGRAPHY

See *Actuarial Analysis; Animal Ecology; Life Tables; Multistate Demography; Renewal Theory and the Stable Population Model; Simulation Models; Stochastic Population Theory*

MICROECONOMICS OF DEMOGRAPHIC BEHAVIOR

This article briefly surveys the intellectual development and empirical implications of the literature on the microeconomic theories of demographic behavior. The behaviors discussed in this article include fertility behavior, investment in the human capital of children, marriage, divorce, non-marital childbearing, and selected aspects of female labor supply. Other demographic variables such as mortality and migration have been analyzed using microeconomic theory, but are not treated in this article. This article begins with fertility, the first of these behaviors to be studied using the microeconomic approach.

Microeconomic Fertility Theory

The view that fertility behavior can be analyzed within the choice-theoretic framework of neoclassical economics originated in a model of fertility by economist Harvey Leibenstein (1922–1994) in 1957 that stressed the importance of intergenerational transfers from children as a form of old age security as a motivation for fertility in developing countries. A far more influential economic model of fertility was presented shortly thereafter in a pioneering paper by economist Gary Becker in 1960. Becker attempted to reconcile the prediction from demand theory that increases in income should raise the demand for children with the facts that income growth has been accompanied by secular decline of fertility and that family income is inversely associated with cross-section differentials in the industrialized countries. Becker sought to address this apparent paradox by applying the theory of the consumer to show that these secular changes and cross-sectional differences in the completed family sizes of households in developed countries were the result of variations in family incomes and the *prices,* or opportunity costs of children.

In his 1960 paper, Becker introduced two key elements of all microeconomic theories of household behavior: preferences and constraints. A household consisting of a husband and wife is assumed to have preferences for goods and services that contribute their own adult standard of living and, crucially, also to have preferences for children. The household faces a budget constraint determined by its lifetime resources and market prices or opportunity costs of these resources. Using terminology introduced by economist Pierre-Andre Chiappori in 1992, Becker

assumed a *unitary* model of the household in which a husband and wife behave as if their preferences are described by a single household utility function. This common utility function might be justified by assuming that the husband and wife have identical preferences or that one of them controls the household's resources and has the power to dominate household decisions. Later, this article will consider "collective" household models in which husbands, wives, and even children all have their own preferences and household behavior that reflects the interaction of these actors within some kind of bargaining model. Meanwhile, the unitary model is utilized as a convenient simplifying assumption to be replaced by more appropriate assumptions when the question under analysis requires separate consideration of the interests of the husband and wife as, for example, when considering the formation or dissolution of the household through marriage and divorce, the decision of whether to bear children within marriage, or out of wedlock, or how the allocation of resources to children may vary with the resources owned by the father and mother.

Quality versus Quantity of Children

In conventional economic theory, the demand function for a given good can be derived by assuming that a household maximizes its utility subject to its budget constraint. Hypotheses about observable behavior are then developed from *comparative static* analysis that shows how demand varies as the budget constraint shifts due to changes in income, the price of the given good, or prices of related goods. When this methodology is applied to fertility behavior, Becker noted an apparent conflict between the predictions of theory and empirical evidence. As income rises, theory predicts that the quantity of most goods should increase, with the exception of "inferior" goods that tend to be inferior members of a class—the potato as an inferior form of food is a common textbook example. Empirically, Becker noted that fertility had been declining secularly at the same time that incomes had grown enormously and, in cross-sections, that there appeared to be a negative correlation between family incomes and number of children.

Becker rejected the two most obvious ways to reconcile theory and data. He argued that the true effect of income on the demand for children is unlikely to be negative because children are not inferior members of some broader class of goods. He also rejected the idea that the *price* of children is higher because more is spent on them when incomes are high or in higher compared with lower income families. All families in a given market face the same prices regardless of their income. Expenditures on children are a matter of choice, not an exogenous component of the budget constraint.

Becker then introduced the important idea that the demand for children has a qualitative as well as a quantitative dimension such that total expenditures on children are equal to the number of children multiplied by quality per child and by a price index reflecting the cost of inputs into children relative to adult goods. Within the quality–quantity model, expenditures on children tend to increase with income, implying that children are normal goods, but most of the increase is due to rising child quality while fertility does not vary strongly with income.

Further analysis of the quality–quantity model by economist Robert Willis and by Becker and economist H. Gregg Lewis, all in 1973, provided an underlying reason for the differential magnitude of the income effects on the number and quality of children. Within this model, the marginal cost of an additional child is proportional to its quality while the marginal cost of an addition to quality per child is proportional to the number of children. It follows that the relative marginal cost of quantity to quality is equal to the ratio of quality to quantity. As income increases, the relative marginal cost of quantity to quality therefore must shift in favor of whichever of these aspects of children has the larger income elasticity, causing a substitution effect that reinforces the change in that attribute. Thus, if the *true* income elasticity of quality is larger than that of quantity, an increase in income causes an income effect plus an induced substitution effect tending to raise quality per child and an income effect minus an induced substitution effect that may even cause a reduction in fertility.

Household Production and Allocation of Time

The next major steps in the development of a microeconomic model of fertility involved a more careful specification of a household's resource constraints, a correspondingly richer definition of the cost of children, and a linkage of fertility to other household behaviors, especially female labor supply.

The key idea in these developments is to consider the household as a productive unit as well as a consumption unit. In the first application of this idea to fertility behavior in 1963, economist Jacob Mincer argued that the mother's time was a crucial input to childcare and that the opportunity cost of this time is measured by the woman's potential market wage. Given that the husband's income and the wife's earnings potential tend to be positively correlated, the marginal cost of children will tend to be higher in higher income families, thus suggesting another reason for a negative correlation between family income and fertility. In a groundbreaking paper on married women's labor supply in 1962, Mincer argued that the productivity of nonmarket time for women led both to a lower level of market labor supply than for men and to greater responsiveness of labor supply to increased real wages than is true for male labor supply. Greater responsiveness arises from the high degree of substitutability between market and nonmarket goods ultimately satisfying the same needs (e.g., home-cooked meals vs. restaurant meals) whereas the relevant margin for male labor supply is more likely between goods and leisure, which are less substitutable. Secular growth of real market wages thus could consistently explain both the secular increase in female labor supply and secular decrease in male labor supply. Labor supplies of both sexes are reduced by the gain in real income and associated increase in the demand for leisure caused by rising real wage rates; however, the substitution effects in favor of work caused by higher real wages tend to outweigh the income effect for married women and to be outweighed by the income effect for married men.

In 1965 Becker produced a formal model of household production and time allocation in which he assumed that all commodities that a household ultimately values appear in the household's utility function. These are produced with inputs of purchased goods and time according to household production functions that reflect technology as distinct from the utility function that reflects taste. Within this framework, for example, differences in household demand for heating oil in Miami, Florida, and Minneapolis, Minnesota, are derived from the demand for the nonmarket household commodity, "comfortable temperature and humidity," which appears in the utility function. This approach provides a useful heuristic device for developing models of related investments such as furnaces and insulation or the study of the impact of air conditioning on the development of the U.S. Sunbelt.

More generally, the household production model, with its emphasis on time allocation, and its capacity to incorporate technological, environmental, and biological variables into economic models of household decisionmaking, has had broad influence on research on demographic behavior. Willis presented a model of fertility behavior that synthesizes the quality–quantity model of Becker using the concepts of household production and human capital investment. It emphasized the role of female time allocation between market and home work based on the earlier work of Becker in 1964 and 1965 and Mincer in 1963. The model assumes that the wife's time is combined with goods purchased in the market to produce two distinct household commodities: adult standard of living and child services where child services are the product of quality per child and number of children. A key technological assumption is that children are intensive users of female time relative to the adult standard of living from which it follows that increases in the marginal value of female time cause an increase in the ratio of the marginal cost of children to the marginal cost of adult standard of living. Increases in the cost of female time therefore tend to cause substitution effects weighted against children which, it is argued, will tend to induce quality–quantity interactions that reduce fertility while perhaps even raising quality per child.

Cost of Time and the Fertility Transition

The cost-of-time hypothesis is one of the leading hypotheses advanced to account for secular fertility decline and for the negative cross-sectional relationship between fertility and potential female market wage rates, often proxied by female education. Empirical tests of this hypothesis have been complicated by the fact that, according to the theory, variables such as the wife's labor supply and her market wage are chosen simultaneously with fertility and expenditures on children and that crucial prices that determine decisions are not directly observable. A woman will enter the labor force if her market wage exceeds the shadow price of time, an unobservable quantity that measures the marginal value of her time in household production, and, given that children are relatively time intensive, is positively related to the shadow price of children—another unobservable quantity. Women who do enter the labor force adjust their labor supply until the shadow price of time

is equal to the market wage. Hence, the market wage, which is observable, can be used as a measure of the price of time and, indirectly, of the marginal cost of children. However, the value of time remains unobservable for nonworking women and, worse, these women are a self-selected non-random sample of all women so that the wage rates of observationally similar working women may not provide a suitable estimate of the time value of nonworking women. Methods to allow econometric estimation of theoretically relevant behavioral relationships in this situation were pioneered by economist James Heckman (1974a).

Another important issue, first analyzed by Mincer and economist Solomon Polachek in 1974, is that the value of a woman's time in market work depends on the human capital she acquires through labor market experience. Willis's 1973 study suggests that the dependence of the value of time on market experience may promote "corner solutions" in which some women pursue careers and remain childless while other women have large families and remain out of the labor force. In part, the tension between allocating time to children or to career development may be resolved through the purchase of childcare services in the market, as first analysed by Heckman in 1974. To the extent that market childcare can substitute for the mother's care, the household technology of families of high wage women may actually become relatively *goods intensive*. This is consistent with the declining negative correlation between market work and fertility, noted by economist V. Joseph Hotz, and his fellow researchers, in 1997, that has accompanied the dramatic increase in female labor force participation of mothers with young children.

If children are relatively goods intensive among high wage women who substitute market childcare for their own care, then increases in female wages reinforce income effects and the correlation between income and fertility may become positive in such groups. To the extent that lower wage women supply market childcare, however, the overall opportunity cost of children will increase over time as the real wage of women increases. An analysis by economist Dianne J. Macunovich in 1996, however, suggests that the real female wage, holding education constant, has not increased since the mid-1970s nor has U.S. fertility experienced major changes although rates of childlessness have increased and the mean age of childbearing has also increased.

Dynamic Models

The static models of fertility behavior described so far in this article make the highly unrealistic assumption that decisions about fertility, work, and other household life cycle decisions are made simultaneously at the beginning of marriage with perfect foresight. Recognizing this limitation, economists began to build dynamic models of fertility decision-making under uncertainty, shortly after static models had been introduced. An initial application to imperfect fertility control and contraception by Heckman and Willis, in 1975, built on stochastic models of reproduction developed in 1964 by biostatisticians Edward Perrin and Mindel Sheps with further developments described in more detail by Hotz, Jacob Klerman, and Willis in 1997. While dynamic models make more realistic assumptions, they can also be analytically intractable. In an important advance in the use of dynamic models in 1984, economist Kenneth I. Wolpin showed how numerically specified structural dynamic models of demographic behavior could be estimated and the estimates used to answer counterfactual policy questions. In 2002, economist Marco Francesconi provided an example of a dynamic model of the interaction between fertility and work decisions by married women.

Divergent Interests of Husband and Wife

An important limitation of the theories discussed so far is their assumption that the unit of analysis is a unitary household in which the interests or preferences of the husband and wife are not distinguished. As noted earlier in this article, this assumption must be abandoned before it is possible to analyze the formation and dissolution of households through marriage and divorce or a variety of questions concerning the division of labor, the allocation of household resources and the distribution of welfare among household members. Becker, as usual, made seminal contributions with his theories of marriage and divorce. In these theories, the household is viewed as a productive partnership. For a given marriage to be formed or maintained, each partner must perceive himself or herself to be better off than they could be in an alternative arrangement as single person or in another potential match. Becker shows that a marriage market equilibrium will result in an efficient assignment of males and females such that no alternative assignment could make any individual or set of individuals better off without making some others worse off.

These models allow analysts to address a number of new questions. One concerns sorting in marriage markets. Under what conditions does like marry like or, alternatively, do unlikes marry? One possibility analyzed by Becker emphasizes gains to specialization in market or nonmarket labor, reinforced by incentives to invest in acquiring skills that are proportional to the time spent in market or nonmarket activities. These incentives, Becker argues, lead to a sexual division of labor within the household and to a pattern of negative assortative mating in the marriage market such that the market wage rates of husbands and wives would be negatively correlated. Although a sexual division of labor within households is almost universally in evidence, there are few if any empirical instances of negative assortative mating either on actual market wages or on potential wages as measured by education. A theoretical explanation for this puzzle was provided by economist David Lam in 1988. Lam argued that economies of scale in household production, including the important special case of *household public goods,* create gains to positive assortative mating which, under plausible conditions, more than offset the gains from negative assortative mating associated with specialization of household labor. Evidence presented by demographers Lisa K. Jepsen and Christopher A. Jepsen in 2002, comparing the matching patterns of married couples, opposite-sex cohabiting couples, and same-sex couples, is broadly consistent with Lam's analysis. They found positive assortative mating on all traits for all couple types, but stronger correlations for nonmarket traits than for market traits and stronger correlations for married couples than opposite-sex couples and the weakest correlations for same-sex couples. Lam's model rationalizes these correlations because children are the most prominent examples of household public goods and match-specific investments in other collective household goods tend to be larger for more durable unions.

Divorce and Child Support

Models that allow for separate interests of men and women can help explain phenomena such as the failure of divorced fathers to pay child support and the rise of out-of-wedlock childbearing.

In 1985, Willis and economist Yoram Weiss showed that, relative to marriage, divorce reduces the incentives of both parents to devote resources to their children. In particular, it may cause a non-custodial father who served as an exemplary bread-winner for his wife and children during marriage to become, upon divorce, a "deadbeat dad" who fails to pay child support. This change in behavior upon divorce occurs even if it is assumed that the strength of the father's concern for his children's welfare remains unchanged.

The key assumption underlying their analysis is that children are "collective goods" from the standpoint of their parents because each parent values the welfare of the children. Because an additional expenditure on a child by one parent benefits the other parent, there is a potential gain to both parents in sharing in the cost of the child. The optimal level of child expenditure occurs when the sum of the marginal values of a dollar spent on the child of each parent is equal to one dollar.

Marriage provides an institutional setting that facilitates a cooperative allocation of resources to children. However, non-cooperative behavior by divorced parents tends to reduce child expenditures below the optimal level. For example, consider a divorced couple with one child in the mother's custody. Using only her own resources, the mother will spend on the child up to the point at which the marginal value of a dollar of expenditure equals one dollar. The father may endeavor to increase child expenditures by providing child support payments to the mother. Assuming the mother treats child support payments as ordinary income, she will tend to increase expenditures on both the child and her own consumption. For instance, suppose she receives one hundred dollars in child support leading her to increase expenditures on the child by twenty dollars and on her own consumption by eighty dollars, a response consistent with an analysis of household expenditures by economists Edward Lazear and Robert T. Michael in 1988. In this case, it will cost the father five dollars to increase expenditures on his child by one dollar as compared to a cost equal to a fraction of a dollar when he and the mother cooperatively shared child costs within marriage. Weiss and Willis's theory implies that the increased cost of children caused by non-cooperative behavior in divorce leads to a reduction in child well-being, as measured by total expenditures by both parents, and may also lead to an unwillingness of the non-custodial father to pay any child support voluntarily, thus tending to shift cost of children onto the custodial mother. In 1999, Willis extended this analysis to show how these factors may lead to out-of-wedlock childbear-ing among low income women under conditions in which such women are economically able to support children with their own resources (including receipt of welfare payments) and when they outnumber men in the marriage market.

See also: *Becker, Gary S.; Easterlin, Richard A.; Economic-Demographic Models; Family Bargaining; Intergenerational Transfers; Leibenstein, Harvey; Partner Choice.*

BIBLIOGRAPHY

Becker, Gary S. 1960. "An Economic Analysis of Fertility." In *Demographic and Economic Change in Developed Countries.* Princeton, NJ: Princeton University Press, National Bureau of Economic Research.

———. 1964. *Human Capital* New York: Columbia University Press.

———. 1965. "A Theory of the Allocation of Time." *Economic Journal* 75: 493–517.

Becker, Gary S., and H. Gregg. Lewis. 1973. "On the Interaction between the Quantity and Quality of Children." *Journal of Political Economy* 81 (Suppl.): S279–S288.

Chiappori, Pierre-Andre. 1992. "Collective Labor Supply and Welfare." *Journal of Political Economy* 100(3): 437–467.

Francesconi, Marco. 2002. "A Joint Dynamic Model of Fertility and Work of Married Women." *Journal of Labor Economics* 20(2) pt 1: 336–380.

Heckman, James J. 1974a. "Shadow Prices, Market Wages and Labor Supply." *Econometrica* 42: 679–694.

———. 1974b. "The Effect of Day Care Programs on Women's Work Effort." *Journal of Political Economy* 82 (Suppl.): S136–S163.

Heckman, James J., and Robert J. Willis. 1977. "A Beta-logistic Model for the Analysis of Sequential Labor Force Participation by Married Women," *Journal of Political Economy* 85(1): 27–58.

Hotz, V. Joseph, Jacob Klerman, and Robert J. Willis. 1998. "Economics of Fertility in Developed Countries: A Survey." In *Handbook of Population Economics*, 1A., ed. M. Rosenzweig and O. Stark. Amsterdam, Netherlands: North-Holland.

Jepsen, Lisa K., and Christopher A. Jepsen. 2002. "An Empirical Analysis of the Matching Patterns of Same-Sex and Opposite-Sex Couples." *Demography* 39(3): 435–453.

Lam, David. 1988. "Marriage Markets and Assortative Mating with Household Public Goods: Theoretical Results and Empirical Implications." *Journal of Human Resources* 23: 462–487.

Lazear, Edward, and Robert T. Michael. 1988. *Allocation of Income within the Household.* Chicago: University of Chicago Press.

Leibenstein, Harvey. 1957. *Economic Backwardness and Economic Growth.* New York: Wiley.

Macunovich, Dianne J. 1996. "Relative Income and Price of Time: Exploring Their Effects on U.S. Fertility and Female Labor Force Participation." In *Fertility in the United States: New Patterns, New Theories.* Suppl. to *Population and Development Review*, Vol. 22, pp. 223–257.

Mincer, Jacob. 1962. "Labor Force Participation of Married Women." In *Aspects of Labor Economics,* ed. H. Gregg Lewis. Princeton: Princeton University Press.

———. 1963. "Market Prices, Opportunity Costs, and Income Effects." In *Measurement in Economics: Studies in Mathematical Economics in Honor of Yehuda Grunfeld.* Stanford: Stanford University Press.

Mincer, Jacob, and Solomon Polachek. 1974. "Family Investments in Human Capital: Earnings of Women." *Journal of Political Economy* 82 (Suppl.): S76–S108.

Perrin, Edward, and Mindel C. Sheps. 1964. "Human Reproduction: A Stochastic Process." *Biometrics* 20: 28–45.

Willis, Robert J. 1973. "A New Approach to the Economic Theory of Fertility Behavior." *Journal of Political Economy* 81 (Suppl.): S14–S64.

———. 1999. "A Theory of Out-of-Wedlock Childbearing." *Journal of Political Economy* 107(6) Part 2: Symposium on the Economic Analysis of Social Behavior in Honor of Gary S. Becker, S33–S64.

Wolpin, Kenneth I. 1984. "An Estimable Dynamic Stochastic Model of Fertility and Child Mortality." *Journal of Political Economy* 92(5): 852–874.

ROBERT J. WILLIS

MICROSTATES, DEMOGRAPHY OF

Attempts to define microstates are fraught with problems. There are no evident breaks in the size distribution of states, whether by population or by land area. Nor do population and area necessarily go together: States may be small in area but large in population (like Singapore) or large in area and small in population (like Greenland).

Somewhat arbitrarily, it is common to define microstates as political units with a population of less than 1 million. The definition of what constitutes a political unit for this purpose is also somewhat arbitrary: the notion of "state" in this context is by convention expansively interpreted. Microstates may be fully independent, or just have distinct geographic-territorial identities, with their political status ranging from full home rule (for instance, Greenland, a part of Denmark) to gradations of autonomy, as exemplified by such "microstates" as Gibraltar (formerly a British Crown Colony, now a dependent territory of the United Kingdom) or Martinique and Guadeloupe (overseas departments of France). The combination of a demographic criterion—a population below 1 million in 2000—and an expansive notion of what constitutes a state yields more than 70 such states: about a quarter of the "states" of the world. Some 38 of these microstates are formally fully-sovereign states, as signaled by membership in the United Nations. The most recent of these in the early twenty-first century is East Timor, with a population of around 750,000. Many of the UN member states have populations much smaller than that: Nauru and Tuvalu each has an estimated 11,000 people and some 11 others have populations of less than 100,000 each. The rest of the microstates are dependent territories. Most microstates are islands. Most are relatively poor.

Diversity characterizes the economies of microstates, though small size, isolation, fragmentation, limited diversification, and distance from markets are commonly a hindrance to economic growth. Several dependent territories have benefited from substantial metropolitan aid and they and most continental microstates have high income levels as a consequence of being economically well-integrated with affluent neighbors. Some of these, and also some formerly poor island states, achieved success with the new economies of banking and finance.

Various microstates that enjoy attractive climate and topography as well as stable administration, especially those in the Caribbean, have vibrant tourism economies.

With few exceptions the populations of microstates, in the early twenty-first century, are as large as they have ever been and, despite declines in fertility, growth rates usually remain at high levels. By global standards, population densities, especially on islands, are also high, and most microstates—other than the minority experiencing significant economic growth—are characterized by emigration, though only rarely is there absolute population decline. Economically successful continental microstates, such as Monaco and Liechtenstein, are characterized by both population growth (at least, as measured in de facto rather than de jure terms) and high levels of international commuting.

Fertility

Microstates have generally, if sometimes belatedly, experienced the significant fertility declines that occurred in most developing countries in the last half of the twentieth century. A number of countries have, since the 1980s, entered the demographic transition, such as those in Melanesia (Vanuatu and the Solomon Islands), the Comoros, Equatorial Guinea, and the Marshall Islands, retaining annual growth rates of over 2.5 percent. States where fertility has not fallen significantly tend to be poorer and have higher death rates. High rates of natural increase are usually associated with poverty, but also with the possibility of emigration, which is widely regarded as both a safety valve and a means of securing economic growth through remittances.

Many microstates have responded to high population growth rates by adopting family planning policies, but few of their family planning programs have been effective, especially in the African and Pacific island states. Total fertility rates remain very high in several states; in the Marshall Islands, Vanuatu, and the Solomon Islands they have fallen below six children per woman only since the 1990s. Much the same is true of Djibouti and the Maldives. Rates of natural increase are generally highest among Pacific island states, but are also very high in the Comoros, Equatorial Guinea, and the Maldives. The limited recourse to family planning reflects the continued economic value of children, the inclination of wives to comply with their husbands' preferences, the prevalence of adoption, and limited access to family planning services, especially where most populations are rural. However, acceptance of the small family system is more common in the Caribbean and in continental microstates. In a number of microstates, including Barbados, Luxembourg, Malta, and Martinique, total fertility rates are well below two children per woman.

Mortality

Good information on mortality in many microstates is limited. Crude death rates are generally low, reflecting a young age structure in many states. But age-specific mortality rates are often also low: Indeed Andorra, Iceland, Malta, and the French Antilles (Guadeloupe and Martinique) are among the places with the highest life expectancies in the world. The mortality rates in dependent territories tend to be lower than those in independent states, because of superior access to health services. Health services are least adequate and mortality rates highest in microstates that are classified as least developed, including Cape Verde, the Comoros, the Maldives, and East Timor. Life expectancy is below 50 years in the African state of Djibouti and in East Timor.

Mortality rates, especially infant mortality rates, everywhere fell rapidly in the second half of the twentieth century. This decline was associated with the epidemiological transition from infectious and parasitic diseases to chronic non-communicable diseases. The transition occurred in the Caribbean microstates prior to occurring in the Pacific. Indeed, in some Pacific microstates, such as the Solomon Islands, the decline in mortality may have stopped as a result of reduced access to health services.

Migration

In continental microstates such as Monaco and Gibraltar populations have long been urban. Most other microstates are becoming increasingly urbanized. Only in the smallest microstates does more than a quarter of the population live in rural areas. In most cases rapid urban growth followed increased post-World War II and post-independence expansion of government activity and spending and the growth of bureaucracies. Urban bias in resource allocation is fairly prevalent. Natural increase is now more significant than rural migration as a contribution to urban growth, posing economic, environmental and social problems in urban centers. Efforts to decentralize populations have occasionally had partial success, such as in Kiribati, but by and large have failed.

A number of continental, politically dependent, and resource rich microstates have experienced substantial immigration. The populations of oil-rich Bahrain and Brunei almost tripled in the last quarter of the twentieth century, through labor migration; the Netherlands Antilles, Turks and Caicos, the Cayman Islands, San Marino, Andorra, and the Channel Islands have also experienced rapid growth through tourism and finance. Several political dependencies, including Guam, Ceuta and Melilla, Mayotte, and the French Caribbean islands have experienced similarly rapid immigration from nearby but impoverished independent states.

A number of mainly small and remote island microstates have experienced sustained emigration, notably Pitcairn (which may become totally depopulated), Niue, the Cocos (Keeling) Islands, and Montserrat. A few dependent territories, notably the United States Virgin Islands, Guam, the Northern Marianas, and American Samoa, have become stepping stones for onward migration to affluent metropolitan states, usually the United States. In each of these territories, population growth has also been very rapid.

In most island microstates, international population flows are the major regulators of demographic change. Emigration characterizes many states, especially such Pacific states as Tonga, Samoa, Tokelau, and the Cook Islands. In those states and elsewhere migration is oriented to former or existing colonial powers and is primarily due to economic reasons. Remittances, from migrants in metropolitan states, sometimes sustained over generations, are the main source of national income—often contributing more than foreign aid and exports combined. Remittances are primarily directed toward consumption rather than investment, although less so than formerly, and thus tend to reinforce dependency. The rise in the significance of migration and remittances in several microstates has caused them to be characterized as MIRAB economies, an acronym referring to their heavy dependence on Migration, Remittances, and Aid, thereby promoting a Bureaucratic form of development.

In several states, such as Tokelau, Niue, Anguilla, and Montserrat, the majority of citizens live outside the country. International migration is selective by age and skills, and has caused a skill-drain from many states. Return migration has been small and is usually dominated by those in unproductive age groups. Despite limits imposed by destination countries, hope of opportunities for emigration in most island states remains undiminished. In some atoll states, concerns over rising sea levels are a further stimulus to emigration.

Achieving sustainable development is a formidable challenge for most microstates, especially the smaller, more remote island states. Young populations place strains on land and other resources, and on education systems, employment, and social organization. Some states are experiencing a fall in the standard of living and a rise in crime rates. Development in most states will be increasingly urban, is unlikely to be self-sustaining, especially if aid fatigue occurs, and will continue to be linked to migration. Yet there is no single observable pattern for the future: Microstates are enormously diverse, demographically as well as in other respects. They represent every global extreme.

See also: *States System, Demographic History of.*

BIBLIOGRAPHY

Aldrich, Robert, and John Connell. 1998. *The Last Colonies.* Cambridge, Eng.: Cambridge University Press.

Bertram, Geoff, and Ray Watters. 1985. "The MIRAB Economy in South Pacific Microstates." *Pacific Viewpoint* 26: 497–519.

Caldwell, John, Graham Harrison, and Pat Quiggin. 1980. "The Demography of Microstates." *World Development* 8(12): 953–968.

Connell, John. 1988. "The End Ever Nigh: Contemporary Population Change in Pitcairn Island." *Geo Journal* 16: 193–200.

———. 1999. "Environmental Change, Economic Development and Emigration in Tuvalu." *Pacific Studies* 22: 1–20.

Connell, John, and Dennis Conroy. 2000. "Migration and Remittances in Island Microstates: A Comparative Perspective on the South Pacific and the Caribbean." *International Journal of Urban and Regional Development* 24(1): 52–78.

Connell, John, and John Lea. 1992. "My Country Will Not Be There: Global Warming, Development and the Planning Process in Small Island States." *Cities* 9: 295–309.

―――. 2002. *Urbanisation in the Island Pacific. Towards Sustainable Development*. London: Routledge.

JOHN CONNELL

MIGRATION

See *Forced Migration; Immigration, Unauthorized; Immigration Policies; Immigration Trends; Internal Migration; International Migration; Labor Migration, International; Refugees, Demography of; Resettlement; Temporary Migration; Trans-Atlantic Migration; Urbanization*

MIGRATION MODELS

Decisions about migration are shaped by economic, social, and cultural factors. Migration models formalize these determinants. They also may describe the effects of migration at its origin and destination and the interactions between those effects.

Economic Determinants

Most formal migration models focus on economic determinants: opportunities and constraints on income at migrant origins (limited capital and technology, scarcity of employment, imperfect market environments), income opportunities at migrant destinations (demand for migrant labor in urban centers), and migration costs (travel costs, networks of contacts at prospective migrant destinations, border policies). Not all context variables are exogenous to migration; some may be influenced by migration decisions, as occurs when migrant remittances create labor scarcities or loosen financial constraints on production in migrant-sending areas, with ramifications for both migrant and nonmigrant households. A growing body of migration research attempts to elucidate these indirect or feedback effects of migration.

Although the results of sociological research usually agree that migration is the result of rational decisions by individual actors, such research often adds noneconomic variables to the list of determinants, viewing migration as a social process. Anthro-

pological research generally deemphasizes formal or quantitative modeling in favor of ethnographic research, viewing migration within a cultural, historical, and political-economic context. This article focuses on formal approaches that employ quantitative and statistical methods to model migration phenomena.

Objectives

The primary objective of migration models is to provide an analytic structure through which the direct and indirect influences on migration are identified, migration trends are charted, and the impact on migration of exogenous shocks, including policy changes, are predicted. Statistical models are used to test specific hypotheses derived from migration theories and estimate the magnitude of migration determinants and impacts. Estimated models, along with programming techniques, are used to explore or simulate the effects of policy and other influences on migration decisions. Simulations alter exogenous context variables, which are the only variables that researchers and policy makers are free to change directly.

The evolution of migration theory shapes both models and data collection. The earliest migration models are rooted in the theory of the geographer E. G. Ravenstein (1834–1913), who proposed 11 laws of migration based on the observation of migration patterns in Great Britain and, later, the United States. He proposed that although most migrants travel short distances, longer-distance migrants prefer to go to centers of commerce or industry; each stream of migration produces a counterstream; large towns owe more of their growth to migration than to natural increase; the volume of migration increases with the development of industry and commerce and as transportation improves; most migration is from agricultural areas to centers of commerce and industry; and the main causes of migration are economic. These observations motivated a plethora of quantitative models of migration flows and the aggregate variables that affect those flows.

Gravity Models

Ravenstein's (as well as Newton's) influence is clear in gravity models, which posit that migration between place i and place j, M_{ij}, is a positive function of repulsive forces at i (R_i) and attractive forces at j (A_j) and is inversely related to the "friction" or distance between i and j (D_{ij}):

$$M_{ij} = f(R_i, A_j)/g(D_{ij})$$

In practice, most formulations of the gravity model simply assume that migration between i and j is directly proportional to the product of the two places' populations and inversely proportional to the intervening distance ($M_{ij} = P_i P_j / D_{ij}$). Stouffer (1940) extended gravity models by introducing the notion of intervening opportunities: Migration over a given distance is held to be directly proportional to the number of opportunities at that distance and inversely proportional to the number of possible alternative migration destinations between i and j. In this approach the nature of particular places may be more important than distance in determining where migrants go.

These aggregate models, particularly gravity models, had the advantage of being simple to estimate, but they offered no insight into who migrated and who did not; how changes in policies, markets, and trade affected migration; or the social process of migration. Distance and population alone were not sufficient to explain migration behavior. Lee (1966) hypothesized that both the destination and the origin have characteristics that attract or repel migrants and that perceptions of these characteristics differ between migrants. The complexity of migration models has increased as research has evolved to address these and other questions.

Table 1 summarizes different migration models in terms of the variables included. The models range from early formulations, which included only a few variables, to new economics of labor migration (NELM) models, which contain many variables at the individual, household, and community levels, as well as policy instruments to influence migration.

The Models of Lewis and Schultz

In the 1950s and especially the 1960s economic models assumed a central role in migration research. W. Arthur Lewis's (1954) dual economy model of economic development with unlimited supplies of labor was not an explicit model of migration. Nevertheless, in this model migration is the means by which surplus labor in the traditional (agricultural) sector is redeployed to fill rising modern (urban) sector labor demands. Migration is demand- or employment-driven rather than being driven by wages, which are assumed to be fixed. The Lewis model assumes that a labor surplus exists. Thus, the loss of

TABLE 1

Variables Included in Migration Models

Migration Model	Population	Distance	Place Characteristics	Migration Costs	Individual Human Capital	Migration Networks	Source-Household Variables	Remittances and Their Use	Nonremittance Expenditures	Community Variables	Policy Focus to Influence Migration
Gravity	X	X									NA
Stouffer	X	X	X								Create intervening opportunities
Neoclassical wage-driven			X	X							NA
Todaro			X	X							Create jobs in migrant-source areas
Cumulative causation			X	X	X	X					NA
Human capital			X	X	X	X					NA
Remittance-use							X	X			NA
New economics of labor migration	X	X	X	X	X	X	X	X	X	X	Alleviate market imperfections in source areas

Note: NA: not applicable either because policy variables are not included (e.g., gravity models) or because, in light of the model's assumptions, the social welfare rationale for policy interventions is not evident (e.g., neoclassical wage-driven models). Many studies employ a mixture of the models in this table.

SOURCE: Compiled by author.

labor to migration does not reduce agricultural production or affect wages. This assumption, which accords with a classical economic perspective, was called into question by some economists, most notably Theodore W. Schultz (1964).

Once migration eliminates rural labor surpluses, urban wages must rise to lure additional workers from the rural sector. Wages adjust to ensure that both rural and urban labor markets clear. This is the essence of neoclassical migration models, which are of the form:

$$M_{ij} = f(W_i, W_j, C_{ij})$$

where W_i denotes wages at place i; W_j denotes wages at place j, and C_{ij} denotes migration costs.

In neoclassical models, intersectoral wage differentials are the primary factors driving migration. Population and distance play a role only insofar as they influence or are "proxies" for wages or migration costs and condition the scale of the overall process. Empirical models document that migrant flows are usually from low-wage to high-wage places and respond negatively to migration costs. However, wage-driven migration models cannot explain migration in the context of high rates of urban unemployment and explain only a small share of the variation in migration flows.

Alternative Models

Michael P. Todaro (1969) proposed an alternative formulation of neoclassical migration models in which prospective migrants maximize their expected income; in the aggregate migration equation above, W_i and W_j are replaced by expected incomes at places i and j, respectively. Nearly all empirical tests of the Todaro expected-income hypothesis use aggregate data on migration flows and wages and assume a random job-allocation process so that expected income equals the wage times the employment rate (or 1 minus the unemployment rate). The wage-driven neoclassical model may be viewed as a special case of the Todaro model in which the probabilities of employment at migrant destination and origin equal 1.

The power of the Todaro model lies in its ability to explain the persistence of migration in the context of unemployment at migrant destinations. A higher wage in the urban sector than in the rural sector is not a sufficient or even necessary condition for migration because the probability of finding a job at the prevailing wage also matters. Like its neoclassical precursors, expected-income models imply that an equilibrium eventually is reached, after which migration pressures abate. The Todaro equilibrium is where expected incomes (not wages) are equalized across sectors, adjusting for migration costs.

In the 1970s most statistical tests of the Todaro hypothesis used data on aggregate place characteristics and migration flows. They generally supported the hypothesis that migration flows from places where expected incomes are low to places where they are high and that unemployment rates have an effect on migration that is independent of wages. These aggregate models, however, were an uneasy fit with the theoretical models of migration behavior on which they ostensibly were based. They left fundamental questions unanswered: Why do some individuals migrate while others do not? What distinguishes the labor "lost" to migration from that remaining in the rural sector?

Micro Behavioral Models

In the 1980s research emphasis shifted from aggregate to "micro" behavioral models that focus on individuals' migration decisions. Most migration behavior models are based on the assumption that an individual n at place i will migrate to place j if the net benefits from migration exceed the migration costs, that is, if

$$B_j^n - B_i^n > C_{ij}^n.$$

The diversity of migration models in the last two decades of the twentieth century reflects differing hypotheses about what constitutes migration benefits and costs, and those hypotheses in turn reflect evolving theories of migration behavior. For example, in a wage-driven neoclassical model, B_i and B_j are replaced by wages at places i and j, respectively. In a Todaro model, they are replaced by expected wages: $p_i^n W_i^n$ and $p_j^n W_j^n$. (The model posited by Todaro actually was dynamic and hypothesized that individuals migrate if their discounted future stream of urban-rural expected income differentials exceeds migration costs.) Extensions of these models incorporate job search, migration networks, and risk as benefits or costs. In risk models migration benefits are hypothesized to be functions of both expected incomes and income risk.

Methodologically, micro models of migration behavior shift the researcher's focus from aggregate migration flows (estimated by using standard regression techniques) to individual migration decisions (modeled with probit or logit models or other related statistical methods). They require explicit consideration of differences among individuals in terms of migration benefits and costs. Human capital theory had a fundamental impact on migration research by positing that differences in individuals' earnings, and thus the economic returns from migration, can be explained by differences in skill-related attributes across workers, including experience and schooling.

Human capital migration models usually replace migration benefits and costs with human capital and other variables. In a few cases these benefits and costs are explicitly modeled as a function of human capital and other variables and their effects on migration decisions are estimated directly by using simultaneous-equation methods. In addition to human capital, social capital in the form of migration networks, or contacts with family and friends at prospective migrant destinations, plays a key role in some migration models. Migration networks may assist migrants in job searches and reduce migration costs and risks while creating a process of cumulative causation by which past migration makes future movements more likely. Empirically, networks are often the most significant variables explaining migration behavior.

The Impact of Remittances

Models of individual migration behavior do not provide a rationale for continuing interactions between migrants and source households, especially through income remitted, or sent home, by migrants. They also do not provide a useful basis for understanding the impacts of migration and remittances on migrant source areas. In the 1970s and early 1980s some researchers attempted to model the impacts of remittances separately from migration determinants, based on surveys of remittance use for productive investments by migrant source households. However, those studies did not investigate the indirect effects of remittances on migration decisions in the migrant source areas.

The New Economics of Labor Migration

The need to integrate the analysis of migration determinants and impacts stimulated a new genre of migration research in the 1980s and 1990s known as the new economics of labor migration (NELM). NELM models hypothesize that migration decisions are made not by isolated actors but by larger units of related people, typically households or families; that people act collectively not only to maximize income but also to minimize risks and loosen the constraints created by various inadequacies of markets in source areas, including missing or incomplete capital and insurance markets; and that migration decisions may be influenced by the behavior of other actors within the prospective migrant's social group.

In the imperfect-market environments that characterize most migration source regions, migrants create benefits and impose costs that are ignored by individual-decision migration models. In the absence of well-functioning credit and insurance markets, migrants serve as "financial intermediaries," providing source households with capital to invest in local production as well as income insurance (e.g., a promise to remit if a crop or family business fails). NELM theory implies new migration determinants (household capital constraints, risk, and community-level variables), as well as new potential impacts (positive effects of remittances on family production but also negative impacts of losing family labor to migration). It also draws attention to new forms of policy interventions to influence migration. Whereas a Todaro model would call for policy interventions in labor markets to influence migration, NELM modelers emphasize that interventions in capital and insurance markets can provide alternatives to migration as a means for households to obtain investment capital or income security.

A trademark of NELM models is their simultaneous consideration of migration determinants, remittance behavior, and impacts. This makes the application of NELM models relatively demanding in terms of both estimation methods and data needs. Empirical modeling provides evidence that production and incomes in migrant source areas are affected negatively by the loss of labor to migration but positively by migrant remittances and that household and community variables as well as individual variables affect migration and remittance behavior. It also offers support for the hypothesis that the characteristics of social groups, such as average incomes and inequality, both influence and are influenced by migration. Village-wide general-equilibrium models incorporating migration and remittances allow explanation of the effects of policy changes on overall village economic outcomes. These models reveal that many of the determinants and effects of migration are found outside the households that actually send migrants and receive remittances.

See also: *Economic-Demographic Models; Multistate Demography.*

BIBLIOGRAPHY

Knowles, James C., and Richard B. Anker. 1981. "Analysis of Income Transfers in a Developing Country: The Case of Kenya." *Journal of Development Economics* 8: 205–226.

Lee, Everett S. 1966. "A Theory of Migration." *Demography* 3: 47–57.

Lewis, W. Arthur. 1954. "Economic Development with Unlimited Supplies of Labour." *Manchester School of Economic and Social Studies* 22: 139–191.

Lucas, Robert E. B. 1987. "Emigration to South Africa's Mines." *American Economic Review* 77: 313–330.

Massey, Douglas S. 1990. "Social Structure, Household Strategies, and the Cumulative Causation of Migration." *Population Index* 56: 3–26.

Massey, Douglas S., Joaquin Arango, Graeme Hugo, Ali Kouaouci, Adela Pellegrino, and J. Edward Taylor. 1998. *Worlds in Motion: Understanding International Migration at the End of the Millennium.* Oxford: Clarendon Press.

Mincer, Jacob. 1974. *Schooling, Experience, and Earnings.* New York: Columbia University Press.

Oberai, Amarjit S., and H. K. Manmohan Singh. 1980. "Migration, Remittances and Rural Development: Findings of a Case Study in the Indian Punjab." *International Labor Review* 119: 229–241.

Ranis, Gustav, and John C. H. Fei. 1961. "A Theory of Economic Development." *American Economic Review* 51: 533–565.

Ravenstein, Ernest G. 1885. "The Laws of Migration." *Journal of the Royal Statistical Society* 48: 167–227.

Schultz, Theodore. 1964. *Transforming Traditional Agriculture.* New Haven, CT: Yale University Press.

Sjaastad, Larry A. 1962. "The Costs and Returns of Human Migration." *Journal of Political Economy* 70(5): 80–93.

Stark, Oded. 1991. *The Migration of Labor.* Cambridge, Eng.: Basil Blackwell.

Stouffer, Samuel A. 1940. "Intervening Opportunities: A Theory Relating Mobility and Distance." *American Sociological Review* 5: 845–867.

Taylor, J. Edward, and Irma Adelman. 1996. *Village Economies: The Design, Estimation and Application of Village-Wide Economic Models.* Cambridge, Eng.: Cambridge University Press.

Taylor, J. Edward, and Philip L. Martin. 2001. "Human Capital: Migration and Rural Population Change." In *Handbook of Agricultural Economics,* ed. Bruce L. Gardner and Gordon C. Rausser. New York: Elsevier Science.

Todaro, Michael P. 1969. "A Model of Migration and Urban Unemployment in Less-Developed Countries." *American Economic Review* 59: 138–148.

Yap, Lorene. 1977. "The Attraction of Cities: A Review of the Migration Literature." *Journal of Development Economics* 4: 239–264.

J. Edward Taylor

MILL, JOHN STUART

(1806–1873)

John Stuart Mill, English political economist and philosopher, was the son of James Mill, the utilitarian economist, who was responsible for his son's precocious upbringing, described in the latter's autobiography. Much of Mill's career, like his father's, was spent with the East India Company, based in London, in a period when the Company was effectively India's administering authority. From 1865 to 1868 he was a member of parliament. His formal occupations did not greatly interfere with his writing—in the 1820s and 1830s, essays for the *Westminster Review;* then *A System of Logic* (1843); and his major works, *The Principles of Political Economy* (1848) and *On Liberty* (1859). (Page references to the *Principles* below are to the 1965 variorum edition from the

University of Toronto Press.) He was a longtime companion and eventually husband of Harriet Taylor, whose strong stance on women's rights accorded with his own, set out in his essay *The Subjection of Women* (1869).

Mill's views on population issues were in many respects Malthusian, but he went further in approving of contraception within marriage, in promoting the emancipation of women, and in calling for curtailment of population increase on environmental grounds. The combination of utilitarianism, feminism, and environmentalism yielded an outlook that is surprisingly modern.

In his *Autobiography* (1873), Mill describes how the Philosophical Radicals, the group with which he was associated in the 1830s, interpreted T. R. Malthus's principle of population, seeing it not, as most of Malthus's readers did, as an argument against the improvability of human affairs, but "as indicating the sole means of realizing that improvability . . . [for] the whole labouring population through a voluntary restriction of the increase of their numbers" (Mill 1924, p. 74). The later Malthus, of course, also believed in prudential restraint, but more as an exercise of individual virtue than as an outcome of social policy. The policies Mill advocated to promote escape from a low-level Malthusian equilibrium were popular education (convincing people that producing a large family should be "regarded with the same feelings as drunkenness or any other physical excess"—*Principles*, 1965, p. 368); land reform, to establish a system of peasant proprietorship; and subsidized emigration, especially of young couples. But a big push was called for: "Unless comfort can be made as habitual to a whole generation as indigence is now, nothing is accomplished; and feeble half-measures do but fritter away resources" (*Principles*, 1965, p. 378). A further policy measure implied in *The Subjection of Women* was to prevent women being forced into the role of child-producers by "the press-gang of society." In a letter written shortly before his death, Mill agreed with the opinion that "a necessary condition for over-population is woman's subjugation, and the cure is her enfranchisement" (Mill, 1910, vol. 2, p. 303).

Mill was an early, though circumspect, supporter of artificial birth control, presumably under the influence of the radical reformer Francis Place, an associate of his father. He expressed amazement that, in England at least, the idea of voluntarily limiting the size of family after marriage was never mentioned. "One would imagine that children were rained down upon married people, direct from heaven, without their being art or part in the matter" (*Principles*, 1965, p. 369). (Mill is not usually known for a lightness of touch, but in a footnote in the *Principles* [1965, p. 156n] he comments on the relevant proximate determinant: "The most rapid known rate of multiplication is quite compatible with a very sparing use of the multiplying power.")

Most of Mill's views on population and even on women's rights are of interest mainly to historians of ideas. On one issue, however, he is still frequently read and quoted: his vision of the stationary state, set out in Book 4, Chapter 6 of the *Principles*. Classical economists like Adam Smith, James Mill, and David Ricardo saw economic growth leading eventually to stagnation at subsistence wages as profits fell toward zero and consumer demand flagged. This was their view of the stationary state. Mill's stationary state, in contrast, was arcadian—consistent with the prospect of indefinite human improvement in a world without the "unmeaning bustle of so-called civilized existence":

> If the earth must lose that great portion of its pleasantness which it owes to things that the unlimited increase of wealth and population would extirpate from it, for the mere purpose of enabling it to support a larger, but not a better or happier population, I sincerely hope, for the sake of posterity, that they will be content to be stationary, long before necessity compels them to it. (*Principles*, 1965, p. 756)

See also: *Malthus, Thomas Robert; Optimum Population; Population Thought, History of.*

BIBLIOGRAPHY

SELECTED WORKS BY JOHN STUART MILL.

Mill, John Stuart. 1871. *Principles of Political Economy with Some of Their Applications to Social Philosophy.* (1848). 7th edition. London: Parker. A variorum edition appears as volumes 2 and 3 (1965) of Mill's *Collected Works,* published by the University of Toronto Press, 1963–91.

———. 1869. *The Subjection of Women.* 1869. London: Longmans.

———. [1873] 1924. *Autobiography.* New York: Columbia University Press.

———. 1910. *The Letters of John Stuart Mill.* London, Longmans.

SELECTED WORKS ABOUT JOHN STUART MILL.

Himes, Norman E. 1928. "The Place of John Stuart Mill and of Robert Owen in the History of English Neo-Malthusianism." *Quarterly Journal of Economics* 42(4): 627–640.

Hollander, Samuel. 1985. *The Economics of John Stuart Mill.* Oxford: Blackwell.

Ryan, Alan. 1975. *John Stuart Mill.* London: Routledge and Kegan Paul.

GEOFFREY MCNICOLL

MINORITY POPULATIONS

See *African-American Population History; Ethnic and National Groups; Indigenous Peoples; Nomads; Racial and Ethic Composition*

MOHEAU, JEAN-BAPTISTE

(1745–1794)

Jean-Baptiste Moheau was a French proto-demographer. He was born in 1745, and died in 1794; he would not have been thirty years old at the writing of a treatise entitled *Recherches et Considérations sur la population de la France,* published in 1778 under his name. There remains some doubt about the authorship of the work, but it is now proven that Moheau was the personal secretary of Montyon, *Intendant* of the *généralité* of La Rochelle on the Atlantic coast of France, to whom the work was sometimes attributed. It appears that Moheau was substituting for Montyon, and took a special interest in the collection of population statistics that were requested by the royal administration. He made no other contribution to science. The book consists of two distinct parts, probably written by different persons. It is a remarkable achievement for its time, and deserves an important place in the history of demography. The title could be roughly translated, as "Empirical Studies on the Population of France, and their Interpretation." The work is characterized by a dual concern to present hard data and use them to make politically and socially relevant inferences. The first part ("State of the Population") is a demographic monograph, and contains chapters that are strikingly similar to those in any demographic description of a national population of the twenty-first century on the topics of data collection; an estimate of population size; the distribution by age, sex, and social characteristics; fertility; mortality; and migration. Especially noteworthy is the chapter on fertility. Moheau distinguishes fertility from what is now called the birth rate, and marital fertility from overall fertility. He is interested in fertility's variability in space, national and international, urban and rural, and analyzes the seasonality of births.

The second part of the book examines the causes of the progress or decay of the population. This is the part described by the word *considérations* in the title of the book. It distinguishes between physical causes (e.g., climate, food, dangerous occupations) and political, social, or moral causes. The latter factors include the effects of law, government, religion, taxes, war, and the possession of colonies. The most noteworthy passage is the allusion to *funestes secrets* (fatal secrets), a phrase widely quoted by French demographers. It has been often interpreted as a reference to the spread of contraception in marriage. In context, however, it would appear that Moheau had in mind the growing impact of various types of extramarital behavior, both before marriage and in prostitution and adultery.

See also: *Demography, History of.*

BIBLIOGRAPHY

Moheau, Jean-Baptiste. 1994. *Recherches et Considérations sur la population de la France* (1778). Paris: Institut national d'études démographiques, Presses universitaires de France.

ETIENNE VAN DE WALLE

MOMENTUM OF POPULATION GROWTH

Population momentum is the tendency for changes in population growth rates to lag behind changes in childbearing behavior and mortality conditions. Momentum operates through the population age distribution. A population that has been growing rapidly for a long time, for example, acquires a *young* age distribution that will result in positive population growth rates for many decades even if childbearing behavior and mortality conditions imply zero population growth in the very long run. Population momentum is important because of the magnitude and duration of its effects.

An Example

Consider the population of Nigeria, estimated at 114 million persons at mid-year 2000. Life expectancy rose from 36 to 51 years over the preceding half century, while completed family size remained at around six children per woman. In consequence, population grew very rapidly, with an average annual growth rate of 2.7 percent. (Statistics here and below are from United Nations 2000 projection series unless otherwise indicated.)

Rapid population growth implies a young age distribution because larger numbers of persons were born in the recent past than in the more distant past. During the period 1995 to 2000, for example, 22 million children were born in Nigeria, as compared with only 8 million from 1950 to 1955. Even if everyone in the earlier cohort had survived, there would have been far fewer persons aged 45 to 49 years than persons aged 0 to 4 in the year 2000.

Because of this young age distribution, the population of Nigeria will tend to grow rapidly in the future even if fertility declines rapidly to replacement level. The relatively large numbers of women and female children in and approaching reproductive age will generate large numbers of births, while the smaller numbers of persons at older ages will generate small numbers of deaths. The resulting population growth will slow as the population ages, but this will occur only over the many decades it takes for young persons to become old.

The United Nation's "instant replacement" population projections show that even with two-child families from the year 2000 forward, the population of Nigeria would grow from 114 million in 2000 to 183 million persons in 2050, an increase of 60 percent. The same projections show that the less developed world as a whole would grow from 4.9 to 7.1 billion persons, an increase of 2.2 billion persons, even with an immediate fall of fertility to replacement level in 2000.

Momentum and World Population Growth

The importance of momentum as a cause of future world population growth has increased as fertility levels throughout the world have declined. In 1994, John Bongaarts estimated that population growth due to momentum could account for nearly half of world population increase during the twenty-first century. He pointed out that this growth could be reduced without any change in completed fertility by raising the average age of childbearing. This is a consequence of the *tempo effect* identified by Norman Ryder, whereby shifts in the timing of births result in a bunching up or thinning out of births during the years in which the shifts occur.

For populations with very young age distributions, however, reducing population growth due to momentum may lead to undesirable changes in the population age distribution. The *constant stream of births* model proposed by Li Shaomin in 1989 is useful in this connection. Fertility declines that produce a constant stream of births will result in age distributions for which numbers of persons decline slowly with increasing age through old age. More rapid fertility declines will result in age distributions in which numbers of young persons in younger age groups are lower than numbers of persons in older age groups.

Returning to the example of the population of Nigeria, suppose that fertility declines after 2005 in such a way as to maintain numbers of births constant at the level observed during the period 2000 to 2005. On this assumption, the population would grow from 114 million persons in 2000 to 250 million in 2050. The later number is not much less than the United Nations medium-variant projection of 279 million. Further reduction in population growth would require more rapid fertility decline.

To eliminate growth during the period 2005 to 2010, for example, it would be necessary to reduce the number of births from the 26 million projected in the medium variant to 8.4 million, the projected number of deaths. This precipitous decline in births would be followed by similarly precipitous falls in the numbers of persons entering primary school (after a delay of 5 or 6 years), in numbers of persons entering the labor force (after a delay of 15 or 20 years), and so on through the life cycle.

Some decline in numbers in these age groups might be advantageous, but such extreme declines would be problematic. Any sustained fertility decline will yield an age distribution with a larger proportion of old persons relative to those at working ages, but the momentum effect—although ultimately transient—will greatly accentuate this dependency burden for a period of many decades.

Generality of the Momentum Concept

Population momentum is most often thought of in the context of fertility declining to replacement level, but the concept applies to all changes in childbearing behavior and mortality conditions. Consider for example a population that has a very old age distribution as a result of an extended period of population decline resulting from below replacement fertility. Should fertility rise to and remain at replacement level, population decline would nevertheless continue for many decades. Large numbers of persons in post-reproductive ages would generate relatively large numbers of deaths, because death rates in old age are high, but no births. Population decline would slow only as the large cohorts of older persons die out, so that the population age distribution ceases to be old.

To illustrate momentum resulting from changes in mortality conditions, imagine a hypothetical population in which 1,000 children are born every year and in which everyone dies on reaching their 60th birthday. Total population is the product of the annual number of births and life expectancy at birth, 60,000 persons. Suppose that at some time t mortality conditions change in such a way that persons alive at time t die only when they reach their 70th birthday. Then no deaths will occur for 10 years, during which period the population will grow from 60,000 to 70,000 persons. This growth is due to population momentum.

The constant-stream-of-births model may be used to generalize the concept of momentum to populations that do not reproduce biologically. Consider for example the population of PhD degree holders in the United States, for which new PhDs constitute "births" and "age" may be understood as time since PhD. According to the U.S. Bureau of the Census, the number of degrees granted annually grew from 1 in 1870 to just under 30,000 in 1970, with an average annual growth rate of 7 percent. Because of this very rapid growth, the population of PhD holders in 1970 had a very young age distribution, and therefore a strong tendency to future growth. On the assumption that there were 330,000 PhD holders in 1970 (the precise number is not pertinent for this example), holding the annual number of degrees constant at 30,000 after 1970 would result in a population of about 1.2 million PhD holders in 2010, an increase of over 360 percent.

Definition of Population Momentum

The definition of population momentum requires three concepts from stable population theory. First, a population that experiences fixed age schedules of fertility and mortality will over time approach a stable state in which the age composition (the proportions of persons in each age group) and the population growth rate (which may be positive, zero, or negative) are constant. Second, this age composition and growth rate are determined by the age schedules of fertility and mortality. They do not depend on the initial population age distribution. Third, two age distributions (giving numbers of persons in each age group) are *asymptotically equivalent* with respect to given age schedules of fertility and mortality if the ratio $P_1(t)/P_2(t)$ approaches 1 as t gets large, where $P_1(t)$ and $P_2(t)$ are the total populations projected from the two age distributions.

Given any age distribution and any age schedules of fertility and mortality, two stable age distributions may be calculated, both with the age composition implied by the age schedules of fertility and mortality, but with different total populations. Let the total population for the first stable distribution equal the total population for the given age distribution, and denote this number by P_1. Let the total population for the second stable distribution be chosen so that the second stable distribution is asymptotically equivalent to the given age distribution. Let this population be denoted P_2. The *momentum* of the given age distribution with respect to the given age schedules of fertility and mortality is the ratio P_2/P_1. This formulation was first stated by Paul Vincent in 1945, following Alfred Lotka's seminal 1939 monograph on stable population theory.

A necessary condition for momentum effects to exist is that risks of birth or death vary with age. If age schedules of birth and death are constant over age, the age distribution does not influence numbers of births and deaths and population dynamics are fully described by crude birth and death rates. The population growth rate will equal zero (assuming no migration) for any period in which birth and deaths rates are equal.

See also: *Keyfitz, Nathan; Population Dynamics; Projections and Forecasts, Population; Renewal Theory and Stable Population Model.*

BIBLIOGRAPHY

Bongaarts, John. 1994. "Population Policy Options in the Developing World." *Science* 263: 771–776.

Keyfitz, Nathan. 1971. "On the Momentum of Population Growth." *Demography* 8(1): 71–80.

Li, Shaomin. 1989. "China's Population Policy: A Model of a Constant Stream of Births." *Population Research and Policy Review* 8: 279–300.

Lotka, Alfred J. 1939. *Théorie Analytique des Associations Biologiques.* Paris: Hermann et Cie.

Preston, Samuel H., Patrick Heuveline, and Michel Guillot. 2001. *Demography: Measuring and Modeling Population Processes.* Oxford: Blackwell.

Ryder, Norman B. 1983. "Cohort and Period Measures of Changing Fertility." In *Determinants of Fertility in Developing Countries*, Vol. 2, ed. Rudolfo Bulatao and Ronald D. Lee. New York: Academic Press.

United Nations. 2001. *World Population Prospects: The 2000 Revision.* CDROM. New York: United Nations. Sales No. E.01.XIII.13

United States Department of Commerce. 1975. *Historical Statistics of the United States, Colonial Times to 1970.* Part I. Washington, D.C.: U.S. Government Printing Office.

Vincent, Paul. 1945. "Potentiel d'accroissement d'une population." *Journal de la Société de Statistique de Paris* 86(1–2): 16–39.

GRIFFITH FEENEY

MORBIDITY

See *Disease, Burden of; Disease and History; Disease, Concepts and Classification; Diseases, Chronic and Degenerative; Diseases, Infectious; Epidemics; Epidemiological Transition*

MORTALITY, AGE PATTERNS OF

The risk of death varies markedly with age. The death rate is high in the first month after birth, declines during the rest of infancy and childhood, remains low during adolescence and young adulthood, and then rises gradually in middle age and steeply in old age (see Figures 1A and 1B). The decrease and increase in mortality reflect the rise of physiological abilities and disease resistance during child development and their decline during senescence. This basic pattern has been observed for most human populations in different historical eras, for both males and females.

The age pattern of death rates determines the age distribution of the number of deaths and the age trajectory of the number of survivors. Because the death rate declines during childhood and rises later in life, the age distribution of the number of deaths usually has two peaks, one in the first year of life, and the other in old age (Figure 1C). The later peak is usually between 70 and 90 years of age in modern human populations, but it is estimated to have been between 20 and 40 years in Stone Age populations.

The number of individuals who survive from birth to a given age x is a decreasing function of x. Usually, the number of survivors plummets during infancy and early childhood, decreases gradually at young adult and middle ages, and then falls steeply at old ages (Figure 1D).

Mathematical Regularities

Because of the universality of this fundamental age pattern and the smoothness of mortality curves, several mathematical models have been developed for expressing mortality as a function of age. Generally these mathematical models fit observational data well.

Some of these models (including the Thiele model, the Siler model, and the Heligman-Pollard model) cover the entire life span by combining separate components that represent mortality patterns in different stages of life. For example, in the Siler model, the death rate (or force of mortality) at exact age x, denoted by $m(x)$, is expressed as the sum of three terms: $m(x) = ge^{-hx} + c + ae^{bx}$ where g, h, c, a, and b are parameters of the model. The three components (ge^{-hx}, c, and ae^{bx}) represent mortality decline in childhood, stable mortality during adoles-

FIGURE 1

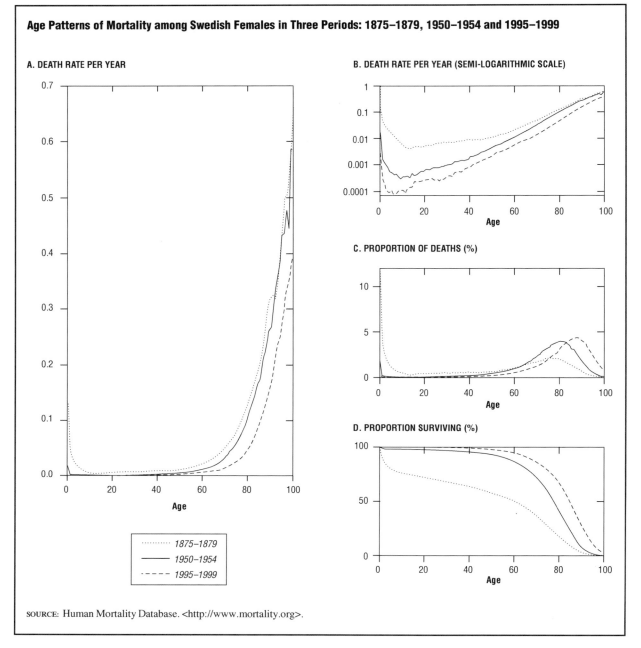

Age Patterns of Mortality among Swedish Females in Three Periods: 1875–1879, 1950–1954 and 1995–1999

A. DEATH RATE PER YEAR

B. DEATH RATE PER YEAR (SEMI-LOGARITHMIC SCALE)

C. PROPORTION OF DEATHS (%)

D. PROPORTION SURVIVING (%)

········· 1875–1879
——— 1950–1954
– – – – 1995–1999

SOURCE: Human Mortality Database. <http://www.mortality.org>.

cence and young adulthood, and mortality rise at middle and old ages, respectively. The three components can be additively combined because in each life stage one of the three components largely determines the age-specific death rate with only small numerical contributions from the other two terms.

Most other models (including the Gompertz model, the Makeham model, the Weibull model, and different versions of the logistic model) are con-

cerned with describing adult mortality only. The rising mortality curve at middle and old ages appears fairly straight on a semi-logarithmic scale (Figure 1B), suggesting that the death rate increases nearly exponentially with age. This exponential rise was discovered by the British actuary Benjamin Gompertz (1779–1865) in the early nineteenth century. In the Gompertz model, the death rate at exact age x is expressed simply as: $m(x) = ae^{bx}$ where a and b

are parameters of the model. The Gompertz model appears as one of the three components of the Siler model.

The parameter b of the Gompertz model, the slope of the logarithmic mortality curve, is called the Gompertzian rate of aging. In biodemographic research, the Gompertz model has been applied to mortality data of various species, and the Gompertzian rate of aging is widely used for comparing the pace of senescence among species, and also for studying effects of genetic and environmental factors on senescent processes.

Mortality Deceleration at Older Ages

The exponential increase of adult mortality tends to slow at very old ages, as illustrated in Figure 2. Thus the logistic equation, which sets an upper limit to mortality rise, usually fits observed death rates at very old ages more closely than the exponential equation does. This mortality deceleration is observed in most large human populations as well as in several non-human animal species (including fruit flies, earthworms, wasps, and beetles) for which old-age mortality patterns have been examined in detail. Although the slowing-down of mortality increase can be clearly seen in human populations, it is less pronounced than in the non-human species. Some fruit fly populations even exhibit notable age-related *declines* of mortality at very old ages.

In modern human populations, the deceleration can be visually detected in the data for mortality above age 90, but age-specific rates of relative mortality increase (called *life table aging rates*) indicate that the slowing-down actually starts earlier, typically between ages 75 and 80. In populations with lower levels of old-age mortality, the deceleration tends to be delayed to higher ages.

The reason for the mortality deceleration is not fully known. One possible explanation is selective survival. Because less-healthy individuals are more likely to die at younger ages, survivors to older ages tend to have favorable health endowments and/or healthy lifestyles. This selection process could slow down the age-related increase in the death rate in the *population* data. Another possible explanation is that the age-related increase of mortality risk in each *individual* may slow down at old ages for physiological reasons.

FIGURE 2

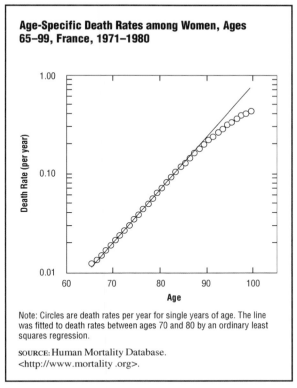

Age-Specific Death Rates among Women, Ages 65–99, France, 1971–1980

Note: Circles are death rates per year for single years of age. The line was fitted to death rates between ages 70 and 80 by an ordinary least squares regression.

SOURCE: Human Mortality Database. <http://www.mortality.org>.

Orchestrated Variations of Mortality Schedule

A *mortality schedule* is a set of age-specific death rates observed during a given period or over the lifetime of a cohort. As described earlier, empirical mortality schedules generally exhibit a three-phase pattern (downward, stable, and upward). Thus it might seem reasonable to expect mortality schedules that produce the same life expectancy at birth to be similar. However, very different combinations of age-specific death rates (e.g., a combination of relatively high child mortality and low adult mortality and a combination of relatively low child mortality and high adult mortality) can show the basic three-phase age pattern and produce the same life expectancy. Various hypothetical mortality schedules with the same life expectancy could be generated by adjusting the parameter values of, for example, the Siler model.

Nevertheless, data from various areas and countries in different periods suggest that age-specific death rates tend to change over time and vary among populations in fairly orchestrated ways. Death rates at even widely different ages are strongly positively

FIGURE 3

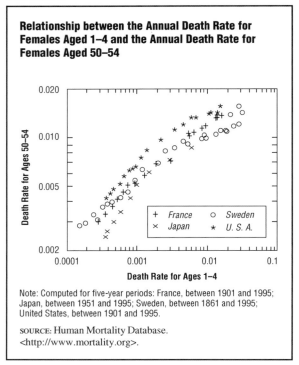

Relationship between the Annual Death Rate for Females Aged 1–4 and the Annual Death Rate for Females Aged 50–54

Note: Computed for five-year periods: France, between 1901 and 1995; Japan, between 1951 and 1995; Sweden, between 1861 and 1995; United States, between 1901 and 1995.

SOURCE: Human Mortality Database. <http://www.mortality.org>.

(though not linearly) correlated with each other (Figure 3). The reason that mortality schedules vary in orchestrated ways is probably that the overall level of socioeconomic and technological development in the population is reflected in various determinants of health and survival, including the standard of living, nutritional status, available medical technologies, and level of public health services. These factors, in turn, affect death rates of all age groups simultaneously.

High correlations among age-specific death rates make it possible to construct a set of *typical* mortality schedules corresponding to different levels of life expectancy. Such a typical schedule is called a model life table. Two well-known systems of model life tables are the Coale-Demeny model life tables and United Nations (Heligman-Preston) model life tables; both are widely used. The most typical patterns in the two systems are called the West model life tables in the Coale-Demeny system and the General Pattern in the U.N. system. Not surprisingly, the West life tables and General Pattern life tables are very similar.

However, some empirical mortality schedules depart systematically (though not greatly) from these typical patterns, probably reflecting mortality impacts of different natural and cultural environments. Thus both the Coale-Demeny and U.N. systems include additional sets of model life tables to describe these departures.

Demographers have developed several mathematical formulations of the relationships among age-specific death rates. These are called "relational models" and include the Brass logit model, the Heligman-Preston principal-component model, the Lee-Carter model, and Azbel's "law of survival." For example, in the Lee-Carter model, the death rate at age x and time t, denoted by $m(x, t)$, is expressed as:

$$log\ m(x,t) = a(x) + k(t)b(x)$$

where $a(x)$, $k(t)$, and $b(x)$ are estimated from a set of observed age-specific death rates for multiple periods. This implies that logarithms of age-specific death rates are linear functions of each other. The Lee-Carter model has been shown to closely fit mortality schedules of the United States between 1933 and 1987 and those of the G-7 countries (Canada, France, Germany, Italy, Japan, United Kingdom, and United States) during the second half of the twentieth century.

Historical Changes in Mortality Schedules

Two major health transitions affected age patterns of mortality differently. In Figure 1, these two transitions are illustrated by changes in Swedish female mortality from 1875–1879 to 1950–1954 and changes from 1950–1954 to 1995–1999. The first type of transition (called the epidemiological transition) is the significant reduction of mortality from highly contagious infectious diseases, nutritional disorders, and complications of pregnancy and childbirth. In many countries that are at high levels of economic and technological development, this transition occurred mainly in the nineteenth century and the first half of the twentieth century. Early childhood mortality fell considerably, but old age mortality declined only modestly (Figure 1A). Because the relative reduction of adult mortality was greater at younger ages, the slope of the logarithmic mortality curve became steeper (Figure 1B).

The epidemiological transition greatly reduced the proportion of deaths in early childhood and concentrated deaths into a relatively narrow range of old age. Thus the earlier peak in the distribution of deaths fell and the later peak rose (Figure 1C). The transition made the survival curve more rectangular. The survival curve has become fairly flat from birth to middle age because of the low mortality in this age range, and slopes steeply downward in old age because of the high concentration of deaths (Figure 1D).

The second transition is the substantial decline of mortality from degenerative diseases, including heart disease, stroke, and chronic kidney disease. In economically developed countries, this change started in the third quarter of the twentieth century. The absolute reduction of mortality was greater at older ages (Figure 1A), and the relative reduction of mortality was fairly constant over adult ages, producing a nearly parallel downward shift of the logarithmic mortality curve without appreciably changing the slope (Figure 1B). Because of the decline of old age mortality, the peak of the distribution of adult deaths moved toward older ages instead of rising higher (Figure 1C), and the downward slope of the survival curve shifted horizontally to the right without becoming noticeably steeper (Figure 1D).

Age Patterns of Cause-Specific Mortality

The age pattern of mortality differs among major causes of death. The differentials help in investigating the relationships between disease development and age-associated physiological changes, particularly the processes of senescence. Some typical age patterns of cause-specific mortality are shown in Figure 4. They are shown on a semi-logarithmic scale, because notable differences are found in the patterns of relative (rather than absolute) changes of mortality with age. Figure 4 displays data for France, but similar patterns are observed in other low mortality countries.

Above age 85, the curvatures of most cause-specific trajectories are concave (i.e., the gradients of the curves diminish with age), as seen for the four causes of death in Figure 4. Under age 85, the patterns are more variable. The death rate from cardiovascular diseases keeps rising steeply and exponentially throughout the adult ages. The death rate from cancers increases sharply at middle ages (the 30s and 40s), but slows down markedly at older ages, making the mortality curve of adult cancers concave already from around age 40. Most site-specific cancer death

FIGURE 4

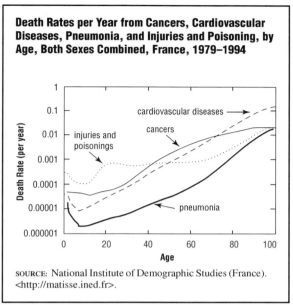

Death Rates per Year from Cancers, Cardiovascular Diseases, Pneumonia, and Injuries and Poisoning, by Age, Both Sexes Combined, France, 1979–1994

SOURCE: National Institute of Demographic Studies (France). <http://matisse.ined.fr>.

rates follow this pattern as well. In contrast, the death rate from pneumonia increases relatively slowly around age 30 but the increase accelerates at old ages. Thus the mortality curve for adult pneumonia tends to be convex in the entire adult age range below 85.

Concave and convex curvatures on a logarithmic scale indicate deceleration and acceleration, respectively, of age-related relative increases in mortality. Overall, the curvature of the mortality age-pattern seems related to the selectivity of the disease. Concave patterns are likely to be seen for diseases that develop in persons with specific genetic, environmental, and lifestyle risk factors. Convex curvatures tend to be found for diseases to which most persons are vulnerable when they become old and frail. Concave patterns are seen for acute myocardial infarction, hemorrhagic stroke, and chronic liver diseases. In addition to cancers, convex patterns are observed for congestive heart failure, infarctive stroke, chronic kidney diseases, and some infectious diseases such as influenza and septicemia.

A very different pattern is seen for mortality from injuries and poisoning, including accidents, homicide, and suicide. The death rate remains stable from age 20 to 60. In this age range, the risk of external injury is strongly related to behavioral patterns but not directly to physiological changes in the processes of senescence. At older ages the death rate from injury and poisoning increases fairly rapidly. This is mainly due to rising mortality from accidents such as falls and the inhalation or ingestion of harmful substances, reflecting the weakening of the musculoskeletal system and diminishing effectiveness of neural control of the body.

See also: *Aging and Longevity, Biology of; Causes of Death; Epidemiological Transition; Gompertz, Benjamin; Life Tables.*

BIBLIOGRAPHY

Azbel, Mark Y. 1999. "Empirical Laws of Survival and Evolution: Their Universality and Implications." *Proceedings of the National Academy of Sciences of the United States of America* 96(26): 15368–15373.

Coale, Ansley J., and Paul Demeny. 1983. *Regional Model Life Tables and Stable Populations,* 2nd edition. New York: Academic Press.

Finch, Caleb E. 1990. *Longevity, Senescence, and the Genome.* Chicago: University of Chicago Press.

Gage, Timothy B. 1990. "Variation and Classification of Human Age Patterns of Mortality: Analysis Using Competing Hazards Models." *Human Biology* 62(5): 589–617.

Gavrilov, Leonid A., and Natalia S. Gavrilova. 1991. *The Biology of Life Span: A Quantitative Approach.* Chur, Switzerland: Harwood.

Heligman, Larry, and John H. Pollard. 1980. "The Age Pattern of Mortality." *Journal of the Institute of Actuaries* 107: 49–80.

Horiuchi, Shiro, and John R. Wilmoth. 1997. "Age Patterns of the Life-Table Aging Rate for Major Causes of Death in Japan, 1951–1990." *Journal of Gerontology: Biological Sciences* 52A: B67–B77.

Horiuchi, Shiro, and John R. Wilmoth. 1998. "Deceleration in the Age Pattern of Mortality at Older Ages." *Demography* 35(4): 391–412.

Kohn, Robert R. 1985. "Aging and Age-Related Diseases: Normal Processes." In *Relations Between Normal Aging and Disease,* ed. Horton A. Johnson. New York: Raven Press.

Lee, Ronald D., and Lawrence R. Carter. 1992. "Modeling and Forecasting U.S. Mortality." *Journal of American Statistical Association* 87: 659–671.

United Nations. 1982. *Model Life Tables for Developing Countries.* New York: United Nations.

Vaupel, James W., et al. 1998. "Biodemographic Trajectories of Longevity." *Science* 280(5365): 855–860.

Vaupel, James W., Kenneth G. Manton, and Eric Stallard. 1979. "The Impact of Heterogeneity in Individual Frailty on the Dynamics of Mortality." *Demography* 16: 439–454.

Wilmoth, John R., and Shiro Horiuchi. 1999. "Rectangularization Revisited: Variability of Age at Death within Human Populations." *Demography* 36(4): 475–495.

Shiro Horiuchi

MORTALITY, INFANT AND CHILD

See *Infant and Child Mortality*

MORTALITY DECLINE

One of the greatest human achievements has been the decline in mortality that has occurred during the modern era. This article describes major trends in human mortality and longevity, especially during the nineteenth and twentieth centuries. The data are derived mostly from detailed mortality statistics collected by national governments. Prior to 1950 reliable information of this kind was collected by only a small number of countries, mostly in Europe, North America, and East Asia. As leaders in industrialization and other forms of social change during this period, these areas have also led the mortality decline and offer valuable statistical documentation of historical trends.

Substantial mortality decline in other parts of the world is a more recent phenomenon, sharply accelerating after 1950, although demographic data to document these trends are deficient in many cases. Similar changes in society and technology underlie mortality declines in all parts of the world, although there are also some regional patterns and exceptional trends.

TABLE 1

Life Expectancy and Infant Mortality throughout Human History

	Life expectancy at birth (in years)	Infant mortality rate (per 1000 live births)
Prehistoric Era	20–35	200–300
Sweden, 1750s	37	210
India, 1880s	27	230
United States, 1900	48	133
France, 1950	66	52
Japan, 1999	81	3

SOURCE: Wilmoth (2002, updated); Bhat (1989).

Sources of Information

It is not known with accuracy how long individuals lived before 1750. Around that time the first national population data were collected for Sweden and Finland. After 1750 and even now in the twenty-first century there is extensive and highly reliable mortality information for only a subset of national populations. For many less developed countries modern mortality estimates are based on sample surveys or other study designs that do not include the entire population and, especially for adults, are not highly reliable.

For the period from around 1500 to 1750 there are several examples of reliable mortality data referring to municipal populations, members of the nobility, and other groups that cannot be considered representative of the total population. For the Middle Ages and earlier periods mortality levels have been estimated through the use of data gleaned from tombstone inscriptions, genealogical records, and skeletal remains. Such estimates are prone to various forms of error but provide a useful description of the general contours of human mortality before the great mortality decline of the modern era.

Mortality data often include information on the cause of death, although this concept is difficult to define and measure consistently. Data on the cause of death always must be analyzed with great caution: Although some trends are irrefutable such as the historical decline of infectious disease, others appear to be influenced by changes in diagnostic procedures and reporting practices (e.g., cancer trends, especially among older persons).

Historical Trends

Historical changes may be described along various dimensions. The following sections examine the rise of life expectancy, changes in the age pattern of human mortality, and trends in extreme longevity.

Life expectancy. Most scholars agree that life expectancy at birth (or $\mathring{e}_0$, in the notation of demographers and actuaries) was probably in the 20s among early human populations (Table 1). Some less fortunate populations may have had life expectancies below 20 years. If early levels of life expectancy at birth were around 20–30 years compared to 75–80 years in the early twenty-first century in some countries, one may conclude that there has been roughly a tripling over the course of human history in the average life span that can be attained by large populations. Much of this increase has been due to the near elimination of infant and childhood deaths. In early human populations the available evidence suggests that around a quarter of all babies died in the first year of life. In the early twenty-first century in the most advanced countries, less than half a percent of infants meet a similar fate.

Most of the increase in human longevity is recent. By 1900 the average newborn in Australia and New Zealand could be expected to live about 55 or 57 years, respectively, based on mortality levels in those countries, which were the lowest in the world at that time. In 2000 the world's healthiest nation, Japan, had a life expectancy at birth of around 81 years. Thus, in the leading countries almost half the historical increase in human life expectancy occurred during the twentieth century.

The rise in life expectancy at birth probably began before the industrial era in some parts of Europe and North America. By the 1750s, when data for national populations first became available, life expectancy in some areas of northern Europe was already in the high 30s. Over the next century or more the increase in life expectancy was slow and irregular. After about 1870, this increase became stable and more rapid, especially during the first half of the twentieth century. Since 1950 the rise in life expectancy has slowed somewhat in those areas that led the longevity revolution, such as Europe and North America.

Figure 1 shows trends in life expectancy at birth for males and females in France since 1806. This graph summarizes key aspects of French mortality history over the nineteenth and twentieth centuries. First, life expectancy increased from the high 30s at the beginning of the nineteenth century to the 70s or 80s at the end of the twentieth. Second, the im-

FIGURE 1

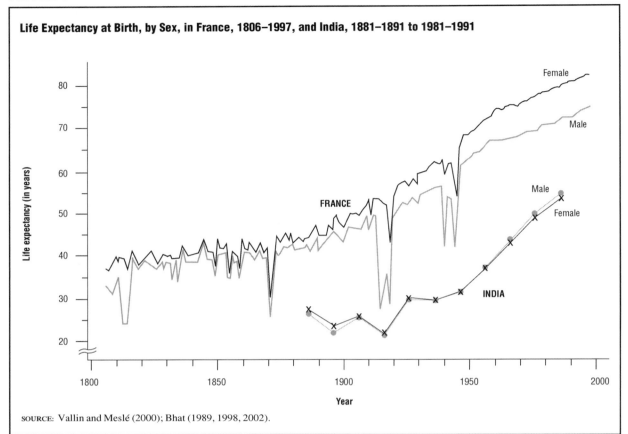

Life Expectancy at Birth, by Sex, in France, 1806–1997, and India, 1881–1891 to 1981–1991

SOURCE: Vallin and Meslé (2000); Bhat (1989, 1998, 2002).

pact of various wars was different for the sexes. The Napoleonic wars and World War I were fought mostly at the front and thus affected male life expectancy strongly, but their effect was minor on females in most parts of the country. On the other hand, the Franco-Prussian war and World War II involved widespread occupations of the French territory by enemy forces and thus affected men and women in a similar fashion. Third, a large male–female gap in life expectancy emerged even during peacetime, increasing from a difference of less than two years at the beginning of the period shown to around eight years at the end.

The mortality decline of the modern era began in countries that were leaders in the process of industrialization, but it has spread across the entire world. Alongside the trend for France mentioned earlier, Figure 1 also shows the rise in life expectancy at birth for India from the 1880s until the 1980s. As in most of the poorer regions of the world, the majority of this increase has occurred since around

1940. Fragmentary evidence suggests that life expectancy in the period 1935–1939 was around 30 years in Africa and Asia and 40 years in Latin America. Around 2000, estimates for these regions were much higher at 53, 67, and 71 years, respectively, as summarized in Table 2.

Many factors have contributed to the rise of life expectancy all around the world. Prior to the last decades of the nineteenth century most of the reduction of mortality rates in the early industrializing countries was likely the result of improved living conditions (e.g., better nutrition, shelter, and clothing) made possible by the increased wealth brought about by industrialization. In addition, confirmation of the germ theory of disease in 1882—as a result of Koch's rigorous identification of the bacillus that cause tuberculosis—led to a flourishing of public health measures (e.g., anti-malarial programs, immunization campaigns, and other government health initiatives) and associated improvements in personal health practices. Such developments were

TABLE 2

Life Expectancy at Birth for Major World Regions and Selected Countries, around 2000

Region/Country	Life expectancy at birth (in years)	Region/Country	Life expectancy at birth (in years)
World	67	Europe	74
More developed	76	France	79
Less developed	65	Germany	78
Africa	53	Italy	80
Congo, Dem. Rep. of	49	Poland	74
Egypt	66	Russia	65
Ethiopia	52	Ukraine	68
Nigeria	52	United Kingdom	78
South Africa	51	Latin America & Caribbean	71
Tunisia	72	Argentina	74
Zimbabwe	38	Brazil	69
Asia	67	Chile	77
Bangladesh	59	Colombia	71
China	71	Cuba	76
India	63	Guatemala	66
Indonesia	68	Haiti	49
Iran	69	Mexico	75
Japan	81	North America	77
Laos	54	Canada	79
Pakistan	63	United States	77
Philippines	68	Oceania	75
Turkey	69	Australia	80
Vietnam	68	Papua-New Guinea	57

Note: Following the U.N. classification, "more developed" regions include all of Europe, North America, Japan, Australia, and New Zealand. All other areas are classified as "less developed."

SOURCE: Population Reference Bureau (2002).

probably the major factor in mortality reduction, in both rich and poor countries, from the late-nineteenth century until the 1960s. As discussed below, the main contributions of therapeutic medicine to the historical mortality decline arrived relatively late in this process: antibacterial drugs from the 1930s and 1940s onward, and improved management of cardiovascular disease beginning around 1970.

Although the general trend toward lower mortality and higher life expectancy has become worldwide, there are a few notable exceptions. During the 1990s the major exception was a stagnation and even reversal of earlier progress in parts of Africa because of the AIDS epidemic and in parts of the former Soviet Bloc (especially Russia) resulting from social disruptions and instability.

Age pattern of human mortality. The age pattern of human mortality can be characterized in various ways. Age-specific death rates depict the changing risks of mortality over the life course. During the historical mortality decline, death rates typically have fallen much more rapidly at younger than at

older ages. A complete set of age-specific death rates implies a particular distribution of deaths by age for a cohort of individuals. Because mortality decline has been more rapid at younger ages, the distribution of ages at death has become more concentrated at older ages. Thus, not only is life longer on average, but also the age range in which most deaths occur has been reduced substantially.

One measure of variability in the timing of death is the interquartile range of ages at death, thus the age span of the middle 50 percent of deaths over the life course of a cohort. The calculation is most simply done for the synthetic cohort of a period life table. During the late-eighteenth century in Sweden, the life-table interquartile range was around 60 to 65 years, since more than one quarter of infants died before age 5, while another quarter survived to age 65 or older. The distribution of age at death was compressed over the next two centuries. In the 1950s the life-table interquartile range in the industrialized countries was around 15 to 20 years. Since 1960 there has been little further reduction in the variability of age at death in the developed world, even

FIGURE 2

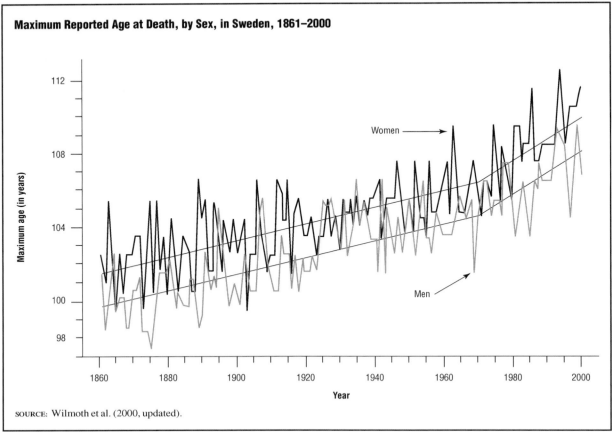

Maximum Reported Age at Death, by Sex, in Sweden, 1861–2000

SOURCE: Wilmoth et al. (2000, updated).

though the average age at death (as reflected in life expectancy at birth) has continued to increase.

Extreme longevity. It is difficult to study trends in extreme longevity because of frequent errors in the age at death reported for very old individuals. For this specialized purpose the longest available series of reliable data begins in the 1860s for Sweden. Figure 2 shows the trend in the maximum age at death for men and women over the period 1861–2000. The trend is clearly upward, especially from about 1970. The maximum age rises by 0.44 years (of age) per decade prior to that date and by 1.1 years per decade since then. More than two-thirds of this increase can be attributed to reductions in death rates above age 70, with the rest being due to the fact that more people reach old age (and thus have a chance to die at a very old age) as a result of mortality decline at younger ages and a modest increase in the size of birth cohorts.

These Swedish data provide the best available evidence for the gradual extension of the maximum

human life span that has occurred over this time period. Similar trends are evident for other countries as well, although problems of age misreporting complicate the task of interpretation.

Components and Causes of Mortality Decline

The mortality decline of the last two centuries has many components and causes. Two major components of the trend are discussed below: (1) the decline of infectious disease, known as the epidemiologic transition, and (2) the decline of old-age mortality in more recent years. In both cases the causes of the change are complex and can be linked to socioeconomic conditions, public health measures, individual behaviors, and medical interventions.

Epidemiologic transition. The epidemiologic transition is the most important historical change that has affected the level and pattern of human mortality. The transition refers to the decline of acute, infectious diseases and the rise of chronic, degenerative conditions. This shift does not necessarily imply that degenerative diseases became more common for individuals of a given age. It merely means that infectious diseases nearly disappeared, and so something else had to take their place as the major cause of death.

Increasingly, people survived infancy and childhood without succumbing to measles, tetanus, whooping cough, diphtheria, and other infectious causes of juvenile mortality. Once people pass these critical early years, survival to advanced ages is much more likely, and at older ages various degenerative diseases present mortality risks even when infections are well controlled.

The cause of the historical decline of infection-related mortality has been a topic of much discussion. It has become widely acknowledged that most of this decline occurred before the availability of effective medical treatments: In the wealthy countries that industrialized early a substantial reduction had occurred by the 1930s and 1940s, the period when effective antibacterial drugs (sulfanomides and antibiotics) were introduced. Instead, the decline can be attributed mostly to the general improvement in living standards that accompanied industrialization (food, housing, clothing, etc.) and to public health measures that helped control the spread of germs (sanitation, clean drinking water, education about hygiene, quarantine, etc.).

In the countries of Europe and North America this process of epidemiologic transition began during the nineteenth century and was completed mostly before 1960. A similar process began later in the economically less advantaged regions of the world. Mortality decline began in the early-twentieth century in some parts of Latin America and East Asia. In sub-Saharan Africa, in contrast, there is little evidence of mortality reduction before the late 1940s. Even in the early twenty-first century residents of poor countries bear an undue burden of mortality linked to infection. In these cases the successes brought about by organized public health campaigns have not been matched by comparable improvements in the general standard of living.

Mortality decline among the elderly. By around 1960 mortality resulting from infectious diseases had been reduced to very low levels in industrialized countries, and it appeared to many observers that a further extension of the human life span was

unlikely. Few people anticipated the coming reduction in old-age mortality that would prolong the historical trend toward longer life into the twenty-first century. Before the late 1960s death rates at older ages seemed to have declined slowly, if at all, and rates of mortality decline were much higher at younger ages than at older ages.

In wealthy nations of the late twentieth century, the most significant change affecting life expectancy was mortality decline among the elderly. The decade of the 1960s marked a turning point from an earlier era of longevity increase caused primarily by the decline of acute, infectious diseases among children and young adults to a more recent era characterized by the decline of chronic, degenerative diseases among the elderly.

Mortality decline at older ages in the last decades of the twentieth century was linked mainly to the reduction of deaths resulting from cardiovascular disease (CVD)—essentially, heart disease and stroke. For the United States it is estimated that 73 percent of the decline in the total death rate from 1950 to 1996 was due to a reduction in CVD mortality. Although the exact cause of this decline is open to debate, several factors have been proposed: (1) a decline in cigarette smoking among adults; (2) a decrease in mean blood pressure levels; (3) changes in diet, especially a reduction in the consumption of saturated fat and cholesterol; and (4) improvements in medical care, including better diagnosis and treatment of heart disease and stroke, the development of effective medications for hypertension and hypercholesterolemia, and an increase in coronary-care units and emergency medical services for heart disease and stroke.

A rapid decline in old-age mortality beginning in the late 1960s has been observed for many industrialized nations. Given the precipitous onset of this decline, which occurred simultaneously across a broad age range, it is plausible that improvements in medical therapy were responsible at least for the initiation of the new trend. Landmark investigations such as the Framingham Heart Study that began in the late 1940s provided significant breakthroughs in the scientific understanding of cardiovascular disease during the 1960s, leading to more effective medical prevention and management. Since modifications in diet and lifestyle should have led to a more gradual pattern of mortality change, it seems unlikely that such factors have been the main cause of the

TABLE 3

Summary of Major Trends in Human Longevity in Industrialized Countries

Indicator	Before 1960	After 1970
Average life span (life expectancy at birth)	Increasing rapidly because averted deaths are among younger people. Very rapid reduction in infant/child mortality linked mostly to effective control of infectious diseases.	Increasing moderately because averted deaths are among older people. Accelerated reduction in old-age mortality linked mostly to better management of cardiovascular disease.
Maximum life span (observed and verified maximum age at death)	Increasing slowly due mostly to gradual reductions in death rates at older ages.	Increasing moderately due almost entirely to accelerated reduction in death rates at older ages.
Variability of life span (standard deviation, interquartile range, etc.)	Decreasing rapidly due to reductions in mortality at younger ages.	Stable, because death rates at older ages are decreasing as rapidly as at younger ages.

SOURCE: Author.

recent decline in old-age mortality. Nevertheless, it is possible that behavioral changes or other factors have reinforced a trend that was set in motion initially by improvements in medical therapy.

After CVD, cancer is the most important cause of death in low-mortality countries of the twenty-first century. In most of these countries cancer mortality began to decline in the late 1980s, although the change has been less rapid and more varied than the trend in CVD mortality. Cancer occurs in many different forms, and trends vary greatly by the site of the primary tumor. For example, lung cancer has become more common over time as a result of increased cigarette smoking, whereas the incidence of stomach cancer has declined. Among women mortality from cervical cancer has fallen markedly as a result of successful medical intervention (screening and early treatment), whereas breast cancer has been on the rise apparently as a result of a number of interrelated factors, such as lower and later fertility and changes in diet and lifestyle.

Summary of Major Trends in Low-Mortality Countries

A summary of major trends in human longevity in industrialized countries is presented in Table 3. Amid the remarkable detail available in historical mortality statistics two major epochs are discernible: before 1960, and after 1970. The driving force in the earlier period was a rapid decline in mortality from infectious diseases, which had an impact across the age range but a much larger effect at younger ages. The sharp reduction in infant and child mortality led to a rapid increase in average life span and a marked

reduction in the variability of age at death. It did not, however, have a major impact on the maximum life span, which rose very slowly as a result of the more gradual improvement in death rates at older ages.

From the mid-1950s to the late 1960s mortality trends in industrialized countries seemed to stabilize. Then, starting from about 1970, death rates at older ages entered a period of unprecedented decline. Compared with the earlier era of rapid reductions in infant and child mortality, these changes yielded a slower increase in life expectancy at birth. However, the rise in the maximum life span accelerated, driven by a more rapid decline in death rates at older ages. The variability of the life span tended to stabilize during this period, as the entire distribution of ages at death—now concentrated at older ages—moved upward in a parallel fashion. The difference between these two eras is illustrated in Table 4 for Sweden.

Prospects for the Future

The rapid rise in life expectancy before 1950 and its subsequent deceleration are linked to trends in mortality at young ages. By around 1950 infant mortality in wealthy countries was in the range of 20 to 30 per 1,000 births, compared with perhaps 200 to 300 per 1,000 births historically. Since that time infant mortality has continued to decline, and early in the twenty-first century it is below 4 per 1,000 births in the healthiest parts of the world. As babies were saved from infectious disease, their chances of survival to old age improved considerably. Once mortality at young ages was reduced substantially, improvements in life expectancy caused by the reduction of mortality in this age range had to slow down, and further gains had to come mostly from mortality reductions at older ages.

The rise of life expectancy in the leading industrial countries was slower during the second half of the twentieth century than during the first half because it depended on the reduction of death rates at older ages rather than in infancy and childhood. Put simply, saving an infant or child from infectious disease, who then lives to age 70, contributes much more to the average life span than does saving an adult of 70 years from heart disease, who may then live another 10 years. Thus, the deceleration in the historical rise of life expectancy is a product of the J-shaped age pattern of human mortality: relatively high in infancy and childhood, low through adolescence and early adulthood, and rising steeply after age 30. Gains in life expectancy at birth that result from reducing mortality among the young are large, whereas gains resulting from a reduction in old-age mortality are necessarily much smaller.

It is a common mistake to assert that deceleration in the rise of life expectancy at birth, $\mathring{e}_0$, reflects a slowdown in progress against mortality. In fact, the reduction of death rates changed its character in the late-twentieth century, but it did not slow down. At older ages the decline of mortality has accelerated since around 1970. As long as the decline of old-age mortality continues, life expectancy will continue to increase, driven now by the extension of life at older ages rather than by saving juveniles from premature death.

The historical rise in human longevity is the result of a complex set of changes that began several centuries ago. Before the 1930s most of this decline was due to factors other than medical therapy and is generally attributed to improvements in living conditions and public health. With the advent of antibacterial drugs in the 1930s and 1940s, medical treatment began to play an important role in these changes. The role of medicine expanded in the late-twentieth century because of interventions in cardiovascular disease and cancer that have contributed to the rapid decline of old-age mortality. It is important to keep this complex causality in mind when speculating about future trends in human mortality.

It seems reasonable to expect that future mortality trends in the most advanced countries will resemble past changes. Although the focus of efforts to improve health will evolve, the net effect on death rates

TABLE 4

Average Change (in Years per Decade) in Key Mortality Indicators, Sweden

Indicator	1861–1960	1970–2000
Average life span (life expectancy at birth)	3.1	1.8
Maximum life span (max. reported age at death)	0.4	1.5
Interquartile range (of deaths in life table)	−5.3	−0.4

Note: The average change shown here equals the difference between mean values for the last and first 10-year periods (within the indicated time interval) divided by the number of years in between.

SOURCE: Author.

probably will be similar. Most extrapolations of past trends for the leading industrial countries yield predictions of life expectancy at birth for the sexes combined of around 85 to 87 years by the middle of the twenty-first century. Unexpected events could change the course of these trends. Nevertheless, the historical stability of mortality trends over at least the twentieth century offers strong support for the belief that trends in the twenty-first century will be similar in character.

See also: *Causes of Death; Demographic Transition; Epidemiological Transition; Health Transition; Life Span; Maternal Mortality; Oldest Old.*

BIBLIOGRAPHY

Acsádi, György, and János Nemeskéri. 1970. *History of Human Life Span and Mortality.* Budapest: Akadémiai Kiadó.

Bell, Felicitie C., Alice H. Wade, and Stephen C. Goss. 1992. Life Tables for the United States Social Security Area. Actuarial Study No. 107, Social Security Administration Pub. No. 11–11536.

Bhat, Mari P. N. 1989. "Mortality and Fertility in India, 1881–1961: A Reassessment." In *India's Historical Demography: Studies in Famine, Disease and Society,* ed. Tim Dyson. London: Curzon Press. pp 73–118.

———. 1998. "Demographic Estimates for Post-independence India: A New Integration." *Demography India* 27(1): 23–57.

———. 2002. "Completeness of India's Sample Registration System: An Assessment Using the General Growth Balance Method." *Population Studies* 56(2): 119–134.

Centers for Disease Control. 1999. "Decline in Deaths from Heart Disease and Stroke—United States, 1900–1999." *Morbidity and Mortality Weekly Report* 48: 649–656.

Crimmins, Eileen M. 1981. "The Changing Pattern of American Mortality Decline, 1940–77, and Its Implications for the Future." *Population and Development Review* 7: 229–254.

Davis, Kingsley. 1951. *The Population of India and Pakistan.* Princeton, NJ: Princeton University Press.

McKeown, Thomas. 1979. *The Role of Medicine: Dream, Mirage, or Nemesis?* Oxford: Basil Blackwell.

Population Reference Bureau. 2002. *World Population Data Sheet.* Washington, D.C.: Population Reference Bureau.

Preston, Samuel H. 1980. "Causes and Consequences of Mortality Decline in Less Developed Countries during the Twentieth Century." In *Population and Economic Change in Developing Countries,* ed. Richard Easterlin. New York: National Bureau of Economic Research.

Riley, James C. 2001. *Rising Life Expectancy: A Global History.* Cambridge, Eng.: Cambridge University Press.

Tuljapurkar, Shripad, Nan Li, and Carl Boe. 2000. "A Universal Pattern of Mortality Decline in G7 Countries." *Nature* 405: 789–792.

Vallin, Jacques, and France Meslé. 2000. *Tables de Mortalité Françaises 1806–1997.* Paris: INED.

Wilmoth, John R., and Shiro Horiuchi. 1999. "Rectangularization Revisited: Variability of Age at Death within Human Populations." *Demography* 36: 475–495.

Wilmoth, John R., Leo J. Deegan, Hans Lundström, and Shiro Horiuchi. 2000. "Increase of Maximum Life Span in Sweden, 1861–1999." *Science* 289: 2,366–2,368.

Wilmoth, John R. 2002. "Human Longevity in Historical Perspective." In *Physiological Basis of Aging and Geriatrics,* 3rd edition., ed. Paola S. Timiras. Boca Raton, FL: CRC Press. pp. 11–24.

INTERNET RESOURCE.

Human Mortality Database. <http://www.mortality.org>.

JOHN R. WILMOTH

MORTALITY DIFFERENTIALS, BY SEX

Sex differences in mortality have varied in different countries, historical periods, and age groups (see Figure 1). During the last quarter of the twentieth century, males had higher mortality than females at all ages in all developed countries and in most less developed countries. However, higher mortality for females was relatively common among young children in less developed countries. During the mid-twentieth century, females also had higher mortality among older children, teenagers, and/or young adults in some less developed countries, particularly in South Asia.

Because males generally had higher mortality than females, males had shorter life expectancies than females in most countries during the period 1950–2000. During the late 1990s, male life expectancy at birth was shorter than female life expectancy by approximately eight years in Europe, six years in North America, seven years in Latin America and the Caribbean, three years in Asia, and two years in Africa. Sex differences in life expectancy varied for different countries within each continent. Probably the largest recorded male disadvantage was in Russia during the late 1990s, when male life expectancy was more than twelve years shorter than female life expectancy. In contrast, males had longer life expectancies than females in some South Asian countries during the mid-twentieth century. For example, in India in the period 1950–1975 male life expectancy was one to two years longer than female life expectancy.

Causes of Death

Major contributors to higher male mortality include coronary heart disease (also known as ischemic heart disease) and injuries, suicide, and homicide (known collectively as external causes of death). For coronary heart disease and for the external causes of

FIGURE 1

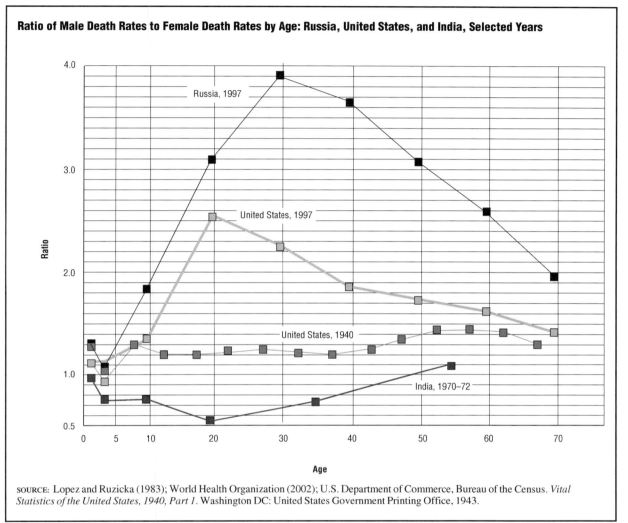

Ratio of Male Death Rates to Female Death Rates by Age: Russia, United States, and India, Selected Years

SOURCE: Lopez and Ruzicka (1983); World Health Organization (2002); U.S. Department of Commerce, Bureau of the Census. *Vital Statistics of the United States, 1940, Part 1*. Washington DC: United States Government Printing Office, 1943.

death, males have had higher mortality than females at all ages in all or almost all countries and time periods. Often male death rates have exceeded female death rates by 100 to 300 percent for these causes of death.

Sex differences in cancer mortality and infectious diseases mortality have varied, depending on the specific type of cancer or infectious disease as well as the age range, country, and time period considered. For example, males have had higher lung cancer mortality, but females have much higher breast cancer mortality. Males have often had higher infectious disease mortality than females, particularly in developed countries and among infants and older adults. However, females have had higher infectious disease mortality for chil-

dren and/or young adults in some less developed countries.

Variation in sex differences in total mortality has been due to variation in the sex differences for specific causes of death and variation in the relative importance of the different causes of death. For example, higher total mortality for females has been observed most often among children and young adults in less developed countries where infectious disease mortality is more likely to show a female excess and where infectious diseases and maternal mortality make substantial contributions to total mortality. In contrast, these causes of death are less important in developed countries where the dominance of external causes of death, coronary heart disease, and lung cancer in total mortality results in males having consistently higher total mortality than females.

Biological, Behavioral, and Environmental Causes

Sex differences in mortality have been influenced by the interacting effects of multiple biological and environmental factors, including the effects of sex hormones on physiology and behavior, as well as cultural and social influences on sex differences in behavior and access to health-promoting resources. The following paragraphs illustrate the diversity of causal factors that have influenced sex differences in mortality for different causes of death.

Males' higher mortality for accidents, suicide, and homicide has been due primarily to a variety of sex differences in behavior and life roles, including males' higher rates of gun use, heavy drinking, physical risk taking in recreation, employment in physically hazardous occupations, and speeding and other risky driving practices. These behaviors have been more expected and accepted for males, and cultural and social influences on sex differences in behavior have contributed to males' higher mortality for the external causes of death. In addition, males' brains are exposed to higher testosterone levels in utero as well as after birth, and this may predispose males to more vigorous physical activity and physical aggressiveness, which contribute to males' higher mortality for the external causes of death.

The consistent male excess in coronary heart disease mortality appears to be due in large part to biological sex differences, including males' greater propensity to accumulate abdominal fat and the apparently protective effects of females' natural sex hormones. These biological effects have been reinforced by males' greater risk as a result of higher rates of tobacco use, especially cigarette smoking, in most countries and time periods.

Sex differences in cigarette smoking have been the main cause of sex differences in lung cancer mortality. In many developed countries in the twentieth century sex differences in smoking increased initially as males adopted cigarette smoking earlier and in greater numbers than did females; subsequently, sex differences in smoking decreased as female smoking became more common and male smoking rates decreased. These trends in sex differences in smoking have been followed by corresponding initial increases and subsequent decreases in sex differences in lung cancer mortality. The delay between the trends in smoking and lung cancer is explained by the substantial lag between initial smoking adoption and the consequent lung cancer mortality.

Sex differences in mortality resulting from infectious diseases have been influenced by multiple and sometimes counteracting biological and environmental factors. Hormonal and genetic effects appear to contribute to lower immune function and greater vulnerability to infectious diseases among males. However, in some regions, especially in South Asia, girls may receive less medical care for infectious diseases, and this may increase their risk of infectious disease mortality. The factors that influence sex differences in infectious disease mortality vary for different types of infectious diseases. For HIV/AIDS, biological sex differences result in a greater female risk of infection as a consequence of heterosexual intercourse with an infected partner, but a greater male risk of infection as a consequence of homosexual contacts. In addition, in many societies males have greater exposure to HIV infection because of greater use of intravenous drugs and multiple sexual partners. Thus, both biological factors and culturally influenced behavioral differences influence sex differences in HIV/AIDS infection and mortality rates.

Trends

Historical data for economically developed countries that are economically developed at the beginning of the twenty-first century show that sex differences in mortality have varied substantially in magnitude and have even reversed direction in some cases in which higher mortality for females during earlier periods was subsequently replaced by higher mortality for males. Higher mortality for females was relatively common among children, teenagers, and/or young adults during the late-nineteenth and/or early-twentieth century. Contributing causes appear to have included higher infectious disease mortality for females and maternal mortality. By the mid-twentieth century these causes of death had become less important and females' status and life circumstances had improved, and so females had lower total mortality than males did at all ages.

By the late-twentieth century in economically developed countries, external causes of death became the largest contributor to total mortality for teenagers and young adults, so in this age range males had much higher mortality than females. The male mortality disadvantage also increased among older adults during the mid-twentieth century, partly as a result of the delayed harmful effects of males' early and widespread adoption of cigarette smoking. As a result of all of these mortality trends, the male disadvantage in life expectancy increased from approximately zero to four years around 1900 to approximately five to nine years in the late 1970s.

During the last few decades of the twentieth century, sex differences in mortality showed contrasting trends in different developed countries. The male mortality disadvantage began to decrease in the United States and some Western European countries, but it increased substantially in Russia and some other Eastern European countries. The increasing male mortality disadvantage in Russia was due primarily to increasing male death rates for external causes of death and cardiovascular diseases, apparently partly as a result of increased binge drinking and other harmful effects of the substantial social and economic disruptions during this period.

In light of the many different interacting factors that influence sex differences in mortality and the difficulty of predicting future trends in many of those factors, it is not surprising that there is a wide range of predictions concerning future trends in sex differences in life expectancy. For example, for developed countries different researchers have predicted increasing or decreasing sex differences in life expectancy during the early decades of the twenty-first century. For Asia and Africa there appears to be a more general agreement that sex differences in life expectancy will show a growing female advantage during the early-twenty-first century, repeating the experience of developed countries during the mid-twentieth century. However, uncertainty concerning future trends in the HIV/AIDS epidemic contributes to uncertainty concerning future trends in sex differences in life expectancy in Asia and Africa.

See also: *Biology, Population; Causes of Death; Infant and Child Mortality; Sex Ratio; Tobacco-Related Mortality.*

BIBLIOGRAPHY

Bobadilla, Jose Luis, Christine A. Costello, and Faith Mitchell, eds. 1997. *Premature Death in the New Independent States.* Washington, D.C.: National Academy Press.

Feachem, Richard G. A., Tord Kjellstrom, Christopher J. L. Murray, Mead Over, and Margaret A. Phillips. 1992. *The Health of Adults in the Developing World.* Washington, D.C.: Oxford University Press.

Lopez, Alan D., and Lado T. Ruzicka, eds. 1983. *Sex Differentials in Mortality: Trends, Determinants and Consequences.* Canberra: Australian National University, Miscellaneous Series No. 4.

United Nations. 1998. *Too Young to Die: Genes or Gender?* New York: United Nations.

———. 2000. *The World's Women 2000: Trends and Statistics.* New York: United Nations.

———. 2001. *World Population Prospects: The 2000 Revision,* Vol. 1: *Comprehensive Tables.* New York: United Nations.

Weidner, Gerdi, Maria Kopp, and Margareta Kristenson, eds. 2002. *Heart Disease: Environment, Stress and Gender.* Amsterdam: IOS Press.

Wizemann, Theresa M., and Mary-Lou Pardue, eds. 2001. *Exploring the Biological Contributions to Human Health: Does Sex Matter?* Washington, D.C.: National Academy Press.

INTERNET RESOURCE.

World Health Organization. 2002. *1997–1999 World Health Statistics Annual.* <http://www3.who.int/whosis/whsa>.

INGRID WALDRON

MORTALITY DIFFERENTIALS, SOCIOECONOMIC

Research on differential mortality generates answers to questions such as the following: To what extent are there within-country differences in mortality between subpopulations defined by area of residence, socioeconomic status, marital status, and other variables? What are the causes of such differences? How and why does the extent of the differences change in time and vary between countries?

The answers to these questions are important from a social and health policy perspective because mortality differentials are useful indicators of the health and well-being of population groups. Studies on differential mortality also contribute to the understanding of the determinants of mortality levels and trends in national populations. For epidemiologists cause-specific mortality differences provide clues to the etiology of diseases.

Research on differential mortality has long traditions. As early as 1901 the Danish researcher Harald Westergaard published a 700-page treatise that summarized the results of hundreds of studies carried out in the nineteenth century. The book by Evelyn M. Kitagawa and Philip M. Hauser published in 1973 is a classic American study on this topic.

This article discusses mortality differentials by socioeconomic status, racial/ethnic group, marital status, geographic area, and rural-urban division. The article focuses on developed countries. The data and research on less developed countries are relatively scarce and mainly concern infant and child mortality.

Mortality Differentials by Socioeconomic Status

Several indicators, such as occupational class, level of education, and income, have been used in studies of socioeconomic differentials in mortality. Information about these differentials usually is not available in regular statistics because the ordinary sources of mortality statistics do not include reliable information on the socioeconomic characteristics of deceased persons. Most knowledge about socioeconomic differences in mortality comes from studies for which data have been specifically collected for an analysis of socioeconomic differences.

Despite the measurement problems there is abundant evidence from different periods and countries showing that persons in lower socioeconomic positions die on average younger than do those in higher socioeconomic positions. For example, Eileen M. Crimmins and Yasuhito Saito (2001) estimated that the difference in life expectancy at age 30 between persons with 13 or more years of schooling and those with less than nine years was 6.7 years among white men and 3.8 years among white women in 1990 in the United States. Among African Americans these differences were, respectively, 11.8 years and 10.5 years.

Many hypotheses about the causes of socioeconomic mortality differences have been offered, but experts differ about their validity. Some hypotheses emphasize the causal effects of differences between classes in working and living conditions, health-related behaviors (e.g., smoking, alcohol use, diet), the prevalence of psychosocial stressors, or access to health services. According to other hypotheses, poor health and certain characteristics of individuals (e.g., social background and intelligence) may affect both their socioeconomic position and their risk of premature death.

Cross-national variation in the extent of socioeconomic differences in mortality in the 1980s was studied in a large project coordinated by John P. Machenbach and Anton E. Kunst from the Erasmus University Rotterdam (1997). Data for thirteen European countries and the United States were used. The mortality of men in manual occupations was higher than that of men in nonmanual occupations in all those countries. The relative excess mortality of the manual class was remarkably similar (ranging from 32% to 44%). However, larger differences were observed for France, the Czech Republic, and especially Hungary.

The results for mortality by cause of death showed that the mortality of manual workers was higher than that of nonmanual employees for nearly all the causes of death distinguished in the study. There was, however, an interesting exception: No class difference was found in mortality from ischemic (coronary) heart disease in France, Switzerland, Italy, and Spain. In Portugal mortality rates were higher in the nonmanual classes than in the manual classes. However, socioeconomic gradients in mortality from causes other than ischemic heart disease were steeper in southern European than in northern European countries.

Socioeconomic differences in mortality have widened in almost all the countries for which data are available, including the United States. The main reason for the increase has been a more rapid than average decline in mortality from cardiovascular diseases among persons with high socioeconomic status.

Differentials by Race/Ethnicity

Few countries report mortality differences by race or ethnicity, but in the United States the white-black division has been used as a standard classification for more than a hundred years. The life expectancy of the black population has always been lower, but the size of the difference has varied. It narrowed from 15.8 years in 1900 to 5.7 years in 1982, increased to 7.1 years in 1993, and declined to 6.0 years in 1998. The increase in the gap from 1983 to 1993 was largely the result of increases in mortality among the black male population caused by HIV infection and homicide.

Since the 1990s more detailed classifications than the white-black dichotomy have been used. For example, Richard G. Rogers and colleagues (2000) studied mortality differences among adult Americans in the period 1989–1995 by using seven race/ethnicity groups. The age- and sex-adjusted excess mortality of African Americans compared to white Americans was found to be 41 percent, but after controlling for social and economic factors (education, income, employment status, and marital status) the excess mortality was only 17 percent. Sixty percent of the excess thus was due to the difference in the composition of the two groups. The mortality of Asian Americans was 31 percent lower than that of white Americans and remained 19 percent lower after controlling for nativity and social and economic factors. The four Hispanic groups distinguished in the study displayed varied mortality levels.

Marital Status

Hundreds of studies since the nineteenth century have shown that married persons live longer than do single, divorced, and widowed persons. One cause for the longer life of married persons is the selection of healthier than average persons into the married state. Selection also occurs on the basis of personal characteristics that affect the risk of death, such as level of education, psychological characteristics, and drinking habits. Another reason for the longer life of married persons is the protective effect of the married state associated with psychosocial factors (less stress and more social support), financial circumstances (more income and better housing conditions), and health behavior (healthier diet, less smoking and alcohol consumption). The adverse effects of divorce and loss of a spouse account for part of the excess mortality of divorced and widowed persons.

A comparative study of seventeen countries from the 1950s to the 1980s by Yuanreng Hu and Noreen Goldman (1990) showed that unmarried (single, divorced, and widowed) men of working age had a clear excess mortality (100% on average) com-

pared to married men in all countries. In most countries divorced men had the highest death rates among the three unmarried groups. Unmarried women also had excess mortality compared with married women, but the excess was smaller (50% on average) than it was among men.

There is variation in the size of marital status differences between both countries and time periods. A general tendency has been an increase in the relative excess mortality of the unmarried groups. As shown by Tapani Valkonen (2002), this increase was particularly pronounced among elderly women in Western and Northern European countries as well as in Canada.

Geographic Differentials and Rural-Urban Differentials

Statistics on mortality for areas within countries, such as states, provinces, municipalities, and neighborhoods, usually show more or less systematic geographic variations. For example, life expectancy is several years higher in southern than in northern regions in many European countries, such as the United Kingdom, Russia, France, and the Scandinavian countries. In the United States there is a zone of low mortality in the north-central part of the country (e.g., Minnesota, North Dakota, and Iowa had life expectancies above 77 years in 1990) and a zone of high mortality in the southeastern region (e.g., Missouri, Louisiana, and South Carolina had life expectancies of 73.5 years or less).

Geographic differentials in mortality can be accounted for partly by differences in the composition of the population by occupational class, education, race/ethnicity, and other characteristics of individuals, but they are not due only to population composition. A large number of studies have shown associations between the level of mortality and a multitude of characteristics of areas, such as climate, mineral content of drinking water or soil, environmental pollution, quality of health services, dietary traditions, income inequality, and social cohesion. The causal interpretation of these results is, however, controversial.

Statistics on mortality by rural-urban division are available for relatively few countries. In the United States mortality is higher in urban than in rural areas. James S. House and colleagues (2000) have shown that this difference cannot be accounted for by differences in the socioeconomic and racial composition of the population. The age-adjusted mortality of city residents was found to be 60 percent higher than that of residents of small towns and rural areas and 40 percent higher than that of suburbanites after the effects of differences in population composition were adjusted for. In Russia and most other former socialist countries mortality is higher in rural than in urban areas. For the Western European countries the evidence is scarce, but it seems that rural-urban differences are small and that their direction varies from country to country.

The size and direction of the rural–urban mortality gap are determined by the balance of the influence of two factors. The higher average income and educational levels favor the urban areas, but the risks connected with urban life (environmental pollution, social stress, violence, smoking, and the use of alcohol and drugs) reduce the positive effects of higher living standards.

See also: *Alcohol, Health Effects of; Causes of Death; Epidemiological Transition; Health Transition; Infant and Child Mortality; Mortality Decline; Tobacco-Related Mortality.*

BIBLIOGRAPHY

Crimmins, Eileen M., and Yasuhiko Saito. 2001. "Trends in Healthy Life Expectancy in the United States, 1970–1990: Gender, Racial, and Educational Differences." *Social Science and Medicine* 52: 1,629–1,641.

House, James S., James M. Lepkowski, David R. Williams, Richard P. Mero, Paula M. Lanz, Stephanie A. Robert, and Jieming Chen. 2000. "Excess Mortality among Urban Residents: How Much, for Whom, and Why?" *American Journal of Public Health* 90(12): 1,898–1,904.

Hu, Yuanreng, and Noreen Goldman. 1990. "Mortality Differentials by Marital Status: An International Comparison." *Demography* 27(2): 233–250.

Kitagawa, Evelyn M., and Philip M. Hauser. 1973. *Differential Mortality in the United States: A Study in Socioeconomic Epidemiology.* American Public Health Association. Vital and Health Statistics Monographs. Cambridge, MA: Harvard University Press.

Kunst, Anton E. 1997. "Cross-National Comparisons of Socio-Economic Differences in Mortality." Ph.D. diss., Erasmus University, Rotterdam.

Machenbach, John P., Anton E. Kunst, Adriënne E. J. M. Cavelaars, Fejke Groenhof, José J. M. Geurts, and the EU Working Group on Socioeconomic Inequalities in Health. 1997. "Socioeconomic Inequalities in Morbidity and Mortality in Western Europe." *The Lancet* 349: 1,655–1,659.

Pickle Linda W., Michael Mungiole, Gretchen K. Jones, and Andrew A. White. 1996. *Atlas of United States Mortality.* Hyattsville, MD: National Center for Health Statistics.

Preston, Samuel H., and Irma T. Elo. 1995. "Are Educational Differentials in Adult Mortality Increasing in the United States?" *Journal of Aging and Health* 7(4): 476–496.

Rogers, Richard G., Robert A. Hummer, and Charles B. Nam. 2000. *Living and Dying in the USA: Behavioral, Health, and Social Differentials of Adult Mortality.* San Diego, CA: Academic Press.

Valkonen, Tapani. 2001. "Trends in Differential Mortality in European Countries." In *Trends in Mortality and Differential Mortality,* ed. Jaques Vallin, France Meslé, and Tapani Valkonen. Population Studies No. 36. Strasbourg: Council of Europe Publishing, pp. 185–328.

Williams, David R., and Chiquita Collins. 1995. "U.S. Socioeconomic and Racial Differences in Health: Patterns and Explanations." *Annual Review of Sociology* 21: 349–386.

World Health Organization. 1997. *Atlas of Mortality in Europe: Subnational Patterns, 1980/1981 and 1990/1991.* World Health Organization Regional Publications, European Series, No. 75.

TAPANI VALKONEN

MORTALITY-FERTILITY RELATIONSHIPS

It is axiomatic that, once death rates in a population have fallen steeply and irreversibly, birth rates must eventually follow. The alternative is rapid population growth that is unsustainable in the long term. However, the characterization of the link between mortality and fertility in classic statements of demographic transition theory has differed. As described in the pioneering 1953 study of the population scientist Frank Notestein, societal modernization was the common cause of declines in both mortality and fertility, though falls in death rates preceded falls in birth rates. In his view, improved survival was a contributory cause of fertility reduction, among many others. By contrast, in 1963, Kingsley Davis the eminent demographer, saw improved survival as the central cause of such decline—both necessary and sufficient. To Davis, societal modernization was largely irrelevant; the effect of improved survival was as strong in subsistence, agrarian societies as in more urban, industrialized settings.

Since these early theoretical contributions, scientists have accumulated a great deal of empirical evidence on the mortality–fertility link at the societal and family level. It has become clear that the relationship is not a simple mechanical one. Though it remains true that mortality decline has always preceded secular declines in fertility, the degree of prior mortality improvement, the absolute level and age pattern of mortality at the onset of fertility decline, and the time lags involved vary widely among societies.

In Europe, improvement in life expectancy typically started in the eighteenth century with the gradual elimination of mortality crises. In the latter half of that century and the early decades of the nineteenth century, gains in life expectancy appear to have been widespread; but this period was followed in some countries by an era of stabilization before further and more pronounced improvements started at the end of the nineteenth century, when the onset of fertility decline also occurred. In much of Europe, declines in childhood mortality preceded falls in infant mortality: Indeed, large improvements in infant survival coincided with fertility decline in many provinces. In some Northern European countries, the crude death rate had fallen to 15 per 1,000 population and infant mortality to about 100 per 1,000 births by the start of fertility transition. Conversely, the crude death rate was about 30 and infant mortality over 250 in much of Eastern Europe and Germany when their fertility transitions started.

In the developing regions, the prior imprint of mortality decline was much more substantial than in Europe. In Asia and Latin America, by 1960, which broadly marks the onset of fertility transition in these regions, mortality at all ages, including infancy

and childhood, had been falling sharply for several decades, mainly in response to public health initiatives rather than improved living standards. As a consequence, and also because the pre-transition levels of the crude birth rate were higher than were those in Europe, rates of natural increase were much higher than in Europe at the end of the nineteenth century. In sub-Saharan Africa, large gains in life expectancy occurred a decade or so later, as did the onset of fertility decline. But even in the developing world, societal levels of mortality varied widely at the onset of fertility decline—for instance, ranging from life expectancies of 67 and 60 years in Costa Rica and China to 47 and 45 years in Bolivia and Bangladesh.

These irregularities in the mortality–fertility relationship do not disprove the existence of a strong underlying causal connection between the two. Rather, they may reflect the influence on reproductive behavior of many intervening factors— economic, cultural, and political—that mediate its response to improved survival. Opinion on the causal centrality of the relationship is divided and the difference in emphasis between Notestein and Davis is not yet reconciled. The main reason for this continued uncertainty is the failure to identify strong and convincing linkages between improved survival and fertility.

Family-level Links

Possible links between mortality decline and fertility are depicted in Figure 1. Four main links at the family level have been identified. One of these is physiological. Early death of a child necessarily stops breastfeeding; thus lactational protection against conception is lost and the interval to next birth shortened. Moreover, in societies where the custom of prolonged sexual abstinence during lactation is observed, the death of a child may trigger the resumption of intercourse, also contributing to a shortening of the next birth interval. Ample evidence confirms that, in societies characterized by prolonged breastfeeding, reductions in infant mortality will act to lengthen birth intervals and hence reduce the frequency of childbearing. However the effect on fertility of even major reductions in infant mortality in these societies is minor.

Improved survival of children reduces any tendency to replace children who have died and thus represents a second possible pathway of influence. Intentional replacement of children who have died

FIGURE 1

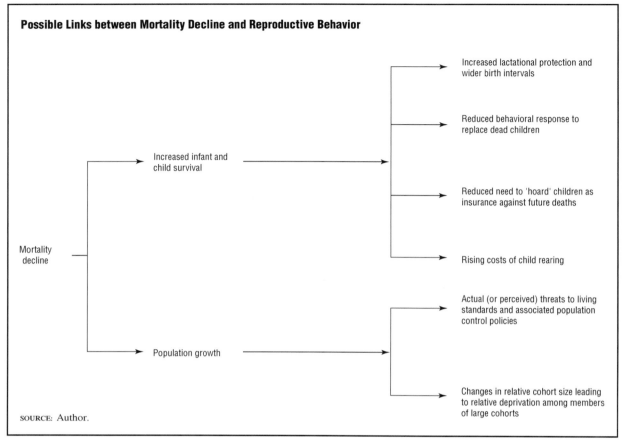

Possible Links between Mortality Decline and Reproductive Behavior

SOURCE: Author.

can only be an important consideration in societies where birth control is widely practiced. But, of course in most of these societies, child mortality is already low and any need to replace dead children is uncommon. In a synthesis of evidence from a variety of transitional and low fertility societies, the demographer Samuel Preston concluded that parents who had lost a child were only 20 to 30 percent more likely to proceed to the next birth than other parents. This effect is also too small to constitute an important part of any overall explanation.

The theory that parents insure against possible future deaths of children by having more children than they would otherwise want is highly plausible. When life expectancy is 30 years (typical of many pre-transitional societies), 4.5 births are required to ensure that two children, on average, survive to the next generation. When life expectancy has risen to 65 years, only a fraction over two births are required to achieve the same outcome. All that is required to imbue this *insurance hypothesis* with causal force is

for the adult generation to perceive that survival has improved and to respond by bearing fewer children. Surprisingly, the actualization of this hypothesis has little empirical support. An individual's perception of mortality change corresponds weakly with actual change, and perceptions correlate poorly with reproductive behavior. Moreover, improved child survival is rarely proffered by parents as a reason for having fewer births.

The last of the four family-level links between mortality decline and fertility concerns rising costs of childbearing. To understand the potential explanatory power of this factor, some characteristics of pre-transitional societies need to be outlined. In such societies, only two children per family survived to adulthood per family on average but there was wide inter-family variability. Parents with many children alleviated the costs of nurture by transferring *surplus* offspring to those with few or no children: by fostering, adoption, or offering them as servants or apprentices, for instance. Such redistributive mechanisms appear to have been a common feature in most traditional societies.

Consider the effects of a sustained decline in mortality. The number of surviving children per family doubles, ratcheting up expenditures on food, clothing, education, and so on. At the same time opportunities for children to be adopted by the childless decrease. Moreover, parents themselves survive longer, thus delaying inter-generational transfer of assets. In short, improved survival places a strain on families. Emigration represents a possible, but typically short-term, solution. Sooner or later, reproduction itself is modified, perhaps by postponement of marriage but ultimately by birth control within marriage. This characterization is the kernel of Kingsley Davis's theory.

Several features of this proposed link, between higher survival and lower reproduction, need to be stressed. Unlike the insurance mechanism, it does not depend on accurate perceptions of changes in mortality. The pressure on families does not suddenly appear. Rather it increases gradually but relentlessly. The increase in numbers of surviving children is experienced first by relatively privileged urban sectors of society, the very groups most concerned with providing children with sufficient means to maintain the social position of the family.

This theory is consistent with evidence that, even in subsistence economies, children consume more than they produce until at least the early teenage years. It is also consistent with the most commonly cited reason for wishing to reduce childbearing, namely that childrearing costs are too high. The demographer John Cleland claims that the theory provides coherence to an otherwise baffling body of evidence. Improved survival is the most plausible common underlying cause of the fertility declines that have arisen over a relatively short period (1950–2000) in most developing countries despite their wide economic, cultural, and political diversity. This interpretation, however, is not amenable to empirical appraisal and offers a less compelling explanation of the earlier transition in Europe, when fertility fell in the context of more modest mortality improvements.

Societal Links

Identification of the main societal link between mortality and fertility decline is attributable to English economist T. R. Malthus who claimed that population growth, resulting from an imbalance between death and birth rates, would drive down living standards and thereby produce a resurgence of mortality (the positive check) or a lowering of fertility (the preventive check). The role of such homeostatic forces has been a major theme of historical demography and assumed a new relevance in the context of rapid population growth in the latter half of the twentieth century. In the 1960s, a broad—but by no means universal—consensus arose that rapid population growth posed a serious threat to development goals in Asia, Latin America, and Africa. The main policy response took the form of state-sponsored family planning programs. Such policies have facilitated reproductive change in many developing countries (particularly in Asia), played a minor role in others (particularly in Latin America), and of course played no role at all in the European transition.

The fact that government policies, driven by neo-Malthusian concerns, do not constitute a central part of the mortality–fertility relationship, does not necessarily imply that a Malthusian perspective is invalid. Yet the thesis that negative feedback from population growth, at a societal level, can trigger a fertility response has little support. Fertility has declined in buoyant economies (e.g., Republic of Korea) and stagnant ones (e.g., Kenya), in densely populated countries (e.g., Bangladesh) and in ones with abundant under-utilized land (e.g., Colombia). Nor, despite intensive empirical investigation, is there decisive evidence that rapid population growth has had negative effects on improvements in living standards. Whatever threats further population growth in the twenty-first century may bring, the twentieth century has seen unprecedented improvement in living standards in parallel with unprecedented population growth, the exact opposite of Malthusian predictions.

Relative, rather than absolute, deprivation resulting from the effect of mortality decline on age structure is a further possible link. The central idea, derived from the economist Richard Easterlin, is that the economic and social fortunes of a cohort tend to be inversely proportional to its size relative to other cohorts. Mortality decline at younger ages results, some 20 years later, in an increase of young adults relative to older generations. Compared with their parents, these young adults are vulnerable to relative deprivation: The labor market becomes saturated leading to stagnation in wage increases and family assets have to be divided among more survivors. In short, the natural desire of the younger generation to maintain or improve upon the living standards of its parents is jeopardized and this pressure stimulates a reduction in childbearing. In a simple statistical test using data from 184 countries, economist Diane Macunovich found that increases in the ratio of males aged 15 to 24 years to males aged 25 to 59 were more strongly predictive of declines in fertility than were declines in infant mortality. Pending further assessment of such linkages, this thesis remains an interesting possibility.

Conclusion

Mortality decline must remain at the center of attempts to understand the fertility transition of the past 120 years. Steep declines in childbearing from over five births to around two births per woman were only possible in the context of vastly improved survival. Beyond this obvious truth, few other generalizations can be stated with confidence. Because fertility decline occurs under widely differing mortality conditions, it is clear that improved survival, while it is probably the underlying cause, is not the sole nor, in the short term, necessarily the dominant influence.

See also: *Demographic Transition; Fertility Transition, Socioeconomic Determinants of.*

BIBLIOGRAPHY

Cleland, John. 2001. "The Effects of Improved Survival on Fertility: a Reassessment." *Population and Development Review* 27(Supplement):60–92.

Davis, Kingsley. 1963. "The Theory of Change and Response in Modern Demographic History." *Population Index* 29: 345–366.

Macunovich, Diane H. 2000. "Relative Cohort Size: Source of a Unifying Theory of Global Fertility Transition." *Population and Development Review* 26(2): 235–261.

Notestein, Frank W. 1953. "Economic Problems of Population Change." In *Proceedings of the Eighth International Conference of Agricultural Economists.* Oxford: Oxford University Press.

Preston, Samuel H. 1978. "Introduction." *The Effects of Infant and Child Mortality on Fertility,* ed. Samuel H. Preston. New York: Academic Press.

van de Walle, Francine. 1986. "Infant Mortality and the European Demographic Transition." In *The Decline of Fertility in Europe,* ed. Ansley J. Coale and Susan Cotts Watkins. Princeton, NJ: Princeton University Press.

JOHN G. CLELAND

MORTALITY MEASUREMENT

This article gives a nontechnical account of the principal indexes used by demographers to measure the level of mortality in a population. For each index, the main advantages and disadvantages are also noted.

Crude Death Rate

The crude death rate is the number of deaths in a population during a specified time period divided by the population "at risk" of dying during that period—that is, for a time period measured in years, the number of person-years lived during the period. For a one-year period, the population at risk is simply the average population size over the year; for a calendar year, the mid-year population is usually taken. By convention, the resulting fraction is applied to a standard-sized population of 1,000, thus making the crude death rate the number of deaths per 1,000 population per year. The adjective "crude" is used since none of the structural characteristics of the population that might affect the number of deaths that occur in the time period—in particular the age distribution—is taken into account, only total population size.

The crude death rate is normally calculated for a single calendar year, although in order to smooth out year-to-year fluctuations, published estimates often give an average rate over several years—typically a five-year period. Calculation of the crude death rate for France in 2000 is shown in Item 1 of the Formula Table.

Pros: It requires less detailed data than other mortality measures, and uses data that are more likely to be available for a very recent time period. The crude death rate is needed for calculation of the rate of natural increase (the crude birth rate minus the crude death rate).

FORMULA TABLE

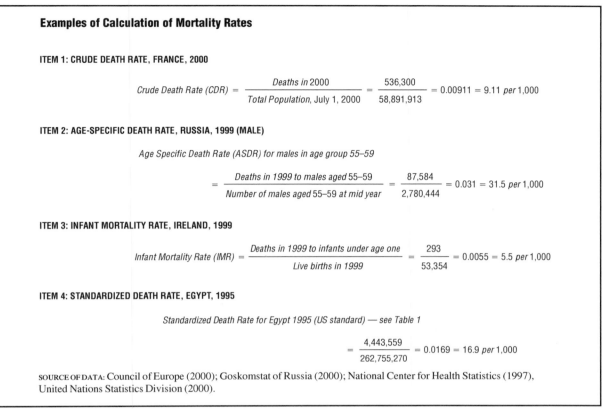

Examples of Calculation of Mortality Rates

ITEM 1: CRUDE DEATH RATE, FRANCE, 2000

$$\text{Crude Death Rate (CDR)} = \frac{\text{Deaths in 2000}}{\text{Total Population, July 1, 2000}} = \frac{536,300}{58,891,913} = 0.00911 = 9.11 \text{ per } 1,000$$

ITEM 2: AGE-SPECIFIC DEATH RATE, RUSSIA, 1999 (MALE)

Age Specific Death Rate (ASDR) for males in age group 55–59

$$= \frac{\text{Deaths in 1999 to males aged 55–59}}{\text{Number of males aged 55–59 at mid year}} = \frac{87,584}{2,780,444} = 0.031 = 31.5 \text{ per } 1,000$$

ITEM 3: INFANT MORTALITY RATE, IRELAND, 1999

$$\text{Infant Mortality Rate (IMR)} = \frac{\text{Deaths in 1999 to infants under age one}}{\text{Live births in 1999}} = \frac{293}{53,354} = 0.0055 = 5.5 \text{ per } 1,000$$

ITEM 4: STANDARDIZED DEATH RATE, EGYPT, 1995

Standardized Death Rate for Egypt 1995 (US standard) — see Table 1

$$= \frac{4,443,559}{262,755,270} = 0.0169 = 16.9 \text{ per } 1,000$$

SOURCE OF DATA: Council of Europe (2000); Goskomstat of Russia (2000); National Center for Health Statistics (1997), United Nations Statistics Division (2000).

Cons: It is affected by the population age structure—in particular, by the proportions of elderly, who have a higher than average probability of dying in any given period. For that reason, the crude death rate is not a good indicator of overall mortality for comparisons among countries or regions with differing age structures. For example, the crude death rate of Sweden in 2000, 11 per 1,000 population, is much higher than that of Venezuela, 5 per 1,000. But Sweden had a proportionately much larger elderly population than Venezuela: 17 percent of the population of Sweden was aged 65 and over, compared to only 5 percent in Venezuela. By the measure of life expectancy at birth, Sweden has the lower mortality: its life expectancy in 2000 was 80 years, compared to Venezuela's 73 years.

Age-Specific Death Rates

Age-specific death rates (or age-specific mortality rates) (ASDR) are similar to the crude death rate, but calculated for a individual age groups, typically five-year groups. If calculated for a single year, the numerator of the rate is the number of deaths to persons in the age group during the year and the denominator is the average population in the age group during the year (or the mid-year population). Age-specific death rates are often calculated for each sex separately.

Age-specific death rates normally have a J-shaped distribution over the age range. Death rates are relatively high for infants and young children, low for older children and from the young adult years to middle age, and then become higher with increasing age. (Countries with severe AIDS epidemics are an exception to this pattern: AIDS mortality among young adults and persons of middle age has created a sharp rise in age-specific mortality rates in those ages.) Calculation of the age-specific death rate for Russia in 1999 is shown in Item 2 of the Formula Table.

Pros: It allows analysis of mortality patterns by age and sex. Age-specific death rates are required for the calculation of life tables.

Cons: It requires detailed data on deaths by age group, data that are often not available in developing countries.

TABLE 1

Comparison of Death Rates in Egypt and in the United States, 1995

Age group	US population thousands	US ASDRs (x 1000)	Egypt ASDRs (x 1000)	Actual US deaths in 1995	US deaths in 1995 if Egypt's ASDRs applied
0–4	19,595	1.836	8.1	35,976	158,718
5–9	19,188	0.197	0.9	3,780	17,269
10–14	18,886	0.255	0.8	4,816	15,109
15–19	18,071	0.835	1.0	15,089	18,071
20–24	17,885	1.071	1.0	19,155	17,885
25–29	19,012	1.193	1.3	22,681	24,715
30–34	21,874	1.603	1.6	35,064	34,998
35–39	22,253	2.089	2.4	46,487	53,408
40–44	20,219	2.759	3.5	55,783	70,765
45–49	17,448	3.761	5.8	65,623	101,200
50–54	13,630	5.677	8.6	77,377	117,217
55–59	11,085	8.718	13.9	96,641	154,085
60–64	10,046	13.823	25.0	138,871	251,159
65–69	9,928	20.583	40.9	204,347	406,053
70–74	8,831	31.314	68.2	276,543	602,294
75+	14,773	82.138	162.5	1,213,436	2,400,613
Total	**262,755**			**2,311,669**	**4,443,559**

Note: ASDR is age-specific death rate.

SOURCE: U.S. Census Bureau (www.census.gov); National Center for Health Statistics. 1997. Report of Final Mortality Statistics, 1995; United Nations Statistics Division (2001).

Infant Mortality Rate

The infant mortality rate (IMR) is the proportion of infants who die in their first year. It is conventionally calculated as the number of deaths under age one in a given year divided by the number of live births, with the result expressed per 1,000 births. Calculation of the infant mortality rate for Ireland is shown in Item 3 of the Formula Table.

To be strictly accurate, the IMR in this case should be the number of deaths before age one to infants born in 1999 divided by the number of live births in 1999. This formula would relate infant deaths to the population at risk—in this instance, comprising the births among which such deaths could occur. (It is equivalent to the life table death rate between age zero and exact age one.) The practical problem this precise formulation raises is that deaths under age one from among births in a given calendar year consist of some fraction of infant deaths during the calendar year in question and some fraction of infant deaths that occur in the following calendar year. Hence the precise IMR calculation would require information about infant

deaths in two calendar years, and the deaths would need to be classified by the double criterion of age and year of birth. Such detail is rarely available.

Pros: The infant mortality rate is usually considered a good indicator of overall health conditions in a country, particularly child health. Frequently it is used to infer ("impute") the entire age schedule of mortality, using a set of model life tables.

Cons: Accurate registration data on births and infant deaths are unavailable in many countries. (In the absence of such data, estimates of IMR—and of proportions of births surviving to later ages of childhood—at a period several years in the past can be derived from retrospective survey data on survivorship rates of children. Demographic surveys routinely ask women how many children they have had and how many are living.)

Standardized Death Rate

The standardized death rate of a population is the death rate that it would have if the population had the age distribution of some different specified population—the "standard." The concept can be explained in terms of weighted averages. The crude death rate of a population can be represented as the weighted average of the prevailing age-specific death rates, the weights being the proportions of the population at each age. If the weights used in the calculation are instead taken from the age distribution of some different population, chosen as the standard, the resulting weighted average is the standardized (or strictly, the age-standardized) death rate.

For comparisons of death rates among populations, standardization (with the same standard used throughout) removes the effects of the different actual age distributions on the rates. In the example in Table 1, standardization is used to compare the mortality of Egypt and the United States in 1995, using the U.S. age distribution as the standard. In 1995 the United States had 2.311 million deaths in a population of 262.755 million, giving a crude death rate of 8.8 per 1000. The corresponding crude death rate for Egypt was 6.5. The lower level of mortality in Egypt by this measure, however, is an artifact of the age distribution: Egypt's life expectancy at birth, about 65, is some twelve years less than that of the United States. Since reported age-specific death rates of reasonable quality for Egypt are available, it is possible to calculate the number of deaths the United States would have if it had the reported age-specific death rates of Egypt. Table 1 compares the number of deaths at each age using ASDRs of both Egypt and the United States applied to the U.S. age distribution. The deaths that would have occurred in the United States if it experienced Egypt's mortality at each age are about 4.4 million, compared to the 2.3 million deaths that did occur. The resulting death rate for Egypt in 1995, standardized on the U.S. population, is 16.9 per 1,000 population rather than 6.5. (See Item 4 in the Formula Table.)

The technique of standardization is much more general than this example may suggest. Death rates can be standardized by other characteristics than age, or by other characteristics as well as age, the choice depending on the intended comparison.

Pros: Standardization by age allows comparison of death rates abstracting from influences of differences in age distributions.

Cons: It requires data on deaths or death rates by age for both countries and the age distribution of one country. The comparison depends to some degree on the choice of the standard.

Life Expectancy

Life expectancy at any given age is the average number of additional years persons of that age would live under the mortality conditions prevailing at the time. Most frequently, life expectancy is quoted in terms of life expectancy at birth: the number of years a newborn infant can be expected to live under mortality rates at each age existing at the time of its birth.

Life expectancy at age x is calculated in a life table by summing the number of survivors at each single year of age above x (which gives the total person-years lived beyond x in the life table population) and dividing by the number at age x. It is most commonly calculated from age 0, giving the expectation of life at birth.

Pros: Life expectancy at birth is the single best summary measure of the mortality pattern of a population. It translates a schedule of age-specific deaths rates into a result expressed in the everyday metric of years, the average "length of life."

Cons: It requires a full schedule of age-specific death rates. Since mortality typically declines over time, a calculated life expectancy, derived from cross-sectional mortality data, understates the true expected length of life. Subtracting actual age from life expectancy at birth is often erroneously interpreted as giving average remaining years to live.

See also: *Actuarial Analysis; Fertility Measurement; Life Tables; Maternal Mortality; Mortality, Age Patterns of; Population Dynamics.*

BIBLIOGRAPHY

Bogue, Donald J., Eduardo E. Arriaga, and Douglas L. Anderton, eds. 1993. "Readings in Population Research Methodology," Vol. 2: *Mortality Research.* Chicago: United Nations Population Fund and Social Development Center.

Coale, Ansley J., and Paul Demeny. 1983. *Regional Model Life Tables and Stable Populations,* 2nd edition. New York: Academic Press.

Council of Europe. 2000. *Recent Demographic Developments in Europe 2000.* Strasbourg: Council of Europe.

Goskomstat of Russia. 2000. *The Demographic Yearbook of Russia 2000.* Moscow: Goskomstat of Russia.

Lancaster, Henry O. 1990. *Expectations of Life.* New York, Berlin, Heidelberg: Springer-verlag.

National Center for Health Statistics. 1997. *Report of Final Mortality Statistics, 1995.* Hyattsville, MD: National Center for Health Statistics

Pressat, Roland. 1972. *Demographic Analysis: Methods, Results, Applications.* London: Edward Arnold.

Ruzicka, Lado, Guillaume Wunsch, and Penny Kane. *Differential Mortality, Methodologocal Issues and Biosocial Factors.* Oxford: Clarendon Press.

Shryock, Henry S., Jacob S. Siegel, and Associates. 1976. *The Methods and Materials of Demography,* condensed edition. New York: Academic Press.

United Nations Statistics Division. 2001. *Demographic Yearbook 1999.* New York: United Nations.

Vallin, Jaques, Stan d'Souza and Alberto Palloni. 1990. *Measurement and Analysis of Mortality, New Approaches.* Oxford: Clarendon Press.

Carl Haub

FIGURE 1

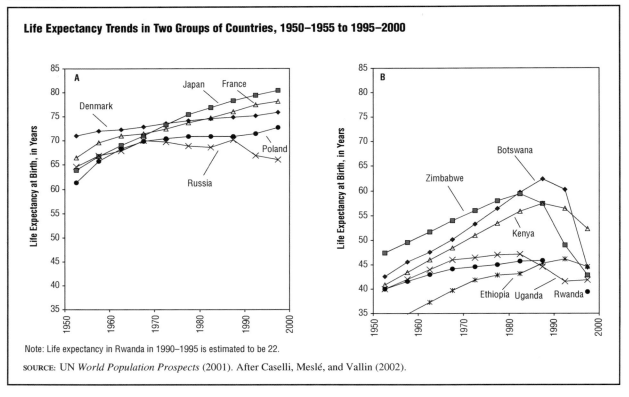

Life Expectancy Trends in Two Groups of Countries, 1950–1955 to 1995–2000

Note: Life expectancy in Rwanda in 1990–1995 is estimated to be 22.

SOURCE: UN *World Population Prospects* (2001). After Caselli, Meslé, and Vallin (2002).

MORTALITY REVERSALS

Declining mortality has long been a routine expectation in most of the world, aside from wartime interruptions. Many forecasts envisage a global convergence to low mortality over coming decades. Mortality reversals refer to exceptions to this long-run trend—situations in which the decline ceases or is even reversed.

Until the last decades of the twentieth century, significant mortality reversals were nearly unknown. The only example occurred in Europe in the first half of the nineteenth century during the early stages of the industrial revolution. Since the 1970s, however, many countries have experienced mortality reversals—most remarkably in Eastern Europe, where mortality increased from the 1970s through the 1990s, and in sub-Saharan Africa, with rising AIDS-related mortality beginning in the 1980s. In both regions, adult-age mortality was much more affected than was the mortality of children or the elderly.

Figure 1 displays trends in life expectancy for two groups of countries. Panel A illustrates a widening of the life expectancy gap between Russia and Poland and selected high-income countries.

Panel B shows striking cases of abrupt drops of life expectancy to extremely low levels in Africa.

Mortality Reversals in Eastern Europe

Panel A in Figure 1 shows that converging trends in life expectancy between East and West were observed only in the 1950s and the early 1960s. Later the trends in the former Communist countries diverge from those in the market-economy countries. Most remarkably, Russia (and other countries of the former Soviet Union) experienced a gradual decline in life expectancy in the 1970s and a further drop in the 1990s to a low of 66 years. In the 1990s, a previously small gap between Russia and Poland widened, reflecting the probable emergence of a new mortality divide between the former Soviet Union and the rest of Eastern Europe.

The health crisis in Eastern Europe and the former Soviet Union has been analyzed extensively. The effects were seen predominantly in the male population. In the year 2000 male life expectancy at birth in Russia was 59 years—below its level of 60 years in 1955–1956. The corresponding figures for the female population were 72 and 68 years, respec-

FIGURE 2

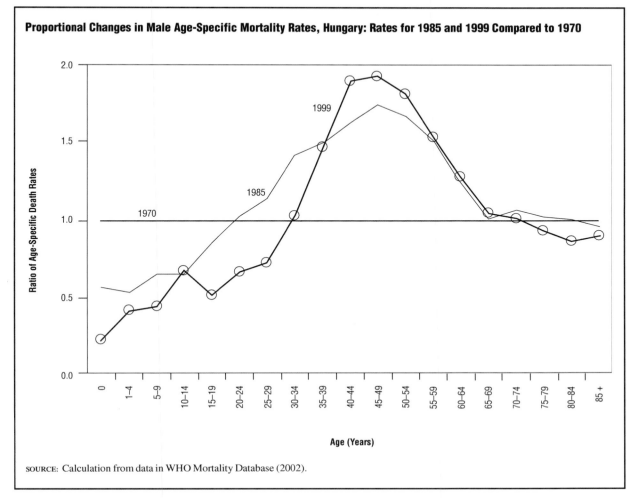

Proportional Changes in Male Age-Specific Mortality Rates, Hungary: Rates for 1985 and 1999 Compared to 1970

SOURCE: Calculation from data in WHO Mortality Database (2002).

tively. The gender gap in life expectancy varies from 8 to 13 years across the Eastern European region. The concentration of increasing mortality at adult ages is shown for Hungary in Figure 2. In Russia in 2000, men aged 20 had only a 45 percent probability of surviving to age 65; the equivalent probability in Western Europe was about 80 percent.

At the same time, in contrast, child mortality in Eastern Europe has been continuously decreasing. Cardiovascular disease, lung cancer, liver cirrhosis, and other behaviorally-linked diseases and injuries were contributing to the mortality increase at adult ages. In countries of the former Soviet Union, mortality from accidents and violence had reached very high levels by the late 1970s and increased through the 1990s. In the 1990s in Russia, mortality attributed to homicide approached the world's highest levels.

Excess mortality in Eastern Europe has been increasingly concentrated among manual workers and low education groups. It is important to note that the worst patterns of excess mortality affecting population groups in Western countries are quite similar to those in Eastern Europe according to age and cause-of-death structures.

The factors underlying the unfavorable mortality trends probably include lack of preventive health programs and inadequate quality of medical services; smoking and alcohol abuse; general neglect of individual health and other individual societal values; and stress, whether caused by a lack of life choices under the former Communist regimes, or by unemployment, relative deprivation, and inability to cope with the economic challenges of post-Communist times.

FIGURE 3

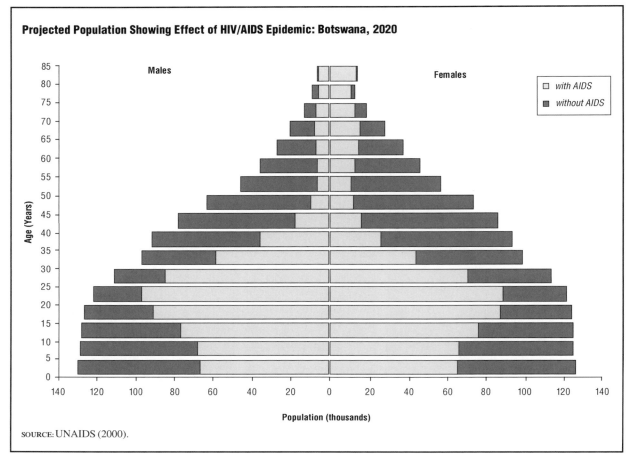

Projected Population Showing Effect of HIV/AIDS Epidemic: Botswana, 2020

SOURCE: UNAIDS (2000).

Mortality Effects of Infectious Disease in Sub-Saharan Africa

Panel B in Figure 1 shows the UN estimates of decreases in the African life expectancies after the late 1980s. Losses are especially high in Zimbabwe and Botswana, bringing life expectancy down to levels not seen in these countries since the 1950s. In Rwanda, the natural trend in life expectancy was severely disrupted by the 1994 genocide and subsequent civil war.

Regular mortality statistics are generally unavailable in the region. Existing estimates are based on household surveys or censuses that include questions about recent household deaths, orphanhood, and survival of children, and *verbal autopsy* questions on causes of death. Mortality increases are found mostly among young adults. The male probability of death between ages 15 and 55 in Zimbabwe increased from 0.15 in the mid-1980s to 0.5 in the late 1990s. The probability of dying between ages 20

and 60 doubled in Uganda and Zambia. In rural Uganda, mortality rates among HIV-positive adults were 15 times higher than those among HIV-negative adults and the probability of death between ages 20 and 60 was about 0.5. Adult mortality rose substantially in East, Central, and Southern Africa; adult mortality also rose in West Africa, but to a far lesser extent. Survey data also show increases in child mortality in countries with the highest prevalence of HIV.

High levels of adult-age mortality and consequent drops in the number of children born will result in profound changes in future population size and age structure, as indicated in the projections for Botswana given in Figure 3.

The factors facilitating a rapid spread of HIV/AIDS in the region are poverty, lack of education, spread of violence, increased spatial mobility (inducing greater promiscuity), gender inequalities, and inadequate health systems.

Poverty increases the risk of infectious diseases in general. Low education is an obstacle to promoting healthy behavioral patterns.

Wars, which have affected many countries in the region, spread HIV through increased prostitution and sexual violence. HIV transmission may also be promoted by polygyny, extramarital sex, and sex between teenage girls and older men.

Economic hardships and an already high burden of infectious diseases account for a lack of access to medical care, resulting in untreated sexually transmitted diseases, unchecked mother-to-child HIV transmission, and a lack of treatment of AIDS-related illnesses.

Conclusion

The experience of the last several decades of the twentieth century suggests that health progress does not continue automatically. Certain combinations of epidemiological situations, socio-economic and socio-psychological conditions, and cultural and behavioral patterns can cause significant mortality reversals.

See also: *AIDS; Alcohol, Health Effects of; Mortality Decline.*

BIBLIOGRAPHY

Caselli, G., F. Meslé, and J. Vallin. 2002. "Epidemiologic Transition Theory Exceptions." *Genus* 58(1): 9–51.

Cockerham, William C. 1999. *Health and Social Change in Russia and Eastern Europe.* New York: Routledge.

Corina, G.A., and R. Paniccià. 2000. "The Transition Mortality Crisis: Evidence, Interpretation and Policy Responses." In *The Mortality Crisis in Transitional Economies,* ed. G. A. Cornia and R. Paniccià. Oxford: Oxford University Press.

Leon, D. A. 2000. "Common Threads: Underlying Components of Inequalities in Mortality Between and Within Countries." In *Poverty, Inequality and Health,* ed. D. A. Leon and G. Walt. Oxford: Oxford University Press.

Quinn, T.C. 2001. "AIDS in Africa: A Retrospective." *Bulletin of the World Health Organization* 79(12): 1156–1158.

Shkolnikov, V. M., F. Meslé, and J. Vallin. 1996. "Health Crisis in Russia I. Recent Trends in Life Expectancy and Causes of Death from 1970 to 1993." *Population: An English Selection* 8: 123–154.

Timæus, I. 2001. "Impact of the HIV Epidemic on Mortality in Sub-Saharan Africa: Evidence from National Surveys and Censuses." *AIDS* 12: S15–S27.

UNAIDS. 2000. *Report on the Global HIV/AIDS Epidemic. June 2000.* Geneva. Joint United Nations Programme on HIV/AIDS.

VLADIMIR M. SHKOLNIKOV

MULTIPLE BIRTHS

Nearly one in every hundred deliveries is a twin birth. Triplet, quadruplet, and higher order deliveries occur far less frequently—only 1 in 10,000 deliveries. This article concerns only twins.

Twins are of two kinds: identical and fraternal. Biologists call the former monozygotic twins and the latter dizygotic twins, in reference to their different origins.

Identical (monozygotic) twins derive from a single fertilized egg, or zygote, that has divided in two in the course of its development. The two resulting embryos are genetically identical, which explains the close resemblance of monozygotic twins. They are always of the same sex.

Fraternal (dizygotic) twins derive from the ovulation and fertilization of two different ova during the same menstrual cycle. Each of these ova is fertilized by a spermatozoon and the twins resulting from these two eggs or zygotes are no more similar, from a genetic point of view, than ordinary brothers and sisters. Fraternal twins can be of the same sex or male and female, both variants occurring with equal frequency.

Fraternal and identical twins thus correspond to two distinct biological processes, and their incidence depends on different factors.

The Twinning Rate

The twinning rate is the proportion of twin deliveries in the total number of deliveries.

FIGURE 1

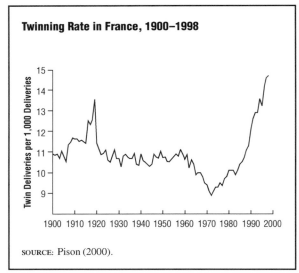

Twinning Rate in France, 1900–1998

SOURCE: Pison (2000).

Identical twin deliveries occur at the rate of 3.5 to 4 per 1,000, regardless of the mother's age, birth order, or ethnic or geographic origin. The same proportion has been observed among all mammals, except for some armadillos that systematically give birth to monozygotic quadruplets or octuplets. All women seem to run the same risk of having identical twins, whether or not they have previously given birth to twins.

In contrast to identical twin births, the proportion of fraternal twin births is extremely variable. The main factors influencing these variations are as follows.

Age of the mother. Beginning with a near zero level at puberty, the proportion steadily increases up to age 37, where it reaches its maximum level, then rapidly decreases back to zero level by the time of menopause. This variation corresponds to that of the Follicle Stimulating Hormone (FSH), which ensures the development of the ova. (The drop in the fraternal twin rate after the age of 37 could be due to weaker ovarian function and to the higher mortality of fertilized eggs as menopause draws nearer.)

Order of birth. Controlling for age of mother, the fraternal twinning rate increases with every childbirth. Birth order is nevertheless less influential than age.

Geographic or ethnic origin. The same variations by mother's age and order of birth are observed everywhere, but the frequency of twinning differs by region. Controlling for age and birth order, the fraternal twinning rate in sub-Saharan Africa is two times higher than in Europe, and four to five times higher than in China or Japan. These differences are partly linked to hormonal differences of genetic origin. Hence, for example, the twinning rate of African-Americans in the United States lies between the European and the African rates.

Individual and family characteristics. Some women may have several sets of fraternal twins; this predisposition to twin pregnancies is partly genetic and can be observed among the sisters and daughters of women who have had twins.

The Influence of Sterility Treatments

In France, in the first half of the twentieth century, the incidence of twin deliveries was about 11 per 1,000, a proportion which did not significantly vary, except during World War I, when the twinning rate temporarily rose. (See Figure 1.) In the 1960s, the proportion of twin deliveries declined, reaching a low 8.9 per 1,000 in 1972. The rate then began to climb again and by 1987, it had risen back to the level of the first half of the century. However, the upward trend did not stop there, and even gained momentum: By 1998, the twinning rate had reached 14.7 per 1,000, a 65 percent increase from 1972. The same downward and upward trends were observed in most developed countries.

A partial explanation for these trends is variation in the mean age of mothers. In France in the 1950s, for example, the mean age was close to 28; it fell to 26.5 in 1977. A rapid increase followed and, by the end of the 1990s, it exceeded 29. However, the most important factor in the steep rise in twinning rates since the 1970s has been the expanded use of sterility treatments. Twinning rates rose especially in developed countries, where such treatments are most available, and particularly among older women, who are more likely to utilize them.

French physicians began to prescribe hormones to stimulate ovulation in 1967. The treatments became so popular that by 2000 some 400,000 menstrual cycles were being stimulated each year. By comparison, the total number of births in France in 2000 was 780,000. In addition, at the beginning of the twenty-first century some 40,000 in vitro fertilization (IVF) procedures are performed per year. In order to improve the likelihood of IVF success, physicians often implant several ova or several embryos at once—2.5 on average in 1997—resulting in a high probability of multiple births. Almost one out of four IVF pregnancies leads to the birth of twins, as opposed to one in 100 for natural pregnancies.

Mortality of Twins

In all parts of the world, the mortality rate of twin babies is much higher than that of singletons, due to their often low birth weight, their tendency to be premature, and more frequent complications at birth. The risk of giving birth to a stillborn twin is three to four times as high as that for a singleton. The mortality rate of twins born alive is also higher than that of singletons. In the first month following birth, the mortality rate for a twin is five to seven times higher than for a singleton, both in countries where infant mortality rates are high and in countries where the rate is low. After the first month, the gap decreases, but, regardless of the overall level of mortality, the mortality rate of twins remains two to three times that of singletons through the first year of life and continues to exceed that of singletons throughout childhood.

See also: *Reproductive Technologies: Modern Methods.*

BIBLIOGRAPHY

Bulmer, M. G. 1970. *The Biology of Twinning in Man.* Oxford: Clarendon Press.

FIVNAT. 1995. "Grossesses Multiples." *Contraception Fertilité Sexualité* 23(7–8): 494–497.

FIVNAT. 1997. "Bilan Général Fivnat, 1997." *Contraception Fertilité Sexualité* 26(7–8): 463–465.

Institut National de la Statistique et des Études Économiques (INSEE). Various years. *La Situation Démographique.* Paris: INSEE.

Office for National Statistics, Great Britain. 1995. *Mortality Statistics in England and Wales. Childhood, Infant and Perinatal.* London: The Stationery Office.

Pison, Gilles. 1992. "Twins in Sub-Saharan Africa: Frequency, Social Status and Mortality." In *Mortality and Society in Sub-Saharan Africa,* ed. Etienne van de Walle, Gilles Pison, and Mpembele Sala-Diakanda. Oxford: Clarendon Press.

INTERNET RESOURCE.

Pison, Gilles. 2000. "Nearly Half of the World's Twins Are Born in Africa." *Population et Sociétés* 360: 1–4. <http://www.ined.fr/englishversion/publications/pop_et_soc/index html>.

GILLES PISON

MULTISTATE DEMOGRAPHY

Multistate demography is the study of populations stratified by age, sex, and one or several attributes, such as region of residence, marital status, number of children, living arrangement, employment status, occupation, and health status. A population that is stratified is a multistate population, and people who occupy the same state constitute a subpopulation. The dynamics of multistate populations are governed by differential fertility and mortality, the transfer of individuals between subpopulations.

A Brief History

Multistate demography was pioneered by Andrei Rogers in the 1960s and 1970s. Rogers's aim was to generalize classical demographic models—the life table, population projection models, the stable population model—from two states (alive and dead) to multiple states of existence. As a specialist in urban and regional planning, Rogers's interest was mainly in regional population dynamics and migration, and the generalization was to a system of regions: a multiregional system. His first results appeared in *Demography* in 1966 and in book form in 1975. The book covers the multiregional life table, the continuous and discrete models of multiregional demographic growth (the Lotka and Leslie models), and the estimation of multiregional demographic measures from incomplete data. Rogers demonstrated that the generalization of demographic techniques to multiple states is relatively straightforward. Changes in multiregional populations are described by systems of simultaneous linear equations, conveniently represented in matrix notation. The broadening of multiregional demography into multistate demography was triggered by Robert Schoen's treatment of a population stratified by marital status (Schoen 1975).

In England, the geographer Philip Rees developed an accounting system for multiregional populations, pursuing some ideas from Rogers and having been influenced by earlier work of the economist Richard Stone (1913–1991), who initiated economic and social accounting in the early 1960s (Rees and Wilson, 1977). Accounts—in this case comprising population stocks and flows—have a great advantage: They must balance. Differences in data type, inconsistencies, and other data problems are easily identified.

From their beginning, multistate models followed the accounting tradition prevailing in demography and the actuarial sciences. Multistate models, and in particular the multistate life table, however, could also be viewed as applications of mathematical statistics, based in probability theory. Supporters of this perspective—Jan M. Hoem, Michael T. Hannan, and others—identified common features of the questions demographers try to answer using the life table and those addressed in the fields of survival analysis and event-history analysis with their focus on models of duration dependence. Age is viewed as a duration variable. The two distinct traditions persist (see Bogue et al. 1993, Chapters 21-22 for an accessible introduction).

Multistate Models

At any point in time, an individual occupies a state, and the distribution of people over the various states determines the population structure. State occupancies change over time as a result of (1) interstate transitions people experience—for example, from being single to being married, from being diseased to being healthy, or from being a resident of one region to being a resident of another region, and (2) differential entries from and exits to the rest of the world. The multistate life table describes how the size and composition of a (synthetic) cohort change over time. Multistate projection models describe how the population structure (stock) at a given time depends on the initial population and the transitions people make (flows).

The dynamics of a multistate population—a cohort or an age-graded population—are based on transition rates and transition probabilities. Rates relate the number of transitions people make to the *duration* at risk of a transition. Probabilities relate transitions to the *population* at risk at the beginning of an interval.

Transition rates and transition probabilities are estimated from the data. The estimation of probabilities directly from the data is complicated in the presence of censoring (i.e., if individuals enter or leave the population during the period of observation for a reason unrelated to the transitions being studied). In survival analysis, the concept of *risk set* has been introduced to distinguish the population at risk of experiencing an event during an interval from the population present at the beginning of that interval. The estimation of rates does not present that problem since the transitions are related to the time spent in the origin state during the interval. In this approach, people may enter and/or leave a state during an interval. Transition rates must be converted into probabilities. The task is straightforward if the rates vary between age intervals but not within age intervals, or when the transitions that occur during an interval are uniformly distributed.

Applications

Early applications considered populations stratified by age and region of residence. The life table was used to estimate the regional distribution of members of a synthetic cohort and the number of years spent in the different regions. For example, using data from the 1980 census and vital statistics, Rogers (1995, p. 91) found that a person born in New York and subjected to migration and mortality patterns of the late 1970s, may expect to live 74 years, of which 18 years are in the South including 3 years in Florida. The period in the South is concentrated at higher ages. The life table also gives the number of migrations cohort members may experience in a lifetime. Rogers and Frans Willekens (1986) present multiregional life tables for several countries. Multiregional population projections are used widely because regional populations change more in response to migration than to fertility or mortality. A multiregional model is the only one that considers migration by origin and destination.

Another popular area of application is family and household demography. The life table produces indicators such as the probability that a marriage ends in a divorce, the mean age at divorce, the expected duration of marriage at divorce, and the expected number of divorces in a lifetime. It also reports the probability that a married woman at a given age, 32 (for example), will experience a divorce within 10 years and the probability that she will be divorced at age 60 (for example). The multistate life tables follow women and men through their marital careers. The text *Family Demography* (1987), edited by John Bongaarts, Thomas Burch, and Kenneth

Wachter, which includes descriptions of the marital careers of American women, children's experiences with different types of families, and the family types generated over the life course of a cohort, has stimulated the development and application of multistate models. Multistate projection models allow researchers to move beyond the widely used headship rate method and to consider changes in the number and types of families and households in terms of the demographic events people experience and the transitions they make to new family or household types.

Epidemiology and public health are other important areas of application of the multistate models. The state space distinguishes states of health and may consider specific diseases, impairments, disability or handicaps. The life table estimates the probability that a person of a given age develops a disease over a period of 5 years, 10 years, or a lifetime, and adds the probability of recovery if data permit. It also yields estimates of expected duration of the disease. Kenneth Manton and Eric Stallard (1988) developed multistate life tables for chronic diseases. Historically, multistate models have been applied and further developed in epidemiology and public health, in particular to assess the length of healthy life and the effect of risk factors on morbidity and mortality. A review by D. Commenges (1999) reveals, however, that many studies using multistate models do not stratify the population by age and do not use a multistate life table. Commenges concludes that "the strong effect of age is not very well taken into account" (1999, p. 332). The situation is changing, however, age is becoming a significant time scale in epidemiology and is leading to the new subfield of life-course epidemiology. A paper on the cardiovascular life course by Anna Peeters and others (2002) illustrates how the multistate life table may be used to describe a particular disease history of a cohort and how the life table may be used to improve the estimates of lifetime risk of the disease and years with the disease attributable to risk factors.

As the area of application is extending into new fields of research, the multistate life table is developing into a technique that moves beyond the description of a (synthetic) cohort into a method that accounts for intra-cohort variation. Two developments are currently under way. The first considers the effect of covariates on transition rates and probabilities. The multistate life table with covariates generalizes the semiparametric Cox model and parametric duration models to multiple and transient states. This change is a movement toward the construction of synthetic individual biographies rather than cohort biographies. That action requires techniques of microsimulation to produce samples of individual life histories on the computer that are consistent with the empirical evidence on life histories. The second development results in probabilistic multistate life tables that account for the effects of sampling variation. The most modern procedure is to produce probabilistic life tables using bootstrapping.

The prediction of individual life histories combining data on the individual and on people with similar characteristics, and accounting for the uncertainties involved, may initiate a new era in which the multistate life table becomes an instrument for life planning and contingency analysis.

See also: *Event-History Analysis; Life Tables; Migration Models; Renewal Theory and the Stable Population Model; Stochastic Population Theory.*

BIBLIOGRAPHY

Bogue, Donald J., Eduardo E. Arriaga, and Douglas L. Anderton, eds. 1993. *Readings in Population Research Methodology.* Chapter 21: "Survival and Event History Methods"; Chapter 22: "Multistate Methods." Chicago: Published for the United Nations Population Fund by Social Development Center.

Bongaarts, J., T. Burch, and K. Wachter, eds. 1987. *Family Demography.* Oxford: Clarendon Press.

Commenges, D. 1999. "Multi-state Models in Epidemiology." *Lifetime Data Analysis* 5: 315–327.

Hannan, Michael T. 1984. "Multistate Demography and Event History Analysis." In *Stochastic Modeling of Social Processes,* ed. A. Diekmann and P. Mitter. Orlando, FL: Academic Press.

Hoem, Jan M., and U. F. Jensen. 1982. "Multistate Life Table Methodology: A Probabilist Critique." In *Multidimensional Mathematical Demography,* ed. K. C. Land and A. Rogers. New York: Academic Press.

Manton, K. G., and E. Stallard. 1988. *Chronic Disease Modelling: Measurement and Evaluation of the Risks of Chronic Disease Processes.* London: Charles Griffin.

Peeters, A., A. A. Mamun, F. Willenkens, and L. Bonneux. 2002. "A Cardiovascular Life History:

A Life Course Analysis of the Original Framingham Heart Study Cohort." *European Heart Journal* 23: 458–466.

Rees, Philip, and A. Wilson. 1977. *Spatial Population Analysis.* London: Edward Arnold.

Rogers, Andrei. 1975. *Introduction to Multiregional Mathematical Demography.* New York: Wiley.

———. 1995. *Multiregional Demography: Principles, Methods, and Extensions.* New York: Wiley.

Rogers, Andrei, and F. Willekens, eds. 1986. *Migration and Settlement: A Multiregional Comparative Study.* Dordrecht, Netherlands: Reidel.

Schoen, Robert. 1975. "Constructing Increment-Decrement Life Tables." *Demography* 12: 313–324.

———. 1988. *Modeling Multigroup Populations.* New York: Plenum Press.

FRANS WILLEKENS

N

NATIONAL SECURITY AND POPULATION

National security issues can be defined narrowly as immediate threats of violence to a society—terrorism, war, revolution, ethnic/religious/regional conflicts. National security issues can also be defined more broadly to include diffuse and non-violent threats to the well-being of a society, such as damage to the environment, problems of disease and public health, and reductions in present or future economic welfare. Demography is relevant to both kinds of national security. Under certain conditions, as Myron Weiner and Sharon Stanton Russell (2001) have shown, demographic changes can increase both the risks of violence, and the degree of diffuse and non-violent threats to well-being.

Demographic Variables and National Security

Scholars such as Thomas Homer-Dixon and Jessica Blitt (1998) have pointed to a number of demographic variables as relevant to issues of national security. These include the size and density of a country's population and its rate of growth; the proportion of population that is urban and the urban growth rate; the age structure of the population; the rates of internal and international migration; the internal composition of the population with regard to ethnicity, regional identity, or religion; the rates of social mobility, literacy, and education; infant mortality and life expectancy; and the distribution of income.

However, few of these variables have simple, uniform effects on national security across time and space. To understand their impact requires careful examination of how they interact with, or exacerbate, other factors leading to violent conflict or diffuse harm.

Violent Environmental and Demographic Security Threats

Because populations must exist in a physical space, from which they draw the resources to survive and reproduce, the effects of demographic structure and change in any population are inextricably bound up with the conditions of the environment, particularly the flows and stocks of renewable and non-renewable resources available either within the national boundaries of the population in question or through exchanges with other populations. Changes in population that affect the ratios of population (or population segments) to key resources generally have impacts on national security, as do changes in key resources on which the population (or population segments) depends. The term "environmental and demographic security threats" recognizes this intertwining.

Violent environmental and demographic security threats (VEDS) arise when the relationship between a population (or populations) and its environment increases the risks of war, revolution, terrorism, and ethnic or other violent conflicts. A number of demographic variables seem to be correlated with such conflicts. Countries with larger and denser populations appear to have more civil conflicts and greater involvement in international wars. In addition, the proportion of men aged 15 to 24 in the total population aged 15 and above correlates with the frequency and magnitude of war conflicts. Countries with higher rates of infant mortality also appear to have a higher rate of revolutions and ethnic/religious/regional conflicts.

However, many of these relationships are simple correlations—that is, there is a relationship between demographic conditions and violence, but that relationship could be due to other combinations of factors than simply population characteristics. For example, if some of the world's most populous countries (e.g., China, India, Indonesia, Nigeria, Pakistan) are also very poor, and poor countries have more conflict, then cross-national studies would show a correlation between population size and conflict, even though that relationship may actually be due to another causal relationship. To test such relationships, political scientists have subjected VEDS issues to multivariate analysis.

So far, multivariate studies such as those by Nils Petter Gleditsch (1998) and by Wenche Hauge and Tanja Ellingsen (1998) have tended to undermine most of the claims made for the importance of VEDS threats. Population pressure on resources does *not*, in general, lead to war or other violent conflicts. For example, one of the most obvious needs of populations is for fresh water, and there are many areas in the world where large populations in arid or semi-arid regions seem poised to clash over control of river basins. Yet as Aaron Wolf (1999) has pointed out, examining numerous cases of potential water-related conflicts, wars over water have almost never occurred. Rather, countries find it preferable to negotiate water rights rather than engage in costly military strife, simply because the costs of water conservation and negotiated agreement are almost always far less than the costs of armed conflict.

In addition, population size, density, growth rates, and age-structure have been shown in some studies, such as that of Jack Goldstone and colleagues (2000), to have no effect on the risks of violent internal conflicts when one controls for such other factors as regime type, involvement in international trade, and the presence of conflicts in neighboring countries. Such studies have shown that whether or not conflicts have "pass[ed] the threshold of violence definitely depends on *sociopolitical* factors and not on the degree of environmental degradation as such" (Baechler 1998, p. 32; emphasis in original).

Thus, there are no simple and direct effects of population characteristics on violence. Nonetheless, under certain conditions, demographic considerations do affect violence. This depends on the degree to which political elites use demographic factors as a basis for mobilizing populations for conflict.

Political violence is rarely a simple response to poverty or religious or ethnic differences. Such violence is the result of the inability of government institutions to diffuse and channel conflicts into constructive efforts for change, and more specifically the result of a choice by elites to mobilize populations or particular groups for organized violence against others. Where demographic factors produce violence, it is through their impact on state capacity, and on elite interests and choices. The demographic and political characteristics and the related material interest of elites are important elements in conflict, as are conditions that affect the opportunities for elites to mobilize followers for violence.

The ability of the state to manage growing populations is a key factor. Where a country's population grows faster than the government's revenues, administration and welfare provision become increasingly difficult. Criticism of the state is likely to mount along with state debts, and elites are more prone to oppose a decaying government. Among elites, if their numbers are growing rapidly relative to the growth of the economy, and hence of jobs suitable for elites, they are more likely to become polarized and initiate violent conflicts over control of the government and resources. In addition, where elites are drawn from all major ethnic or religious groups in a society, there seems to be less violence. However, where elites are concentrated in one dominant ethnic or religious grouping that excludes and discriminates against other groups, violent conflict is a greater risk. Finally, countries with greater material deprivation (as indicated by higher rates of infant mortality, or scarcity of land or jobs for peasants and workers) often have large populations that can readily be tempted by elite promises of better material conditions in return for enlisting in campaigns of violence. This is especially true in societies with larger proportions of urban population, and of young men, as such societies have potentially more people who are concentrated and easily mobilized for group violence. Goldstone (1991) has shown how these effects contributed to numerous rebellions and revolutions throughout history, including the English and French Revolutions, and the Taiping Rebellion in China.

Because certain demographic conditions can create opportunities favorable for elites to mobilize populations for violence, researchers examining particular cases of conflict often find demographic preconditions such as rapid population increase, high rates of urban growth, and large youth cohorts. However, this does not mean that *in general* such conditions conduce to violence. Rather, population growth can lead to violence where state revenues, economic growth, and the expansion of elite positions fall behind the demands created by population increase. Countries with fiscally sound governments, strong economic growth, and stable elites can avoid violent conflicts regardless of demographic conditions.

It is also notable that several of the demographic conditions often associated with violence—mass migrations, poverty, and religious/ethnic concentrations—are more often the *result* of violent conflicts than their cause.

Non-violent Environmental and Demographic Security Threats

In contrast to violence, the range of non-violent environmental and demographic security (NEDS) threats is widespread; but doubts about the severity of these problems remains high. Damage to the atmosphere—mainly in regard to ozone destruction and global warming—has led to extensive international negotiations and treaties, although thus far these have only been effective with regard to controlling ozone depletion. Debates on the magnitude of the threat to global well-being from climate changes due to human activity continue to hamper political agreements. Other areas of international conflict and negotiations over environmental and demographic threats noted by Goldstone (2001) include concerns over the extinction of species; loss of tropical and temperate forests; the generation of acid rain or particulates; over-fishing of oceans or estuaries that depletes fish stocks; the spread of harmful biological agents, such as pathogens or perhaps undesirable genetic elements from genetically-modified biota; and environmental damage to agrarian regions or other population/resource imbalances that lead to large and unexpected international migrations.

All of these NEDS threats are affected by changes in the size, density and geographic distribution of populations. In particular, larger populations, dispersed over larger areas, generally increase their use of energy for production and transportation, and destroy habitat and spread pathogens.

Population changes thus tend to increase NEDS threats if their consequences are not appropriately controlled.

However, control of such threats is often difficult because actions and events in one country can create NEDS threats in others. Acid rain and particulates are carried thousands of kilometers by high altitude winds; over-fishing affects all countries that exploit a given fishery; carbon emissions or forest destruction affect global and not just local atmospheric and weather conditions. Efforts to deal with NEDS threats often stumble on the need to build complex international agreements that meet the needs of countries at vastly different levels of economic development and with very different degrees of responsibility for the creation of such threats.

In sum, the relationships between demographic variables and national security are varied and complex. Simple and direct relationships are absent; rather, contingent and indirect relationships dominate. In the area of VEDS threats, demographic conditions generally facilitate, rather than cause, political violence, creating more or less fertile ground for elites to mobilize groups for violent action. Yet elite conditions and motivations, and the political institutions that regulate elite interaction, are the key factors that determine whether violence will arise. For the more diffuse NEDS threats, dealing with the impact of population growth and dispersion seems critical. However, political factors again are key, for the international agreements that seem necessary to regulate NEDS threats have been difficult to achieve, given the varied goals and prospects of different countries.

See also: *Ethnic Cleansing; Forced Migration; Geopolitics; Lebensraum; Refugees, Demography of; War, Demographic Consequences of.*

BIBLIOGRAPHY

Baechler, Günther. 1998. "Why Environmental Transformation Causes Violence: A Synthesis." *Environmental Change and Security Project Report of the Woodrow Wilson Center* 4: 24–44.

Gleditsch, Nils Petter. 1998. "Armed Conflict and the Environment." *Journal of Peace Research* 35: 381–400.

Goldstone, Jack A. 1991. *Revolution and Rebellion in the Early Modern World.* Berkeley: University of California Press.

———. 2001. "Demography, Environment, and Security." In *Environmental Security,* ed. Paul Diehl and Nils Petter Gleditsch. Boulder, CO: Westview Press.

Goldstone, Jack A., Ted Robert Gurr, Barbara Harff, Monty Marshall, Robert Bates, Tom Parris, Colin Kahl, and Marc Levy. 2000. *State Failure Task Force Report: Phase III Findings.* McLean, VA: Science Applications International Corporation.

Hauge, Wenche, and Tanja Ellingsen. 1998. "Causal Pathways to Conflict." *Journal of Peace Research* 35: 299–317.

Homer-Dixon, Thomas, and Jessica Blitt. 1998. *Ecoviolence: Links Among Environment, Population, and Security.* Lanham, MD: Rowman & Littlefield.

Weiner, Myron, and Sharon Stanton Russell. 2001. *Demography and Security.* Oxford: Berghahn Books.

Wolf, Aaron T. 1999. "'Water Wars' and Water Reality." In *Environmental Change, Adaptation, and Human Security,* ed. Steve Lonergan. Dordrecht, Netherlands: Kluwer.

JACK A. GOLDSTONE

NATURAL FERTILITY

The concept of natural fertility was first defined by the French demographer Louis Henry (1911–1991) in the 1953 study, "Fondements théoriques des mesures de la fécondité naturelle," to refer to the fertility of a population not practicing any form of birth control. In 1961, he gave a more precise definition in two papers. In "Some Data on Natural Fertility," published in *Eugenics Quarterly,* and frequently quoted, Henry stated clearly that he preferred the qualifier *natural* to *physiological* or *biological* because "social factors may also play a part—sexual taboos, for example, during lactation" (Henry 1961, p. 81). He also suggested a simple means for separating controlled fertility from natural fertility: "control can be said to exist when the behavior of a couple [at a given age or marriage duration] is bound to the number of children already born and is modified when this number reaches the maximum which the couple does not want to exceed" (p. 81).

The role of marriage—a typical non-biological variable—was implicit in this definition because Henry was in fact interested in marital fertility: Out-of-wedlock births were rare in the France of the *ancien régime* (the fifteenth through eighteenth centuries). Even with this restriction, the levels of natural fertility that he found exhibited a wide range, varying by a factor of two. The highest recorded total fertility in a population is around ten children per woman; but in some parts of seventeeth-century France fertility—also taken to be natural—was below five children per woman. This variation is due to both behavioral factors (age of marriage, sexual behavior, duration of breastfeeding) and biological factors (fecundability, the post-partum non-susceptible period, the rate of fetal wastage—which vary both among individuals and among populations). It has been estimated that a woman who is continuously in a sexual union between the ages of 15 and 50 years, not breastfeeding her children, and not practicing any form of birth control, would bear 15 children on average.

Although age-specific marital fertility rates may vary among natural-fertility populations, the age profile of these rates is characteristic. This property has been used to develop models of fertility (for example, the Coale-Trussell model) which, fitted to the observed fertility schedule from any given population, can give an indication of how far the observed rates are from the standard profile, and thus how far fertility in that population is from a natural regime. The widely-used decomposition of fertility into its proximate determinants, the framework developed by John Bongaarts, also owes much to the scheme developed by Henry.

The concept of natural fertility is explicitly based on the absence of attempts by couples to *limit* the number of their children, not on the absence of efforts to *space* them. Strictly speaking, spacing behavior that was independent of the number of children born could not be detected. It is however, very unlikely that a population would develop an effective form of spacing behavior that was independent of any limiting intentions. Breastfeeding could be construed to be such a practice. However, its primary aim is to help the child survive and grow; it is impossible to separate this purpose from a possible attempt by the mother to space her births as a way of controlling their final number.

See also: *Fecundity; Fertility, Proximate Determinants of; Fertility Control, Indirect Measurement of; Henry, Louis.*

BIBLIOGRAPHY

Coale, Ansley J., and James Trussell. 1974. "Model Fertility Schedules: Variations in the Age-Structure of Childbearing in Human Populations." *Population Index* 40(2): 185–258.

Henry, Louis. 1953. "Fondements théoriques des mesures de la fécondité naturelle." *Revue IIS* 21(3): 135–151.

———. 1961. "Some Data on Natural Fertility." *Eugenics Quarterly* 8(2): 81–91.

Leridon, Henri. 1989. "Fécondité naturelle et espacement des naissances."*Annales de démographie historique 1988*, pp. 21–34.

Leridon, Henri, and Jane Menken, eds. 1979. *Natural Fertility/Fécondité Naturelle.* Liège, Belgium: Ordina.

HENRI LERIDON

NATURAL RESOURCES AND POPULATION

Human survival in places with clement climate requires only a constant supply of oxygen and drinkable water and digestible food; no more was available to human's earliest hominin ancestors. Subsequent evolutionary processes, marked by extraordinary increase of brain capacity and resulting in the worldwide radiation of human species, extended the human need for natural resources to phytomass and zoomass (poles, branches, leaves, fibers, skin, sinews, furs, bones) used to construct simple shelters, clothes, and tools. Transition from migratory foraging to sedentary existence based on permanent agriculture expanded the requirements to a much greater variety of resources that were increasingly subjected to some kind of processing—relatively simple milling and fermenting of grains, more complicated firing of clays to produce bricks and ceramics, or elaborate smelting and forging of a growing array of metals.

Acquisition and Use of Resources

This trend of widening resource acquisition and more sophisticated processing has been accelerating since the mid-nineteenth century. It has become difficult to think about any part of the Earth's natural capital that is not either already exploited or seen as a potentially useful input into some process or service. And human ingenuity keeps creating new resources even from the oldest and simplest materials. Sand (silica dioxide) got its first upgrade more than 2 millennia ago when the Roman engineers began using it to make concrete. The second, unheralded, elevation of sand came in 1918 when Jan Czochralski discovered how to grow large silicon crystals. Half a century later his process was deployed on an industrial scale to produce thin semiconductor wafers for photovoltaic cells that power satellites and that may, within a few generations, produce a large share of electricity.

Determining the Magnitude of Resource Bases

Resource base is the totality of a commodity present in the biosphere and in the Earth's crust. Although this changes naturally only over long periods of evolution, measuring it is seldom easy. Resource base quantification is relatively straightforward only for such entities as the total volume of surface water, the area of potentially arable land, or the aggregate volume of wood in a particular forest biome. In contrast, it is very difficult to measure not just minerals in the Earth's crust but also such diffuse and mobile living resources as ocean fish and marine mammals. Not surprisingly, these uncertainties lead to recurrent disputes about the ultimate amounts of globally recoverable fossil fuels and ores (engendering periodic "running out" scares) and make the management of ocean fisheries or conservation of endangered marine mammals a matter of continuing controversy (American estimates of whale numbers are much below Japanese estimates).

Renewable and Nonrenewable Resources

Moreover, the distinction between renewable and nonrenewable resources is not as clear as it may seem at first. Clearcutting of forests on steep slopes, overgrazing of pastures, and improper agronomic procedures are among common malpractices that open the way for excessive soil erosion, loss of organic matter and plant nutrients, decline in soil's moisture-storing capacity, and, in arid areas, an often irreversible desertification. These environmental changes may make it impossible to restore the forest or to sustain highly productive grazing and crop cultivation. Similarly, excessive withdrawals of surface water for irrigation and industrial and urban uses can eliminate (entirely or seasonally) previously copious river flows; neither the Colorado River nor the Huanghe (Yellow River) now reach, respectively, Baja California and Bohai Bay for most of the year. They can also deplete aquifers—such as the great Ogallalla reservoir that underlies the croplands of the Great Plains or the huge aquifers under the Saudi Arabian sands whose water irrigates wheat in the midst of a desert—at rates far exceeding the pace of their slow natural recharge.

Historical Debates on Resource Scarcity

Concerns about the balance between human numbers and natural resources have exisited ever since the beginning of modern industrial expansion when, in 1798, they were eloquently formulated by T. R. Malthus (1766–1834) in the first edition of his *An Essay on the Principle of Population.* Malthus's pessimistic conclusions—that "the power of population is indefinitely greater than the power in the earth to produce subsistence for man" and that "this natural inequality . . . appears insurmountable in the way to the perfectability of society"—have been surely among the most cited sentences of the nineteenth and twentieth centuries. In the second (1803) and subsequent editions of the essay, however, Malthus was more sanguine. In fact, the true Malthusian bequest is not a message of despair but a judicious mixture of understandable concern about the human future and confident hope for progressive solutions, a judgement that continues to be vindicated by gradual improvements of the human condition.

The economist David Ricardo (1772–1823) raised another concern regarding agricultural resources in *The Principles of Political Economy and Taxation,* published in 1817. He argued that the new land brought into cultivation as population grows will be steadily less fertile, and thus its produce increasingly costly. Within a few generations these worries had receded, thanks to the unprecedented availability of extrasomatic energies. Massive flows of fuels and electricity that are used to produce and to power the field and processing machinery and to synthesize agricultural chemicals have virtually eliminated hard physical labor in modern food production and turned the farmers in affluent countries into mere controllers of inanimate energy flows. The same process is underway in all rapidly modernizing low-income countries.

A third kind of worry was about running out of mineral resources. In 1865 William Stanley Jevons (1835–1882), one of the leading economists of the Victorian era, published *The Coal Question,* in which he rightly connected the rise of British power with the widespread use of coal converted to the mechanical energy of steam but wrongly concluded that coal's exhaustion must spell an inevitable demise of national greatness. In forecasting coal demand he made the two perennial errors of long-range forecasting by vastly exaggerating future demand for the fuel and grossly underestimating human inventiveness. After examining all supposed substitutes for coal (wind, water, tides, atmospheric electricity, peat, and petroleum) he concluded that it is "of course . . . useless to think of substituting any other kind of fuel for coal" and that future advances in science "will tend to increase the supremacy of steam and coal."

As it turned out, his worries were groundless. During the first years of the twenty-first century, rapidly dwindling numbers of British miners are extracting less coal every year than does Colombia or Turkey, not because the United Kingdom has no coal left (its remaining reserves are a hefty 1.5 billion tons), but because the country has little need for it as it has become the world's ninth largest producer of crude oil and the fourth largest producer of natural gas and a substantial exporter of both of these hydrocarbons.

Future Resource Supplies

But these realities do not mean that concerns about the scarcity of natural resources and about their role in economic growth have disappeared; they receded during the last decades of the nineteenth and during the first half of the twentieth century, but its second half was punctuated by flare-ups of such worries even as the costs of all basic commodities were steadily declining or, at worst, remained fairly stable. These apprehensions ranged from the 1952 warning by the Paley Commission that the United States does not have all of the material resources necessary for its development to the latest round of predictions about an imminent peak (before 2010) of global oil extraction and the subsequent inexorable decline of world oil supplies. Most famously, in 1973 the modeling study *Limits to Growth* predicted that, according to its "standard" world model run, the global economy and the Earth's population will collapse "because of nonrenewable resource depletion" and an unbearable spike in environmental degradation well before the end of the twenty-first century.

New discoveries, resource substitutions, technical innovation, economic adjustments, and extensive global trade in relatively scarce commodities have repeatedly turned these catastrophically framed scenarios into yet another set of failed forecasts. Britain's experience is an excellent example of a universal trend of resource substitutions evident not only in transitions to new sources of energy (the post-1850 sequence being wood, coal, crude oil, natural gas, new renewables) but also in shifts in using structural materials (in machine construction: wood, iron, steel, aluminum, composites; in buildings: wood and stone, bricks, concrete, steel and glass) or in the ways people communicate across long distances (running messengers, horse riders, wired telegraphy, wireless broadcasting). The last sequence is a perfect example of dematerialization, a broad civilizational trend toward using smaller specific amounts of resources.

Evidence of this admirable trend is everywhere, whether measured in macroeconomic terms (e.g., consumption of primary energy or basic metals per unit of GDP) or expressed as resource needs for particular products or services (engine mass/installed automobile power; gasoline consumed/distance; irrigation water or nitrogen fertilizer per unit of crop yield). And in some instances the need for a particular resource has entirely disappeared; reserves of copper ore deposits and the price of the metal used to be a recurrent worry for a society depending on highly conductive wires—but they are of little concern for cellular telephony, satellite TV, and the Internet. Innovative substitutions have not been the only means of dematerialization and of allaying concerns about the exhaustion of mineral resources: higher efficiencies of resource use and increasing rates of recycling have extended the available supplies and helped to lower the cost of virtually every mineral resource.

As a result, and in spite of growing populations and advancing economies, national and global consumption of some key resources has actually declined in absolute terms. Perhaps the most surprising example in this category has been the decline in water withdrawals in the United States; between 1980 and 1995 the U.S. GDP expanded by nearly 55 percent (in real terms) while the country's total water use fell by 10 percent. However, for many resources, from aluminium to urea, the trend of relative dematerialization has been going hand in hand with increasing rates of absolute consumption.

Even so, there have been hardly any exceptions to the long-term secular decline of inflation-adjusted commodity prices. No insurmountable shortages of nonrenewable resources are foreseen during the twenty-first century, which should be marked by the necessarily slow but epochal transition to renewable sources of energy and by a slow shift toward many bioengineered materials.

The main resource challenges of the twenty-first century will be concerned with environmental impacts of resource use rather than with resource availability. The most intractable global concern is the loss of those natural resources that are critical for maintaining irreplaceable environmental services. Destruction of tropical and marine biodiversity and large-scale transformation of remaining natural ecosystems due to human interference in grand biospheric cycles are high on this list of worries. Combustion of fossil fuels and deforestation alter the global carbon cycle; applications of nitrogen fertilizers and emissions of nitrogen oxides from combustion introduce large amounts of reactive nitrogen into the biosphere; sulfur, and nitrogen, oxides are the principal cause of acidifying deposition. A dire but conceivable environmental scenario would have the biosphere experiencing more pronounced and faster global warming than at any time during the last 1 million years.

Regional Resource Scarcities

There are justifiable local and regional concerns about the future availability of some key resources. The most acute of these is the availability of water in some 40 arid African and Asian countries extending from Mali to Iran. As with nearly every other perceived resource scarcity, a large part of the solution to water shortages lies not in tapping new sources but in reducing considerable waste (caused by low and subsidized prices and by poor efficiencies of water use due to improper irrigation, outdated industrial processes, and leaky urban distribution) and by deploying available techniques that allow for virtually perfect water recycling.

Another effective solution to these local and national resource scarcities is through trade based on comparative advantage. As production of a kilogram of grain needs more than 1000 kilograms of water, rainy and fertile places have an obvious comparative advantage in grain production. In a rational world there would be no wheat produced in Saudi Arabia, nor any alfalfa in California. Unfortunately, extensive government subsidies (amounting globally to more than $1 billion per day for agricultural production alone) lead to an enormous misallocation and waste of resources. Even a very conservative appraisal of the world's natural resources cannot find any reasons why they could not support dignified life for a population that may be finally approaching the global plateau and that may avoid yet another doubling. But given the naturally uneven geographic distribution of every major resource it would be impossible to achieve that goal through national and regional autarky.

Cornucopians and Catastrophists

Cornucopian dismissal of any concerns about the quantity and quality of the world's natural resources derives from the record of indisputably admirable innovation, technical fixes and socioeconomic adjustments that have been able, so far, to prove all modern Cassandras wrong. Indicators that matter point in the right direction as resources have been able to support a higher quality of life for larger populations: infant mortality is down, life expectancy, income, and schooling rates are up. In contrast, catastrophists see the emerging scarcities of some natural resources, and equally indisputable examples of worldwide environmental change and degradation, as harbingers of worse things to come. Some important indicators that matter point in the wrong direction: the Earth's biodiversity is declining, simplification and homogenization of ecosystems is progressing, and the signs that the biosphere is in trouble can be found anywhere from the rapidly rising incidence of childhood asthma to the fact that the 1990s were the warmest decade since the beginning of instrumental records.

Both the cornucopians and the catastrophists are right—and they are both wrong. The historical record is both inspiring and discouraging; the future looks very promising but also quite perilous. The civilization of the early twenty-first century would not be the first whose mismanagement of resources (as opposed to their actual availability) would be the cause of its decline or even of its demise. But our innovative drive, our technical prowess, and our understanding of how the biosphere works gives us the capacity to avoid that fate. The outcome is not preordained one way or the other but will be determined by our choices.

See also: *Carrying Capacity; Deforestation; Ecological Perspectives on Population; Energy and Population; Food Supply and Population; Land Use; Limits to Growth; Sustainable Development; Water and Population.*

BIBLIOGRAPHY

Coyne, Mark S., and Craig W. Allin, eds. 1998. *Natural Resources.* Pasadena, CA: Salem Press.

Dahlberg, Kenneth A., and John W. Bennett, eds. 1986. *Natural Resources and People: Conceptual Issues in Interdisciplinary Research.* Boulder, CO: Westview.

McLaren, Digby J., and Brian J. Skinner, eds. 1987. *Resources and World Development.* Chichester, Eng.: Wiley.

Simon, Julian L., ed. 1995. *The State of Humanity.* Oxford: Blackwell.

Smil, Vaclav. 1994. *Global Ecology.* London: Routledge.

———. 2002. *The Earth's Biosphere: Evolution, Dynamics, and Change.* Cambridge, MA: MIT Press.

Vaclav Smil

NITROGEN CYCLE

Only three elements cycled through the biosphere form stable compounds that can be transported both in water and air: carbon, sulfur, and nitrogen (N). The N cycle is peculiar, not only because the element's largest biospheric reservoir (nitrogen gas, N_2, in the atmosphere) exists in an unreactive form, but also because it is largely mediated by bacterial metabolism. A small number of bacterial species are the only organisms that can fix N—that is, convert it from inert N_2 to reactive ammonia (NH_3). Bacteria also convert NH_3 to soluble nitrates (nitrification), which are the main source of the nutrient for plants; decompose organic matter (ammonification); and close the N cycle by reducing nitrates back into N_2 (denitrification). N, together with phosphorus and potassium, is one of the three plant macronutrients and its shortages were the most common cause of low crop yields in all pre-industrial agricultures. N is also a key constituent of amino acids, the building blocks of proteins, adequate intake of which is essential for human growth and health.

Traditional farmers could supply the nutrient by either recycling organic materials (crop residues, manures, human waste) or by planting leguminous crops, which contain symbiotic *Rhizobium* bacteria, and can break down the inert atmospheric N_2 and synthesize reactive ammonia, NH_3. However, even the most assiduous recycling of organic wastes and the highest practicable planting of legumes in climates that allow year-round cultivation would result in crop yields that could support no more than five or six persons per hectare on an almost totally vegetarian diet. Guano and Chilean nitrate, commercially introduced after 1840, offered only a limited expansion of supply of reactive N.

The barrier to agricultural productivity growth, and hence to population carrying capacity, imposed by limits on the availability of nitrogen was broken by German chemist Fritz Haber's discovery of the synthesis of NH_3 from its elements (in 1909) and its speedy conversion to a large-scale industrial process by the BASF (Badische Anilin & Soda Fabrik) chemical company under the leadership of German industrial chemist Carl Bosch (in 1913). Thereafter, production of synthetic nitrogenous fertilizer became a major worldwide industry. Widespread use of N fertilizer accelerated after the mid-1960s with the introduction of new high-yield varieties of wheat and rice. American agronomist Norman Borlaug, one of the key architects of this Green Revolution, concluded that N fertilizer was responsible for its forward movement.

In the early twenty-first century, nearly 90 million tons of nitrogen are applied to crops each year, mostly to cereals and other annuals. In affluent nations, these applications help to produce an excess

of food in general, and of animal foods in particular, and they boost agricultural exports. At least one-third of the world's population is alive at the beginning of the twenty-first century because of the additional food produced by application of N fertilizers—the nitrogen in the world's population dietary proteins comes from inorganic fertilizers. Moreover, given the balance of population numbers and cultivable land, and disregarding food imports from other countries, most of the anticipated future population growth in Asia could not take place without proteins synthesized by using N from urea, the world's leading N fertilizer.

The rising dependence on inorganic N represents the most pronounced human interference in the biospheric N cycle. More than half of all N fertilizer leaches into waters, volatilizes as NH_3, or is denitrified before it can be assimilated by plants. Environmental consequences of these losses include eutrophication of both aquatic and terrestrial ecosystems, contamination of waters with nitrates, and generation of nitrous oxide, a potent greenhouse gas, from imperfect denitrification. These effects can be reduced by adopting appropriate agronomic practices, as well as by more efficient feeding of animals, proper treatment of urban sewage, and reduction of the intake of animal foods.

See also: *Food Supply and Population; Land Use; Sustainable Development.*

BIBLIOGRAPHY

Smil, Vaclav. 2000. *Cycles of Life.* New York: Scientific American Library.

VACLAV SMIL

NOMADS

Nomads are people who move in order to survive. True nomads have mobile housing and no settlements, although many mobile populations group together for parts of the year and many have some form of fixed settlement. There are three main types of nomads: hunter-gatherers, livestock herders, and travelers (Roma, or gypsies). Few demographic data are available for any of these groups for a variety of reasons: They are often despised minorities, their mobility hinders demographic data collection, they usually live in low-density remote areas, and they frequently refuse to provide information.

Nomads are found throughout the Old World. It is impossible to quantify their numbers past or present, although these populations probably decreased substantially throughout the twentieth century as a result of forced (e.g., Iran, Mongolia, China) or voluntary (Middle East, Africa) sedentarization. Many nomads still live in central Asia and Africa, with a few reindeer herders living above the Arctic circle and a few Bedouin residing in the Middle East.

Pastoral nomadism, whatever the animal species kept, is highly specialized and, at least in more recent decades, usually exploits environments that are unsuitable for agriculture. However, all pastoralist populations depend substantially on mutual exchanges with agricultural and urban communities, and the boundaries between them are often blurred; this hinders the study of the demography of nomads. People and communities may slip in and out of nomadic lifestyles, depending on particular political, economic, or climatic situations.

African Pastoral Nomads

This article focuses on African pastoral nomads, the only populations for which reasonable demographic data are available. African pastoralists move throughout the year, as the essential resources required for their herds fluctuate over time and space. A range of theories have been developed about the demography of African pastoral nomads, and this may explain the relative wealth of data on them.

Colonial administrators were interested in the demography of their subject populations as sources of labor and for purposes of taxation. That colonial understanding of nomad demography continues to influence perceptions of nomads' demographic behavior. Nomads were thought to have low fertility, high mortality, and often a high prevalence of sexually transmitted diseases. These ideas were rarely based on reliable data and reflected a mistrust of these populations, with their uncontrollable mobile lifestyle. The belief that nomads had low fertility probably was a result of colonial administrators' inability to find and count mobile people; however, the perception of low nomad fertility and relatively low population growth rates persists today.

Traditional pastoral nomads have decreased in number over recent decades, although mobility remains an integral part of survival strategies for many groups. The nomadic proportion of the population has declined as a consequence of sedentarization, diversification out of pastoralism, government pressure, droughts, war, and impoverishment. With the exception of Mauritania and Somalia, African pastoral nomads are national minorities and are usually both politically and spatially marginal, living far from capital cities in low-population-density environments where the provision of public services is poor. Low educational opportunities and participation have reinforced their marginalization. Largely untouched by family planning and health interventions, they represent some of the few "natural fertility" regimes left in the world.

This marginalization has repercussions for researchers understanding of their demography, as nomadic populations are frequently excluded from demographic sample surveys: Sampling frames for them are difficult to establish, and interviewing is expensive. Census data on nomads are also poor. For example, in Mali most nomads live in the northern regions of the country, which have been omitted or only fractionally covered in all principal demographic surveys since 1963. In Kenya the 1998 Demographic and Health Survey excluded the seven districts dominated by nomadic pastoralists. Demographic data for these nomadic and seminomadic pastoralist groups usually come from small community studies.

Environment and Mobility

Contemporary African nomadic pastoralists generally live in semiarid areas that are unsuitable for agricultural production and have extreme seasonal variation. This spatial peripheralization has been exacerbated in the last half of the twentieth century by population growth and expansion of agricultural areas, pushing nomadic pastoralists farther toward arid areas where extensive livestock production is the only way of exploiting the erratic rainfall.

The disease burden might be expected to be low because of low population density, fewer problems of fecal disposal, less water-borne disease (especially malaria), and population groups of insufficient size to maintain disease epidemics. That may have been the case in the past. However, because of scant investment in health, education, and transport infrastructure, most nomadic populations in the early twenty-first century are severely disadvantaged in terms of health and related services relative to countrywide averages, and this is likely to be reflected in their morbidity and mortality. Strong seasonal variation in energy balance (nutritional intake and energy expenditure) has a substantial impact on conception rates of the Turkana (Kenya) and the nutritional status of the WoDaaBe (Niger). R. A. Henin (1968) suggests that the physical demands of mobility may lead to an increased incidence of miscarriages.

Constraints of a Pastoral Economy

Unlike subsistence agriculture, pastoralism can achieve substantial economies of scale; therefore, there may be few economic benefits to having many children, although this depends on both herd composition and herding strategies. A nomadic pastoral economy has to balance human population growth with herd growth; this is difficult to achieve when animals reproduce relatively slowly and are subject to rapid fluctuations in a risky environment. Various strategies for coping with this problem have been documented: maintaining low fertility through delayed marriage and social acceptance of many divorcees and widows (Tuareg, Maure, Rendille, Baggara), although other regimes appear to maximize fertility (Turkana, Maasai); out-migration; and economic transformation and sedentarization of surplus population (Tuareg, Rendille, Turkana, Fulani, WoDaaBe, Maasai). Out-migration or economic transformation can provide immediate responses to population—resource imbalances; fertility reduction is a longer-run adjustment. Until recently some West African low-fertility pastoral nomads (Tuareg, Maures) had substantial dependent slave populations who provided labor that otherwise might have been performed by children. In subsistence crises slaves could be jettisoned.

Fertility and Mortality

Aside from the questionable colonial reports mentioned above, there is little evidence that East African nomads have low fertility. Data from 1998 for the Maasai in Kenya and Tanzania show very high levels of fertility (total fertility rates of 8.2 and 6.4, respectively). In Kenya the more nomadic pastoral Maasai had higher fertility than did the sedentary agropastoral Maasai; the opposite was true in Tanzania. Completed fertility for the Turkana, another Kenyan nomadic group, in the 1980s was around 6.6, with

substantial variation according to whether the population was going through a good (high fertility) or a poor (low fertility) climatic period. In East Africa nomadic pastoral production is relatively labor-intensive and women contribute substantially to the household economy, and there are economic advantages to men in having many wives and offspring. Among Sudanese and some West African nomadic pastoralists fertility may be lower. However, the few studies that allow a comparison of the fertility of nomadic and nonnomadic groups of the same ethnic origins show inconsistent patterns; for example, the nomadic Fulani of Burkina Faso had higher fertility (completed parity 8.0 compared to 6 to 7 in sedentary groups), whereas the Sudanese Baggara and Khawalha nomads had lower fertility than did the corresponding sedentary groups.

Nomadic pastoralists' nuptiality regimes often have a significant fertility-reducing impact. Tuareg and Maures have relatively high proportions of women who never marry and substantial numbers of widowed and divorced women at reproductive ages. In the Rendille traditional marriage system one-third of women are not permitted to marry and reproduce until all their brothers are married, a practice that is rationalized in terms of herd management and raiding but that has long-term consequences for population growth. In contrast, Maasai marriage patterns maximize the time women spend reproducing.

Comparatively little is known about nomads' mortality. Data problems are compounded by the fact that many nomadic groups, particularly Maasai and Samburu, have strong taboos against discussing dead people. Paul Rada Dyson-Hudson and Peggy Fry (1999) put together a series of estimates (direct and indirect) of child mortality in East and West African pastoral populations spanning 40 years, finding probabilities of death up to age 5 ($_5q_0$) ranging from 0.21 (for Turkana and Rendille in the 1990s) to 0.48 (FulBe in the Malian inner delta, an exceptionally unhealthy environment). In Burkina Faso overall Fulani $_5q_0$ was about 0.23 in the 1990s, but that of the more nomadic population was substantially lower than that of the sedentary. Recent studies of previously nomadic Tuareg in Mali suggest that $_5q_0$ declined substantially from about 0.35 in the 1970s to around 0.2 in the late 1990s. This variability indicates that there is not a single nomadic mortality regime but context-specific mortality, a conclusion confirmed by the existence of substantial mortality differentials by Tuareg social class.

Data are even scarcer for adult mortality. Indirect estimates from 1981–1982 data based on orphanhood proportions show extremely high adult mortality for Tuareg (Mali) men and women compared to neighboring sedentary populations but with substantial differences both within and between Tuareg groups. A later restudy (2001) of the same Tuareg population suggests little improvement in adult female mortality in the interim and an estimated lifetime risk of dying from maternal causes of one in eight.

Despite limited and low-quality data, the picture of African nomad demography is one of "natural fertility" populations in which nuptiality is the main factor constraining fertility. As would be expected in isolated populations with little formal education and limited access to health services, mortality is relatively high. The substantial variation between and within nomadic populations suggests that this is not a consequence of nomadism per se, although a contributory factor is the fact that a nomadic economy in the early twenty-first century is possible only in marginal isolated zones.

See also: *Hunter-Gatherers; Indigenous Peoples.*

BIBLIOGRAPHY

Hampshire, Kate, and Sara Randall. 2000. "Pastoralists, Agropastoralists and Cultivators: Interactions between Fertility and Mobility in Northern Burkina Faso." *Population Studies* 54(4): 247–261.

Henin, Roushdi A. 1968. "Fertility Differences in the Sudan." *Population Studies* 22(1): 147–164.

Little, Michael A., and Paul W. Leslie, eds. 1999. *Turkana Herders of the Dry Season Savanna.* Oxford: Oxford University Press.

Muhsam, H. V. 1966. *Beduin of the Negev: Eight Demographic Studies.* Jerusalem: Academic Press.

Randall, Sara. 1993. "Issues in the Demography of Mongolian Nomadic Pastoralism." *Nomadic Peoples* 33: 209–230.

Randall, Sara C. 1994. "Are Pastoralists Demographically Different from Sedentary Agriculturalists?" In *Environment and Population Change,* ed. B. Zaba and J. Clarke. Liège, Belgium: Ordina editions.

SARA RANDALL

NOTESTEIN, FRANK W.

(1902–1983)

Frank Notestein was born in Alma, Michigan, the son of the Dean of Alma College. He attended Wooster College in Ohio, graduating with a degree in economics. He received a Ph.D. in social statistics from Cornell University in 1927, where he was a student of Walter Willcox, one of America's leading demographers. After a brief stint in Europe studying occupational mortality, Notestein took a position as a research associate at the Milbank Memorial Fund in 1928. The Fund, formerly interested primarily in public health issues, was expanding its focus to general population concerns, especially fertility trends. Notestein spent his eight years at the Fund studying class differences in fertility and the role played by birth control in inducing fertility decline. He was present at the establishment of the Population Association of America in 1931, being one of its charter members. His research on birth control culminated in the publication of *Controlled Fertility* (1940), coauthored with Regine Stix, which concluded that fertility declined when the motivation to have children underwent a change. They found that an increased desire for small families stimulated the desire for more contraceptive use and better contraceptives, not the reverse.

In 1936 Frederick Osborn, convinced of the need for a formal training center in demography, persuaded Albert G. Milbank to fund the establishment of the Office of Population Research at Princeton University. Notestein became the director of this first center at a major U.S. university offering graduate training in demography. His recruitment of Irene Taeuber, Frank Lorimer, Dudley Kirk, Kingsley Davis, Ansley Coale, Wilbert Moore, John Hajnal, Robert Potter, and Charles Westoff over the early years as staff members or associates provided demography with an entree into the academy that helped establish it as an accepted academic discipline. Notestein's initial research agenda at Princeton was the study of Europe's interwar population trends, undertaken at the request of the League of Nations—later extended, at the instigation of the State Department, to Asia. In the course of projecting future European demographic trends, the Princeton demographers observed that the population dynamics of Eastern and Southern Europe were similar to those of Western and Northern Europe at an earlier time, and Notestein argued that a "vital revolution" was sweeping Europe. (Adolphe Landry had earlier used essentially the same term.) In 1945 Notestein made this revolution worldwide in his classic elaboration of transition theory, "Population: the long view." "High growth potential" populations would become "transition growth" ones as modernization began to affect their fertility. When industrialization and urbanization became commonplace fertility would reach low levels and the population would enter into the stage of "incipient decline." At the time Notestein clearly foresaw the possibility that not all "high growth potential" populations would experience the entire vital revolution, especially those under colonial domination. Many of these populations were experiencing public health advances and improved agricultural productivity that lowered their mortality, but not the urbanization and industrialization that would lower their fertility. Notestein suggested that their period of population expansion could end in catastrophes and increased mortality. He directed his scholarly and practical energies over the rest of his career to preventing such an eventuality.

Partly at Notestein's initiative, one of the early offices established by the United Nations Secretariat, in 1946, was a Population Division, and he became its first director. He set the division on the path of objective, informed documentation and analysis of demographic trends that it has subsequently followed.

In 1948 John D. Rockefeller 3rd invited Notestein to be part of a four-person team to travel to six East Asian countries and appraise their population problems. The team reported that birth rates were "resistant to change" and were producing a situation where the gains in production were being consumed by increasing numbers. Although the political sensitivities surrounding the birth control issue prevented the conservative Rockefeller Foundation from acting on this report at the time, it induced Rockefeller to sponsor a conference on population problems in 1952 that resulted in the establishment of the Population Council. Notestein was one of the original four trustees of this unique non-profit organization focused on population issues, and became its third president in 1959. Under Notestein's leadership the Council conducted biomedical and demographic research and sponsored graduate training in these fields; it also became the key organization offering technical assistance to developing countries wishing to establish family planning programs well before the United States and the United Nations began offering such assistance. He retired in 1968.

A bibliography of Notestein's writings appears in Population Index, 49 (Spring 1983), pp. 7–12.

See also: *Demographic Transition; Demography, History of; Population Thought, Contemporary.*

BIBLIOGRAPHY

SELECTED WORKS BY FRANK W. NOTESTEIN.

Notestein, Frank W. 1936. "Class Differences in Fertility." *Annals of the American Academy of Political and Social Science* 188: 26–36.

———. 1943. "Some Implications of Population Change for Post-War Europe." *Proceedings of the American Philosophical Society* 87, no. 2 (August): 165–174.

———. 1945. "Population—The Long View," In *Food for the World,* ed. Theodore W. Schultz. Chicago: University of Chicago Press.

———. 1964. "Population Growth and Economic Development." Colombo. Reprinted in *Population and Development Review* 9 (1983): 345–360.

———. 1967. "The Population Crisis: Reasons for Hope." *Foreign Affairs* 46(1): 167–180.

———. 1982. "Demography in the United States: A Partial Account of the Development of the Field." *Population and Development Review* 8: 651–687.

Stix, Regine K., and Frank W. Notestein. 1940. *Controlled Fertility: An Evaluation of Clinic Service.* Baltimore: Williams and Wilkins.

SELECTED WORKS ABOUT FRANK W. NOTESTEIN.

Coale, Ansley J. 1979. "Notestein, Frank W." In *International Encyclopedia of the Social Sciences:*

Biographical Supplement, ed. David L. Sills. New York: Free Press. Reprinted in *Population Index* 49(1), 1983.

Ryder, Norman B. 1984. "Obituary: Frank Notestein (1902–1983)." *Population Studies* 38(1): 5–20.

DENNIS HODGSON

NUPTIALITY

See *Marriage*

NUTRITION AND CALORIE CONSUMPTION

Net nutrition (diet in relation to claims made on food intake by basal metabolism, physical activity, and disease) is an important influence on overall health. Poor nourishment impairs child growth and development, which in turn increases the risk of mortality, raises morbidity, and reduces physical capacity. These consequences are not limited to the growing years, and adversely affect adults who had poor nutritional experiences as children. Numerous debates and controversies surround the study of nutrition. These controversies historically have been fed by a lack of scientific knowledge, by varying goals and methods for studying nutritional needs, and by the confusion arising from simplifying complex material for a wide audience.

Dietary Standards

A brief history of the evolution of approaches to calibrating requirements for human nutrition can illuminate some of the central issues around dietary standards. The nutritional values of certain foods—such as limes in combating scurvy—have been known for over two centuries, but it was food shortages associated with World War I that established the need for dietary standards in planning food shipments. In the 1930s the League of Nations issued a series of reports on nutrient needs according to age, sex, and activity patterns; these were later drawn on in responding to the food crises created by World War II. Beginning in the late 1940s the United Na-

tions, the League's successor, coordinated a program of nutritional requirement reports produced by individual countries. These reports were often local adaptations of Food and Agriculture Organization/World Health Organization recommendations, but they varied widely on some components.

Research on dietary standards began with tabulations of average intakes of nutrients thought essential to life among "healthy" people. Over time this list expanded from items such as energy and carbon to include protein, iron, zinc, and a host of other ingredients. Scientific studies that varied or observed these intakes across people, looking for readily observable effects on health (such as growth failure or specific signs of disease), found both systematic patterns and also considerable differences in individual needs. Biochemical markers later provided a means to identify subclinical deficiencies.

An important question to ask of dietary recommendations is how they are to be used. The standards may differ widely depending on whether they are used to implement a program of organizing food shipments to address a crisis; to protect against obvious deficiency diseases in the vast majority of a population that is relatively sedentary; or to insure against any subclinical deficiencies for all people in a physically active group.

Assessment Strategies

Another area of concern in the field of nutrition is assessment, or measuring dietary intake in relation to dietary standards. Several approaches historically have been used, but each has limitations. Under the "disappearance" method, human consumption is a residual calculated as the supply of food (production, plus beginning stocks, plus imports) minus utilization (the sum of exports, ending stocks, nonfood uses, feed, spoilage, and seed). This method ignores the unequal distribution of food across regions, families, and individuals, and so malnutrition may exist even though per capita amounts are adequate. In addition, methods of preservation and cooking affect food's nutritional value. These changes are not acknowledged by the disappearance method of nutritional assessment.

Surveys are another method of assessment. While much has been learned through dietary surveys, one may question their accuracy as they are affected by the limited window of time during which food intakes are observed. Because diets vary by season, it is desirable to gather information throughout the year, but this takes time and imposes high costs. Moreover, even well constructed studies across seasons cannot detect annual fluctuations. Surveys conducted through recall methods may undercount or misreport consumption. This can be remedied in principle by placing an observer in the household; however, the family may then try to impress the observer by preparing unusually good meals (a situation that is analogous to the Heisenberg principle).

Anthropometric Measures

Anthropometric approaches to measuring nutritional status have the virtue of accounting for biological individuality while simultaneously measuring net nutrition, or dietary intake minus claims made by work and by disease. Disease is too seldom recognized as a factor in nutritional status. A person's need for iron in the diet, for example, is very much a function of exposure to hookworm and other parasites. Similarly, gastrointestinal diseases may divert dietary intake, resulting in malnutrition even though disappearance methods or dietary surveys would indicate that food supplies or intake were adequate. Anthropometric measures consider biological performance or failure to thrive as motivating principles.

Numerous studies of height and weight of healthy groups around the world suggest that a wide variety of human populations have a similar potential for growth. Therefore, if a particular group falls substantially below standard, one may infer that components of net nutrition are inadequate. The two most widely used anthropometric measures are height and weight-for-height (sometimes expressed as the body mass index, which is weight in kilograms divided by the square of height in meters). Height is an indicator of a person's net nutrition from conception through the growing years, which if poor, results in "stunting." Weight-for-height is a measure of recent nutritional status, which if poor, results in "wasting." If it can be established that a particular group's potential for growth differs from commonly used norms, it may be appropriate to utilize other standards.

A significant advantage of anthropometric measures is their low cost of collection. They are also broad-spectrum measures, incorporating a wide variety of factors that affect height and weight. This has the advantage of reflecting all variables that affect growth, but complicates the analysis of results. Simply identifying groups that fail to grow adequately does not provide information on causes or remedies. Other detective work (and expense) may be required.

Under- and Overnutrition

Historically a major challenge facing humans has been acquiring enough food. In the early twenty-first century, however, the world faces two food problems: undernutrition and overnutrition. The first is primarily, but not exclusively, an issue for poor countries, many of which have low agricultural productivity yet limited capacities to pay for food imports. Nutritional problems can be made worse by policies that artificially reduce prices received by farmers, thereby discouraging production and agricultural innovation. Wars and rivalries within and across countries can be significant in interrupting the delivery of food that would alleviate malnutrition. The largest regions of contemporary nutritional distress are found in Africa and Asia. Pockets of malnutrition are widely distributed and can be found throughout the world, even among some subpopulations in industrialized countries.

Obesity is a growing problem in developed countries, and is especially noteworthy in the United States. In more recent years, some children in some developing countries also have acquired this "disease." Two causes are widely cited: the declining cost of food and sedentary lifestyles. Rapid increases in agricultural productivity have occurred since the 1950s, and the price of food has fallen relative to income and many other commercial goods, which tempts people to consume more. Evidence for sedentary lifestyles is less well established, in part because energy expenditure is difficult and expensive to measure. But the growing use of automobiles to replace walking or cycling, falling demand for manual labor, and a host of household conveniences do make a case for reduction in calorie expenditures. Against this one may cite growth of health clubs and the rise of recreational sports played by a segment of the population. If these trends continue, the populations within industrialized countries may become divided increasingly on the basis of weight and physical fitness.

See also: *Anthropometry; Food Supply and Population.*

BIBLIOGRAPHY

Beaton, George H. 1999. "Recommended Dietary Intakes: Individuals and Populations." In *Modern Nutrition in Health and Disease,* 9th edition, ed. Maurice E. Shils, James A. Olson, Moshe Shike, and A. Catharine Ross. Baltimore, MD: Williams and Wilkins.

Eveleth, Phyllis B., and J. M. Tanner. 1990. *Worldwide Variation in Human Growth,* 2nd edition. Cambridge, Eng.: Cambridge University Press.

Steckel, Richard H. 1995. "Stature and the Standard of Living." *Journal of Economic Literature* 33: 1903–1940.

RICHARD H. STECKEL

O

OCCUPATION AND INDUSTRY

Occupation and industry are key variables needed to describe and analyze the world of work experienced by men, women, and sometimes children in nations around the world and the changes that occur in this experience over time. These variables are also indispensable in describing the structure of national economies and their temporal dynamics. Briefly, occupation describes the type of work a person does and industry describes the main activity of the establishment in which the work is done (e.g., *rice farmer* in *agriculture*). Statistics on occupation and industry are usually collected by the official statistical organizations of individual countries through censuses or surveys designed to meet national needs for monitoring the economy and shaping economic policies. The range of activities defined as work affects the scope of statistics that will be collected by these organizations. Coverage of such statistics is typically limited to persons who were employed during some reference period, such as the week preceding the census or survey, although usual occupation is sometimes reported for the unemployed. Occupations of persons who are employed intermittently (such as poll workers on election days), are temporarily out of the labor force, or are producing goods and services for their own consumption only usually will not be included. These persons are often disproportionately women.

National statistical organizations in many countries have collected industry and occupation data in censuses and surveys for many years. In the United States decennial census, for example, questions on industry date back to 1820 and regarding occupation to 1850.

Industry and Occupation Classification

Once the agencies have collected information about the industry in which respondents work and the occupations they report, they must classify these responses into industry and occupational categories. While the industry and occupation classifications adopted are necessarily country-specific, there has been considerable progress over the last 50 years toward also ensuring international comparability of such statistics.

Industry

An industry category is designed to describe the activity of the establishment in which employed or self-employed persons worked during a specified reference period. It describes what the establishment does rather than what the individual does while employed there. Industry statistics have been collected in censuses and employment surveys in many countries, usually in response to questions regarding where a person works (including name and address of the establishment), or what the main products or functions of the establishment are. In order to facilitate comparisons of different data sources and data from different countries, it is desirable to have an internationally comparable industry classification. This type of classification scheme has been in existence since 1948 and is periodically revised. The United Nations Statistics Division recommends that countries code and tabulate industry data ". . . according to the most recent revision of the International Standard Industrial Classification (ISIC) of All Economic Activities" (United Nations, Principles and Recommendations for Population and Housing Censuses, Revision 1.1998, p. 86). Many other classification schemes exist, however.

TABLE 1

United States Civilian Labor Force in 2000, by Industry

Industry	Number (thousands)	Percent Female
Total Employed	135,208	46.5
Agriculture	3,305	26.4
Mining	521	13.7
Construction	9,433	9.7
Manufacturing	19,940	32.5
Transportation, communication, and other public utilities	9,740	28.7
Wholesale and retail trade	27,832	47.2
Wholesale trade	5,421	30.4
Retail trade	22,411	51.2
Financial, insurance, real estate	8,727	58.5
Services	49,695	62.1
Business and repair services	9,661	37.4
Advertising	280	55.2
Services to dwellings and buildings	862	51.6
Personnel supply services	1,063	59.9
Computer and data processing	2,496	31.8
Detective/protective services	574	25.6
Automobile services	1,626	14.9
Personal services	4,515	70.0
Private households	894	92.1
Hotels and lodging places	1,443	57.9
Entertainment and recreation	2,582	42.3
Professional and related services	32,784	70.0
Hospitals	5,028	76.3
Health services, except hospitals	6,569	79.7
Elementary, secondary schools	7,629	76.0
Colleges and universities	2,903	54.3
Social services	3,519	81.9
Legal services	1,362	58.5
Public administration	6,015	44.9

SOURCE: U. S. Census Bureau (2001).

The North American Industry Classification System (NAICS) was adopted by the United States, Canada, and Mexico, and used in their 2000 round of censuses. The overall structure of the classification is the same in all three countries, though the details differ. The United States version of NAICS, used to code Census 2000 industry responses, is a complete revision of the 1990 census classification and differs from the ISIC. The 1990 census published data under 13 major industry groups and 243 detailed industries; for Census 2000 there are 15 major groups and 265 detailed industry categories.

Occupation

In any complex economy, people work in a wide variety of occupations. A classification scheme for occupations, similar to that devised for industries, must be adopted. The many existing schemes used by different governments all seek to organize the actual jobs people do into clearly defined groups, according to the tasks performed and/or the skills required. They provide guidelines as to how the jobs people report are to be classified into detailed occupational groups and how these detailed groups are to be aggregated into broader groups. Many national classifications are designed to be similar to or comparable with the International Standard Classification of Occupations (ISCO).

The version of ISCO employed in the early twenty-first century, ISCO-88, was developed by the Fourteenth International Conference of Labor Statisticians in 1987 and adopted by the International Labor Organization (ILO) in 1988. It consists of four levels of aggregation: 10 major groups; 28 sub-major groups; 116 minor groups, and 390 detailed occupational unit groups. The ILO, as custodian of ISCO-88, provides advice and assistance to countries in developing common classifications based on that classification system. The UN Statistics Division recommends that countries prepare tabulations of census data in accordance with ISCO-88 to facilitate international comparisons and communication among users of the data.

Full international comparability has not yet been achieved. An ILO review of 1990 census-round practices in 115 countries found that 65 countries could link their occupational data to ISCO-88, and another 33 to an earlier version of that system; others used national classification systems which were not comparable. In the 2000 round of censuses, many countries still used occupational classifications that were not directly comparable with ISCO-88.

In the United States until the 1970s, government agencies, notably the Department of Labor (and its Bureau of Labor Statistics) and the Census Bureau, used different and noncomparable occupational classifications. The 1980 U.S. Standard Occupational Classification (SOC) was developed concurrently with the 1980 Census Occupational Classification with the expectation that it would be phased in and used by all agencies. A secondary consideration in its development was comparability with ISCO-68. A major revision of the SOC was undertaken prior to the 2000 census, with many occupational categories added, deleted, or changed. There are now over 800 detailed categories. In the final Census 2000 Occupational Index these were aggregated into 509 detailed occupations, which are not directly comparable with those in the 1990 census or with ISCO-88.

History of Industry and Occupation Statistics

Statistics on industry and occupation are needed to monitor social and economic trends and to inform related policies. In the United States the census was mandated primarily to establish the basis for apportioning the House of Representatives. Yet, as early as the first census in 1790, the debates about its content reflected a view that governments at all levels need more detailed knowledge about the social and economic characteristics of the population. Several proposals on industry/occupation categories were made, including some by the future presidents James Madison and Thomas Jefferson. Eventually, a three-way classification was adopted, and applied in the census of 1820: agriculture, commerce, and manufactures. Today these would be viewed as industrial classifications. No occupational information was collected in 1830 but the question was included again in 1840. By this time the number of categories had been extended to seven: mining; agriculture; commerce; manufactures and traders; ocean navigation; navigation of canals, lakes, and rivers; and learned professions and engineers. While these categories gave a fuller depiction of the work people were doing than did the previous three, the categories still combined industry and occupation and omitted servants, government officials, clerks, and others.

The increasing division of labor in American society can be observed by noting the occupational classifications of each progressive census. The census of 1850 shifted from family to individual enumeration and separate schedules were provided for free persons and slaves. Information on occupation was acquired only for free males over 15 years old but greater occupational detail was collected. In 1850, 323 specific occupational categories were created under ten headings. In 1860 women as well as men over 15 years old were asked their occupations and the increasing complexity of the economy was reflected in the list of 584 possible choices. Between 1870 and 1930, persons ten years old and over were included in the occupational inquiry, reflecting the prevalence of child labor in the United States. In 1940 and later the age limit was 14 years old and over, reflecting the effect of child labor laws enacted in the early part of the century that prohibited or limited the paid work of children. Separate questions on occupation and industry were introduced in 1910, and the number of occupational categories

TABLE 2

Percent Distribution of the Civilian Labor Force by Industry in Selected High-Income Countries, 2000					
Industry	US	Australia	Japan	Germany	Italy
Agriculture, forestry, fishing	3	5	5	3	6
Mining and construction	7	8	10	10	8
Manufacturing	15	13	21	24	25
Services	75	74	64	64	62
Total	100	100	100	100	100

SOURCE: U. S. Census Bureau (2001).

changed each decade: 303 in 1900, 469 in 1950, 509 in 2000.

Trends in Occupation and Industry Composition

These changes in coverage and in occupational categories reflected an expanding economy, greater division of labor, emergence of new jobs, and shifts in broad occupational areas, as well as major changes in the status of women and African Americans. In 1790, the nation was predominantly agricultural. By the mid-twentieth century, it had become predominately industrial and commercial. At the end of the twentieth century it was largely a service economy.

The census occupational data reveal a number of other striking changes over the course of the twentieth century. In addition to the movement from farm to non-farm work, the composition of non-farm work changed: The number of laborers declined, operatives and craftsmen increased, as did those in the service trades. The most significant twentieth century increase was observed in "white-collar" occupations, which went from about 18 percent of workers in 1900 to over 40 percent by 1980. According to the U.S. Department of Commerce in 2001, figures indicated that by 2000, white collar workers represented about 59 percent of the total employed.

Occupational trends were usually described in detail only for men until the last several decades when the increasing participation of women in the labor force required attention to their roles also. Trends in the distribution of occupations for women differed somewhat from men. There was a notable drop in private household workers throughout the twentieth century and significant declines in the operatives category as well. In contrast, trends for women were similar to those for men with respect to the number of farm workers and other types of manual work. Some convergence in occupational distributions was evident by 1980 although many more women were still in clerical and service work whereas men predominated in managerial and craft occupations. The convergence continued through 2000, though a substantial degree of occupational clustering by sex remains a characteristic of the labor force.

Industry Composition in 2000

In 2000 the total U.S. population was 281 million. Of this, the civilian non-institutional population aged 16 years and older was 209.7 million: 100.7 million males and 109 million females. The total number of employed persons was 135.2 million, or 64.5 percent of the total, of which 72.3 million were males and 62.9 million were females. A concise description of the industrial composition of the 135.2 million figure just cited is presented in Table 1. For each category, the proportion of females is also shown.

As Table 1 shows, by the beginning of the twenty-first century, the proportion of people employed in agriculture was only 2.4 percent of total employment—considerably less, for example, than persons employed in hospitals, 3.7 percent. Women had a share of employment that ranged from less than 10 percent in construction to 81.9 percent in social services—an industry in which total employment was also larger than the total employment in agriculture.

The radical transformation of the industrial-occupational structure away from agriculture, first toward manufacturing and then from manufacturing toward service industries, is also reflected in the statistics of other high-income countries, although to a lesser degree than in the United States. Table 2 presents the broad distribution of the civilian labor force by major industrial sectors in selected high-income countries.

See also: *Census; Labor Force.*

BIBLIOGRAPHY

Bradley, Dana and Katharine Earle. 2001. "Developing and Explaining the Crosswalk between Census 1990 and 2000 Industry and Occupation Codes." *Proceedings of the Annual Meeting of the American Statistical Association* August 5–9, 2001. American Statistical Association.

International Labour Office. 1990. *International Standard Classification of Occupations: ISCO–88.* Geneva, Switzerland: International Labour Office.

International Labour Office. 1996. "Sources and Methods: Labour Statistics." *Total and Economically Active Population, Employment and Unemployment,* 2nd edition. Geneva, Switzerland: International Labour Office.

International Labour Office. 2001. "Asking Questions on Economic Characteristics in a Population Census." *STAT Working Papers, No. 2001–1* pp. 4–48. Prepared by R. Gilbert. Geneva, Switzerland: International Labour Office, Bureau of Statistics.

Nam, Charles B. and Mary G. Powers. 1983. *The Socioeconomic Approach to Status Measurement.* Houston, TX: Cap and Gown Press.

United Nations. 1998. *Principles and Recommendations for Population and Housing Censuses,* revision l. Statistical Papers. Series M No. 67. New York: United Nations.

U. S. Census Bureau. 2001. *Statistical Abstract of the United States: 2001* Washington, D.C.: U.S. Government Printing Office.

MARY G. POWERS

OLDEST OLD

The term "oldest old" refers to persons at the upper segment of the age pyramid. By a conventional demographic definition those age 80 years and older are included in the oldest-old population, although, as noted below, alternative definitions are also in use. Since the end of World War II, in most countries the oldest old has been the fastest growing component of the population at large. This trend will almost certainly continue in the decades to come, with improving survival rates at very high ages.

The relationship between indicators of average lifespan, such as life expectancy at birth, and the age structure of populations is often misunderstood by statisticians, policymakers, journalists, and other users of demographic data. Increases in life expectancy are welcomed as a sign of progress and improvement in living conditions. The countries that are most advanced in the demographic transition are proud that their life expectancy at birth exceeds 80 years, at least among women (who, especially in low-mortality countries, enjoy an appreciable advantage over men). This was the case by the end of the twentieth century in Japan (the country which in the period from 1995 to 2000 had the highest female life expectancy at birth: 83.8 years) and in Hong Kong; in Finland, Norway, and Sweden; in most countries of southern and western Europe; and in Canada and Australia. (In the United States, female life expectancy during the period from 1995 to 2000 was, at 79.4 years, slightly short of this mark.) On the other hand, increases in the numbers of nonagenarians and even octogenarians are often viewed with alarm, as portending an increase in the burden of health care and old-age support. Most people, of course, do not die in the years narrowly bracketing the average life expectancy at birth.

The increasing number of old people is not a new phenomenon, although some still find it surprising. One reason for this is the way in which a final open-ended age group is used in tabulating age distributions and mortality rates: in the past, 65 years and over; now, 85 years and over. But 65 years and over or 85 and over tends to be popularly interpreted as approximately 65 years and approximately 85 years, not age brackets ranging from 65 or 85 to 100 or 110 years. The upper end of the distribution, the oldest-old population, is thus incorrectly visualized.

The Problem of Definition

The oldest old as an identifiable category within human populations always existed even if its definition in terms of biological, social, or chronological age was varying and fuzzy. During the seventeenth century, the absence of a concept of the oldest old was not very important because with life expectancy at birth at levels of 30 to 35 years, only a small minority—about 10 to 15 percent—of the population reached the age of 70.

The three great ages of humankind—youth, adulthood, and old age—correspond to the history of life from a biological point of view, with youth a phase of growth and development, adulthood a phase of reproduction and childrearing, and old age a phase of physical decline, beyond the selective pressures of evolution. The division also corresponds to the economic and social organization of the industrialized countries during the twentieth century around school, work, and retirement, reflected in the three broad age ranges of many statistical tables: 0 to 14 years; 15 to 64 years; 65 and over. But these socioeconomic ages have little reality for most developing countries, where very few old people enjoy retirement. And in the developed countries furthest advanced in the demographic transition, the period of old age, as defined by lessened or no economic activity, lengthens at both ends—as labor force participation tends to decline above the age 50 and as life expectancy at age 65 increases. This explains the logic of dividing old age into two parts: the "young old" and the "oldest old."

But on what criteria? Chronological age is a rather crude marker here. Everyone can agree that those aged 60 to 70 are "young old" and that those over 85 are oldest old, but what about those between 70 and 85? Criteria other than age might be considered.

Biodemographic approach. A simple biodemographic classification would consist of numbered generations or "ages": a child belongs to the first age, parents to the second age, grandparents to the third age, and great-grandparents (the oldest old in this scheme) to the fourth age. But this simple classification presumes reproductive success and a high degree of uniformity in the reproductive life cycle.

Functional approach. An approach largely popularized by the historical demographer Peter Laslett (1996) is that the fourth age—the age of the oldest old—starts when a person becomes physically dependent on another. Thus the third age starts when the person is released from the constraints of adulthood (paid work and education of children) and finishes when the loss of physical independence begins, without precise age limits. Indeed, the concept of loss of autonomy of old people is not easily pinned down as it involves three main criteria: physical dependence—the need for the assistance of another to perform the activities of daily life; cognitive autonomy—the capacity to make decisions for oneself; and social integration—the capacity to remain integrated in a community. Three indicators of life expectancy by health status (active life expectancy, dementia-free life expectancy, and institution-free life expectancy) are helpful in defining the boundary of the fourth age congruent with this approach.

Gerontological approach. In their model of successful aging, John Rowe and Robert Kahn (1997) distinguish four states, namely the absence of appreciable risk of degenerative disease or disability, the presence of risk, the presence of actual degenerative disease, and the presence of disability. Successful aging would imply prolongation of the period without accumulation of the risk of developing a degenerative disease or becoming disabled. The third age is generally associated with successful aging and the fourth age with unsuccessful aging. The fourth age would begin with the accumulation of risks of degenerative diseases and disability. The risk of "unsuccessful" aging is an important concept in gerontology, drawing on the concept of frailty.

Demographic approach. A definition of oldest old based on loss of autonomy faces the difficulty that a large minority of older people will never lose their autonomy. Demarcating the category of oldest old by setting a plausible if necessarily arbitrary age when persons are thought to enter it, such as age 80 or 85, is an approach commonly used by demographers. It should be remembered, of course, that an arbitrarily selected advanced age does not have the same connotations in the early twenty-first century as it did in the past when attainment of that age was exceptional. Nor does it have the same meaning for men as for women. Other demographic definitions of the oldest old, or the fourth age, would be in terms of the proportion of survivors—the highest age reached by at least 25 percent of the population; or in terms of life expectancy—the age at which there remains ten years of expected life. The nominal ages corresponding to these criteria, however, would vary depending on the level and pattern of mortality; hence, they differ from one country to another and from one time to another.

Numbers and Trends

In virtually all countries the populations at ages beyond 80 years—the oldest old—have strongly increased in size since 1950. This is a consequence of declining mortality and also of the fact that as time passes the oldest old consist of survivors of increasingly larger birth cohorts (groups of individuals born at the same time). The proportions of the oldest old within the overall population have also been increasing, in part as a result of declining fertility,

TABLE 1

The Oldest-Old Population by Age Group and Proportions Aged 80 and Over, Selected Countries, 2000 and 2050 (Numbers in Thousands)

Age	United States	European Union (15 countries)	India	China
		Year 2000		
80–84	4,900	6,997	4,264	7,826
85–89	2,673	4,865	1,472	2,818
90–94	1,160	1,847	328	743
95–99	371	376	44	127
100+	75	37	3	12
All ages	283,230	376,502	1,008,937	1,275,133
Ages 80+	9,179	14,122	6,111	11,526
Percent 80+	3.2	3.8	0.6	0.9
		Year 2050		
80–84	12,676	18,152	28,313	56,986
85–89	9,662	12,740	13,881	28,214
90–94	5,377	6,423	4,783	10,201
95–99	1,969	2,331	1,039	3,286
100+	473	534	142	471
All ages	397,063	339,314	1,572,055	1,462,058
Ages 80+	30,157	40,180	48,158	99,158
Percent 80+	7.6	11.8	3.1	6.7

SOURCE: United Nations (2001). Estimates and medium-variant projections.

which narrows the base of the age pyramid. Thus, for example, in the 15 countries of the European Union the proportion at ages 80 and older was 1.2 percent in 1950 and 3.8 percent in 2000 (more than tripling). In the United States the corresponding percentages were 1.1 and 3.2.

Within the oldest old, the number and proportion in the higher ages increased especially rapidly. In 1995 James W. Vaupel and Bernard Jeune showed that in Western countries the number of centenarians doubled approximately every ten years starting in 1950; the doubling time for the number of people 105 years old was just a little shorter. Of course, in 1950, although the numbers of those over 80 were already numerous, few were over 90, very few were centenarians, and almost none had reached 105. In the lowest-mortality countries, such as France and Japan, in the early twenty-first century, the fall in mortality at old ages appears to be accelerating and the "centenarian doubling time" is becoming shorter. As a consequence of these changes, the maximum reported age at death has been strongly increasing. The longest reliably recorded human lifespan (for the French woman Jeanne Calment, who died in 1997) is 122 years.

These trends are likely to continue in the coming decades. Table 1 shows the size of the oldest-old population in 2000 in the three most populous countries of the world and in the 15-nation European Union and the proportions of the oldest old within the total population. The table also includes anticipated figures of the oldest old in the year 2050, as projected by the United Nations (UN) on rather conservative assumptions as to the future evolution of mortality. Note that the absolute numbers of the oldest old in 2050 are affected only by mortality (and to a degree also by future international migration), because those aged 80 years and older will be survivors of persons already alive (survivors of those aged 30 years or older in 2000). The future proportions of the oldest old within the total population are of course affected by future fertility as well as mortality. The projected proportions shown in the table are based on the UN's "medium fertility" assumptions.

As the table indicates, the rapid expansion of the oldest-old population is not limited to the Western world. Developing countries are also faced with greatly increased numbers over age 80. In China, for example, during the first half of the twenty-first century the number of oldest old is expected to grow nearly ninefold, in contrast to a 15 percent increase of the total population. By 2050, the oldest-old population of China is expected to be some 99 million. As a proportion of the total population that number would represent 6.7 percent—well above the corresponding proportions in 2000 in the United States or in the European Union.

Women invariably represent a high percentage of the oldest old. For example, in the United States in 2000, some 67 percent of those above age 80 were women. And among centenarians, women accounted for 87 percent of the total. In these conditions, further calculations of health expectancies (for example, active life expectancy and disability-free life expectancy) are more and more relevant. They suggest an increase in healthy life expectancy in some — but not all — countries such as the United States and France. In Austria, for instance, life expectancy in good perceived health at age 80 increased by 1.3 years between 1978 and 1998, going up from 2.8 to 4.3 years.

See also: *Aging and Longevity, Biology of; Aging of Population; Disability, Demography of; Health Transition; Life Span; Mortality Decline.*

BIBLIOGRAPHY

Doblhammer, Gabriele, and Josef Kytir. 2001. "Compression or Expansion of Morbidity? Trends in Healthy-life Expectancy in the Elderly Austrian Population between 1978 and 1998." *Social Science and Medicine* 52: 385–391.

Laslett, Peter. 1996. *A Fresh Map of Life,* 2nd edition. Houndmills, Basingstoke, Eng.: Macmillan.

Robine, Jean-Marie, Isabelle Romieu, and Emmanuelle Cambois. 1999. "Health Expectancy Indicators." *Bulletin of the World Health Organization* 77: 181–185.

Rowe, John W., and Robert L. Kahn. 1997. "Successful Aging." *Gerontologist* 37: 433–440.

Thatcher, A. Roger. 2001. "The Demography of Centenarians in England and Wales." *Population* 13(1): 139–156.

United Nations. 2001. *World Population Prospects: The 2000 Revision,* Vol. II: *Sex and Age.* New York: United Nations.

Vaupel, James W., and Bernard Jeune. 1995. "The Emergence and Proliferation of Centenarians." In *Exceptional Longevity: From Prehistory to the Present,* ed. Bernard Jeune and James W. Vaupel. Odense, Denmark: Odense University Press.

JEAN-MARIE ROBINE

ONE-CHILD POLICY

The People's Republic of China (PRC) is the world's most populous country, comprising 21 percent of the global population. After almost three decades of radical Maoist Communism and nearly a decade of increasingly compulsory family planning, China, in 1978, launched both its market-oriented economic reform era and its unique one-child policy. These two plans appear to be contradictory in that the economic reforms loosen the prior meticulous government controls on people's lives under the planned economy, while the one-child policy micro-manages the most intimate parts of marital and family life. Yet China's political leaders and its educated elite generally saw both economic reform and the one-child policy as important, even essential, means toward the goal of rapidly raising per capita living standards in China. Market reforms partially unleashed the previously suppressed and frustrated entrepreneurial, ambitious spirit in Chinese culture, bringing about the world's most rapid macroeconomic growth, while the one-child policy sharply reduced population growth. Very rapid economic growth and unusually slow population growth in combination have yielded the remarkable upsurge in per capita income that China has experienced.

Origin of the One-Child Policy

Mao Zedong had suppressed the field of demography—and population studies in general—from the time of the founding of the PRC in 1949. In the late 1970s, after China tried to impose a two-child limit, a team of natural scientists (non-demographers) prepared a population projection showing, correctly, that China's population would continue to grow rapidly for decades even if all couples had no more than two children. This result shocked China's political leaders, who wanted to stop population growth immediately; they quickly announced a one-child limit for all urban and rural couples, except for the six percent of the population in non-Han Chinese minority groups. At the time, the leadership and scholars apparently were unaware that successful implementation of the one-child policy would speed the emergence of a new problem, the rapid aging of China's population structure.

Implementation of the One-Child Policy

The one-child policy was imposed in 1979 and was carried out with increasing coercion in urban and rural areas. The stated policy was (and, generally speaking, remained) that after one child, a woman was required to have an intrauterine device (IUD) inserted; if the couple already had two children, the woman (or, infrequently, the man) was required to be sterilized; and all pregnancies that had not received prior official approval were to be aborted. Coercive mass campaigns became widespread in the early 1980s and recorded their worst abuses in 1983. Statistics on birth control operations showed a sharp peak in sterilizations (1982: 5 million; 1983: 21 million), abortions (1981: 8.7 million; 1982: 12.4 million; 1983: 14.4 million), and IUD insertions (1981: 10.3 million; 1982: 14.1 million; 1983: 17.8 million) that year.

The one-child policy, from its inception, has also included *disincentives* for births beyond the approved number. Disincentives vary by place and can include severe fines, appropriation or destruction of family homes or possessions, political or physical harassment, work penalties or loss of employment, and the required adoption of officially controllable and long-term birth control techniques. The one-child policy has also always included *incentives* reserved for couples who agree to stop childbearing after one child and who sign a *one-child pledge*. The incentives can take the form of regular payments to the couple for the single child's benefit, priority in access to health services and public childcare and education, hiring priority in desired job categories for the parents and single child, and political praise. However, penalties strongly overshadow incentives in the enforcement of birth restrictions in China.

The one-child policy remained in force in the early twenty-first century. The PRC government, in March 2000, issued a document mandating that there be no change in the overall population targets, fertility controls, or means of enforcement. In December 2001, the National People's Congress passed a law on population and birth planning, thus creating, after much delay, a formal legal basis for the policy.

Compliance and Non-Compliance

At the time the one-child policy was adopted in 1978, the urban population of China had been living with a strict two-child policy since the mid-1960s. Urban conditions such as overcrowding and the greater autonomy of women encouraged voluntary low fertility. In addition, the urban social safety net (allocated housing, free or inexpensive medical care, pensions, subsidies) made families less dependent on their children for old-age support than rural couples. Thus, the one-child policy, aggressively implemented throughout urban China, was successful from its inception. A large proportion of urban couples in childbearing ages sign the one-child pledge, even though China's urban couples, like their rural counterparts, usually say they would prefer two or more children if this were an option. The urban total fertility rate (TFR) is only 1.4 births per woman or lower, well below replacement level. The urban population constitutes 36 percent of the total population of the PRC.

Rural China has consistently resisted the one-child policy, because there is essentially no social support system for rural families to substitute for the support of children, and especially sons, when they are grown. Daughters marry out of their villages (the marriage system is patrilocal), while sons continue to live with or near their parents and each son brings in a wife who helps him support his parents in their old age. Accordingly, preference for male progeny remains strong. Given peasant resistance, the government modified the one-child policy for rural China starting in 1984. In 18 provinces (more than half the total), rural couples are allowed to bear a second child if the firstborn is a girl, but remain subject to the one-child policy if the firstborn is a boy. Five provinces allow all rural couples to have two children and the provinces with populations dominated by minority groups allow rural couples two or three children. The four province-level municipalities and also Jiangsu and Sichuan provinces continue the one-child limit for all urban and rural Han couples. China's exact rural TFR is not known, but it is estimated to be about 2.0 births per woman, slightly below replacement level or lower.

Effects of the One-Child Policy

China's one-child policy has held both urban and rural fertility down to levels well below what they would otherwise have been during the decades since 1978. This has reduced China's population growth rate and, all else being equal, has increased per capita income. Such low fertility has also reduced the number of pregnancies and births per woman, and thereby helped to reduce maternal mortality. The one-child policy has greatly changed family structure and raised the perceived value of each child as the number of children per couple has declined. In cities, the one-child policy may have helped elevate the status of daughters, because almost half the time an only child is a girl. But elsewhere, the one-child policy or its modifications have exacerbated life-threatening discrimination against female infants and very young girls, and brought about a worsening problem of sex-selective abortion of female fetuses. In addition, reproductive rights have been largely denied to China's women who, in most of the country, continue to bear the burden of required use of IUDs, frequent inspections to confirm that the IUD is still in place, required abortions of noncompliant pregnancies, compulsory sterilization, and often, harm to their marriages and family relations if they do not bear a son. Finally, the strong contraction of fertility has distorted China's age structure and set in motion a process of rapid and extreme population aging.

China's one-child policy is, therefore, partly beneficial and partly detrimental to the quality of life of China's people.

See also: *Communism, Population Aspects of; Population Policy.*

BIBLIOGRAPHY

Aird, John S. 1996. "Family Planning, Women, and Human Rights in the People's Republic of China." In *International Conference on Demography and the Family in Asia and Oceania, September 1995, Proceedings.* Taipei: Franciscan Gabriel Printing Company.

Banister, Judith. 1987. *China's Changing Population.* Stanford, CA: University Press.

Chinese Communist Party, Central Committee. 2000. *Document No. 8: Decision of the Central Committee of the Communist Party of China and the State Council on Enhancing Population Work and Ensuring Stable and Low Levels of Births.*

Croll, Elisabeth, Delia Davin, and Penny Kane, eds. 1985. *China's One-child Family Policy.* New York: St. Martin's Press.

Feeney, Griffith, et al. 1989. "Recent Fertility Dynamics in China: Results from the 1987 One Percent Population Survey." *Population and Development Review* 15(2): 297–322.

Greenhalgh, Susan. 1986. "Shifts in China's Population Policy, 1984–86: Views From the Central, Provincial, and Local Levels." *Population and Development Review* 12: 491–515.

Hardee-Cleveland, Karen, and Judith Banister. 1988. "Fertility Policy and Implementation in China, 1986–88." *Population and Development Review* 14(2): 245–286.

Short, Susan E., and Zhai Fengying. 1998. "Looking Locally at China's One-Child Policy." *Studies in Family Planning* 29(4): 373–387.

Wang Feng. 1996. "A Decade of the One-child Policy: Achievements and Implications." In *China: The Many Facets of Demographic Change,* ed. Alice Goldstein and Wang Feng. Boulder, CO: Westview Press.

Winkler, Edwin A. 2002. "Chinese Reproductive Policy at the Turn of the Millennium: Dynamic Stability." *Population and Development Review* 28: 379–418.

Xie Zhenming. 2000. "Population Policy and the Family Planning Program." In *The Changing Population of China*, ed. Peng Xizhe with Guo Zhigang. Oxford: Blackwell.

JUDITH BANISTER

OPTIMUM POPULATION

In casual discourse it seems obvious that a population of some geographically delimited entity—a village, a city, a country, the world—can be too small or too large. People can be too few to sustain a productive economy or creative culture; or so many that congestion effects and environmental degradation detract from present and future well being. Hence, there must be some intermediate population (or population range) that is in some sense *best* or optimal. Unfortunately, translating this simple idea into a coherent and useful concept has proved elusive—to the extent that in the early twenty-first century the term is rarely used in writings on demography or population policy. Some of the difficulties encountered are discussed in this article.

Increasing and Diminishing Returns

The idea that there was some size of population under which, other things being equal, per capita economic wellbeing was maximized, was implicit in the writings of the classical economists in the nineteenth century, particularly John Stuart Mill (1806–1873). Economic (at the time meaning agrarian) output per head was seen as determined by the off-setting forces of diminishing returns to labor (as more labor was applied to the same amount of land) and technological progress. At a given technological level, as the number of workers increased, the output per worker might initially rise, for example, as a result of the division of labor. But as more workers were added, output would ultimately fall. The labor input at the point of peak average productivity corresponded to what came to be called the optimum population.

In more complex economies it is possible to make an analogous argument, although the diminished significance of natural resources and the options for trade and other factor flows make it much less cogent. The pervasiveness of technological change as a source of economic growth undermines the usefulness of the stipulation that other things are equal, which is needed to define an optimum. There was a period of enthusiasm for the concept of an optimum population in the early decades of the twentieth century, starting with English economist Edwin Cannan (1861–1935), which dissipated as its difficulties became apparent. French demographer Alfred Sauvy (1898–1990) made some use of the term, and defined a *power optimum* as distinct from the economic optimum.

The Social Welfare Function

The simplest economic growth models take income per capita as the measure of wellbeing. A straightforward generalization would add numerous other components to the welfare criterion aside from income. Some ethicists (including Peter Singer)—and a few economists (including the Nobelist James Meade)—have argued, following English philosopher Jeremy Bentham (1748–1832), that a more appropriate measure of social wellbeing is average wellbeing multiplied by the size of population. This is called the total welfare or Benthamite criterion. Under it, if everyone in a society enjoyed a given level of happiness, overall wellbeing would be improved by having more people to enjoy it. An optimum population under the Benthamite criterion would be much larger than under the per capita welfare criterion. Most people, however, strongly prefer the per-capita form. This issue is treated at length by the philosopher Derek Parfit. Related theoretical concerns are discussed in a literature in welfare economics on what may be called normative population theory—for example, by economists such as Partha Dasgupta and Charles Blackorby.

If the welfare criterion attaches a strong value to preservation of the natural environment the optimum population may be substantially diminished. This is the basis of the call by some environmentalists for a reduction of world population. However, global averages have little meaning for most such calculations in view of the great diversity of country and local situations. In more constricted regions, the disamenities that may be associated with continued population growth are clearer. For example, various modeling exercises have sought to calculate optimum city sizes under welfare criteria that take into account density and congestion costs. Purely qualitative assessments of diminution of the quality of urban environmental amenity as population increases are also frequently made, albeit confounding the effects of scale with those of public expenditure and aesthetic standards.

No reasonable welfare function should be timeless. Conditions change, and researchers know at least some things about the directions of change. Hence, the welfare function that is to be maximized is usually expressed formally as an integral over time:

$$\int_0^\infty e^{-rt} U(c,t)\, dt ,$$

where $U(c,t)$ is the level of welfare at time t, c is a vector of components of wellbeing, and e^{-rt} is a discounting factor to reflect a bias toward the near term by downweighting future welfare at a rate of r (a necessity if one is to ensure that the integral converges). A plausible welfare function might include the population growth rate or the age structure among its arguments as well as population size: People might reasonably prefer not to live in an excessively elderly population that would eventually be produced by very low fertility. Thus, there may be a conflict between a population size goal and an age-structure (hence population growth) goal, calling for specification of preferred trade-offs between them.

Optimal Population Trajectories

Population growth and economic growth are interrelated, and the combined system can be modeled. The models can be extremely simple, like the Solow neoclassical model, or extremely elaborate, like the large-scale economic-demographic planning models in vogue in the 1970s. The models could have been (although usually they were not) optimized over alternative feasible population trajectories—either analytically or numerically. Incorporating a cost of control is mathematically straightforward. Optimal steady-state solutions for simple classical and neoclassical growth models with age-structured populations are discussed in a 1977 article by W. Brian Arthur and Geoffrey McNicoll. Other formulations are examined by Paul A. Samuelson and Klaus F. Zimmermann.

A striking real-world application of optimal control theory to population lay behind the design of China's radical one-child policy that was introduced in 1979. In work done during the 1970s, Song Jian and his colleagues, systems engineers by train-

ing, calculated that the long-run sustainable population of the country was 700 million. They then formulated the population policy problem in control-theory terms: How should fertility evolve if the population is eventually to stabilize at 700 million, the peak population is not to exceed 1.2 billion, there are pre-set constraints on the acceptable lower bound of total fertility (a one-child average) and the upper bound of old-age dependency, and there is to be a smooth transition to the target population while minimizing the total person-years lived in excess of 700 million per year? The resulting optimized policy called for fertility to be quickly brought down to the allowable minimum, held there for 50 years (producing negative population growth), then allowed to rise back to replacement level. Notably not a part of the technical deliberations—or of the actual policy that was adopted—was consideration of the human costs that attainment of such a trajectory would entail.

Central planning has deservedly lost favor in the economic realm, *a fortiori* in the demographic. But the general issue of achieving balance between human population numbers and the natural world remains relevant, as does the issue of striking a balance between the benefits to a society of a desired demographic outcome and the costs to the society of achieving it. But before these matters can be usefully expressed in the language of optimization, there are important surrounding problems of values, levels of analysis, and delimitation of boundaries to be resolved—areas where most of the meat of the issue is likely to be found. Real-world population policy easily eludes formal characterization.

See also: *Cannan, Edwin; Carrying Capacity; Limits to Growth; Mill, John Stuart; Population Policy.*

BIBLIOGRAPHY

Arthur, W. Brian, and Geoffrey McNicoll. 1977. "Optimal Growth with Age Dependence: A Theory of Population Policy." *Review of Economic Studies* 44(1): 111–123.

Blackorby, Charles, Walter Bossert, and David Donaldson. 1995. "Intertemporal Population Ethics: Critical-level Utilitarian Principles." *Econometrica* 63: 1,303–1,320.

Meade, James. 1955. *Trade and Welfare.* New York: Oxford University Press.

Parfit, Derek. 1984. *Reasons and Persons.* Oxford: Clarendon Press.

Robbins, Lionel. 1927. "The Optimum Theory of Population." In *London Essays in Economics in Honour of Edwin Cannan,* ed. T. E. Gregory and Hugh Dalton. London: Routledge.

Samuelson, Paul A. 1975. "The Optimum Growth Rate for Population." *International Economic Review* 16: 531–538.

Sauvy, Alfred. 1969. *General Theory of Population,* trans. Christophe Campos. New York: Basic Books.

Song, Jian, Chi-Hsien Tuan, and Jing-Yuan Yu. 1985. *Population Control in China: Theory and Applications.* New York: Praeger.

Zimmermann, Klaus F., ed. 1989. *Economic Theory of Optimal Population.* Berlin: Springer-Verlag.

GEOFFREY MCNICOLL

ORGANIZATIONS, DEMOGRAPHY OF

Research on organizations (for example, firms, voluntary associations, political movements) has become increasingly more focussed on demographics and ecology. The research strategy of organizational demography has several noteworthy features that resonate with practice in the study of human demography. This research examines the *full* histories of organizational populations, because early events have been shown to have lasting consequences for population dynamics. It also gathers life history data on all organizations in the population(s), including the large and famous as well as the small and insignificant—this is crucial for avoiding problems of selectivity bias. Organizational demography records detailed information about the ways in which organizations enter and leave and investigates organizational populations. Finally, it uses event-history methods to estimate the effects of characteristics of organizations, populations, and environments on vital rates in populations of organizations.

Differences between Human and Organizational Demography

The fact that organizations are constructed social entities, not biological organisms, has major implications for their demography. In 2000 sociologists Glenn R. Carroll and Michael T. Hannan enumerated several important differences between organizational and human demography. First, organizations come into existence and disappear due to a wider range of events including founding, merger, spin-out, and secession. Their lives as independent corporate actors can end by dissolution, acquisition, or merger. Second, an organization can exist long after its initial members have departed; it is not unreasonable to characterize organizations as, potentially, *immortal.* Third, organizations often do not have obvious parents. Therefore, organizational demography treats the *population of organizations* as the unit at risk of experiencing entries. Fourth, organizations can have multilayered structures, each level of which might operate relatively autonomously. These structures range from establishments (physical sites) to business groups such as the Korean *chaebol.* Many other possible configurations lie between these extremes. Most research, in this area, focuses on the autonomous organization. Fifth, organizational populations generally possess great heterogeneity in size and other characteristics.

Density Dependence

A major discovery of organizational demography is a regular pattern of density dependence in rates of founding and disbanding. As the number of organizations in a population (density) rises, founding rates first rise and then fall as density increases and mortality rates fall initially and then begin to rise. The standard explanation for this pattern is based on the opposing effects of legitimation (taken-for-grantedness) and diffuse competition, each of which depends upon density, but in characteristically different ways. Several parametric models of these relationships are well established from research on many diverse populations. In their 2000 book Carroll and Hannan review this evidence.

Several important variations on the basic pattern have been identified. First, density has a "delayed" effect, as was noted by human demographer P. H. Leslie in his analysis of cohort differences in mortality in human populations. The population density at time of entry has a persistent positive effect on an organization's mortality hazard. Second, density-dependent competition is generally more localized than density-dependent legitimation, presumably because cultural information diffuses more readily.

Resource Partitioning

Another major focus of organizational demography has been endogenous processes of segmentation in organizational populations. The best developed research program builds on resource-partitioning theory, developed by Glenn R. Carroll in 1985, which concerns the relationship between increasing market concentration and increasing proliferation of specialist organizations in mature industries with heterogeneous consumers. Specialist organizations are those that focus on narrow, homogeneous targets, whereas generalist organizations aim at broad, heterogeneous targets. If there is an advantage of scale (in production, marketing, or distribution), then competition is most intense in a resource-dense center, which generally becomes dominated by large generalist organizations. The failures of smaller generalists free some resources near the center, but large generalists can rarely secure all of the newly freed resources due to constraints imposed by organizational identities. Therefore, as concentration (the share of the market held by the largest firms) rises, the viability of specialist organizations increases as well: Founding rates rise and mortality rates fall.

Age and Size Dependence

In 1965 sociologist Arthur L. Stinchcombe observed that organizations experience a liability of newness, that age dependence in the mortality hazard is negative. A great deal of early research confirms this pattern. Some later research found a liability of adolescence: The hazard rises during the early portion of the lifespan—that is, while initial stocks of endowments are being exhausted—before declining. Much of this latter research did not control for age-varying organizational size, which is important because age and size are correlated and mortality hazards fall sharply with increases in size. More recent research, using designs that measure age-varying organizational size, has produced mixed evidence in favor of *positive* age dependence. Two interpretations of this pattern have been proposed. If inertial forces are strong, then the possibility of adapting to changing environments is limited and older cohorts of organizations have lower fitness—there is a liability of obsolescence. Alternatively, the accumulation of rules and routines impedes adjustment to environmental change—the liability is one of senescence. Theoretical research by logician László Pólos and Michael T. Hannan has sought to unify these seemingly irreconcilable theory fragments.

Inertia and Selection

Important inspiration for developing a demography and ecology of organizations comes from Stinchcombe's 1965 conjecture that new organizations get *imprinted* by their environments. Because entrants get tested against taken-for-granted assumptions that vary over time, organizations that pass such tests reflect the social structure of the time of entry. Imprinting requires both a mapping of environmental conditions onto organizations and inertia in the imprinted characteristics.

Organizational demography and ecology emphasizes inertial forces. According to structural-inertia theory, inertia prevails as an inadvertent by-product of a selection process that favors the properties of reliability (low variance in the quality of performance) and accountability (the ability to construct rational accounts for actions). Achieving these properties depends on structures being reproduced faithfully over time. Yet, high reproducibility means that structures resist transformation. Therefore, this selection process inadvertently favors corporate actors with strong inertial tendencies.

Fundamental change in technologies and environments presumably diminishes reliability and accountability. Old loses value, and new processes must be learned. Vestiges of the old system conflict with the emerging new one. Thus, even if fundamental change has long-term benefits (the new form might be better aligned with environments and internal processes), change might increase mortality hazards over the short term. If this is indeed the case, reorganization-prone organizations have a lower probability of representation in future populations.

Substantial research has tested the implications of this argument. Most well designed studies have determined that changing core structures increases the hazard of mortality in the short term, often substantially. Moreover, the magnitude of this effect increases with organizational age.

See also: *Event-History Analysis; Human Ecology.*

BIBLIOGRAPHY

Carroll, Glenn R. 1985. "Concentration and Specialization: Dynamics of Niche Width in Organizational Populations." *American Journal of Sociology* 90:1,262–1,283.

Carroll, Glenn R., and Michael T. Hannan. 2000. *The Demography of Corporations and Industries.* Princeton, NJ: Princeton University Press.

Carroll, Glenn R., and Anand Swaminathan. 2000. "Why the Microbrewery Movement? Organizational Dynamics of Resource Partitioning in the U.S. Brewing Industry." *American Journal of Sociology* 106: 715–762.

Hannan Michael T., and John Freeman. 1989. *Organizational Ecology.* Cambridge, MA: Harvard University Press.

Leslie, P. H. 1959. "The Properties of a Certain Lag Type of Population Growth and the Influence of an External Random Factor on the Number of Such Populations." *Physiological Zoölogy.* 3:151–159.

Pólos, László, and Michael T. Hannan. 2002. "Reasoning with Partial Knowledge." *Sociological Methodology 2002.* ed. Ross M. Stolzenberg. Cambridge, Eng.: Blackwell.

Stinchcombe, Arthur L. 1965. "Social Structure and Organizations." *Handbook of Organizations,* ed. James G. March. Chicago: Rand McNally.

MICHAEL T. HANNAN

OUTER SPACE, COLONIZATION OF

Human beings have established settlements in places as varied as the frigid and dry arctic tundra of northern Canada and the hot and wet Amazon rain forest. Clearly, humans are remarkable creatures. But can humans extend the frontier of settlement into an even less hospitable place, the cold vacuum of outer space? More than forty years after the launch of *Sputnik,* how far off is the colonization of outer space?

Low Earth Orbit

The first human went into space in the early 1960s. From then until the 1990s, a few astronauts—or, to use the even more grandiose Russian label, cosmonauts—episodically "populated" near-Earth space. Groups of such travelers rocketed into space, stayed a few days or months, and then returned to Earth. In the 1990s the space station Mir, assembled by the Soviet Union and operated by Russia, was continuously inhabited for several years by rotating crews of cosmonauts. The station aged and was abandoned in 1998 after Russia, the United States, and many other international partners began work on the International Space Station.

A demographic regime in space may have begun on October 31, 2000, when the three-person crew of *Expedition 1* began its four-month stay in orbit on the space station. The U.S. National Aeronautics and Space Administration (NASA) claims that there will always be a crew in the space station. If this turns out to be right, then the dawn of the third millennium will mark the beginning of a permanent space population, a milestone in space similar to that for Antarctica marked by the International Geophysical Year of 1957.

Water—The Liquid of Life

Are Mir and the International Space Station the first steps toward the human colonization of the solar system? Russian space pioneer Konstantin Tsiolkovsky (1857–1935) wrote that "the Earth is the cradle of humanity, but one cannot live in the cradle forever." It is hard for human beings to leave their literal cradles for the Earth beyond them, because the Earth contains what is needed to sustain life: air, food, and water. Outer space is airless, foodless, and most importantly, waterless.

A single human being needs about eight pounds of water per day, including wash water, to live. It takes a ton of water to sustain an eight-person space station for a month if each drop of water is used by a human being only once. On earth, all of this water is recycled, filtered, and purified by the water cycle. In existing space stations, aerospace engineers have made some progress in closing the water loop, by recycling cabin moisture into drinking water. If large-scale, free-floating space colonies—like those proposed by the Princeton physicist Gerard K. O'Neill (1927–1992) in the 1970s—were to become real, 100 percent of the water, including urine, has to be recycled.

In the past few years space enthusiasts have looked more to the planets as possible future homes for humanity. The discoveries of substantial amounts of water on the planet Mars and on Jupiter's satellite Europa have suggested that it might be more feasible to consider colonizing these places, instead of dealing with the tough (though technically solvable) water problem of space stations. Just as settlers in the American West followed great rivers like the Missouri westward, humans may follow the trail of water, which probably would lead to the surface of Mars. And planets like Mars can not only supply space travelers with water to drink; Martian materials can also provide rocket fuel for the trip home. American engineer Robert Zubrin incorporates the use of Martian materials into his revolutionary and important "Mars Direct" plan, proposed in 1996, which cuts the travel time to Mars from nine months to six and permits astronauts to spend much more time on the Martian surface.

Terraforming Mars

Could humans establish a colony on Mars? The Red Planet is far from being Earthlike. Could it be *terraformed*, or altered in order to make it habitable by humans? Scholars Joseph A. Burns, Martin Harwit, and Carl Sagan were the first to suggest terraforming in a mainstream scientific journal in 1973. In broad terms, to terraform Mars, colonists would need to darken the surface so it absorbs more sunlight, and find a way to release the water and carbon dioxide that exists underground so that the atmosphere will become thicker and will trap solar heat by the greenhouse effect.

Thirty years after its initial suggestion, the idea of terraforming is still intellectually alive. It has been discussed in mainstream scientific reviews by such writers as Martyn J. Fogg (1998), as well as in science fiction novels that occasionally delve quite deeply into scientific issues, such as Kim Stanley Robinson's 1994 novel *Green Mars*. But the obstacles to terraforming Mars are formidable. Once enough volatile material (like water and dry ice) is found to create a massive atmosphere, there is still a need to get the gas mixture right. Scuba divers occasionally experiment with breathing oxygen-rich or nitrogen-poor air, and have established that humans need something close to the 4:1 mix of nitrogen to oxygen that humans breathe on Earth. So it may be that nitrogen, the "inert" ingredient in Earth's atmosphere, will limit humans' ability to terraform Mars.

Beyond the Solar System

For a species which has just stuck its toes in the oceans of space, humans have a wonderful capacity to dream. A surprisingly large literature deals with interstellar space flight. *Interstellar Migration and the Human Experience*, a remarkable book edited by Ben R. Finney and Eric M. Jones (1986), provides an inspiring introduction. Perhaps the most visionary of thinkers is the physicist Freeman Dyson, who suggested in 1979 that very advanced civilizations could construct spherical absorbers that would permit them to harness 100 percent of the energy output from an individual star. Can human beings or other intelligent creatures move from one star to another? While the technical challenges are extreme, it is not impossible.

Whether any such dreams will turn into reality is a matter for the future. Some writers like Dyson and Zubrin believe that the allure of the space frontier by itself is enough to propel humanity—in significant numbers—toward the stars. Others, like Harry L. Shipman and many of the authors in *Interstellar Migration and the Human Experience*, take a more cautious approach, suggesting that some kind of return on investment, whether it be through space industrialization or space tourism, must provide a political and economic push. Whatever the future brings, space colonization is a fun and mind-expanding concept to dream about.

Will space colonization ever reach a scale at which number of colonizers could make a significant difference to demographic trends on Earth? It seems unlikely in the foreseeable future. Even Antarctica, where there is a large supply of water (in the form of ice) and air, can only support a year-round population of a few hundred. The most optimistic visions of space colonies, whether free-floating or Martian, postulate populations of tens of thousands. A significant effect on terrestrial population requires space for at least a few tenths of a billion inhabitants. Although outer space is vast, the environment may not be entirely hospitable.

See also: *Extinction, Human; Literature, Population in.*

BIBLIOGRAPHY

Burns, Joseph A., and Harwit, Martin. 1973. "Towards a More Habitable Mars, or The Coming Martian Spring." *Icarus* 19: 126.

Dyson, Freeman J. 1979. *Disturbing the Universe.* New York: Harper and Row.

Finney, Ben R., and Jones, Eric M., eds. 1985. *Interstellar Migration and the Human Experience.* Berkeley: University of California Press.

Fogg, Martyn J. 1998. "Terraforming Mars: A Review of Current Research." *Advances in Space Research* 22(3): 415–420.

Freeman, Marsha. 2000. *Challenges of Human Space Exploration.* Berlin: Springer-Praxis.

O'Neill, Gerard K. 1982. *The High Frontier: Human Colonies in Space.* Garden City, NY: Anchor Books.

Robinson, Kim Stanley. 1994. *Green Mars.* New York: Bantam.

Sagan, Carl. 1973. "Planetary Engineering on Mars." *Icarus* 20: 513.

Shipman, Harry L. 1989. *Humans in Space: 21st Century Frontiers.* New York: Plenum.

Zubrin, Robert, and Wagner, Richard. 1996. *The Case for Mars: The Plan to Settle the Red Planet and Why We Must.* New York: Simon and Schuster Touchstone.

INTERNET RESOURCES.

British Interplanetary Society. 2002. <http://www.bis-spaceflight.com>.

Fogg, Martyn J. 2002. "The Terraforming Information Page." <http://www.users.globalnet.co.uk/~mfogg/index.htm>.

National Aeronautics and Space Administration. 2002. <http://science.ksc.nasa.gov/history/A97>.

Robinson, Kim Stanley. "The Red, Green, and Blue Maps Site." 2002. <http://www.xs4all.nl/~fwb/rgbmars.html>.

HARRY L. SHIPMAN

P

PALEODEMOGRAPHY

Paleodemography attempts to reconstruct past population structure using samples of human skeletons, either freshly excavated or stored in museum collections, from archaeological sites. Its chief claim to legitimacy is that it provides demographic information—albeit of a limited, indirect, and uncertain sort—about the many human populations in the past that left no written records. In principle, paleodemography also allows the reconstruction of demographic trends over time spans that are unattainable by any other branch of population science. Because of persistent methodological problems, however, paleodemographic analysis has achieved only limited credibility among mainstream demographers. Yet while it is fair to say that past paleodemographic analyses were often too crude to be believable, it is also true that recent methodological advances, not yet known to most demographers, have moved paleodemography to a firmer scientific footing. The most important such advances have been in the areas of age estimation, mortality analysis, and adjustments for the effects of demographic non-stationarity on skeletal age-at-death distributions.

Age Estimation

Osteologists have made great progress in identifying reliable skeletal markers of age. Information on age at death is provided by skeletal features such as dental development, annual increments in dental cementum, closure of long-bone epiphyses and cranial sutures, and changes in the articular surfaces of the pelvis. Ages based on such features are subject to differing degrees of error arising from the inherent variability of the underlying processes of maturation and senescence. The age of juveniles can be estimated much more reliably than that of adults, and younger adults more reliably than older adults. But all paleodemographic age estimates are inherently error-prone and always will be. However much osteologists work to reduce these errors and identify new age indicators, a large degree of aging error will always be a part of paleodemography.

The most difficult problems of paleodemographic age estimation are statistical rather than purely osteological. In addition to a *target sample* (the archaeological skeletons whose ages are to be estimated), the paleodemographer needs access to a *reference sample* of skeletons whose ages at death are known. Several well-known reference samples—for example, the Hamman-Todd and Terry Collections—provide reasonably accurate data on the joint distribution of c and a, where c is a vector of skeletal traits that provide information on age and a is age itself. For the target sample, however, researchers know only the marginal distribution of c, from which they hope to estimate the marginal distribution $\Pr(a)$ of ages at death. One of several parametric or non-parametric methods can be applied to data from the reference sample to estimate the conditional probability density or mass function $\Pr(c \mid a)$. If these estimates are to be used in estimating ages of archaeological skeletons, one needs to make an "invariance assumption" that the joint distribution of c and a is identical in the two populations from which the reference and target samples were drawn. It is by no means clear that this assumption is warranted for many skeletal traits, and an ongoing goal of paleodemography is to identify indicators that are both informative about age and reasonably invariant across human populations.

Insofar as the invariance assumption is correct, it would seem to make sense to combine data on $\Pr(c)$ in the target sample and the joint distribution of a and c in the reference sample to estimate $\Pr(a \mid c)$ for each individual skeleton. But according to Bayes' theorem:

$$\Pr(a \mid c) = \frac{\Pr(c \mid a)\, \Pr(a)}{\int_0^\infty \Pr(c \mid x)\, \Pr(x) dx}$$

where $\Pr(a)$ is the age-at-death distribution in the *target* sample, which is unknown.

A procedure for estimating $\Pr(a)$ was recently developed by Hans-Georg Müller and his colleagues (2002). Briefly, $\Pr(a)$ is specified as a Gompertz-Makeham or similar parametric model, $\Pr(a \mid \theta)$, with parameters θ which can be estimated from the reference sample using a maximum-likelihood technique. Once the parameters of $\Pr(a \mid \theta)$ have been estimated, the expected ages of individual skeletons can be found by a straightforward application of Bayes's theorem. This approach to age estimation is called the *Rostock protocol* because it grew out of a series of workshops held at the Max Planck Institute for Demographic Research in Rostock, Germany.

It will seem strange to orthodox paleodemographers that they need to estimate the entire age-at-death distribution before they can estimate individual ages—the reverse of their usual procedure. But the Rostock protocol actually solves a number of problems that have long plagued paleodemography, including the "age mimicry" problem first noted by Jean-Pierre Bocquet-Appel and Claude Masset in 1982. In addition, the method can be used to obtain not just point or interval estimates of age, but the entire error structure of the age estimates. Important statistical problems remain to be solved, such as whether to use discrete categories or "staged" traits versus more continuous age indicators, and how best to use multivariate skeletal data when traits are correlated in their age trajectories. But these problems can all be attacked within the framework of the Rostock protocol.

Mortality Analysis

For years paleodemographers have used skeletal age-at-death data to compute life tables based on some simple modifications of conventional life-table techniques originally developed by the Hungarian demographer and archeologist Gy. Acsádi and J. Nemeskéri. Though this approach is still a common one, the paleodemographic use of life tables can be criticized on several grounds. First, paleodemographic studies do not produce the kinds of data needed to compute life-table mortality rates using standard methods—specifically, paleodemographers lack the numbers of deaths among people at each (known) age and the number of person-years of exposure to the risk of death at that age during some well-defined reference period. Second, the use of fixed age intervals in the life table implies that the ages of all skeletons are known within the same margin of error, including those of fragmentary skeletons that exhibit only a few unreliable indicators of age. Third, the life table is a wasteful way to use the small samples typical of paleodemographic studies—samples that are often on the order of a few dozen or a few hundred skeletons. In computing a life table demographers need to estimate one parameter (an age-specific mortality rate) for every age category by sex in the table. Few paleodemographic samples will support such a data-hungry approach to estimation.

The Rostock protocol supports an alternative approach to paleodemographic mortality analysis. If unbiased estimates of the parameters of $\Pr(a \mid \theta)$ can be obtained for the target population of interest—and if the effects of demographic non-stationarity can be removed (see below)—the parameter estimates can be used to derive the survival function, the age-specific probability of death, life-expectancies, and anything else one might hope to learn from life-table analysis.

Demographic Non-stationarity

Another shortcoming of traditional paleodemographic life-table analysis is that it assumes that the population under investigation was stationary: that it was closed to migration, and had an intrinsic rate of increase equal to zero, age-specific schedules of fertility and mortality that were unchanging over time, and a balanced age distribution generated by those age-specific birth and death rates. Only in this special case is the empirical age distribution of skeletons expected to have a simple, straightforward relationship to the cohort age-at-death column in the life table. This problem was recognized by Larry Angel, one of the early practitioners of paleodemography, and remains a concern.

As demographers have long realized, the age structure of a non-stationary population—and thus the number of its members at risk of death at each age—is more sensitive to the level of fertility than to the level of mortality. Thus, age-at-death distributions from different populations are at least as likely to reflect fertility differences as genuine differences in mortality. This incontrovertible fact of demography has given rise to the odd notion that paleodemographic age-at-death estimates are more informative about fertility than mortality. In fact all demographers can ever hope to estimate about fertility from such data is the crude birth rate, which is scarcely a measure of fertility at all. But if paleodemographers could correct for demographic non-stationarity, they could extract quite a bit of information about age-specific mortality from skeletons, and perhaps even estimate the population's growth rate.

Let $f_0(a)$ be the expected age-at-death distribution for a single birth cohort in the target population. If the target population was stationary, the same distribution holds for all deaths occurring in the population. But even if the population cannot be assumed to have been stationary, it may be reasonable to assume that it was *stable*. That is, demographers may be able to make all the assumptions listed above for the stationary population, with the exception that they should allow for the possibility of a non-zero growth rate. (The assumption of stability is much less restrictive than that of stationarity: even when fertility and mortality rates are changing and migration is occurring, most human populations still closely approximate a stable age distribution at any given time.) In a stable but non-stationary population, the age-at-death distribution is only partly a function of age-specific mortality; it is also influenced by the number of living individuals at risk of death at each age, which is influenced in turn by population growth. More precisely, the probability density function for ages at death in a stable population with growth rate r, $f_r(a)$, can be expressed in terms of the target population age-at-death distribution, $f_0(a)$, by:

$$f_r(a) = f_0(a)e^{-ra} \Big/ \int_0^\infty f_0(x)e^{-rx}\,dx$$

As David Asch showed in 1976, this expression also applies to all the skeletons accumulated by a stable population over some more or less extended span of time—for example, the period over which skeletons were deposited in a cemetery. In principle, then, $f_r(a)$ can be treated as the $\Pr(a \mid \theta)$ function in the Rostock protocol, and r can be estimated as an additional parameter of the model, if the population can be assumed to be stable. And if it was *not* stable, at least approximately, paleodemographers have probably reached the limits of what they can ever hope to learn about age-specific mortality from skeletal samples.

Prospects

The most important recent developments in paleodemography from the perspective of the early twenty-first century have been methodological, not substantive. But now that paleodemographic methods have become more sophisticated, there is every reason to expect that important empirical results will be forthcoming. It is likely, too, that the findings of paleodemography will be strengthened by the study of DNA extracted from ancient bones—a field that is already starting to provide insights into the ancestry and kinship structure of past populations, as well as the pathogens that infected them. There is also a new and encouraging movement to bring archaeological settlement studies, long an established approach to past population dynamics, into the purview of paleodemography. Another useful development has been the study of historical graveyards where cemetery records or parish registers exist to cross-check the osteological results. While mainstream demographers were once justified in dismissing the field of paleodemography, it may be time for them to rethink their skepticism.

See also: *Archaeogenetics; Evolutionary Demography; Prehistoric Populations.*

BIBLIOGRAPHY

Acsádi, G., and J. Nemeskéri. 1970. *History of Human Life Span and Mortality*. Budapest: Akadémiai Kiadó.

Angel, J. L. 1969. "The Bases of Paleodemography." *American Journal of Physical Anthropology* 30: 427–438.

Asch, D. L. 1976. *The Middle Woodland Population of the Lower Illinois Valley: A Study in Paleode-*

mographic Methods. Evanston, IL: Northwestern University Press.

Bocquet-Appel, J. P., and C. Masset. 1982. "Farewell to Paleodemography." Journal of Human Evolution 11: 321–333.

Hoppa, R. D., and J. W. Vaupel, eds. 2002. Paleodemography: Age Distributions from Skeletal Samples. Cambridge: Cambridge University Press.

Horowitz, S., G. Armelagos, and K. Wachter. 1988. "On Generating Birth Rates from Skeletal Samples." American Journal of Physical Anthropology 76: 189–196.

Iscan, M. Y., ed. 1989. Age Markers in the Human Skeleton. Springfield, IL: C. C. Thomas.

Kolman, C. J., and N. Tuross. 2000. "Ancient DNA Analysis of Human Populations." American Journal of Physical Anthropology 111: 5–23.

Konigsberg, L. W., and S. R. Frankenberg. 1992. "Estimation of Age Structure in Anthropological Demography." American Journal of Physical Anthropology 89: 235–256.

Konigsberg, L. W., and S. R. Frankenberg. 1994. "Paleodemography: 'Not Quite Dead.'" Evolutionary Anthropology 3: 92–105.

Meindl, R. S., and K. F. Russell. 1998. "Recent Advances in Method and Theory in Paleodemography." Annual Review of Anthropology 27: 375–399.

Milner, G. R., J. W. Wood, and J. L. Boldsen. 2000. "Paleodemography." In Biological Anthropology of the Human Skeleton, ed. M. A. Katzenberg and S. R. Saunders. New York: Wiley-Liss.

Müller, H. G., B. Love, and R. D. Hoppa. 2002. "Semiparametric Method for Estimating Paleodemographic Profiles from Age Indicator Data." American Journal of Physical Anthropology 117: 1–14.

Paine, R. R., ed. 1997. Integrating Archaeological Demography: Multidisciplinary Approaches to Prehistoric Population. Carbondale: Southern Illinois University Press.

Sattenspiel, L., and H. C. Harpending. 1983. "Stable Populations and Skeletal Age." American Antiquity 48: 489–498.

Stone, A. C. 2000. "Ancient DNA from Skeletal Remains." In Biological Anthropology of the Human Skeleton, ed. M. A. Katzenberg and S. R. Saunders. New York: Wiley-Liss.

Wood, J. W., G. R. Milner, H. C. Harpending, and K. M. Weiss. 1992. "The Osteological Paradox." Current Anthropology 33: 343–370.

JAMES W. WOOD

PARENTHOOD

Throughout history, pregnancy and parenthood were uncontrollable hazards of life for sexually active women. This changed from the 1960s onwards, as the contraceptive revolution allowed sexual activity to be divorced from reproduction. For women, the most important technical innovation of the twentieth century was the contraceptive revolution: the development of coitus-independent and reliable methods of contraception that can be controlled, or chosen, by women themselves. The three principal methods are the contraceptive pill, the IUD or coil, and sterilization. These modern methods of contraception give women control over their own fertility. For the first time in history, parenthood became a voluntary act, rather than the inevitable outcome of marriage. In countries where women can choose if, and when, to become parents, fertility levels have declined sharply, making it clear that the high fertility levels observed in the past were not entirely chosen, even if accepted by couples.

Social Impact of the Contraceptive Revolution

The contraceptive revolution produced two social developments in modern societies: the rise of voluntary childlessness, and the polarization of lifestyles between couples with and without children. In the past, childlessness was generally due to infertility of one or both partners, and childless couples were pitied. Childless women were often stigmatized as social and physical failures, or as unnatural. In countries where the contraceptive revolution has been fully implemented, voluntary childlessness typically rises to around 20 percent of the adult population. People in this group have a distinctive lifestyle, focused on careers, leisure, and intensive consumption. In contrast, couples with children invest a substantial proportion of their resources in the education and socialization of their offspring. Smaller numbers of children mean that greater effort is put into the care and education of each child. The total volume of parenting work thus grows even though the number of children per family declines. In countries where child mortality remains high, parents have less incentive to invest substantial resources in any individual child. Public concern over child labor, child abuse, and children's education are characteristic of societies where family sizes and child mortality are low.

Economics of Parenthood

The nature of parenting changes as the economic relationship between parents and offspring changes. In less developed countries, children are important contributors of labor to the family enterprise, or they contribute earnings from independent jobs, from an early age. Parents also rely on their offspring for financial and social support when they become infirm or old. In effect, the family provides mutual welfare services, and within-family transfers between generations are balanced. Parenting is thus an economic investment with a clear long-term benefit. In modern societies, the principal within-family income transfer is from the older generation to the younger generation, from parents to their offspring, so that children become consumption goods. It is in this sense that having children becomes a lifestyle choice in modern societies, rather than being an absolute necessity for parents' own survival.

The cost of children, as consumption goods, rises steadily as their dependence on their parents is extended beyond early adolescence—initially to late adolescence, then into early adulthood, then into prime adult age, due to the gradual prolongation of full-time education. In 1999 the average age of leaving the parental home in the European Union was 23 for women and 25 for men. However it was markedly higher in southern Europe: 27 for women and 30 for men in Italy, 28 for women and 29 for men in Spain. In prosperous modern societies, parenting is no longer concentrated exclusively on the early years of a child's life.

Parenting Work

Throughout history, mothers have always worked. Survival depended on it. The non-working wife (or concubine) in a single-earner family has always been an indicator of prosperity and higher social status, in all societies. For most women, productive and remunerative work had to be combined with childcare and other family work. For the space of less than 100 years, in the nineteenth and twentieth centuries, women were "domesticated": western European and north American societies promoted the idea of the single earner model of the family as the ideal to aim for in all social classes. Many achieved the goal of one full-time homemaker, for at least part of the family life-cycle. By the end of the twentieth century, women had returned to the labor market in most modern societies, and the dual-earner family was being re-established as the dominant pattern. Nonetheless, mothers retain a much greater attachment to their children, especially during early childhood, which some claim to be the result of evolutionary development rather than the childbearing process.

The majority of mothers in modern societies thus reduce their involvement in paid work when their children are very young. Some women abandon their jobs to become full-time mothers and homemakers on a permanent basis. Sociologist Catherine Hakim (2000) estimates this choice is made by one-fifth of all adult women. Another minority (about one-fifth) contracts out virtually all parenting work—either to state nurseries and schools, or to private nannies and boarding schools. Most women are able to combine childcare with some type of involvement in paid work. The most popular arrangement is the part-time job, which leaves plenty of time for parenting and family work. Seasonal work, term-time work, and temporary jobs are also used to fit paid work around mothers' parenting responsibilities. In countries where part-time jobs are in short supply (such as the United States and southern Europe), mothers are obliged to choose between a full-time job and no paid work at all. Mothers who choose full-time jobs then complain about their "double shift" as sociologist Arlie Hochschild (1990) described it.

In modern societies, many parenting activities are transferred from families to the state. The most obvious example is the formal education and socialization of children. In many countries, the state also provides informal socialization, through clubs and associations, free or subsidised sporting facilities, and cultural activities. The one enduring and irreplaceable contribution of parents seems to be the emotional and social development of young children. Children deprived of one or both parents are more likely to develop antisocial attitudes and behaviors, and be less successful in adult life. There is, apparently, no substitute for parental love and care in the early years. In the early twenty-first century, this seems to be the permanent obstacle to the mass-production of humans outside the family envisaged by Aldous Huxley in his classic novel *Brave New World.*

See also: *Childlessness; Cost of Children; Family Life Cycle; Family Policy; Grandparenthood.*

BIBLIOGRAPHY

Hakim, Catherine. 2000. *Work-Lifestyle Choices in the 21st Century: Preference Theory.* Oxford: Oxford University Press.

Hochschild, Arlie. 1990. *The Second Shift: Working Parents and the Revolution at Home.* London: Piatkus.

Huxley, Aldous. 1932 (1994). *Brave New World.* London: Flamingo.

Rogers, Barbara. 1981. *The Domestication of Women: Discrimination in Developing Societies,* London: Tavistock.

Westoff, Charles F., and Ryder, Norman B. 1977. *The Contraceptive Revolution.* Princeton NJ: Princeton University Press.

CATHERINE HAKIM

PARETO, VILFREDO

(1848–1923)

Italian economist and sociologist Vilfredo Pareto was classified by Joseph A. Schumpeter, the development economist who integrated sociological understanding into economic theory, as one of the great economists. In 1893, Pareto became Professor of Political Economy at the University of Lausanne, occupying the chair formerly held by Léon Walras, the founder of modern theory of general economic equilibrium. He used his background in mathematics and engineering to study human society, adapting the principles of the physical sciences to economic theory. He understood the latter as a science of people's *logical actions* in the use of means for achieving particular ends.

In Pareto's general system of economic equilibrium, the demographic component is the first variable considered. It is the subject of the lengthy first chapter of volume 1 of his *Cours d'économie politique* (1897), entitled "Personal Capital." His statement that, "Political economics must first of all take into account the composition of the population," was an unusual emphasis to find in an economic text (Pareto, p.96 in the Italian edition: *Corso di economia politica, Giulio Einaudi Editore, Torino,* 1949.). According to Pareto (and also English economist T. R. Malthus [1766–1834], from whom Pareto distanced himself by assessing social organization to be much more important in influencing behavior than the principle of moral restraint), the equilibrium between population and subsistence is caused by the mutual interaction between the two components, in much the same way that the movement of a planet is the result of the combined action of the centrifugal force, which tends to drag it away from its orbit, and the centripetal force, pulling it toward the sun. Analogously, a population would tend to grow constantly, under the effect of the *generative force,* were it not restricted by subsistence: hence an equilibrium caused by two disequilibria. Pareto analyzed the state and movement of populations using the formal paradigms of Luigi Perozzo, Italian mathematical demographer, and Wilhelm Lexis, German statistician, and explored the effects of economic factors (particularly those linked to class differences) on natality and mortality.

There is also a demographic element to Pareto's view of sociology, that was considered as a science of humanity's non-logical actions. Pareto's theory maintains that, in an ideal society, a continued and regular change of the ruling class is a necessary condition for a dynamic equilibrium: This is his theory of the circulation of elites, or more accurately, the downward social mobility of less able members of the upper classes, compensated by the rise of lower class members.

See also: *Social Mobility*

BIBLIOGRAPHY

SELECTED WORKS BY VILFREDO PARETO.

Pareto, Vilfredo. 1893. "La mortalità infantile e il costo dell'uomo." *Giornale degli Economisti* (November): 451–456.

———. 1897. *Cours d'économie politique.* Lausanne, Switzerland: F. Rouge.

———. 1906. *Manuale di Economia Politica* [Manual of political economy]. Milan: Societa Editrice. English translation. 1971. New York: A. M. Kelley.

———. 1916. *Trattato di Sociologia Generale* [The mind and society: A treatise on general sociology]. 4 Vols. Florence, Italy: G. Barbèra. English translation. 1935. New York: Harcourt Brace.

———. 1966. *Sociological Writings,* Selected and Introduced by S. E. Finer. New York: Praeger.

———. 1966. *Sociological Writings,* The Robert J. Le Fevre Collection. Selected and Intro. S. E. Finer, trans. Derick Mirfin. New York: Praeger.

———. 1968. *Rise and Fall of the Elites: An Application of Theoretical Sociology.* Totowa, NJ: Bedminster Press.

SELECTED WORKS ABOUT VILFREDO PARETO.

Schumpeter, Joseph A. 1951. *Ten Great Economists, from Marx to Keynes.* New York: Oxford University Press.

Spengler, Joseph J. 1972. "Pareto on Population." In *Population Economics.* Durham, NC: Duke University Press.

ITALO SCARDOVI

PARTNER CHOICE

There are many systems of partner choice, but all tend to produce a high degree of "assortative mating," that is a pattern in which individuals choose partners who are similar to themselves. This pattern also has been called *homogamy* and has been described as "like marries like." Assortative mating has been observed in a wide range of societies, though numerous exceptions have always been found.

Several theories have been advanced to explain the origins of assortative mating. The most common view starts from a rational actor/exchange perspective in which individuals search among potential partners and seek to maximize their gains from an alliance. Because each individual is likely to reject anyone with characteristics less desirable than his or her own, all are likely to wind up with individuals very much like themselves. An alternative view stresses the noneconomic aspects of status and sees the process as a search for a partner with the same culture and values. In both perspectives assortative mating links individuals who are similar on a number of ascribed (i.e., determined by birth) and achieved characteristics and thus perpetuates the prevailing system of social stratification.

The numerous exceptions to assortative mating also require explanation. Limitations imposed by the pool of possible partners are a potentially important factor. A second factor is that individuals typically have personal, emotional, and idiosyncratic partner preferences. Still, there is good reason to believe that many exceptions to homogamy reflect social structural factors.

Traditionally, women have sought men who can fulfill a breadwinner role, and in contemporary Western societies a man's steady job is still very important. Although women's employment outside the home is growing in importance in many societies, men traditionally have emphasized a woman's social characteristics: poise, charm, attractiveness, and other noneconomic attributes. As a result, mutually beneficial exchanges can occur between a man's economic characteristics (e.g., education, income, and occupation) and a woman's noneconomic characteristics (including age and race/ethnicity). A classic explanation along those lines is that most (two-thirds or more) black-white marriages in the United States involve black men and white women because they represent an exchange between a black man's greater economic resources and a white woman's superior social status.

Although the significance of exchanges in the overall context of partner choice remains a matter of dispute, exchanges involving a number of female noneconomic and male economic characteristics have been found in analyses of marriage data. Marriages that cross major social divisions also reflect the social distance between those groups. When dominant and subordinate groups are involved, such intermarriages are simultaneously a reflection of the acceptance of the subordinate group and a threat to that group's cohesion and distinctiveness.

One characteristic of Western and some non-Western societies since the mid-twentieth century is a trend toward a greater emphasis on achieved characteristics and a deemphasis of ascribed traits. For example, in the United States educational homogamy has grown in importance while religious homogamy has declined. The rise of cohabitation in many Western societies raises additional issues because if cohabitation is a distinct institutional form, patterns of partner choice could differ. There is some evidence that compared with marriages, cohabitations are more assortative in regard to achieved characteristics and less in regard to ascribed ones. Cohabitations are less permanent than marriages and thus are less likely to emphasize long-term, familistic considerations. However, since cohabitation is frequently a prelude to marriage, the increased frequency of cohabitation may accentuate the shift away from ascribed characteristics. Little is known about the nature of assortative mating in same-sex unions.

As societies change their institutional forms and beliefs, the criteria that guide mate selection are transformed. However, despite much individual variation, partner choice has always reflected the prevailing social structures and values.

See also: *Cohabitation; Family Bargaining; Marriage.*

BIBLIOGRAPHY

Davis, Kingsley. 1941. "Intermarriage in Caste Societies." *American Anthropologist* 43: 376–395.

DiMaggio, Paul, and John Mohr. 1985. "Cultural Capital, Educational Attainment, and Marital Selection." *American Journal of Sociology* 90: 1,231–1,261.

Edwards, John N. 1969. "Familial Behavior as Social Exchange." *Journal of Marriage and the Family* 31: 518–526.

Gordon, Milton M. 1964. *Assimilation in American Life.* New York: Oxford University Press.

Schoen, Robert, and Robin M. Weinick. 1993. "Partner Choice in Marriages and Cohabitations." *Journal of Marriage and the Family* 55: 408–414.

Schoen, Robert, and John Wooldredge. 1989. "Marriage Choices in North Carolina and Virginia, 1969–1971 and 1979–1981." *Journal of Marriage and the Family* 51: 465–481.

ROBERT SCHOEN

PEARL, RAYMOND

(1879–1940)

Raymond Pearl was an American biologist, geneticist, biometrician, and eugenicist. He was also a professor of Biometry and Vital Statistics at Johns Hopkins University (1918–1940) and the first president of the International Union for the Scientific Investigation of Population Problems (IUSSP's predecessor). Pearl studied under the statistician Karl Pearson (1857–1936) in London and subsequently applied statistical methods to the analysis of human populations, concentrating on longevity, fertility, and the patterns of population growth. The value used in the medical sciences to rate the effectiveness of a birth control method bears his name (*Pearl Index*). Following the lead of the eugenicist Francis Galton and Pearson, Pearl tried to create a new branch of mathematical biology—the "biology of groups"—based on the population as the unit of analysis.

Under the influence of Pearson, Pearl started out as a strong advocate of eugenics. However, in the course of his active life, he relaxed his views, arguing against the class bias that pervaded the eugenics movement. Much to the chagrin of the eugenicists he asserted that the higher reproduction rate of the lower classes need not be feared: the lower classes often produced superior individuals who, given the opportunity for social mobility, would become valuable members of society.

In 1920 Pearl, together with Lowell J. Reed, rediscovered the "logistic curve" of population growth, which had been first formulated by the Belgian mathematician Pierre-François Verhulst in 1838. Initially, Pearl tended to interpret the logistic curve in a deterministic way as a general biological "law," holding for both human and non-human populations. In his view the theoretical basis for this was to be found in natural causes—biological, physical or chemical. The relevance of the logistic curve as a theory of population growth was widely questioned by those who thought that such growth depended largely upon cultural, social, and economic changes. Later, Pearl moved away from determinism.

Both Pearl and his law of logistic population growth were prominent at the World Population Conference in Geneva in 1927. Throughout the 1920s the merits of the logistic curve as a tool for estimating and projecting population growth were debated and juxtaposed with those of the cohort component approach then being introduced. The latter method was favored by most European statisticians and economists, and subsequently became the dominant mode of population forecasting. In 1932 Alfred Lotka reconciled the two approaches by constructing a unified formal model that integrated the logistic and cohort-component characteristics of population growth.

See also: *Demography, History of; Lotka, Alfred; Projections and Forecasts, Population; Verhulst, Pierre-François.*

BIBLIOGRAPHY

SELECTED WORKS BY RAYMOND PEARL.

Pearl, Raymond. 1924. *Studies in Human Biology* Baltimore, MD: Williams & Wilkins.

———. 1926. *The Biology of Population Growth.* London, Williams and Norgate.

———. 1928. *The Rate of Living: Being an Account of Some Experimental Studies on the Biology of Life Duration.* New York: Alfred A. Knopf.

———. 1939. *The Natural History of Population.* New York: Oxford University Press.

Pearl, Raymond, and Lowell J. Reed. 1930. *The Logistic Curve and the Census Count of 1930.* New York: Science Press.

SELECTED WORKS ABOUT RAYMOND PEARL.

De Gans, Henk A. 2002. "Law or Speculation? A Debate on the Method of Forecasting Future Population Size in the 1920s." *Population* 57(1): 83–108.

Kingsland, Sharon. 1988. "Evolution and Debates Over Human Progress from Darwin to Sociobiology." In *Population and Resources in Western Intellectual Traditions,* ed. Michael S. Teitelbaum and Jay M. Winter. Supplement to *Population and Development Review,* Vol. 14, pp. 167–189.

Lotka, Alfred J. 1932. "The Structure of a Growing Population." In *Problems of Population.* London: George Allen and Unwin Ltd.

HENK A. DE GANS

PEOPLING OF THE CONTINENTS

From Africa, humans migrated to Asia and Europe and, later, settled the Pacific islands and the Americas. Successive waves of migration have covered the habitable world with self-sustaining settlements. The geographical patterns of peopling are the result of two closely related processes: migration and endogenous growth associated with contextual living conditions. Robust endogenous growth is seldom found in isolated and sparse settlements unless the population reaches critical levels of density that make the division of roles and functions and the emergence of agriculture possible. With the neolithic revolution—about 10,000 years ago in the Middle East and China, and later in the Americas—endogenous growth accelerated, providing an additional impetus for successive waves of settlement in empty or sparsely settled regions of the world. As early as 2000 years ago, with a total population of between 250 and 350 million, most regions of the world were well settled with populations expanding by natural growth rather than by migration.

The growth performances of the various continents and regions have differed widely during the last two millennia. In approximately 1500, the population of Europe was double that of Sub-Saharan Africa; in 1900 it was four times larger; and in 2000 the populations were nearly equal. In 1500 the Americas—according to William Denevan's 1992 estimate—had approximately the same population as Africa; in 1800 it was one-half Africa's size; and in 1900 it was larger than Africa's population by 50 percent. Migration flows and differential natural growth are the proximate determinants of these highly varied performances, but the remote determinants are much more complex and rooted in differential command of technology and knowledge, resilience of social texture, and environmental characteristics.

Africa

Oddly enough, Africa, the continent of humanity's origin, has the least understood demographic history. Over the last millennium, the population growth of sub-Saharan Africa was associated with the expansion of Bantu populations, sustained by the use of iron, and by the extension and intensification of agriculture in the tropical forests of Central Africa and in the savannas of East and Southern Africa. Coinciding with this expansion was the southward movement of Nilo-Saharan populations from the eastern part of the continent. The population of North Africa, which at the peak of Roman power matched the size of that in the Sub-Saharan region, fell to perhaps one-fourth of that amount by the middle of the last millennium.

There is a great deal of information available about the slave trade and the forced abduction of millions of Africans, who were taken mainly from the west coast of the continent and transported, in major part, to the Americas, beginning in the late-fifteenth century. The total number of people who were forcibly moved to the Americas is believed to be about 8 million between 1500 and the end of the trade in the mid-nineteenth century. Another flow, of lesser magnitude, followed Arab trading routes to the north. It is generally thought that the slave trade had little or no effect on the growth of Africa's population, which was approaching 50 million at the beginning of the relevant period. A strict Malthusian interpretation of these events is that the population drain might have improved the chance of survival of those remaining behind by lessening the pressure on resources, while the revenues of the slave trade improved the standard of living. But this view must be balanced by the fact that slaves were typically in the prime productive years of their lives, families were separated, and communities were deeply wounded. The negative demographic effects on the areas from which the slaves came must have been considerable.

The Americas

The size of the population of the Americas at the time of the first European contact is a matter of controversy, with many ideological connotations. Influential estimates made by scholars in the last 50 years vary between a low level of 13 million by Angel Rosenblat in 1954 to a high of 113 million by Henry F. Dobyns in 1966, with more recent reassessments taking a middle course: 54 million according to William M. Denevan in 1992. However, the negative impact of contact and conquest is not in dispute: By the early seventeenth century the population had declined to just above 10 million and a sustained recovery took place only during the eighteenth century with the contribution of European and African immigration.

The steep decline in the century after the European arrival has been traditionally explained by the violent shift of power that ensued and the consequences of wars, forced labor, displacement, and violence. These were the ingredients of the *black legend* of the Conquest, first discussed in the writings of the settler-turned-Dominican friar, Bartolomé de Las Casas (1484–1566), and expanded to include anti-Spanish and anti-Catholic attitudes by later writers. Later revisionism, while raising the initial estimates of the indigenous population, attributes the main cause of the demographic catastrophe to diseases—such as smallpox, measles, or influenza—imported from Europe into a population with no immunity. However, the epidemiological explanation fails to take into account the complexity of the changes brought about by the European conquest and settlement. To assess the mix of factors that led to population decline or outright depopulation calls for careful analysis of each area and society. In the Greater Antilles, for example, local Taino Indians had almost disappeared by the mid-sixteenth century and were already much reduced in numbers by 1518 when the first epidemic of smallpox reached the New World from Europe. Earlier negative effects on survival and fertility may be traced to the economic displacement and confiscation of labor by the new masters, which eroded the standard of living in the local subsistence economy, the disruption of traditional social hierarchies, the fragmentation of families and clans, and the absorption of Taino women into the European reproductive pool. In other places, and particularly in the areas of densest settlement, it is likely that imported diseases were the principal cause of population decline.

Some population historians, including Sherburne Cook and Woodrow Borah, demonstrated that population decline was more severe in the areas with low density—for instance, in the coastal lowlands of the Gulf of Mexico—than in the more densely-settled plateaus and highlands—such as those making up the core of the Aztec empire. This argument, if correct, is at odds with the epidemiological explanation: The transmission of new pathologies would have been easier, and would have had deadlier effect, where the population was densely settled. Another nonepidemiological factor in depopulation must have been the displacement of native populations under the pressure of European settlement, as happened, for instance, along the coast of Brazil.

European populations thrived everywhere. The population of French origin in Québec in 1800, was seven times larger than the total inflow of immigrants from France up to that time; the population of Iberian and British origin was three to four times the cumulated immigration from their areas of origin. Compare this pattern of growth with the mere doubling of the European population from 1500 to 1800. European settlers had ample access to land; they found favorable climatic conditions and a more benign pathological environment; and plants and livestock imported from Europe flourished.

In the Americas as a whole, a cumulative total of some two million European immigrants, who had arrived by 1800, had grown into a population (not counting *mestizos*) of around seven million, equally divided between north and south. The population of European origin approached the size of the indigenous population, the descendants of the estimated 54 million of 1500. In contrast with the European immigration, the population of African origin (slave and nonslave) suffered heavy losses due to adverse living and working conditions, restrained family formation, and other consequences of slavery. In 1800 the African population in the Caribbean was perhaps 50 percent of the total inflow of enslaved people that arrived from Africa, while in Brazil the same population approximated the cumulated inflow. These two destinations accounted for 80 percent of the slave trade. A continuous inflow of slaves was needed in order to compensate the negative natural growth of the African population.

In the following century and a half, the population of the Americas increased rapidly due to the pressure of mass European immigration pushing the frontier of settlement westward and southward. Between 1840 and 1940, immigration accounted for 60 percent of natural growth in Argentina, 40 percent in the United States, and 20 percent in Brazil and Canada. Mexico, by far the most populous country of the Americas up to the eighteenth century, was the destination of only modest inflows of immigrants and slaves; Mexico was surpassed in population size by the U.S. in 1800 and by Brazil in around 1850.

Europe

The peopling of Europe is relatively well understood. In prehistoric times agriculturists from Asia Minor progressively migrated northwest into Europe, bringing new settlements and cultivation techniques and causing, or at least encouraging, the neolithic revolution there. The great blending of populations caused by migration from outside the continent increased with the fall of the Roman Empire and continued until the end of the ninth century when nomadic people, today's Hungarians, coming from the Euro-Asian steppes settled in the Carpathian Basin. Immigration continued to the open areas in the east of the continent and with the ebb and flow of Turks in the Balkans. Nevertheless, major immigration into Europe basically ended by the end of the Middle Ages.

The early centuries of the second millennium saw sustained population movement to the east of the continent, a settlement process that continued, in spite of the demographic decline caused by the Black Death in the fourteenth century, with varying rhythm until the nineteenth century. Much of this movement consisted of Germanic groups that gradually settled in territories east of the river Oder, which had been occupied by ethnic Slavs during the preceding millennium, and later in the southeast in territories taken back from the receding Ottoman Empire. The numbers of migrants were relatively small (perhaps a few hundred thousand), but improved technology, good organization and planning, and abundant land created conditions that both favored the natural growth of settlers and generated new waves of migration. In addition to this major eastern thrust, there were also lesser migrations in other directions: Spaniards and Portuguese toward the south, following the Reconquista of the Iberian peninsula (the fifteenth century expulsion of the Arabs); northward by the Scandinavians; and Slavs southward in Russia in search of more stable borders.

After two centuries of moderate but significant migration from Europe to the Americas, Iberian and British imperialists had established the political, economic, and demographic basis for mass migration. The availability of land in the Americas and to a lesser degree in Oceania, combined with an expanding demand for labor in these new societies, created the conditions for massive outflow from Europe. The industrial revolution and the acceleration of population growth in Europe pushed an increasing number of peasants out of their traditional occupations, making them candidates for emigration. Between 1846 and World War II, over 60 million Europeans emigrated, 50 percent of them from the British Isles and Italy; 60 percent of this flow went to North America, and another 25 percent to Latin America. (Many emigrants eventually returned to their home countries.) Another steady outflow—exceeding five million in total—was from European Russia to Siberia and Central Asia in the second half of the nineteenth century and the first half of the twentieth century.

In the first 15 years of the twentieth century the annual rate of European emigration exceeded three per thousand, one-third of the rate of natural increase. In spite of this drain, Europe accounted for about one-fourth of the world population by the onset of World War I, as compared to less than one-fifth in 1750. In part because of this drain, the Americas's share of the world population increased from 2.3 percent in 1750 to 11 percent in 1914.

Asia

The population of Asia is so large that growth of the largest countries has been mainly endogenous, migration playing only a minor role, at least in modern times. In China, with the Ming dynasty replacing the Mongol dynasty in the fourteenth century, the depopulated north was the destination of substantial migration from the Yangtze area. In the nineteenth century and at the beginning of the twentieth century, Chinese migrants went to other southeast-Asian countries—Malaysia, Indonesia, Indochina, Thailand—as well as to the Americas. Indian labor, after the end of the slave system, emigrated to places such as Natal in South Africa, Mauritius, and Trinidad. But the quantitative impact of these flows on the populations of origin was very small, and the decreased weight of Asia on world population, from around 66 percent in 1800 to 55 percent in 1900, is due to natural increase in Asia that was lower than was then prevailing in the rest of the world. Over the same period, the combined weight of Europe and of the Americas on world population increased from 23 to 36 percent, while that of Africa declined from 11 to 8 percent. During this period the West, in full demographic transition, reached the zenith of its weight in world population.

The Twentieth Century

In the twentieth century waves of migration were important locally but, with the steep drop in European emigration in the third decade of the century, changes in the distribution of population among the continents and regions of the world were mainly due to differences in natural increase. This rate declined in the West, with the nearing completion of its demographic transition, and soared in the other continents with the mid-century onset of their respective transitions. For the world as a whole, the number of migrants in relation to the total population has become relatively small: in the second half of the twentieth century the foreign born made up little more than 2 percent of the total population. By 2000, the weight of Europe had declined to 13 percent, about half the level it reached in 1900.

See also: *Prehistoric Populations; Trans-Atlantic Migration; World Population Growth.*

BIBLIOGRAPHY

Biraben, Jean-Noël. 1979. "Essai sur l'évolution du nombre des hommes." *Population* 34(1): 13–25.

Cavalli-Sforza, Luca Luigi, Paolo Menozzi, and Alberto Piazza. 1994. *The History and Geography of Human Genes.* Princeton: Princeton University Press.

Cook, Sherburne, and Woodrow Borah. 1971. *Essay in Population History: Mexico and the Caribbean.* Berkeley: University of California Press.

Curtin, Philip D. 1969. *The Atlantic Slave Trade. A Census.* Madison: University of Wisconsin Press.

Denevan, William M. 1992. *The Native Population of the Americas in 1492.* Madison: The Wisconsin University Press.

Dobyns, Henry F. 1966. "Estimating Aboriginal American Population: An Appraisal of Techniques with a New Hemispheric Estimate." *Current Anthropology* 7(4): 395–416.

Durand, John D. 1977. "Historical Estimates of World Population." *Population and Development Review* 3(3): 253–296.

Livi-Bacci, Massimo. 2000. *The Population of Europe: A History.* Oxford: Blackwell.

———. 2001. *A Concise History of World Population.* Oxford: Blackwell.

Maddison, Angus. 2001. *The World Economy: A Millennial Perspective.* Paris: OECD.

McEvedy, Colin, and Richard Jones. 1978. *Atlas of World Population History.* Harmondsworth, NY: Penguin.

Reinhardt, Marcel, André Armengaud, and Jacques Dupâquier. 1968. *Histoire de la population du monde.* Paris: Montchrestien.

Rosenblat, Angel. 1954. *La población indígena y el mestizaje en América.* Buenos Ayres: Editorial Nova.

Massimo Livi-Bacci

PETTY, WILLIAM

(1623–1687)

Sir William Petty was born in London in very modest circumstances, the son of a clothmaker. After some years in the navy of King Charles I, he studied medicine in the Netherlands; in Paris, where he became a friend of the philosopher Thomas Hobbes; and at Oxford. In 1650, at the age of twenty-seven, he became professor of anatomy at Oxford, resigning the next year when he was appointed physician-general to Cromwell's army in Ireland.

Much of the rest of Petty's life was spent in Ireland in various capacities. He organized a major topographical survey that was needed for the redistribution of the forfeited property of Catholic landowners; after the restoration of Charles II he was a member of parliament for Ireland and was engaged in managing an industrial colony on the estate he had acquired in County Kerry. In his London life he was one of the group of philosophers and scientists, including Robert Boyle and John Graunt (1620–1674), who founded the Royal Society. He was knighted in 1661.

Petty's major intellectual contributions to both economics and demography fall under the broad rubric of political arithmetic, a term he invented. This was the application of Francis Bacon's (1561–1626) methods of natural philosophy to understanding social conditions and economic life—on the assumption that the *body politik* could be studied quantitatively in the same manner as the *body natural*. In his account of Petty in *Brief Lives* (c. 1690), John Aubrey concisely, if somewhat dismissively, characterized the approach as "reducing polity to numbers." Petty's work laid the foundations for the development of systematic social and economic statistics by subsequent scholars such as Charles Davenant (1656–1714) and Gregory King (1648–1712). On the basis of his pamphlet *Verbum Sapienti* (1690, a posthumous publication, like most of Petty's writings)

Richard Stone (1997) calls Petty "the originator of national accounting." This general perspective and its influence on the thinking of his contemporaries and successors is the main reason Petty has a place in the history of demography: Population dynamics were to him an integral part of social accounting.

Petty also made specific demographic contributions, in particular in estimating mortality and population size, chiefly of major cities. He played a role, most likely minor, in the preparation of Graunt's pathbreaking *Observations* on the (London) bills of mortality (1662). Petty has sometimes been credited with virtual authorship of this work, but a detailed investigation by his later editor Charles Henry Hull found little evidence to support that contention. Stone agrees that such an attribution is baseless. Petty admired Graunt's work and drew on it in his own studies, especially of the Dublin bills of mortality.

His estimates of city sizes—based on calculations such as the number of burials divided by the supposed death rate or the number of houses multiplied by the average household size (guessed)—he recognized as highly conjectural, needing to be replaced by independent enumerations. (His population of London was much too large, that of Paris too small.) At the end of his *Observations on the Dublin Bills* (1683), he wrote: "Without the knowledge of the true number of the people, as a principle, the whole scope and use of keeping bills of birth and burials is impaired; wherefore by laborious conjectures and calculations to deduce the number of people from the births and burials, may be ingenious, but very preposterous." Petty's land survey of Ireland, the results of which were published in his *Political Anatomy of Ireland* (1691), was effectively Ireland's first census (1659).

See also: *Demography, History of; Graunt, John; King, Gregory; Population Thought, History of.*

BIBLIOGRAPHY

SELECTED WORKS BY WILLIAM PETTY.

Petty, William. 1686. *An Essay Concerning the Multiplication of Mankind: Together with Another Essay in Political Arithmetick, Concerning the Growth of the City of London: with the Measures, Periods, Causes, and Consequences thereof, 1862.* 2nd edition. London: Mark Pardoe. Excerpted in *Population and Development Review* 10(1984): 127–133.

———. 1690. *Political Arithmetick, or, A discourse concerning the extent and value of lands, people, buildings, husbandry, manufacture, commerce, . . . , as the same relates to every country in general. . .* London: Robert Clavel and Hen. Mortlock.

———. 1691. *The Political Anatomy of Ireland. . . To which is added Verbum sapienti, or, An account of the wealth and expences of England, and the method of raising taxes in the most equal manner. . .* London: D. Brown and W. Rogers. Facsimile edition: Shannon, Ireland: Irish University Press, 1970.

———. [1899] 1964. *The Economic Writings of Sir William Petty,* ed. Charles H. Hull. 2 vols. New York: A. M. Kelly.

SELECTED WORKS ABOUT WILLIAM PETTY.

Aubrey, John. 1898. *Brief Lives . . . Set Down between the Years 1669 & 1696.* Oxford: Clarendon Press.

Hull, Charles H. 1900. "Petty's Place in the History of Economic Theory." *Quarterly Journal of Economics* 14(4): 307–340.

Stone, Richard. 1997. *Some British Empiricists in the Social Sciences 1650–1900.* Cambridge, Eng.: Cambridge University Press.

GEOFFREY MCNICOLL

POPULATION

In modern usage the word population, means "the total number of persons inhabiting a country, town, or other area," or "the body of inhabitants" (*Oxford English Dictionary [OED]*). The two meanings seem much the same and are often conflated, but conceptually they are distinct—the first, the number of persons, is the demographer's stock in trade; the second, the body of inhabitants, is the stuff of social science generally. The word derives from the Latin *populare,* "to populate, to people," and the late Latin noun *populatio.* Curiously, in classical times the verb more commonly meant to lay waste, plunder, or rav-

age, and *populatio* was a plundering or despoliation. Both meanings entered English. The usage of population as devastation, however, had become obsolete by the eighteenth century.

The word's first recorded use in a modern sense, according to demographer Adolphe Landry, is in an essay by the philosopher Francis Bacon from 1597. Another Bacon essay, cited by the *OED* in a 1625 edition, already gives the term a distinctive Malthusian flavor: "It is to be foreseene, that the Population of a Kingdome, (especially if it not be mowen downe by warrs) doe not exceed, the Stock of the Kingdome, which should maintain them." But at this time, and for most of another two centuries, population retained its gerund-like connotation of process—the process of populating or peopling. That usage appears in the 1776 Declaration of Independence of the United States, where one of the particulars among the "abuses and usurpations" charged against George III was: "He has endeavoured to prevent the Population of these States; for that Purpose obstructing the Laws for Naturalization of Foreigners; refusing to pass others to encourage their Migrations hither, and raising the Conditions of new Appropriations of Lands."

Adolphe Landry, in his *Traité de démographie* (1945) traces the parallel shifts in usage in French. He notes the early use of *dépopulation,* in the sense of devastation, and in the eighteenth century the gradual loss of the connotation of population-as-peopling. The new meaning was affirmed when the statesman Comte de Mirabeau could title his 1757 work *L'ami des hommes, ou traité de la population.* A fuller account is contained in Hervé Le Bras's *L'Invention des populations* (2000).

The main demographic interest in population is as a simple magnitude: population size. Well before Bacon there was of course a need to talk about numbers of inhabitants in a particular territory. In English, for example, the word "souls" in the sense of enumerated individuals was used from the fourteenth century or even earlier. But for most purposes the egalitarianism implied by weighting individuals equally would have been seen as distorting reality. Nobles and commoners, or citizens and noncitizens, could not be simply added together. Women and children might count for little; slaves for nothing. Plato's optimal size of a city-state, 5040, referred to the number of citizens—a category that excluded women, children, and slaves. The actual population corresponding to this figure would have been ten or twelve times the size. The *populus* of republican Rome, in the phrase *Senatus populusque Romanus* (SPQR) displayed by its legions and on present-day Rome's manhole covers, were the freeborn citizens—far fewer than the population.

In later times it was the disadvantaged in the society, potentially a charge on the exchequer, that might need to be enumerated. Here, the word "populace" could be employed—in its meaning, dating from the sixteenth century, of riffraff or rabble, to be distinguished from the gentry. In early modern England, a significant motivation for measures to record population numbers was to identify those receiving assistance under the Poor Law.

In England, the subsequent emergence of the word population, qua population size, can be traced in the documents assembled by the demographer David Glass on the history of census-taking. A 1753 bill (not enacted) called "for Taking and Registering an annual Account of the total Number of People, . . ." The term population did not appear, the text constantly referring to the total number of persons or inhabitants. Within two decades the word was in use. English agriculturalist Arthur Young's pamphlet of 1771 advocating a census was entitled *Proposals to the Legislature for Numbering the People. Containing Some Observations on the Population of Great Britain, and a Sketch of the Advantages that would probably accrue from an exact Knowledge of its present State.* Population was used repeatedly in the text, unitalicized and with minimal echoes of its origins as process. The 1800 law establishing the British census was called simply *An Act for taking Account of the Population of Great Britain, . . .*

The application to nonhuman collectivities dates at least from T. R. Malthus's *Second Essay* (1803), where Malthus wrote: "The population of the tribe is measured by the population of its herds." Straightforward extensions of usage cover sets of inanimate objects, especially where age or vintage is a member characteristic. Often demographic analysis finds immediate application to such collectivities—for instance, deriving life tables for stocks of forest trees or automobiles, or investigating birth and death processes for organizations. In the field of genetics, a population is a collection of organisms as opposed to a collection of genes, giving rise to the contrast between *genetic* processes and *population* (or sometimes, *demographic*) processes (see, for ex-

ample, Young and Clarke 2000). *Metapopulation,* a term used in ecological studies, is a system of local populations connected by dispersing individuals (see Gilpin and Hanski 1991).

In both ordinary English usage and in demographic analysis, population refers to a well-defined set, with clear-cut membership criteria. Thus, to take a common example, the population of the United States as identified in the 2000 census—281,421,906—refers to the residents (legal and illegal) of the 50 states and assorted territories plus U.S. military and civil officials stationed abroad, as of April 1, 2000. Conceptually, the membership criteria are clear, even if the resulting number inevitably has a margin of error—by Census Bureau estimates, for example, the 1990 U.S. census missed about 8.4 million persons and double-counted 4.4 million. In some other cases, the concept of population to be applied is itself fuzzy. Consider, for example, the population of a city. The boundaries of an urban agglomeration defined by some specified array of functional characteristics may bear scant relationship to a city's administrative borders, the former being more than a little arbitrary and the latter reflecting historical contingency. Even if there are agreed physical boundaries, the number of legal residents may differ greatly from the number of *de facto* residents, and there is an evident fringe or penumbra of membership beyond both, comprising persons with lesser degrees of attachment. The actual number of people within a city's defined borders varies greatly by time of day, day of the week, and season.

See also: *Census; Demography, History of; Organizations, Demography of.*

BIBLIOGRAPHY

Gilpin, Michael E., and Ilkka A. Hanski, eds. 1991. *Metapopulation Dynamics: Empirical and Theoretical Investigations.* London: Academic Press.

Glass, David V., ed. 1973. *The Development of Population Statistics.* Farnborough, England: Gregg International Publishers.

Landry, Adolphe. 1945. *Traité de Démographie.* Paris: Payot.

Le Bras, Hervé. 2000. "Peuples et populations." In his *L'Invention des populations: Biologie, idéologie et politique.* Paris: Odile Jacob.

Young, Andrew G., and Geoffrey M. Clarke, eds. 2000. *Genetics, Demography and Viability of*

Fragmented Populations. New York: Cambridge University Press.

GEOFFREY MCNICOLL

POPULATION BIOLOGY

See *Animal Ecology; Biodemography; Biology, Population; Evolutionary Demography*

POPULATION DECLINE

Population decline was a frequent experience until the nineteenth and twentieth centuries, when population growth became the norm. By the beginning of the twenty-first century, that era of growth was ending. In Europe, population decline is expected to become general by the mid-twenty-first century, and by the end of the century, global population itself may be falling.

Dynamics of Population Decline

Fewer births, more deaths, and net emigration can each provoke population decline: the basic "balancing equation" can be expressed as:

Population Change =

Births − Deaths ± Net Migration

With modern mortality, where most children survive, each woman needs to produce on average just over two children to replace the population over a generation (25 to 30 years). Average family size is measured by the *Total Fertility Rate* (TFR), the number of children which the average woman would have over her fertile lifetime (conventionally, ages 15 to 49), given current fertility rates at each age. A TFR of 2.11 implies that women would have, on average, 2.11 children at current rates—1.03 girls and 1.08 boys (assuming the sex ratio at birth to be 1.05). If the female survival rate to the end of the childbearing period is 0.97, women would have, on average, exactly 1.0 surviving daughter to replace them: the *Net Reproduction Rate* (NRR) is 1.0. Other things being equal, below-replacement fertility—an NRR below 1.0 or, roughly, a TFR below 2.1—implies population decline in the long run.

In the industrial world since the 1970s, and increasingly in the developing world, the TFR has fallen below 2.1 and the NRR below 1.0. Yet most of these populations continue to grow, partly because of immigration (e.g., Germany and Italy). However, most Western countries still have a positive natural increase (excess of births over deaths). Births can exceed deaths for a time, even when the TFR is less than 2.1, if the number of women in their reproductive years is exceptionally high as a legacy of past population growth or bulges such as the "baby boom" cohorts of the 1960s. Only when this structural anomaly ceases will deaths finally exceed births. This delay is known as *population momentum.* It can sustain growth only for a few decades; the population momentum was ending in most Western populations by the beginning of the twenty-first century (Table 1).

Momentum operates in both directions. A declining population with a structure aged through years of below-replacement fertility would continue to decline in numbers for some years, even if fertility increased to replacement rate (this is the case, for example, in Germany).

Population Decline in the Past

For millennia, until the eighteenth century, average long-term rates of human population growth must have been close to zero. Periods of mild population decline would have been almost as normal as periods of population growth, and except for crisis years, no more perceptible. "Normal" processes served to regulate populations through alternating periods of mild growth and decline, as in early modern Western Europe. There fertility could respond to hard times through delayed marriage, as first described by the English political economist T. R. Malthus (1766–1834).

Deleterious changes (e.g., human mismanagement of resources) can reduce carrying capacity through deforestation or the exhaustion or salination of soils, as in ancient Sumer, the Mayan regions of Central America, and Easter Island. Exogenous climate change helped to eliminate the medieval Vinland and Greenland colonies and almost did the same to Iceland. Other crises were provoked by institutional collapse, new diseases, or warfare, which reduced population irrespective of carrying capacity. Epidemics and famines provoked frequent, sharp but often transient turndowns in population in Eu-

TABLE 1

Population Size, Rates of Change, Total Fertility Rate, and Net Reproduction Rate: Europe and the United States, 2000

Country	Population 2001 (millions)	Annual Rate of Population Growth/ Decline (%)	Annual Rate of Natural Increase (%)	Annual Rate of Net Migration (%)	Total Fertility Rate (TFR)	Net Reproduction Rate (NRR)
Ukraine	49.0	**-0.85**	**-0.76**	**-0.09**	...	...
Latvia	2.4	**-0.58**	**-0.50**	**-0.08**	1.24	0.59
Russian Federation	144.8	**-0.52**	**-0.66**	0.14	1.21	0.57
Bulgaria	8.1	**-0.51**	**-0.51**	0.00	1.26	0.60
Hungary	10.0	**-0.38**	**-0.38**	0.00	1.32	0.63
Estonia	1.4	**-0.37**	**-0.39**	0.02	1.39	0.67
Belarus	10.0	**-0.29**	**-0.41**	0.12	1.31	0.63
Lithuania	3.7	**-0.16**	**-0.13**	**-0.03**	1.27	0.61
Czech Republic	10.3	**-0.11**	**-0.18**	0.06	1.14	0.55
Romania	22.4	**-0.11**	**-0.09**	**-0.02**	1.31	0.62
Poland	38.6	**-0.02**	0.03	**-0.05**	1.34	0.64
Germany	82.2	0.04	**-0.09**	0.13	1.36	*0.66*
Slovakia	5.4	0.07	0.04	0.03	1.29	0.62
Spain	40.1	0.12	0.02	0.10	1.24	0.58
Finland	5.2	0.19	0.14	0.05	1.73	0.83
Greece	10.6	0.21	**-0.02**	0.23	1.29	*0.62*
Japan	126.9	0.21	0.18	0.03	1.36	0.65
Austria	8.1	0.23	0.02	0.21	1.34	0.65
Belgium	10.3	0.24	0.11	0.12	1.66	...
Sweden	8.9	0.24	**-0.03**	0.28	1.54	0.75
Italy	57.8	0.28	**-0.04**	0.31	1.23	*0.57*
Denmark	5.3	0.36	0.17	0.19	1.77	0.85
United Kingdom	59.9	0.40	0.12	0.28	1.65	0.79
France	59.0	0.50	0.41	0.09	1.89	*0.86*
Switzerland	7.2	0.55	0.22	0.33	1.50	0.72
Norway	4.5	0.56	0.34	0.22	1.85	0.89
Portugal	10.2	0.63	0.14	0.49	1.50	0.73
Netherlands	16.0	0.77	0.42	0.36	1.72	0.83
United States	275.3	0.89	0.60	0.29	2.13	1.03
Ireland	3.8	*1.07*	*0.58*	*0.49*	1.89	0.91
Iceland	0.3	1.53	0.87	0.67	2.08	1.01

Note: Countries are listed in ascending order by rate of population growth. Negative rates are in bold. 1999 data in italics. Population sizes are as of January 1, for Europe, mid-year for U.S.

SOURCE: Council of Europe (2001), national demographic yearbooks. Ireland, Spain: growth, natural increase and net migration data from Eurostat.

rope, China, India, Japan, and elsewhere. Disease usually kills most of the victims of famine. The destruction by blight of the Irish potato staple in 1846 left 1 million dead. Two million Irish emigrated, inaugurating a new regime of emigration in which Ireland was the only major European area to lose population in the nineteenth century, its size falling from 8 million to 4 million. However, massive famines of the twentieth century, causing population decline if only for brief periods, were mostly the result of human actions: China's Great Leap Forward of 1958–1961 led to some 30 million excess deaths; the Ukraine collectivization famine of 1932 caused 7 million deaths. The globalization of disease can radically reduce population size. Europe's population fell to two-thirds of its previous level after the Black Death of 1348. The Aztec population was at least halved in the sixteenth century, partly through new diseases.

In simple societies, depopulation can result from genocidal conflict. Attrition by nomads on the settled populations in Eurasia suppressed the latter's populations for a thousand years. Europe lost about a quarter of its population in the centuries following the end of the Western Roman Empire, and China may have lost a quarter of its population in its unsuccessful resistance to Mongol invasion in the thirteenth century. The 30 Years War (1618–1648) inflicted similar proportionate losses on much of Northwestern Europe. In the twentieth century, the near-total destruction of Europe's Jews was the worst of a number of genocidal episodes. Enslavement often followed conquest in earlier epochs, but in some cases enslavement was the aim. The effect of slavery on the populations of tropical Africa cannot be known exactly, but in some areas it may have reduced population to a marked degree.

Contemporary Population Decline

As a broad generalization, in the 1930s the developed world reached a two-child family norm. In 2000, the average TFR in the developed world was 1.6. The United States is the only developed country with fertility approximately at replacement level. By the turn of the twenty-first century, the developed world also faced population decline. Countries with *natural decline* (deaths exceeding births) as of 2001 included Italy (−0.08% per year), Germany (−0.09%), most countries in Eastern and Central Europe, and all of the European states of the former Soviet Union. Natural decline is fastest in the Russian Federation (−0.63%), Ukraine (−0.60%), and Bulgaria and Hungary (−0.48%). However, births in France, the Netherlands, and Norway still exceed deaths (their natural increase is over 0.3% per year; in the United States it is 0.3%). Positive natural increase also continues in the United Kingdom, Denmark, and Finland. East of the river Elbe, population decline is exacerbated by persistent high mortality. Population decline in Italy and Germany is only averted by immigration from Eastern European and non-European countries.

Future trends depend primarily on birth rates and migration. According to the United Nations' medium projections made in 2000, France's population is expected to grow to 62 million by 2050 from 59 million in 2000. Germany, however, is projected to decline from 82 to 71 million, Italy from 58 to 43 million, Japan from 127 to 109 million, and Russia from 146 to 104 million. However, it is difficult to accurately predict population change so many years in the future. The low fertility rates in Russia and Eastern Europe in 2000 were deflated by widespread postponement of childbearing, and may recover substantially. By contrast, in the developing world where fertility in many regions is still relatively high, birth rates may not cease to decline once they reach replacement level, as many projections have assumed. But the possibility or even likelihood of global population decline beginning within a century has become accepted by demographers. Figure 1

shows total population estimates and projections from 1950 to 2050.

Political Economy of Population Decline

Fear of population decline, and policy designed to avert it, are almost as old as states themselves. In the distant past, population was, with land, the chief factor of production. Population increase was encouraged, often by means of conquest and enslavement; its diminution to be avoided at all costs. Mercantilist emphasis on population size, even at the cost of individual standards of living, was reinforced by concerns about the size of armies and the security of territory. Some classical economists assumed that Malthusian population checks and diminishing returns imply an early end to economic and population growth, leading to a stationary population. Others, however, including Adam Smith, saw substantial further growth through productivity driven by technology. He saw population growth as desirable: It would expand markets and encourage division of labor. Larger populations permitted economies of scale and increasing rather than diminishing returns, even though resource constraints imposed ultimate limits to growth.

Economic analysis of the consequences of declining population (e.g., the work of William B. Reddaway) began when birth rates first fell to replacement rate in the 1930s. In 2002, conventional economic opinion was almost unanimous in believing that population decline would remove the guarantee of future customers that underwrites future investment, diminish the size of markets, and reduce productive capacity as the workforce falls and as the stimulus for innovation declines. The economist Ester Boserup feared, at the extreme, that some economies would decline to a more extensive, less specialized level. For Julian Simon, population was the "ultimate resource": Fewer people means fewer geniuses.

In Western democracies, France has shown the most consistent policy response to the fear of population decline, nurtured by the stagnation of its population in the nineteenth century. France, which began the nineteenth century as Europe's demographic, military, and economic superpower, ended it just on a par with the United Kingdom and Germany. Near-defeat in the First World War reinforced fears about declining power and population. The official Institut national d'études démo-

FIGURE 1

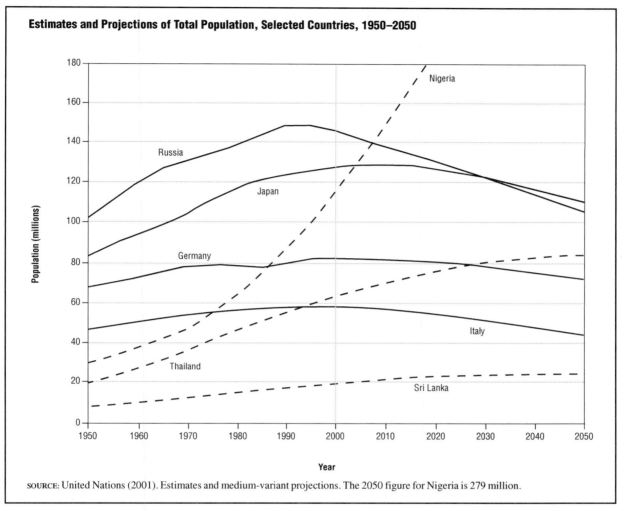

Estimates and Projections of Total Population, Selected Countries, 1950–2050

SOURCE: United Nations (2001). Estimates and medium-variant projections. The 2050 figure for Nigeria is 279 million.

graphiques (INED) was set up to analyze population trends and develop effective pro-population policies. Its first director, the demographer Alfred Sauvy (1898–1990), was an indefatigable analyst of the economic and social evils of depopulation and population aging.

With low vital rates, population decline goes hand-in-hand with population aging. The latter, however, provokes different concerns: of excess consumption by an increasing proportion of elderly dependents, rather than the under-consumption arising from population decline feared by English economist John Maynard Keynes.

Other considerations can prevail in crowded Europe. The United Kingdom's Royal Commission on Population (1949) and its Population Panel (1973) felt that the end of population growth would

moderate problems of food imports and balance of payments. It concluded that "our analysis . . . leads to the conclusion that Britain would do better in future with a stationary rather than an increasing population" (Population Panel, p. 6). The Netherlands has long considered itself overpopulated; up to the 1950s it sought, like the United Kingdom, to encourage emigration to ease domestic population pressure. That remains part of the rationale for contemporary policies seeking to discourage immigration. Even in the United States, the 1972 concluding report of the Commission on Population Growth and the American Future saw an end to U.S. population growth—although not a decline—as, on balance, advantageous. Population growth is commonly regarded as a major cause of environmental degradation, the reduction of biodiversity, and the destruction of countryside; on environmental grounds, the prospect of population decline is usually welcomed. An "optimum" population size has been proposed for countries such as the United Kingdom of a third or less of the existing total (20 million). Australian environmentalists, arguing from considerations of sustainable "environmental footprint" (the area of land needed to sustain the current consumption or lifestyle of an individual, community, or country), desire a population for Australia of 10 million, half its 2002 size.

While population decline brings problems, it may be argued that a smaller but stable population has advantages. Problems of overcrowding are ameliorated and the environment is potentially better protected. Unsatisfactory infrastructure, hastily constructed to cope with growth, can be demolished. Labor shortage may reduce unemployment and moderate inequality, and should promote capital substitution as wages rise. Depopulation after the Black Death in Europe helped to end feudalism and ushered in the "golden age of the peasant." With international trade and alliances, markets and security transcend frontiers; in Western Europe there is no relationship between the standard of living and population size or rate of population change. Some European countries have lost territory and (in most cases) inhabitants over the last century (United Kingdom, Germany, Austria), without harming their standard of living. The universal loss of colonies has been a beneficial relief to the former colonizers.

Policies Affecting Fertility and Population

Continental European countries took fright at the below-replacement fertility of the 1930s and instituted wage supplements, loans, and cash benefits to promote family life and the birth rate. In the post-World War II West (except in France), explicit pronatalist measures were discredited by their enthusiastic adoption by pre-war Fascist regimes and were rendered moot, at least temporarily, by the baby boom. Post-war communist regimes in Eastern Europe, faced with rapid falls of fertility, espoused similar policies, which helped to preserve a birth rate around the replacement rate until the collapse of communism. Pronatalist polices to avert impending population decline and moderate population aging in Japan, in Singapore, and elsewhere since the 1970s have so far lacked conspicuous success.

Twenty-first century Western European policies for child and family welfare are little different from pronatalist policy, except that the demographic rhetoric is lacking and with few exceptions (e.g., France) there are no special benefits for higher-order children. Measures include cash transfers and tax relief for parents, priority to families with children for subsidized housing, paid parental leave, and subsidized child care. The effects these policies have on birth rates are not easily demonstrated, but in Northwestern European countries, where they are best developed, both female workforce participation and birth rates are relatively high, at least in comparison to countries where such policies are absent, as in the more "familist" Southern Europe and East Asia. Central, Southern, and Eastern European and East Asian countries face the prospect of the sharpest population declines.

In the latter part of the twentieth century, European countries had tended to adopt restrictive immigration policies. But by the end of the century, European political and media opinion tended to see immigration as salvation from population decline and population aging. The notion that immigration can solve population aging can quickly be dismissed: preservation of current support ratios—that is, the ratio between persons of labor force age and persons of retirement age—would require very high levels of immigration, generating wholly infeasible rates of population growth. In the case of the Republic of Korea, according to a United Nations calculation, that country would require 6.2 billion immigrants (equaling the world's population as of 2002) by 2050. Future population decline could be averted by more modest, but substantial and fluctuating, levels of immigration: an average of 324,000 persons per year to Germany and 312,000 to Japan, a total inflow of some 16 or 17 million each by 2050. In the end, however, immigration cannot substitute for reduced birth rates. Any population trying to maintain its numbers by importing people to compensate for below-replacement fertility would eventually be replaced by the new immigrants.

See also: *Family Policy; Fertility, Below-Replacement; Keynes, John Maynard; Momentum of Population Growth; Population Policy; Projections and Forecasts, Populations.*

BIBLIOGRAPHY

Chesnais, Jean-Claude. 1996. *La crepuscule de l'occident.* Paris: Robert Laffont.

Courtoise, Stephane, et al. 2000. *The Black Book of Communism: Crimes, Terror, Repression,* trans. J. Murphy and M. Kramer. Cambridge, MA: Harvard University Press.

DaVanzo, Julie, and Gwendolyn Farnsworth, eds. *Russia's Demographic "Crisis."* Santa Monica, CA: Rand.

Demeny, Paul. 1997. "Replacement-level Fertility: The Implausible Endpoint of the Demographic Transition." In *The Continuing Demographic Transition,* ed. Gavin Jones et al. Oxford, Eng.: Clarendon Press.

Glass, David Victor. [1940] 1967. *Population Policies and Movements in Europe.* London: Oxford University Press.

Keynes, John Maynard. 1937. "Some Economic Consequences of a Declining Population." *The Eugenics Review* 29: 13–17.

Lutz, Wolfgang, Warren Sanderson, and Sergei Scherbov. 2001. "The End of World Population Growth." *Nature* 412: 543–545.

McEvedy, Colin, and Richard Jones. 1978. *Atlas of World Population History.* Harmondsworth, NY: Penguin.

Reddaway, William. 1939. *The Economics of a Declining Population.* London: Allen and Unwin.

Sauvy, Alfred. 1969. *General Theory of Population,* trans. Christophe Campos. New York: Basic Books.

Teitelbaum, Michael, and Jay Winter. 1985. *Fear of Population Decline.* London: Academic Press.

Thornton, Russell. 1997. "Aboriginal North American Population and Rates of Decline ca. A.D. 1500–1900." *Current Anthropology* 38(2): 310–315.

United Nations. 2000. *Expert Group Meeting on Policy Responses to Population Ageing and Population Decline.* New York: United Nations.

———. 2001. *World Population Prospects: The 2000 Revision.* Vol. 1. New York: United Nations.

DAVID COLEMAN

POPULATION DYNAMICS

Population dynamics refer to the way in which the size and age structure of populations change over time and the characterization of that change in mathematical terms. This article is a basic introduction to the topic, largely avoiding the mathematics.

Population Growth/Decline

Population growth (or decline) is the net balance of births, deaths, in-migration and out-migration. If growth is assumed to occur on a discrete basis, usually annually, and if the rate of growth is constant, population size at a future time t, $P(t)$, can be related to population size at time 0, $P(0)$, by the geometric equation $P(t) = P(0)(1 + r)^t$ where r is the rate of growth. In practice, demographic events are spread throughout the year so that growth is usually smooth enough to be described by a continuous variable over time. If the rate of growth is constant, $P(t)$ can be related to $P(0)$ by the simple exponential equation $P(t) = P(0)e^{rt}$.

A convenient measure of population growth is doubling time, or the time that would be needed for population size to double at the current rate of growth. The doubling time is calculated by solving the above equation for t in the case where $P(t) = 2P(0)$. Hence the doubling time is the natural logarithm of 2 (about 0.693) divided by the rate of growth (equivalent to dividing 69.3 by the percentage rate of growth). For example, if the annual rate of growth is 2 percent, the doubling time is 69.3 ÷ 2 or just under 35 years. The higher the rate of growth, the shorter the doubling time.

Balance Equation

Changes in population size are a function of the three constituent components of population change: birth, death, and migration. Change is expressed in discrete terms by the *balance equation*:

$$P(t+1) - P(t) = B(t, t+1) - D(t, t+1)$$
$$+ I(t, t+1) - O(t, t+1)$$

where $B(t, t+1)$ is the number of births occurring during the interval t to $t+1$ (usually a year), and D, I, and O are corresponding numbers of deaths, in-migrants, and out-migrants. When age is taken into account, this equation expresses the changes occurring to cohorts (persons of the same age in years at time t) alive at time t. For example, the number of children in the cohort aged 2 at time $t+1$ will be equal to the number aged 1 at t, minus deaths occurring to the cohort during the interval from t to $t+1$, plus net migrants of the same age cohort arriving or departing during this interval (note that B is zero). These demographic accounting equations are used in assessing data quality, in estimating net migration, and, in populations closed to migration, as the basis for demographic estimation using indirect methods.

Age Structure

The age structure of a population is determined by the relative size of past successive cohorts at birth and subsequent changes in size because of death and migration. The numbers of births, deaths, and migrants in the present year (or other time interval) are determined by prevailing fertility, mortality, and migration rates and the existing age structure of the population, which in turn is a result of previous demographic rates and structures. Thus the present age structure is a function of current and past demographic rates—that is, of the population's demographic history. Past changes in demographic rates lead to changes in age structure over time.

Usually, the most significant factor in determining population structure is fertility and, in particular, changes in fertility over time. High-fertility populations are characterized by a population pyramid with a wide base relative to older ages, whereas low-fertility populations have a much narrower base. A rapid change in fertility, whether an increase or a decrease, can lead to dramatic changes in both population structure and growth. An example of such a change is the post–World War II increase and subsequent decrease in fertility in many Western countries, resulting in the period of large birth cohorts known as the "baby boom." A large birth cohort appears as a bulge that "ripples" through the population age structure toward older ages over time. As this cohort passes through the childbearing ages, it produces a secondary large birth cohort (large relative to adjacent cohorts and for given fertility rates), which will itself produce a further large cohort a generation later. The effect—sometimes described as an echo—is progressively dampened as a consequence of the wide age range of childbearing and gradually disappears. Thus, through the initial effect on population structure, an increase in fertility, even if temporary, affects population size and structure for many years into the future.

More permanent changes in fertility and changes in mortality and migration have similar effects. Age- and sex-specific effects caused by war, major epidemics, and large-scale migration can have a marked effect on population structure, with consequent effects on future births and hence on population growth and structure.

Population Momentum and Aging

The effect of age structure on population growth is referred to as *population momentum*. Even if fertility were to change immediately to the level that would just ensure the replacement of each generation (that is, a net reproduction rate of 1), the population would continue to grow (or decline) for as long as structural effects remain in force. Thus, for populations that experienced fertility declines from high levels to near replacement levels in the latter decades of the twentieth century, the age structures are such that substantial further growth will occur for many decades into the twenty-first century. (Momentum effects can also perpetuate population decline, despite a fertility increase, after a long period of below-replacement fertility. This has not yet been observed.)

A consequence of changing age structure is uneven growth across age groups. This is easily seen in the ripple effect of the baby boom. In many populations, past declines in fertility accompanied by increases in longevity have resulted in the aging of the population. An aging population experiences increases in the size of the older population (for example, persons aged 65 and over) relative to the total. In contrast, population rejuvenation occurs when the younger population (for example, persons aged 0 to 14) increases in relative size, normally because of falling infant and child mortality or increased fertility. Growth in the size of different age groups can be compared across ages and populations. For example, during the period from 1950 to 2000, the population of India aged 0 to 14 years increased by a factor of 2.5 compared with a factor of 3.8 for the population aged 65 and over, while the total population increased by a factor of 2.8. This compares with the more rapidly aging population of Singapore, which has corresponding factors of 2.1 at age 0 to 14, 12.0 at age 65 and over, and 3.9 for the total population. By 2050, the populations aged 65 and over in India and Singapore are expected to have increased (since 1950) by factors of 18 and 55 respectively, compared with factors of only 4 or 5 for the total populations, illustrating both the magnitude of growth at this age and the wide variation between populations. The disparity is caused by the different speeds at which fertility declined and mortality improved in the two populations: rapidly in Singapore and only moderately in India.

See also: *Aging of Population; Age Structure and Dependency; Baby Boom; Estimation Methods, Demographic; Fertility Measurement; Momentum of Population Growth; Mortality Measurement; Renewal Theory and the Stable Population Model.*

BIBLIOGRAPHY

Chesnais, Jean-Claude. 1990. "Demographic Transition Patterns and their Impact on the Age Structure." *Population and Development Review* 16: 327–336.

Preston, Samuel H., Patrick Heuveline, and Michel Guillot. 2001. *Demography: Measuring and Modeling Population Processes.* Oxford: Blackwell.

Shryock, Henry S., and Jacob S. Siegal. 1973. *The Methods and Materials of Demography.* Washington, D.C.: U.S. Government Printing Office.

HEATHER BOOTH

POPULATION GEOGRAPHY

See *Geography, Population; Geopolitics*

POPULATION GROWTH

See *Peopling of the Continents; World Population Growth*

POPULATION ORGANIZATIONS

NATIONAL AND INTERNATIONAL AGENCIES	Alphonse L. MacDonald
PROFESSIONAL ASSOCIATIONS	John C. Caldwell
RESEARCH INSTITUTIONS	John Haaga
UNITED NATIONS SYSTEM	Joseph Chamie

NATIONAL AND INTERNATIONAL AGENCIES

This article provides an overview of international, national, governmental, and nongovernmental organizations, including foreign assistance agencies, that work in the field of population.

Intergovernmental Organizations

Many intergovernmental organizations that are active in the population field are part of the United Nations (UN) system discussed in a subsequent article. Some regional intergovernmental organizations are active in advocacy and policy promotion, but most are reluctant to infringe in areas that are seen as national prerogatives. Europe is the principal exception.

The Council of Europe is a human rights–based intergovernmental organization. Any European state can become a member if it accepts the principle of the rule of law and guarantees human rights and fundamental freedoms to any person under its jurisdiction. The council's European Population Committee monitors demographic trends in the member states and advises them on demographic policies. The Parliamentary Assembly, which consists of representatives of the national parliaments, considers European and international problems and proposes solutions. One of its specialist committees deals exclusively with migration, refugees, and demography. The resolutions adopted by the assembly provide guidance to the member states and have considerable influence on national policies.

The International Organization for Migration (IOM), the most important intergovernmental organization dealing with migration, also has European origins. It was established in 1951 as the Provisional Intergovernmental Committee for the Movement of Migrants from Europe (PICMME) to deal with emigration from Europe to non-European destinations after World War II. It became the IOM in 1989, when its constitution was modified to broaden its objectives and scope of operation. The IOM has evolved into a forum for governments, a research institute, a technical advisory center, and a program manager. It continues to deal with national migration programs, including labor migration and the transfer and repatriation of refugees and internally displaced persons. It focuses on migratory movements caused by emergencies, including irregular migration and trafficking in humans, and on post-conflict interventions. It also deals with issues of migrants's health, with an emphasis on the needs of women.

International Nongovernmental Organizations

The International Planned Parenthood Federation (IPPF) is the second largest international nongovernmental organization, after the International Federation of Red Cross and Red Crescent Societies (IFRC). The IPPF was created in 1952 by eight national family-planning associations and has members in over 180 countries. The IPPF and its members are committed to promoting the rights of women and men to decide freely the number and spacing of their children. They also promote sexual and reproductive health. They consider that a balance between the world's population size and its natural resources is a necessary condition for improving the quality of life worldwide. To achieve its aims, the IPPF carries out advocacy campaigns to influence policymakers and public opinion, sets standards for contraceptive safety, and offers a wide range of reproductive health services, with special attention to the needs of adolescents and young people.

Although it is not a population organization, since 1995 the IFRC has paid more attention to public health issues, including reproductive health. Some of its members provide reproductive health services, with an emphasis on the prevention of sexually transmitted diseases, including HIV/AIDS. Together with UN and nongovernmental organizations it offers basic health services to refugees and internally displaced persons.

National Governmental Organizations

A wide range of national governmental organizations deal with population issues. Developed countries do not have explicit comprehensive population policies: In those countries population concerns are dealt with by ministries or specialized agencies. Where needed, policy coordination is the responsibility of the ministry of labor, health and social welfare, or the interior. In the United States the Bureau of Population, Refugees, and Migration of the Department of State formulates and coordinates that country's policies on international population issues.

In developing countries, national governments are responsible for the formulation, implementa-

tion, and monitoring of population and development policies. Following the recommendations of various international population conferences (Bucharest 1974, Mexico City 1984, Cairo 1994), many developing countries created special organizations to deal with population issues. In some cases these are ministries; in other cases they are national population boards or commissions that function as independent units or are attached to a ministry or planning authority.

Reliable and timely population statistics are needed for the formulation, monitoring, and evaluation of population policies. Population statistics are collected and collated by national statistical offices, national census organizations, and civil registries. Several governmental agencies carry out specialized population surveys. All the developed countries have well-established national systems of population statistics. In the United States the main source of population data is the Bureau of the Census, which is constitutionally mandated to carry out the decennial census. The National Center for Health Statistics (NHCS), which is part of the Centers for Disease Control and Prevention of the Department of Health and Human Services, is the principal federal health and vital statistics agency.

Migrant-receiving countries such as the United States, Canada, Australia, and New Zealand have explicit policies that regulate the inflow of migrants. Those policies are developed and implemented by specialized government agencies. In the United States the Immigration and Naturalization Service and its successor agencies within the Department of Homeland Security are entrusted with the administration of the immigration laws. In Canada a special ministerial-level agency, Citizenship and Immigration Canada, is responsible for the development and implementation of immigration and citizenship policies: It controls movement across the border, promotes the integration of migrants, and conducts research on immigration issues. Most developing countries, even those with a large number of foreign residents and continued immigration, do not have explicit migration policies or specialized migration agencies.

National Nongovernmental Organizations

Since the 1970s there has been a rapid increase in the number and variety of nongovernmental organizations (NGOs) that deal with population. Organizations in developing countries tend to be modest in size and to deal with a single issue and often depend on foreign support. A number of NGOs in developed countries are active both in their own countries and overseas. All the service-providing NGOs also have a strong advocacy component. A selection of these organizations is listed below:

Population Action International, a U.S.-based organization concerned exclusively with enhancement of public awareness in support of worldwide population programs based on human rights.

The Planned Parenthood Federation of America, an organization that provides a wide range of reproductive health services that complement those provided by governments.

Marie Stopes International, a United Kingdom–based reproductive health organization that provides information, training, technical assistance, and services to people in 40 countries and promotes research.

Family Health International, a U.S.-based organization that is active in 40 developing countries and attempts to improve reproductive health services worldwide through innovative health service delivery interventions, training, and information provision as well as through biomedical and social science research.

Japanese Organization for International Cooperation in Family Planning, an organization created to share Japan's experience in family planning and maternal and child health that works in 26 developing countries by means of community-based interventions.

Population Reference Bureau, a U.S.-based organization that provides objective and timely information on U.S. and global population trends and their implications.

Helpage International, a United Kingdom–based global network of not-for-profit organizations that works in 39 countries to improve the quality of life of disadvantaged older people.

African Gerontological Society (AGES International), an organization with members in 16 African countries whose main objective is to sensitize African governments and the public at large to issues of aging.

Foreign Assistance Agencies

Before the 1970s technical assistance in regard to population was provided mainly by U.S.-based foundations such as the Rockefeller Foundation and the Ford Foundation. Since that time nearly all developed country governments have provided technical and financial support for population as part of their foreign assistance activities. Donor countries and organizations provide foreign assistance through a special unit in the ministry of foreign affairs or an independent technical assistance agency. The U.S. Agency for International Development, which was created in 1961, is the principal federal agency responsible for U.S. assistance to foreign countries. It is an independent agency that receives policy guidance from the Secretary of State. The EuropeAid Co-operation Office is responsible for the coordination of the technical assistance activities of the European Union, including population assistance, to developing countries and countries in transition.

See also: *Bibliographic and Online Resources; Conferences, International Population.*

BIBLIOGRAPHY

Ducasse-Rogier, Marianne. 2001. *The International Organization for Migration 1951–2001.* Geneva: International Organization for Migration.

European Commission. 2000. "Partnership Agreement between the Members of the African, Caribbean and Pacific Group of States of the One Part, and the European Community and Its Member States, of the Other Part, Signed in Cotonou on 23 June 2000–Protocols–Final Act–Declarations." *Official Journal of the European Communities,* L 317 15.12.2002: 3–353.

Hyde, Sarah, Costanza de Toma, and Giorgiana Rosa, eds. 2000. *Handbook on European Community Support for Population and Reproductive Health,* 2nd edition. Garden City, NY: Waterside Press.

International Federation of Red Cross and Red Crescent Societies. 2000. *World Disaster Report 2000: Focus on Public Health.* Geneva: International Federation of Red Cross and Red Crescent Societies.

Maas, Jörg, and Mirja Rothschädl. 1999. *Guide to European Population Assistance: An Orientation*

Guide for Institutions in Developing Countries on Funding for Population and Reproductive Health. Hannover, Germany: Balance Verlag.

United Nations, Department of Economic and Social Affairs, Population Division. 2000. *Charting the Progress of Populations.* New York: United Nations.

United Nations Population Fund. 2000. *Financial Resource Flows for Population Activities in 1998.* New York: United Nations Population Fund.

INTERNET RESOURCES.

African Gerontological Society (AGES International). 2003. <http://www.geocities.com/csps_ghana/>.

Bureau of the Census. 2003. <http://www.census.gov>.

Citizenship and Immigration Canada. 2003. <http://www.cic.gc.ca>.

Council of Europe. 2003. <http://www.coe.int>.

EuropeAid Co-operation Office. 2003. <http://europa.eu.int/comm/europeaid/index_en.htm>.

Family Health International. 2003. <http://www.fhi.org>.

Ford Foundation. 2003. <http://www.fordfound.org/>.

Helpage International. 2003. <http://www.helpage.org/>.

International Federation of Red Cross and Red Crescent Societies (IFRC). 2003. <http://www.ifrc.org>.

International Organization for Migration (IOM). 2003. <http://www.iom.int>.

International Planned Parenthood Federation (IPPF). 2003. <http://www.ippf.org>.

Japanese Organization for International Cooperation in Family Planning. 2003. <http://www.joicfp.org/eng/>.

Marie Stopes International. 2003. <http://www.mariestopes.org.uk/>.

National Center for Health Statistics (NHCS). 2003. <http://www.cdc.gov/nchs/>.

Planned Parenthood Federation of America. 2003. <http://www.plannedparenthood.org>.

Population Action International. 2003 <http://www.populationaction.org>.

Population Reference Bureau. 2003. <http://www.prb.org>.

Rockefeller Foundation. 2003. <http://www.rockfound.org/>.

United States Agency for International Development. 2003. <http://www.usaid.gov/>.

United States Bureau of Population, Refugees, and Migration of the Department of State. 2003. <http://www.state.gov/g/prm>.

United States Department of Homeland Security, 2003. <http://www.whitehouse.gov/deptofhomeland/sect3.html#3-2>.

ALPHONSE L. MACDONALD

PROFESSIONAL ASSOCIATIONS

In the population field, as in other areas of learning, professional associations have helped to define the field and to bring practitioners into a network of persons with similar interests. Researchers were originally so few in number that a single national organization could cover all disciplines, as did the Royal Society of London, chartered in Britain in 1662, and the Académie Royale des Sciences, established in France in 1666. In the eighteenth and nineteenth centuries similar organizations appeared in much of Europe and the United States. The nineteenth century saw the coming into existence of the first national disciplinary organizations, followed by the first international ones. This was the outcome of the growth of research and advanced teaching in a world becoming wealthier and more specialized. The strongest international demand in each field was usually for conferences, and their organization frequently preceded the establishment of associations.

History

In the early years of the Royal Society there was a marked interest in population promoted by such members as John Graunt, William Petty, and Edmund Halley. It was not sustained: not until years from 1965 to 1970, during the presidency of Howard Florey, was that interest briefly revived. In the late nineteenth and early twentieth centuries, demographers were still so few in numbers that their needs were met by membership in organizations most suited to their substantive interests in such areas as statistics, economics, geography, or health. Demography achieved explicit recognition at the International Conferences of Hygiene, the Fourth of which (Geneva 1882) included demography as a defined section; the Fifth (Hague 1884) and subsequent meetings included "Demography" in the conference title. Demographers also attended the International Statistical Congress from its inauguration in 1853 and belonged to the International Statistical Institute from its establishment in 1885. In 1922 the International Geographical Union was founded, the first international association in any of the social sciences and one with population interests.

Population soon acquired its own association, apparently the second international social science association to be established. Its origin lay in the World Population Conference (WPC) organized by the American feminist Margaret Sanger (1879–1966) and held in Geneva in 1927. This meeting included some academic demographers, but they were outnumbered by others from biology, medicine, statistics, and economics, many of whom were attracted by eugenics or Malthusianism, prominent topics on the program. WPC discussions led to the creation the following year of the International Union for the Scientific Investigation of Population Problems (IUSIPP). IUSIPP's membership was made up of national committees, none of which existed when it was formed. In America, Britain, France, Germany, Italy, and elsewhere in Europe these committees, numbering 14 in all and consisting largely of delegates to the WPC, were set up between 1928 and the first IUSIPP Conference in Rome in 1931. Opposition to racial eugenics and ideology-laden concepts such as *lebensraum* caused some national delegations to boycott the conference and others to withdraw from it, leading to an alternative meeting in London. Similar friction arose at the second conference in Berlin in 1935.

Except in the United States, the establishment of IUSIPP national committees did not lead to the formation of national population associations. In America it did so, with the Population Association of America (PAA) coming officially into being at its first conference in May 1931. The growth of the demographic profession in the United States can be gauged by the attendance at its annual conferences: 38 in 1931, 155 in 1936, 300 in 1946, 500 in 1957, over 1,000 in 1964, over 2,000 in 1971, and over

2,600 in 1975. Then numbers leveled off for almost 20 years, climbing again in the mid-1990s to pass 3,000 in 1996.

IUSIPP was reorganized in 1947 as the International Union for the Scientific Study of Population (IUSSP), with a membership of individual scholars rather than national committees. It displayed disciplinary maturity by omitting "problems" from its title. On the other hand, it retained "scientific," unlike other disciplinary associations—evidence of demographers's wariness of the effect on population research of the ideologies surrounding eugenics, population control, and the promotion of higher fertility. In 2002, the Union had about 1900 members in 130 countries.

As the field expanded after World War II, more national societies, with memberships mostly below 500, came into existence: in Japan in 1948; in West Germany in 1953; in several countries in Latin America in the 1960s; in France, Britain (the British Society for Population Studies), India, and Pakistan in the 1970s; and in Australia, New Zealand, China, and Thailand in the early 1980s. Pan-continental organizations also appeared: the European Association for Population Studies (EAPS) in 1983 and the Union for African Population Studies (UAPS) in 1984.

Roles of Population Associations

The role of population associations is generally similar to that of other learned bodies. Among international associations the IUSSP is distinctive in having a substantial number of its members coming from developing countries and a large proportion of its conference proceedings and research workshops being focused on these countries. This emphasis can be explained by the international interest in the consequences of rapid developing-world population growth during the second half of the twentieth century and the consequent funding the IUSSP could obtain from international organizations and foundations. In most of the world demographers are still few and scattered, and membership in the IUSSP has compensated for the lack of a demography department or faculty. Only in America is the position different, and this explains why the PAA has a greater membership than the IUSSP and attracts greater numbers to its conferences. The majority of PAA members are involved in research focused on America.

Associations have been necessary to promote disciplines and define their boundaries. The definition of *demography* and even the broader *population studies* is a continuing problem, and there has been a tendency to define it by the use of its core methodology and techniques so that many demographers belong both to a population association and to another learned body covering the substantive area from which they draw their methodology (e.g., sociology, economics, anthropology, history, public health, statistics, biostatistics). The definition may also proceed to producing an agreed terminology and publishing dictionaries as the IUSSP does. The IUSSP is an elective organization, supposedly for those who have distinguished themselves in the field although in practice no longer very restrictive. Most national associations admit all interested persons and have membership ranging from academia to the bureaucracy and beyond. Associations facilitate communications by publishing (or placing on the Web) information about members, including in the IUSSP's case (and befittingly as demographers) their exact dates of birth. All this is facilitated by a permanent head office, located in Liège, Belgium, from 1969 to 1999, and transferred to Paris in the latter year.

Most associations produce peer-reviewed journals and newsletters and organize conferences. IUSIPP published *Population* from 1932 to 1939. IUSSP, almost uniquely, does not have a journal, but for many years helped support and distribute *Population Studies* (Britain), *Population* (France), *Population Index* (USA), and *Genus* (Italy). PAA published a bibliographical journal, *Population Literature,* from 1934 (taken over by Princeton University's Office of Population Research in 1936 and becoming *Population Index*), and from 1964 published the journal *Demography*. English-language journals are published by the Indian Association for the Study of Population *(Demography India)*, the Australian Population Association *(The Journal of Population Research)*, the Population Association of New Zealand *(The New Zealand Population Review)*, EAPS *(European Journal of Population,* in part also in French) and UAPS *(The African Population Review)*.

Most national population associations hold annual or biennial conferences. The IUSSP organizes four-yearly general conferences and occasional regional meetings. In 1953 (Rome) and 1965 (Belgrade) it organized international population conferences in conjunction with the United Nations Population Division and it has been a co-sponsoring body for subsequent UN conferences (Bucharest 1974, Mexico City 1984, Cairo 1994). Some associations help give direction to research—notably the IUSSP, through its scientific committees and their workshops. Some award prizes, as IUSSP has done annually since 1991 and PAA for a longer period. Many act as lobbying organizations for the recognition and support of the discipline of demography, and many also raise funds for programs. IUSSP has been particularly active in the latter area.

See also: *Conferences, International Population; Demography, History of; Journals, Population; Population Thought, History of.*

BIBLIOGRAPHY

Grebenik, Eugene. 1991. "Demographic Research in Britain, 1936–1986." *Population Research in Britain,* Supplement to *Population Studies* 45: 3–30.

Hodgson, Dennis. 1991. "The Ideological Origins of the Population Association of America" *Population and Development Review* 17(1): 1–34.

Lunde, Anders S., Frank W. Notestein, and Frank Lorimer. 1981. "The PAA at 50." *Population Index* 47(3): 479–494.

Notestein, Frank W. 1982. "The Development of Demography in the United States." *Population and Development Review* 8(4): 651–687.

Sanger, Margaret, ed. 1927. *Proceedings of the World Population Conference.* London: Edward Arnold.

JOHN C. CALDWELL

RESEARCH INSTITUTIONS

Population research is in many ways an inherently collective enterprise. For many reasons—the need to create and manage large data sets, the value of collaborative projects covering broad geographic areas, and the need to borrow theories and methods from other disciplines—the institutional setting has always been important to population studies.

Early Institutions

Before World War II, there were few specialized institutions for research and training in demography, although small research groups often coalesced in population units of government statistical bureaus or around professorial posts in universities. As a formal university-based unit, the Office of Population Research (OPR) at Princeton University, founded in 1935, was an influential pioneer, training many of those who built other institutions in the United States, Europe, and eventually Asia and the Americas. Funding for OPR came from the Milbank Memorial Fund and the Scripps Foundation for Research in Population Problems, and later from the Rockefeller Foundation. For the League of Nations, OPR undertook four book-length studies of the population of Europe and the Soviet Union, which were published from 1944 to 1946. On the initiative of the U.S. Department of State, then concerned with postwar planning, these studies were extended to include Asia, resulting in influential reports on Japan and India. But even for these, funding came from private sources.

In Europe, early research institutions were created with public funding. The Institut national d'études démographiques (INED) was founded in Paris in 1945, building to some extent on a predecessor set up by the Vichy government. Ever since, INED has maintained a prominent role as a major center of demographic research. Demographic research and training, especially the study of mortality in former colonial regions, was a specialty of several health institutes in France, Belgium, and the Netherlands, and at the Universities of London and Liverpool in the United Kingdom. The immediate postwar period also saw the establishment of a department of demography at the Australian National University.

The Population Council, set up by John D. Rockefeller 3rd in 1952, became an important center for research, a source of fellowships for many people who later became leaders in the field in newly independent countries, and a progenitor of research institutes around the world. One of Rockefeller's motives was frustration at the reluctance of large foundations to work directly on population issues because of controversy surrounding the ethics of contraception and the stigma of demography's past connection with eugenics. The council, based in New York, received a large grant from the Ford Foundation, followed by grants from other foundations, and from the late 1960s on it received funding from the U.S. Agency for International Development and aid agencies of other governments. Its programs span laboratory research and clinical trials, social sciences, and field research on programs in developing countries.

Research Centers Funded in the 1960s and 1970s

Many of the largest and most productive research centers are based at universities in the United States. Most trace their origin to Ford Foundation grants in the 1960s and 1970s. Oscar Harkavy, Ford's program officer in population, saw a need for training population researchers and program administrators in poor countries. It is inappropriate to see the foundation's motivation solely as a concern to staff family planning programs. Harkavy and officers of other foundations also wanted population issues to be incorporated into development planning, and they hoped to train demographers who could lead research institutions in their home countries. The centers funded faculty research projects and travel, development of new courses, fellowships for foreign students, and other institutional needs. Foundation grants also sustained collaborations between U.S. universities and institutions in other countries, notably India, Indonesia, the Philippines, Thailand, and Taiwan.

Ford Foundation grants went to the Universities of Michigan, Pennsylvania, and Chicago in the early 1960s. Beginning in the mid-1960s, grants were made to schools of public health at Johns Hopkins and Harvard Universities, the University of North Carolina, and the University of Michigan, and to the department of demography at the University of California, Berkeley. Ford grants also went to the London School of Economics and the Australian National University to help internationalize existing programs.

The university centers varied in their emphases and the intensity and scope of their international connections. Compared to those located in social science faculties, those based at public health schools tended to place greater emphasis on training for family planning program management and evaluation.

The focus on family planning programs and their needs intensified when the Agency for International Development began to fund population research in 1967. The director of the agency's office of population, Reimert Ravenholt, was able to secure funds for innovative and complex research ventures, notably the World Fertility Survey. But Ravenholt's interest in research (and research results) chiefly as a support for family planning program activities fueled the suspicions of those who feared loss of objectivity and independence from reliance on funding from a "mission agency."

Demography was not alone in suffering deep divisions in the late 1960s. Criticism of collaboration with government programs and policy, lack of sympathy with the growing feminist movement, unequal cooperative arrangements with researchers in "underdeveloped countries," scant involvement of members of racial minorities in research at home, perceived obsession with maintenance of academic standards—these criticisms were aimed at research institutes and professional associations in many disciplines. The population research institutes survived in better shape than some other multidisciplinary institutions (created in many cases by grants to the same universities from the same foundations), such as area studies centers and development studies centers. The greater durability of population research institutes may be due both to the existence of a scientific core in demography and to the growth of new funding agencies with a more purely research orientation.

NIH Grants and Foundation Funding

Beginning in the 1970s, the largest sources of funding for population research have been divisions of the U.S. National Institutes of Health (NIH): the National Institute of Child Health and Human Development (NICHD) and the National Institute on Aging (NIA). Through its Demographic and Behavioral Sciences Branch, NICHD began funding social science research on fertility and family demography as an adjunct to clinical research on contraception. Research on longevity and the effects of an aging population were natural extensions of the health portfolio of the NIA. NIA's budget grew especially rapidly during the 1990s, in part because of the increasing salience of population aging as a demand on government budgets. Demography, as Samuel H. Preston pointed out in a 1997 article, has been the only social science to have a "secure foothold" at the NIH, a great advantage because "cost-conscious legislators continue to place medical research, and NIH in particular, near the top of their priority lists" (p. 236).

NIH grants are made on a highly competitive basis, with committees of non-government scientists playing a crucial role in selection. In 2000 NICHD funded 13 population research centers with program grants, four centers for international training, and 12 training grants to institutions. A number of institutions receive both research and training grants as centers, and also numerous individual project grants for their researchers. NIA funds ten centers for economic and demographic research on aging, often at the same universities that house the NICHD centers.

In the United States, as in other anglophone countries, most population institutes are connected to universities, with research and training closely linked. There are also productive centers based at nonprofit research organizations, such as RAND, the Urban Institute, and Battelle Memorial Institute; much of the work at these centers is concerned with analysis of social, health, and income support policies in the United States.

Foundations have remained a vital source of funding. The Andrew W. Mellon Foundation and the William and Flora Hewlett Foundation provide flexible funding to centers, particularly valuable to centers seeking to maintain international connections. The Mellon Foundation has emphasized support for anthropological demography, the study of urbanization, and refugee studies. The Hewlett Foundation emphasizes reproductive health. The Wellcome Trust, based in the United Kingdom, began in the 1990s to fund several centers in Asia and Africa. Newer foundations, such as the David and Lucile Packard Foundation and the Bill and Melinda Gates Foundation, have also become active in funding.

Organizational Structure

Successful population research centers in the United States are complex organizations requiring entrepreneurial skill as well as intellectual leadership. One research group may include senior demographers with their own individual research grants from NIH, research assistants with stipends paid through foundation postdoctoral fellowships, and visiting scholars whose expenses are paid with NIH center funds, all of whom are supported by administrative staff whose salaries typically are paid from general university funds. Their colleagues may include faculty members performing contractual research for a state health department and graduate students with unrestricted university fellowships. This diversity creates work for accountants but also provides continuity, autonomy, and protection from shifting priorities of funding sources.

A small number of research institutes account for much of the scholarly output in the field. During the 1990s, 44 percent of all first authors of articles in the leading U.S. journal *Demography*, published by the Population Association of America, were affiliated with just ten institutions (all located in the United States). During that decade, all non-U.S. institutions together accounted for fewer first authors of articles in *Demography* than the University of North Carolina alone. This reflects the prominence of U.S. institutions, although perhaps also a degree of insularity among both those who submit articles and the journal editors or the methodological emphases of American demography.

Non-U.S. Institutions

Regional demographic institutes covering major world regions have had partial success in countering the great hindrances to research in poor countries: low salaries, the lack of a critical mass of population scientists in individual countries, and a tradition of hostility between government and universities, especially social science faculties. The United Nations (UN) Secretariat proposed such regional centers for demographic research and training in 1955. The Centro Latinoamericano para demografía (now the Centro Lationamericano y Caribeño de demografía) was founded in Chile in 1957 and the Cairo Demographic Centre in 1963. India under its first prime minister, Jawaharlal Nehru, was determined to create and maintain its own world-class research institutes, mainly in the laboratory sciences and engineering but also in the social sciences. The Government of India and the Tata Trust endowed what became the International Institute of Population Sciences (IIPS) in Bombay. IIPS took on a regional training role beginning in the 1950s, with support from the UN. Sub-Saharan Africa has had several centers that have been important providers of training for statistical services but has had few regional research centers. The two most significant are the UN's Regional Institute for Population Studies at the University of Ghana and the Institut de formation et de recherche démographiques at the University of Yaounde II, Cameroon. Two recently established centers, set up with foundation funding, are the African Population and Health Research Center in Nairobi, Kenya, and the Africa Centre for Health and Population Research in Durban, South Africa.

In Asia and Africa, research groups have grown up around the sites of longstanding health and demographic surveillance systems. The oldest, in Matlab in what is now Bangladesh, was originally a site for cholera vaccine trials conducted by the International Centre for Diarrhoeal Disease Research, Bangladesh (now the Centre for Health and Population Research), which has had many demographers on its staff or as visiting scholars. Other surveillance sites, such as the British Medical Research Council site in Gambia, research sites in West Africa funded by the French government through the Institut de recherche pour le Développement, and the Agincourt site in South Africa, also began as field stations for vaccine trials or community health research. The Navrongo field station in Ghana studies alternative forms of family planning and health services for rural Africa. These centers for demographic surveillance form a network, sharing expertise and software.

The International Institute for Applied Systems Analysis (IIASA) is a unique international institution, created originally to bring together scientists from Western and communist countries to work cooperatively on global problems, and located in Austria on the then frontlines of the cold war. Its population program has included studies in multistate mathematical demography, population projections, and other topics. Perhaps the most significant institutional development in the 1990s was the founding of the Max Planck Institute for Demographic Research, part of the Max-Planck-Gesellschaft through which the German government funds research in the natural and social sciences. It planned a staff of 150 by 2002, which would make it the world's largest single center for demographic research. The institute, which is located in Rostock, has particular strengths in aging, biological demography, mathematical demography, and European and Asian population studies.

Trends and New Developments

Universities are conservative institutions. Population research institutes have proven durable and attractive to several generations of scholars and students. There is no lack of interesting problems (with practical consequences) for which the population sciences provide useful tools for analysis and solution. The largest funders of research give a major role in allocation of resources to committees of scientists who themselves were trained in and work in the existing research centers. Thus the safest prediction is that the population research centers will continue to exist in much the same form as at the beginning of the twenty-first century.

But some potentially important changes are discernible. The development of the Internet has made communication and sharing of files easier. The Wellcome Trust is supporting an Asian Meta-Centre for Population and Sustainable Development Analysis, linking six university-based centers and IIASA, a potential prototype for "virtual" centers linking smaller institutions in neighboring countries. Particularly interesting is the growth of Internet networks such as H-Demog for historical demographers, which is funded by the National Endowment for the Humanities. More formal networks have been created on an experimental basis, for example, the Family and Children Well-Being Research Network funded by the NICHD. One will no longer have to live near and work for a large university in a rich country to benefit from frequent interaction with colleagues with related interests.

Advances in decentralized computing have also reduced the need to be connected to a major research center. Most demographers have in their own homes far more computing power than was available at the facilities lavishly described in funding proposals for center grants in the 1970s. Commercial statistical packages offer online support services and training. Data sets and documentation are increasingly available on the Internet.

The Internet and decentralized computing could lead to new versions of the scientific networks of the early modern era, when the Royal Society and other "invisible colleges" flourished, and scholars of all nations exchanged letters in Latin and gave seminars even in countries at war with their own. Twenty-first-century globalization in science, as in other fields, is in part a return to a golden past.

There are countervailing forces, however. One is the increasing concern in Europe and North America for data privacy. The very factors that have made analysis easier have also heightened concern about confidentiality. A durable function of research institutes may be to guarantee security of data on individuals. Institutes may also expand their roles as data producers, as demographers and other social scientists increasingly rely on complex longitudinal data sets. Keeping in touch with a cohort of respondents in a mobile society through successive rounds of data collection requires continuity and a scale of effort hard to assemble on a short-term basis. Data analysis may be decentralized, but survey management may remain lodged in experienced institutions. Finally, research centers may still be needed as the nurturers of intellectual companionship.

The balance of centrifugal and centripetal forces may favor researchers who can function on multiple levels: as members of a traditional university department, as members of a localized population research center, and as members of networks and "virtual centers" for collaboration with scientists around the world. Demographers will likely adapt to this new world more easily than scientists trained in more self-contained disciplines.

See also: *Bibliographic and Online Sources; Demography, History of; Journals, Population; Population Thought, Contemporary.*

BIBLIOGRAPHY

Caldwell, John C., and Patricia Caldwell. 1986. *Limiting Population Growth and the Ford Foundation Contribution.* London: F. Pinter.

Donaldson, Peter. 1990. *Nature Against Us: The United States and the World Population Crisis, 1965–1980.* Chapel Hill: University of North Carolina Press.

Greenhalgh, Susan. 1996. "The Social Construction of Population Science: An Intellectual, Institutional, and Political History of Twentieth-Century Demography." *Comparative Studies in Society and History* 38: 26–66.

Preston, Samuel H. 1997. "Where Is U.S. Demography Headed?" In *Les contours de la démographie: Au seuil du XXIe siècle,* ed. Jean-Claude Chasteland and Louis Roussel. Paris: Institut national d'études démographiques.

INTERNET RESOURCE.

Comité International de Cooperation dans les Recherches Nationales en Démographie. 2002. *Directory of Population Research Centers.* <http://www.cicred.ined.fr/acerd>.

JOHN G. HAAGA

UNITED NATIONS SYSTEM

Prior to the establishment of the United Nations in 1945, the League of Nations, in existence from 1919 to 1946, had taken a number of initiatives aimed at improving population statistics and information among its member countries. Many of these initiatives have played an important role in the work of the United Nations in the population field. In particular, the League focused on the compilation and publishing of national statistics, including demographics. The *International Statistical Yearbook,* starting with the year 1926, included data on population, births, deaths, growth, age structure, occupational groups, and unemployment. In addition to the *Yearbook,* the League published the *Monthly Bulletin of Statistics,* which contained current national population statistics.

Within the United Nations system, various bodies share responsibility for population issues—at UN headquarters, in the regional commissions, in programs and funds set up under the General Assembly, and in the specialized agencies. Brief descriptions of the population activities of these bodies are given below, based on mission statements and related official information.

The Population Information Network, POPIN, established in 1979 and maintained by the United Nations Population Division, makes population information from all UN sources easily available to the international community. Details of UN publications from each agency can be found at their respective Web sites or through POPIN.

UN Headquarters

The two primary offices concerned with population matters at UN Headquarters are the Population Division and the Statistics Division, both of which are within the Department of Economic and Social Affairs (DESA). In addition, a number of other divisions within DESA have work programs that touch upon aspects of population. In particular, the Division for Social Policy and Development deals with the issue of aging and the Division for the Advancement of Women deals with gender issues.

The Population Division began its work in 1946 as the secretariat to the Population Commission, which was established in the same year as a subsidiary body of the Economic and Social Council. The Division is responsible for monitoring and appraisal of the full range of areas in the field of population, including outcomes of UN global conferences on population and development—notably the Program of Action of the 1994 International Conference on Population and Development. The Division provides substantive support to the Commission on Population and Development (formerly the Population Commission), as well as to related work of the General Assembly and the Economic and Social Council.

The Population Division also facilitates access by governments to information on population trends and their interrelationships with social and economic development as an input to government policy and program formulation. One important activity in this area is the preparation of population estimates and projections for all countries and areas of the world, as well as for urban and rural areas and major cities. These data serve as the standard and consistent set of population figures for use throughout the United Nations system.

The Statistics Division began its work in 1946 as the secretariat to the Statistics Commission established in the same year as a subsidiary body of the Economic and Social Council. The Statistics Division promotes the development of national statistics and the improvement of their comparability. It provides central statistical services to the UN Secretariat and promotes the coordination of the statistical work of the specialized agencies, including the improvement of statistical methods in general.

Within the Statistics Division, population issues fall primarily within the responsibility of the Demographic and Social Statistics Branch. The Branch collects, compiles, and disseminates official national population statistics from censuses, surveys, and vital registration systems and prepares methodological reports and guidelines for the coordination of data collection. Its best-known publication is the *Demographic Yearbook,* issued since 1948.

Regional Commissions

The United Nations has five regional commissions, which as part of their activities deal with population matters. They are: the Economic Commission for Africa (ECA); the Economic and Social Commission for Asia and the Pacific (ESCAP); the Economic Commission for Europe (ECE); the Economic Commission for Latin America and the Caribbean (ECLAC); and the Economic and Social Commission for Western Asia (ESCWA). In the past, most commissions had population divisions, but these have merged with other offices. The commissions promote dialogue among the governments of their respective regions on various aspects of population change and related issues, such as food security, sustainable development, and poverty reduction. They also coordinate regional activities dealing with data collection and research relating to population matters.

Funds and Programs

UNICEF. The United Nations Children's Fund (UNICEF) was established in 1946 as a temporary body to provide emergency assistance to children in war-ravaged countries. In 1953 the General Assembly placed the Fund on a permanent footing and charged it with assisting in the development of permanent child health and welfare services, particularly in developing countries.

UNICEF's mandate is to protect children's rights and promote their welfare. It is guided by the Convention on the Rights of the Child, which seeks to establish children's rights as enduring ethical principles and to support international standards of behavior toward children. UNICEF also monitors the implementation of the World Declaration on the Survival, Protection and Development of Children.

UNFPA. In 1967 the United Nations established a Trust Fund for Population Activities. In 1969 the Trust Fund was renamed the United Nations Fund for Population Activities (UNFPA). In 1987 its name (but not its acronym) was again changed, to the United Nations Population Fund.

UNFPA is the largest international source of population assistance. About a quarter of all population assistance from donor nations to developing countries is channeled through it. It has three main program areas: reproductive health, including family planning and sexual health; population and development strategies; and advocacy in support of its goals. UNFPA is guided by the principles, recommendations, and goals of the Program of Action of the 1994 International Conference on Population and Development—the Cairo conference.

UNHCR. The office of the United Nations High Commissioner for Refugees (UNHCR) was established by the United Nations General Assembly in 1950, one of several initiatives by the international community to provide protection and assistance to refugees. Initially, UNHCR was given a limited three-year mandate to help resettle some 1.2 million European refugees left homeless in the aftermath of World War II. However, as other refugee crises emerged around the globe, UNHCR's mandate was extended and has continued to be extended every five years.

UNHCR promotes international refugee agreements and monitors government compliance with international refugee law. Its principal functions are to provide international protection to refugees, seek durable solutions to their plight, and furnish material assistance. Protection involves preventing *refoulement*—that is, the forcible return of a refugee to a country where he or she may have reason to fear persecution. In addition, UNHCR provides material assistance to refugees in the form of shelter, food, medical aid, education, and other social services.

UN-Habitat. The United Nations Human Settlements Programme, UN-Habitat, formerly known as the UN Centre for Human Settlements (UNCHS-Habitat), was established in 1978. UN-Habitat aims to promote the socially and environmentally sustainable development of human settlements and the attainment of adequate shelter for all. On population issues, UN-Habitat's work is particularly relevant in the areas of urbanization and internal migration. A key element in its work is the implementation of the Habitat Agenda—the global plan of action adopted at the 1996 Habitat II Conference in Istanbul.

UNAIDS. The Joint United Nations Programme on HIV/AIDS, UNAIDS, is the leading coordinator of worldwide action against HIV/AIDS. Its mission is to lead, strengthen, and support an expanded response to the epidemic that will prevent the spread of HIV; to provide care and support for those infected with the disease; to reduce the vulnerability of individuals and communities to HIV/AIDS; and to alleviate the socioeconomic and human impact of the epidemic. UNAIDS is sponsored by the World Health Organization (WHO), the UN Development Programme, UNFPA, UNICEF, UNESCO, the World Bank, and the UN Drug Control Programme. UNAIDS compiles data and statistics on HIV/AIDS globally and undertakes studies addressing the determinants and consequences of the epidemic.

Specialized Agencies

WHO. The World Health Organization was established as a specialized agency of the United Nations in 1948. WHO maintains an international surveillance system to investigate, provide early warning, and respond to epidemics of newly emerging and re-emerging diseases. The agency compiles a variety of health- and mortality-related statistics and conducts research on a broad range of health issues. It coordinates international efforts to eliminate or eradicate some infectious diseases. In 1980, for example, WHO certified the global eradication of smallpox—the first disease to be eradicated by the human race. WHO also works to prevent and control major chronic non-communicable diseases that strike people later in their lives.

WHO has a program in the area of reproductive health, including family planning and safe motherhood, sexually transmitted diseases, and HIV/AIDS.

ILO. The International Labour Organization (ILO) was established in 1919, its constitution forming a part of the Treaty of Versailles, which brought the League of Nations into being. In 1946, ILO became the first specialized agency of the United Nations. Although mainly concerned with employment conditions and industrial relations, ILO also compiles employment statistics, which are fundamental to many population and development analyses.

World Bank. Founded in 1944, the World Bank is the world's largest source of development assistance. The Bank provided U.S.$17.3 billion in loans to its client countries in fiscal year 2001. The Bank emphasizes the need for investing in people, particularly through basic health and education; focusing on social development, inclusion, governance, and institution-building as key elements of poverty reduction; and strengthening the ability of the governments to deliver high-quality services efficiently and transparently. In undertaking its development assistance, the Bank collects an extensive range of demographic and related statistics and conducts numerous studies relating to population and development issues.

UNESCO. Established in 1945, the United Nations Educational and Scientific and Cultural Organization (UNESCO) promotes collaboration among nations in the fields of education, science, culture, and communication. In particular, it compiles educational enrollment and attainment statistics for countries and regions—a crucial element in many analyses of population and development.

FAO. The Food and Agriculture Organization of the United Nations (FAO) was founded in 1945 with a mandate to raise levels of nutrition and standards of living, to improve agricultural productivity, and to improve the conditions of rural populations. A specific priority is encouraging sustainable agriculture and rural development—a long-term strategy for increasing food production and food security while conserving and managing natural resources.

FAO compiles extensive international statistics relating to the rural environment, food production, and population.

See also: *Bibliographic and Online Resources; Conferences, International Population.*

BIBLIOGRAPHY

INTERNET RESOURCES.

International Labour Organization (ILO). 2002. <http://www.ilo.org/>.

Joint United Nations Programme on HIV/AIDS (UNAIDS). 2002. <http://www.unaids.org/>.

United Nations Children's Fund (UNICEF). 2002. <http://www.unicef.org/>.

United Nations Department of Economic and Social Affairs (DESA). 2002. <http://www.un.org/esa/>.

United Nations Division for Social Policy and Development. 2002. <http://www.un.org/esa/socdev/>.

United Nations Division for the Advancement of Women. 2002. <http://www.un.org/womenwatch/daw/>.

United Nations Food and Agriculture Organization of the United Nations (FAO). 2002. <http://www.fao.org/>.

United Nations Economic and Social Commission for Asia and the Pacific (ESCAP). 2002. <http://www.unescap.org/>.

United Nations Economic and Social Commission for Western Asia (ESCWA). 2002. <http://www.escwa.org.lb/>.

United Nations Economic and Social Council. 2002. <http://www.un.org/depts/unsd/>.

United Nations Economic Commission for Africa (ECA). 2002. <http://www.uneca.org/>.

United Nations Economic Commission for Europe (ECE). 2002. <http://www.unece.org/>.

United Nations Economic Commission for Latin America and the Caribbean (ECLAC). 2002. <http://www.eclac.cl/>.

United Nations High Commissioner for Refugees (UNHCR). 2002. <http://www.unhcr.ch/>.

United Nations Human Settlements Programme (UN-Habitat). 2002. <http://www.unhabitat.org/>.

United Nations Educational and Scientific and Cultural Organization (UNESCO). 2002. <http://www.unesco.org/>.

United Nations Population Division. 2002. <http://www.unpopulation.org/>.

United Nations Population Fund (UNFPA). 2002. <http://www.unfpa.org/>.

United Nations Population Information Network (POPIN). 2002. <http://www.popin.org/>.

World Bank. 2002. <http://www.worldbank.org/>.

World Health Organization (WHO). 2002. <http://www.who.int/>.

JOSEPH CHAMIE

POPULATION POLICY

Population policy may be defined as deliberately constructed or modified institutional arrangements and/or specific programs through which governments influence, directly or indirectly, demographic change.

The generality of the definition lends itself to varying interpretations. For any given country, the aim of population policy may be narrowly construed as bringing about *quantitative* changes in the membership of the territorially circumscribed population under the government's jurisdiction. Additions to membership are effected only through births and immigration, losses are caused by emigration and by deaths. Concern with this last component is usually seen as a matter for health policy, leaving fertility and migration as the key objects of governmental interest in population policy.

More broadly, policy intent may also aim at modification of *qualitative* aspects of these phenomena—fertility and international migration—including the composition of the population by various demographic characteristics and the population's spatial distribution.

Furthermore, governments' concern with population matters can also extend beyond the borders of their own jurisdictions. International aspects of population policy have become increasingly salient in the contemporary world.

Population Control in Traditional Societies

Rulers of any political unit have a stake in the size and composition of the population over which they have authority, hence an incentive to try to influence demographic change in a desired direction. Thus "population policy" may be said to have a long history, starting at least with the empires of the ancient world. Greater numbers tended to connote greater wealth and power, at least for those at the apex of the social pyramid. Measures encouraging marriage and sometimes immigration testify to the prevailing populationist sentiment among rulers throughout history.

But the leverage of the weak premodern state over fertility in traditional societies was necessarily limited. The dominant influence setting the patterns of reproduction was located, instead, in a deeper layer of social interaction. Births, the key element affecting population change, are produced by individual couples—seemingly an intensely private affair yet one in which the immediate kin group and the surrounding local society in which that group is embedded have a material stake. All societies, if at varying degrees, grant a measure of self-sovereignty to their members. An individual has certain rights over his or her direction in life. But this is always subject to some constraints, not only biological but also social. Well before rights and obligations are formally codified in legal terms, they are established through spontaneous social interaction—a self-organizing process. Restrictions on freedom to act take the form of social expectations and pressures that individuals can ignore only at considerable personal costs to themselves. Typically, there is strong expectation that men and women should marry and have children. Parental and kin obligations in the matter of bringing up children are well understood by all adults and informally enforced by the community. In most societies there is the expectation that children are to be born to married couples only; that a man can have one wife at a time; that a husband is obligated to support his wife and a father his children; and that he can expect reciprocal services from them. And informal rules shaped by community interest tend effectively to regulate the entry of foreigners.

The fabric of such demographically relevant behavioral stances, supported by internalized personal norms and buttressed by religious injunctions, is a product of social evolution; how effective such institutions are becomes an important determinant of societal success. As a classic statement of the British demographer Alexander Carr-Saunders (1922, p. 223) put it, persons and groups of persons:

> are naturally selected on account of the customs they practise, just as they are selected on account of their mental and physical characters. Those groups practicing the most advantageous customs will have an advantage in the constant struggle between adjacent groups over those that practise less advantageous customs. Few customs can be more advantageous than those which limit the number of a group to the desirable number . . . .[In the traditional society] there would grow up an idea that it was the right thing to bring up a certain limited number of children, and the limitation of the family would be enforced by convention.

Given the harsh biological and economic constraints premodern societies invariably experienced, that "desirable number" presupposed fairly high fertility; high enough to provide a sufficient margin of safety over mortality. Successful societies—societies that survived to the dawn of the modern era—thus obeyed the biblical injunction to be fruitful and multiply, even though such multiplication as a matter of historical record was necessarily very slow. But traditional demographic regimes resulting from spontaneous social interaction achieved modest growth rates at varying levels of fertility and mortality. Early modern Western Europe succeeded in maintaining a relatively low average level of mortality by means of keeping birth rates low, primarily by means of a fairly high average age of marriage and substantial proportions that remained permanently single. A contrasting pattern, such as in India, combined early and universal marriage and a consequent high level of fertility with slow population growth by virtue of

death rates that were also high, approximating the level of the birth rate. With respect to the rate of population growth these different combinations of birth and death rates in traditional societies were very similar. The potential for rapid population growth that might be triggered by a fall of mortality was, however much higher when the premodern equilibrium was the result of a combination of high mortality and high fertility.

Rationale for Population Policy

Modernity—the rise of democratic state formations reflecting the public interest and the emergence of rapid economic development—brought about the realistic promise of realizing age-old human aspirations for a better life. The state increasingly came to be seen as an institution created by the voluntary association of free individuals to further their interests. The central function of the state was to produce public goods—goods that individuals cannot secure for themselves. The U.S. Constitution, promulgated in 1789, articulated key items in the collective interest concisely and with universal validity. The aim of the Union formed by the People was, in the words of the Constitution's Preamble, to "establish Justice, insure domestic Tranquility, provide for the common defence, promote the general Welfare, and secure the Blessings of Liberty to ourselves and our Posterity." In pursuing such goals, regulation of immigration into a state's territory is clearly defined as a public good, thus delineating a particular role for population policy. And aggregate fertility may also be construed a public good, if its level as determined by spontaneous social interaction is too high or too low in terms of the collective interest.

The potential role of the state in regulating immigration is straightforward: individuals wishing to restrict or promote it cannot set up their own border patrols or issue entry visas. Individual preferences in the matter, however, are likely to differ. It is the task of the government to weigh and reconcile conflicting individual desires and come up with a policy deemed the best under the accepted rules of the political process.

To claim a role for the state in the matter of fertility is more problematic. Additions to the population are the result of a multitude of individual decisions concerning childbearing. Within the constraints of their social milieu, these decisions reflect an implicit calculus by parents about the private costs and benefits of children to them. But neither costs nor benefits of fertility are likely to be fully internal to the family: they can also impose burdens and advantages on others in the society. Such externalities, positive and negative, do represent a legitimate concern for all those affected. An individual's influence on the fertility of other families, however, is very limited: there are no private markets offering preferred patterns of aggregate demographic processes to individual buyers. Remedying such market failure may then be attempted through intervention by the state so as to affect individual behavior in order to best serve the common good—the good of all individuals.

The earliest clear formulation of the population problem as a problem of coordination among individual preferences, hence establishment of the rationale for potential state intervention in the matter of fertility, was given by William Foster Lloyd, an Oxford mathematician and economist, in an essay published in 1833. In the spirit of the Malthusian concerns of his time, Lloyd (1833/1968, pp. 22–23) envisaged the possibility of overpopulation even under conditions when all families have only the children they actually want and suggested the direction in which remedy ought to be sought:

> The simple fact of a country being overly populous . . . is not, of itself, sufficient evidence that the fault lies in the people themselves, or a proof of the absence of a prudential disposition. The fault may rest, not with them as individuals, but with the constitution of society, of which they form part.

Population policy should therefore strive toward institutions and incentive systems—a constitution of society—that provide signals to individuals guiding them to behave in harmony with the collective interest.

Population Policy in the Liberal State

Technological progress and consequent improvements in the standard of living in modernizing societies result in a far more effective control of mortality than was possible in the traditional society. But the fall of the death rate accelerates the rate of population growth which, in turn, could strain the capacity of the economic system to accommodate the increased population numbers. Falling living standards then would once again increase death rates, reestablishing an approximate balance be-

tween births and deaths at a low standard of living. This was the pessimistic central vision of T. R. Malthus's 1798 *Essay*. But this outcome, although held to be highly probable, was, according to Malthus, avoidable. Given sound public policies, there was an alternative to subsistence-level equilibrium, both agreeable and achievable.

A salient element in the 1798 *Essay*, and in subsequent writings influenced by it, was disapproval of the schemes for poor relief prevailing in Britain and elsewhere in Europe—on the grounds that they were likely to encourage irresponsible reproduction. Efforts of the paternalistic state to reduce poverty were held to be misguided; by stimulating fertility, hence population growth, such efforts would generate only more misery. Malthusians argued that the state's correct stance in demographic matters, as in the economy at large, was *laissez faire*. This would foster the prudential habits among the general population similar to those that already existed among the propertied classes. It would do so by assuring that the costs of childbearing were not shared by society at large but were primarily borne by the individual couples having children.

Heeding such a prescription did not imply that the state was to play a passive role in demographic matters. Malthus's own writings, most clearly his 1820 tract *Principles of Political Economy* (1989, pp. 250–251), spell out a broad agenda which expresses the philosophy that came to be dominant in the liberal states of the West in the nineteenth century. Material improvements, such as higher wages for labor, could indeed be defeated if they would be "chiefly spent in the maintenance of large and frequent families." But Malthus also envisaged a different, happier possible outcome: "a decided improvement in the modes of subsistence, and the conveniences and comforts enjoyed, without a proportionate acceleration of the rate of [population] increase."

The possibility of such diametrically different responses to the stimulus of higher wages suggests a large element of indeterminacy in fertility behavior. To Malthus, the causes of these divergent responses were to be found in the circumstances, social and political, in which people lived—in particular, whether those circumstances hindered or rewarded planning for the future. From his analysis he derived a prescription for a population policy that would yield the hoped-for demographic outcome:

Of all the causes which tend to generate prudential habits among the lower classes of society, the most essential is unquestionably civil liberty. No people can be much accustomed to form plans for the future, who do not feel assured that their industrious exertions, while fair and honourable, will be allowed to have free scope; and that the property which they either possess, or may acquire, will be secured to them by a known code of just laws impartially administered. But it has been found by experience, that civil liberty cannot be secured without political liberty. Consequently, political liberty becomes almost equally essential. (ibid.)

During the long nineteenth-century—that may be thought of as stretching to the outbreak of the First World War—the politics in Europe and in its overseas offshoots favored, even if imperfectly, the development of institutional and legal frameworks in harmony with such principles. This, in interaction with economic and cultural changes shaped by the industrial revolution, created a milieu that fostered the prudential habits of parents, rendering the micro-level calculus of the costs and benefits of children increasingly salient. Rising demand for labor, including greater use of child labor, and rising income levels tended to sustain high fertility or even to stimulate it. But rising material expectations, broadening opportunities for social mobility, and the patterns and circumstance of urban living pulled in the opposite direction. This was powerfully reinforced by some programmatic activities that were consistent with the limited role the liberal state claimed in managing the economy. These included public health programs and projects aimed at improving basic infrastructure for transport and communication. And most importantly, the state, or local government, assumed a key role in fostering, organizing, and financing public education. At basic levels school attendance was made mandatory and enforced and, in parallel, labor laws curtailed the employment of children.

Reflecting long-standing cultural values and religious injunctions, and contrary to laissez-faire principles, the liberal state generally banned the spreading of contraceptive information and the sale of contraceptive devices and made abortion illegal. Such restrictions typically remained in effect well into the twentieth century. But by all evidence, any upward pressure on fertility from these restrictions was swamped by the downward pressure on parental demand for children resulting from the state policies and programs just mentioned. By the last quarter of the nineteenth century birth rates were falling rapidly in the countries of the West. In many cases, rates of population growth fell also, despite continuing improvements in mortality. In Europe this trend was facilitated by emigration, which both sending and receiving countries—notably the United States, Canada, and Australia—either positively encouraged or at least permitted.

The stance of the liberal state on population policy thus brought about the prospect of a new demographic equilibrium in the West that could be consistent with continuing material progress: achievement of a stationary population at low levels of fertility and mortality and allowing freedom of movement internationally.

Population Policy between the World Wars

The massive losses of life resulting from World War I and from the influenza pandemic at its immediate aftermath, and the sharp drop in the number of births during the war years, were temporary disruptions in the steadily declining trends of fertility and mortality characterizing the prewar decades in the West. Those trends soon made it evident that there is no built-in guarantee that the sum total of individual fertility decisions will eventually settle at a point at which, in the aggregate, the rate of population growth will be exactly zero or fluctuate tightly around a zero rate. Although, owing to relatively youthful age distributions, the rate of natural increase remained positive, by the late 1920s demographers realized that fertility rates in several Western countries had fallen to such a low level that, in the longer term, natural increase would become negative. This trend became more accentuated and more general under the impact of the Great Depression. Some observers foresaw a "twilight of parenthood."

Just as excessive reproduction called for corrective public policies, there were calls for corrective action achieving the opposite result: enhancing fertility so as to assure at least the simple maintenance of the population. In some countries the ban on contraceptives was tightened and the penalties on abortion were increased. These measures had little effect. So did, predictably, governmental exhortation appealing to families to have more children.

The most promising avenue for population policy seemed to be to use the instruments available to the state for redistributing income so as to reward demographic behavior considered socially desirable (and to discourage contrary behavior). By the 1930s such pronatalist policies came to be fairly widely if rather tight-fistedly applied in a number of countries. Among Europe's emerging democratic welfare states Sweden and France were pioneers in providing financial rewards and services in kind to families with children, especially to larger families. (Sweden, however, also allowed liberal access to contraception.) Similar policies were applied with equal or greater vigor in fascist Italy and Germany.

Invariably, the proponents of such policies claimed some results in terms of birth rates somewhat higher than would have been expected in their absence. But the latter quantity is a hypothetical one, which introduces a necessary caution to such claims. More pertinently, when average fertility is low, the birth rate in any given year is an unreliable measure of long-run fertility. Couples have considerable latitude to time the birth of their children earlier or later, without affecting the number of children they ultimately wish to have. Logically, pronatalist policies seek to affect that lifetime total rather than aiming at temporary increases in the birth rate.

International Population Policy after World War II

In the countries that the United Nations categorizes as less developed, population policy issues attracted little attention until the middle of the twentieth century. Fertility remained high, more or less at its premodern level. Population growth was slowly increasing, however, as a result of improvements in mortality. Following the end of World War II, mortality decline accelerated greatly and as a result so did population growth. In 1950 the world population was 2.5 billion. Some 1.7 billion of that total was in countries classified as less developed, with an average annual birth rate of 44 per 1000 population—twice as high as in the more developed group. Unless a decline of the birth rate got under way fairly rapidly, an unprecedentedly large expansion of human numbers was inevitable.

Although the trigger of such population growth was a welcome development—falling death rates—growth rates that would double or even treble a population within a generation seemed a major obstacle to development. And the large and widening differential between the more developed and the less developed countries in terms of population size and average income levels was seen as holding out the prospect of major dislocations and long term instabilities within the international system. As a result, in the 1950s an intense debate started on what policies could reduce fertility in the less developed world. This policy debate was primarily Western, much of it American, just as the diagnosis of the problem itself had been. The proposals that emerged were to be applied in countries representing a large and growing share of the global population. Population policy became international.

The West of course already had relatively low fertility, and with it much historical experience on why birth rates fell. Social science analysis was virtually unanimous in interpreting this experience. The explanation centered on the role of changing structural conditions of the economy, conditions to which micro-level units of the population tended to respond, in demographic as well as in other matters. Demand for smaller families was seen as the primary force determining birth rates; the means by which couples regulated their fertility was not unimportant, but seen as a distinctly secondary factor. If the demand was strong enough, fertility would be low, even if birth control technology was primitive. A transition to low fertility presupposed changing preferences, and such preferences were responses to market signals. If policy was to have an explicit role, it would be through reinforcing those signals.

In the experience of past fertility transitions four components of the incentive structure seemed especially pertinent: (1) the direct costs parents must incur in bringing up children; (2) the opportunity costs of children to parents; that is, the earnings a couple must forgo because of children; (3) the contribution of children to family income through labor services; and (4) the contributions of children to parents' economic security in old age, in comparison to alternative sources of security.

Fertility declines when shifts in these components make family limitation advantageous to couples, overcoming cultural resistance supporting traditional behavior. Patterns of development generate that effect when at least some, but especially when all of the following conditions are fulfilled: (1) social expectations and formal institutional arrangements place on parents the major financial responsibility for raising their own children, including much of the cost of education and health care; (2) women have access to income-earning opportunities in the labor market, including jobs not easily compatible with childbearing and childrearing; (3) social institutions make formal education (primary and early secondary) compulsory and effectively enforce school attendance; (4) child labor is made illegal; (5) effective legal guarantees of property rights, legal enforcement of private contracts, and the development of public and private insurance and pension schemes provide attractive and comparatively secure alternatives to children as a source of old-age security.

Social and institutional conditions that make such changes potent generators of fertility decline include the following: (1) emphasis on personal economic contribution (rather than, for example, class status or political loyalty) as the primary factor determining a person's earnings, thus providing an incentive for increased investment in human capital; (2) systems of promotion that provide opportunities for upward social mobility according to merit and tolerate downward social mobility; (3) openness to outside influences that create rising expectations with respect to material standards of living; and (4) emphasis not only on the rights but also on the social and economic responsibilities of the individual.

Some of the factors that prompted the fall of fertility in the West also became potent in the less developed countries as concomitants of successful economic and social progress. International conferences, for example the 1974 Bucharest conference on population, spelled out many of the essential socioeconomic changes necessary for fertility to shift from high to low levels. But assembling the instruments so identified into a coherent development strategy of institutional-structural reforms, reforms justified also by demographic objectives, remained an elusive task. In promoting development governments came to see their roles not in supporting institutions harnessing the market, but replacing the market in key developmental tasks through specific goal-oriented categorical programs. In the matter of population policy, the rapid postwar progress in the technology of birth control provided an appealing apparent short-cut for achieving fertility decline through programmatic means. Markets, it was held, could not be relied on to bring that technology to those wishing to practice birth control. Governments could, instead, organize free delivery of birth control information, and provide effective means for preventing

births to all those, primarily (it was assumed) women, who wished to plan their families. Surveys indicated that there existed a substantial latent demand for such services. Satisfied customers, in turn, would serve as role models, bringing new clients to the program.

By the mid-1960s, in programmatic terms the international population policy debate on the relative importance of demand versus supply was essentially decided in favor of the latter. For the next quarter century, population policy in the developing world became essentially synonymous with family planning programs.

Financial and administrative limitations within developing countries necessitated the heavy involvement of foreign assistance in launching and sustaining family planning programs. Although donor countries' own domestic experience in this area was practically nonexistent, such aid, justified by the seriousness of the "population problem" (a problem whose cause was defined in terms of aggregate indexes of population growth) was readily forthcoming, partly in the form of bilateral assistance and partly through international aid institutions.

The cost of birth control technology was, in itself, relatively modest. But sustaining an effective delivery service did represent significant claims on scarce human and material resources. Declared demand for birth control does not necessarily translate into effective willingness to practice it: conflicting desires may interfere. Weakness of measures of latent demand, or "unmet need," is reflected in the requirements that programs are supposed to satisfy if they are to be successful. These typically included such items as "doorstep accessibility of quality services," "broad choice of contraceptive methods," "forceful IEC [information, education, and communication] programs," "sound financing strategies," "sound management with proper logistics," "evaluation systems," "a continuous process of strategic thinking, planning and management," and "staff leadership for program parameters" (Mahler 1992, p. 5).

The effectiveness of family planning programs in reducing fertility remains a matter of controversy. According to international guidelines, programs recruit their clients on a strictly voluntary basis. By accepting the service voluntarily, the individual acceptor demonstrates that she values that service. But some of the more successful programs, notably in

Asia, tended to increase acceptance by often heavy-handed methods of persuasion, and, in the especially important case of China, by coercion backed by legal sanctions. Where fertility fell in less developed countries with active family planning programs, it is typically found that program-provided free services account for a large percentage of those practicing contraception. This non-surprising result is then often taken as an indicator of success in reducing aggregate fertility. But what would have happened in the absence of the program is conjectural, hence routinely ignored. Some less developed countries that lacked government programs also experienced major falls of fertility: Brazil is a conspicuous example. Similarly, if programs have seemingly only minor success in reducing fertility, this can be taken as evidence that the program is inadequately financed, organized, and managed: greater efforts would have led to better results.

Family planning programs as they were commonly conceived had a strong resemblance to health programs. But given the special priority accorded to family planning services in foreign assistance, typically they were organized as a separate "vertical" program, or kept administratively distinct within the broad health program. The justification for such treatment was that while acceptors of family planning services are recruited because the program satisfies their individual need, the program also serves a national developmental need by helping to reduce aggregate population growth, hence deserves priority. Once a family planning program is organized, its managerial and professional cadres form a natural advocacy group strongly interested in the program's sustenance. Invoking the public interest in lowered fertility, as distinct from simply serving the needs of the clients of the program, has long served as a key supporting argument in that endeavor.

Over time, this developmental prop has eroded. This was in part a result of criticisms of the intrinsic scientific merit of the argument but most of all a reflection of the extensive decline of fertility that has occurred, a decline often attributed to the success of the family programs themselves. At the eve of the 1994 International Conference on Population and Development, a review, considered highly respectful of the importance of fertility decline for successful development, reached the guarded conclusion that the evidence on the subject "mostly support the view that rapid population growth in poor countries under conditions of high fertility is inimical to many

development goals"—with stress on the qualifying words "mostly," "high fertility," "many development goals," and "rapid," and with the last-mentioned term defined as "in excess of 2 percent annually" (Cassen 1994, p. 13). By that time, among world regions, only Africa and West Asia had a population growth rate meeting that criterion.

Accordingly, the development rationale of family planning programs was gradually dropped and was replaced by the argument that the programs satisfy important health needs and help people exercise a fundamental human right. The Cairo conference formalized this shift: even though the name of the conference for the first time included a reference to development, scant attention was paid to that concept. Family planning programs were redefined, instead, as reproductive health programs, responding to a broader range of women's health needs, such as prevention of unsafe abortions and sexually transmitted diseases, including HIV/AIDS. But beyond this, new emphasis was put on some requirements that would contribute to women's empowerment: reduction of infant and maternal mortality and improvement in girls' education and women's opportunities for employment and political participation. Although the connection was not highlighted, these are conditions that are likely to help reduce the birth rate through stimulating the demand for smaller family size. The Cairo conference, in effect, reverted to some key elements of a demand strategy for reducing birth rates.

The future of family planning service programs are thus left in a somewhat tenuous status. Without invoking a collective interest in a wider practice of birth control, it is not clear what level of priority should be accorded to such programs as just one part of publicly financed health programs, or indeed relative to many other social welfare programs that also serve demonstrable human needs. Not surprisingly, there are increasing efforts in national programs to rely on the market in enhancing access to contraceptives and to provide program services on a fee-for-service basis.

Population Policy in Response to Below Replacement Fertility

During the second half of the twentieth century debates about population policy, and consequent programmatic action, were centered on the issue of rapid population growth in the less developed world.

Toward the end of this period, however, a quite different demographic phenomenon has begun to attract increasing attention: aggregate fertility levels that are inadequate for the long-run maintenance of the population. Analytically, the potential population policy issue raised by low fertility is identical to the problem inherent in rapid population growth: it is caused by the disjunction between the sum total of individual reproductive decisions and the collective interest in a long-run demographic equilibrium. But this time individual aspirations generate a deficit rather than an excess in population growth. The syndrome, as was noted above, is not entirely novel: it was detectable in fertility trends in the West, especially in Europe, in the 1920s and 1930s, and in some instances, notably in France, even earlier. But in the decades immediately following World War II the baby boom seemed to make the issue of low fertility moot. Indeed, by any historical standard, population growth was rapid during the second half of the twentieth century even in the developed world. Europe's population, for example, grew during that period from 550 million to about 730 million.

The baby boom was, however, a temporary interruption of the secular downward trend in fertility. By the 1970s the net reproduction rate was at or below unity in most countries in Europe and also in the United States. In the U.S. fertility stabilized at or very close to that rate, but in Europe fertility continued to decline. By the beginning of the twenty-first century, the average total fertility rate was 1.4. Such a level, if maintained indefinitely, would result in a population loss of one-third from generation to generation, that is, roughly, over each period of some 30 years. Some countries, notably in Southern, Central, and Eastern Europe, period fertility rates were at low levels without historical precedent for large populations. If continued, in the absence of large compensatory immigration this would not only lead to rapid population decline but also result in very high proportions of the population at old ages. It might be expected that in the affected countries such prospects would generate not only concern, but also vigorous remedial policy action.

By and large, however, this response has not been evident. Most governments as well as the general public tend to view below-replacement fertility with an equanimity quite unlike the alarmed reaction that the same phenomenon elicited when it first emerged between the two World Wars. And explicit pronatalist policies, common in the 1930s, are conspicuous by their absence. There are a variety of reasons explaining this indifference.

First, the preeminent population issue confronting policymakers in the post–World War II period was rapid global population growth. Programs aimed at moderating fertility in the developing world received assistance or at least encouragement from the rich, low-fertility countries. Although the rationale was modified over time, such assistance and encouragement has continued, as indeed substantial further population increase in the less developed countries is still anticipated in the early decades of the twenty-first century. Even though population issues tend to be *sui generis,* reflecting differences in demographic behavior country-by-country, there was, and remains, a perceived dissonance between fertility-lowering assistance to other countries and engaging in action at home serving the opposite aims. Faulty logic notwithstanding, the international terrain has not been favorable for domestic pronatalism.

Second, the natural rate of increase—the difference between the number of births and the number of deaths—is still positive in many of the countries with fertility well below replacement. This is the result of age distributions that reflect past fertility and mortality, and notably the effects of the postwar baby boom, that still favor population growth. While this momentum effect is temporary, the longer-term implications for population decline and population aging are only dimly perceived by the general public and provide an excuse for inaction on the part of policymakers.

Third, when those longer-term demographic effects are understood, a calmer attitude still prevails. There is an inclination, reinforced by increasing concern with the quality of the natural environment, to regard a degree of demographic "decompression" as a not necessarily unwelcome prospect, especially in countries with an already dense population. And it is assumed that the economic and social disadvantages that might be imposed by a declining population can be effectively dealt with through institutional adjustments and social policy measures other than measures aiming for a higher birth rate. A demographic policy often regarded as potentially helpful in this regard is encouragement of immigration. That willing immigrants are available to compensate for low birth rates is taken for granted—a realistic assumption in high-income countries.

Fourth, there is a vague expectation that the population decline, impending or already begun, will in due course trigger corrective homeostatic mechanisms, leading to a spontaneous rebound in the level of fertility. Another baby boom may not be in the offing, but fertility may rise sufficiently to once again reach or at least approximate replacement level. Governments, it is assumed, would be ill-advised to interfere with this natural process by trying to increase birth rates and then seek to fine-tune them at the desirable steady-state level. According to this view, a laisser-faire fertility policy is justified since, apart from broad upper and lower limits, governments are not competent to determine what constitutes an optimal fertility rate, or growth rate, or population size in any given year, decade, or even longer time interval.

Finally, even if the will were there, there is a paucity of effective pronatalist policy instruments. Exhortation from governments are not promising, and in any case unlikely to be tried in a democratic polity. Restrictions imposed on access to modern contraceptive technology are not politically acceptable; they would be also certain to prove a failure. This leaves the traditional levers of social policy: dispensing material incentives and disincentives so as to increase the willingness of couples to have children. Such incentives can be engineered by the government through fiscal measures, such as differential taxation, and/or through provision of services in kind. This approach was tried in the interwar years, but, as noted above, with at best limited success. After World War II many similar measures continued to be applied; in fact, with the steadily expanding welfare state, they were often upgraded and their scope, too, was extended. However, they were no longer considered "pronatalist" but were absorbed within the more encompassing frames of family and general welfare policy. The new label partly reflected a political-ideological preference, but in part also the fact that some distinctive features of pronatalism—such as differential rewards that favored large families, and non-means-tested or even regressive allocation of family and child benefits—were generally no longer acceptable.

Although the redistributive policies of the contemporary welfare state are biased in favor of the elderly and the poor, government-organized transfers to parents of children, or to children directly (such as through publicly financed day-care services and free or subsidized education often beyond the sec-

ondary school level, which lessen the cost of children to parents), are substantial in all low fertility countries. Indeed, it is typically assumed that existing family and welfare policies sustain fertility above a level that would ensue in their absence. Accordingly, making these policies more generous—socializing an even larger share of child costs—is often seen as a means toward increasing fertility, whether as an outright policy objective or, more in the prevailing spirit of the time, as an unintended but welcome by-product. Such extension, however, is difficult, given the fiscal constraints of already overcommitted welfare states. And more to the point, the net effect of family-friendly redistribution of incomes and provision of services is uncertain. It is notable that in the United States, where such schemes are distinctly less well funded than, for example, in Western Europe, fertility is, nevertheless, relatively high.

In recent decades, in modern industrial economies, participation of women in the formal labor force expanded rapidly. This tendency, reflecting market forces but also encouraged by government policy (partly as an antidote for deteriorating dependency ratios as the population becomes older), is likely to continue. Among the factors explaining the low level of fertility despite general material affluence, many observers point to the double burden on women of both raising children and working outside the home. To the extent that higher birth rates are seen to be socially desirable, the derived policy prescription is to adopt measures that make motherhood and women's labor force participation more compatible. The higher fertility in countries (notably in Scandinavia) where such measures are strongly applied, compared to countries (especially those in Southern Europe) where they are largely absent, suggests that enhanced compatibility (through day-care services, flexible work-hours, liberal sick-leave allowances, and the like) is an effective pronatalist policy even if motivated by other considerations. But it is far from clear whether the fertility differential so generated is high enough to bring the total fertility rate back to replacement level. Steady labor force participation of women during the childbearing years can certainly be made compatible with having one child or even two. It is likely to be far less compatible with sustaining, or even increasing, the proportion of women who have more than two children. Many career-oriented women voluntarily remain childless; many others prefer a single child. It follows that, to achieve average replacement-level fertility, the proportions of such women need to be counterbalanced by high enough proportions of women who have chosen third-, fourth-, or even higher-order births. There is little indication at present that policies directed at enhanced compatibility achieve that result.

When fertility is high, as it still is in most developing countries, it is a safe prediction that with economic development it will eventually decline, at least to replacement level. In the longer term, apart from outmigration, the only alternative is higher mortality. The record of the high-income countries indicates, however, that replacement level fertility is not a necessary resting point. Once fertility is lower than that, predictions become highly hazardous. European, and also East Asian experience suggests that fertility has a tendency to settle below an average of two children per woman, hence a tendency toward sustained population decline. The question, to which no good answers exist at the dawn of the twenty-first century, is "how far below?" "Scandinavian"-style family policies may stabilize fertility only modestly below replacement—such as around a total fertility rate of 1.8. That would imply a fairly moderate relative shortfall of births compared to deaths, and population stability in rich countries with such vital rates could be fully or nearly compensated with a modest level of controlled immigration. Population aging would be then kept within relatively narrow limits, which postindustrial economies could readily adjust to. The demographic weight of such countries within the global total in the foreseeable future would continue to shrink, raising possible problems of a shifting geopolitical balance. Still, such demographic configurations would be likely to push the day of demographic reckoning beyond the policy horizons that governments feel an obligation to be actively concerned with. Pronatalist interventions would find at best a marginal place on governments' policy agendas.

On the other hand, fertility levels in the lowest-fertility countries—countries with a total fertility rate of 1.3 or below around the turn of the century—might stabilize at that level, or even shrink further, reflecting the decentralized and uncoordinated decisions of individuals and individual couples. Such an outcome might also foreshadow future reproductive behavior in countries in which fertility is still fairly close to replacement level. This would create a qualitatively different demographic situation for which there are few precedents in modern history. It would

represent a clear threat to the continuing viability of the countries affected. Compensatory immigration flows would have to be so large as to be inconsistent with any reasonable degree of cultural and ethnic continuity. Alternatively, population aging in the absence of immigration would create virtually unsolvable challenges, and there would be a likely drastic loss of relative geopolitical status. Spontaneous homeostatic mechanisms may not come into play to save the day, or may do so too sluggishly to matter. A radical rethinking of fertility policy would then become a necessity for social—and national—survival.

See also: *Eugenics; Family Policy; Immigration Policies; One-Child Policy; Reproductive Rights.*

BIBLIOGRAPHY

Bauer, P. T. 1981. *Equality, the Third World, and Economic Delusion.* Cambridge, MA: Harvard University Press.

Berelson, Bernard. 1969. "Beyond Family Planning." *Studies in Family Planning* No. 38.

Blake, Judith. 1972. "Coercive Pronatalism and American Population Policy." In U. S., Commission on Population Growth and the American Future, *Aspects of Population Growth Policy,* Vol VI of Commission research reports, pp. 85–109, ed. Robert Parke, Jr. and Charles F. Westoff. Washington, D.C.: Government Printing Office.

Bongaarts, John. 1994. "Population Policy Options in the Developing World." *Science* 263: 771–776.

Carr-Saunders, A. M. 1922. *The Population Problem: A Study in Human Evolution.* Oxford: Clarendon Press.

Cassen, Robert, and contributors. 1994. *Population and Development: Old Debates, New Conclusions.* Washington, D.C.: Overseas Development Council.

Casterline, John B., and Steven W. Sinding. 2000. "Unmet Need for Family Planning in Developing Countries and Implications for Population Policy." *Population and Development Review* 26: 691–723.

Chesnais, Jean-Claude. 1996. "Fertility, Family, and Social Policy in Contemporary Western Europe." *Population and Development Review* 22: 729–739.

Cross, Máire, and Sheila Perry, eds. 1997. *Population and Social Policy in France*. London and Washington: Pinter.

Davis, Kingsley. 1967. "Population Policy: Will Current Programs Succeed?" *Science* 158: 730–739.

Davis, Kingsley, Mikhail S. Bernstam, and Rita-Ricardo-Campbell, eds. 1987. *Below-Replacement Fertility in Industrial Societies: Causes, Consequences, Policies*. Cambridge: Cambridge University Press.

Demeny, Paul 1986. "Population and the Invisible Hand." *Demography* 23: 473–487.

———. 1988. "Social Science and Population Policy." *Population and Development Review* 14: 451–479.

———. 1992. "Policies Seeking a Reduction of High Fertility: A Case for the Demand Side." *Population and Development Review* 18: 321–332.

Donaldson, Peter J. 1990. *Nature Against Us: The United States and the World Population Crisis, 1965–1980*. Chapel Hill, NC: The University of North Carolina Press.

Finkle, Jason L., and Barbara B. Crane. 1975. "The Politics of Bucharest: Population, Development and the New International Economic Order." *Population and Development Review* 1: 87–114.

Finkle, Jason L., and C. Alison McIntosh, eds. 1994. *The New Politics of Population: Conflict and Consensus in Family Planning*. Supplement to Vol. 20 of *Population and Development Review*.

Glass, D. V. 1940. *Population: Policies and Movements in Europe*. Oxford: Clarendon Press.

Gwatkin, Davidson R. 1979. "Political Will and Family Planning: The Implications of India's Emergency Experience." *Population and Development Review* 5: 29–59.

Hardin, Garrett. 1968. "The Tragedy of the Commons." *Science* 162: 1,243–1,248.

Hartmann, Betsy. 1995. *Reproductive Rights and Wrongs: The Global Politics of Population Control*, Rev. edition. Boston: South End Press.

Hodgson, Dennis. 1983. "Demography as Social Science and Policy Science." *Population and Development Review* 9: 1–34.

Johansson, S. Ryan. 1991. "'Implicit' Policy and Fertility during Development." *Population and Development Review* 17: 377–414.

Lloyd, W. F. 1968 (1833). "Two Lectures on the Checks to Population." In *Lectures on Population, Value, Poor Laws and Rent*. New York: Augustus M. Kelley.

Mahler, Halfdan. 1992. "Our Next Forty Years." *People* 19: 3–6.

Malthus, T. R. 1820. *Principles of Political Economy*. London: John Murray.

McIntosh, C. Alison, and Jason L. Finkle. 1995. "The Cairo Conference on Population and Development: A New Paradigm?" *Population and Development Review* 21: 223–260.

McNicoll, Geoffrey. 1975. "Community-level Population Policy: An Exploration." *Population and Development Review* 1: 1–21.

———. 2001. "Government and Fertility in Transitional and Post-transitional Societies." *Population and Development Review* Supplement to vol. 27, pp. 129–159.

Myrdal, Alva. 1941. *Nation and Family: The Swedish Experiment in Democratic Family and Population Policy*. London: Routledge.

National Research Council. 1986. *Population Growth and Economic Development: Policy Questions*. Working Group on Population Growth and Economic Development. Committee on Population. Washington, D.C.: National Academy Press.

Olson, Mancur Jr. 1965. *The Logic of Collective Action*. Cambridge, MA: Harvard University Press.

Pfenning, Astrid, and Thomas Bahle, eds. 2000. *Families and Family Policies in Europe: Comparative Perspectives*. Frankfurt am Main: Peter Lang.

Pritchett, Lant H. 1994. "Desired Fertility and the Impact of Population Policies." *Population and Development Review* 20: 1–55.

Teitelbaum, Michael S., and Myron Weiner, eds. 1995. *Threatened Peoples, Threatened Borders: World Migration and U. S. Policy*. New York: W. W. Norton.

Teitelbaum, Michael S., and Jay M. Winter. 1985. *The Fear of Population Decline*. San Diego: Academic Press.

United Nations, Department of Economic and Social Affaires, Population Division. 1999. *Below Replacement Fertility. Population Bulletin of the United Nations*. Special Issue, Nos. 40/41.

———. 2001. *Replacement Migration: Is It a Solution to Declining and Ageing Populations?* New York: United Nations.

———. 2002. *National Population Policies 2001.* New York: United Nations.

United States National Academy of Sciences. 1971. *Rapid Population Growth: Consequences and Policy Implications.* Washington, D.C.: National Academy Press.

Warwick, Donald P. 1982. *Bitter Pills: Population Policies and Their Implementation in Eight Developing Countries.* New York: Cambridge University Press.

Winckler, Edwin A. 2002. "Chinese Reproductive Policy at the Turn of the Millennium: Dynamic Stability." *Population and Development Review* 28: 379–418.

PAUL DEMENY

POPULATION QUALITY

See *Quality of Population*

POPULATION REGISTERS

A population register, broadly interpreted, is a list of persons who belong to a predefined group, containing information identifying the members in a unique way. In that broad sense, a list of members of a club, union, or society could be called a population register if it contains some characteristics like name, address, and date of birth which (in combination) provide unique identifications.

In a more formal sense, the term population register denotes a list (register) of persons who are citizens or residents of (or in some other sense "belong to") a country or a sub-national region. That list typically includes each person's name, current address, and date of birth as an external identifier, and a personal identification number as an internal identifier. This identifier should be unique.

Brief History and Status

Population registers in the more formal sense of the term have been known for several centuries. The parish registers found in many European countries are an example. Local civil registers were established with the development of social security and similar programs at the end of the nineteenth century, when municipal and other authorities needed lists of persons under their responsibility. The demand for national registers intensified in northwest Europe after World War II, with the development of the welfare state. For some countries, that meant a fully centralized register; in others local registers were maintained but under central leadership and coordination (to ensure that every person was included in only one local register).

Since the 1960s, registers have normally been kept in an electronic format, at local and/or national level. This format makes for greater usefulness but is not a prerequisite for a well-functioning population register.

As of the 1990s, most European countries had some sort of population register, local or central or both, and assigned some kind of personal identification numbers. Ireland and Romania are exceptions. Aarno Laihonen's 1998 article provides an overview of the situation. Many less developed countries either already have some kind of population register or are planning to develop one. In Eastern Europe during the Communist period, population registers were used for control as well as administrative purposes, and the successor regimes for the most part have not maintained them. The U.S. lacks any sort of national population register.

The use of registers and identification numbers for statistical and analytical purposes, and the laws regulating this use, vary greatly by country. The Nordic states, the Netherlands, and Belgium have fully centralized registers available for analytical purposes. Israel and Slovenia have similar systems; Austria has one under development.

Content and Linking

The number and nature of variables included in a population register are determined by the political and administrative intention for use. The normal identifiers are name, date of birth, and sex; marital status is recorded; information on children and family may be included, and in some countries, ethnic group. Address or locality information makes it possible to combine regional registers or integrate them at the national level. Some registers on principle include as little information as possible, to avoid items that change frequently. Sex, age, marital status, and a numerical identifier are probably the minimum for a basic register. Other registers that may be linked to it would include the variables needed for specific purposes, like address, births, or co-residence. A register with such variables will have to be updated often.

The key determinant of the ease of use of a register is whether or not it assigns a personal identification number (PIN-code) to each name. Such a number is typically made up of digits indicating date of birth and a sequence number, a code for sex, and one or more control digits. The encoded information should not, of course, include items than may change.

Use of PIN-codes makes it easy to link information from different registers, so the content of any particular register is less important. The variables in the whole cluster of registers can be used simultaneously. For example, in the 2001 Norwegian census about 30 registers were combined.

Where two or more registers of the same population can be linked, the system of registers permits refined analysis of population processes in combination with a broad range of covariates (Aukrust and Nordbotten (1973), Statistics Denmark (1995)). Indeed, linked systems are like social and demographic surveys, but without the surveys' response problems and sampling errors. Ideally, a register keeps a record of all previous variable values, along with the date of change. This is important for historical studies and for longitudinal micro-level analyses with time-varying covariates.

Administrative Registers

Population registers belong to a broader family of administrative registers. These may be numerous, often including employment and unemployment registers, income registers, social security registers, registers of criminality, education registers, etc. Because they are established and run for administrative purposes, their content may not always be well-suited for scientific purposes. For instance, analysts of internal migration may prefer a different definition of place of residence than the one used by tax authorities. However, both the responsible authorities and the researchers share a common interest in appropriate definitions and timely updating.

Quality Aspects

The main advantage of an administrative register is quality. A register run for purely statistical or scientific purposes, can seldom keep high enough quality. Those registered will not have serious interests in informing the register about every change of status. An administrative register is often linked to, and uses administrative routines, which also can be used for controlling the register content. It will often be in the interest of both the registered persons and the users to keep the register correct. Neither register users nor the registered persons can accept that important decisions are based on registers with wrong information. Frequent use increases the possibility to detect mistakes.

A population register adds persons at birth or at entry and deletes them at death or departure. Coverage problems mainly concern migration. There may be a strong personal interest in not having a correct register status. In Scandinavia, however, there are probably more persons (but still below one percent of the total population) who have left the country without notification than are persons living there illegally. Remaining clandestinely in highly regulated countries like the Nordic states without being registered is very difficult.

Internal migration causes particular problems for local registers, due to delayed or completely missing migration notifications. Moreover, for researchers, the rules for registration of place of residence may be ill-suited to demographic analysis. The more actively the register cooperates with other institutions (mail and telephone systems, electricity, schools, health care, etc.), the better its quality.

Statistics based on population registers share some of the same problems as those based on sample surveys. Persons who want to hide themselves or their characteristics will probably not be better covered by sample surveys than by registers. The two sources can, however, be combined. Registers can be used as a sampling frame for a survey, or certain pieces of information can be taken from the register instead of bothering the respondent. In addition, having a register linked to a survey allows survey non-response to be properly analyzed; whereas in a register-based system non-response is virtually non-existent. If variables needed for some purpose are not included in the register, or included with unacceptable definitions, sample surveys or other direct methods of data collection may be necessary.

Data Protection and Privacy

Linking of registers provides information of potentially great value to government, but also great potential for misuse. The same is true for social scientist users of these data. In both cases, confidentiality and protection of privacy have to be properly taken care of. Virtually every country with register systems that allow linking has a Data Surveillance Authority or equivalent agency with the aim of strict enforcement of privacy requirements. These usually specify that information should never be available for identifiable persons; individual data are to be available only for making statistical tables or estimates. In Europe, this work is regulated by the European Union (EU 1995).

See also: *Census; Data Collection, Ethical Issues in; Demographic Surveillance Systems; Family Reconstitution; State and Local Government Demography; Vital Statistics.*

BIBLIOGRAPHY

Aukrust, Odd, and Svein Nordbotten. 1973. "Files of Individual Data and their Potentials for Social Research." *Review of Income and Wealth* 19(2): 189–201.

European Union (1995): Directive 95/46/EC of the European Parliament and of the Council of 24 October 1995 on the protection of individuals with regard to the processing of personal data and on free movement of such data. Brussels, Belgium.

Laihonen, Aarno, Ib Thomsen, Elisabetta Vassenden, and Britt Laberg. 1998. *Final Report from the Development Project in the EEA: Reducing Costs of Censuses through use of Administrative Registers.* Documents 98/1. Oslo: Statistics Norway.

Statistics Denmark. 1995. *Statistics on Persons in Denmark.* ECSC-EC-EAEC. Brussels-Luxembourg.

LARS ØSTBY

POPULATION THOUGHT, CONTEMPORARY

Population thought is the body of work that reflects on the causes and consequences of demographic change. Drawing on studies whose aim is to analyze population trends accurately, it primarily includes works that specify the problematic nature of population trends and works that attempt to induce desired population trends. Individuals with a concern about population, a group far broader than academic demographers, have produced the bulk of twentieth-century population thought so defined.

During the twentieth century most countries have experienced dramatic changes in both the number and the composition of their populations. Many observers have judged that these demographic changes have made the accomplishment of a variety of goals more difficult, whether enhancing national power, maintaining ethnic or cultural hegemony, improving the economy, preserving the environment, or attaining gender equity. These observers have produced a stream of policy-oriented works that highlight an assortment of population problems and argue for a variety of population policies. A chronological treatment of contemporary population thought therefore largely reflects the changing concerns of twentieth-century policymakers.

Academic analyses of twentieth-century population trends both reflected current population concerns and influenced the development of population thought. Demography as an activity has historically contained elements both of a social science and a policy science, and demographers have been motivated both by a desire to understand population trends and a desire to influence them. For instance, the worrisomely low fertility evident throughout much of Europe and the United States during the 1930s clearly influenced the Italian demographer Corrado Gini (1884–1965), who developed a cyclical theory of the rise and fall of population, and the French demographer Alfred Sauvy (1898–1990), who adopted a life-long anti-Malthusianism and a concern for population aging and decline, and the American economist Joseph J. Spengler, who contended that children had become "commodities" like "automobiles" that only would be produced in greater numbers by applying "the economic principles of price." After the baby boom made its appearance during the 1950s the American economists

Gary Becker and Harvey Leibenstein (1922–1994) actually viewed children as a special kind of commodity and elaborated a "new home economics," a key component of which was a sophisticated micro-economic model of fertility. The economist Richard Easterlin, studying the long swings in the growth of population and the economy uncovered by the economist Simon Kuznets (1901–1985), produced a macro-economic explanation of developed societies' fertility trends that focused on the influence played by shifts in cohort sizes over time.

At mid-century, though, rapid population growth in the less developed world attracted the most attention from academic demographers. Frank Notestein (1902–1983) was so alarmed by this population crisis that he left his position as director of Princeton University's Office of Population Research and became president of the Population Council. The Princeton economist Ansley J. Coale (1917–2002) helped convince world leaders of the need for fertility control programs by specifying the economic consequences of rapid population growth. The American demographer Donald Bogue even called for the establishment of a new discipline of family planning research that would have the explicit goal of lowering fertility. Not all academic demographers adopted a neo-Malthusian stance. Alfred Sauvy was a voice of skepticism, and the Danish economist Ester Boserup (1910–1999) argued that increases in population densities historically had been the chief stimulus to the adoption of more productive agricultural methods. The American sociologist Kingsley Davis (1908–1997), believing that a society's fertility level was the result of complex institutional arrangements within its social system, doubted that high fertility could be easily lowered by simply providing individuals with contraceptives. Later in the century Ron Lesthaeghe would take a similar position when examining the potential of increasing the below-replacement fertility of European countries. The American demographer Ronald Freedman and the Australian demographer John C. Caldwell, while believing that fertility levels were largely determined by socio-cultural factors, contended that government policy initiatives to influence fertility ought, themselves, to be considered significant components of the socio-cultural determinants of fertility. Clearly, academic demographers actively participated in twentieth century population debates and both reflected and helped to mold the broader stream of population thought.

The Goal of Population Thought

Twentieth-century students of population had an overarching disciplinary goal: to summarize accurately the mortality and fertility transitions that accompanied the agricultural, industrial, and political revolutions of the modern era and predict their future course. Their analyses more often than not aroused the concern of policymakers. The provisional nature of demographic knowledge played a role in this process, as did the tendency to project trends to the point where problems would be produced. For instance, as the twentieth century began, students of population were attempting to make sense of a number of demographic trends. What was most notable to Walter Willcox (1861–1964) in 1906 was the "enormous" increase in the world's population from 1 billion in 1750 to 1.5 billion in 1900. Willcox attributed almost the entire increase to the "expansion of Europe" as increased agricultural and industrial productivity brought death rates down both in Europe and in "Europe overseas." He did note, however, that fertility had begun to decline throughout most of that of region and predicted that it would continue to do so.

Causes of Fertility Decline

What captured the attention of Western policymakers were not descriptions of 150 years of substantial population growth but instead predictions of continued fertility decline. By the turn of the twentieth century a consensus had emerged among students of population that fertility decline was due to individuals voluntarily controlling their fertility in response to pressures created by changing economic and social conditions. As Arsène Dumont (1849–1902) posited in his 1890 "social capillarity theory," individuals attempting to improve their social position in increasingly stratified societies had come to view children as encumbrances. They therefore lowered their fertility rate to improve their chances of upward mobility.

Statistics on fertility differentials by class, education, and occupation were just beginning to be compiled in the early 1900s, and the trends they revealed worried the elites. In the United States the sons and daughters of New England's oldest families were delaying and forgoing marriage to such an extent that as the century began, their fertility was barely at replacement levels. President Theodore Roosevelt railed against such "race suicide" and declared that "the greatest problem of civilization is to be found in the fact that the well-to-do families tend to die out; there results, in consequence, a tendency to the elimination instead of the survival of the fittest"(Roosevelt, p. 550).

The Social Darwinist Perspective

The social Darwinist belief that competition and natural selection produce beneficial change within human societies had become nearly universal among the educated in the late nineteenth and early twentieth centuries. When they used social class and race as surrogate measures of biological quality, as they were inclined to do, differential fertility assumed supreme importance. In the United States the declining fertility of old-line Americans and the influx of prolific and presumedly "inferior" peoples from southern and eastern Europe came to be viewed as a national catastrophe, a "degradation" of the race.

One policy response to this crisis was the passage in the 1920s of national origin quota acts that severely restricted the entry of supposedly "inferior" immigrant groups. During the first third of the twentieth century many Western nations also passed laws requiring the sterilization of various "defective" groups. In Germany eugenic attempts at race purification eventually led to the implementation of Nazi selective breeding programs and campaigns to eradicate undesired minorities.

The Neo-Malthusian Movement

Early in the twentieth century a neo-Malthusian movement had a very different perspective on fertility decline. Neo-Malthusians believed that growing populations are a major cause of poverty and that lowering fertility by making contraception more accessible facilitates prosperity. The movement originated in Great Britain early in the nineteenth century and had spread throughout Europe by 1900, when the first International Neo-Malthusian Conference was held in Paris.

The Eugenicist and Birth Control Perspectives

By 1900, however, much of the initial concern about population growth had dissipated as fertility decline spread throughout Europe. Neo-Malthusians might praise fertility decline and contraception, but eugenists successfully fought to restrict access to contraceptives, contending that their use harmed the commonwealth since only the "more fit" classes were sufficiently disciplined to use them. Into the fray stepped Emma Goldman (1869–1940), Margaret Sanger (1883–1966), and Marie Stopes (1880–1958), seeking to establish feminist-oriented "birth control" movements in the United States and Great Britain. During a period when high-ranking politicians were publicly reminding educated women of their patriotic duty to marry and have children, these advocates of birth control began mobilizing citizens to legalize a woman's access to contraception.

With most academic population experts at the time siding with the eugenists, advocates of birth control had to work hard to develop convincing counterarguments proving that legalized contraception would be socially beneficial. Margaret Sanger was the most successful, fashioning a case for a woman's right to access to birth control by deftly weaving together eugenic and neo-Malthusian themes: Restrictive laws could not keep contraception out the hands of the educated classes and only served to slow the adoption of birth control among the less motivated "inferior" classes, an adoption that would benefit both the individual and the society.

The Pronatalist Position

Fertility decline did spread throughout the classes in many Western populations during the 1910s and 1920s, even in places where access to contraceptives was legally restricted. It reached such a high level that fears of actual depopulation developed, and with them a backlash against the birth controllers' message. France, for example, had an active birth control movement in the early twentieth century, the production and sale of contraceptives were legal, and the national fertility level was low. After the devastating military losses of World War I, however, worry grew among French leaders over what population decline might mean for the nation's competitiveness.

In 1920 the French government, advised and aided by French population experts, enacted a strongly pronatalist population policy that sought to encourage fertility through a combination of positive programs that enhanced couples' ability to care for children and repressive programs that limited couples' access to contraceptives and abortion. The law of February 13, 1920, made manufacturing, selling, or advocating the use of contraceptives illegal, punishable by fines or imprisonment. The French birth control movement found itself under a systematic attack and without much public support.

In the United States Louis Dublin (1882–1969) and Alfred Lotka (1880–1949) developed "intrinsic" vital rates that controlled for the influence of the age structure on crude birth rates and dramatically announced that the average American woman in 1920 was having only half a child more than was needed to maintain a stationary population. P. K. Whelpton (1893–1964) devised the cohort-component method of population projection in 1928 and forecast a significant slowdown in U.S. population growth. Dublin followed with a call for more "birth release" and less "birth control." U.S. leaders began worrying less about declining population quality and more about declining numbers.

The Effects of Fertility Decline

By 1930 a number of Western countries had ended their modern period of population expansion as their fertility rates reached the low levels already achieved by their mortality rates. At that time students of population in the United States (Warren Thompson [1887–1973]), France (Adolphe Landry [1874–1956]), and Great Britain (A. M. Carr-Saunders [1886–1966]) brought forth very similar summations of modern population dynamics.

Generalizing from the Western experience, they all contended that a shift from high to low vital rates was associated with the transformation of agrarian societies into industrial societies. Because mortality declined earlier and more quickly than did fertility, a period of population growth accompanied the shift. The United States and Western Europe had already experienced this "demographic revolution," eastern and southern Europe and Japan were in the middle of their expansion stage, and much of the rest of the world had just begun the revolution.

This summary of modern population dynamics, which reemerged after World War II as demographic transition theory, represented a great achievement for academic demographers. However, its appearance in the 1930s proved troublesome. Germany and Japan both were engaged in imperialist moves into their neighbors' lands that they claimed were necessitated by their growing populations. Western policymakers rejected the legitimacy of such moves. They also largely ignored these early transition treatments of modern population movements that seemingly imparted scientific legitimacy to such *lebensraum* rationales for Axis expansionism.

In general, the 1930s was a period when nationalistic chauvinism made any examination of international population trends controversial. The International Union for the Scientific Investigation of Population Problems (IUSIPP), launched in 1928, planned to hold its first meeting in Rome in 1931. Hints that the meeting would be used to promulgate Mussolini's racial theories caused the IUSIPP's leadership to convene a hastily planned counter-conference in London. The IUSIPP's next official meeting was held in Berlin in 1935, and several national committees that correctly feared that it would be used to spread Nazi racial theories boycotted that meeting.

Postwar Developments

Among countries engaged in World War II older mercantilist notions that equated larger populations with enhanced state power tended to reemerge immediately after entry into the conflict and to remain in place until the war ended. The period after World War II was one of dramatic change in both population trends and population concerns. The unexpected baby boom that occurred in many Western low-growth populations ended fears of depopulation. The enormity of the Holocaust dissipated any remaining enthusiasm for eugenics. The removal of German and Japanese military threats broke the association between transition accounts of modern population dynamics and population-pressure rationales for territorial expansion. In fact, the transition framework in the postwar world was a valuable tool for Western policymakers, serving as a way to interpret the unprecedented demographic changes arising in the world's "underdeveloped" regions during the 1950s and 1960s.

The use of newly developed antibiotics and the application of effective methods for eliminating malaria produced unprecedented mortality decline throughout much of the "Third World," an entity engendered by postwar decolonization. The resultant rapid population growth was problematic for both political and demographic reasons. From the perspective of postwar versions of demographic transition theory put forward by population experts working at Princeton's Office of Population Research, the economic strains associated with rapid population growth might prevent the transformation of traditional agrarian societies into modern industrial societies. Rapid population growth in the Third World might forestall the very socioeconomic changes—industrialization and urbanization—that would induce fertility decline and complete the demographic transition. Without fertility decline, the Third World's period of population expansion would come to an end with mortality rising as starvation and disease increased.

The Populating Dilemma of the Third World

Politically, the Third World was a Cold War battleground where the United States and the Soviet Union fought for supremacy. Starvation, economic stagnation, and growing poverty were judged to be propitious for the spread of communism. There appeared to be only one way to humanely resolve the Third World's emerging population dilemma and, incidentally, the geopolitical threat to the free world: inducing fertility decline in societies that were still agrarian.

American population experts expounded this vision of the postwar global population situation, and by the early 1950s, John D. Rockefeller 3rd and the leadership of the Ford and Rockefeller foundations had accepted its validity. They began establishing a neo-Malthusian movement with a global focus. Their goal was to lower fertility and lessen population growth throughout the Third World by setting up family planning programs. They recognized that only governments could implement effective family planning programs, and their immediate task became to convince policymakers in both the First World and the Third World that high fertility was a major social problem that required state intervention.

At first the population crisis appeared to be a peculiarly "Asiatic problem" to those foundations. Would food and natural resource supplies be adequate to feed, clothe, and shelter increasingly large and dense populations? By the end of the 1950s, however, the crisis had grown in their minds to include all countries with high population growth rates. Any population with a 3 percent annual rate of growth of its population would need an equally high rate of growth in the economy simply to assure that its current standard of living would not slip even lower and a much higher rate to experience significant economic development. Simulation models to quantify the economic benefits of lowering fertility were developed. They found the benefits to be substantial, and movement advocates used those findings to persuade many Third World leaders to adopt antinatalist policies.

Opposition to Neo-Malthusianism

There were voices in opposition to this global neo-Malthusian movement. At the first United Nations-sponsored population conference, which was held in Rome in 1954, the Soviet delegation presented a Marxist critique: Poverty and lack of development were caused by imperialism and colonialism, not population growth. In France a long-standing pronatalist tradition among demographers and government leaders produced skepticism about the validity of neo-Malthusian precepts. Many Third World leaders, especially in low-population-density regions of Latin America and Africa, believed that population growth would aid their countries' development, not detract from it. Finally, the Roman Catholic Church strongly objected to neo-Malthusians' advocacy of "artificial" birth control. With the development of new nonbarrier contraceptives in the late 1950s, especially the birth control pill and the intrauterine device, neo-Malthusians hoped that Catholic opposition might end, but Pope Paul VI's 1968 encyclical on the regulation of birth, *Humanae Vitae*, contained no change in the church's position even though it recognized the existence of a "population problem."

The Neo-Malthusian Movement in the 1960s and 1970s

In the 1960s the global neo-Malthusian movement developed deeper roots among First World policymakers and the public, especially in the United States. In 1965 the U.S. government, at the direction of President Lyndon Johnson, began offering family-planning aid to developing countries and quickly became the major source of such funds. In 1968 Paul Ehrlich published a neo-Malthusian tract, *The Population Bomb*, that sold over 3 million copies. In the same year Zero Population Growth was founded, an organization committed to bringing about global population stabilization; within three years its membership had exceeded 30,000. The Commission on Population Growth and the American Future, established by U.S. President Richard Nixon, issued a 1972 report advocating population stabilization for the United States itself.

A somewhat different course of events, however, was occurring in the Third World. Beginning in the mid-1960s, a variety of First World institutions began pressuring Third World governments to adopt population control policies. Family-planning programs were one activity for which Third World governments could easily find First World monetary support. Such advocacy produced a growing list of leaders who nominally endorsed the need for population control, but those leaders were suspicious of the donors' motives. This ambivalence was evident at the 1974 United Nations World Population Conference held in Bucharest. Delegates from Third World countries refused to ratify a proposed plan of action that called for a united global effort to lower fertility. They countered that "development is the best contraceptive" and called for a "new international economic order" that would entail a redistribution of global power and wealth. If First World governments wished to slow Third World population growth, they should do so by appropriating the significant funds needed to foster comprehensive development, not the modest funds needed to establish family planning clinics.

The conference finally adopted a developmentalist plan of action, although the implementation of the plan after the conference was not without ironies. Although developmentalist rhetoric became obligatory among movement population experts, the Third World countries that led the developmentalist fight at Bucharest, India and China, proceeded to implement coercive "beyond family planning" fertility control programs at home, indicating a deep acceptance of neo-Malthusian precepts that belied their rhetoric at the conference. Accounts of Indian teenagers being forcibly given vasectomies and Chinese women, seven months pregnant, being badgered into accepting abortions would help fracture what had been solid U.S. government support for the neo-Malthusian agenda. After the U.S. Supreme Court's 1973 *Roe v. Wade* decision legalizing abortion, right-to-life advocates began mobilizing around a conservative reproductive agenda and skillfully used those accounts to further their efforts.

During the decade that followed the 1974 conference the neo-Malthusian movement experienced some advances: Family-planning programs expanded their range, communist opposition to neo-Malthusianism lessened considerably, and significant fertility decline occurred in much of the Third World. However, there also were setbacks: Public alarm over the "population bomb" diminished, and the movement's major private sources of funds, the Rockefeller and Ford foundations, significantly reduced their allocations for population-related work. Although the U.S. Congress steadily increased funding for international family planning programs, the media attention paid to coercive fertility control efforts, especially those employing abortion, made American politicians hesitant about offering unqualified support for population control.

The 1980s

Abortion politics eventually fueled a dramatic reversal in U.S. population policy with Ronald Reagan's election as an anti-abortion president. In 1984, a re-election year for Reagan, another United Nations conference on population was to be held in Mexico City. Anti-abortion social conservatives would interpret any talk of population problems by Reagan-appointed delegates as justification for abortion and state-mandated contraception.

Motivated by domestic politics, Reagan appointed U.S. conference delegates who declared that there was no international population problem, only an international abortion problem. They voted with the Vatican to amend that conference's plan of action to prohibit the promotion of abortion "as a method of family planning" and used the occasion to announce a new U.S. "Mexico City policy" aimed at curtailing the global spread of abortion. Julian Simon (1932–1998), an American economist, had written several "revisionist" works that questioned Malthusian assertions about the deleterious effect of rapid population growth on countries' economic development efforts, going so far as to argue that population growth stimulates economic growth. U.S. delegates adopted his revisionist thought to justify their dismissal of a population problem.

Concern over global population growth continued to lessen as the 1980s progressed. Population growth was decreasing, the Cold War ended, and many of the northern countries' political fears surrounding population growth dissipated. Moderate revisionist thought became more respectable as a 1986 study by the U.S. National Academy of Sciences concluded that any deleterious of effect of population growth on development was modest.

The 1990s

The global neo-Malthusian movement reacted to declining interest in its agenda by pragmatically looking for new issues and allies. The environmental movement seemed to be an obvious source for both.

One branch of the movement had begun emphasizing the need for developing countries to direct their development efforts away from maximizing economic growth and toward achieving "sustainable development," a key element of which was curbing population growth. However, these efforts to rejuvenate the neo-Malthusian movement by giving it an environmental focus provoked opposition. At the 1992 United Nations Conference on Environment and Development held in Rio de Janeiro a number of factions, chief among which were delegates from the southern countries and feminists, objected vigorously to considering population a significant cause of environmental degradation. Overconsumption by the rich, not the prolific reproduction of the poor, was the cause of environmental problems. The final Rio Declaration on the environment and development contained only an oblique mention of population.

The 1990s began with an international population agenda that had lost its clear neo-Malthusian focus. At the 1994 United Nations Conference on Population and Development in Cairo a new feminist-oriented population agenda made its debut. Despite a long feminist tradition of viewing all population policies as inherently coercive toward women, a group of reproductive health feminists united with what remained of the neo-Malthusian establishment to form a "common ground" alliance. The program of action adopted at Cairo embodied its major terms: Redressing gender inequities is needed for lasting fertility control, and women have reproductive rights to determine their reproductive destinies. With surprisingly few reservations delegates endorsed this essentially feminist agenda. Countries pledged themselves to eliminate social, cultural, political, and economic discrimination against women as the central component of an effort to balance population and available resources.

The Twenty-first Century

At the start of the twenty-first century most policymakers and population experts assumed that nearly every population would complete its mortality and fertility transitions, most likely by mid-century. Already a commonality of population trends is present: population aging in nearly every region, below-replacement fertility in much of the North, and declining population growth in much of the South. These trends are producing a new set of population concerns. In countries with extremely low fertility

questions exist about the ability of the working-age population to provide adequately for the growing elderly population, and many people wonder if economic prosperity is possible with a declining population. Unlike the case a century earlier, no state is likely to restrict access to contraception as part of its pronatalist policy; such an affront to women's reproductive rights would no longer be tolerated.

More states are offering monetary inducements to spur childbearing, but the efficacy of such policies is unclear. "Replacement immigration"—filling the void left by declining native births by accepting migrants from countries with surplus populations— is being discussed seriously, but opposition to this strategy is strong. In Europe the compositional concerns of a hundred years ago are reemerging in public debates over whether an Algerian, a Turk, or a Pakistani can be "French," "German" or "British." Which concern—declining numbers or changing composition—will prove more influential in shaping tomorrow's population policy is unclear. Population thought, however, will continue to evolve as the proponents of each position make their cases.

See also: *Becker, Gary S.; Caldwell, John C.; Conferences, International Population; Davis, Kingsley; Demographic Transition; Demography, History of; Ecological Perspectives on Population; Eugenics; Landry, Adolphe; Lebensraum; Notestein, Frank W.; Sanger, Margaret; Sauvy, Alfred; Simon, Julian L.; Thompson, Warren S.*

BIBLIOGRAPHY

Becker, Gary. 1960. "An Economic Analysis of Fertility." In *Demographic and Economic Change in Developed Countries*. National Bureau of Economic Research. Princeton, NJ: Princeton University Press.

Boserup, Ester. 1965. *The Conditions of Agricultural Growth; The Economics of Agrarian Change under Population Pressure*. Chicago: Aldine Publishing.

Caldwell, John C. 1976. "Toward a Restatement of Demographic Transition Theory." *Population and Development Review* 2(3/4): 321–366.

Carr-Saunders, A. M. 1936. *World population*. Oxford: Clarendon Press.

Coale, Ansley J., and Edgar M. Hoover. 1958. *Population Growth and Economic Development in Low-income Countries: A Case Study of India's*

Prospects. Princeton, NJ: Princeton University Press.

Dublin, Louis, and Alfred Lotka. 1925. "On the True Rate of Natural Increase." *Journal of the American Statistical Association* 20(150): 305–339.

Dumont, Arsène. 1890. *Depopulation et civilisation: étude démographique.* Paris: Lecrosnier et Babe.

Ehrlich, Paul. 1968. *The Population Bomb.* NY: Ballantine Books.

Gini, Corrado. 1930. "The Cyclical Rise and Fall of Population." In *Population,* ed. Corrado Gini et al. Chicago: University of Chicago Press.

Goldman, Emma. 1916. "The Social Aspects of Birth Control." *Mother Earth* 11(12): 468–475.

Landry, Adolphe. 1934. *La révolution démographique; études et essais sur les problèmes de la population.* Paris: Sirey.

Lesthaeghe, Ron. 1980. "On the Social Control of Human Reproduction." *Population and Development Review* 6(4): 527–548.

National Research Council. 1986. *Population Growth and Economic Development: Policy Questions.* Washington, D.C.: National Academy Press.

Roosevelt, Theodore. 1907. "A Letter from President Roosevelt on Race Suicide." *American Monthly Review of Reviews* 35(5): 550–551.

Sanger, Margaret. 1919. "Birth Control and Racial Betterment." *Birth Control Review* 3(2): 11–12.

Sauvy, Alfred. 1969. *General Theory of Population,* trans. Christophe Campos. New York: Basic Books.

Simon, Julian. 1981, 1996. *The Ultimate Resource.* Princeton, NJ: Princeton University Press.

Spengler, Joseph J. 1932. "The Birth Rate — Potential Dynamite." *Scribner's Magazine* 92 (July): 6–12.

Stopes, Marie. *Contraception (Birth Control) Its Theory, History and Practice: A Manual for the Medical and Legal Professions.* London: J. Bale, Sons & Danielsson.

Thompson, Warren S. 1929. "Population." *American Journal of Sociology* 34(6): 959–975.

U.S. Commission on Population Growth and the American Future. 1972. *Final Report.* Washington, D.C.: U.S. Commission on Population Growth and the American Future.

Whelpton, P. K. 1928. "Population of the United States, 1925 to 1975." *American Journal of Sociology* 34(2): 253–270.

Willcox, Walter. 1906. "The Expansion of Europe and Its Influence upon Population." In *Studies in Philosophy and Psychology.* NY: Houghton Mifflin.

DENNIS HODGSON

POPULATION THOUGHT, HISTORY OF

This article discusses European thinking on human population from the early modern period to the end of the nineteenth century. Later developments are treated in the article entitled "Population Thought, Contemporary."

European traditions of population thought began to take their definitive modern form in the sixteenth and seventeenth centuries. Some components that came together to bring about this transformation had much longer histories. Rudimentary census lists, for example, appear in Egypt as early as the eleventh century B.C.E.; developed subsequently in many places, their use remained no more than an adjunct of taxation and conscription for nearly three millennia. Reasoned accounts of population size and growth appear in treatises on government as early as the fourth century B.C.E. Plato and Aristotle, observing that republics and monarchies differ in their aims and capacities, argued that each type of government has an optimum population size. They proposed, in other words, that means used to regulate human numbers should be consistent with moral and political systems. By the Middle Ages, systematic theology carried this a step further. Theologians of the time argued that population size and growth can only be influenced by humans in accordance with God-given laws of nature (*lex naturalis*). As divine law cannot be apprehended directly, the role of the Church is to interpret scriptural evidence (*lex divina*) so that princes may rule legitimately (*lex civilis*). In this doctrine, the divine right of kings determines population movements either directly by policies of war, colonization, and trade, or indirectly by provoking divine judgment (epidemics, infertility, famines).

The Church's claim to sole authority collapsed in the sixteenth century, but the quest for a cohesive system uniting natural principles and human government remained. With the Reformation, the competition of religions undermined the supposed natural and divine legitimacy of kings. The foundations of human society and government could begin to be located more directly in the population of a state as a whole, or in ideas of natural law binding a ruler to the people. Humanist writers from Niccolo Machiavelli (1469–1527) to Thomas Hobbes (1588–1679) took a crucial step: in different ways, they faced up to the realpolitik that states often do not act in conformity with morality and nature. In their search for principles of effective and legitimate government, population obtained a twofold, generative, role and became integral to the modern theory of the state. First, population came to be seen as the natural source of a state's power in the sense that human fecundity produces the people that are the source of productive energies for all purposes; and second, a population was understood as the collective entity of individuals and groups whose interaction generates a political and moral community. In this view, power no longer resides in the natural and divine sanctions a prince imposes on his subjects, but in the members of that population acting individually and collectively. The quest for principles of legitimate government and conformity with nature thus converged on the problem of how to control, or at least manage, the generative capacities inherent in a population. Put another way, the relative greatness of states—including the size and growth of their population—depends on effective membership: whether people act (or can be constrained to act) cohesively.

An important point in sixteenth- and seventeenth-century writings was that the generative capacities of population are not necessarily positive, especially as they may lead to conflict. On one hand, larger, more populous states may decimate smaller ones. On the other, a large population does not necessarily make for a secure state. People commonly differ in their actions and interests. A governing elite composed of competing nobles, and sometimes merchant families, will form shifting alliances, each able to draw on a wider multitude of common people. Such competing memberships were difficult to control in a large population and, as Machiavelli observed, usually tended toward dissent and sedition.

Internal struggles acted, in turn, as a drain on the exchequer. Hence states, even when well-endowed with people and other natural resources, could be defeated in war and surpassed in trade by less-endowed but more cohesive neighbors.

As princes turned to merchants for loans, an active body of mercantilist writings grew up. These writings urged that deficient state revenues could be made good only where policies promoted trade. Mercantilist writers argued that the greatness of states depends on a large population, and governments could achieve this by encouraging people into occupations and places where greater profits could be made. Trade would then flourish and growth would be sustained as more land came into cultivation, producing more raw materials for manufacture, raising merchants' profits, employment, and tax revenues. Once again, the size and growth of a population depend on how well its members are ordered: The second generative role of population takes priority over the first.

An important implication of this priority was that bad government was itself a major check on population. Where princes were badly advised, weak, or corrupt, people would feel insecure, and conflicts would inevitably ensue. Members would form themselves into opposing factions, or ally themselves with other states. Even authors sympathetic to republics like Jean Bodin (1530–1596), Hobbes, Machiavelli, and Charles de Secondat baron de Montesquieu (1689–1755) regarded a just sovereign or prince as best able to direct people's conflicting capacities. The idea that the generative powers of population and its growth are never entirely within princely control here became an important argument against tyranny. Rulers must attend justly to the needs of the population, otherwise the population will not grow and may even decline. Where, in contrast, a sovereign's rule was acceptable, then positive effects of cohesive membership would come to the fore. Merchant, political, and religious arguments agreed, advising princes to promote population growth by inducements to marriage, procreation, immigration, increased production and trade, and justice ensuring continued loyalty. But Giovanni Botero (1540–1617) speculated that in such circumstances there could conceivably be too many people relative to subsistence.

The Emergence of Population Arithmetic

One of the far-reaching changes induced by early modern reflection on population membership was the altered role of measurement. The need to recognize the members of a population and, if possible, control their aggregate dynamics made more systematic knowledge of human numbers desirable, and stimulated lines of questioning leading far beyond the ancient problems of raising armies and state revenue. Humanist and scientific developments were closely allied in the sixteenth and seventeenth centuries, opening the order of nature to question by direct, numerical observation. These developments were synthesized in Francis Bacon's (1561–1626) influential program for the systematic reform of knowledge. Methods of scientific observation were not, however, considered directly applicable to problems of government until the first essay in "population arithmetic," John Graunt's (1620–1674) *Natural and Political Observations* (1662). Graunt's work, written explicitly to carry out Bacon's program, showed how merchant accounting arithmetic could be combined with direct observation and the humanist methodology of language and rhetoric to develop a natural history of populations. Scientific approaches to population begin with Graunt, and his candor and critical approach to the quality of quantitative evidence are still considered outstanding. Many fundamentals of population research were treated cohesively and quantitatively by Graunt for the first time, including ratios of births, deaths, and sexes, the structuring of a population by age, urban and rural differences, proportionate changes over time in causes of death, and possible implications of all of these factors for the greatness of states.

For Graunt, scientific measurement belonged to natural history, but its applications embraced policy. The order of nature is intrinsically mathematical, and recurring balances in human numbers belong to this order. This approach enabled his political framework to remain outwardly conventional: population arithmetic, by revealing proportions and disproportions in the members of the body politic, would help princes to rule in conformity with natural and divine balances. Graunt also made clear, however, that population policy is not solely for princes to decide: His method showed pointedly how all readers may make calculations of their own. Rulers and citizens alike were thus enjoined to examine evidence of the quantitative impact of epidemics, the implications of unhealthy urban conditions for reproduction, and other problems of personal and collective concern. This evidence could be used to identify problems needing good government, and to ascertain whether a prince's policies really did anything to help people. For the first time, the search for unifying principles of legitimate government and laws of nature was posed in terms of sustained numerical observation and analysis.

Population arithmetic was not, however, integrated easily into government or daily life. The attitudes of the *ancien régime,* or of European government generally before the end of the eighteenth century, stressed deference to hereditary rights and the divine basis of monarchy, both strongly backed by religious teaching. This attitude prevailed in the eighteenth century, and in many places well into the nineteenth. Princes, while often conscious of the need to improve institutional capacities of government, remained wary of the implications of population arithmetic. Vital data were sensitive, as they indicated the capacities of states and the efficacy of governments. Where states made sustained attempts to collect these data, as in Prussia, Sweden, and France, access to the results was restricted.

Graunt's persuasive rationale nonetheless enabled individuals' quantitative inquiries (frequently critical of contemporary regimes) to be tolerated within this broadly authoritarian world view. His work was taken up enthusiastically across the whole range of contemporary opinion: by royalists and republicans; priests, dissenters, and atheists; merchants and ministers of state; physicians and philosophers; surveyors and tradesmen. Contemporary mathematical and scientific elites were involved in Holland (Jan DeWitt [1625–1672], Johannes Hudde [1628–1704], Christian Huygens [1631–1699], Nicolaas Struyck [1687–1769]), England (Abraham De Moivre [1667–1754], Edmund Halley [1656–1742], Richard Price [1723–1791]), France (Georges Louis Leclerc, comte de Buffon [1707–1788], Jean-Antoine-Nicolas Caritat, Marquis de Condorcet [1743–1794], Jean le Rond D'Alembert [1717–1783], Joseph Louis Lagrange [1736–1813], Pierre Simon de LaPlace [1749–1827], Antoine Laurent Lavoisier [1743–1794]), America (Benjamin Franklin [1706–1790] Thomas Jefferson [1743–1826]), Germany (Gottfried-Wilhelm Leibniz [1646–1716]), Sweden (Pehr Wargentin [1717–1783]), and Switzerland (Leonhard Euler [1707–1783], Jacob Bernoulli [1654–1705]). Population thought continued to develop significantly in advance of institutional realities until the nineteenth century.

Elements of Population Theory in the *Ancien Régime*

During the period historians have called the long eighteenth century (1660–1830), individual inquiries made for lively, if inconclusive, debates. Demographers and statisticians have sometimes dismissed the period as one of confusion and even stagnation, yet the end of this era witnessed the two restatements of Graunt's project that still shape most people's understanding of population: T. R. Malthus's *Essay* and the promulgation of statistics as a universal basis of government and national development. Both depended on the foundation laid in the sixteenth and seventeenth centuries. Given that good government and the population trends depend on a state's ability to balance the divergent capacities of populations, discussion turned to the implications of population arithmetic: Which specific proportionalities should a state maintain, and what means are best suited to this objective? Graunt's arithmetic implied not only that particular balances but also ratios of relative improvement or decline could be specified. Differing ratios, in turn, implied different population sizes and structures, and recourse to different mechanisms of control. Much further work was necessary for these implications to be formulated explicitly. Three developments of population arithmetic on which Malthus and statistics depended emerged in the century and a half following Graunt. Population arithmetic became central to separate developments in the calculus of probability, in attempts to conceptualize relations between labor and wealth, and in registration as an administrative procedure in many institutions.

Pioneers of mathematical probability—including Huygens, Leibnitz, and Bernoulli—found in Graunt's mortality arithmetic instances of what was later called the "law of large numbers." They conceived probability as a general method of social reasoning that could reduce the uncertainty of moral, political, and economic affairs to a single workable logic. Sex ratios, smallpox vaccinations, and life expectation provided the only empirical series with which to explore this logic. Their ambitions, although not realized, gave rise to the first and enduring formal model of population, the life table, which quickly passed into the wider literature on population arithmetic. In the most widely read application, Johann Peter Süssmilch's (1707–1767) *Die Göttliche Ordnung* (1765), age structures of death provided new and formidable evidence of God's laws indispensable to improved government.

Süssmilch's great volume, together with Jean-Baptiste Moheau's (1745–1794) treatise of 1778, mark the arrival of essays in population arithmetic on a scale that would now be called general social theory. Written in the service of powerful princes like Frederick II and Louis XVI, their works brought quantitative evidence to bear on the main traditions of political theory. More particularly, these thinkers set out to refute the contention of major eighteenth-century works critical of princely rule, like those of Montesquieu, Victor Mirabeau [1715–1789], and Jean-Jacques Rousseau [1712–1778], that prevailing monarchies fostered depopulation. Interestingly, arithmeticians like Moheau could disagree with Montesquieu over forms of government and their effects, but were in substantial accord that population growth or decline depended on the moral and political condition of citizens. In principle, only state policies that were consistent with natural rights to personal liberty, security, and livelihood would promote population growth.

Major economic contributors, notably François Quesnay (1694–1774), Du Pont de Nemours (1739–1817), and Anne Robert Jacques Turgot (1727–1781), could likewise disagree over the virtues of princely rule while developing Montesquieu's lead that *ancien régime* policies of taxation, trade, labor, and war had crippling effects on the security of ordinary citizens, and hence on their willingness to marry and have children. Moheau, like Montesquieu, considered that the dire effects of bad government on population proceeded largely via *moeurs,* that is, customs of marriage, procreation, inheritance, and other aspects of family life through which economic factors acted on social status. Where insecurity became entrenched in customs, the decline of reproduction could take centuries to reverse. Debates over depopulation were also prominent in Britain, addressed variously to ancient populations (David Hume [1711–1776], Robert Wallace [1773–1855]) and modern (Richard Price, William Wales [1734–1796], and Arthur Young [1741–1820], among many others). The republican Richard Price, the most formidable English probabilist and practitioner of population arithmetic in the later eighteenth century, came down firmly on the side that argued that modern populations were decreasing.

The numerical approach employed in these controversies was sometimes called "political arithmetic," following the phrase coined in the 1670s by Graunt's friend, William Petty (1623–1687). As the phrase suggests, the natural historical component of Graunt's method was dropped, and with it the need for practitioners to present calculations and evidence in a way that would enable readers to evaluate them independently. What remained were the multipliers and other proportional devices merchants used to abridge accounts in the absence of full information. Without doubt, the arithmeticians faced a serious difficulty. The general importance of population arithmetic could only be broached in terms of general population totals necessary to calculate vital and economic measures. Careful proposals for national censuses were duly put forward, notably by Sébastien le Prestre de Vauban (1633–1707), but not enacted. Without them, only the partial enumerations provided by parish records, bills of mortality, lists of annuitants, and local censuses, were extant. Petty therefore made multipliers central to his approach, and their use greatly expanded in the eighteenth century. In effect, political arithmetic made a virtue of necessity by aiming at reasonable orders of magnitude rather than systematic accounting. Typical methods took the number of households (usually estimated, or derived from a local list) and multiplied it by a postulated average household size; or the proportion of births to population in a local census would be applied to estimates of annual births at wider levels of aggregation. As late as 1814, LaPlace could argue that multipliers were superior for government purposes to the inaccurate figures any census would provide.

As a reliable aid to the economics and health of population, however, political arithmetic was always open to question. Petty's predominant interest lay in economic policy, and he used population multipliers to attempt pioneering estimates of national income, the distribution of labor, and surplus productive capacity. Like mercantile writers before him, he treated a growing population as conducive to the national wealth that is the possession of the prince and the elite. His methods were viewed critically in his own time by Gregory King (1648–1712) who, in gaining privileged access to tax records and applying Graunt's scrutiny to them, initiated the empirical study of national income and its distribution. King's arithmetical analyses were not prepared for publication, and were known only in brief excerpts given by

Charles Davenant (1656–1714). The interrelation of population and economy as a unified system begins properly with Richard Cantillon (1697–1734), who turned his back on political arithmetic in two major respects: first, although quantitative (i.e., proportional) reasoning was instrumental to his logic, analysis of numerical records was secondary, and merely illustrative; second, the natural resource of a state is identified primarily not with population but with land, and secondarily with manufactures and trade. In his account, which shaped later work by Adam Smith (1723–1790), T. R. Malthus (1766–1834), Quesnay, and Turgot, Cantillon argued that population growth tends naturally to rise to the limits of subsistence; what checks it directly are those *moeurs* pertaining to age at marriage and procreation that regulate social status, and which make men and women attentive to their economic situation. Cantillon also broke new ground by developing his account of economics and *moeurs* within a clearly articulated social structure, divided simply into a small class of proprietors and a multitude of laborers. Proprietors, in their differing tastes for goods and services, determine the demand for labor, the way resources in land are utilized, and the balance of manufactures and raw materials in trade. His analysis made the relationship of subsistence and population central while retaining merchants' characteristic view that such factors become important to a nation's wealth chiefly as a support to trade.

Early economic writings, from mercantilism through political arithmetic to Cantillon, had generally assumed that populations would continue to grow while workers' wages remained at subsistence level. In other words, the ideal of a well-ordered polity in which a cohesive and growing population generates rising profits, taxes, and trade presupposed the brute fact that producers' wages would be kept at a minimum. A sophisticated discourse on population and agricultural economy that questioned this premise grew up in France after Cantillon. This discourse considered the condition of the poor to be a major source of depopulation and recognized its potential as a source of disorder. Physiocratic authors following Quesnay developed an analysis of economic classes that finally gave preeminence to relations between agricultural resources and population. Merchants might assume the natural capacity of population to increase whenever demand for labor rises, but the consequences for producers could not be taken for granted. The Physiocrats therefore reasserted the principle that legitimate government is based on populations endowed with natural rights, notably producers with rights to economic liberty and material security. For Turgot, every man has a fundamental right to work and to basic support, if not to indiscriminate charity. As the benefits of a growing population would nonetheless accrue chiefly to upper classes, Jacques Necker (1732–1804) argued that government has a critical role to play in ensuring justice.

The conceptual shift that made land the intrinsic source of wealth and state power thus did not devalue population. Rather, it focused attention more closely on population and resources within the state considered as a more or less fixed domain. If, as many writers seriously believed, countries well-endowed with resources like France and England were losing population, then the role of subsistence in limiting human numbers could not be put down to brute material want. Explanations continued to point to bad government as the key problem, but examined its implications in terms of variations in the demand for labor and of wages, in relations between mortality and living conditions, and in the strong role of custom in determining acceptable minimal living standards. Population arithmetic, carefully applied at the local level by Jean Muret, John Heysham (1753–1834), Vauban, and Antoine Deparcieux (1703–1768), among others, demonstrated convincingly that a range of factors (including infant mortality, epidemics, and emigration) exercised a major check on particular parishes. Such factors underlined the vulnerability of the poor.

A considerable body of British essays in the later eighteenth century by Smith, James Steuart (1712–1780), Young, Joseph Townsend (1739–1816), and others shared French concern over the moral and economic condition of the poor. Adam Smith, for example, took the view that population was in general kept down by high mortality as an inevitable consequence of economic adjustments. Increased demand for labor might improve living standards for a time, but it also tended to increase reproduction; in the absence of continuing improvements in land management or technology, the supply of labor could then exceed demand, and the infants of poor people without jobs would die. Turgot, in contrast, is indicative of more hopeful Enlightenment ideals that gained ground in continental writings. One of the first to formulate the law of diminishing returns, he strikingly did not consider its application impor-

tant to population, at least in France. Population growth tends to rise or fall with changes in subsistence levels, but the crucial issue is to ensure that producers always make a small profit for themselves. Without this margin, people would choose not to marry, or would emigrate or remain indigent. Population then declines. In contrast, economic adjustment in a justly-governed population should follow a virtuous natural cycle in which producers' modest margin or profit sustains population growth, encouraging more land into cultivation, increasing subsistence, and driving down the price of provisions, thus enabling benefits to spread ever more widely.

Population and the Emergence of the Modern Nation-State

Thus, by the late eighteenth century a growing body of theory had emerged in which alternative proportional logics were used to explain how population levels rise and fall systematically in relation to political, economic, and moral values. Ironically, the debates over depopulation that did so much to stimulate interest belonged to an era that was later shown to have experienced population growth. Contemporaries would certainly have appreciated the irony. Reflecting the ideology of Enlightenment, many analysts viewed history as a progressive application of human reason. As rational government implied comprehensive and reliable information, the absence of national enumerations became a recurring issue from the 1740s.

Necker, as minister of finance to Louis XVI, was one of several senior officials who found their plans to improve national enumerations frustrated by the conservatism of the *ancien régime*. The arithmeticians, economists, and *philosophes* prominent in debates included local officials who were well aware of the limitations of the estimates they provided. In Prussia, rational government's basis in population knowledge became integral to cameralism (a prevalent political theory emphasizing bureaucratic management of the state's property) in writings put forward by government ministers like Johann Heinrich Gottlob von Justi (1720–1771) and Ewald Friedrich von Hertzberg (1725–1795). "Statistics" was proposed by Gottfried Achenwall (1719–1772) in 1768 as a general term and program of government, acquiring its specifically numerical associations in works by L. Schloezer (1735–1809), John Sinclair (1754–1835), Jacques Mourgue (1734–1818),

Jacques Peuchet (1758–1830), and others at the turn of the eighteenth century. In England the need for censuses was argued as early as Petty, and reached parliamentary debate by the 1750s; censuses remained unacceptable, however, as they implied enfranchisement of dissenting religious and political opinion. Thus, even as population became the focus of sustained discussion of glaring differentials in living conditions and rights, the old order persisted in its attitude toward vital data as secrets of state.

Population knowledge remained integral to the theory of the state, however, erupting with the revolutions of the late eighteenth century. In the United States, the census was written into the constitution as a mechanism of apportioning political representation. In France, proposals impossible for Necker to effect in 1784 were redeveloped by Lavoisier and quickly passed by the National Assembly in 1791. Arguments for enumeration spread widely in the first decades of the nineteenth century, reiterating seventeenth- and eighteenth-century ideals. Following the French Revolution, natural rights of equality and liberty were linked directly to the need to establish public records detailing vital and civil status (for example, in relation to property). Yet the old order was not silenced so easily. Attempts to establish a general statistical office in France were taken over by Napoleon for imperial purposes, and then abandoned in 1812. American enumerations became the basis of political compromises in which Southern states counted slaves for congressional representation without having to enfranchise them. Statistics as a new governmental norm was adopted by established monarchies as well as new republics, often as a concession to reform, with controlled access to records. By the time Louis-Philippe re-established the French statistical bureau in 1833, national offices had spread to Prussia (1805), Bavaria (1808), Tuscany (1818), Holland (1828), Austria (1829), Belgium (1831), Saxony (1831) and the smaller German states, to be followed shortly by Norway (1833) and England (1837).

The continuity of population measures carried over from the *ancien régime* was strong, the "new" vital statistics drawing its ratios and life table techniques directly from population arithmetic. The rebirth of population arithmetic as statistics, however, radically altered its scope and potential influence. Censuses, registrations, and related statistical inquiries reconstituted the state as an empirical domain bounded and structured by its population. The early

nineteenth century witnessed an explosion of enumerations detailing national production, commerce, health, and other factors to which population data were integral. The humanist and scientific ideal that population arithmetic is a critical foundation of government at last achieved centralized institutional form, and population statistics accordingly became a major platform for proposed social reforms. Three implications of this reconfiguration of population thinking deserve note.

First, the conduct and scale of enumerations gave them a much-vaunted objective value. Population arithmetic was no longer applied to partial records underwritten by the presumed rationality of enlightened opinion. Statisticians, applying mathematical procedures to uniformly collected, comprehensive enumerations, claimed that their methods and results possessed an empirical value both unique and completely general. On one hand, ratios or frequencies were measures of material facts in which local variations and other biases were averaged out among the great mass of data. On the other, the explosion of compilations on seemingly all topics meant that states, provinces, and localities could now be examined in their specificity as discrete empirical domains, in each of which population characteristics could be revealed in relation to other variables in exhaustive detail. This methodology was supposed to guarantee that data at whatever level stood above subjective estimates and political interests. Regularities repeatedly observed in national populations were taken to be instances of general and deterministic social laws comparable to those of the natural sciences.

Second, population statistics became integral to the growing professional ideology of government. New statistical bureaus were able to draw on a considerable body of experience from institutions like hospitals, insurance companies, prisons, the military, and some manufacturing. Even as the *ancien régime* had continued to view population arithmetic with caution, these institutions were developing comprehensive registration systems for local administrative purposes. In hospitals, registration functioned beyond clinical purposes as an encompassing regimen of patient and staff discipline, and as evidence securing financial support. Vital records kept by insurance companies provided a corporate data base on which actuarial observation and experience grew. The influence of nationally prominent physicians and actuaries like Benjamin Gompertz (1779–

1865), Louis Villermé (1782–1863), John Finlaison (1783–1860), William Farr (1807–1883), Joshua Milne (1776–1851), Rudolph Ludwig Karl Virchow (1821–1902), and Alexandre-Jean-Baptiste Parent-Duchâtelet (1790–1836) generalized the experience of reasoning quantitatively in terms of limited institutional domains to the national level.

Third, the finite empiricist approach implied a major reconfiguration of the way natural and political dimensions of population are related. From Machiavelli to Turgot, thinkers assigned primacy to the second of the two generative capacities of population that sixteenth- and seventeenth-century authors made fundamental to population thought: population as the source of political and moral community. In this way of thinking, nature would be amenable as long as human government observed inherent principles, whether conceived as matters of divine or natural right, moral tradition, or inherent balances between trade, people, and subsistence. A just government would enable population to grow in proportion to a state's needs. The emphasis on a cohesive, growing membership as essential to internal and external security as well as trade, is a reminder that in the *ancien régime* the limits of states and populations were not assumed to be fixed. Population arithmetic, however, notably failed to define the population balances proper to cohesive government with any precision.

However, once states, populations, and resources began to be conceived in finite, empirical terms, the room available to states for maneuver began to appear seriously circumscribed. The unhealthy environments, excess reproduction, limitations of technology and ecology that statistics documented constituted endemic constraints that the best efforts of a government might not be able to remedy. Not only resource imbalances but also manifest disproportions among class, ethnic, and regional identities (often attributed at the time to inherent natural characteristics), likewise came to be understood as a quantitatively demonstrable reality. In short, the way was opened to reexamine the potential power of the first generative role of population enunciated by sixteenth- and seventeenth-century thinkers: the capacity of population as a natural force to act on other resources independently of governmental control.

The Emergence of Demography

The six editions Malthus prepared of his *Essay on the Principle of Population* (1798–1826) belong to the early period of statistics' rise. In his work, finite population reasoning attained its most influential general statement. Malthus's analysis depended on prevailing premises of late-eighteenth-century population reasoning: that population tends to rise automatically with subsistence; that its growth, although a positive force for a time, can exceed the demand for labor, with dire consequences for the poor; that the way people respond to imbalances of population and subsistence depends on prevailing moral values; that civil liberty is essential to moral and national improvement; and that governments have a role to play in assisting the poor. The "principle of population" reformulated these ideas in a closed, deterministic framework. Malthus postulated that the constant passion of the sexes, if unchecked, tends to increase population geometrically; the maximum growth of agricultural production is, in contrast, limited to an arithmetical rate by the law of diminishing returns. The natural capacities of population and subsistence thus tend inevitably to conflict. Human societies are likely to experience high rates of mortality and suffering unless some means is available to check population. The window of hope Malthus offered was "moral restraint": the practice of delayed marriage and strict abstinence outside marriage. Malthus saw moral restraint not only as a response to threatened impoverishment, but as opening opportunities for the laboring poor to retain a higher standard of living instead of continued childbearing. In later editions of the *Essay,* Malthus wrote a comprehensive survey of historical and modern societies that showed the extent to which each relied on moral restraint, or was subject to the "positive checks" of disease, famine, and war. As he saw the evidence, moral restraint was commonly practiced only in northwest Europe, and even there insufficiently. Malthus famously opposed any use of contraception.

Malthus's principle quickly met with controversy, reflecting his apparent reversal of three established tenets of Western thought on population. First, the inherent quantitative regularity of nature was no longer assumed to be benign, or at least reasonably responsive to just government. Malthus argued in his first edition that God imposes suffering as a "partial evil" to induce men to foresighted action. Restraint of passion is difficult and means of subsistence are scarce because God meant to focus men's minds on moral behavior; only the higher classes of society, however, can be expected to show prudence at any given point in time. A second and parallel reversal, particularly with regard to preceding French population thought, was that any right to subsistence is not natural, but earned. Third, it followed that the role of the state in assisting the poor must be limited strictly to measures that encourage prudence. Malthus here emphasized education together with restricting assistance to the very poor on terms that proscribe procreation. The severity of Malthus's system is a compound of the strictures of his morality, limitations placed on state intervention, and the determinism of his laws.

All three aspects had been substantially rejected by the third quarter of the nineteenth century. The changes in European government informed by population statistics increased rather than reduced the scope for state intervention, while social changes encouraged the spread of contraception and revealed the limitations of deterministic laws. Malthus's *Essay* remains important in the study of pre-industrial family systems in Europe, although his postulated upper limit for agricultural output is insufficient. More influential in the history of population thought, however, are two refinements Malthus introduced. Since Graunt, the unity of natural principles and human government devolved on knowledge and just management of the inherent proportional regularity of population. Malthus, agreeing that the generative capacities of population require control if civil society is to be maintained, showed first that this central theme of modern population thought could be narrowed to a single issue: the quantitative regularity of individuals' decisions to marry and have children. Second, as E. A. Wrigley has observed, Malthus constructed a homeostatic model in which the primacy of these decisions becomes the crucial arbiter of the dynamics of population and subsistence. Reproductive checks are not just individuals' moral response to hard times, but part of a series of adjustments to potential or actual economic recession. Moral restraint checks population increase, enabling the demand for labor to rise. Rising demand in turn stimulates wages to rise, and the need for moral restraint lessens. An oscillation may then begin as marriage age falls, population growth resumes, and diminishing returns again drive down the demand for labor. Or, people may continue to exercise moral restraint, locking in their improved

incomes. Malthus's system revealed that previous proportional logics in which population increase simply perpetuates economic growth apply only to one phase in a cycle.

"Demography" as a general term was introduced by Achille Guillard (1799–1876), who defined the field as population statistics in its broadest sense, giving pride of place to the vast body of data emerging from the new state statistical bureaus. Noting that the scale of compilations was particularly suited to probabilistic analysis, he nonetheless inclined to the prevailing period view that a science of population is anchored not in abstract mathematics, but in comprehensive enumeration and the law-like relationships that it describes. Indeed, historians have remarked that the enduring importance of nineteenth-century population thinking lies in the program established for recording mass vital and social characteristics. This way of reasoning was in practice more reliant on models like the life table than Guillard allowed. Nor did its practitioners' belief that classification and enumeration are a purely empirical exercise reflect their strategic use of the program to change the way society and its problems are defined. Population statistics, in developing occupational, cause of death, and other standard classifications, and tabulating them with age/sex structures, vital rates, and other measures, successfully named and codified a tremendous range of hitherto unspecified populations and population characteristics. New quantitative entities were brought into existence not as mere physical distributions, but as normative social phenomena. Statistical reformers like Villermé, Farr, and Adolphe Quetelet (1796–1874) followed Malthus in considering constants found in such data as evidence of inevitable moral and natural causes. Passionately committed to using population thinking to improve human government, these men used the new capacity to codify and distinguish sub-populations to identify problem groups, particularly amongst the poor. Their work greatly enlarged the view that the quantitative regularity of population legitimizes specific policies and interventions. Population differentials became staple formulae underlying *laissez faire*, socialist, and cooperative proposals.

The Problem of Determinism

In its earliest appearance, then, demography aspired to incorporate deterministic analysis into its empirical and governmental roles. The attempt to formulate general laws on the basis of crude quantitative regularities provoked debates that lasted throughout the nineteenth century. These may be grouped into four related developments.

First, vital statisticians used public data sources to construct new measures of health and the strength of the state, or "indices of salubrity." These statisticians, for example, argued that life tables demonstrated determinant laws of mortality at national and local levels. The main approach refined classifications and measures of mortality and localized them to specific urban, occupational, class, and other groups. Mortality differences were then attributed to variations of income, moral traits, or social and environmental conditions which new data sources provided on these groups. Like Malthus, vital statisticians saw individual moral choice as a crucial arbiter of demographic change, but considered hygiene a precondition. Many reformers, like Virchow, Parent-Duchâtelet, and Farr, argued that people have a right to good health; public provision of sanitation, instruction, and urban planning are necessary if individuals are to take control of their lives. Statistics on the impact of epidemic and endemic diseases, and of age, sex, and occupational patterns of mortality, provided an overpowering rationale for sewerage, piped water, factory reform, and other public works. For some vital statisticians, like Villermé, the association between poverty and high mortality supported a Malthusian view that a residual population of suffering and improvident poor would always remain. The moral and physical character of this residuum, like the positive checks that controlled its numbers, was regarded as natural, and began to be attributed to heredity. New classification schemes enabled a line of social demography from Quetelet to Emile Durkheim (1858–1917) to isolate populations of suicides, prostitutes, and criminals, and to argue that deviant groups are inevitable and statistically normal elements of all societies. As concern mounted in the later nineteenth century regarding fertility declines and continuing high levels of infant mortality, new reproductive indices were developed by James Mathews-Duncan (1826–1890), Jacques Bertillon (1851–1919), and József Kőrösi (1844–1906). Such measures were widely interpreted as indicating a decline in morality (especially of mothers) and the loss of national strength.

Second, Malthus's "principle" proved to be too broad, and the function of moral restraint too narrow, to be useful as general laws. Although methods were developed—by Ernst Engel (1821–1896) and

Frédéric LePlay (1806–1882), for example—that explored the equilibrium of poverty and population in data on laborers' family budgets, population statistics remained largely unintegrated with economic theories of population. Instead, all manner of alternative laws to Malthus's proliferated. A diverse body of population thought from his contemporaries Thomas Rowe Edmonds and Archibald Alison (1792–1867) to demographers at the end of the century, like Emile Levassure (1828–1911) and Paul Leroy-Beaulieu (1843–1916), considered technological improvements, increased division of labor, and resulting economic growth capable of postponing subsistence crises indefinitely. Revisionist hypotheses from Nassau William Senior (1790–1854) to Arsène Dumont (1849–1902), and including those of neo-Malthusian writers, reasoned that workers would control their fertility to preserve living standards more readily than Malthus believed possible. By the end of the century, the decline in fertility was widely accepted as proof. A differing continuity with eighteenth-century population thought characterized other writers, notably Jean-Baptiste Say (1767–1832) and John Stuart Mill (1806–1873), who argued that unequal distribution of income remained a major check on population. Alternatively, for Karl Marx (1818–1883) such inequalities increased population size. Marx reasoned that each stage of society has its own population laws. In capitalist modes of production, population is regularly stimulated to exceed the demand for labor; the resulting surplus ensures that employment is insecure, wages low, and capital accumulation is confined to the upper classes. These and other deterministic hypotheses of nineteenth-century economic demography could not be reconciled, and by the turn of the century began to be bypassed by the new marginal analysis that did not require specific hypotheses about population growth.

Beneath the period passion for laws lay the deeper fascination with the stability of population series which, since Huygens's reading of Graunt, made population arithmetic the proving ground of probability theory. Public sources of mass population data opened up an apparently limitless horizon in which instances of the "law of large numbers" could be explored. A third attempt to develop deterministic laws of population was Quetelet's "social physics." Quetelet showed how error theory used by astronomers to reconcile observational variations could be used to express the regularity long observed in mortality and other vital series. For Quetelet, all material and moral aspects of society took the form of normal distributions around a hypothesized "average man," the statistical composite of all that is good in a given population. Changes over time in average tendencies reveal natural laws of social development, which Quetelet regarded as material, supra-individual forces. His ambition was to expand population thinking into an all-embracing, probabilistic social science, in effect reversing Malthus's attempt to show that the fundamental unity of nature and society comes down to individual agency. Variation, instead of being determined by singular moral choices, became deviance from aggregate natural forces. The role of a science of society based on population was to identify central tendencies and policies that allow causes thus established to take their course. Social physics implied *laissez faire*. Quetelet's program acquired immense prestige, but had very few applications and produced no general theory of development. Its importance in population thought owes, rather, to two very different critical responses it generated. These two responses may be considered a fourth development of the problem of determinism, which focused in different ways on the statistics of variation.

Wilhelm Lexis (1837–1914), Georg Friedrich Knapp (1842–1926), and other population theorists of the German historical school, in demonstrating that Quetelet's supra-individual statistical forces are imaginary, showed that the critical problems of explanation lie in patterns of variation, not central tendencies. Objecting strongly also to Malthus, these writers argued that quantitative regularities may be considered only *indicative* of natural laws, as they deal with distributions of events, not causes. Variations are at base historical and cultural; the nature of society, as a union of free persons, depends as much on people's differences as similarities.

This reassertion of the theme that population is fundamentally a common community did not prevail in demography. Health and economy predominated in the programmatic compilation of mass population data, and the importance of studying variation as a cultural and mathematical question appeared technically difficult and secondary. It is noteworthy, however, that the need to standardize data for comparative purposes led to eight international statistical congresses in the second half of the nineteenth century, in which officials from state statistical bureaus, vital statisticians, and economists agreed on protocols not only on matters like cause of death classification, but criteria detailing linguistic, religious, ethnic, and other populations. With the rise of nationalism and imperial conflicts, such criteria became controversial as grounds constituting rights of distinctive cultural groups. Henceforth population data on cultural variation appeared to question the legitimacy of modern states, just as population arithmetic had troubled the *ancien régime*. Congress criteria were ignored outside of Austria-Hungary, Russia, and in areas under British colonial administration.

The study of variation developed, instead, as population thinking became a common ground of theories of biological and social evolution. The second critical response to Quetelet, associated particularly with the work of Francis Galton (1822–1911), embraced the search for supra-individual forces, attributing them to heredity. The decisive role Malthus had assigned to reproduction was reinterpreted as the cornerstone of eugenics, the doctrine that social development depends on scientific control of human breeding. Malthus's idea that the pressure of population generates a struggle for existence influenced evolutionary theory even before Charles Darwin (1809–1882) developed his ideas of natural selection on the basis of the "principle of population." Herbert Spencer's (1820–1893) paper of 1852, for example, and a wide range of scientific and social opinion later called "Social Darwinism," saw population density as stimulating competition in which the socially and biologically fittest would dominate. For Spencer, the development of human intelligence was a part of this process, and would lead to declines in fertility, resolving Malthus's dilemma. Darwin, in emphasizing intra-species competition, drew further on Malthus's stress on the strategic role of marriage (or, in species terms, of mating). Reflecting on the problem of moral restraint, Darwin realized that controls over *which members* of a species are allowed to reproduce determines natural selection, as dominant members will be more likely to pass genetic characteristics to future generations. Evolution was generally conceived in terms of species and race progress, but Darwin conceded the point of William Rathbone Greg (1809–1881) and Alfred Russel Wallace (1823–1913) that in modern society the poor and improvident outbreed frugal and virtuous members of society, which in time could bring about degeneration. Similar hereditarian concerns were often expressed by demographers, from the vital statistics of Farr to the economics of Leroy-Beaulieu and Adolphe Landry (1874–1956). The decline of fertility in late nineteenth-century Europe appeared to add force to such concerns. Advanced civilizations again came to be associated with depopulation. Eugenicists went further: as fertility declines were much greater in the middle and upper classes, they concluded that a larger and larger proportion of the population was being produced from inferior genetic stock.

The view that laws of heredity determine social relations, however, presupposed simple answers to a difficult question that Darwin and modern genetics have yet to resolve: Which traits are transmitted through the selective effect of marriage on reproduction? Galton recognized that Quetelet's reformulation of error theory could be used to open up a new evolutionary demography: the possibility of defining genetic types by quantifying the range and variability of traits. The concepts of statistical correlation and regression he pioneered have, with time, become principal means of associating fertility and mortality trends with social and economic variables. But Galton's own applications, developed and extended by Karl Pearson (1857–1936), were vitiated by his assumption that social class is indicative of genetic worth. Although discredited by later developments, eugenics nonetheless exercised a continuing influence on twentieth-century occupational and other classification schemes.

Conclusion

The generative capacities of population and knowledge of them have occupied a critical position in attempts to define and govern human society since the sixteenth century. The prevailing view into the early nineteenth century conceived population primarily in terms of membership of a state, the fruits of members' interaction (moral, political, and economic), and the natural rights inherent in such association. In this view population trends, although subject to divine and natural forces outside human control, depend on the limitations and strengths of individual will and collective human government. In the course of the nineteenth century, a sustained but inconclusive effort was made to constitute a deterministic science of population based on systematic quantitative measurement. Major achievements of this era include the pervasive role population thinking acquired in public institutions; the myriad populations, trends, and differentials its methodology

constructed; and the instrumental role it began to play in improving public health. Population statistics provided effective means of demonstrating major economic, social, and cultural divisions in society, and of differentiating and sometimes stigmatizing subpopulations. The traditional view of population as based in common membership, although reaffirmed at times, generally receded as much greater energy went into trying to identify determinants of enduring population differences. With this shift, nineteenth-century population thinking brought to the fore generative capacities of population, notably reproduction and its relation to other natural resources, which had previously been secondary to cohesive membership. As the century proceeded, the implications of statistical trends for government were increasingly seen in evolutionary and biological terms, with extreme interpretations (depopulation, degeneration, the disappearance of national cultures) leading to calls for selective action in favor of some populations over others. The need to reconcile concepts of population based in common membership with those emphasizing potential natural constraints, particularly of fertility, remained pressing as population thinking entered the twentieth century.

See also: *Bertillon, Jacques; Botero, Giovanni; Cantillon, Richard; Condorcet, Marquis de; Darwin, Charles; Demography, History of; Dumont, Arsène; Eugenics; Euler, Leonhard; Farr, William; Galton, Francis; Gompertz, Benjamin; Graunt, John; King, Gregory; Kőrösi, József; Landry, Adolphe; Literature, Population in; Malthus, Thomas Robert; Marx, Karl; Mill, John Stuart; Moheau, Jean-Baptiste; Petty, William; Quetelet, Adolphe; Süssmilch, Johann.*

BIBLIOGRAPHY

PRIMARY.

Botero, Giovanni. [1589–1596] 1956. *The Reason of State*, trans. P. J. Waley and D. P. Waley. London: Routledge and Kegan Paul.

———. [1588] 1956. *The Greatness of Cities*, trans. R. Peterson. London: Routledge and Kegan Paul.

Cantillon, Richard. 1755. *Essai sur la nature du commerce en général*. Paris. [Written originally in English between 1730 and 1734; only the French translation survived. English transl: *Essay on the Nature of Commerce in General*. New Brunswick, NJ: Transaction Publishers, 2001.]

Condorcet, Jean-Antoine-Nicolas de Caritat, marquis de. [1767–89] 1994. *Arithmétique politique: textes rares ou inédits,* ed. B. Bru and P. Crépel. Paris: l'Institut national d'études démographiques.

Franklin, Benjamin. 1755. "Observations Concerning the Increase of Mankind and the Peopling of Countries." Reprinted in *Population and Development Review* 11(1) 1985: 107–112.

Graunt, John. 1662. *Natural and Political Observations Made upon the Bills of Mortality.* London. (Reprinted 1973 in *The Earliest Classics: Pioneers of Demography,* ed. P. Laslett. Farnborough, Hants: Gregg International.)

Guillard, Achille. 1855. *Eléments de statistique humaine ou démographie comparée.* Paris: Guillaumin et Cie.

Hume, David. 1752. "Discourse Concerning the Populousness of Ancient Nations." In *Political Discourses.* Edinburgh: Sands, Murray and Cochran.

King, Gregory. 1696. *Natural and Political Observations and Conclusions upon the State and Condition of England.* (Reprinted 1973 in *The Earliest Classics: Pioneers of Demography,* ed. P. Laslett. Farnborough, Hants: Gregg International.)

Malthus, T. R. 1986. *Works,* ed. E. A. Wrigley and D. Souden. London: William Pickering. *Vol. I: An Essay on the Principle of Population* (1798); *Vol. II: An Essay on the Principle of Population* (1826, with variants from the 2nd ed. of 1803).

Moheau, M. 1778. *Recherches et considérations sur la population de la France.* (Reprinted 1994, ed. E. Vilquin. Paris: Institut national d'études démographiques and Presses Universitaires de France.)

Montesquieu, C. L. Secondat, Baron de. 1964. *Oeuvres Complètes.* Paris: Seuil.

Petty, William. 1690. *Political Arithmetic.* (Reprinted 1899 in *The Economic Writings of William Petty,* ed. C. H. Hull. Cambridge, Eng.: Cambridge University Press.)

Spencer, Herbert. 1852. "A Theory of Population, Deduced from the General Law of Animal Fertility." *Westminster Review* 57: 468–501.

Steuart, James. 1770. *Principles of Political Oeconomy.* Dublin: James Williams.

Süssmilch, Johann Peter. 1765 *Die Göttliche Ordnung.* Berlin: Realschule. French transl., *L'Ordre Divine, traduction orignale, avec des études et commentaires rassemblés par Jacqueline Hecht.* trans. J. Hecht, 3 Vols. Paris: Institut national d'études démographiques, 1979.

Wallace, Robert. 1753. *A Dissertation on the Numbers of Mankind in Ancient and Modern Times.* Edinburgh.

SECONDARY.

Bourguet, Marie-Noëlle. 1989. *Déchiffrer la France. La statistique départmentale à l'époque napoléonienne.* Paris: Editions des archives contemporaines.

Desrosières, Alain. 1993. *La politique des grands nombres. Histoire de la raison statistique.* Paris: Éditions La Découverte.

Dupâquier, Jacques, and Michel Dupâquier. 1985. *Histoire de la Démographie.* Paris: Libraire Académique Perrin.

Glass, David V. 1973. *Numbering the People.* Farnborough, Hants: Saxon House.

Hacking, Ian. 1990. *The Taming of Chance.* Cambridge, Eng.: Cambridge University Press.

Hecht, Jacqueline, 1987. "Johann Peter Süssmilch: A German Prophet in Foreign Countries." *Population Studies* 41(1): 31–58.

Hutchinson, Edward Prince. 1967. *The Population Debate: The Development of Conflicting Theories up to 1900.* Boston: Houghton Mifflin Co.

Kreager, Philip. 1991. "Early Modern Population Theory: A Reassessment." *Population and Development Review* 17(2): 207–227.

———. 1992. "Quand une population est-elle une nation? Quand une nation est-elle un état? La démographie et l'émergence d'un dilemme moderne, 1770–1870." In *Population: 1639–1656.* Paris: Institut National D'Études Démographiques

MacKenzie, Donald A. 1981. *Statistics in Britain 1865–1930.* Edinburgh: Edinburgh University Press.

Porter, Theodore M. 1986. *The Rise of Statistical Thinking, 1820–1900.* Princeton, NJ: Princeton University Press.

Rohrbasser, Jean-Marc, and Jacques Véron. 2001. *Leibniz et les raisonnements sur la vie humaine.*

Paris: Institut national d'études démographiques.

Spengler, Joseph J. 1942. *French Predecessors of Malthus.* Durham, NC: Duke University Press.

Stangeland, Charles. 1966. *Pre-Malthusian Docrines of Population* (1966). New York: A. M. Kelly.

Szreter, Simon, ed. 1991. "The General Register Office of England and Wales and the Public Health Movement 1837–1914." Special issue of *Social History of Medicine* 4(3): 401–537.

Teitelbaum, Michael S., and Jay M. Winter, eds. 1989. *Population and Resources in Western Intellectual Traditions.* In *Population and Development Review,* Suppl. to Vol. 14.

Wrigley, E. A. 1989. "The Limits to Growth: Malthus and the Classical Economists." *Population and Development Review,* Suppl. to Vol. 14.

PHILIP KREAGER

POVERTY AND INCOME DISTRIBUTION

Poverty and income distribution have risen to the top of the list of social issues in many countries. Since the 1970s the United States and United Kingdom have experienced increases in both poverty and economic inequality. But these countries are not unique; many developed countries have experienced at least modest increases in the inequality of income. As economies and labor markets become more international and countries wrestle with the social and economic consequences of aging populations, increased market work by women, and marital dissolution, public interest has come to focus on how successfully different social policies cope with inequality, poverty, and joblessness.

Definitions and Measurement

Poverty is measured by a lack of resources relative to needs. Resources can be measured by consumption, assets, or income, though most analysts prefer income because of the availability and comparability of relevant statistics. Needs measures can be either relative or absolute. Relative deprivation is almost always the preferred measure, both nationally and cross-nationally, because it examines deprivation subject to a household's social and economic context. There is no single best measure of absolute poverty for precisely this reason. Depending on the country, period, and context, the World Bank uses poverty lines of US $1.00, $2.00, or $3.00 per person per day. In contrast, the "official" poverty line for the United States is set at a level of $10.00 to $15.00 per person per day (depending on household size). Relative poverty can be defined using any of a variety of measures. The United States' "absolute" poverty line is approximately 40 percent of the median household income. Most international analysts, and many governments, choose a poverty line of 50 percent of the median. The European Union has chosen a line of 60 percent of the mean for measuring deprivation.

Since there are economies of scale in the consumption of most household goods, income and other measures of resources are usually adjusted for these differences by means of an equivalence scale. The equivalence scale measures the cost of providing an equal level of living for households that differ by characteristics such as household size or age of members. For instance, household size raised to the power 0.5 is a common equivalence scale adjustor. This adjustment says that if a single person needs 100 monetary units to be non-poor, a consumption group of four persons needs $100 \times 4^{(.5)}$ or 200 monetary units to be non-poor. Measures of poverty include the head count (the fraction poor), the poverty gap (the average additional income of those below the poverty line needed to bring them up to that line, and more sophisticated measures.

Income inequality refers to the distribution of income among households or persons. But the distribution of what, measured when, and among whom? Most analysts of inequality use a measure of *disposable money income*. For most households, the primary income source is market income, which includes earned income from wages, salaries, and self-employment, and other cash income from private sources such as property, pensions, alimony, or child support. In calculating disposable income, governments add public transfer payments (e.g., retirement, family allowances, unemployment compensation, welfare benefits) and deduct income tax and social security contributions from market income. Most analysts measure income on an annual basis. This may be too long an accounting period for families that are severely credit-constrained and too short for those that can smooth consumption over several years, but almost all available surveys report income for the calendar year.

The usual answer to the question "distribution among whom?" is "among individuals." Most surveys focus on the individual as the unit of analysis and the household as the unit of income sharing. A household is defined as all persons sharing the same housing unit, regardless of any familial relationship. One therefore estimates individual disposable income by aggregating the income of all household members and using an equivalence scale to arrive at individual equivalent income per person equivalent income. Equal sharing of incomes within the household is assumed.

There exist many different summary measures of inequality, most of them based on the Lorenz curve, or other variants. Their usage is demonstrated below.

Databases for Measuring Poverty and Inequality

A heightened interest in poverty and inequality has led to greater efforts to assemble comparable cross-national measures of economic inequality—not an easy task, because the data that exist are not uniform in nature or purpose. Some national surveys are designed to collect income data and some to collect expenditure data. Some are longitudinal household panel surveys, while others are cross-sectional income or labor force surveys. For some countries, data are derived from income tax or administrative records. Despite the difficulties, projects such as the Luxembourg Income Study (LIS) and, to a lesser extent, the International Social Survey Program (ISSP) are helping create a richer body of comparative economic studies. It has become possible to provide a more complete picture of cross-country differences at many points in the income distribution, instead of merely providing snapshot comparisons of the "average" or "typical" family in different countries. Researchers have not only been able to address the factual question of whether inequality has grown in a particular country, but also to start to probe more deeply into the factors explaining changes in economic inequality.

The LIS provides standardized measures of poverty and inequality for a set of 25 high-income countries over the period from 1979 to 1999. These fig-

ures can be found on the Internet. As of 2002 it is the only such database. Data on poverty and inequality compiled from a number of different country sources are typically not fully comparable. Trend data, which rely on changes in the same measure within a single country, are likely to be more reliable, assuming that there is no substantial change in survey design or measures. The set of estimates briefly summarized in Figure 1 is based on the LIS.

Relative Differences in Poverty and Inequality Across Nations

A large body of research has documented comparative levels of poverty and inequality among countries and also the substantial increases in inequality in many countries over time. How do countries measure up? Figure 1 compares the distribution of disposable income in 22 countries for various years around 1995. It highlights the relative differences between those at the bottom and those at the top of the income distribution. It shows the ratio of the income of a household at the 10th percentile (P10) and a household at the 90th percentile (P90) to median income for each country. This indicates how far below or above the middle of the distribution the poor and the rich are located on the continuum of income. Figure 1 also shows the ratio between the incomes of those at the 90th and 10th percentiles (the "decile ratio"). This illustrates the size of the gap between the richest and the poorest in each country. LIS also uses the most common (Lorenz curve-based) measure of inequality—the Gini coefficient.

Most measures of inequality, including those presented in Figure 1, are conducted on a relative basis within nations. (With careful use of Purchasing Power Parties, one may also be able to compare income distributions and percentiles of the distribution among similarly developed countries in real income terms.) The measures describe relative social distance. They are easy to understand but focus on only a few points in the distribution of income.

Figure 1 shows that the United States has an exceptionally large gap between the rich and the poor when compared to other advanced market economies. A low-income American at the 10th percentile in 1997 had an income that was 38 percent of median income, whereas a high-income American in the 90th percentile had an income that was 214 percent of the median. The high-income American had an income nearly six times as much as the low-income

FIGURE 1

"Social Distance": Relative Income Comparisons Across 22 Countries, Mid-1990s

(Adjusted Disposable Income)

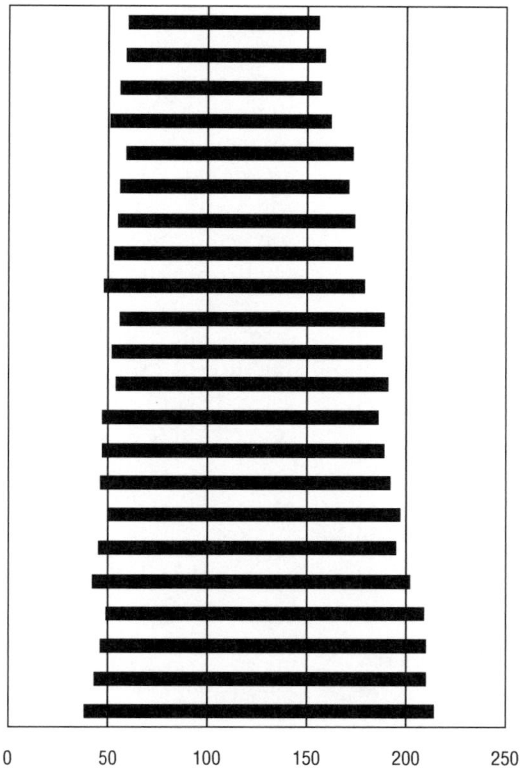

Country and Year	P10 (Low)	Length of bars represents the gap between high and low income individuals	P90 (High)	P90/P10 (Decile Ratio)	Gini Index
Sweden 1995	60		156	2.61	0.221
Finland 1995	59		159	2.68	0.226
Norway 1995	56		157	2.83	0.238
Denmark 1997	51		162	3.15	0.257
Luxembourg 1994	59		173	2.92	0.235
Netherlands 1994	56		171	3.07	0.253
Germany 1994	55		174	3.18	0.261
Belgium 1997	53		173	3.26	0.255
Austria 1995	48		179	3.73	0.277
Taiwan 1995	56		189	3.38	0.277
Switzerland 1992	52		188	3.62	0.307
France 1994	54		191	3.54	0.288
Canada 1997	47		186	4.00	0.291
Poland 1995	47		189	4.04	0.318
Japan 1992	46		192	4.17	NA
Spain 1990	50		197	3.96	0.303
Australia 1994	45		195	4.33	0.311
Italy 1995	42		202	4.77	0.342
Ireland 1987	49		209	4.23	0.328
United Kingdom 1995	46		210	4.57	0.344
Israel 1997	43		210	4.86	0.336
United States 1997	38		214	5.57	0.372
		0 50 100 150 200 250			
Simple Average	51		185	3.75	0.288

Note: Numbers for P10 and P90 are percent of median in each country.

SOURCE: Authors' calculations from LIS data and LIS "Key Figures" (http://www.lisproject.org/keyfigures.htm). Japan taken from Ishikawa (1996).

American, even after adjustment for taxes, transfers, and family size (the decile ratio is 5.63). In contrast, in the other countries in Figure 1, the income of the poor averaged 51 percent of the median income; that of the rich, 184 percent. The average rich person in these countries had only 3.6 times the income of the average poor person.

The countries in Figure 1 fall into clusters. Inequality is lowest in Northern Europe (the Scandinavian countries and Finland, and also Luxembourg and the Netherlands), where the income of those at the 10th percentile averages 57 percent of the median. A number of Central and Western European countries come next (Germany, Belgium, Austria, Switzerland, and France—plus Taiwan, included for comparison). Israel and the United Kingdom have the highest levels of inequality outside the United States. In some countries—Italy, Ireland, Israel, and the United Kingdom—the incomes of the richest people, those at the 90th percentile, are more than 200 percent of median income. This is not very different from the United States; the United States differs, above all, in the relative disadvantage of its poorest residents.

Table 1 shows poverty rates (fraction of persons below 50 percent of median income) in these same

TABLE 1

Percent Living in Poverty in the Total Population, among Children, and among the Elderly, in 20 Developed Countries, mid–1990s

Country	Year	Total Population	Children	Elderly
Luxembourg	1994	3.9	4.5	6.7
Finland	1995	5.1	4.2	5.2
Sweden	1995	6.6	2.6	2.7
Taiwan	1995	6.7	6.2	21.7
Norway	1995	6.9	3.9	14.5
Germany	1994	7.5	10.6	7.0
France	1994	8.0	7.9	9.8
Netherlands	1994	8.1	8.1	6.4
Belgium	1997	8.2	7.6	12.4
Denmark	1997	9.2	8.7	6.6
Switzerland	1992	9.3	10.0	8.4
Spain	1990	10.1	12.2	11.3
Austria	1995	10.6	15.0	10.3
Poland	1995	11.6	15.4	8.4
Canada	1997	11.9	15.7	5.3
United Kingdom	1995	13.4	19.8	13.7
Israel	1997	13.5	13.3	26.4
Italy	1995	14.2	20.2	12.2
Australia	1994	14.3	15.8	29.4
United States	1997	16.9	22.3	20.7
Simple Average		9 9	11.3	12.1

Note: The poverty line is defined as 50 percent of the median disposable income (adjusted) in each country.

SOURCE: Authors' calculations from LIS data and LIS "Key Figures" (http://www.lisproject.org/keyfigures.htm).

countries for all persons, children, and the elderly. Once again, these figures show that the United States stands apart from the other countries in the study, with the highest levels of poverty for the total population (16.9%) and for children (22.3%). In fact, more than one child in five fell below the poverty line in the United States in 1997. Only Australia had a higher percentage of elderly persons below the poverty line (nearly 30% of elderly Australians were living in poverty in 1994). At the other extreme, only 3.9 percent of Luxembourgers (1994), 2.6 percent of Swedish children (1995), and 2.7 percent of elderly Swedes were below the poverty line in their countries. Average 1990s poverty rates for the Table 1 countries apart from the United States are 9.5 percent for the total population, 10.8 percent for children, and 11.6 percent for the elderly.

Poverty and inequality measures differ across countries (e.g., compare the extremes, Luxembourg and the United States, in Figure 1). However, the Northern European countries tend to have the lowest levels of poverty, followed by Central Europe and then Southern Europe and the English-speaking countries (United States, United Kingdom, and Australia).

Extensions and Summary

Poverty and income distribution are concrete and valid measures of economic status. Broader measures of well-being may also include such items as health status and literacy, and are especially appropriate for developing countries. An example of such a measure is the Human Poverty Index, published in the United Nations Human Development Report. A broader analysis of global poverty is contained in the 2000/2001 World Development Report, issued by the World Bank. The effect of inequality and poverty on economic growth, crime, and related social outcomes is also a growing field of inquiry. Using measures such as those described above, and developing more datasets like the LIS, should provide a clear picture of how well the world does in combating poverty and in understanding the effects of both poverty and inequality on social well-being.

See also: *Cost of Children; Development, Population and; Economic-Demographic Models; Education; Residential Segregation.*

BIBLIOGRAPHY

Atkinson, Anthony B., Lee Rainwater, and Timothy M. Smeeding. 1995. "Income Distribution in OECD Countries: Evidence from the Luxembourg Income Study (LIS)." *Social Policy Studies* 18.

Gottschalk, Peter, and Timothy M. Smeeding. 2000. "Empirical Evidence on Income Inequality in Industrialized Countries." In *Handbooks in Economics,* Vol. 1: *Handbook of Income Distribution,* ed. Anthony B. Atkinson and François Bourguignon. Amsterdam: North-Holland.

Ishikawa, Tsuneo. 1996. Data runs conducted by the Ministry of Welfare, Japan.

Jäntti, Markus, and Sheldon Danziger. 2000. "Income Poverty in Advanced Countries." In *Handbooks in Economics,* Vol. 1: *Handbook of Income Distribution,* ed. Anthony B. Atkinson and François Bourguignon. Amsterdam: North-Holland.

Smeeding, Timothy M., Lee Rainwater, and Gary Burtless. 2002. "United States Poverty in a Cross-National Context." In *Understanding*

Poverty, ed. Sheldon H. Danziger and Robert H. Haveman. New York and Cambridge, MA: Russell Sage Foundation and Harvard University Press.

INTERNET RESOURCES.

Smeeding, Timothy M., and Lee Rainwater. 2001. "Comparing Living Standards Across Nations: Real Incomes at the Top, the Bottom and the Middle." Syracuse, NY: Luxembourg Income Study. <http://www.lisproject.org/publications/liswps/266.pdf.>.

United Nations Development Programme. 2001. "Human Development Report 2001." <http://www.undp.org/hdr2001/>.

World Bank. 2000. "World Development Report 2000/2001: Attacking Poverty." <http://www.worldbank.org/poverty/wdrpoverty/>.

DAVID K. JESUIT
TIMOTHY M. SMEEDING

PREHISTORIC POPULATIONS

INTRODUCTION

Human prehistory is treated regionally in the series of articles that follow. The discussion mainly pertains to the modern (and only surviving) human species, *Homo sapiens,* which emerged little more than 100,000 years ago; however, other hominid species—ancestral or cognate lines of the genus *Homo*—are also referred to. Humans in this generic sense emerged over 2 million years ago. Depending on how human origin is defined, human prehistory thus covers all but a small fraction (95–99.7 %) of the duration of human existence.

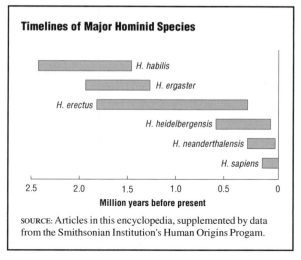

FIGURE 1

Timelines of Major Hominid Species

SOURCE: Articles in this encyclopedia, supplemented by data from the Smithsonian Institution's Human Origins Progam.

An approximate time line of major hominid species is shown in Figure 1. The dating and in some cases even the species identifications are tentative, subject to revision as research progresses. The associated phylogeny—the relationships among these species—is even less securely founded.

AFRICA

The ancestors of modern human populations separated from those of humankind's nearest primate relatives some 5 million years ago on the African continent and by 2.5 million years ago were making stone artifacts that can be recognized as tools. Slightly less than 1.5 million years ago those kinds of tools appear outside Africa, marking the latitudinal expansion of people from the subtropics to more temperate zones. By 100,000 years ago African descendants of the earliest people were skeletally modern, and soon after that time they were marking stone, bone, and ostrich eggshell in ways that obviously are symbolic, if not artistic, long before such behavior was evident elsewhere.

Less than 50,000 years ago modern people began a further expansion, again emanating from Africa, crossing land bridges, occasionally making sea crossings, and entering arid, cold, and seasonal environments in a wave or waves that would eventually result in a nearly global distribution. Most of the early experiments in the domestication of plants and animals, metallurgy, urban development, and intercontinental trade seem to have originated outside Africa, but starting 500 years ago Africa experienced a return of its progeny in an extended colonial period whose effects have not yet been shaken off.

Several billion stone tools litter the African landscape, but of a billion or more African people who were alive during the period from 5 million to 0.5 million years ago there are the fragmentary skeletal remains of about 500 individuals at most. Only from the last 10,000 years is there anything approximating a decent sample, no more than a thousand or two individuals. Palaeoanthropologists refer to up to 15 species of hominids and 5 genera but rarely agree on the correct assignation of most fragments, and only in very rare cases are there nearly complete individuals, let alone useful numbers of contemporary conspecifics.

The discovery of ancient hominid remains in the currently desert environment of Chad, several thousand kilometers away from any other contemporary locality, has underlined the fragility of the current understanding of hominid distribution patterns. Are researchers looking merely at the absence of evidence rather than the evidence of absence? The sampling, dating, and empirical constraints on reconstructing African Pleistocene populations are so severe that anthropologists rarely mention issues such as population sizes, birth or mortality rates, life expectancy, life history patterns, and biogeographical range shifts, except in the most general terms. Demographic research requires much better observations.

Conclusions Drawn from Genetics and Morphology

There are, however, some interesting generalizations that can be made, although some of them depend as much on genetic and linguistic patterns or primate analogues as they do on skeletal or archaeological remains. In different ways genetic and linguistic patterns among current African populations reflect past movements, isolations, and distributions. History is written in the diversity of traces on the physical and social landscape. The application of sophisticated genetic techniques to fossil or subfossil hominid remains, though in its infancy, promises to expand considerably the conclusions that can be drawn from artifact distributions and morphological comparisons.

First, there is nearly universal agreement that through the Pleistocene African populations were becoming increasingly modern and formed the core group from which both archaic and modern people emerged. Although it is possible that early hominids are almost uniquely represented in the dolomite caverns of the south and the rift valley lake beds of the east purely because of good preservational circumstances, stone tool distributions offer an opportunity free of such taxonomic limitations.

African archaeologists now have a good idea of the technological and formal development as well as the approximate dating of artifact assemblages. All the earliest stone tool assemblages come from riverside or lakeside camps in savanna landscapes with moderate to low rainfall, whereas occupations in demonstrably arid, humid, rugged, or forested regions come much later. The savanna hypothesis for the origins of hominid adaptation, however, may have overestimated the terrestrial habit of early hominids at the expense of riverine fringe resource use. Presumably, early populations were expanding into more difficult resource areas, a movement that was facilitated by technological and social innovations and fueled by a growing intellectual capacity. Brain-specific nutrition, such as the fatty acids so abundant in freshwater and marine ecosystems, probably underwrote sustained, and energetically expensive, brain growth. Eventually, certainly by 1.5 million years ago, populations reached the boundaries of the continent in the Mediterranean climates of the north and the south. Only the route to the north led elsewhere.

Movement Out of Africa

The earliest human skeletal remains from outside the African continent date from a little more than 1 million or perhaps 1.5 million years ago in southern Europe and southwestern and southeastern Asia. These sites mark the first out-of-Africa movement, perhaps along productive and nutritionally rich coastal plains, although evidence is scarce. Palaeoanthropologists disagree on whether there were several later movements or a more or less continuous diffusion of population out of Africa after that time, but most support at least one recognizable expansion between 100,000 and 50,000 years ago.

Skeletal remains more or less indistinguishable from the modern form are found around the coastal fringes of southern Africa soon after 100,000 years ago, but their rarity at contemporary sites farther north could as easily be preservational, or even terminological, as evidential. It is possible that modern people evolved throughout Africa. Outside Africa almost all human populations after about 30,000 years ago are described as modern and appear to be ancestral to recent local populations. It appears increasingly likely that whereas African populations were evolving toward the modern condition, the archaic humans already living in Europe and Asia were not, though the significance of genetic separation and the potential for genetic reincorporation are controversial issues.

If these southern African populations really are part of the ancestral stock from which all modern humans evolved, their descendants soon became isolated by extreme aridity in the midlatitudes. By 70,000 years ago both the Saharan and the Kalahari-Namib arid landscapes had expanded under the influence of global glacial expansion, altered atmospheric circulation, and oceanic cooling. This diminished genetic and cultural links between equatorial and Mediterranean African groups at either end of the continent. At the Cape and in the Mediterranean, with similar latitudes and climates, people drifted genetically away from their subtropical relatives until terminal Pleistocene climate changes allowed more substantial connections across shrinking aridity barriers.

The implications of this for Cape populations at the southern tip of the continent are of course profound and quite different from those for their northern relatives living on the fringe of Eurasia. The blood group and other genetic parameters that distinguish broad groups of Africans seem to have been the result of late Pleistocene extreme aridity. As the glaciers melted, previously isolated groups began to reestablish contact, resulting in the complex social, linguistic, genetic, and political landscape that exists in the early twenty-first century.

During the Holocene period population movements within the African continent seem to have been associated with the sub-Saharan spread of farming and metallurgy during the last three millennia. In the early Holocene domesticated plants and animals in Africa were limited to the Mediterranean Basin, where the domestication process began, and to winter rainfall domesticates. Once the idea of domestication had been transferred to subtropical crops, probably in the highlands of Ethiopia, a process of diffusion to the south began. Although the Mediterranean domesticated animals remained the important ones, new plant species, significantly

forms of millet and sorghum, were added to the domestic suite.

It was only after the conjunction of domesticated plants, animals, and metallurgy some 2,500 years ago that any kind of rapid population movement can be detected. This is most obviously reflected in the distribution of languages of the Niger-Congo family in western, eastern, and southern Africa. Within this grouping languages spoken by people separated by thousands of kilometers remain linguistically similar, suggesting a recent common ancestry. The most parsimonious explanation is one of recent rapid population movement, bringing Niger-Congo-speaking, metal-using farming communities east and then south through the parts of sub-Saharan Africa suited to millet and sorghum farming.

Understandably, many parts of the subcontinent were unattractive to people with domestic stock or crops, leading to the survival of hunting and gathering communities in regions that were too arid, rugged, or forested for some version of agriculture or pastoralism. Farmers moved preferentially into lands that were easily tilled without machinery, naturally watered, and suited to the requirements of both domesticated animals and cultivated crops. The wide distribution of very similar ceramic forms and decorative motifs from the Great Lakes region to the eastern parts of South Africa from about 2,500 to 1,500 years ago mimics the pattern of language similarities and almost certainly supports the notion of a rapid population movement.

Several hundred small, encapsulated groups of hunter-gatherer communities survived across Africa to provide case studies for nineteenth- and twentieth-century ethnographers. The most substantial residual hunting and gathering populations remained in place in the southwestern corner of the continent until very recently in the form of people referred to as bushmen or San. Their nearest geographic, cultural, and genetic relatives, the pastoralist Khoe or Quena (derogatively known as Hottentots), have been the focus of much debate. It appears likely that Khoe pastoralists were former San hunters and gatherers who had gained access to stock through contact with Niger–Congo-speaking mixed farmers who were penetrating the former San regions of southernmost Africa. They were subsequently able to replace or incorporate hunter-gatherer groups in areas where stock, particularly the fat-tailed sheep they herded, could thrive. This process, which essentially was confined to the arid western parts of the subcontinent, was contemporary with the spread of mixed farming in the east, where better rainfall and deeper soils made crop farming viable. These two expansions were complementary and effectively defined the population structure of modern southern Africa.

The Earliest Moderns?

What makes this historically and evolutionarily interesting is the confluence of linguistic, behavioral, and genetic patterns in the geographically well-defined Khoe and San people. Leaving aside earlier theories of the existence of a "Capoid race," it is surely significant that groups formerly dominant south of the Kalahari-Namib arid zone exhibit biological and cultural signs of extreme and long-lasting isolation. Implosive consonants ("clicks"), a highly noticeable feature of Khoesan languages, are unknown in regular speech anywhere else in the world; geneticists have detected ancient mitochondrial DNA lineages among modern Khoe and San people; and the survival of San hunter-gatherers into recent times coincides geographically with the distribution of the best evidence for early modern humans.

It is tempting to write a history of human populations at the Cape that views them as the earliest moderns, subsequently isolated from their relatives elsewhere, allowed by environmental factors and geographic marginality to remain relatively unaffected. It is appropriate that they should have survived to become the best ethnographically studied examples of a formerly pan-human hunting and gathering lifestyle. They are certainly not living fossils, but their study has unlocked the secrets of precolonial rock paintings, provided models for archaeological reconstructions, and graphically illustrated the details of a genocidal colonial era.

See also: *Archaeogenetics; Environmental Impact, Human; Evolutionary Demography; Hunter-Gatherers; Indigenous Peoples; Paleodemography; World Population Growth.*

BIBLIOGRAPHY

Klein, Richard. 1999. *The Human Career: Human Biological and Cultural Origins.* Chicago: University of Chicago Press.

Klein, Richard, and Edgar Blake. 2002. *The Dawn of Human Culture.* New York: Wiley.

JOHN PARKINGTON

ASIA

The vast majority of the paleoanthropological evidence from Asia, particularly most of the geologically-early evidence, derives from East and Southeast Asia, especially mainland China and Java. Relatively early fossil evidence has also been recovered from Narmada, India. South Asia—including Ceylon, Pakistan, Bangladesh, and especially India—has also played an important role in interpretations of Asian paleolithic archaeology as a whole. West Asia has yielded archaeological and fossil evidence of Neanderthals, early anatomically-modern *Homo sapiens,* and possibly *Homo erectus.*

Regional Continuity or Replacement Model Interpretation of Modern Asian Humans

There are two major antithetical theories about the origins of modern Asian populations. One theory, called *Replacement Theory* or "Out of Africa Theory," maintains that modern Asian populations descended from a geologically recent (ca. 100,000 to 50,000 years ago) migration from Africa that resulted in the total replacement of the indigenous hominids who had occupied Asia from close to or more than one million years ago. The Replacement Theory is based on mtDNA (mitochondrial DNA) studies that purport to show that all modern humans are descended from a single African female, "Eve," as she has been termed in the press. Diametrically opposed to this interpretation is the *Regional Continuity Theory,* which maintains that Asian *Homo erectus* evolved into the anatomically modern Asian *Homo sapiens.* Both theories agree that all hominids originated in Africa; they disagree about when hominids first left Africa and when extant populational distinctions originated.

Replacement proponents have argued that the "crude" nature of the Far East Asian tool kit is the product of the evolutionarily stagnant species *Homo erectus.* In this scenario, suggested by scholars such as Christopher Stringe and Bernard Wood, *Homo erectus* left Africa before the development of more sophisticated stone technologies such as the Acheulean "hand axe" and became a genetically-isolated evolutionary dead end, never passing beyond the technological sophistication of the earliest and most crudely made Oldowan artifacts of Africa. But neither the Asian paleontological evidence nor the paleolithic record documents morphological or cultural stagnation. Indeed, there is evident morphological change in the fossil record in the direction of modern Asians. Scholars such as Geoffrey Pope, Mulford Wolpoff and many others assert that both the archaeological and hominid fossil records support evolutionary continuity in Asia.

Culture and Technology

In the 1940s the archaeologist Hallam Movius (1907–1987) pointed out that there is a "line" of demarcation between hand axes of prehistoric South Asia and the crude, so-called "chopping-chopper" tools of the Far East. He believed that places like China and Java were cultural backwaters where human-like technology never evolved beyond the most simplistic levels. His work led to the concept of the "Movius Line," which has been used to demarcate evolving humanity from populations that had somehow become "stuck in time." Very few hand axes have ever been found in China despite long and concerted searches. L. Binford and Nancy Stone (1987) suggest that there is very little reliable evidence for any human-like culture in the artifact assemblages of ancient Asians.

In 1989, Pope countered Movius's resurrected argument with the observation that the "crude" Far Eastern tools coincide with the distribution of bamboo and a wealth of other non-lithic resources. The Pleistocene inhabitants of the region most certainly utilized these resources. Since *Homo erectus* (i.e., early to middle Pleistocene *Homo* in East Asia) was the first hominid to colonize both temperate (including seasonally frigid) as well as tropical environments and given its long presence in the region, it seems more reasonable to interpret the simple stone technology of Pleistocene Asia as complementary to sophistication in non-lithic resource utilization. The seemingly unchanging Asian paleolithic record, described (tongue in cheek) by one archeologist as "crude, colorless and unenterprising" (White 1977), is more parsimoniously attributed to an emphasis on non-lithic technology such as bamboo and other organic resources.

Agriculture in Asia seems to have developed independently at about 10,000 years ago in both China and northwest India. Mesopotamian agriculture may also have been of independent origin from the Fertile Crescent in Iraq. Some archaeologists have suggested that rice cultivation and pottery and/or polished stone tools seem to have diffused from China to other circum-Pacific regions. Similar diffusion processes may have existed for other cultigens in South and West Asia.

Hominid Morphology

The history of Far Eastern paleoanthropology begins in 1891 when Eugene Dubois (1858–1940) discovered the first *Homo erectus* skull cap and femur at Trinil, Java. Subsequent discoveries of other Javanese and Chinese hominids confirmed the hominid status of *Homo erectus*, as did the many discoveries made at the famous "Peking (Beijing) Man" site of Zhoukoudian Locality 1 in China. These finds are now considered to be representative of *Homo erectus*.

Anatomically, *Homo erectus* is defined primarily by its extremely thick cranial bones, a projecting and continuous brow ridge above the eye orbits, a sagittal "keel" of thickened bone running from the top of the skull to the back of the cranium, a thickened and angular occipital region, and a generally robust skeleton. These features are expressed most strongly today among indigenous populations of the southwest Pacific. *Homo erectus* also displays a much-debated dental anatomy including what have been called "shovel shaped" incisors, a trait that is most prevalent in modern "Mongoloid" and Mongoloid-derived populations. As Pope (1992) pointed out, other facial features also appear to connect this extinct species with modern East Asian and Native American populations.

Such morphological evidence is discounted by proponents of the Replacement Model, who point instead to the biomolecular results of mtDNA studies as an indication that this species and others from East Asia went extinct with the arrival of anatomically-modern *Homo sapiens*. These DNA interpretations can in turn call into question the many genetic assumptions which the model makes.

A number of anatomically more modern-looking hominids have also been recovered from both Java and China. Only one early hominid specimen has also been recovered from Narmada, India. "Archaic or Pre-modern" hominids all have larger cranial capacities than is typical of *Homo erectus*, as well as other features reminiscent of fully modern humans. The Solo (Ngandong) crania from Java look very much like scaled-up versions (in terms of cranial capacity) of *Homo erectus*. Whether these crania should be classified as *Homo erectus* or *Homo sapiens* is a matter of continuing debate, but they provide strong evidence of continuity between fossil and modern hominids.

By definition, separate species cannot interbreed and produce fertile offspring. Classic reasons for such barriers are geographical separation, anatomical–behavioral incompatibility, temporal separation, genetic incompatibility, or a combination of all or some of these factors. In Asia geographically-widespread hominids give rise to a number of specimens which look anatomically distinct from one another. Whether these differences represent species difference or an increase in variation within a species, is not known. In Pleistocene Asia, variation in appearance seems to increase over time. Since paleoanthropologists have only the bones and stone to study, they cannot tell if the morphological differences in fossils indicate species barriers that would prevent interbreeding or are reproductively unimportant. New forms may have arisen through interbreeding of once far-flung and isolated populations that came into contact again. In short, the relation between morphology and breeding can never be known for certain in fossil paleospecies.

Geography and Climate

The geography and climate that helped shape the anatomical traits and paleoecological adaptations of *Homo erectus* resulted in a large extent from the continuing tectonic collision of the South Asian Plate with the underbelly of the Asian mainland. This continuing collision produced the vast Himalayan mountain system that, in combination with the equatorial monsoons, has had a strong influence on hominid evolution in Asia. Worldwide climatic fluctuation, while no doubt influential in the formation of climates and topographies, did not, except indirectly, have the profound ecological influence on Asian climates that it had in glacial Europe. However, indirect influence in the form of the development of the loess areas of North China and the rise and fall of sea levels surrounding and alternately isolating and connecting the present islands of the Sunda Shelf certainly affected hominid evolution and dispersal.

The effects of the Himalayan uplift are also responsible for the modern loess plateaus, grabens, and mountains that form the past and present biogeographic regions, barriers, and biogeographic dispersal routes of Asia. Early hominids seem to have been confined to relatively low and thus warmer altitudes, where all of the early hominid finds in Asia have been located. Although the long and repeated occupation of sites such as Zhoukoudian Locality 1 testify to the ability of *Homo erectus* to endure marked seasonal fluctuations, it seems that cold temperature altitude was a definite limiting factor in the distribution of this species. Over the course of a million years, however, *Homo erectus* had become adapted to a number of varying environments. It is difficult to imagine that a tool-dependent hominid could have been completely replaced by invaders in all these ecological settings, which it had occupied for approximately one million years.

The influence of the Himalayan uplift also influences researchers' understanding of prehistoric archaeology in Asia. In South Asia and Western Asia, the run-off and resulting detritus from the Himalayan system may be the principal reason that only one early Pleistocene hominid (Narmada) has been recovered from South Asia.

Archaeologists have yet to discover the presence of early (Early Late Pleistocene) hominids in other countries of the Far East, such as the islands of Southeast Asia and Taiwan (and possibly Japan) that were periodically connected by land bridges at times of low sea level. Australia was never connected to Asia, and therefore its first colonization by around 40,000 or more years ago must have been over water.

Gene Flow

As early as 300,000 years ago, hominids that were physically very different from each other were living in the same geographic regions. This also happened in Europe, where Neanderthals lived side by side with modern humans for as much as 60,000 years and also shared (to judge from their artifacts) many of the same cultural attributes. It is rare, if not unknown, for modern hunters and gatherers to exchange only culture and not genes. Furthermore, there is no well-established evidence for one group of hunters and gatherers ever having completely replaced another. It is in this light that the later evolutionary evidence from Asia must be interpreted.

In China, recent finds of pre-modern *Homo sapiens* (such as Dali and Jinniushan) show a remarkable degree of variation that, on the basis of archaeologists' current knowledge, seems to exceed differences in other geographic areas. One interpretation, strongly supported by Pope and others, is that gene flow across Eurasia became increasingly more common as hominids increased in cultural complexity and technological prowess.

More generally, in the closing phases of the Pleistocene it seems likely that increased gene flow occurred between the eastern and western edges of Eurasia and the continent of Africa. The morphological "sameness" which has often been perceived in *Homo erectus* culminates in a variety of morphologies that indicate gene flow. Many scholars believe that the much more recent changes in lithic technology may indicate continued and even increased gene flow across the top of Eurasia, primarily proceeding in directions along an East-West axis, but also along a North-South axis.

Conclusion

To explain the origin of modern Asian peoples, one needs to recognize both indigenous development and transcontinental gene flow, and not simple regional continuity or replacement by geologically recent Africans. Physically, Asians are impossible to define as a single group unified by any ubiquitous morphologies. There are clines of differences such as in skin color, facial characteristics, or body type, reflecting regional adaptations. Repeated genetic exchange occurred from both near and far.

From the standpoint of physical anthropology and archaeology, anatomically modern Asian populations are the product of both local indigenous adaptation and extraregional gene flow. From a cultural standpoint, modern Asian groups result from continuing and ancient overlays of culture, religion, and ecological adaptations. Neither the fossil nor the archaeological evidence points to a single geographical or temporal origin of Asians.

See also: *Archaeogenetics; Paleodemography; World Population Growth.*

BIBLIOGRAPHY

Bellwood, Peter. 1994. "An Archaeologist's View of Language Macrofamily Relationships." *Oceanic Linguistics* 33: 392–406.

Binford, L. R, and Nancy M. Stone. 1987. "On Zhoukoudian. Reply to Comments." *Current Anthropology* 28(1): 102–105.

Cann, Rebecca L. 1988. "DNA and Human Origins." *Annual Review of Anthropology* 17: 127–143.

Jia, Lanpo, and Weiwen Huang. 1990. *The Story of Peking Man*. Beijing: Foreign Language Presses and Oxford University Press.

Keates, Susan. 2000. *Early and Middle Pleistocene Hominid Behavior in Asia*. Oxford: BAR International Series 863.

Movius, Hallam. 1944. "Early Man and Pleistocene Stratigraphy in Southern and Eastern Asia." *Papers of the Peabody Museum of American Archaeology and Ethnology* 19(3): 1–125.

Pope, Geoffrey G. 1984. *Hominid Evolution in East and Southeast Asia*. Ann Arbor: University Microfilms.

———. 1992. "The Craniofacial Evidence for the Origin of Modern Humans in China." *The Yearbook of Physical Anthropology* 35: 243–298.

———. 1997. "Asian Paleoanthropology." In *The History of Physical Anthropology, An Encyclopedia*, ed. Frank Spencer. New York and London: Garland Publishing.

———. 1997. "Java." In *History of Physical Anthropology, An Encyclopedia*, ed. Frank Spencer. New York and London: Garland Publishing.

Pope, Geoffrey, and Susan Keates. 1994. "The Evolution of Human Cognition and Cultural Capacity: A View from the Far East." In *Integrative Pathways to the Past,* ed. Robert Corrucini and Russel L. Ciochon. Englewood Cliffs, NJ: Prentice Hall.

Stringer, Christopher. 1992. "Replacement, Continuity and the Origin of Homo sapiens." In *Continuity or Replacement? Controversies in Homo sapiens Evolution*, ed. Günter Brauer and Fred H. Smith. Rotterdam: Balkama.

Swisher III, Carl, et al. 1994. "Age of the Earliest Known Hominids in Java, Indonesia." *Science* 263: 1,118–1,121.

Tungsheng, Liu, et al. 1985. *Loess and the Environment*. Beijing: China Ocean Press.

Turner, Christy G. 1990. "Major Features of Sundadonty and Sinodonty." *American Journal of Physical Anthropology* 82(3): 295–317.

von Koenigswald, Gustav H. R. 1962. *The Evolution of Man.* Ann Arbor: University of Michigan Press.

Wolpoff, Milford. 1999. *Paleoanthropology.* Boston: McGraw Hill.

Wood, Bernard. 1994. "Taxonomy and Evolutionary Relationships of Homo erectus." *Courier Forschunginsitut Senckenberg* 171: 159–165.

GEOFFREY G. POPE

AUSTRALIA AND THE PACIFIC

Although hominids have been present on Sunda, the continental shelf of what are now islands in Southeast Asia, for more than 800,000 years, they appear to have been unable to regularly cross water barriers. *Homo erectus* traversed small ocean gaps to reach Flores in Indonesia, but was absent from islands further east. Consequently Australia and the Pacific islands were first colonized by modern humans. This observation has often been used as a measurement of the greater organizational capacity of *Homo sapiens* during the last 40,000 to 60,000 years, perhaps reflecting enhanced language abilities. Populating the Pacific required human groups to have adequate seacraft, but more importantly to have the means of storing and transmitting information about new environments. In each part of the Australian-Pacific region the first evidence of human occupation not only implies extensive seafaring skills but also includes the archaeological residues of complex social behavior: art and ornaments, burials, and well-organized settlement structures.

Exploration of the Australian continent and Pacific islands was a prolonged process, taking many millennia to complete. The colonizing process began in the west, and terminated in the remote eastern and southern Pacific Ocean. Australia is the landmass in the region with the earliest dates for human occupation.

Australia

Homo sapiens colonized the Australian continent more than 40,000 years ago, although there is extensive debate as to whether humans arrived as early as about 55,000 to 60,000 years before the present (abbreviated B.P.), or as late as 40,000 to 45,000 B.P. This debate hinges on different opinions as to the ve-

racity of alternative dating techniques, as well as uncertainty about the extent of disturbance processes in early archaeological sites. Claims for occupation substantially earlier than 60,000 B.P. have been shown to be spurious. The uncertainty about the date of colonization makes reconstructions of the first settlement systems tenuous. For instance, if colonization took place prior to 40,000 B.P., so few sites are known that discussions of settlement are insubstantial. Furthermore, dating uncertainties make it impossible to evaluate the actual rate of colonization within Australia.

Some scholars have suggested that early settlement may have focused on coastal resources, but this seems unlikely in view of the growing evidence of occupation in arid and semi-arid inland landscapes. Lake Mungo is the most famous example of inland occupation, but hundreds of sites now reveal Pleistocene-era occupation, more than 10,000 years old, in a diverse range of inland landscapes. It is clear that people at least occasionally occupied many environments within Australia, and it is thought that population densities were higher in the zones of higher rainfall around the periphery of the continent. Early models of population change hypothesized fixed patterns of settlement during the Pleistocene, such as continuously low or high numbers of people in the arid core of Australia. These models have more recently been replaced by an image of fluctuating population in response to changing resource availability and discontinuous settlement in at least some landscapes. This is most dramatically illustrated in the glacial uplands of Tasmania, where humans abandoned the region permanently in the terminal Pleistocene, and in some arid landscapes, where some regions were abandoned during the glacial maximum, 14–18,000 B.P., while in other regions with favorable resource bases occupation continued throughout the glacial maximum.

During the late Holocene period (3000 B.P. to present), a larger number of archaeological sites were occupied in many regions of Australia, coastal and inland, islands and mainland. There was also an increase in the number of sites and the number of artifacts in many of those sites. Many archaeologists have interpreted this pattern as a reflection of population increase during the later prehistoric period in Australia. However, the magnitude of any population change has been difficult to evaluate. Calculations of the annual increase in site numbers and the rate of artifact discard show that both measures, in all regions, were well below 0.1 percent per year. It is feasible that this might be the approximate rate of population change, in which case the scale of change would be something like a tripling or quadrupling of population between 4000 and 1000 B.P.. The absolute size of the population during this period cannot be calculated.

Increases of population may have been greater in some regions than in others. For example, in the southeast (particularly in the densely populated Murray River Valley), high levels of anemia, parasitism, and infectious diseases have been inferred from skeletal markers, and perhaps indicate higher densities of people in these lands. This conclusion is consistent with the discovery of many densely-packed cemeteries in this region. Some researchers have therefore suggested that the river valleys of the southeast were more densely populated, but if so these regions also show the same archaeological evidence for increased site and artifact abundance.

If these archaeological patterns indicate minor but sustained population growth, the causes are unclear since this period was one of drier and variable climatic conditions. Some researchers have suggested that intensification of production driven by social competition led to population increase, but there is little support for this theory in the archaeological evidence. However, the cause of population change in this period need not be a dramatic process, since the growth rate discussed here would represent a minor departure from a long-term balance between births and deaths. Moreover, a number of archaeologists have cautioned that the change in the quantities of archaeological material (numbers of sites and artifacts) is probably not a reliable indicator of the magnitude of population change. The quantity of archaeological material preserved from any period is a reflection of many factors in addition to group size, including the destruction of sites and the wastefulness of the production system creating artifacts. Such factors would have exaggerated the observable abundance of material in the recent past. Consequently, while many archaeologists have concluded there were population increases in the late Holocene, the nature and size of those changes remains poorly defined.

Melanesia

Melanesia is that area of the western Pacific that includes New Guinea and a series of large and small islands stretching eastward. Lower sea levels during the Pleistocene meant that New Guinea was connected to northern Australia by an exposed portion of the shared continental shelf, and it is not surprising that the human occupation of New Guinea is thought to be of comparable antiquity to that of Australia. Archaeologists have dated the subsequent colonization of the islands to the east of New Guinea to more than 35,000 years ago, based on a series of archaeological sites in New Britain and New Ireland such as Buang Merabak, Yombon, and Matenkupkum. By about 30,000 B.P. people had reached the Solomon Islands, but here the colonization process halted for 25,000 years. This distribution of archaeological sites in Pleistocene Melanesia is limited to those islands separated by a water barrier of less than 250 kilometers, a distance that perhaps indicates the limits of the maritime journeys of the day. However, within the colonized zone of Melanesia there appears to have been considerable maritime interaction, including possible trade, which implies that longer oceanic journeys may not have been impossible. For whatever reason, more isolated islands were not colonized until much later, with the spread of people archaeologists call *Lapita*.

Lapita is a distinctive archaeological complex, marked in many sites by elaborate dentate stamped pottery, and by diverse economic practices including but not limited to the use of domesticated plants (yams, taro, banana, etc.) and animals (chicken, pig, dog). This archaeological material first appears in the Bismarck archipelago, east of New Guinea, about 3500 B.P. and spreads eastward throughout Melanesia within a short time. The proliferation of the Lapita Complex is likely to have involved not only the colonization of distant islands of Melanesia but also a region-wide increase in population.

Late Holocene increases in population size in many parts of Melanesia are often thought to reflect the introduction of agriculture that accompanied Lapita. However, the late Holocene population changes in Australia, where agriculture was never established, and the obvious late Holocene growth of populations on Polynesian islands, where agricultural abilities were known to the founding groups, represent parallel demographic trends. These similarities are as yet unexplained but imply processes other than or additional to the introduction of agriculture.

Polynesia

Polynesia is the vast expanse of the central Pacific Ocean covering nearly 30 million square kilometers. Within this area are a number of island groups, from Samoa and Tonga in the west to the Hawaiian Islands in the north, Easter Island in the east, and New Zealand in the southwest. The spread of people across this vast region appears to have taken place in a number of stages. Excavations on many islands suggest humans moved from the Samoa and Tonga island groups eastward into the central Polynesian region about 2200 years ago. After building an economic and demographic base in the Marquesas and Society Islands, people migrated northward to Hawaii and further east to Easter Island approximately 1500 to 1700 years ago. Still later, only within the last 800 years, another migration to the south produced the colonization of New Zealand. These movements of people were sometimes single, one-way voyages, but there is also evidence of return voyaging and secondary migrations, making the colonization process a complex one.

Population change in the Pacific islands has been measured by charting alterations in the abundance of dated habitation sites. For example, on a number of the Hawaiian Islands analysis of this archaeological evidence reveals an S-shaped population curve: there were few habitation sites dated to the period prior to 800 B.P. (1200 C.E.), then a tenfold increase in habitations during the period from 800 to 400 B.P. (1200–1600 C.E.), followed by a stabilizing or even decline in their number. The period of rapid increase is thought to have been caused by the development of intensive forms of food production such as irrigated field systems and fishponds. The cessation of population growth may have been a result of limits to agricultural intensification in some regions and of European contact and diseases. Population growth in the Hawaiian Islands is also entangled with sociopolitical change. In Hawaii's hierarchical political structure, the increased pools of labor could be directed by chiefs to create large-scale infrastructure projects that increased resources for the expanding population. As this process continued, the distinctions of rank and power became exaggerated. Warfare appears to have increased in frequency and severity as struggles over power and resources became more intense. This pattern of increasing warfare, sometimes accompanied by declining populations as human-induced environmental changes occurred, is a common one.

European Contact

In many areas of the Pacific and Australia, the introduction of diseases such as smallpox at the time of European contact led to marked reduction of population and subsequent reorganization of social, political, and economic practices. For this reason it is accepted that many historical observations of population density are poor indicators of precontact demographic conditions. It is likely that population densities in Australia and the Pacific during the late Holocene were substantially higher than observed historically, a pattern that matches well with archaeological evidence.

See also: *Archaeogenetics; Hunter-Gatherers; Paleodemography; World Population Growth.*

BIBLIOGRAPHY

Fagan, Brian. 1996. *The Oxford Companion to Archaeology.* New York: Oxford University Press.

Flood, Josephine. 1995. *Archaeology of the Dreamtime,* 3rd edition. Sydney: Angus and Robertson.

Kirch, Patrick Vinton. 1985. *Feathered Gods and Fishhooks.* Honolulu: University of Hawaii Press.

Irwin, Geoffry. 1992. *The Prehistoric Exploration and Colonisation of the Pacific.* Cambridge, Eng.: Cambridge University Press.

Meehan, Betty, and Neville White, eds. 1991. *Hunter-gatherer Demography: Past and Present.* Sydney: University of Sydney.

Spriggs, Matthew. 1997. *The Island Melanesians.* Oxford, Eng.: Blackwell Publishers.

PETER HISCOCK

EUROPE

Europe was the last continent of the Old World to be inhabited by modern humans, but the demographic prehistory of Europe is as long, as rich, and a lot better known that that of any other continent. In spite of the short history of human occupation in Europe, some of the most important evolutionary demographic events took place there.

The First Europeans

About 1.7 million years before present (B.P.), *Homo ergaster,* the earliest hominid species known in Europe, reached the Caucasus. However, it was a descendant of this species, *Homo heidelbergensis* that about 500,000 B.P. became the first true European. These hominids had a lasting influence, as can be seen from the morphological similarity between European *Homo heidelbergensis* and the Neanderthals who inhabited most of Europe between 250,000 and 30,000 B.P. Anatomically modern humans—*Homo sapiens sapiens*—only arrived in the region around 40,000 B.P. The Neanderthals adopted some technological skills from the anatomically modern human population, which indicates that the two groups of humans met and exchanged knowledge and probably genes as well.

There were never many Neanderthals in Europe—100,000 individuals at any one time is probably an absolute maximum size of the population. But the few specimens of identified Neanderthal DNA indicate that the size of the breeding population of Neanderthals was as large as that of anatomically modern humans, as shown by John Relethford (2001). The overall number of Neanderthals probably fluctuated along with changes in mean temperature during the glacial cycles. Eric Trinkaus, in his 1995 study, has concluded, based on a small sample, that the pattern of mortality was similar to that found in prehistoric anatomically modern groups, although the Neanderthals experienced a higher level of young adult mortality.

Anatomically modern man and Neanderthals coexisted in Europe for around 10,000 years. Around 30,000 B.P. the Neanderthals ceased to exist as a culturally and biologically distinct group. What happened to them is a source of considerable debate, but the available evidence is slightly in favor of the survival of some Neanderthal genes in the present European population, according to Relethford.

Anatomically modern man appeared in Europe at the beginning of the Upper Palaeolithic period—about 35,000 B.P.—a period marked by many new and well-made stone and bone tools. The rate of cultural innovation increased markedly at that time, making it possible to date archaeological sites more accurately than those of earlier times. Thus it is possible to track fluctuations in population size through the last stages of the last Ice Age. Climatic changes were the main driving force for changes in population size and distribution. The close association between the area occupied and climate indicates that human adaptive strategies remained basically un-

changed over the 25,000 or more years (from around 35,000 to 10,000 B.P.) of the Upper Paleolithic. Only at the end of the Upper Paleolithic is there evidence for the use of a broader array of foods and environments, foreshadowing the subsequent early postglacial Mesolithic period.

Economic Transitions

Since the end of the Ice Age (roughly 10,000 years ago) Europe has experienced two fundamental economic transitions. The first transition, the Neolithic Revolution, saw the earlier hunting-and-gathering way of life of the Mesolithic era replaced by subsistence agriculture as the dominant mode of production. In well-dated areas, such as southern Scandinavia, this transition took place over many centuries. Agriculture, which had originated in the Middle East, spread to Europe from east to west along the Mediterranean and southeast to northwest through Central Europe to the plains of Northern Europe. Agricultural communities appeared in Scandinavia some 3000 years after they first were seen in Greece. This peasant agricultural era spans much of the Neolithic and the Bronze and Iron Ages; it can be termed the Peasant Age.

The second transition was from subsistence to market production. This also took several centuries. It was marked by the development and growth of urban centers.

All parts of Europe have gone through Neolithic Revolutions and market transitions, and these transformations, not the absolute dating of various events, define the demographic prehistory of Europe. For example, the Sami of northernmost Europe entered the first transition at a time when the central parts of the Roman Empire were already entering the second transition.

Prehistoric Mortality

All post-glacial periods have yielded extensive cemeteries, the skeletal remains from which allow estimation of age at death distributions. Very rough rates of infant mortality, average late childhood (age 5 to 18 years) mortality rates, and levels of life expectancy can be inferred.

Table 1 summarizes the broad trends in European mortality in terms of the three indicators from the Mesolithic through the Neolithic revolution, the Peasant Age, and the market transitions to contemporary Europe, partly based on skeletal data from

TABLE 1

Levels and Patterns of Mortality in Europe, by Era

Era	Infant mortality (%)	Average late childhood mortality age 5 to 18 (%)	Life-expectancy, at birth (years)
Mesolithic	10–20	<0.5	35
Neolithic revolution	15	1.0	<35
Peasant Age	15	1.5	30
Early market transition	15	2.5	<25
Late market transition	25	1.0	35
Modern Europe	<5	<0.1	>70

SOURCE: Paine and Boldsen (2002).

Richard Paine and Jesper Boldsen published in 2002. Infant mortality is not as high during the Peasant Age as it later becomes. There is a significant increase in late childhood mortality across the Neolithic Revolution, a high plateau during the Peasant Age, and a decline when trade and urban communities became common.

In Scandinavia the change from subsistence to market production took place very late and can therefore be better described. The process seems to have gone through two steps. First there was a sharp increase in late childhood mortality when the market still was peripheral to the local rural communities, followed by a rapid decline as these communities became fully integrated in the network of market towns and trade relations, according to a 1997 study by Boldsen.

The Driving Force of Demographic Evolution

Although much remains to be learned about European population prehistory, it is clear that fluctuations were common. Phases with relatively steady growth were separated by episodes of collapse, when the population had exceeded the carrying capacity of the environment at the existing technological level. Over the millennia, Europe's population grew along with its technology.

When people became settled during the Neolithic Revolution, local environments became much more polluted with human and animal waste, which increased the risk of infection with gastrointestinal diseases. Such infections tend to affect people of all ages, not only infants and the elderly, and are the reason for the initial increase of late childhood mortality. Some infections left definite signs on skeletons but most did not.

With the growth of trade relations and urban centers, new avenues for the spread of infections were opened. Viral infections such as the great killers, measles and smallpox, could spread widely. These are diseases that leave a lasting immunity in survivors, so large human (host) populations are needed to sustain them as endemic or frequently recurrent diseases. However, all segments of the population were not at equal risk of exposure to the relevant pathogens. In small and relatively isolated rural communities, these crowd infections would die out, only to be reintroduced at a later time when the populations no longer had immunological experience with them. Viral infections striking such virgin populations tend to affect people at all ages and cause widespread mortality. Eventually, as contact with the trade network intensified, the reservoir for the pathogens expanded virtually region-wide and what had been the great killer diseases changed to the childhood diseases that affected European populations within living memory.

See also: *Climate Change and Population: History; Disease and History; Paleodemography; World Population Growth.*

BIBLIOGRAPHY

Boldsen, Jesper. 1997. "Patterns of Childhood Mortality in Medieval Scandinavia." *Revista di Antropologia* 74: 147–159.

Paine, Richard, and Jesper L. Boldsen. 2002. "Linking Age-at-Death Distributions and Ancient Population Dynamics: A Case Study." In *Paleodemography: Age Distributions from Skeletal Samples,* eds. Robert. D. Hoppa and James. W. Vaupel. Cambridge, Eng.: Cambridge University Press.

Relethford, John. 2001. *Genetics and the Search for Modern Human Origins.* New York: Wiley-Liss.

Trinkaus, Eric. 1995. "Neanderthal Mortality Patterns." *Journal of Archaeological Science* 22: 121–142.

JESPER L. BOLDSEN

THE AMERICAS

Unlike the Old World, where modern humans and their ancestors evolved and underwent a variety of demographic processes over a long period of time, the presence of *Homo sapiens* in the New World is a relatively recent occurrence, with the first migrations having taken place well after the emergence of anatomically-modern humans in the Old World. When these earliest migrations occurred, however, remains the subject of debate, particularly with respect to how and when people migrated to areas south of northwestern North America.

The Peopling of the New World

Researchers generally agree that the first humans in the New World came from Asia. Evidence for this movement comes from the analysis of biological traits such as tooth morphology and blood types as well as from linguistic relationships between contemporary and historical populations. The traditional assumption is that humans traveled from Siberia to Alaska over a land bridge that is now submerged beneath the Bering Strait.

During periods of glaciation, the last of which occurred about 10,000 years ago, this area, called Beringia, would have been dry land. Based on paleoclimatic reconstructions, it is known that Beringia was exposed from about 60,000 years ago to 18,000 years ago. However, that does not indicate when the first human populations migrated into North America or whether current North American aboriginal populations are descended from the early migrants or from subsequent waves of population movement. There is evidence of human occupation on the southern tip of South America from at least 12,500 years ago and perhaps even earlier; this means that the earliest movements into the New World through Alaska must have occurred substantially earlier than this date.

It is possible that humans came to the New World by water, but there is no evidence for this hypothesis. If this occurred, there should be coastal sites, now submerged under higher seas, that show evidence of human occupation.

Early sites of occupation. The evidence for early human migration into the New World comes from a few archaeological sites. On the basis of those clues, most researchers concede that humans were not present south of Alaska until after about 15,000

years ago. Although there may have been an ice-free corridor during the earliest period of migration into the New World, conditions were not suitable for big-game hunting, which would have been necessary for human survival, until after about 14,000 years ago. As a result, researchers have suggested that migrations southward via this ice-free corridor were not likely until that time.

A possible early human occupation site in the Yukon has been dated to between 12,000 and 27,000 years ago; it would be the oldest known human habitation site in the New World. Nearby, the Bluefish Caves site, also in the Yukon Territory, indicates human occupation through the presence of skeletal remains of mammoth, horse, bison, and caribou in association with stone tools. Radiocarbon dating for this site suggests a date between 15,000 and 12,000 years ago.

Linguistic evidence. Linguistic evidence has been used by Joseph Greenberg and Merritt Ruhlen (1992) to argue that there were three successive waves of migration into the New World. By examining and grouping hundreds of contemporary languages from both North America and South America, those researchers determined that there are three distinct language families. The first group is the Amerind family, which is found throughout Central America and South America and much of North America. The second is the Na-Dené family, which today includes Haida on the northwestern coast of Canada as well as Navaho and Apache in the southwestern United States and various Athapaskan languages. The third is the Inuit-Aleut family. These researchers have suggested that since each of these three groups has a closer relationship to an Asian language family than to any language families in the New World, there were three distinct migrations to the New World from Asia, with the Inuit-Aleut language reflecting the last migration, perhaps some 4000 years ago.

Biological and genetic evidence. Biological evidence from teeth has supported Greenberg and Ruhlen's hypothesis. Christy G. Turner (1989) looked at a variety of morphological aspects of teeth from various New World populations. He noted the presence of common Asian traits, such as shovel-shaped incisors—where the lingual side of the central teeth has a scooped-out or shovel-like appearance—in many New World populations. On the basis of population grouping of similarities, Turner suggested that the distribution of traits fell into the same three distinct groupings identified by Greenberg and Ruhlen from the linguistic evidence.

Genetic analyses have been used to shed light on early migrations. Some have suggested that the Inuit-Aleut population group may in fact have split from Na-Dené in the New World. A number of studies of the distribution of mitochondrial DNA groups and of Y-chromosome haplogroups have suggested that there were one or two major migrations to North America from Asia. However, the distribution of genetic patterns in contemporary New World populations is complicated by admixtures with European and other groups in more recent historical times. This can make it difficult to distinguish ancestral but rare traits from recent rare traits without some collaborative evidence (for example, the interactions of indigenous groups with Europeans) from ethnohistorical sources.

Early Peoples of the New World

The first undisputed human populations in North America are referred to as the Palaeo-Arctic tradition. The earliest well-documented Palaeo-Arctic sites have been identified from stone tools and date to between 8000 B.C.E. and 5000 B.C.E. Human populations reflecting the Palaeo-Arctic tradition occur throughout Alaska, the southwestern Yukon, and the Queen Charlotte Islands in British Columbia. Next there is the movement of human populations into the eastern Canadian Arctic and Greenland, sites denoted archaeologically as the Arctic Small Tool tradition. This tradition evolved into the Norton tradition in Alaska and the Dorset culture in the eastern Arctic. The later Thule tradition developed from the Norton tradition in the area around the Bering Strait. It is the Thule tradition that subsequently spread across the entire Arctic region with the exception of the Aleutian Islands.

By 11,000 years ago the evidence that humans were living in North America south of Canada is clear. Archaeological evidence for the Clovis tradition, named after the first site identified near Clovis, New Mexico, can be found in many areas of North America. After that time there is also some evidence from human skeletal remains. One site has been argued to be pre-Clovis: the Meadowcroft Rockshelter in Pennsylvania, where the lower stratum dates between 19,600 and 8,000 years ago. There are clear indications of human occupation at that site that date to about 12,800 years ago.

Archaeological evidence in the form of tools found in association with the remains of butchered animals provides some clues that can help reconstruct these early populations. For example, the Olsen-Chubbuck site in Colorado is a bison kill site that is reflective of a highly organized population. Joe Wheat (1978) has estimated that the nearly 200 bison remains would have produced as much as 25,000 kilograms (55,500 pounds) of meat and may have been recovered from one kill—enough to feed almost 2,000 people for a month. However, these early populations did not continue to subsist on large mammals.

The archaeological evidence for these earliest Paleo-Indian populations in North America before about 8000 B.C.E. remains sparse, and reconstructions point to very small groups of a few adults and children with low population densities. Their survival depended on their dispersal over large territories, with these groups slowly moving into territories farther east. However, it is known through the presence of trade goods and large-scale kill sites that groups would have come together on a regular basis, forming long-term social networks with each other. Sites, such as Debert in Nova Scotia, that date to around 8600 B.C.E. suggest a group size of fifteen to fifty people who probably subsisted on caribou and sea mammals.

In later times, in conjunction with climatic change and perhaps extinctions of many of the larger mammals in the New World, there is evidence of populations exploring new subsistence strategies. Nevertheless, bison remained an important source of food among the plains populations, with archaeological sites such as Head-Smashed-In in Alberta showing that bison drives were used over a 7000-year span. Although the decreasing availability of big game may have been a factor, population growth may have put additional pressure on food sources. Stress on local carrying capacity probably resulted in the frequent fission of groups that dispersed into new territories. This rapid expansion of Paleo-Indian populations is reflected archaeologically by rapidly diversifying cultural assemblages. Survival would have been heavily dependent on game resources for subsistence, and although it fluctuated locally with irregular peaks, overall population growth would have been steady, with regional differences from western to eastern North America.

Mark Nathan Cohen (1989) has argued that the world was increasingly filling up with hunter-gatherer populations, and this may have forced them to exploit other, less desirable sources of food. Many researchers have argued, however, that the bulk of population growth throughout the world came about after people began to settle down and develop an agricultural subsistence base. Some support for this theory comes from anthropological studies of contemporary groups that show a reduction in the typical birth spacing in sedentary populations compared with nomadic populations.

The Paleo-Indian populations gave way to Archaic populations after about 8000 B.C.E. For many thousand years after that time North American groups continued to develop as regionally distinct populations. Early large-scale settlements in North America are best exemplified by the Mississippian culture after about 200 C.E., which evolved from the earlier Archaic groups in the Midwest and the South. Characteristic of these early chiefdoms are the large earthenworks and burial mounds associated with their permanent, sedentary communities. Although many were networks of smaller communities, a few settlements, such as Cahokia and Moundville, represent large political centers in the region, housing at their peak perhaps as many as 30,000 inhabitants. Within three centuries the area had been abandoned.

Large-scale population centers emerged in Mesoamerica later than they did in the Old World; this probably was related to the later development of agriculture in the New World. About 500 B.C.E. in the Valley of Oaxaca in southern Mexico there was a unification of individual villages to form larger centers. For example, the city of Monte Albán grew to house about 30,000 people. Slightly later the city-state of Teotihuacán in northeastern Mexico emerged, reaching its height around 2000 years ago. Again, this center probably developed from small, scattered farming villages on the slopes south of the Teotihuacán Valley that were inhabited by a few hundred people each.

Around 500 B.C.E. there seems to have been a population shift to settlements on the floor of the valley, with the emergence of distinct centers within the next few centuries. Between about 150 B.C.E. and 500 C.E. the population of the region grew rapidly from several thousand individuals to well over 100,000. Using skeletal samples, Rebecca Storey (1986) has argued that infant and childhood mortality in Teotihuacán was high, with over one-third of

infants dying before age one year. This pattern is consistent with large, overcrowded preindustrial urban centers in Europe, where a variety of diseases had become endemic within the population.

Somewhat later the Mayan city of Copán emerged in what is now Honduras, with classic plazas, pyramids, and temples spanning an area of 30 acres. Estimates have suggested that it experienced rapid population growth, doubling in size every hundred years. Reaching its height between 700 and 850 C.E., Copán would have been home to perhaps 20,000 people. Several other Mesoamerican state societies also developed in the highlands and lowlands of what are now Guatemala and the Yucatán Peninsula. Although they once were thought to be less densely populated than Teotihuacán, it is now believed by archaeologists that the extent of Mayan culture has been underestimated, largely because of the dense tropical forest that now covers much of the remains of Mayan civilization.

Between 800 and 1000 C.E. many lowland Mayan cities were abandoned. The reasons for this collapse are unclear; suggestions include population pressure and resource depletion. Others believe that disease played a role, including an increased incidence of yellow fever as a result of deforestation creating larger breeding grounds for mosquitoes.

Large sedentary populations emerged in South America around 8000 years ago along the coast of Peru. Although estimates of population size vary, archaeological evidence points to long periods of high population density in some areas followed by demographic collapse and decline before the arrival of Europeans. Reconstructions of demographic patterns suggest very high infant and childhood mortality, with up to 50 percent of all children dying under 15 years of age. At its height the Incan empire of Peru had a population of some six million to 13 million people. This population was reduced drastically after European contact in the mid-sixteenth century.

Depopulation

Epidemic diseases introduced by Europeans, such as measles and smallpox, probably played a major role in causing a drastically increased level of mortality among New World populations. Estimates of the scale of depopulation depend on estimates of the total population of the New World before European contact, which range from eight million to over 100 million people. The overall distribution of populations throughout the New World varies, but estimates would place a large portion (over half and as much as three quarters) of the total in Mesoamerica.

Although European contact was certainly devastating, many New World populations had already reached a size at which they could support a variety of endemic diseases. Increased population densities and poor sanitation in many large urban centers, such as Cahokia in North America and the Maya city-states in Mesoamerica, would have imposed on them a variety of health burdens, much like their European counterparts. However, rapid colonization and new diseases, in conjunction with warfare, resulted in extremely high mortality and drastic depopulation among many New World peoples.

See also: *Archaeogenetics; Climate Change and Population: History; Environmental Impact, Human; Hunter-Gatherers; Paleodemography; World Population Growth.*

BIBLIOGRAPHY

Adovasio, James M., with Jack Page. 2002. *The First Americans: In Pursuit of Archaeology's Greatest Mystery.* New York: Random House.

Cohen, Mark Nathan. 1989. *Health and the Rise of Civilization.* New Haven, CT: Yale University Press.

Crawford, Michael. 1992. *The Origins of Native Americans: Evidence from Anthropological Genetics.* Cambridge, Eng.: Cambridge University Press.

Fagan, Brian.1987. *The Great Journey: The Peopling of the New World.* London: Thames and Hudson.

————. 1991. *Ancient North America.* London: Thames and Hudson.

Fiedel, Stuart J. 1992. *Prehistory of the Americas.* Cambridge, Eng.: Cambridge University Press.

Greenberg, Joseph H., and Merritt Ruhlen. 1992. "Linguistic Origins of Native Americans." *Scientific American* (November) 94–99.

Kirk, Robert, and Emőke Szathmáry, eds. 1985. *Out of Asia: Peopling of the Americas and the Pacific.* Canberra, Australia: Journal of Pacific History.

Larsen, Clark Spencer. 1997. *Bioarchaeology: Interpreting Behavior from the Human Skeleton.* Cambridge, Eng.: Cambridge University Press.

Paine, Richard R., ed. 1997. *Integrating Archaeological Demography: Multidisciplinary Approaches to Prehistoric Population.* Occasional Paper 24. Carbondale: Center for Archaeological Investigations, Southern Illinois University at Carbondale.

Steckel Richard H., and Jerry C. Rose, eds. 2002. *The Backbone of History: Health and Nutrition in the Western Hemisphere.* Cambridge, Eng.: Cambridge University Press.

Storey, Rebecca. 1986. "Perinatal Mortality at Pre-Columbian Teotihuacán." *American Journal of Physical Anthropology* 69: 541–548.

Szathmáry, Emőke J. E. 1993. "Genetics of Aboriginal North Americans." *Evolutionary Anthropology* 1: 202–220.

Turner, Christy G., II. 1989. "Teeth and Prehistory in Asia." *Scientific American* 260(2): 88–91, 94–96.

Verano, John W., and Douglas H. Ubelaker, eds. 1992. *Disease and Demography in the Americas.* Washington D.C.: Smithsonian Institution Press.

Webster, David, and Ann Corinne Freter. 1990. "The Demography of Late Classic Copan." In *Precolumbian Population History in the Maya Lowlands,* ed. T. P. Culbert and D. Rice. Albuquerque: University of New Mexico Press.

Wheat, Joe. 1978. "Olsen-Chubbuck and Jurgens Sites: Four Aspects of Paleo-Indian Bison Economy." *Plains Anthropologist* 23: 82(2): 84–89.

Robert D. Hoppa

PRIMATE DEMOGRAPHY

Primate demography is the study of population processes in species most closely related to humans. Primates include the prosimians (lemurs, lorises, galagos, etc.) and the anthropoids (monkeys and apes). Prosimians differ from the rest of the primate order in their largely nocturnal habits, reliance on smell rather than vision, and because they generally live in smaller groups. For these reasons and for human relevance this article is focused on the anthropoid primates. Knowledge of primate demography provides the context for understanding how human demography is constrained by general mammalian and ancestral primate patterns of birth, death, and movement. Some of these patterns are specific to primates and some reflect broader mammalian patterns. Primate demography provides a backdrop against which uniquely human characteristics may be discerned. Human lineage probably diverged from that of the other great apes some five to six million years ago. Humans and chimpanzees, however, still share many life history traits such as male philopatry (females leave their natal home range at maturity while males remain) and prolonged post-weaning dependency of young on their mother. Humans differ from chimpanzees in that humans have longer pre-reproductive periods than would be expected for a mammal of similar body size, delayed reproductive maturity for body size, relatively short interbirth intervals, and have probably always had a sizeable proportion of individuals with long post-reproductive life spans. While quantitative demographic information on wild primate populations is limited, there is a useful literature on primate life history that relates to demographic processes.

Life history traits are suites of co-evolved traits affecting reproduction, growth and development, patterns of social organization, and mortality. Just as the sources of mortality and physiological constraints on reproduction strongly influence life history, life history also affects birth and death rates and patterns of movement.

Although primates are mammals and share many demographic patterns arising from the constraints of mammalian reproduction (e.g., lactation leads to primarily maternal care of infants in most mammals, larger species tend to live longer and reproduce more slowly, etc.), their demography differs in many ways. The origin of primates in the tropical forests, their frugivorous (fruit eating) diets, evolution of larger brains, and complex social groupings, resulted in divergence from mammalian norms. Primates live longer than expected for mammals of similar body size and have low reproductive rates due to delayed maturity, singleton births, and prolonged dependency of young. Primates exemplify what Harvey and Promislow termed the "slowed down" life histories that are unusual for mammals and thus require special explanation. Primates as a group have larger brains than expected in a mammal of their body size. Within the order, positive selec-

tion for brain size is indicated by the fact that brain size increased faster than body size—a relationship that is not observed in most orders of mammals.

Social Organization

With a few exceptions (some prosimians, orang-utans) primates live in long-term social groups that are kin-based. Polygyny is the most common mating system, but monogamy (a single male mates with a single female), polyandry (one female mates with multiple males) and polygynandry (multiple females mate with multiple males) are also represented within the order. In most Old World monkeys, males disperse while females remain in their natal groups. Apes show the full range of sex-differential dispersal: Both sexes leave natal home ranges among the monogamous lesser apes (gibbons), the solitary orangutans, and the polygynous gorillas; while female chimpanzees most often disperse. Dispersal patterns are even more varied among New World monkeys with long-lived Cebus (capuchin monkeys) demonstrating many of the life history traits—including female emigration—more common among Old World monkeys. Essentially all primate groups are dominance structured. Group size, composition, and social status are often related to both reproductive success and mortality. In 2001, Carey and Judge proposed that reduced levels of mortality and fertility are related through increased intergenerational transfers.

Fertility

Birth of singleton young is the ancestral primate norm. Singleton births of slow growing young take place at annual or longer intervals that correlate with body size. Young are most commonly carried in the mouth (prosimians), cling ventrally, or ride on the back of the mother. Primate fertility increases with age to a peak after the first reproduction and subsequently shows senescent decline. However, as in the vast majority of mammals, true menopause is absent in nonhuman primates studied to date.

Several small bodied groups of prosimians and New World monkeys have secondarily evolved litter sizes of two to three young that are produced at less than annual intervals. In the small New World marmosets and tamarins, group members, other than the mother, most frequently carry the multiple infants and juveniles, thus facilitating the ability of the females to produce two litters per year, which is a substantially higher reproductive rate than observed in larger primate species.

Most of the fertility data for New World monkeys come from captive marmosets and tamarins (Callithricidae). As noted, the members of these groups are small bodied and unusual in terms of litter size (greater than 1), early reproduction (beginning at approximately 1 year of age), short interbirth intervals (less than one year), and also in the predominance of allomaternal care (care by group members other than the mother). These traits are not characteristic of most of the New World monkeys and, thus, the demography of New World monkeys is ripe for additional research.

The models for Old World monkeys are based on several species of macaques. These monkeys begin to reproduce at the age of two years and produce one offspring every one to two years. In most species, female offspring remain in a natal troop of dominance ranked matrilines (a grouping of related female lineages) and male offspring disperse at adolescence. In contrast, apes have longer immature periods after controlling for body size, which is related to the four to five year length of their interbirth intervals. Unlike other apes, human interbirth intervals are not long given their body size. Hawkes, O'Connell, and their colleagues related this to the prevalence of allomaternal care, mainly by older female relatives, especially grandmothers. Gage estimated total fertility for all three groups of non-human anthropoid primates at approximately six—similar to that of contemporary populations of humans in developing countries prior to the fertility transition.

Sugiyama's 1994 study of demographic patterns in a wild female population of common chimpanzees in Bossou suggested similarities in reproductive parameters to those of humans in some hunter-gatherer populations. Age at first birth varied between 12 and 14 years and fertility increased to peak at an average of 0.33 per year at 20 to 23 years of age. Mothers over 40 years of age produced very few infants, none of whom survived. The mean interbirth interval after a surviving offspring was 5.1 years. Gage suggests that the earlier age, compared to humans, of first reproduction and the similar age-related decline in fertility mean that chimpanzees have longer reproductive life spans than do humans and that this is probably related to different patterns of immature mortality.

Mortality

Primates demonstrate many aspects of the mammalian pattern of high neonatal mortality, followed by a mortality decline to a pre-reproductive lifetime minimum, after which mortality rises at an increasing rate into old age. Human mortality departs from that of non-human primate patterns in the relatively low immature mortality achieved as a result of lower infant mortality and a more rapid decline in age-specific mortality of human juveniles relative to infants. Mortality increases at sexual maturity and there is evidence, especially in low mortality populations, of an early-adulthood mortality hump both among non-human primate and human males, often attributed to accidents. In Bossou, Guinea, 73 percent of chimpanzee infants survived to age four, 71 percent survived from age four to age eight, and 22 percent survived from age eight to age 12. The last of these values suggests unusually high mortality that may be conflated by female outmigration. But this is not entirely an artifact of measurement: In all natural populations, outmigration from the natal home range is associated with an increase in age-specific mortality in early adulthood.

While models suggest that life expectancy is quite low among wild chimpanzees and that life expectancy at sexual maturity is only an additional 15 years on average (with approximately 35 years of age as the outside age limit), these models are based on increasing mortality rates with age. There is evidence, however, that mortality rates of non-human primates as well as of humans level off, rather than continuing to increase, in very old age; indeed, there are numerous chimpanzees in the wild that are estimated to be well past 45 years of age. Clearly there is much yet to be learned about the mortality scenarios of older primates in natural populations.

New World monkeys generally have the shortest lives and the earliest reproduction, with the important exception of the genus Cebus. Old World monkeys both live, and delay maturity, longer than New World monkeys. The apes, all of which are Old World, exceed Old World monkeys in life span and in age at maturity; the longest lived and latest maturing primate after controlling for body size is the human. The survivorship curves become increasingly rectangular (i.e., exhibit prolonged survivorship followed by rapid decline at old age) over the same phylogenetic gradient. This picture is undoubtedly over-simplified if for no other reason than the paucity of data and the limited New World taxa for which demographic data are available.

Migration

Male emigration from natal groups, similar to that in most mammals, is temporally associated with increases in mortality. This mortality may be due to risks associated with poorer knowledge of resource distribution in new areas, with greater vulnerability to predators, and with intraspecific competition, particularly male–male competition in polygynous species. Research regarding sex-specific mortality associated with emigration in male versus female philopatric species is needed. Even in semi-captive groups of female philopatric species, young adult males are more likely to disappear from censuses than are other age classes or females. Unlike most mammals, female rather than male chimpanzees emigrate at puberty or early adulthood; interestingly, high-status female chimpanzees do not necessarily leave their natal ranges. Demographic research on New World species will be enlightening since females, or both sexes, emigrate in many of these groups. The common human practice of female outmarriage (the practice of women moving further from their natal family than men at marriage) often results in females leaving their natal communities at sexual maturity; however, sex differentials at young adult ages among humans still exhibit excess male mortality. Sources of mortality risks in young adulthood may include ecological (resource levels, predation risks) and social (e.g., male–male competition for mates) factors.

See also: *Animal Ecology; Evolutionary Demography.*

BIBLIOGRAPHY

Austad, Steven N., and Kathleen E. Fischer. 1992. "Primate Longevity: Its Place in the Mammalian Scheme." *American Journal of Primatology* 28(4): 251–261.

Carey, James, and Debra Judge. 2001. "Life Span Extension in Humans is Self-reinforcing: A General Theory of Longevity." *Population and Development Review* 27(3): 411–436.

Caro, Tim M., Daniel W. Sellen, et al. 1995. "Termination of Reproduction in Nonhuman and Human Female Primates." *International Journal of Primatology* 16(2): 205–220.

Dunbar, Robin I. M. 1984. *Reproductive Decisions: An Economic Analysis of Gelada Baboon Social Strategies.* Princeton, NJ: Princeton University Monographs.

Fedigan, Linda M., and S. Zohar. 1997. "Sex Differences in Mortality of Japanese Macaques: Twenty-one Years of Data from the Arashiyama West Population." *American Journal of Physical Anthropology* 102: 161–175.

Gage, Timothy B. 1998. "The Comparative Demography of Primates: With Some Comments on the Evolution of Life Histories." *Annual Review of Anthropology* 27: 197–221.

Harvey, Paul H., Daniel E. L. Promislow, et al. 1989. "Causes and Correlates of Life History Differences among Mammals." In *Comparative Socioecology,* eds. V. Standen and R. A. Foley, Oxford, Eng.: Blackwell Scientific Publications 305–318.

Hawkes, Kristen, James F. O'Connell, et al. 1998. "Grandmothering, Menopause, and the Evolution of Human Life Histories." *Proceedings of the National Academy of Sciences USA* 95(3): 1336–1339.

Hill, Kim, Christopher Boesch, et al. 2001. "Mortality Rates among Wild Chimpanzees." *Journal of Human Evolution* 40: 437–450.

Judge, Debra S., and James R. Carey. 2000. "Postreproductive Life Predicted by Primate Patterns." *Journal of Gerontology: Biological Sciences* 55A: B201–B209.

Kappeler, Peter M., and E. W. Heymann. 1996. "Nonconvergence in the Evolution of Primate Life History and Socio-ecology." *Biological Journal of the Linnean Society* 59(3): 297–326.

Pusey, Ann, J. Williams, et al. 1997. "The Influence of Dominance Rank on the Reproductive Success of Female Chimpanzees." *Science* 277: 828–831.

Sugiyama, Y. 1994. "Age-specific Birth Rate and Lifetime Reproductive Success of Chimpanzees at Bossou, Guinea." *American Journal of Primatology* 32: 311–318.

DEBRA S. JUDGE

PROJECTIONS AND FORECASTS, POPULATION

Population size and structure can be projected into the future based on current knowledge about population size; age and sex composition; and rates of birth, death, and migration; and on assumptions about how these rates may change over time. The projection may cover very different geographic areas, time horizons, or population characteristics, and they may be targeted for a number of different uses. Spatial dimensions can range from local areas such as counties or cities to the entire world. Local-area projections tend to use shorter time horizons, often ten years or less, whereas national and global projections typically extend decades into the future—in some cases, for more than a century. Short- and medium-term projections are more likely than long-term (50-plus-year) projections to include more detail than just the size and age and sex composition of the future population. They may project such socioeconomic characteristics as educational and labor force composition, ethnicity, urban residence, or household type.

While individual researchers and national statistical institutions have made significant contributions to the methods used to project population, especially at the national level (or below), global projections have been the province of relatively few institutions: principally, the United Nations (UN) Population Division, the U.S. Bureau of the Census, the World Bank, and the International Institute for Applied Systems Analysis (IIASA). These institutions have different ways of dealing with uncertainty, make varying assumptions about future fertility, mortality, and migration trends, and begin with slightly different estimates of current population size

Projection Techniques

While some projections for individual countries or regions have been made with other techniques, long-term global population projections commonly employ the cohort-component method. Initial populations for countries or regions are grouped into cohorts defined by age and sex, and the projection proceeds by updating the population of each age- and sex-specific group according to assumptions about the three components of population change: fertility, mortality, and migration. Each cohort is "survived" forward to the next age group according to assumed age-specific mortality rates. Five-year age groups (and five-calendar-year time steps) are commonly used (although IIASA uses single years of age and time) for long-range projections. As an example, the number of women in a particular population aged 20 to 25 in 2005 is calculated as the number of women aged 15 to 20 in 2000 multiplied by the assumed probability of survival for women of that age over the period from 2000 to 2005. This calculation is made for each age group and for both sexes and is repeated for each time step as the projection proceeds. Migration can be accounted for by applying age- and sex-specific net migration rates to each cohort as well, and, in the case of global projections, by ensuring that immigration equals emigration when summed over all regions. The size of the youngest age group is calculated from the number of births during the most recent time period by applying an appropriate survival rate. For example, those under age five in 2005 will be the survivors of births during the preceding five years. Births are calculated by applying assumed age-specific fertility rates to female cohorts in the reproductive age span. An assumed sex ratio at birth is used to divide total births into males and females.

Development of this approach was a major innovation in the evolution of projection methodology, bringing it beyond the mere application of growth rates to an unstructured population. It was first proposed by the English economist Edwin Cannan in 1895. The technique was elaborated by demographer Pascal K. Whelpton in the 1930s, and the method was first employed in producing a global population projection by demographer Frank W. Notestein in 1945. Prior to the mid-twentieth century, the few global population projections that had been made were based on extrapolations of the population growth rate applied to estimates of the total population of the world or by application of some mathematical formula, such as the logistic function.

Since Notestein's 1945 projection, the cohort-component method has become the dominant means of projecting population and has remained essentially unchanged, except for extensions to multistate projections and innovations in characterizing uncertainty. The cohort-component method is nothing more than a particularly useful accounting scheme: It works out the numerical consequences of the size and age structure of the population at the beginning of the period and the fertility, mortality, and migration rates assumed to prevail over the projection period. This was once a laborious operation, but computers have greatly simplified the mechanics of preparing projections. The real work in producing projections lies not in carrying out the necessary calculations but in estimating the population size and age structure in the base period and in selecting appropriate assumptions for specifying future trends of fertility, mortality, and migration. Demographers can draw on specialized knowledge of each of these components of population change to inform projections, and institutions therefore normally project trends in vital rates based on expert opinion. Often, however, it has been difficult to determine precisely how knowledge has been applied in making the assumptions for such projections.

In general, fertility has the greatest effect on the trajectory of a population over time because of its multiplier effect: Children born today will have children in the future, and so on. The fertility component of population projections is summarized by the total fertility rate (TFR), the average total number of children a woman will have assuming that current age-specific birth rates remain the same throughout her childbearing years. In long-term projections the TFR generally reflects the assumption that fertility will eventually stabilize at a specific level in a country or region and an assumption about the time path the TFR will follow in reaching that level. Once fertility stabilizes at that level, assuming mortality and migration rates also remain the same, the population age structure will eventually stabilize as well. Thereafter, the population size will change at a constant rate. If there is no net migration (that is, if the number of in-migrants is canceled out by the number of out-migrants), and the TFR stabilizes at replacement level (when mortality is low, a little more than two children per woman), the growth rate will eventually be zero. Both the projected pace of fertility decline and the assumed eventual fertility level are important in determining trends in population size and age structure. The two factors also interact: The lower the assumed eventual fertility level, the more important the pace of fertility decline becomes in determining the long term projected population size.

Mortality projections are based on projecting life expectancy at birth—that is, the average number of years a child born in a given year can expect to live if current age-specific mortality levels continued in the future. Projections of mortality must specify how the distribution of mortality over different age and sex groups may change over time. Changes in mortality at different ages have different conse-

quences for population growth and age structure. When child and infant mortality decline, for example, a greater proportion of babies will survive to adulthood to have their own children and contribute to future growth. Mortality declines among the older population have a smaller effect on population growth because the survivors are already past reproductive age.

Future international migration is more difficult to project than fertility or mortality. Migration flows often reflect short-term changes in economic, social, or political factors, which are impossible to predict. And, because no single, compelling theory of migration exists, projections are generally based on past trends and current policies, which may not be relevant in the future.

Projection Results and Uncertainty

Projection results are generally produced in one of three forms: as a single projection, as a set of scenarios, or as probability distributions. Many projections present to their users just one path of future population, which is considered most likely at the time of the production. Population projections according to alternative scenarios, called variants in some cases, show what the future population would be if fertility, mortality, and migration follow different paths. Some scenarios are purely illustrative—such as the UN's constant fertility scenario, which projects world population assuming that fertility remains constant at its current level. In other cases, users are given a "plausible" range as indicated by some high and low scenarios or variants. The best known among such projections are those of the UN (revised every two years), which are elaborated in three variants: "medium," "high," and "low." Figure 1 shows the results of these three variants (along with the constant-fertility scenario) on the global level for the period 2000 to 2050 as progressively divergent continuations of the estimated 1950 to 2000 trend. In these UN projections, the four population paths differ only by the fertility trends assumed while disregarding mortality and migration uncertainty. Users of population projections sometimes require projections that conform to various "story lines." For example, population projections might form just part of a scenario of future energy use and greenhouse gas emissions that presuppose particular socioeconomic, technological, or political developments.

Presenting just one best guess projection (e.g., as done by the World Bank and the U.S. Bureau of

FIGURE 1

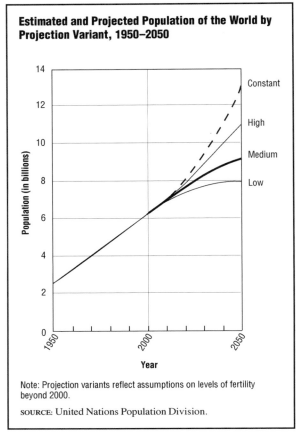

Estimated and Projected Population of the World by Projection Variant, 1950–2050

Constant

High

Medium

Low

Note: Projection variants reflect assumptions on levels of fertility beyond 2000.

SOURCE: United Nations Population Division.

the Census) may satisfy the needs of most users, but it does not convey the message that this future path is uncertain. The scenario approach also has several weaknesses. The most important is that users cannot interpret the probability that population will actually follow a higher or lower scenario or lie within that range. The UN provides little information about the likelihood of a particular scenario, except that it suggests that both the high and low scenarios are unsustainable over the very long run. These scenarios produce a global population that doubles or is halved every 77 years. Theoretically, they would eventually lead to implausible crowding or to extinction. In the real world, however, fertility will almost certainly not stay constant over extended period but rather show some ups and downs.

Another shortcoming of scenario approaches lies in the fact that they have usually been used to represent the uncertainty induced by only one of the three components, mostly fertility. But mortality and migration uncertainties also significantly influence population outcomes. For example, Figure 2

shows IIASA probabilistic projections for the proportion above age 80 in Western Europe over 2000–2100, taking into account uncertainty in fertility, mortality, and migration. The proportion is not expected to change much over the first two decades but, after 2030, it increases significantly while at the same time the uncertainty range widens dramatically, with the 95 percent uncertainty interval covering a range from 3 to 43 percent aged 80+ by 2100, due mainly to high uncertainty in the future path of old age mortality. In contrast, the most recent UN long range projections for 2100 foresee a proportion above age 80 that ranges from 7 percent in the high scenario to 17 percent in the low scenario, with the other UN scenarios all lying within this narrow interval. Because the UN projections do not include mortality uncertainty, they significantly underestimate the uncertainty in the number of elderly.

Finally, aggregation of the low and high scenarios to regional and global totals is typically based on the highly unlikely assumption that these extreme paths occur in all countries of the world simultaneously, an approach termed probabilistically inconsistent by the U.S. National Research Council (NRC).

An alternative way to communicate the uncertainty in population projection results is to derive probability distributions for the projected size and characteristics of a population by using a range of different fertility, mortality, and migration rates. There have been three main bases for determining the probabilities associated with vital rates: expert opinion, statistical time series analysis, and analysis of errors in past projections.

Researchers at IIASA pioneered a methodology for assessing uncertainty in population projections based on asking a group of experts to give a likely range for future fertility, mortality, and migration rates—that is, that the vital rates for a given date would be within the specified range 90 percent of the time. Thousands of cohort-component projections are then produced, drawing from these distributions. Unlike other methods, this approach is also applicable in geographic areas where data on historical trends are sparse.

The expert opinion approach has several drawbacks. For example, the task of deciding who constitutes an expert will always be problematic, and research has shown that, on average, experts tend to be too conservative in their expectations for future

FIGURE 2

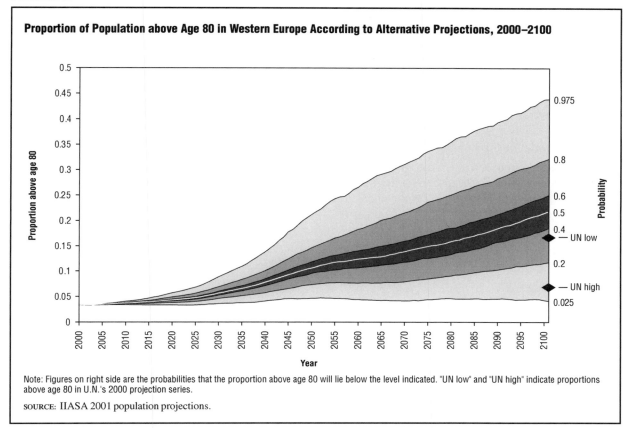

Proportion of Population above Age 80 in Western Europe According to Alternative Projections, 2000–2100

Note: Figures on right side are the probabilities that the proportion above age 80 will lie below the level indicated. "UN low" and "UN high" indicate proportions above age 80 in U.N.'s 2000 projection series.

SOURCE: IIASA 2001 population projections.

changes. Demographer Ronald D. Lee has questioned whether experts can meaningfully distinguish between different confidence levels they may place on estimates of future vital rates. He also argued that the original IIASA methodology, which was based on (piece-wise linear) random scenarios, excluded the possibility of fluctuations in vital rates that deviate from a general trend, which could underestimate uncertainty in outcomes.

Statistical analysis of historical time series data can be used either to project population size directly or to generate probability distributions for population size or vital rates assuming no structural changes. While statistical methods also employ expert judgment, they do not rely on it as much as the purely expert-based method. Statistical analysis methods based on times series have been applied to some national projections but not to global projections because their wide application is severely constrained by lack of data.

Population projections made in the past can be evaluated for how well they forecast the actual popu-

lation, and these errors—the difference between the projected and actual population size—can be used to calculate probability distributions for new projections. An NRC report issued in 2000 calculated probability distributions from the errors of UN medium-variant projections for 2000 that were made between 1957 and 1998. The NRC found the UN was somewhat more likely to overestimate than to underestimate future population size at the world level, although the size of the error was small. Errors were much greater for projections of country populations, but these errors tended to cancel out over the long term at the global level. The average error in UN projections for individual countries varied from 4.8 percent for five-year projections to 17 percent for 30-year projections, according to the NRC report.

In general, projections of population size tend to be more uncertain, or less accurate, under particular circumstances. They are less accurate for:

1. Less developed countries than for more developed countries, partly because less developed countries tend to have limited and

less reliable data and, because they are still in the process of demographic transition, their demographic outlook is very sensitive to the timing of fertility decline;

2. Smaller countries than for larger ones, perhaps stemming in part from the greater attention devoted to larger countries and from greater heterogeneity within large countries, which allows errors at the level of sub-populations to cancel;

3. Younger and older age groups than in middle age groups, because incorrect assumptions about fertility and mortality have a greater effect at older and younger ages; and

4. The country level than at regional or global levels, because errors at the country level partly cancel each other when aggregated to regions or to the world.

These three methods of producing probabilistic projections are not mutually exclusive. Early-twenty-first-century projections from IIASA combine all three elements: Expert opinion is used to define a central path for fertility, mortality, and migration in all world regions. It is also used, in conjunction with historical errors, to define the uncertainty ranges for these values. Time series methods are used to generate paths for each variable that can show realistic short-term fluctuations over time.

Current Projections

Given the difficulties of estimating baseline data accurately and the inherent uncertainty in projecting trends in vital rates, different population projections can produce widely varying population sizes, age structures, and distributions. Nevertheless, the U.S. Census Bureau and World Bank projections, the medium or "most likely" projection from the UN, and the median future population from IIASA's probabilistic projection are similar in some respects. The Census Bureau foresees a world population of 9.1 billion in 2050, compared with 9.3 billion for the 2000 medium UN series (reduced to 8.9 million in the 2002 series) and 8.7 billion for the World Bank, while IIASA's median value for 2050 is 8.8 billion.

Differences between the UN medium variant and the median path of IIASA's probabilistic long-range projections increase over time. By 2100, projected world population differs by 11 percent: IIASA projects a median population of 8.4 billion that is al-

ready declining by 2100, whereas the UN projects a population of 9.5 billion that is nearly stable. For total population size, the UN high and low variants span a wide range (of undefined probability) that is also generally higher than the IIASA 95 percent uncertainty range. The UN projects a global population of five billion to 16 billion by 2100, based on its low and high variants, while IIASA projects a 95 percent uncertainty interval of 4.3 to 14.4 billion. IIASA's projections are generally lower primarily because they assume that fertility will, in the long run, fall below replacement level in all world regions.

Projections following different scenarios differ less in the short term than in the long term because they generally start from the same base population, and because it takes years for changes in vital rates to alter the built-in momentum that drives population growth. Momentum refers to the effects of population age structure on demographic trends: In a population with a young age structure, even if fertility falls sharply, the numbers of children will continue to increase for about a generation as the large cohorts of young people pass through their reproductive years. As a result, such populations will continue to grow for decades even if fertility were to be instantly reduced to replacement level. In contrast, some low-fertility industrialized countries are subject to negative population momentum. Because of past fertility decline, their populations have relatively small cohorts under age 30 and, therefore, even if fertility were to rise to replacement level, population size would decline for some time.

Under any plausible scenario for future growth, the world age structure will grow older, greater percentages of people will live in urban areas, and the regional balance will shift. These changes will be more dramatic further into the future. In 2000 the global population below age 15 was about three times the size of the population age 60 or older. The proportion age 60 or older is projected to swell in all scenarios, while the proportion below age 15 shrinks. World population is youngest under the higher fertility rates in the UN high-variant projections. In the UN medium-variant and the IIASA median, the proportion age 60 or older is likely to surpass the proportion below age 15 by the middle of the twenty-first century.

Based on the high and low projections prepared by these institutions, however, the older age group could overtake the below-15 age group as early as

2030 or as late as the twenty-second century. This reflects the uncertainty in the rates of change in each of these age groups considered separately. While in all cases the proportion of the population below 15 is expected to fall, it could reach anywhere from 10 percent to 22 percent of the total population in 2100. Similarly, while the percentage age 60 or older will grow, the figure could be as low as 22 percent or as high as 44 percent of the population by the end of the century.

All of the global projections show that the regional balance of world population will shift over time. Under the UN long-range projections, the share of the global population made up by the current more developed countries of North America and Europe declines from 17.2 percent in 2000 to about 10 percent in 2100. Africa's share of the total grows the most over this period, from 13.1 percent to about 23 percent, while the population share of China actually falls from 21 percent to 14 percent. These conclusions are qualitatively consistent across other scenarios, as well as across institutions.

See also: *Cannan, Edwin; Cities, Future of; Momentum of Population Growth; Multistate Demography; Notestein, Frank W.; Pearl, Raymond; Thompson, Warren S.; Whelpton, P. K.; World Population Growth.*

BIBLIOGRAPHY

Cannan, Edwin. 1895. "The Probability of a Cessation of the Growth of Population in England and Wales during the Next Century." *Economic Journal* 5(20): 505–515.

Frejka, Tomas. 1996. "Long-Range Global Population Projections: Lessons Learned." In *The Future Population of the World: What Can We Assume Today?* 2nd edition, ed. Wolfgang Lutz. London: Earthscan.

Lee, Ronald D., and Shripad Tuljapurkar. 1994. "Stochastic Population Projections for the United States: Beyond High, Medium, and Low." *Journal of the American Statistical Association* 89: 1175–1189.

Leslie, P. H. 1945. "On the Use of Matrices in Certain Population Mathematics." *Biometrika* 33: 183–212.

Lutz, Wolfgang, ed. 1996. *The Future Population of the World: What Can We Assume Today?* 2nd edition. London: Earthscan.

Lutz, Wolfgang, Warren C. Sanderson, and Sergei Scherbov. 2001. "The End of World Population Growth." *Nature* 412: 543–546.

Lutz, Wolfgang, James W. Vaupel, and Dennis A. Ahlburg, eds. 1999. *Frontiers of Population Forecasting,* Supplement to Volume 24 of *Population and Development Review.* New York: Population Council.

National Research Council. Committee on Population. Panel on Population Projections. 2000. *Beyond Six Billion: Forecasting the World's Population,* ed. John Bongaarts and Rodolfo A. Bulatao. Washington, D.C.: National Academy Press.

Notestein, Frank W. 1945. "Population: The Long View." In *Food for the World,* ed. Theodore W. Schultz. Chicago: University of Chicago Press.

O'Neill, Brian C., Deborah Balk, Melanie Brickman, and Markos Ezra. 2001. "A Guide to Global Population Projections." *Demographic Research* 4(8): 203–288.

O'Neill, Brian C., Sergei Scherbov, and Wolfgang Lutz. 1999. "The Long-Term Effect of the Timing of Fertility Decline on Population Size." *Population and Development Review* 25: 749–756.

United Nations. 2001. *World Population Prospects: The 2000 Revision,* Vol. 1: *Comprehensive Tables.* New York: United Nations.

United Nations. Population Division. 2000. *Long-Range World Population Projections: Based on the 1998 Revision.* New York: United Nations.

U.S. Bureau of the Census. 1999. *World Population Profile, 1998.* Washington, D.C.: U.S. Government Printing Office.

Whelpton, Pascal K. 1936. "An Empirical Method of Calculating Future Population." *Journal of the American Statistical Association* 31: 457–473.

World Bank. 2000. *World Development Indicators, 2000.* Washington, D.C.: World Bank.

BRIAN C. O'NEILL
WOLFGANG LUTZ

PROXIMATE DETERMINANTS OF FERTILITY

See *Fertility, Proximate Determinants of*

PUBLIC HEALTH

See *Environmental Health; Health Systems; Health Transition; Mortality Decline; Reproductive Health*

PUBLIC OPINION ON POPULATION ISSUES

Public attitudes toward global population issues have been more closely surveyed in the United States than in other countries; therefore this article focuses on the United States.

An overwhelming majority of the U. S. population correctly perceives the world's population as growing and believes that world population growth is a significant problem. This majority is divided, however, as to how serious and pressing the problem is. There is also evidence of some decline in the sense of urgency. A very strong majority supports the U.S. government providing aid to assist people in poor countries with family planning. Support is more modest, however, when the goal is framed in terms of getting developing countries to reduce their birthrates; Americans are more comfortable with the goal of helping women plan their families.

Perception of the Problem

In a September 1998 Belden and Russonello poll, 83 percent of respondents described the world population as growing. Seventy-one percent agreed (43 % strongly) that "too much population growth in developing countries is holding back their economic development."

But this majority is divided as to how serious or pressing the problem of population growth is. In a June 2002 Chicago Council on Foreign Relations (CCFR) poll, 86 percent thought "world population growth" a threat "to the vital interests of the US in the next ten years." However, that majority was divided between 44 percent who thought the threat "critical" and 42 percent who thought it "important but not critical." Similarly, in an October 1999 Gallup poll, 88 percent said that "population growth internationally" is a problem; 47 percent, however, said it was "a major problem now," while 41 percent characterized it as "not a problem now, but likely to become a problem for the future." In a February 1994 Belden and Russonello poll, 73 percent said that population growth would have a negative impact on the global environment, with 46 percent saying it would have a very negative impact and 27 percent, a somewhat negative impact.

In most cases, a plurality or majority takes the more dire perspective. In an October 1999 Pew poll, which posed a pair of arguments, 56 percent chose the one that said that the growing population "will be a major problem because there won't be enough food and resources to go around"; 42 percent chose the one that said that it "will not be a major problem because we will find a way to stretch our natural resources."

Modest Decline in Sense of Urgency

There is some evidence that the issue of overpopulation evoked less of a sense of urgency at the end of the 1990s than it did in the early 1990s—perhaps because some of the public has become aware that global population growth has slowed in the developed world. In Gallup polls, the proportion saying that population growth is a major problem now dropped from 29 percent in 1992 to 18 percent in 1999. Those holding the less urgent view that it "was not a problem now, but likely to be a problem in the future" rose from 45 percent to 59 percent.

Nevertheless, the argument that birth rates in developed countries have become too low is not popular with the public. Belden and Russonello's 1998 survey tested the statement, "People in the developed, wealthier countries are having too few babies," and found only 22 percent in agreement, with 62 percent disagreeing.

Overwhelming Support for Family Planning

Beldon and Russonello's 1998 survey also indicated that there is broad consensus among Americans that family planning services should be universally available. A near-unanimous 92 percent agreed (69 percent strongly) that "all couples and individuals should have the right to decide freely and responsibly the number, spacing and timing of their children and to have the information and the means to do so." In the same poll, 68 percent agreed with the proposition that family planning services were not "already available to most people in all parts of the world today."

Foreign Aid for Family Planning

A strong majority supports the idea that facilitating family planning is an appropriate purpose for U.S. foreign aid. The Program on International Policy Attitudes reported that, "when asked to rate how high a priority family planning should be in U.S. foreign aid programs on a scale of 1 to 10, with 1 meaning the lowest priority and 10 a top priority, family planning ranked quite high. In a February 2000 poll, the objective of 'making birth control available to people in other countries so they can choose the number of children they have' received a mean rating of 6.9, with 39 percent rating it at 10."

When asked directly about providing aid for family planning, support tends to be very high, especially if it is spelled out that family planning does not include abortion. In a 1998 Belden and Russonello poll, 80 percent said they favored (45% strongly) "the US sponsoring voluntary family planning programs in developing countries" when this distinction was spelled out (18% were opposed). In February 1994, the same question was asked, but the exclusion of abortion was not specified; a much lower proportion, 59 percent, favored such programs, with 37 percent opposed.

In a January 1995 poll by the Program on International Policy Attitudes (PIPA), respondents were given information about the cost of U.S. foreign aid for family planning. The poll found that 74 percent wanted to increase (36%) or maintain (38%) the level of funding.

A majority prefers giving aid for family planning through United Nations (UN) population programs. In October 1999 a NBC/*Wall Street Journal* poll asked if "nations should share resources and information through groups such as the United Nations to promote birth control, or should nations determine their own population and family planning programs?" Only 40 percent chose the statement that nations should determine their own family planning programs, whereas 54 percent preferred the statement that nations should share resources through the UN to promote birth control.

Ambivalence about the Goal of Reducing Birth Rates

While support for assistance for family planning is high, the support for using aid for the goal of reducing birth rates is more mixed. More than 80 percent support aid for family planning, whereas aid for limiting population growth finds a modest majority. The reason for this ambivalence may well be found in the response to a 1998 Belden and Russonello question that asked: "Do you agree more with those who say the United States should encourage developing countries to lower their birthrates, or more with those who say it is inappropriate for us to do this because it may offend other people's cultures?" A slight majority of 52 percent thought it was inappropriate; 42 percent thought it was appropriate.

There is a strong consensus that there should not be any encroachment on the right to have children. In September 1998, 76 percent agreed (50% strongly) with the statement: "People should feel free to have as many children as they can properly raise" (23% disagreed). Presumably the response to this question is colored by a rejection of coercive birth control practices, such as those associated with China's one-child program, but it is also an indication that Americans feel that the United States should not take the position of pressuring individuals to refrain from having children.

Family Planning and Abortion

Most Americans do not make a link between family planning and abortion. A September 1998 Belden, Russonello, and Stewart (BRS) poll asked respondents in open-ended questions what came to mind when they heard the terms "family planning" and "birth control." In both cases, only very small minorities volunteered that these terms included abortion.

The Program on International Policy Attitudes reported that

> Only a small minority thinks that an increase of family planning services in a developing country is likely to lead to an increase in abortions there. The same 1998 BRS poll asked: "If family planning were made widely available in a country where it had not been, would you expect the number of abortions to fall, or to rise, or would having family planning widely available make no impact on abortion rates?" Only 15 per-

cent said they would expect the number of abortions to rise, while a slight majority, 52 percent, said they expected abortions would go down and 27 percent thought it would make no difference ("Americans and the World").

Americans are divided on whether the United States should help fund the performance of abortions abroad. When asked whether they would favor "US aid programs contributing the funding" of "voluntary, safe abortion as part of reproductive health care in developing countries that request it," 50 percent favored this and 46 percent opposed it. Likewise, the public is divided on the question of whether the United States should fund organizations that discuss the option of abortion with their clients. In an April 1998 PIPA poll, 50 percent thought "the US should withhold US funds from family planning organizations that discuss abortion," while 46 percent thought it should not.

A strong majority, however, opposes making the payment of UN dues by the United States contingent on the UN having such a policy. In the PIPA question just mentioned, respondents who said the U.S. Congress should withhold funds (or "don't know") were told there was a good chance that if the restriction was added to the bill to pay U.S. back dues to the UN, the bill would not pass. Twenty-four percent of the total sample shifted to rejecting the restriction, making a total of 70 percent opposed.

See also: *Mass Media and Demographic Behavior.*

BIBLIOGRAPHY

Adamson, David M., Nancy Belden, Julie DaVanzo, and Sally Patterson. 2000. *How Americans View World Population Issues: A Survey of Public Opinion.* Santa Monica, CA: Rand.

INTERNET RESOURCE.

Program on International Policy Attitudes (Stephen Kull, Director). "Americans and the World" website. <http://www.americans-world.org>.

STEVEN KULL

Q

QUALITY OF POPULATION

Population quality is the overall level of certain desirable traits in a specific population. The members of a population do not contribute equally to the size of the next generation: The distribution of births, especially in low-fertility populations, varies markedly across the adult members. Because the data seem to show family resemblances across generations in these traits (the traits are familial whether they are transmitted genetically or socially), the question arises whether their overall level is going up or down as a result of this unequal distribution of births.

Increasing the Incidence of Desirable Traits

In most discussions of population quality the traits in question are health, intelligence, and what the scientist Sir Francis Galton, the coiner of the term *eugenics,* called "moral character"; this is frequently interpreted by modern psychologists as the personality traits of conscientiousness and altruism. However difficult it may be to define and assess such qualities in ways that command wide agreement, let alone consensus, it is obvious that people want to live in a society whose members are healthy, intelligent, conscientious, considerate, and civil toward others and prefer not to live in a society whose members are on the whole unhealthy, unintelligent, dishonest, lazy, and uncivil. The question, then, is how social policies in a specific population could be devised to increase the frequency of members with high amounts of the good traits and decrease the frequency of those with low amounts and whether such policies should even be sought.

A commonly discussed method of increasing the frequency of those with the good traits and decreasing the frequency of those without them is eugenics. Eugenic methods are applicable when the trait in question is inherited in some fashion, and many of those traits seem to be. What Richard Lynn (2001) calls "classical eugenics" seeks to increase the reproductive rates of those with higher levels of the desired traits and decrease the reproductive rates of those without them. This would counteract the tendency, perceived by many observers, of people who are better endowed with intelligence or the personality traits of conscientiousness and civility to replace themselves in the next generation at lower rates than those of people with low intelligence or minimal conscientiousness or civility.

Problems with Eugenics

There are problems with a program of eugenics. Assuming that agreement about desirable and undesirable traits can be reached, probably the most important problem is time. Generation length (the average time between two successive generations) among human beings is between 25 and 30 years, and for males it is often even longer. Because eugenics programs propose changing the frequency of a trait in the next generation, such programs would take 20 or more years to have an effect. This may be too long in comparison to other changes affecting human populations.

The eugenicist Hermann Muller (1890–1967), a Nobel Prize winner in medicine, wrote about this problem, noting the "creeping pace" of dysgenic trends compared to the "fast growing menaces presented by our cultural imbalances" (Muller 1973, p. 128). Konrad Lorenz (1903–1989), also a Nobel Prize winner, worried about the genetic quality of the human species. Late in his life, however, he allowed that cultural deterioration proceeds much more rapidly than does genetic deterioration (Lorenz 1976). This argument against the efficacy of eugenics has not been answered.

Of course, if change in the quality of a population is due in large part to the environment in which the members of that population live, change can take place considerably faster than the slow pace of genetic change. However, Richard Lynn has shown in his books *Dysgenics* (1996) and *Eugenics* (2001) that important traits such as intelligence, conscientiousness, altruism, and a psychopathic personality have significant inherited components. That conclusion strongly suggests that public policies consider eugenic measures despite the problems.

Population quality was a significant concern to an earlier generation of demographers. The goal of the Population Association of America (PAA) is defined in its constitution as the study of population in its "quantitative and qualitative aspects." Many of the founders of the PAA were eugenicists (Kiser 1981). Although the constitution of the International Union for the Scientific Study of Population (IUSSP) does not contain the phrase "population quality," the proceedings of its early conferences indicate a strong interest in the subject (Sanger 1927, Pitt-Rivers 1932). That contraception might be confined to or more prevalent among the more fit was a real concern. Arguably, the problem then identified by some demographers—the low fertility of those with large amounts of desirable traits relative to the fertility of those with low amounts—persists to this day.

The phrase, "population quality," has largely disappeared from recent demographic writings, partly because of its association with Nazi eugenic theories and programs. However, the decline of interest in population quality, and thus in eugenics, began before there was full awareness of what happened in Germany and in German-occupied lands in the Nazi era. Therefore, the reasons for the eclipse of the study of population quality in contemporary demography are not well understood.

Policies and Population Quality

A few countries have instituted demographic policies designed to cause a higher level of population quality. In China mentally retarded persons and those with genetically transmitted diseases are actively discouraged from having children. In Singapore more highly educated women are actively encouraged and given substantial financial incentives to have more children. These policies have been noted in the West but derided and not emulated. In the West persons with mental retardation, which is known to have an inherited component, are not discouraged from having children and highly educated men and women are not encouraged to reproduce.

A host of artificial methods of reproduction are existent or on the horizon, such as embryo selection and genetic engineering, that will allow parents to choose certain genetic qualities of their offspring. So far the high cost and unavailability of these methods have allowed society to avoid confronting the questions raised by what Sinsheimer (1969) calls the "new eugenics": genetic selection governed not by top-down eugenic policies but by the choices of individuals.

However, it is doubtful that consideration of these issues can be avoided much longer. There has never been a technology that has not attracted users. Any country that opted to allow and encourage the widespread employment of such technologies, as Raymond Cattell (1972, 1987) points out, would potentially render itself ascendant in light of what is already known about the heritability of various desirable traits (Lynn 1996, 2001) that are of interest to people. Less desirably, taking that option may create social problems that in the early twenty-first century are only dimly perceived.

See also: *Eugenics; Family Size Distribution; Galton, Francis; Genetic Testing; Reproductive Technologies: Modern Methods, Ethical Issues.*

BIBLIOGRAPHY

Cattell, Raymond. 1972. *A New Morality from Science: Beyondism.* New York: Pergamon.

———. 1987. *Beyondism: Religion from Science.* New York: Praeger.

Galton, Francis. 1869. *Hereditary Genius.* London: Macmillan.

Kiser, Clyde. 1981. "The Role of the Milbank Memorial Fund in the Early History of the Association." *Population Index* 47: 490–494.

Lorenz, Konrad. 1976. "Konrad Lorenz Responds to Donald Campbell." In *Konrad Lorenz: The Man and His Ideas,* ed. Richard Evans. New York: Harcourt Brace Jovanovich.

Lynn, Richard. 1996. *Dysgenics: The Genetic Deterioration in Modern Populations.* Westport, CT: Praeger.

———. 2001. *Eugenics: A Reassessment.* Westport, CT: Praeger.

Muller, Hermann. 1973. "What Genetic Course Will Man Steer?" In *Man's Future Birthright: Essays on Science and Humanity by H. J. Muller,* ed. Elof Carlson. Albany: State University of New York Press.

Pitt-Rivers, George, ed. 1932. *Problems of Population: Being the Report of the Proceedings of the Second General Assembly of the International Union for the Scientific Investigation of Population Problems.* London: George Allen.

Sanger, Margaret, ed. 1927. *Proceedings of the World Population Conference, Geneva.* London: E. Arnold.

Sinsheimer, Robert. 1969. "The Prospect of Designed Genetic Change." *Engineering and Science* 32: 8–13.

Daniel R. Vining, Jr.

QUETELET, ADOLPHE

(1796–1874)

Born in Ghent, Belgium, mathematician and demographer Adolphe Quetelet earned a doctorate in mathematics at the age of twenty-three and was elected, one year later, to the *Académie royale des sciences et belles-lettres.* The Belgian academy became the central place from which Quetelet directed most of his activities for the rest of his life. He worked in a variety of disciplines such as astronomy, meteorology, physical geography, development psychology, demography, and statistics. Quetelet's work was profoundly influenced by early probability theory. From astronomer and mathematician Pierre-Simon Laplace (1749–1827), Quetelet learned that measurement errors are normally distributed around the true value; this information allowed him to detect systematic errors in early social science data. His notion of *l'homme moyen* also stems from Laplace's theory. However, Quetelet was never exclusively preoccupied by averages, and whenever possible he presented complete distributions. One of his contributions to demography is his presentation of age-specific rates for vital events or for other phenomena (e.g., crime), and his construction of time series. In fact, the materials brought together in his *Physique Sociale* (1835) mark the beginning of the statistical study of the life cycle. Quetelet's interpretation of population distributions of social characteristics announced the advent of sociology as a new science, according to which the entity called "society" could be studied and analyzed with objective methods. In contrast to philosopher Auguste Comte (1798–1857), Quetelet never developed a general plan for this new discipline, but his influence on sociology remained strong throughout the nineteenth century, as is evidenced in the work of French sociologist Émile Durkheim (1858–1917).

Quetelet's contribution to demography started in the 1820s. Together with E. Smits, he noted, like several others before him (e.g., French military engineer Sébastien Vauban [1633–1707] and German demographer Johann Peter Süssmilch [1707–1767]) that the numbers and age distributions of vital events in the Low Countries showed a remarkable degree of stability over time. In *Physique Sociale,* Quetelet argued that only major disturbances were capable of producing temporary distortions. By contrast, *les causes constantes* would re-establish the dominant pattern. This is a view similar to that of the homeostatic demographic regime of the economist T. R. Malthus.

Quetelet's other contributions to demography deal respectively with census taking and life table construction. These two areas were intimately related since no direct measurement of probabilities of dying (i.e., the q_x-function of a life table) was available at that time. Hence, like all other investigators before him, Quetelet depended on the stationarity assumption that permitted the linkage of ved age structures to the L_x-function (numbers of person-years lived in an age interval). Quetelet explicitly discussed the properties of stationary populations, and showed that the hypothesis of constant mortality could be relaxed. In fact, he was on the way to showing that there is a *neutral* pattern of mortality decline (i.e., a reduction in age-specific death rates which does not alter the shape of the population age distribution). (For the proof, see A. J. Coale, 1972: 33–36.) Quetelet was never able to develop a model for a stable population with a constant growth rate different from zero. He also failed to recognize the significance of the logistic curve developed by one of his younger colleagues, Belgian mathematician and demographer Pierre-François Verhulst (1804–1849). In actual practice, Quetelet remained a master of comparative statics rather than of social dynamics.

Quetelet did not comment on the numerous social developments in Belgium, which began in the 1860s. After suffering a stroke in 1855, his scientific innovativeness ended. However, until his death in 1874, Quetelet continued to inspire statistical applications in other many fields, and to promote international comparability of statistical information. In the words of mathematician Alain Desrosières, "Quetelet was the orchestra conductor of nineteenth century statistics" (Derosières, p. 95).

See also: *Demography, History of; Life Tables; Population Thought, History of; Verhulst, Pierre-François.*

BIBLIOGRAPHY

SELECTED WORKS BY ADOLPHE QUETELET.

Quetelet, Adolphe. 1835. *Sur l'homme et le développement de ses facultés ou essai de physique sociale.* Paris: Editions Bachelier. English transl.: *A Treatise on Man and the Development of His Faculties.* Edinburgh: Chambers, 1842.

———. 1848. *Du système social et des lois qui le régissent.* Paris: Guillaumin et Cie.

——— 1849. "Nouvelles tables de mortalité pour la Belgique." *Bulletin de la Commission Centrale de Statistique* 4: 1–22.

SELECTED WORKS ABOUT ADOLPHE QUETELET.

Académie Royale de la Belgique. 1997. *Actualité et universalité de la pensée scientifique d'Adolphe Quetelet.* Classe des Sciences, Actes du Colloque 24–25.10.96, Brussels, Belgium.

Coale, Ansley J. 1972. *The Growth and Structure of Human Populations—A Mathematical Investigation.* Princeton, NJ: Princeton University Press.

Desrosières, A. 1993. *La politique des grands nombres—Histoire de la raison statistique.* Paris: Editions La Decouverte. English edition: *The Politics of Large Numbers: A History of Statistical Reasoning.* Cambridge, MA: Harvard University Press. 1998.

Lesthaeghe, R. 2001. "Quetelet, Adolphe (1796–1874)." In *Encyclopedia of the Social and Behavioural Sciences.* Oxford: Elsevier Science Ltd.

RON LESTHAEGHE

R

RACIAL AND ETHNIC COMPOSITION

Ethnicity is a socially important demographic marker throughout the world. In many countries, however, it is not collected or reported in official population statistics, typically for reasons of social policy. *Race* is a concept with a contentious history and is no longer in use in anthropology. But in the United States, both concepts have long been, and continue to be, prominent features of population statistics. This article is therefore focused on the U.S. case.

The racial and ethnic composition of the U.S. population has changed markedly since the founding of the nation as successive waves of immigrants arrived from an ever-shifting array of countries around the world. Classifying persons as members of particular racial or ethnic groups is, however, far from straightforward, not only because of the increasingly complicated mix of identities among children whose parents, grandparents, or great-grandparents were members of different groups, but also because social definitions of race and ethnicity have changed through time. Despite these complexities, it is clear that the racial and ethnic composition of the U.S. population has been becoming increasingly diverse especially since the 1970s, and this trend is projected to continue.

The Racial and Ethnic Classification System

Ethnicity can be defined as a social boundary between groups reflecting distinctions made by individuals in their everyday lives based on cultural differences, such as language, religion, dress and food preferences, and entertainment and artistic expression, as well social and physical differences between members of specific groups. Scientists long ago abandoned the search for rigid biological distinctions between races, but insofar as racial distinctions continue to be drawn in everyday life, race can be viewed as a particular type of ethnicity in which social perceptions regarding physical characteristics play an important role in characterizing group membership.

Reflecting their socially constructed nature, racial and ethnic categories differ substantially across societies, and from time to time within particular societies, as individuals assimilate across boundaries, as boundaries erode with intermarriage or through the adoption of cultural practices across boundaries, or as new groups enter a society through immigration. A long historical perspective on the changing racial and ethnic classification system of the United States is provided in the series of population censuses conducted every ten years. Questions in past censuses designed especially to identify key groups have focused on country of birth (along with year of immigration, citizenship status, and language), ancestry, and race and Hispanic origin.

Cultural differences between the foreign-born and native-born populations have long been prominent. Country of birth was asked in each census since 1850, and mother's and father's countries of birth were asked in the censuses between 1870 and 1970. The latter provide the basis for distinguishing the second generation from the foreign-born and from third- and later-generation Americans. Responding to the great wave of immigration from Europe between 1880 and 1930, the censuses asked additional questions about year of immigration (1890–1930), citizenship status (1900–1950), and language spoken (1900–1940). With the blurring of ethnic distinctions among European Americans who were the grandchildren of those immigrants, questions on father's and mother's countries of birth were replaced with a question on ancestry beginning in the 1980 census. With the second great wave of immigrants after 1960, mainly from Latin America and Asia, questions were reintroduced asking about language spoken (1960–2000), year of immigration (1970–2000), and citizenship (1970–2000).

Questions seeking to ascertain race have the longest history in U.S. census data collection. The censuses from 1790 to 1820 distinguished free whites, other free persons, and slaves; the category "free colored persons" was added in 1830. Whites and blacks (referred to as Negro between 1930 and 1960) were each identified in every census since 1850. The mixed-race category of mulatto was included between 1850 and 1890 and again between 1910 and 1920, while the 1890 census also sought to distinguish among mulatto (a person with three-eighths to five-eighths black ancestry), quadroon (a person of one-quarter black ancestry), and octoroon (a person of one-eighth or any trace of black ancestry). American Indians (Native Americans) have been identified since 1860. With the admission of Alaska and Hawaii as states in 1959, the terms Eskimo and Hawaiian were introduced in 1960, and Aleut was introduced in 1970.

Successive waves of immigrants from Asia and the Pacific islands were identified not only through the country of origin question but also with new explicit racial categories on the census form: Chinese (1860–2000), Japanese (1870–2000), Filipino (1930–2000), Korean (1930–1940 and 1970–2000), and Samoan, Guamanian, and Vietnamese (1980–2000). Asian Indians were distinguished beginning in 1980 but had also been identified in two earlier censuses (1930 and 1940) under the rubric of Hindu. Mexicans were included as a racial category once, in 1930. With increasing immigration from Latin America, ethnic identifiers specific for that region were introduced in census data collection: Spanish surname in 1960 (for the five southwestern states only) and Hispanic origin (with categories including Mexican, Puerto Rican, and Cuban) from 1970 to 2000. (The Hispanic category refers only to Latin American countries.)

Thus, persons of European origin were identified only through country of origin and related questions until the introduction of the ancestry question in 1980. But persons with origins in Africa, Asia, and Latin America have been identified both through immigration-related questions and, typically from early in their presence in substantial numbers in the United States, through questions regarding race or ethnicity. These specific racial or ethnic categories, however, usually refer to countries, such as Mexico, Cuba, China, Japan, the Philippines, or Korea. The most important innovation in the 2000 census was the provision for the choice and reporting of more than one race for an individual, that is, multiple- or mixed-race reporting.

Historical Transformations in Racial and Ethnic Composition

In 1790 more than one-half of the population (56%) within the then geographic boundaries of the United States had origins in Great Britain, and an additional one-fifth (19%) had origins in other northwestern European countries. As the number of immigrants per decade rose steeply from 143,000 in the 1820s to an average of 4.5 million in the 1880s and 1890s, the flow from Britain fell far short of the Irish immigration between 1820 and 1860 and the German immigration between 1830 and 1900. The Irish and Germans were commonly viewed as racially inferior to and/or religiously and linguistically incompatible with the native-born U.S. population of predominantly British origin.

This first great wave of immigration involved a dramatic shift in countries of origin at the end of the nineteenth century. During the two decades from 1900 to 1920, the majority of the 15 million immigrants entering the United States were from southern and eastern Europe. Anthropologists, scientists, and policymakers of the era shared the public sentiment that these southern and eastern European immigrants were racially distinct from earlier arrivals and that they were likely to dilute the racial and the cultural character of the American population of the time with its mainly northwestern European origins. The Irish, Germans, and southern and eastern Europeans were each, in turn, treated with often intense hostility and more than occasional discrimination.

Ethnic assimilation can be defined as a form of ethnic change taking place on one or both sides of the ethnic boundary involving a diminution of cultural, social, or physical distinctions. By the end of the twentieth century differences among European Americans on many measures, including language

FIGURE 1

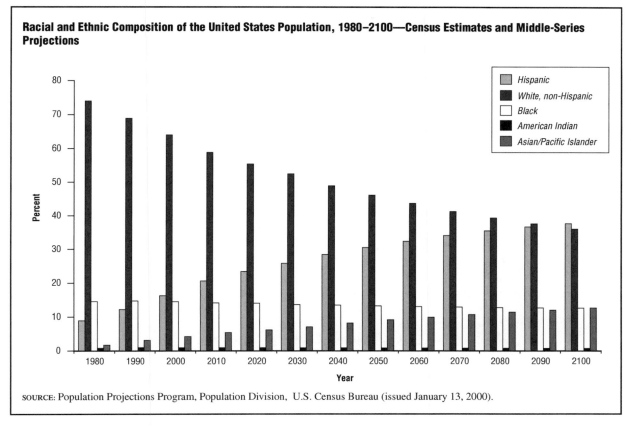

Racial and Ethnic Composition of the United States Population, 1980–2100—Census Estimates and Middle-Series Projections

Legend:
- Hispanic
- White, non-Hispanic
- Black
- American Indian
- Asian/Pacific Islander

SOURCE: Population Projections Program, Population Division, U.S. Census Bureau (issued January 13, 2000).

spoken, fertility, and socioeconomic measures such as educational attainment, had largely disappeared. For European Americans, assimilation occurred as race and ethnic boundaries were blurred, stretched, and otherwise altered through intermarriage and through the expansion of mainstream culture to accommodate cultural differences.

While European-American ethnic groups have maintained some distinctive patterns, these are now slight compared to other, historically long-standing, racial and ethnic boundaries, most notably those separating non-Hispanic whites from American Indians, blacks, and Hispanics. In 1830, whites accounted for about 82 percent of the U.S. population but made up only 65 percent of the population within the territory now encompassed by the continental United States. With the continuing decimation of American Indians, the abolition of slave trade, and increasing immigration from Europe, the proportion of whites in the United States grew to 86 percent in the 34 states constituting the United States in 1860, and to 90 percent during the period from 1920

to 1950. Blacks accounted for most of the remaining 10 to 14 percent during these years.

Recent and Projected Transformations in Racial and Ethnic Composition

Following a sharp drop in the number of immigrants during the Great Depression, steady increases occurred during each decade between the 1940s and 1970s, followed by much larger influxes during the 1980s and 1990s. During the 1960s, 54 percent of immigrants came from Mexico, other western hemisphere countries (excluding Canada), and Asia. This proportion rose to 79 percent during the 1970s and 85 percent during the 1980s. In the 1980s Mexico and other western hemisphere countries (excluding Canada) accounted for 47 percent of all immigrants and Asia for an additional 37 percent. Most of these immigrants and their children are counted among the racial and ethnic minorities of the U.S. population.

Dramatic growth in the number of immigrants and major shifts in countries of origin are rapidly transforming the racial and ethnic composition of the United States. Non-Hispanic whites declined sharply from 83.5 percent to 69.1 percent of the population between 1970 and 2000. Most of this 14 percentage-point-drop is accounted for by the 8 percentage-point-rise in Hispanics, from 4.6 percent to 12.5 percent of the total population. Non-Hispanic Asians and Pacific Islanders also grew substantially, from 1.6 percent in 1980 to 4.1 percent in 2000. Meanwhile, non-Hispanic blacks increased slightly, from 10.9 percent in 1970 to 12.1 percent in 2000, and American Indians continued to account for less than 1 percent of the population. An additional 1.6 percent of non-Hispanics listed two or more races in the 2000 census: These people are not included in the single-race categories noted.

Looking to the future, the U.S. Bureau of the Census projects that most U.S. population growth during the twenty-first century will occur through immigration and births to immigrants and their descendants. Thus the proportion of the population belonging to the current racial and ethnic minorities is projected to continue expanding to about 50 percent by mid-century and 60 percent by century's end, with a corresponding decline in the non-Hispanic white proportion. The emergence of racial and ethnic minorities as (in combination) the majority of the population is occurring most rapidly and will first become a reality among children. Census Bureau projections indicate that the proportion of children who are Hispanic, black, Asian, or of some other racial minority will rise above 50 percent before 2040, up from 31 percent in 1990 (see Figure 1).

Differences in the rates of change by age have important consequences. In 2030 the baby-boom generation born between 1946 and 1964 will be in the retirement ages of 66 to 84 years old. The Census Bureau's projections indicate that by that year, 74 percent of the elderly will be white, non-Hispanic, compared to only 58 percent of working-age adults and 52 percent of children (see Figure 2). The growing elderly population of the predominantly white (non-Hispanic) baby-boom generation will increasingly depend for its economic support during retirement on the productive activities and the civic participation (i.e., voting) of working-age adults who are members of racial and ethnic minorities, many of whom lived in immigrant families as children. Consequently, research and public policy addressing education, the labor force, and health should in-

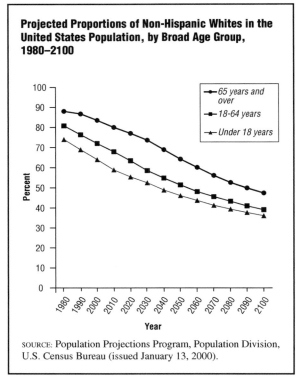

FIGURE 2

Projected Proportions of Non-Hispanic Whites in the United States Population, by Broad Age Group, 1980–2100

SOURCE: Population Projections Program, Population Division, U.S. Census Bureau (issued January 13, 2000).

creasingly attend to the circumstances of racial and ethnic minorities.

To what extent will members of various racial and ethnic minorities, including immigrants and their children, experience economic advance or constitute a permanent underclass during the coming decades? Four major scenarios (pluralist, structural, segmented assimilation, and traditional assimilation) provide different answers to this question. Taken together, these scenarios suggest that the outcomes experienced by racial and ethnic minorities, both as individuals and as groups, will depend on external factors, such as racial and ethnic stratification and discrimination, the availability of economic opportunities, and residential and educational segregation; as well as factors intrinsic to the group, such as the group's human and financial capital, cultural patterns of social relations, and community organization and infrastructure.

Will various racial and ethnic minorities of the twenty-first century experience the improved life chances associated with assimilation that benefited generations of white (non-Hispanic) groups during the twentieth century as the boundaries between these groups and the mainstream blurred? Or will the racial and ethnic minorities of the twenty-first century experience severely constrained opportunities and deprived circumstances similar to those that confronted many American Indians, blacks, and Hispanics throughout the twentieth century? The social, economic, and political future of the United States will be profoundly shaped by the answers to these questions.

See also: *African-American Population History; Census; Chinese, Overseas; Ethnic and National Groups; Immigration Trends; Residential Segregation.*

BIBLIOGRAPHY

Bennett, Claudette. 2000. "Racial Categories Used in the Decennial Censuses, 1790 to the Present." *Government Information Quarterly* 17: 161–180.

Goldstein, Joshua R., and Ann J. Morning. 2000. "The Multiple-Race Population of the United States: Issues and Estimates." *Proceedings of the National Academy of Sciences* 97: 6,230–6,235.

Harrison, Roderick J., and Claudette E. Bennett. 1995. "Racial and Ethnic Diversity." In *State of the Union: America in the 1990s,* vol. 2: *Social Trends,* ed. Reynolds Farley. New York: Russell Sage Foundation.

Heer, David. 1996. *Immigration in America's Future: Social Science Findings and the Policy Debate.* Boulder, CO: Westview Press.

Hernandez, Donald J., and Evan Charney, eds. 1998. *From Generation to Generation: The Health and Well-Being of Children in Immigrant Families.* Washington, D.C.: National Academy Press.

Hernandez, Donald J., and Katherine Darke. 1999. "Socioeconomic and Demographic Risk Factors and Resources among Children in Immigrant and Native-Born Families: 1910, 1960, and 1990." In *Children of Immigrants: Health, Adjustment, and Public Assistance,* ed. Donald J. Hernandez. Washington, D.C.: National Academy Press.

Lieberson, Stanley, and Mary C. Waters. 1988. *From Many Strands: Ethnic and Racial Groups in Contemporary America.* New York: Russell Sage Foundation.

U.S. Bureau of the Census. 1975. *Historical Statistics of the United States, Colonial Times to 1970,* bicentennial edition. Washington, D.C.: U.S. Government Printing Office.

———. 2000. *DP-1 Profile of General Demographic Characteristics: 2000 Data Set,* Census 2000 Summary File. Washington, D.C.: U.S. Government Printing Office.

Zhou, Min. 1997. "Growing Up American: The Challenge Confronting Immigrant Children and Children of Immigrants." *Annual Review of Sociology* 23: 63–95.

INTERNET RESOURCES.

Gibson, Campbell J. 1999. "Historical Census Statistics on the Foreign-born Population of the United States: 1850–1990, Population Division Working Paper no. 29." Washington, D.C.: U.S. Bureau of the Census. <http://www.census.gov/population>.

Yax, Laura K. 2000. "1980–2100 Projections." Washington, D.C.: U.S. Bureau of the Census. <http://www.census.gov>.

DONALD J. HERNANDEZ

RATZEL, FRIEDRICH

See *Lebensraum*

REFUGEES, DEMOGRAPHY OF

According to the 1951 Convention Relating to the Status of Refugees and its 1967 Protocol, a refugee is a person who has:

> a well-founded fear of persecution for reasons of race, religion, nationality, membership [in] a particular social group or political opinion, is outside the country of his nationality and is unable or, owing to such fear, is unwilling to avail himself of the protection of that country; or who, not having a nationality and being outside the country of his former habitual residence as a result of such events, is unable or, owing to such events, unwilling to return to it.

Most refugees flee in large groups to neighboring countries, where they often live in crowded refugee camps. Refugee-receiving states that are party to the convention are obliged to provide protection to refugees until they can safely return to their country of origin, integrate into the host society, or be resettled elsewhere.

Asylum seekers are people who have fled their countries of nationality and are seeking protection and immunity from forcible return by the government of the country in which they request asylum. Put differently, asylum seekers are, for the most part, refugees who are requesting that the authorities of a state grant them the legal status, and rights, of refugees according to the convention. Asylum seekers present themselves individually or as a family group to the relevant national authorities after arrival at the border or on the national territory. Every state has a slightly different application and recognition process, though in general receiving countries require asylum seekers to prove that they have a well-founded fear of persecution in their country of origin, in line with the definition set out above. If the asylum seekers' claims are accepted, they are granted refugee status and all the associated protections under national and international law. If a claim is not accepted, the asylum seeker is either subject to deportation or granted some form of "complementary protection" (where such status exists) allowing legal residence for "humanitarian reasons." Such protection is usually given for a limited period of time and does not grant the full range of rights and protections of "convention" status.

This article outlines the basic demography of refugees and asylum seekers worldwide since the end of World War II. It provides estimates of total numbers and briefly discusses major causation factors and policy changes affecting and resulting from refugee flows.

The 1950s

Immediately following World War II and the communist takeover of Eastern Europe, there were approximately 2.2 million refugees and stateless persons in Europe. These persons were mainly Jews, Roma, and other peoples uprooted during the war or fleeing political or religious persecution. Owing to the nature of the threats from which they fled, these refugees were largely unable and unwilling to return home even after the war had ended or after the Iron Curtain had solidified. In response, in 1950 the Office of the United Nations High Commissioner for Refugees (UNHCR) was established. An inter-

national legal mechanism was also needed to deal with the long-term protection needs of refugees and to allow for interstate understanding of their position. That mechanism was the 1951 refugee convention, which specified that the obligations of signatories extended only to those who became refugees as a result of "events occurring in Europe before 1 January 1951."

The convention fulfilled its intended initial mandate, as most of these refugees were integrated into host societies or resettled in other countries, notably in the United States, Canada, and Australia, by 1960.

The 1960s

By the mid-1960s, however, it became clear that the time and geographical limitations of the refugee convention were no longer sufficient to deal with the issues presented by the "newer" refugees, the vast majority of whom were from countries outside of Europe, particularly developing countries, and who were fleeing persecution for reasons unassociated with World War II. (An exception was the exodus from Hungary of some 200,000 refugees after the defeat of the 1956 uprising and a steady trickle of refugees from East to West Germany. Both resulted in speedy resettlement and integration of the refugees in the receiving Western countries.) By around 1970, there were nearly 1 million refugees fleeing wars of independence and postcolonial civil wars in countries such as Sudan, Ethiopia, Mozambique, Angola, Guinea-Bissau, India, and Pakistan. Therefore a protocol was added to the convention in 1967, removing the time reference and, except for those states that opted to keep them, the geographical specifications of the original convention. Additionally, the worldwide scope of refugee protection was broadened in 1969 by the Convention Governing the Specific Aspects of Refugee Problems in Africa (also called the OAU [Organization of African Unity] Convention), which noted that the increasing numbers of refugees in Africa necessitated that African states not only adhere to the refugee convention and its protocol but also develop common standards for refugee treatment. Additionally, the OAU Convention expanded the definition of a refugee to include:

> every person who, owing to external aggression, occupation, foreign domination or events seriously disturbing public order in either part or the whole of his country of

origin, is compelled to leave his place of habitual residence in order to seek refuge in another place outside his country of origin or nationality.

Together, the protocol and the OAU Convention increased the number of persons considered refugees as they expanded the geographical scope of areas of concern (beyond Europe) as well as the reasons predicating the granting of refugee status (beyond World War II).

The 1970s and 1980s

Three major refugee crises took place between the signing of the 1967 protocol and the end of the Cold War. The first involved the Vietnamese "boat people" who fled their country after the break-up of South Vietnam in 1975. Due largely to their mode of transport as well as direct American involvement in the crisis, the boat people, unlike other, less visible, refugee streams, attracted significant international attention. Beginning in 1975, almost 850,000 people would eventually flee Vietnam claiming political, religious, or ethnic persecution (though by the late 1980s it was clear that many new boat people were in fact economic migrants rather than refugees). Of this total, 250,000 fled to Malaysia, 210,000 to Hong Kong, and 160,000 to Thailand. The Philippines and Brunei also received large numbers. As most of these countries of first asylum were themselves relatively poor countries with their own social tensions, they were unwilling to permanently resettle such large numbers of refugees. As a result, they successfully lobbied the international community, particularly the United States and Australia, to resettle the majority of Vietnamese who had sought refuge on their shores. Between 1975 and 1991, nearly half a million Vietnamese were permanently resettled in industrialized countries.

For various reasons, refugees fleeing Afghanistan after the Soviet invasion of that country in 1979 drew much less international attention than the boat people, and they in fact remained the world's single largest refugee problem 23 years later. Between 1979 and 2002, an estimated one in four Afghans became a refugee. The Afghan refugee emergency had two major peaks, the first between 1988 and 1991, when there were 3.5 million Afghan refugees in Pakistan, 2 million in Iran, and nearly 1 million more in other areas of the world. The crisis subsided for a short while in the early 1990s as many Afghans returned

home after the break-up of the Soviet Union, but the civil war that flared up shortly thereafter caused another mass exodus, totaling approximately 5 million refugees by early 2000.

The third major refugee crisis of the 1980s occurred in Central America as a result of the various wars and political conflicts in Nicaragua, Guatemala, and El Salvador. Though such conflicts did not produce the same numbers of refugees as Vietnam and Afghanistan, they resulted in the creation in 1984 of the Cartagena Declaration on Refugees. Like the OAU Convention of 1969, this nonbinding declaration also expanded the refugee definition, in this case to better suit the nature of refugee problems in Central America, stating that:

> it is necessary to consider enlarging the concept of a refugee . . . the definition or concept . . . to be recommended for use in the region is one which, in addition to containing the elements of the 1951 Convention and the 1967 Protocol, includes among refugees those persons who have fled their country because their lives, safety or freedom have been threatened by generalized violence, foreign aggression, internal conflicts, massive violation of human rights or other circumstances which have seriously disturbed public order.

Post–Cold War Era

The end of the Cold War marked the beginning of "modern" refugee crises as many, mostly developing, countries found themselves embroiled in often violent conflicts after they lost the support of their superpower backer. Most of these conflicts were internal and created huge new (or increased, in the case of Angola and Afghanistan) refugee movements in countries such as Liberia, Bulgaria, and Romania. Other massive refugee crises occurred throughout the 1990s in locations as geographically diverse as Sudan, the Democratic Republic of the Congo (then Zaire), Rwanda, Burundi, Iraq, Indonesia, Ethiopia, Eritrea, and the former Yugoslavia (see Table 1). Further, the political incentive for many Western states to accept refugees was greatly reduced by the end of the Cold War, and it consequently became difficult for many of these states to adjust their policies to accept refugees and asylum seekers in whom they had a less clearly defined political interest. An increase in economic migration from several of the

TABLE 1

Major Refugee Populations and Host Countries, c. 2001

Country of Origin	Main Countries of Asylum	Number of Refugees (thousands)
Afghanistan	Pakistan, Iran	3,580
Burundi	Tanzania	568
Iraq	Iran	512
Sudan	Uganda, Democratic Republic of the Congo, Ethiopia, Kenya, Central African Republic, Chad	490
Bosnia–Herzegovina	Yugoslavia, Croatia, United States, Sweden, Netherlands, Denmark	478
Somalia	Kenya, Ethiopia, Yemen, Djibouti	448
Angola	Zambia, Democratic Republic of the Congo, Namibia	433
Sierra Leone	Guinea, Liberia	401
Eritrea	Sudan	376
Vietnam	China, United States	370

SOURCE: UNHCR, "Refugees by Numbers" (2001).

same countries and regions led many citizens and government officials in receiving countries to question the motives of asylum seekers and therefore be less willing to grant protected status under the terms of the refugee convention. This attitude was perhaps most clearly illustrated by the response of western European states to the Balkan crises of the 1990s. Rather than accepting Bosnian and Kosovar refugees (*prima facie*) as a predetermined group or even allowing them to submit asylum applications, most receiving states granted them only temporary protection, determined that they would be repatriated as soon as conditions in the country of origin allowed.

This combination of larger numbers of refugees and asylum seekers and less willingness on the part of states to accept them has led many to question the continuing effectiveness of the refugee convention. Statistical estimates on the size of refugee and asylum flows between 1980 and 2000 shown in Table 2 suggest the magnitude of the refugee problem and the pressures on the international refugee protection system at the dawn of the twenty-first century.

Refugees in Developing Countries

The vast majority (approximately 95%) of all refugees flee developing countries to seek protection in other developing countries nearby. Thus it is states such as Pakistan—which has hosted the largest refugee population of any country in the world for over a decade—as well as Iran, Jordan, Tanzania, Sudan,

Kenya, India, and many more developing countries as well as the Israel-occupied Palestine territories that bear the brunt of the increased refugee populations, even though such states have limited resources with which to support their new guests who, in turn, often suffer severe and prolonged deprivations materially and by criteria of human rights and dignity. For the most part, countries receive refugees because of geographic proximity and/or cultural and religious ties—for example, most Afghan refugees flee to Pakistan or Iran and most Burundians to Tanzania. Pressures on the receiving states are great, as many struggle to support their native populations and must rely on the international community—mainly through the UNHCR and other governmental or voluntary organizations—to help care for the refugee populations.

Asylum Seekers in Industrialized Countries

Industrialized countries have also seen increases in the number of people seeking protection, most of whom arrive under their own power as asylum seekers rather than as refugees resettled through predetermined government-sponsored programs. Overwhelmed bureaucracies in most industrialized receiving countries were unable to keep up with the increased flow of asylum seekers during the 1990s, often taking so long to process applications that asylum seekers became de facto residents. As a result, many citizens of these host countries came to regard the asylum process as just another form of economic migration. Public frustration with what is often perceived as a "flood" of "bogus" asylum seekers has been the driving factor behind many of the reforms that have been adopted or advocated in countries of asylum since the mid-1990s. In the United States, these reforms entailed delinking the asylum application process from the immediate receipt of a work permit and increasing the numbers of staff assigned to processing asylum-seeking applications. In Europe, however, the changes have meant that fewer and fewer applicants are actually granted—or even allowed to apply for—asylum. Instead, applicants are given some form of temporary protection and may remain in an uncertain legal status for prolonged periods.

Refugees and Displaced Persons in 2001

At the beginning of 2001, nearly 22 million people —approximately 80 percent of whom are women and children; 50 percent of whom are children and adolescents—were classified as "persons of concern" by the UNHCR; roughly one out of every 275 people on Earth. The majority of these people were refugees, asylum seekers, or part of the rapidly growing number of "internally displaced persons" (IDPs). IDPs are people who, much like refugees, have fled their homes because of conflict or persecution. Unlike refugees, however, IDPs have not crossed an international border and therefore do not fall within the scope of the refugee convention. Because of their growing numbers as well as their lack of protection under a single international instrument, IDPs are of increasing concern to many within the refugee protection field, and debate continues as to which international organizations are best equipped and mandated to deal with their particular needs. The largest populations of internally displaced persons are found in Sudan (approximately 4 million in 2001), Colombia (over 2 million in 2001), and Afghanistan (from 750,000 to 1.5 million immediately following the U.S.-led campaign to oust the Taliban regime in 2001–2002).

See also: *Asylum, Right of; Ethnic Cleansing; Forced Migration; Immigration, Unauthorized; Resettlement.*

BIBLIOGRAPHY

Ager, Alistair, ed. 1999. *Refugees: Perspectives on the Experience of Forced Migration.* London: Continuum.

Loescher, Gil. 2001. *The UNHCR and World Politics: A Perilous Path.* New York: Oxford University Press.

Loescher, Gil, and Laila Monohan, eds. 1989. *Refugees and International Relations.* Oxford: Clarendon Press.

Nicholson, Frances, and Patrick Twomey, eds. 1999. *Refugee Rights and Realities: Evolving International Concepts and Regimes.* Cambridge, Eng.: Cambridge University Press.

United Nations. Treaty Series. 1954. "The 1951 Convention Relating to the Status of Refugees." July 28, 1951. *Treaties and International Agreements Registered or Filed or Reported with the Secretariat of the United Nations* 189(2,545).

———. 1969."Convention Governing the Specific Aspects of Refugee Problems in Africa." September 10, 1969. *Treaties and International Agreements Registered or Filed or Reported with the Secretariat of the United Nations* 1001 (14691).

United Nations High Commission for Refugees. 2001. *Asylum Applications in Industrialized Countries, 1980–1999.* Geneva, Switzerland: UNHCR, Population Data Unit.

———. 2001. *Global Report 2000: Achievements and Impact.* Geneva, Switzerland: ATAR Rotopresse.

———. 2001. *The 1951 Refugee Convention: Questions and Answers.* Geneva, Switzerland: UNHCR, Public Information Section.

———. 2001. "Refugees by Numbers, 2001." Geneva, Switzerland: UNHCR, Statistics Division.

———. 2001. "2000 Global Refugee Trends: Analysis of the 2000 Provisional UNHCR Population Statistics." Geneva, Switzerland: UNHCR, Population Data Unit.

U.S. Committee for Refugees. 2001. *World Refugee Survey 2001.* Washington, D.C.: Immigration and Refugee Services of America.

TABLE 2

Asylum Applications in Europe, North America, Australia, New Zealand and Japan, 1980–2000		
Year	Total (thousands) (37 countries)	European Union	North America
1980	180	149	28
1981	199	130	65
1982	140	93	38
1983	115	71	35
1984	160	98	35
1985	203	157	30
1986	247	190	45
1987	254	167	64
1988	353	215	109
1989	439	283	122
1990	573	402	110
1991	661	492	89
1992	856	674	142
1993	769	550	164
1994	515	302	168
1995	529	308	181
1996	465	260	154
1997	530	291	178
1998	577	340	140
1999	652	414	121
2000	569	390	102

SOURCE: UNHCR Statistic Division (2001).

INTERNET RESOURCES.

"Cartagena Declaration on Refugees." November 22, 1984. <http://pbosnia.kentlaw.edu/services/chicago/legal_aid/treaties/cartagena.htm>.

Women's Commission for Refugee Women and Children. <http://www.womenscommission.org/wc_factsheet.pdf>.

ERIN PATRICK

REGISTRATION, POPULATION

See *Population Registers; Vital Statistics*

RELIGIONS, POPULATION DOCTRINES OF

The questions about religious doctrine of interest in the field of population studies have usually been those referring to its effects on reproductive behavior. Two kinds of effects have been studied: the direct effects of doctrines about reproductive behavior itself, and the indirect effects on this behavior of doctrines that concern the status of women. This essay reviews doctrines of both kinds in the five religions that together represent the dominant religious affiliations in countries containing over two-thirds of the world's population. These religions are Judaism, Christianity, Islam, Hinduism, and Buddhism. The first section presents a summary of each religion's doctrine on sexual and reproductive behavior. In each case, this is the version believed to represent the official or conventional doctrine. Often of course this may have little in common with the doctrine understood by lay adherents and even less with their conduct. Each description is preceded by an outline of the origin of the religion and of the core beliefs regarded by those who espouse them as legitimating its doctrines. In subsequent sections, the views of sociologists on the social functions of the doctrines are described.

Doctrines

Introducing an encyclopedia of the world's religions, R. C. Zaehner divides them into two main traditions. *Western* religions—Judaism, Christianity, and Islam—are those that were born in the Near East and owe their origin, directly or indirectly, to the Jews. *Eastern* religions—largely Hinduism and Buddhism—are those that either originated in India or have been profoundly influenced by Indian thought. Zaehner notes the profound difference in content between the two traditions. Each of the Western religions claims that it is a direct revelation of the one true God to humans, that he created the world, that his sovereignty is absolute and his will must be obeyed, that life on this earth is a preparation for an immortal life to come, and that the nature of that life will be determined by God's judgment of the individual's conduct during the life on earth. In contrast, salvation in the Eastern tradition means escape, by one's own efforts or with the grace of a God, from the process of reincarnation. The dominant preoccupation is not with duty to God, but with the deliverance of the immortal soul from the bondage of the body. Given the immense differences between these two worldviews, notable differences might be expected in their doctrines on sexual and reproductive behavior. In the event, it is the similarities that are more striking.

Judaism

Judaism is the religion of Jewish believers in Israel and throughout the world. It also played a formative role in the early history of Christianity and Islam. According to traditional belief, God revealed himself to the ancestors of the people of Israel three and a half millennia ago, using the prophet and leader Moses to communicate teaching and commands that became embodied in the Hebrew bible. Over the centuries, biblical teaching has been interpreted and supplemented by rabbis—Judaism's teachers and scholars—and they continue to be the source of guidance on conduct that will conform to God's will. The diverse and changing circumstances that Jews have encountered, especially since the late-eighteenth century, have led to the creation of separate movements within Judaism that differ in what they will accept as an interpretation of divine will.

The Hebrew Bible idealized a patriarchal and pronatalist model of the family, and this ethos is evident in the contemporary doctrines of orthodox Judaism. It is a religious duty for men (but not women) to marry. The man also bears responsibility for procreation. The couple is expected to have at least one child of each sex, in conformity with the biblical injunction to "be fruitful and multiply."

Premarital sex is forbidden. Adultery is forbidden. Divorce is permitted but requires the husband's consent if sought by a woman. Abortion is permitted to save the life of the mother, but there is contention about other possible justifications; life is considered to begin at birth. Contraception is permitted if the motive is acceptable and if the method (unless used for medical reasons) does not impede full sexual union. On all these issues, non-orthodox movements within Judaism are more permissive than the orthodox and more likely to leave decisions to the individual.

Christianity

Christianity had its origin in a Jewish movement that emerged after the death around 30 C.E. of the Jewish preacher Jesus of Nazareth, later known as Jesus Christ or simply Christ ("Messiah") and believed by Christians to be an incarnation of God. The religious doctrines are based on accounts of the life of Christ written by disciples after his death and forming the core of the New Testament which, with the Old Testament (essentially the Hebrew Bible), became the authorized scripture of Christianity. According to traditional Christian doctrine, the way of securing salvation from the consequences of sin and ensuring that death will be followed by eternal life in paradise is to accept God's grace and to follow the teaching and example of Christ. Essentially this requires the adoption of a way of life dominated by love of God and obedience to his will, and by love of one's fellow human beings. In the early twenty-first century, the main institutions of Christianity—inheritors of the disciples' function of propagating Christ's teaching—are the Roman Catholic Church, the Eastern Orthodox Church, and a large number of Protestant churches.

In most respects, Christianity's early teaching on sexual and reproductive behavior, which was based on the Old and New Testaments, reiterated the traditions of Judaism, though with divorce and remarriage after divorce added to the forms of conduct that were condemned, and with celibacy newly valued as a way of expressing a special devotion to God. Early Christian teaching continues to be endorsed to this day by the Roman Catholic Church. A valid marriage is a divinely established institution and is indissoluble. It is written within marriage that conjugal love achieves its divine purposes, that of uniting the couple and endowing them with children. Premarital sex and adultery are prohibited.

Abortion at any time is prohibited because life is believed to begin at conception. Any act, including sterilization, specifically intended to prevent procreation is prohibited. Periodically these doctrines have been elaborated by holders of the office of Pope, in whom the ultimate authority of the Roman Catholic Church is vested. For example, in his 1968 encyclical *Humanae Vitae*, which was widely greeted with dismay, Pope Paul VI stressed ". . . an act of mutual love which impairs the capacity to transmit life . . . frustrates His [God's] design which contradicts the norm of marriage, and contradicts the will of the Author of life." In an apparent concession to changing times, and one regarded within and outside the Church as a major innovation, couples with acceptable motives for wanting to avoid conception have increasingly been encouraged to restrict intercourse to the infertile period of the menstrual cycle. It is claimed that this method acknowledges the inseparable connection between the unitive and procreative purpose of intercourse, and enriches the couple's relationship by promoting dialogue, mutual respect, shared responsibility, and self control.

In the eleventh century, as a result of doctrinal differences and a refusal by the Eastern part of the church to accept that authority should be vested in a single head, the Eastern and Western parts separated and the former became the Eastern Orthodox Church. Like its Roman counterpart, the Eastern Church maintains a strong commitment to the ideas of the early Church. Great emphasis is placed on the importance of home and family. Sexual intercourse must be confined to marriage. Divorce and remarriage are allowed, but remarriage in church is possible only if church authorities have granted the divorce as well as the state. Abortion and permanent sterilization are condemned. Previously, contraception was also prohibited but the views coming to prevail are that the responsible use of contraception within marriage is acceptable, and that decisions on family size should be left to the individual couple, according to the guidance of their own consciences.

In the sixteenth century, a reform movement within Christianity led to the establishment of a Protestant branch of the religion that rejected the authority of the Roman Catholic Church and many of its beliefs and practices, though not its view that procreation was the principal purpose of marriage. Protestantism spawned many denominations, which differ among themselves and from Catholicism in their population-related and other doctrines. Until the 1930s, the doctrines of Protestantism about contraception had been as rigorous as those of the Roman Catholic Church. The break with tradition started with the Lambeth Conference of the Church of England in 1930, when the use of contraception was allowed if abstinence was not practicable. After another three decades, the 1958 conference rejected the primacy of procreation as the purpose of marriage and approved the use of contraception by methods "admissible to the Christian conscience." Similar changes have since occurred in the doctrines of other mainstream denominations. The Anglican and other denominations have also become more tolerant of divorce and remarriage. Some of the relaxations in doctrine, including those allowing the acceptability of abortion in some cases, have been vigorously opposed by the more conservative denominations.

Islam

Islam was founded by the prophet Muhammad (570–632 C.E.) who reported a series of revelations from God. Embodied in the Quran, these revelations, together with the collected accounts of the Prophet's life and teaching, are the principal source of the beliefs and practices of Muslims. According to the Quran, Muhammad was the last in a line of prophets (that included Moses and Jesus) who, like him, had received revelations from God and had been required to propagate them. As individuals and as a community, Muslims are required to submit to divine will, as revealed (with the help of Muslim scholars) in the Quran and accounts of the prophet's teaching.

Like Judaism and Christianity, Islam in its classical form endorses the biblical injunction to "be fruitful and multiply" and to do so only within marriage, an institution recommended to everyone able to afford it. Sexual intercourse outside marriage is forbidden. A husband may divorce his wife simply by declaration, though he is required to be considerate in his behavior toward her in the process. A wife may obtain divorce with the husband's agreement or by other procedures if he does not agree. Islam allows a man to have up to four wives, but only if he believes he can treat them equitably. Contemporary scholars stress that the teaching did not commend polygyny, but permitted it in some circumstances. It is thought to be a way of providing a husband for a woman who would otherwise be without one, including widows with children.

Birth control is not prohibited and the majority view among contemporary Muslim scholars is that the use of contraception is permissible with the wife's consent. Sterilization is seen as contrary to divine will, and is approved for medical reasons only. According to some scholars, abortion is permitted if it takes place before the fetus acquires a soul or to save the mother's life, but there is disagreement about the stage of fetal development at which ensoulment occurs. Others argue that, in the light of modern scientific knowledge about the early stage at which human life can be recognized in utero, abortion is always unacceptable unless carried out to save the mother's life or prevent the birth of a severely handicapped child.

Hinduism

Hinduism has no single founder and no orthodox version. Instead it comprises a family of related traditions and customs that have developed in the Indian subcontinent over a period of at least 3000 years. It encompasses a wide variety of beliefs and practices, has a vast store of sacred scriptures, and acknowledges numerous deities but (usually) one God as the creator and preserver of the universe. Some core beliefs are common to most versions of Hinduism. The most important is the conviction that all living things (human, animal, insect) have the same kind of soul—one that is destined, when the body dies, to be reborn in a different body. The particular form of the latter will depend on the individual's *karma,* the effect of good and bad deeds in the life that has ended and in previous lives. Accumulating merit by living dutifully increases the probability that the next life will be an improvement on the current one. The ultimate aim is liberation from the cycle of death and rebirth.

Like the religions of near-Eastern origin, Hinduism accords fundamental importance to the family and views it from a male-oriented perspective. Women are regarded as subordinate to men, though Hindu codes urge that women be treated with kindness and respect, especially if they are mothers. Premarital chastity for women is highly valued. Marriage is a sacred and, ideally, indissoluble relationship, but hallowed texts specify various circumstances in which wives may be replaced. Childbearing, especially the bearing of sons, has been accorded importance in the Hindu tradition from earliest times. Traditionally, failure to bear a son was a justification for the husband to take another wife. Because life is believed to begin at conception, abortion is not approved, though it may be permitted if the continuation of the pregnancy would put the mother's health at risk. Hinduism is permissive toward contraception and sterilization. Methods of avoiding conception were mentioned in its earliest texts.

Buddhism

Buddhism was founded in India in the sixth century B.C.E. by Siddhartha Gautama, who later became known as the Buddha ("enlightened one" or "awakened one"). According to the scriptural accounts, the prospective Buddha, like the philosophers of Hinduism, searched for a way of escaping the suffering that the endless cycle of death and rebirth imposed on humankind. Having eventually found it, he undertook to teach others how they too might find enlightenment. To this end he established a monastic order, the members of which continue to act as teachers and advisers to lay Buddhists.

According to the Buddha's teaching, life is permeated with suffering and this is caused by craving. The extinction of craving, and therefore of suffering, can be achieved by adopting a way of life that requires virtuous conduct, meditation, and finally the achievement of the transcendental wisdom necessary for liberation. The process takes numerous cycles of death and rebirth, but serenity and insight can eventually be achieved in a final lifetime, when the notion of the permanent self is seen for what it truly is—an illusion. Death is then followed by *nirvana,* a permanent state of transcendent liberation. Virtuous conduct entails not taking life, avoiding sexual misconduct, and developing ways of thought that will encourage selflessness and moral and compassionate behavior toward others.

It seems to be generally agreed by experts on its doctrines that Buddhism does not regard marriage and childbearing as sacred obligations. On the other hand, the encouragement to act virtuously and the concept of rebirth could help to sanctify the observance of whatever norms of family formation and reproductive behavior prevail in the Buddhist's own social setting. There is no doctrinal bar to contraception and sterilization, but there is contention about abortion. The most common view is that because life (the transmigration of consciousness) begins at conception, abortion entails killing, but other positions have been proposed.

The Social Functions of Religion

The sociology of religion is concerned with the social functions of religious belief and practice. One main tradition of enquiry has focused on the general significance of religion for society. The other main tradition has been concerned with the interaction between religious belief and actual social experience. Both traditions can illuminate the social significance of the doctrines described above.

The first of the traditions mentioned was established by the French sociologist Emile Durkheim (1858–1917). Writing at the end of the nineteenth century, he proposed that the latent function of religious worship in a society was to encourage veneration of society's institutions. In his classic and influential work, *The Elementary Forms of the Religious Life* (1912), he argues that a society necessarily and naturally generates a collective and sacred ideal of itself. This ideal is symbolized and sustained by religion, the doctrines of which express the nature of sacred things and of the relationships they sustain with each other and with profane things. From Durkheim's standpoint, the doctrines described above could be seen as epitomizing religion's function: encouraging veneration of marriage and procreation and a collective commitment to the social order. For him, falling birth rates and rising divorce rates—evidence of the weakening of domestic solidarity and therefore of social solidarity in general—reflected the social malaise that had befallen European societies in the process of their development.

Sociologists who have focused on the relationship between religion and the material conditions of life often have a different perspective on doctrine. In his treatment of the historical development of the family, Friedrich Engels (1820–1895) sees monogamous marriage as closely connected with the emergence of private property, and enforced by religion and law to secure the stable transmission of property between generations. In his study of the relationship between the development of capitalism and Protestant asceticism, Max Weber (1864–1920) emphasized its rigidly biblical view of the purpose of marriage. A contemporary sociologist, Bryan Turner, draws on these and other sources to argue that religion has been important historically for the distribution and control of property in society, and has had its effect by providing beliefs and institutions that support the control of children by parents and women by men. A similar view is taken by those who, on behalf of women, campaign against constraints on their autonomy and status and maintain that religious and related doctrines often serve the interests of men at the cost of women's control over their sexual and reproductive lives.

Procreation and the Sacred in Modern Societies

It is a commonly held view that, with the waning of attachment to traditional doctrines, religion has lost its social significance in modern societies. Against that view, Thomas Luckmann argues that all societies, including modern societies, necessarily generate sacred beliefs that have the social function of explaining the ultimate relevance of the social world and human conduct. From a similar standpoint it can be argued that, because the reproduction of the social world and its sacred beliefs depends on a continuing commitment to procreation, it is reasonable to expect procreation itself to be the subject of sacred beliefs. The form these take in modern societies may continue to owe something to traditional doctrine, but may be experienced primarily as collective reverence for parenthood as a feature of a particular and hallowed way of life.

See also: *Animal Rights; Euthanasia; Future Generations, Obligations to; Induced Abortion: Legal Aspects; Population Thought, History of; Reproductive Rights; Reproductive Technologies: Ethical Issues.*

BIBLIOGRAPHY

Berer, Marge, and T. K. Sundari Ravindran. 1996. "Fundamentalism, Women's Empowerment and Reproductive Rights." (Introduction to collection of articles on this subject). *Reproductive Health Matters* 8: 7–10.

Coward, Howard G., Julius J. Lipner, and Katherine K. Young. 1989. *Hindu Ethics: Purity, Abortion, and Euthanasia.* New York: State University of New York Press.

Dorff, Elliot, and Louis Newman, eds. 1995. *Contemporary Jewish Ethics and Morality: A Reader.* New York: Oxford University Press.

Durkheim, Emile. 1888. "Suicide et natalité: Etude de statistique morale." *Revue Philosophique* 26. Transl. H. L. Sutcliffe 1992: "Suicide and Fertility: A Study of Moral Statistics." *European Journal of Population* 8: 175–197.

Durkhem, Emile. 1912. Les formes élémentaires de la vie religieuse: le système totémique en Australie (Paris: Alcan). Trans. J. W. Swain 1915: *The Elementary Forms of the Religious Life.* London: Allen & Unwin.

Feldman, David M. 1968. *Birth Control in Jewish Law: Marital Relations, Contraception, and Abortion as Set Forth in the Classic Texts of Jewish Law.* New York: New York University Press. (Also in paperback as *Marital Relations, Birth Control, and Abortion in Jewish Law.* New York: Schocken Press.)

Hathout, Hassan. 1991. "Islamic Concepts and Bioethics." In *Theological Developments in Bioethics, 1988–1990,* ed. Baruch A. Brody and B. Andrew Lustig. *Bioethics Yearbook,* Vol. 1. Dordrecht: Kluwer Academic.

Luckmann, Thomas. 1967. *The Invisible Religion.* London: Macmillan.

Maguire, Daniel C. 2001. *Sacred Choices: The Right to Contraception and Abortion in Ten World Religions.* Minneapolis: Fortress Press.

Morgan, Peggy, and Clive Lawton, eds. 1996. *Ethical Issues in Six Religious Traditions.* Edinburgh: Edinburgh University Press.

Noonan, John T. 1986. *Contraception: A History of its Treatment by the Catholic Theologians and Canonists.* Enlarged edition. Cambridge, MA: Harvard University Press.

Omran, Abdel-Rahim. 1992. *Family Planning in the Legacy of Islam.* London: Routledge.

Pope Paul VI. 1970. *On Human Life: Encyclical Letter—Humanae Vitae.* 1968. London: Catholic Truth Society.

Reich, W. T., ed. 1995. *Encyclopedia of Bioethics.* rev. edition. New York: Simon and Schuster Macmillan.

Simons, John. 1999. "The Cultural Significance of Western Fertility Trends in the 1980s." In *Dynamics of Values in Fertility Change,* ed. R. Leete. Oxford: Oxford University Press.

Smith, Janet E. 1991. *Humanae Vitae: A Generation Later.* Washington, D.C.: Catholic University of America Press.

Turner, Bryan S. 1991. *Religion and Social Theory.* 2nd edition. London: Sage.

Ware, Timothy. 1997. *The Orthodox Church.* New York: Penguin.

Zaehner, R. C. 1977. "Introduction." In *The Concise Encyclopedia of Living Faiths,* ed. R. C. Zaehner. London: Hutchinson.

Zaehner, R.C., ed. 2001. *Hutchinson Encyclopedia of Living Faiths.* Oxford: Helicon.

INTERNET RESOURCES.

Hughes, James J., and Damien Keown. 1995. "Buddhism and Medical Ethics: A Bibliographic Introduction." *Journal of Buddhist Ethics* 2: 105–124. <http://jbe.gold.ac.uk>.

Pope Paul VI. 1968. *Humanae Vitae.* Rome: The Vatican. Available at <http://www.vatican.va>.

JOHN SIMONS

RELIGIOUS AFFILIATION

There are estimated to be some 10,000 distinct and separate religions in the early twenty-first century. Information on the size and characteristics of their membership can be drawn from the various religious authorities themselves and from government data.

The Religion Megacensus

Major efforts are put into the collection of statistics by individual religious bodies. For example, Christian denominations periodically undertake a decentralized and largely uncoordinated global census of their members. The most extensive of these inquiries is conducted by the Roman Catholic Church, whose bishops are required annually to submit a detailed statistical report on their work. The entire data collecting operation, performed to some degree by all religious bodies, has been termed the religion megacensus.

Government Censuses

Since the twelfth century, the world's governments also have collected information on religious populations and practice. A question related to religion is asked in the decennial population censuses of over 120 countries (not including the United States and a number of European countries). Before 1990, this number was slowly declining as developing countries began dropping the question because it was deemed too expensive, uninteresting, or sensitive. Subsequently, the trend appears to have reversed. Thus Britain—which produced the world's first national census of religious affiliation (the Compton Census, in 1676)—included a religion question in the census of 1851 but none thereafter, until it reintroduced the question in the 2000 census. The question was considered the best way to get reliable data on non-Christian minorities.

A Summary Global Table

These two approaches, the religion megacensus and government censuses with questions about religious affiliation, produce an enormous volume of data. Table 1 presents a compact global overview derived from these data, showing estimated number of adherents by major religion for 1900, 1970, and 2000.

Categories and Data Problems

The starting point in any analysis of religious affiliation is the United Nations 1948 *Universal Declaration of Human Rights,* Article 18: "Everyone has the right to freedom of thought, conscience and religion; this right includes freedom to change his religion or belief, and freedom, either alone or in community with others and in public or private, to manifest his religion or belief in teaching, practice, worship and observance." Since its promulgation, this group of phrases has been incorporated into the state constitutions of a large number of countries across the world and applied in census-taking practice. If a person states that he or she is a Christian (or Muslim, Hindu, Buddhist, etc.), then no one has a right to say he or she is not. Public declaration or profession must be taken seriously. The result should be a clear-cut assessment of religious profession.

Data on religious affiliation obtained from government censuses can be strikingly different from those collected by the religious bodies themselves. For example, in Egypt, where the great majority of the population is Muslim, in government censuses every 10 years for the last 100 years some 6 percent of the population are reported to be Christians. However, based on church censuses the number of Christians affiliated to churches in Egypt amounts to 15 percent of the population. The main reason for this discrepancy appears to be a misclassification of Christians as Muslims in the government census, perhaps through pressure on the Christian minority.

TABLE 1

Adherents of the World's Major Religions, 1900, 1970 and 2000 (Estimated Numbers and Percentage of World Population)

Religion	1900 Number (million)	%	1970 Number (million)	%	2000 Number (million)	%
Christians	558	34	1236	34	2000	33
Muslims	200	12	553	15	1188	20
Hindus	203	13	463	13	811	13
Chinese folk-religionists	380	24	231	6	385	6
Buddhists	127	8	233	6	360	6
Ethnoreligionists	118	7	160	4	228	4
New-Religionists	6	–	78	2	102	2
Sikhs	3	–	11	–	23	–
Jews	12	1	15	–	14	–
Spiritists	–	–	5	–	12	–
Baha'ís	–	–	3	–	7	–
Confucionists	1	–	5	–	6	–
Other religions	9	1	9	–	14	–
Doubly-counted religionists	–	–	−4	–	−14	–
Nonreligious/atheists	3	–	697	19	918	15
Total	1620	100	3696	100	6055	100

Note: – = less than 0.5 million or less than 0.5%

SOURCE: Barrett and Johnson (2001), p. 384.

Changes in Affiliation

Changes in total numbers of persons by religious affiliation result from the combination of three factors: (1) births and deaths—that is, natural increase; (2) conversion and defection; and (3) population movement.

Natural increase. The primary mechanism of change in religious affiliation globally is births and deaths. Children are usually counted as being of the religion of their parents (this is the law in Norway, among other countries). The change over time in any given community is most simply expressed as the number of births into the community minus the number of deaths. Many religious communities around the world experience little else in the dynamics of their growth or decline.

Conversion and defection. Nonetheless, it frequently happens that individuals (or even whole villages or communities) change allegiance from one religion to another (or to no religion at all). In the twentieth century, this change has been most pronounced in two general areas: (1) Tribal religionists, more precisely termed ethnoreligionists, have converted in large numbers to Christianity, Islam, Hinduism, and Buddhism; and (2) Christians in the Western world have defected in large numbers to become nonreligious (agnostics) or atheists. Both of these trends, however, had slowed considerably by the dawn of the twenty-first century.

Population movement. At the country level, it is equally important to consider the movement of people across national borders. From the standpoint of religious affiliation, migration can have a profound impact. In the colonial era in the nineteenth century, small groups of Europeans settled in Africa, Asia, and the Americas. In the late-twentieth century, people from these regions migrated to the Western world. Thus, in the United States, religions such as Islam, Hinduism, and Buddhism are growing faster than either Christianity or the nonreligious and atheists. This growth is almost entirely due to the immigration of Asians. In the Central Asian countries of the former Soviet Union, Christianity has declined significantly every year since 1990, due to the emigration of Russians, Germans, and Ukrainians.

Methodology Employed

Tables similar to Table 1 but giving more detailed categories, breakdowns of change over time, and projections for several decades ahead have been prepared for every country. These data tables and detailed descriptions of methodology—explaining how the formidable technicalities were resolved—can be found in *World Christian Trends, AD 30–AD 2200* (Barrett and Johnson, 2001) and *World Christian Encyclopedia* (Barrett, Kurian, and Johnson, 2001). The underlying demographic data incorporate the updates (every two years since 1950) of the United Nations population database for all countries from 1950 to 2050, and for some 100 variables each. A summary report on the religion megacensus has been published annually in *Encyclopaedia Britannica's Book of the Year* since 1987.

See also: *Ethnic and National Groups; Languages and Speech Communities.*

BIBLIOGRAPHY

Annuario Pontificio. Annual. Citta del Vaticano: Tipografia Poliglotta Vaticana.

Barrett, David B., and Todd M. Johnson. 2001. *World Christian Trends, AD 30–AD 2200: Interpreting the Annual Christian Megacensus.* Pasadena, CA: William Carey Library.

Barrett, David B., George T. Kurian, and Todd M. Johnson. 2001. *World Christian Encyclopedia: A Comparative Survey of Churches and Religions in the Modern World,* 2nd edition, 2 Vols. New York: Oxford University Press.

Eliade, Mircea, et al., eds. 1986. *The Encyclopedia of Religion.* New York: Macmillan.

Statistical Yearbook of the Church. Annual. Citta del Vaticano: Secretaria Status.

Todd M. Johnson
David B. Barrett

REMOTE SENSING

Information on characteristics of landscape and human settlement can be derived from aerial photography and satellite imagery. The technology and procedures involved are known as remote sensing.

Resolution and Bandwidth

The images produced by remote sensing can be classified by resolution and bandwidth. Resolution refers to the size of the image captured by the smallest pixel (picture element) in the image. The highest resolution data commercially available from satellite-based sensors as of around 2000 is one meter—that is, the smallest pixel in the image corresponds to an area of 1m by 1m on the ground. More detailed imagery typically requires the use of aerial photography. Bandwidth refers to the wavelengths recorded by the sensor. They may be panchromatic (producing black-and-white images) or specific to certain parts of the spectrum, such as visible red, green, blue, and near-infrared bands, or other (longer or shorter) bands that are not visible to the naked eye. If information is recorded for two or more wavelength bands, the image is described as multispectral.

Each of the various land cover categories on the earth's surface, whether natural or built, has a distinctive "spectral signature," the combination of wavelength values characteristic of that category of surface (such as bare soil, a specific type of vegetation, water, or an impervious surface like asphalt or concrete) but not of others. The aim in using remotely sensed data is to associate each pixel with a particular type of land cover. The higher the resolution (i.e., the smaller the pixel size), the more likely it is that the pixel will include only one type of land cover, and hence can be unambiguously categorized. The process of categorization is a crucial operation involving sophisticated statistical procedures, including new approaches drawing on "fuzzy" analysis.

Major producers of high resolution panchromatic and multispectral satellite imagery include the Landsat Thematic Mapper images and IKONOS (USA), Spot (France), Indian Remote Sensing (India), and Spin-2 (Russia). The Earth Observing-1 (EO-1) satellite launched by NASA in 2000 is capable of measuring 220 spectral bands at 30m resolution.

Remote Sensing in Demographic Analysis

For demographic analysis it is necessary to combine the data from remotely sensed images with local-level information from censuses, vital statistics, surveys, or administrative data. This is done within a geographic information system (GIS), which allows the matching of two or more sources of data for each small geographic area such as a census tract.

Remote sensing has been used in a variety of ways in demographic analysis, particularly for estimating population size and distribution, assessing the human impact on the natural environment, and examining characteristics of urban settlement.

A number of remotely sensed characteristics can be used to indicate the spatial distribution of population. The visible and near-infrared emissions of nighttime lights is one such indicator. A broader array of characteristics was drawn on in producing the LandScan Global Population 1998 Database developed by Oak Ridge National Laboratory, Tennessee. This database has a resolution of 30 arc seconds—approximately 1 km². Population data for larger geographic units come from ground-based sources, but the allocation over these 1 km cells is made on the basis of remotely detected characteristics of those cells: land cover, road proximity, slope, and nighttime lights.

Monitoring changes in the natural environment is one of the major uses of remote imagery. Such changes are often linked to expansion of human settlement and economic activity. The important case of deforestation in the Amazon region is explored by Tom Evans and Emilio Moran (2002) and Steven Walsh and Kelly Crews-Meyer (2002).

In urban applications, by use of a variety of indicators remote imaging allows the specification of gradations of "urbanness," avoiding the conventional urban-rural dichotomy. The ways in which remote sensing can be used in urban areas are summarized by Jean-Paul Donnay, Michael Barnsley, and Paul Longley (2001). A case study of Cairo is given by Tarek Rashed and colleagues (2001).

Remote sensing cannot reveal what people on the ground are doing. It offers only clues to that behavior, and proxies for variables such as the level of economic development or degree of urbanization that in turn may be predictors of that behavior. Its usefulness is as a tool that extends the spatial scope of social science analysis.

The value to demography of remotely sensed imagery depends not only on the quality and quantity of data that can be derived but also on the uses to which it can be put. To expand the latter requires further investigation of the connection between built and social environments and a better understanding of the spatial dimensions of human behavior. These are active areas of research. Advances in GIS techniques and applications will also promote greater use of remote sensing. It seems likely that remote sensing imagery will eventually be seen as a routine additional source of demographic information.

See also: *Geographic Information Systems; Geography, Population.*

BIBLIOGRAPHY

Donnay, Jean-Paul, Michael J. Barnsley, and Paul A. Longley. 2001. *Remote Sensing and Urban Analysis.* London: Taylor and Francis.

Entwisle, Barbara, Ronald R. Rindfuss, Stephan J. Walsh, Tom P. Evans, and Sara R. Curran. 1997. "Geographic Information Systems, Spatial Network Analysis, and Contraceptive Choice." *Demography* 34: 171–188.

Evans, Tom P., and Emilio F. Moran. 2002. "Spatial Integration of Social and Biophysical Factors Related to Landcover Change." In *Population and Environment: Methods of Analysis,* Supplement to *Population and Development Review,* Vol. 28, ed. Wolfgang Lutz, Alexia Prskawetz, and Warren C. Sanderson. New York: Population Council.

Jensen, John R., and Dave C. Cowen. 1999. "Remote Sensing of Urban/Suburban Infrastructure and Social-economic Attributes." *Photogrammetric Engineering and Remote Sensing* 65: 611–624.

Liverman, Diana, Emilio F. Moran, Ronald R. Rindfuss, and Paul C. Stern, eds. 1998. *People and Pixels: Linking Remote Sensing and Social Science.* Washington, D.C.: National Academy Press.

Rashed, Tarek, John R. Weeks, M. Saad Gadalla, and Allan G. Hill. 2001. "Revealing the Anatomy of Cities Through Spectral Mixture Analysis of Multispectral Imagery: A Case Study of the Greater Cairo Region, Egypt." *Geocarto International* 16: 5–16.

Sutton, Paul. 1997. "Modeling Population Density with Night-Time Satellite Imagery and GIS." *Computing, Environment and Urban Systems* 21: 227–244.

Walsh, Steven J., and Kelly Crews-Meyer, eds. 2002. *Linking People, Place, and Society.* Boston: Kluwer Academic Publishers.

Weeks, John R., M. Saad Gadalla, Tarek Rashed, James Stanforth, and Allan G. Hill. 2000. "Spatial Variability in Fertility in Menoufia, Egypt, Assessed Through the Application of Remote Sensing and GIS Technologies." *Environment and Planning* A32: 695–714.

INTERNET RESOURCE.

LandScan Global Population Database. Oak Ridge National Laboratory. 1998. <http://www.ornl. gov/gist/projects/LandScan/SIMPLE/ smaps.htm>.

JOHN R. WEEKS

RENEWAL THEORY AND THE STABLE POPULATION MODEL

Deaths deplete a population and births add new individuals, with the overall effect being a renewal of population numbers. A mathematical analysis of this process is called, accordingly, a theory of renewal. At its core, this theory is a bookkeeping scheme to describe changes in a population over time, a goal achieved by tracking the time course of births. Tracking births over time is the same as tracking every cohort, that is, every group of individuals born at the same time. Because the number of individuals of a given age in the population is just the cohort of that age, the theory also tracks the age composition of a population. Finally, the theory combines the age composition (the result of past births) with fertility rates by age to obtain current births, thereby completing the accounting process. As will be seen below, this theory provides a powerful tool for the analysis of population composition and change.

Population renewal theory has origins in the work of the Swiss mathematician Leonhard Euler (1707–1783) in 1760 and the German demographer Johann Peter Süssmilch (1707–1767) in 1761, but its modern form was largely developed by the American demographer and biometrician Alfred Lotka (1880–1949) between 1907 and 1913. Renewal theory has obvious relevance for any collection of things that are created in the manner of a birth and eliminated in the manner of a death, for example, a collection of machinery parts in a factory. A broader theory of renewal for such processes, not discussed here, has been developed for other applications.

Lotka's work provides the basic framework of mathematical demography and is the primary focus of this article. Many applications and extensions of his work have been made as the subject of demogra-phy has blossomed since the 1950s. Some of the more important elements of this newer work as it is used by demographers are summarized below.

Births, Cohorts, and Lotka's Equation

To track births, researchers record the rate at which new individuals are born into a population at each instant of time. They simplify by considering only female births, males being accounted for separately later. At a time denoted by t let the rate at which females are born be denoted by $B(t)$. As time advances these newborns will age, so the cohort of females aged a at time t consists of the survivors among the $B(t - a)$ individuals who were born at the earlier time $(t - a)$. Using the notation $l(a)$ to indicate the fraction of newborn females that survives from birth to age a, one sees that at time t there must be $l(a)$ $B(t - a)$ females aged a. This expression links past births to cohorts and thus to the age composition of the female population.

To obtain current births at time t researchers need the per-capita fertility rate, denoted by $m(a)$ and defined as the rate of female births to a mother at age a. Mothers aged a will together produce female births at a rate $m(a)$ $l(a)$ $B(t - a)$. The total birth rate $B(t)$ in the population is a sum of births to mothers of all ages. Using an integral to indicate the sum yields the first form of Lotka's equation for population renewal:

$$B(t) = \int_{15}^{45} m(a)l(a)\ B(t - a)da \qquad [1]$$

The limits on the integral here are the limits on the reproductive ages of mothers. For human populations, this would typically range from 15 to 45 years. An unfortunate aspect of equation [1] is that to obtain today's birth rate one must know the past birth rate going back at least as far as the oldest reproductive age. This is information researchers rarely have. Instead, in most situations one can specify only the age composition of the population at some starting time (which one labels as time $t = 0$) and would like to use the renewal argument to obtain birth rates $B(t)$ for all later times. Researchers deal with such cases by noting that at time t (after the starting time), births into the population are a sum of (1) births to individuals who were present before the starting time—call these $f(t)$; and (2) births to individuals who were born at or after the starting time.

The latter births must clearly follow from the argument that produced equation [1], so one can write:

$$B(t) = f(t) + \int_0^t m(a)l(a)\, B(t-a)da \qquad [2]$$

In this equation the limits on the integration indicate a sum of the individuals born after the starting time, which implies that the limits are 0 and t. A mathematical expression for $f(t)$ may be written out by applying to the initial population the logic that was used to derive equation [1].

Between the two forms given, Lotka's equation translates a population's past composition into its future. The equations above are written for female births: What about males? In most countries (with some striking exceptions) human births occur with a sex ratio of about 105 male births to 100 female births, and this ratio can be used to infer male births from female. In addition, if male survival rates are available, male cohorts can be tracked just as was shown above for female cohorts.

The Stable Population

Suppose that a population has for many generations followed the renewal process of births and deaths with some fixed schedule of age-specific birth and survival rates. It is reasonable to expect that the population as a whole, and the birth rate in particular, should then experience a steady rate of growth r per unit time. Such steady growth would imply that the birth rate $B(s)$ at some time s and the birth rate $B(s + t)$ at a later time $(s + t)$ would be in the ratio:

$$B(t + s) = B(s)\, e^{rt}$$

Such an exponential ratio of births at different times satisfies equation [1] only if the growth rate r satisfies what is called Lotka's *characteristic equation:*

$$1 = \int m(a)l(a)\, e^{-ra}\, da$$

This equation shows how age-specific fertility and survival determine the unique steady rate of population growth that these rates can support. Among the many important results that flow from this equation, two will be mentioned here. First, the equation im-plies that r will be positive (population increase) or negative (population decline) depending on whether the *net reproduction rate* (NRR), defined by NRR = $\int m(a)l(a)da$, is larger or smaller than one. An NRR equal to one characterizes and defines a population in which $r = 0$. This is called a stationary population. The characteristic equation for this case also defines what is commonly called *replacement fertility*. Second, in populations whose NRR is not far from one, an expansion of the exponential term in the equation yields the useful approximate result that:

$$r \approx \ln(\text{NRR}) / T,$$

in which the quantity T is the average age at childbearing of mothers. This result provides ready insight into the impact of changes in the level and timing of fertility, and of changes in survival rate, on the steady population growth rate.

When births over time grow at a steady rate r, if the total birth rate is $B(t)$ at time t, the population at the same time at any age a can be inferred to be $B(t)l(a)e^{-ra}$. Hence a population in a steady state growing at rate r will have an age composition in which the fraction of the population at age a is proportional to $l(a)e^{-ra}$. The age composition of such a population does not change over time and is known as the *stable population*. The stable population is basic to demographic analysis. It underlies the use and interpretation of population pyramids. For example, the well-known difference between the shapes of the pyramids for rapidly growing (broad-base) versus slowly growing (narrow-base) populations is attributable to the differences in growth rates and survival rates. In population analysis, the stable population provides a ready standard of comparison that yields insights into observed population structures that are rarely stable. (A mathematical note: This discussion glosses over the fact that $B(t)$ is a rate, not a number, and the stable structure as it is written above is a density. Correctly, the density should be integrated over an age interval, such as a calendar year, to obtain the number of individuals in that interval; but there is little danger of error, and greater clarity, in the exposition without introducing this refinement.)

Dynamics of Births

As was shown above, a fixed set of age-specific fertility and survival rates define a stable population. Suppose, however, that at a time $t = 0$ a population has an age composition that is not the stable one, but the fertility and survival rates still remain fixed. Lotka proved that over time the population's age composition will converge toward the stable composition—this is the reason for the adjective *stable*. The mathematical demonstration of this convergence starts with equation [2], in which an arbitrary initial age composition can be used to determine the term $f(t)$. Lotka showed that the birth rates $B(t)$ obtained by solving that equation have the form:

$$B(t) = B_0 e^{rt} + B_1 e^{r_1 t} \cos(\omega t) + B_2 e^{r_1 t} \sin(\omega t) + \textit{etc.}$$

In this series of terms, the first simply represents the stable population, with r being the stable growth rate (as can be seen by omitting all the other terms). The second and later terms (the "etc." in the equation stands for a possibly infinite sequence of similar terms) contain exponents such as r_1 and corresponding sinusoidal terms that are computed as additional solutions—called the *roots*—of the characteristic equation. These additional roots have the property that their exponential parts are smaller than the first exponential r, which implies that stable population dominates the solution as time increases. Each additional term has an oscillatory character indicated by the sine and cosine terms; the second and third terms above have a period of $(2\pi/\omega)$. These decaying cycles are transient aspects of the population that are observed en route to the stable population.

These cycles have real demographic consequence in populations that are far from stability. The many countries (e.g., Japan, China) that experienced rapid fertility declines in the second half of the twentieth century provide striking examples of this phenomenon. After the decline, fertility rates were relatively stable at their new low levels, but the population structure still reflected years of high pre-decline fertility and rapid growth. Age compositions in these populations in subsequent years clearly show Lotka's damped oscillations—they consist of population booms, busts, and echoes. The Lotka solution in this case is also the basis for Nathan Keyfitz's calculation of momentum—the effect on long-run numbers of a sudden transition to replacement fertility. The tendency of a population with fixed fertility and survival rates to gravitate to the stable population structure is an example of *demographic ergodicity*—the convergence of age composition to a stable structure whereby the history of a population's age structure is gradually obliterated by the process of population renewal.

Reproductive Value

The discussion thus far has largely ignored the population's starting age composition except as the term $f(t)$ in equation [2]. But the starting composition is surely relevant to the future population, which leads to the question: If a single female of age a is added to the population, what contribution does she make to the future population? That contribution can be specified by keeping count of her children, her grandchildren, and so on. The issue here is not the total number of these descendants, which might well be infinite if all future generations are counted; rather, the question is how the future contributions of a female depend on her age. In other words, what is the relative contribution to the future population made by females of different ages? This relative contribution was called *reproductive value* by the great statistician and geneticist R. A. Fisher (1890–1962), who introduced the notion in his work on the evolution of reproductive characteristics.

How is reproductive value, denoted by $V(a)$ at age a, to be determined? To make a sensible comparison between ages, the effect of population growth must be discounted and then the contributions made by the female at her current and future ages until death must be added. Doing so produces the expression:

$$V(a) = \left(1/l(a)\right) \int_a^{45} e^{-rx} m(x) l(x)\, dx,$$

with the limits on the integral running from current age a to the maximum reproductive age (45). The reproductive value plays a key role in population momentum, in evaluating the dynamics of a population subject to disturbance, and in evolutionary theory.

Applications of Lotka's Theory

The logic and mathematics of Lotka's theory underlie several methodological developments. The cohort-component method of projecting a population, first used by P. K. Whelpton and now in regular use by forecasters, is an expression of equation [2]. Although equation [2] applies only to populations that are closed to migration, it is easily modified to incorporate births gained or lost via migration. If the net migration flow is constant over time and exhibits some specified age pattern that is also constant over time, the stability properties of equation [2] apply with suitable modification to the equation that includes migration. Such modified equations are commonly used to project and analyze the dynamics of populations subject to significant migration flows.

The mathematical analysis outlined above treats time and age as continuous, hence the integrals. In practice, demographers must work with events observed over discrete intervals, such as one year or five years. The equations carry over fairly directly to the discrete case. For example, in equation [1], if $m(a)$ and $l(a)$ are the rates for a discrete interval with a length of one year, the equation remains the same except that a sum over discrete age intervals replaces the integral.

The tracking of cohorts in Lotka's analysis extends directly to cases in which the growth rate of births or other population segments changes with time and has made possible methods of demographic estimation for unstable populations as developed by Ansley J. Coale, Samuel H. Preston, and others. The characteristic equation highlights the central demographic importance of the age schedules of mortality and survival, which have therefore been the subject of considerable independent study. Coale, Paul Demeny, and James Trussell developed their model demographic schedules of mortality and fertility in the context of renewal theory. Numerous methods of direct and indirect demographic estimation originate in the logic and mathematics of Lotka's analysis.

Demographic Ergodicity and Time-Varying Rates

Perhaps the most obvious limitation of Lotka's equation is that the fertility and survival rates are taken as fixed and known. But derivation of the equation does not require the rates to be fixed: The equations remain valid with time-dependent birth and death rates. Solving them in such cases is harder because Lotka's analysis does not apply, but progress has been made on several fronts. A key feature of Lotka's theory is demographic ergodicity, and, as Álvaro López (1926–1972) first showed, ergodicity also holds for many situations in which rates vary over time. In other words, given a time-dependent sequence of fertility and survival rates, the process

of population renewal causes the population's age composition to converge toward a particular stable (but time-varying) composition. This phenomenon is called *weak demographic ergodicity* and has been shown to hold for many types of temporal change in the rates. Joel Cohen has shown that ergodicity holds for many kinds of random change over time in fertility and survival rates. Aside from this general property, progress has been made in finding some useful explicit solutions to Lotka's equation for time-varying rates, including work by Robert Schoen and Young Kim for cyclically changing rates and by Shripad Tuljapurkar and Nan Li for populations undergoing demographic transitions from old to new rates. The latter work is also the basis for calculations of population momentum when fertility or mortality transitions take place gradually over some years.

Sex and Marriage

Lotka's theory greatly simplifies the real-world situation by using fertility rates for females by age as a proxy for a more realistic accounting of marriage (and, in modern times, cohabitation or simply mating) as a precursor to reproduction. This simplification is serviceable and is surely correct in some aggregate average sense. But demographers have naturally been interested in adding an explicit accounting of marriage to the theory of population renewal. Efforts to do this have not yet been successful in producing what demographers call a *two-sex theory* of population renewal. Some useful work has been done in terms of defining the mathematical structure of a marriage function that translates male and female age compositions into an age composition of married couples. Robert Pollak has established stability properties for some particular forms of two-sex renewal. But a generally useful theory remains elusive. In addition, much of this two-sex theorizing makes little contact with the far more successful theory of the proximate determinants of fertility or of fecundability (the probability of conception). In recent years, this type of theory has attracted new interest among epidemiologists who analyze sexually transmitted diseases and are therefore concerned with tracking the rate of sexual interactions.

Feedback and Nonlinearity

The renewal theory discussed above assumes that fertility and mortality rates are exogenously determined (i.e., by factors such as economics or culture that are not explicitly included in the present analysis), even if they vary over time. Yet there are persuasive arguments that one or both of these rates may be at least partly determined by the state of the population itself. One such line of thought begins with the English economist T. R. Malthus (1766–1834) and continues through more recent and considerably more general arguments for the necessity of homeostasis—a self-regulatory force in human population growth. A different line of thought is exemplified by Richard Easterlin's work on the relationship between cohort size, expectations, and eventual cohort fertility. In either type of argument, a relationship is posited between fertility or mortality and the past time sequence of births; this is called a feedback relationship. If researchers introduce a feedback relationship into equation [2], for example, they make the equation *nonlinear* in the birth rates. A general analysis of the dynamics of such nonlinear equations poses many mathematical challenges. The goal of such an analysis is to produce understanding that parallels the understanding of Lotka's theory—to determine what sustained population trajectories can be maintained by particular types of nonlinearity. Intuitively, negative feedback, in which increasing birth rates act to depress future fertility rates, should lead to population cycles. Various studies show how feedback can maintain population cycles, but they unfortunately also suggest that it is hard to find good specifications of feedback that are consistent with observed population cycles. More complex types of feedback can generate interestingly complex, even chaotic, dynamics in nonlinear models, but the practical usefulness of this work for human demography remains uncertain.

See also: *Actuarial Analysis; Age Structure and Dependency; Coale, Ansley Johnson; Cycles, Population; Euler, Leonhard; Keyfitz, Nathan; Life Tables; Lotka, Alfred; Momentum of Population Growth; Multistate Demography; Projections and Forecasts, Population; Stochastic Population Theory; Süssmilch, Johann.*

BIBLIOGRAPHY

Caswell, Hal. 2001. *Matrix Population Models: Construction, Analysis, and Interpretation.* Sunderland, MA: Sinauer.

Coale, Ansley. 1972. *The Growth and Structure of Human Populations: A Mathematical Investigation.* Princeton, NJ: Princeton University Press.

Keyfitz, Nathan. 1968. *Introduction to the Mathematics of Population.* Reading, MA: Addison-Wesley.

Preston, Samuel H., Patrick Heuveline, and Michel Guillot. 2001. *Demography: Measuring and Modeling Population Processes.* Malden, MA: Blackwell.

Smith, David P., and Nathan Keyfitz. 1977. *Mathematical Demography: Selected Papers.* Berlin: Springer-Verlag.

Shripad Tuljapurkar

REPRODUCTIVE HEALTH

Reproductive health is a concept that came to prominence in international discourse about population issues in the 1990s, especially as a result of the preparatory process leading to the International Conference on Population and Development (ICPD) held in Cairo in 1994. It is defined in Chapter 7, paragraph 2 of the ICPD Programme of Action as follows:

> Reproductive health is a state of complete physical, mental and social well-being and not merely the absence of disease or infirmity, in all matters relating to the reproductive system and to its functions and processes. Reproductive health therefore implies that people are able to have a satisfying and safe sex life and that they have the capability to reproduce and the freedom to decide if, when and how often to do so. Implicit in this last condition are the right of men and women to be informed and to have access to safe, effective, affordable and acceptable methods of family planning of their choice, as well as other methods of their choice for regulation of fertility which are not against the law, and the right of access to appropriate health-care services that will enable women to go safely through pregnancy and childbirth and provide couples with the best chance of having a healthy infant. In line with the above definition of reproductive health, reproductive health care is defined

as the constellation of methods, techniques and services that contribute to reproductive health and well-being by preventing and solving reproductive health problems. It also includes sexual health, the purpose of which is the enhancement of life and personal relations, and not merely counseling and care related to reproduction and sexually transmitted diseases.

From Birth Control to Reproductive Health

The evolution of language referring to fertility policy since the 1950s, from "birth control" to "family planning" to "reproductive health," represents a paradigm shift in theory, policy, and practice. When concerns about the consequences of delayed fertility decline in the demographic transition in the developing world originally emerged, the major focus was on the economic implications of rapid population growth. Logically, this necessitated a better understanding of the factors influencing fertility and reproduction. For example, priority was placed on mapping and measuring the proximate determinants of fertility, and the socioeconomic characteristics of women that influence the proximate determinants. Interest in reproduction in general, and fertility regulation in particular, has gradually evolved into attention to reproductive health. A variety of actors, ranging from demographers to women's health advocates, worked together in the early l990s to propose this new, broader approach. They intended to promote population and development policies and programs that were centered on individual rights, health, and well-being.

The World Health Organization (WHO) defines health as a "state of complete physical, mental and social well-being." The ICPD applied this concept of health to reproduction. WHO promotes, and sets standards for, scientific analysis of reproductive health. Estimates of the "global burden of reproductive ill-health" clearly signal that that burden affects women more than men. (See Table 1) For women of childbearing age in developing countries, the burden of reproductive ill-health is far greater than the disease burden from such important diseases as tuberculosis and respiratory infections. Among women aged 15 to 44 in developing countries, reproductive ill-health is estimated to account for 36 percent of the total disease burden, compared with 12 percent for men.

As advocates of the concept emphasize, reproductive health services are not limited to family planning services, nor is their clientele limited to women in unions. Programs delivering family planning services could be organized as categorical programs; this is more difficult for reproductive health services, which require a broader array of facilities. Reproductive health is not solely a health issue. The concept includes such factors as gender-based violence, power dynamics in sexual relationships, and individuals' subjective assessment and perception of risks involved in contraceptive practice. As stated in a follow-up report on ICPD (ICPD+5), "There is a continuing need to include social, cultural, economic and behavioural dimensions in the planning and implementation of reproductive health policies and programmes. This requires the involvement of many other sectors in a partnership to remove barriers to access and create a more enabling environment" (United Nations Population Fund 1999, paragraph 65).

Reproductive Health Services

The programmatic implications of the goal of improving reproductive health, over and above the provision of contraceptive services, include prevention and treatment of reproductive tract infections, sexually transmitted diseases, including HIV, and reproductive system cancers; counseling or treatment of infertility; pregnancy and delivery care; access to safe, legal abortion; and information on sexuality and sexual dysfunction.

The concept of reproductive health provides a framework to guide program implementation strategies and performance indicators. It emphasizes quality of care for the individual, often neglected in older, target-oriented family planning programs. For example, a client-provider interaction concerned with choosing an appropriate contraceptive can be used for family planning counseling as traditionally practiced (mostly one-way, didactic communication from an authority figure to a passive acceptor about medical aspects of contraception), or it can involve true two-way dialogue, with the provider seeing the client as a partner in solving health problems. The latter model of reproductive health care includes exploring topics such as sexual practices and risks, as well as the gender and power dynamics that affect those risks.

TABLE 1

Selected Aspects of Reproductive Ill-Health: Estimates of Global Incidence (millions), 1990s

Category	Women	Men	Both Sexes
Maternal deaths (annual – 1995) (a)	0.515	–	0.515
Cases of severe maternal morbidity (annual) (b)	30	–	30
Unsafe abortions (annual) (b)	20	–	20
Adults living with HIV/AIDS (c)	17.6	19.6	37.2
Annual adult incidence of HIV infection (c)	1.8	2.5	4.3
Annual incidence of curable STIs (1999) (d)	174.7	164.8	339.5
Prevalence of female genital mutilation (b)	100-140	–	100-140
Percent infertile couples (e)	–	–	8-12%

SOURCES: (a) Maternal Mortality in 1995: Estimates developed by WHO, UNICEF, UNFPA. Geneva, World Health Organization, 2001.
(b) WHO: *HRP Biennial Report 2000–2001*.
(c) UNAIDS: *AIDS Epidemic Update* December 2001.
(d) Global prevalence and incidence of selected curable STIs, WHO/HIV/AIDS/ 2001–2002.
(e) Sciarra, J. (1994). "Infertility: An International Health Problem." *International Journal of Gynecology and Obstetrics*, 46:155–163.

The Future of Reproductive Health

Future improvements in reproductive health call for more research, drawing on both social science methods and "operations research" on the effectiveness and costs of reproductive health interventions. Special attention needs to be paid to promoting evidence-based reproductive health care in developing countries. The WHO and other international agencies have made a major commitment in this area. The WHO Reproductive Health Library (RHL) offers analyses to help ensure that resource allocations and current health care practices are based on scientifically solid and up-to-date information. The RHL aims "not only to prevent the introduction of unsubstantiated health care practices into programmes but also to replace the practices that have been demonstrated to be ineffective or harmful with those based on best available evidence" (Villar et al. 2001). Stronger assessments of the economic value of reproductive health interventions are also needed, so that investments in reproductive health are given their proper priority in health sector reform.

Beyond research, the ICPD and ICPD+5 documents include numerous recommendations for governments, United Nations agencies, donors, and other actors concerning reproductive health. A roadmap for progress has been laid out, ranging from specific "benchmark indicators" in health to suggested changes in policies and resource allocation. The recommendations cover not only specific health topics such as maternal mortality, but also the reproductive health needs of population groups such as adolescents and men, while acknowledging the priority that should be accorded to women and girls.

Commitment to implementing the reproductive health approach requires a clear understanding of how the thinking underlying it differs from the once prevalent "population control" mentality, and the programmatic and policy changes implied by this paradigm shift. The Fourth World Conference on Women summed up the links among reproductive health, human rights, gender equity, and sexuality in its Platform for Action (United Nations 1995, paragraph 96):

> The human rights of women include their right to have control over and decide freely and responsibly on matters related to their sexuality, including sexual and reproductive health, free of coercion, discrimination and violence. Equal relationships between women and men in matters of sexual relations and reproduction, including full respect for the integrity of the person, require mutual respect, consent and shared responsibility for sexual behaviour and its consequences.

See also: *AIDS; Family Planning Programs; Feminist Perspectives on Population Issues; Health Systems; Induced Abortion: History, Prevalence, Legal Aspects; Maternal Mortality; Sexuality, Human.*

BIBLIOGRAPHY

Bongaarts, John, and Robert G. Potter. 1983. *Fertility, Biology, and Behavior: An Analysis of the*

Proximate Determinants. New York: Academic Press.

Campbell, Oona, John Cleland, Martine Collumbien, and Karen Southwick. 1999. *Social Science Methods for Research on Reproductive Health.* Geneva: World Health Organization.

Davis, Kingsley, and Judith Blake. 1956. "Social Structure and Fertility: An Analytic Framework." *Economic Development and Cultural Change* 4(3): 211–235.

Germain, Adrienne, Sia Nowrojee, and Hnin Hnin Pyne. 1994. "Setting a New Agenda: Sexual and Reproductive Health and Rights." In *Population Policies Reconsidered: Health, Empowerment, and Rights,* ed. Gita Sen, Adrienne Germain, Lincoln C. Chen. Boston: Harvard Center for Population and Development Studies.

Helzner, Judith F. 2002. "Transforming Family Planning Services in the Latin American and Caribbean Region." *Studies in Family Planning* 33(1): 49–60.

Jain, Anrudh, and Judith Bruce. 1994. "A Reproductive Health Approach to the Objectives and Assessment of Family Planning Programs." In *Population Policies Reconsidered: Health, Empowerment, and Rights,* ed. Gita Sen, Adrienne Germain, and Lincoln C. Chen. Boston: Harvard Center for Population and Development Studies.

Villar, José, Metin Gülmezoglu, Jitendra Khanna, Guillermo Carroli, Justus Hofmeyr, Ken Schulz, and Pisake Lumbiganon. 2001. "Evidence-based Reproductive Health in Developing Countries." *WHO Reproductive Health Library* 4.

INTERNET RESOURCES.

Health, Action, Empowerment, Rights & Accountability (HERA). 1998. "Action Sheet: Reproductive Rights and Reproductive Health." <http://www.iwhc.org/uploads/HERAactionsheeteng%2Epdf>.

United Nations. 1995. "Beijing Declaration Platform for Action, Fourth World Conference on Women (FWCW)." <http://gopher://gopher.undp.org/00/undocs/gad/A/CONF.177/95_11/20>.

United Nations Population Fund. 1994. "International Conference on Population and Development (ICPD), Programme of Action." <http://www.unfpa.org/ICPD/reports%26doc/icpdpoae.html>.

———. 1999. "International Conference on Population and Development ICPD+5, Implementation of the Programme of Action." <http://www.unfpa.org/icpd/icpdmain.htm>.

World Development Report. 1993. "Investing in Health." <http://publications.worldbank.org/ecommerce/catalog/product?item_id=194651>.

World Health Organization. 1997. "The global burden of reproductive ill-health." *Progress in Human Reproduction* 42: 2–3. <http://www.who.int/hrp/progress/42/prog42.pdf>.

JUDITH F. HELZNER

REPRODUCTIVE RIGHTS

In the early 1990s, there was mounting international recognition that individuals' rights to reproductive integrity and choice required a coherent, unifying context of reproductive and sexual health. Two United Nations (UN) conferences in the mid-1990s propelled an expansive concept of reproductive health as an element of social justice that includes rights both to have children and to enjoy human sexuality without unwanted reproduction. These conferences placed reproduction in its wider setting, as an important aspect but not the sole purpose of human sexuality, equating rights not to reproduce with rights to plan for parenthood.

The International Conference on Population and Development, held in Cairo, Egypt, in 1994, and the Fourth World Conference on Women, held in Beijing, China, in 1995, advanced a common vision of reproductive health that everyone has the same human right to enjoy. Reproductive health, the conferences declared, "implies that people are able to have a satisfying and safe sex life and that they have the capability to reproduce and the freedom to decide if, when and how often to do so." Reproductive rights are understood to be rights that depend on duties to respect, protect, and fulfill human rights to reproductive health.

Sources of Reproductive Rights

The Cairo and Beijing concept of reproductive health, to which everyone is entitled, was built on a foundation of internationally recognized human rights. When the United Nations was established in 1946, its urgent task was to redeem confidence in respect for human rights after the inhumane excesses of the Nazi period and World War II. The UN initiated the Universal Declaration of Human Rights of 1948 to condemn, among other wrongs, the gross denials of reproductive rights during this period, such as forced sterilizations of vulnerable populations and severe punishment of abortion. (In Nazi-dominated Vichy France, a woman had been sentenced to death and executed for terminating her pregnancy.)

The Universal Declaration of Human Rights was described only as a declaration because it did not create any new rights but only declared those that already existed. To reinforce recognition of rights, however, UN member states created a series of legally enforceable international human rights treaties by which states could confirm their commitment. These include the International Covenant on Civil and Political Rights (the Political Covenant), the International Covenant on Economic, Social, and Cultural Rights (the Economic Covenant) and, more specifically, the Convention on the Elimination of All Forms of Discrimination Against Women (the Women's Convention). These international instruments reflect laws that already exist in the legal systems by which many countries conduct their national life, and elevate them to national commitments that states make not only to their own populations but also to each other in international law. That is, states accept international scrutiny of and accountability for their observance of these designated human rights.

Rights to Have and Not to Have Children

The Political Covenant expresses the most traditional of reproductive rights. Article 23 (echoing Article 16 of the Universal Declaration) recognizes "the right of men and women of marriageable age to marry and to found a family" and that "no marriage shall be entered into without the free and full consent" of the intended spouses. The Political Covenant implies that marriage is a precondition to reproduction, because Article 23 opens with the widespread understanding (also included in the Universal Declaration) that "the family is the natural and fundamental group unit of society." This approach reflects the conservative disapproval of reproduction outside marriage.

The UN Charter observes the purpose "to reaffirm faith in fundamental human rights . . . [and] in the equal rights of men and women." The Universal Declaration of Human Rights and the implementing Political and Economic Covenants echo the entitlement to equality of both sexes. Because of human biology, however, reproduction affects the sexes differently. Women's unmarried parenthood is apparent in pregnancy and childbirth, whereas men have traditionally been able to conceal and deny their paternity. Similarly, women can have pregnancy involuntarily imposed by rape and may be subject to laws that deny abortion even on this ground, whereas men can only very rarely be forced to experience sexual intercourse. The biological difference has been translated into discriminatory social sanctions. Men shown to have fathered children outside marriage usually face, at most, financial sanctions of support payments. Women have been and often still are stigmatized, condemned, and severely punished, by family and society, for unwed motherhood and face communal ostracism and judicial penalties—even reaching stoning to death, a sanction still threatened in some communities. The expectation of virginity at marriage applies discriminatorily to brides but not to grooms. Loss of virginity may reduce women's marriage prospects and options.

The Women's Convention requires, in Article 1, that women be entitled to exercise their rights, which include rights to reproductive health, "irrespective of their marital status." Article 12 of the Economic Covenant requires states to recognize "the right of everyone to the enjoyment of the highest attainable standard of physical and mental health." Article 16 of the Women's Convention requires that states ensure that women enjoy with men "the same rights to decide freely and responsibly on the number and spacing of their children and to have access to the information, education and means to enable them to exercise these rights." This convention's Article 12 more explicitly requires states "to eliminate discrimination against women in the field of health care in order to ensure . . . access to health care services, including those related to family planning." Family planning includes planning when and whether to have children. This is the foundation on which the Cairo and Beijing conferences built the concept of the right to reproductive health.

Duties to Respect Reproductive Choice

Rights depend on duties, in that a right is enforceable only against those individuals and governmental and other agencies duty bound to comply with its exercise. States that have ratified one or more of the Political and Economic Covenants and the Women's Convention accept duties not only of compliance but also of periodic reporting to and monitoring by the different bodies these treaties have created to review parties' compliance. Different rights require different responses for compliance, but a general distinction may be drawn between so-called negative and positive rights. Negative rights require state tolerance and passivity when individuals act to enjoy their rights. Negative rights are sometimes expressed as "the right to be let alone," to act as one wishes and is able, without interference by police or other government officers. Positive rights are rights for which a person may need to be provided with the means to exercise them—at least those unable, for whatever reason, to provide such means for themselves.

Reproductive rights have historically been negative rights. Laws may intervene to set minimum ages for marriage and prohibit incestuous unions, but marriage is otherwise a private arrangement, and natural procreation by fertile couples within marriage is even more intimately a matter for the participants alone. Laws prohibiting artificial contraception have now been almost universally discarded, so that in nearly all countries fertile couples can decide whether and when to conceive children without accountability to government officers or agencies.

Negative rights, however, may in practice be rights for those who can provide themselves with contraceptive means or means to promote their fertility when it is impaired, but not for others. In order for all individuals to be able to avail themselves of reproductive rights, states would have to observe them as positive rights and ensure access to necessary services for citizens whether they are rich or poor; fertile, subfertile, or infertile; privileged or disadvantaged.

Some international treaties express the right to family planning services as a positive right, in recognition of the burden on poor women of repeated pregnancy and their vulnerability, particularly in low-income countries, to maternal ill-health and pregnancy-related death. Even in affluent countries, however, medically assisted reproductive services to overcome infertility may be available only as "luxury medicine" and be unavailable to many without unbearable personal expenditure and sacrifice. Article 15 of the Economic Covenant requires states to recognize the right of everyone to enjoy "the benefits of scientific progress and its applications," but it imposes no positive duty on states to fund access to reproductive technologies. Accordingly, reproductive rights remain an ideal, but they are subject in practice to personal and governmental resources and the sense of priority with which they are allocated.

See also: *Conferences, International Population; Family Planning Programs; Feminist Perspectives on Population Issues; Population Policy; Reproductive Technologies: Ethical Issues.*

BIBLIOGRAPHY

Center for Reproductive Law and Policy. 2000. *Reproductive Rights 2000: Moving Forward.* New York: Center for Reproductive Law and Policy.

Cook, Rebecca, ed. 1994. *Human Rights of Women: National and International Perspectives.* Philadelphia: University of Pennsylvania Press.

Cook, Rebecca, and Bernard Dickens. 2000. *Considerations for Formulating Reproductive Health Laws,* 2nd edition. Geneva, Switzerland: World Health Organization.

Cook, Rebecca, Bernard Dickens, and Mahmoud Fathalla. 2003. *Reproductive Health and Human Rights: Integrating Medicine, Ethics and Law.* Oxford: Oxford University Press.

Eriksson, Maja Kirilova. 2000. *Reproductive Freedom: In the Context of International Human Rights and Humanitarian Law.* The Hague, Netherlands, and Boston: Martinus Nijhoff.

Symposium Number. "Conference on the International Protection of Reproductive Rights." 1995. Symposium *American University Law Review* 44: 963–1,475.

REBECCA J. COOK

REPRODUCTIVE TECHNOLOGIES

MODERN METHODS	Luigi Mastroianni, Jr.
ETHICAL ISSUES	Bernard M. Dickens

MODERN METHODS

The medical management of infertility has involved increasingly complex treatment methods. Most of these reproductive technologies employ manipulations of the gametes: sperm and eggs. Most of the newer methods are offshoots of in vitro fertilization systems, although older techniques such as artificial insemination still play an important role.

Artificial Insemination

Artificial insemination has been practiced for more than a century. When done using the husband's semen, it is clinically useful in the management of conditions such as penetration failure, premature ejaculation, and retrograde ejaculation into the bladder. Artificial insemination using a specimen other than the husband's (donor insemination) also has evolved as an acceptable treatment for infertility. Donor insemination is utilized mainly in cases in which the spermatozoa are absent or severely compromised in number and quality.

The donor, who usually is anonymous and is identified only by a third party, is thoroughly screened for general health, genetic abnormalities, and sexually transmitted diseases such as HIV infection. Other characteristics are considered as well. Detailed pretreatment counseling is critical and should include an in-depth discussion with both partners of the acceptability of using a donor. The ethical issues to be considered should include whether the offspring will be informed of the method of conception and the safeguards in place to ensure the long-term availability of genetic information if it becomes medically important in the future. Donor insemination has been extended to single women and lesbian couples in many centers.

Techniques have evolved to concentrate and wash the spermatozoa from the ejaculate so that they can be safely inserted directly into the uterus. Intrauterine insemination (IUI) commonly is combined with the induction of ovulation with gonadotropins, which allows precise timing of the insemination and the development of several egg-containing follicles.

This increase in the number of ovulations improves the success rate. Gonadotropin superovulation combined with intrauterine insemination has proved useful in the management of male infertility as well as unexplained infertility. It has also contributed significantly to an epidemic of multiple pregnancies that are associated with increased prematurity and newborn morbidity. Although the incidence of high multiple pregnancies can be reduced by careful clinical management, it cannot be eliminated completely. For this reason, the approach is gradually being replaced by in vitro fertilization procedures in which the number of embryos transferred into the uterus is more easily controlled.

In Vitro Fertilization/Embryo Transfer

Normal reproduction requires a properly functioning fallopian tube. The fallopian tube captures the egg from the ovulating ovarian follicle, transports it to a point well within its lumen for fertilization, and retains and nurtures the newly dividing embryo for three days, after which, at the eight- to 16-cell stage, it is delivered into the uterus. After approximately three additional days the embryo attaches to the uterine lining (endometrium) in the process of implantation.

Much of the early information on fertilization was derived from observations in marine forms, mainly the sea urchin. The first mammalian in vitro fertilization was carried out in the rabbit in 1952 by M. C. Chang, but it was not until 1980 that Robert Edwards and Patrick Steptoe reported the first successful pregnancy after the in vitro fertilization (IVF) of human eggs. Until their experiment there was reluctance to transfer in vitro fertilized human embryos back into the uterus out of concern that they were abnormal. There is now firm evidence that there is no increased risk of congenital or genetic abnormalities in children born after IVF and embryo transfer.

Multiple ovulations are induced with gonadotropins, follicle-stimulating hormone (FSH) to produce larger number of follicles, and human chorionic gonadotropin (hCG) or luteinizing hormone (LH) to finalize the development of the follicle and egg. The eggs are easily recovered by means of a transvaginal ultrasound probe to facilitate direct aspiration from the mature follicles. Spermatozoa that have been appropriately conditioned are then added to the culture system containing the eggs, initiating the fertilization process.

Within 24 hours, a spermatozoon has penetrated the egg and its nucleus has formed a pronucleus. The nucleus of the egg also forms a pronucleus. The two pronuclei then join, completing the initial phases of fertilization. Within hours there is a first cell division, followed by other cell divisions. Usually on the third day after fertilization embryos are selected for transfer into the uterus. The transfer is carried out with a fine, flexible catheter placed into the uterine cavity transcervically. In the early phases of the development of IVF, it was common to transfer multiple embryos in the hope that at least one would implant. As the quality of the cultured embryos has improved, multiple embryo transfer with its attendant complication of multiple pregnancies has become unnecessary. In some countries the number of embryos transferred is regulated to no more than two, and this is now standard practice in many U.S. centers.

Initially IVF was used solely in patients with damaged, nonfunctioning fallopian tubes. As it became clear that fertilization could be enhanced by using in vitro techniques, IVF became clinically applicable for couples with impaired sperm number or motility. As laboratory and clinical methods have evolved, additional techniques for managing fertilization have been developed that enhance male fertilization potential.

IVF and Male Fertility Potential

In 1992 Gianpierro Palermo, A. Van Steirteghem, and colleagues reported pregnancies after the mechanical injection of sperm directly into the cytoplasm of the egg. This procedure—intracytoplasmic sperm injection (ICSI)—has been applied to clinical situations in which there are a limited number of spermatozoa or in which the spermatozoa are functionally impaired. The egg is held firmly in place under the microscope. A single spermatozoon is aspirated into a fine catheter, and the catheter is inserted directly through the zona pellucida, the protein egg coat, past the egg membrane and into the cytoplasm, where it is released. Thus, the necessity for the spermatozoon to traverse these barriers by normal mechanisms is eliminated. Groups with the most experience with ICSI have reported a slightly increased incidence of genetic abnormalities.

Men with congenital absence of the vas deferens, which transports spermatozoa from the testes, fail to release sperm in the ejaculate. In these cases the epididymis, the storage reservoir of spermatozoa proximal to the vas, contains spermatozoa. These spermatozoa can be aspirated for in vitro fertilization through the use of ICSI. Spermatozoa have also been recovered directly from the testes and used successfully for ICSI. Men with congenital absence of the vas have been shown to be carriers of the cystic fibrosis gene. Pregnancies that might not have been possible otherwise can be produced with ICSI, and although the incidence of abnormalities is increased over that of the general population, the increase is small. Fortunately, when the embryo that is transferred is abnormal, it is destined not to proceed through pregnancy. Generally, grossly abnormal embryos fail to implant or do not develop normally, aborting early in the pregnancy. To address these issues further, techniques for genetic evaluation of the embryo have been developed.

Preimplantation Genetic Diagnosis

As laboratory techniques for in vitro culture of embryos have been refined, systems have been developed to analyze the genetic characteristics of a single cell for preimplantation genetic diagnosis (PGD). PGD involves the removal of a cell from a dividing embryo by micromanipulation for genetic analysis, using probes to identify and assess the normality of individual chromosomes. Only embryos that are deemed genetically normal are transferred into the uterus, and the remainder are discarded. These techniques are particularly useful in couples who are carriers for certain genetic diseases, such as Tay-Sachs disease. This approach is also useful clinically in women over age 35, who are at a greater risk for having a baby with Down's syndrome. Transferring only normal embryos could result in an increased pregnancy rate after in vitro fertilization. The downside is that because the technique involves the removal of a cell from the embryo, there is the possibility that the embryo will be injured, impairing further development. PGD allows the determination of the sex of the embryo, and some have suggested that it be used for prenatal sex selection. This would be clinically applicable in cases in which there is a sex-linked genetic defect that would be present only in an embryo of a given sex (e.g., hemophilia).

Embryo Freezing

The techniques of IVF result in the recovery of numerous oocytes that are then available for fertilization. In contrast to semen, which is readily frozen and stored, techniques for freezing eggs have encountered difficulties. The freezing and storage of embryos, however, is technically feasible and practical. Embryo freezing is most successful when it is carried out at the pronuclear stage shortly after the development of the male and female pronuclei. Freezing of embryos that are not transferred in the treatment cycle allows the opportunity for additional pregnancies without another cycle of stimulation and ovum recovery.

Although offering a significant advantage in terms of the pregnancy rate per couple, the eventual use or disposal of freeze-stored embryos is a matter for careful consideration. In its guidelines, the Ethics Committee of the American Society for Reproductive Medicine strongly recommends that the decision on freezing and eventual disposition of unused embryos be made in advance, after a thorough consultation with both partners. The couple may elect to allow their stored embryos to be used for research. A preliminary decision is also made in advance about the disposition of the frozen embryos in the event of a divorce or the death of one partner. From time to time legal issues arise in this regard that must be resolved in court.

Research utilizing human embryos is controversial. Policies vary from one country to the next. In the United Kingdom research is deemed permissible up to the fourteenth day of development but not beyond that time. This matter is receiving increasing attention as methods are developed to identify and culture embryonal stem cells to provide future treatment options for a number of diseases.

Donor Eggs

The use of an egg donated by another woman is the female counterpart to the use of donor semen for male infertility. The differences, however, are significant. Although small, there are risks associated with the procedures employed to recover the ova. The ovaries can overrespond to the gonadotropin hormones, causing hyperstimulation, a serious medical condition. Rare deaths have been reported from hyperstimulation because of coagulation problems and pulmonary emboli. Infection after ovum recovery, although rare, has been reported.

Ovum donors usually are recruited from among young women, often college or graduate students. Some programs allow a differential in the payment scale when a woman undergoing IVF is willing to release some of her recovered oocytes for the use of an infertile woman who is unable to produce eggs. Obviously, the ethical and social issues surrounding ovum donation are far more complicated than is the case for semen donation. The Ethics Committee of the American Society for Reproductive Medicine has established guidelines for the compensation of ovum donors and has suggested that a woman be paid reasonably for her time and effort.

Recipients of donated eggs are usually women who are unable to produce their own eggs. Ovum donation has been used in postmenopausal women who wish to extend their reproductive life span. Extreme examples include pregnancies in women over age 60, which have been reported in at least three countries. The risk to the mother in those circumstances is not insignificant, and the social and ethical issues surrounding such treatment require careful consideration. Donated embryos genetically unrelated to the couple have also been used.

Conclusion

The development of reproductive technologies has occurred at a breathtaking rate. The net result has been increased opportunity for reproductive choice. These techniques have provided an increased likelihood of pregnancy among women in their late reproductive years. They have allowed men with subfertility or even complete absence of spermatozoa in their ejaculate to establish a pregnancy by using their own genetic material. Concomitant with these dramatic developments has been an increasing concern over ethical issues, and societal norms have been strained. As basic mechanisms of reproductive functions are analyzed and demystified, there will be continued clinical and laboratory innovation not only in the management of infertility but in the development of systems to prevent pregnancy as well.

See also: *Contraception, Modern Methods of; Genetic Testing; Multiple Births; Reproductive Rights.*

BIBLIOGRAPHY

Dohle, G. R., D. J. Halley, J. O. Van Hemel, A. M. van Den Ouwel, M. H. Pieters, R. F. Weber, and L. C. Govaerts. 2002. "Genetic Risk Factors in Infertile Men with Severe Oligozoospermia and Azoospermia." *Human Reproduction* 17: 13–26.

Ethics Committee of the American Society for Reproductive Medicine. 2000. "Financial Incentives in Recruitment of Oocyte Donors." *Fertility and Sterility* 74: 216–220.

Guzick, D. S., S. A. Carson, C. Coutifaris, J. W. Overstreet, P. Factor-Litvak, M. P. Steinkampf, J. A. Hill, L. Mastroianni, J. E. Buster, S. T. Nakajima, D. L. Vogel, and R. E. Canfield. 1999. "Efficacy of Superovulation and Intrauterine Insemination in the Treatment of Infertility." *New England Journal of Medicine* 340: 177–183.

Patrizio P., and L. G. Leonard. 2000. "Mutations of the Cystic Fibrosis Gene and Congenital Absence of the Vas Deferens." In *The Genetics of Male Infertility: Results and Problems in Cell Differentiation,* ed. K. McElreavy. Berlin and Heidelberg: Springer-Verlag.

LUIGI MASTROIANNI, JR.

ETHICAL ISSUES

Reproductive technologies—the manipulation and exchange of gametes (i.e., sperm and ova) and human embryos—were developed to overcome the natural infertility that frustrates individuals' intentions to parent children. The development and application of these technologies raised heated ethical debates at the turn of the twenty-first century. Some condemn these technologies as "unnatural," although many other applications of medical science intended to overcome natural failures in health, such as organ failure or susceptibility to infection, are not ethically condemned.

Ethicists do not agree on the moral status that human embryos deserve. Those who consider them to have high intrinsic worth, as actual or potential human beings, oppose the deliberate wastage of embryos that accompanies the development and application of reproductive technologies. Those who accord embryos respect, but at a lower level than born people or fetuses, assert that embryos may be employed, and their wastage may be responsibly planned, in efforts to assist reproduction. The ethical expectation of tolerance of plurality—that is, the acceptance of different ethical approaches—requires that individuals not be compelled to act against their conscience, and that they not be barred from acting as their conscientious convictions allow, unless there is demonstrable evidence that their actions cause pain to others. Scientists widely accept, for instance, that embryos may ethically be used and be let perish in reproductive research up to fourteen days from their creation, when the "primitive streak," the origin of the brain, appears.

Ethical Acceptance

Reproductive technologies include drug treatments to assist fertility and natural conception. Hormonal stimulation of women's ovulation raises ethical concerns because it may result in hyperstimulation and the natural conception of a high number of embryos in the same reproductive cycle. Pregnancies of four or more fetuses usually jeopardize the health of the mother, and endanger the survival of their fetuses or born children, due, for instance, to low birth weight. Triplet and even twin pregnancies can also present risks. One medical response to high multiple pregnancies is to use techniques that reduce the number of embryos or fetuses growing *in utero*; these techniques raise ethical concerns related to abortion.

People who adhere to religious convictions approach reproductive technologies differently. Some raise few ethical objections, seeing the procedures as expressions of divinely inspired human resourcefulness and proper human collaboration in creation. However, there is considerable religious condemnation of the prospect of human reproduction by cloning. Cloning is the production, by non-sexual means, of a genetically identical cellular structure (a "twin") such as an embryo, from a pre-existing structure. The religious objection to it is that induced human cloning is unnatural, and a human assumption of divine authority to create human life. The Roman Catholic tradition is very conservative regarding almost all reproductive technologies and rejects any procedure perceived as unnatural. Roman Catholic ethics may allow transfer of ova into a woman's reproductive system for natural fertilization there by her husband. The Islamic tradition rejects all gamete and embryo transfer, because of the strong emphasis on the integrity of genetic lineage, but accepts many technologies that equip women to bear their husbands' children. As a secular, pluralistic approach to human behavior, the observance of ethics requires tolerance of diverse opinions about the many forms of consensual reproduction.

Gamete and Embryo Donation and Use

Ethical respect for individuals' self-determination or autonomy requires that gamete and embryo donors give their informed consent. Donors may be required to remain anonymous to recipients, since personal contact may raise concerns about payments, unethical commerce, and treating reproductive materials as marketable commodities. Similar concerns arise when clinics purchase gametes and embryos and pass costs on to recipients the donors do not know. When couples have surplus embryos or gametes from their own *in vitro* fertilization (IVF) treatment, they may donate an embryo or gamete to another couple. If IVF clinics refuse to accept applicants if they will not agree to donate surplus gametes or embryos, they raise issues around the patient-donors' freedom of choice, and clinic operators' conflict of interest. If treatment is unsuccessful, childless donors may face the knowledge that strangers may bear and rear their children when they cannot. If a couple ends IVF treatment because they have separated, one may veto the other's consent to embryo donation. Patients are always ethically entitled to withdraw consent that has been elicited by excessive pressure.

Use of gametes and embryos, by couples themselves or by the recipients of donation, depends on these materials satisfying genetic and other criteria. Ethicists disagree over precisely which characteristics make gametes and embryos unsuitable for use. Gross genetic abnormality, determined by pre-implantation genetic diagnosis (PGD), will clearly negate use, as will racial incompatibility with possible recipients. Mild genetic abnormalities, such as to genetically-inherited but manageable disabilities, may not be an ethical basis of rejection, and some legal systems and ethics codes prohibit decision making on the sole basis of an embryo's sex. Ethical advantages of PGD are that it reduces the incidence of elective abortion due to negatively perceived embryonic or fetal characteristics, and may provide support for initiating pregnancies women would otherwise decline.

Eligibility for Assisted-Reproduction Services

The characteristics that make couples and individuals ineligible to receive technological assistance to become parents are often ethically contentious, since they may reflect negative stereotypes of poor parents that lack evidence, and may violate principles of nondiscrimination. Social justice is denied when low family income excludes couples from access to high-cost assisted reproduction. Couples may also be ineligible for reproductive assistance when one parent has a disability. Denial of assistance to applicants with physical disabilities may be unethical even when disabling conditions may be genetically transmitted, and raises issues of negative eugenics concerning whether conditions such as congenital deafness and short stature truly are disabilities. Negative eugenics is the practice of restricting people considered unfit to transmit their genetic characteristics from having children, which became discredited by association with coercive Nazi practices. Mental impairment may more easily justify ethical denial of assistance, on the grounds that prospective children's interests would be violated, but this claim also requires demonstrated evidence. Ethicists assert that applicants' unmarried status and partnership in same-sex relationships are decreasingly defensible ethical grounds to deny technologically assisted reproductive services, since evidence shows that children brought up in homes of such parents are not significantly different from children reared in more conventional homes.

Since advanced paternal age is not a natural barrier to parenthood, ethicists sometimes question whether age should be a bar to assisted reproduction. Post-menopausal pregnancy is often opposed on grounds that aging mothers are a disadvantage to children, although many children are successfully raised by grandparents. Assisted reproduction in cases of premature menopause raises fewer ethical objections. There is also an ethical debate around assisting widows to conceive children by their deceased husbands, since some consider recovery of sperm while the men are unconscious, dying, or deceased without their clearly given prior consent ethically objectionable.

A surrogate mother is a woman who agrees in advance to gestate a child or children for surrender upon birth to others who requested this service. Such women provide authentic prenatal mothering, whether they are also genetic mothers or receive embryos created by IVF from other women's ova. Ethical concerns around surrogate motherhood include how women are engaged for this role, and whether their consent is adequately informed, freely given, and not unduly induced. Both commercial recruitment and pressuring family members or friends to render unpaid services raise ethical concerns.

Children's Interests

If the experience of human life is considered inherently beneficial, it may be ethically unobjectionable to create a new human life. Some may claim, however, that inappropriate reproductive assistance causes births that violate the interests of particular families, communities, or societies. Human reproductive cloning may ethically be opposed, for instance, with the argument that its safety has not yet been established in animal studies. Objection relies on political or macro-ethical claims, however, which address community-wide interests, rather than micro-ethics, meaning the ethics of individual physician–patient relationships, since within those relationships patients may ethically be assisted to bear children at known risk of adverse health consequences.

Communities are increasingly recognizing the ethical entitlement of children born of gamete and embryo donation to know about their genetic origins. The anticipated growth of genetically based diagnosis, prognosis, and treatment is likely to reinforce claims to this knowledge, particularly as therapeutic drugs begin to be designed to fit the particular features of patients' genetic inheritance. Ethicists differ on how much children should be entitled to learn. At one end of the spectrum are those who argue that information of children's biological parents' genetic deficits and predispositions to illness should be available, so that children may benefit from accessible treatments and be able to avoid diets, lifestyles and, for instance, environments that trigger inherited predispositions to illness. At the other extreme are those who claim that, notwithstanding confidentiality, children have a right to know the personal identities, circumstances and family background of those whose genes they have inherited, and the right to meet them if the children wish and practically can. The ethical basis of this claim is that individuals should not become parents unless they are willing to be responsible to their children. However, social parenthood, meaning accepting continuing responsibility for the welfare and rearing of children, is now distinguishable from medically assisted biological parenthood. Children conceived in casual, perhaps single-instance sexual encounters may not have enforceable claims to know who their fathers are, and it is not ethically established that children of artificial, planned conception have superior rights to those born of natural, unplanned conception.

See also: *Eugenics; Genetic Testing; Quality of Population; Religions, Population Doctrines of; Reproductive Rights.*

BIBLIOGRAPHY

Department of Health and Social Security (U.K.). 1984. *Report of the Warnock Committee of Inquiry into Human Fertilisation and Embryology.* London: Her Majesty's Stationery Office, Cmnd. 9314.

Golombok, Susan, R. Cook, A. Bish, and C. Murray. 1995. "Families Created by the New Reproductive Technologies: Quality of Parenting and Social and Emotional Development of the Children." *Child Development* 66: 285–298.

Harris, John, and Soren Holm, eds. 1998. *The Future of Human Reproduction.* Oxford: Clarendon Press.

New York State Task Force on Life and the Law. 1998. *Assisted Reproductive Technologies: Analysis and Recommendations for Public Policy.* Albany, NY: New York State Task Force on Life and the Law.

Royal Commission on New Reproductive Technologies. 1993. *Final Report: Proceed With Care.* Ottawa: Minister of Government Services, Canada.

Serour, Gamal, and Bernard Dickens. "Assisted Reproduction Developments in the Islamic World." *International Journal of Gynecology and Obstetrics* 74: 187–193.

BERNARD M. DICKENS

RESETTLEMENT

Resettlement of people from one part of a country to another is a specific form of internal migration and is of particular significance in less developed countries. It is usually associated with programs of agricultural settlement carried out under government auspices. There are two main forms of resettlement. The first is a largely voluntary movement, seen as a solution to "overpopulation" in the areas of origin and as a means to increase production in "underused" land in the destination areas. The second form, more forced than voluntary in nature, is settlement of people who have been displaced by environmental events, development projects, or conflict.

The extension of agricultural settlement as older-settled areas fill up has occurred throughout human history, albeit usually on a more-or-less spontaneous basis. In the twentieth century governments often took a hand in the process, opening new areas for closer agricultural settlement and selecting settlers—mainly persons with agricultural backgrounds. While there have been examples of such schemes in developed countries—for example, Donald Rowland (1979) has discussed the returned soldier settlement schemes in Australia following World Wars I and II—the largest resettlement schemes have been initiated by colonial and independent governments in developing countries. Indonesia, Brazil, and China are notable cases in point. Large variations in population density between different parts of the nation are often a reflection of ecological realities (in Indonesia, for example, some 60 percent of the population is in Java, which accounts for only about 6 percent of the country's land area). Nevertheless, comparatively "empty" areas, such as in Indonesia's other major islands, often have some potential for closer settlement.

Land settlement schemes were prominent in the first four decades following World War II in many developing countries. By the mid-1980s, such projects were no longer favored. In a representative comment, Andrei Oberai concluded:

Despite the substantial amounts that have been invested in planned settlement schemes . . . their performance has not been very encouraging. . . . If not complete failures, they have, in almost all parts of the world, given settlement officials and policy makers serious cause for concern. They are costly in relation to the number of persons settled, and frequently suffer from low productivity and high rates of desertion. In some cases they also appear to have created social tensions in the areas concerned (Oberai 1986, pp. 141–142).

As a result of such assessments as well as the decreasing availability of suitable land, the number and scale of settlement programs declined and by the beginning of the twenty-first century few countries had them.

Although they vary by country, land settlement schemes have typically involved governments in selecting potential settlers, assisting and organizing their move to the settlement area, clearing and preparing the land for agriculture, and providing the settlers with housing and other services and economic assistance until their agricultural holdings become established.

The goals of government-sponsored settlement schemes have differed. In Indonesia, the Philippines, and Peru "evening out" the national population distribution has been an important aim. In Brazil, Malaysia, and Sri Lanka the main objective has been regional development. Some schemes have explicit (or implicit) political motives. The "colonization" of Tibet by Han Chinese is one example. Some have suggested that Indonesia's transmigration scheme has sought to establish the dominance of Javanese in the outer islands of Indonesia.

In 1985 Thayer Scudder put forward a four-stage model of the land settlement process: (1) planning and design of the scheme, initial infrastructure development, and the recruitment of settlers; (2) the actual transfer of settlers and their initial establishment in the new environment; (3) economic growth and social progress in the settlement area; and (4) incorporation of the settlement scheme into the existing local and regional structure. There is an additional, fifth stage, however: what may be referred to as the "second generation problem." Once the initial settlers have become established and their children begin to enter the working ages, this second generation puts great pressure on local labor markets, which often cannot absorb the increasing numbers of workers. In some schemes, there is evidence of settlers having higher fertility than their counterparts in origin areas, which exacerbates the problem.

Indonesia's Transmigration Program

Probably the largest single government-organized land settlement scheme has been the transmigration program in Indonesia, which resettled families from Java and Bali in Sumatra, Kalimantan, Sulawesi, and West New Guinea (Papua). As shown in Table 1, the numbers over the twentieth century amounted to about 1.5 million families—or around 8 million people. The Dutch colonial government began the program in 1905, and after independence successive regimes continued carrying it out until it was officially terminated in 2000. As with other settlement

TABLE 1

Indonesian Transmigration in 1905–1998	
Period	Number of Families (thousands)
1905–1968	243
1969–1974	39
1974–1979	55
1979–1984	366
1984–1989	228
1989–1994	247
1994–1998	315
Total	1,494

SOURCE: Mubyarto (2000).

schemes, it also created a parallel flow of spontaneous migrants into the settlement areas or to nearby land, both from Java and Bali and from other parts of Indonesia.

Problems of Resettlement Schemes

Land settlement programs have encountered a range of problems. These have included belated discovery that the settlement land could not support intensive agriculture; insufficient preparation of settlers for farming in a different environment; insufficient early support for settlers and consequent "desertion" of settlers from schemes; social tensions between settlers and the original inhabitants of the settlement areas, often arising from inadequate recognition of the latter's title for the land or from inadequate compensation; and ecological problems created by poor or unsustainable agricultural practices.

The costs of resettlement per family are high in relation to alternative strategies to fight poverty, increase agricultural production, or influence population numbers and distribution. The World Bank, which became involved in supporting some land settlement programs as a development strategy in the 1970s and 1980s, subsequently withdrew most of its support, partly on these grounds.

Forced Internal Resettlement

Forced migrations across national borders have attracted a great deal of research attention, but analogous movements within countries have been substantially greater in size and have been much less studied. The main causes of such forced resettlement are large-scale infrastructure projects, environmental disasters, and political, ethnic, or religious conflict. The bulk of these resettlements occur within less developed countries. In a 2000 report, Michael Cernea and Christopher McDowell maintained that "the most widespread effect of involuntary displacement is the impoverishment of a considerable number of people" (Cernea and McDowell, p. 12).

Dam construction is a major reason for population displacement. It is estimated that around 12 million Chinese were displaced by reservoir and dam construction in the half century following establishment of the People's Republic of China in 1949. The Three Gorges Project, damming the Yangtze River in central China, involves the inundation of almost 30,000 hectares (74,000 acres) of farmland and the resettlement of at least 1.2 million people; it is due to be completed in 2009.

Environmental disasters such as volcanic eruptions, floods, cyclones, tsunami, and droughts can cause massive displacement on both a temporary and permanent basis. South Asia and Africa are the regions most affected. Those displaced are often described as environmental refugees. A 1980s estimate found that in India alone four million persons on average were needing to migrate elsewhere to seek food and shelter each year. The Sahelian drought of the late 1980s saw the displacement of several million people in a number of African countries, including Burkina Faso, Chad, Mali, Mauritania, and Niger.

Internally Displaced Persons

Persons fleeing persecution or threat of violence but who remain within their country (and thus cannot formally be recognized as refugees under the mandate of the United Nations High Commission for Refugees [UNHCR]) comprise another large category of displaced persons. Beginning in the late twentieth century, the UNHCR has identified internally displaced persons (IDPs) as a "group of concern." Although they are outside of the 1951 UN Refugee Convention, the UNHCR defined IDPs as:

> persons or groups of persons who have been forced or obliged to flee or to leave their homes or places of habitual residence, in particular as a result of or in order to avoid the effects of armed conflict, situations of generalized violence, violations of human rights or natural or human-made disasters, and who have not crossed an internationally recognized state border (U.S. General Accounting Office, p. 5).

Figure 1 shows the UNHCR estimates of trends in numbers of IDPs (and the numbers of refugees for comparison). Figure 1 shows that the numbers of IDPs recognized by the UNHCR expanded greatly in the late 1980s and early 1990s with the number of nations with IDPs increasing from 14 in 1985 to 34 in 1996. The increases in numbers were predominantly in Africa (Burundi, Somalia), Europe and the former USSR (Bosnia and Herzegovina, Azerbaijan, Georgia, Cyprus, Russian Federation, Croatia, Armenia) and Asia (Afghanistan, Sri Lanka, Cambodia). The figure of around eight million IDPs globally at the beginning of 2001 underestimates the actual number. For example, it omits 1.3 million IDPs officially identified in Indonesia. Indeed, in 2001 the U.S. General Accounting Office estimated that there were over 20 million IDPs worldwide.

IDPs are often less able to obtain assistance than refugees, because they do not qualify for UNHCR protection and support. They usually are forced to move under conditions of great duress and are often unable to take their possessions with them. The camps they are initially housed in are often overcrowded and suffer from major health and social problems.

Governments seek to return IDPs to their home area if that is possible, but often they are resettled in other parts of the country. In Indonesia, for example, the same government agency that was responsible for transmigration has responsibility for resettling IDPs who are unable to return to their home area. Forced movements within less developed nations appear to be increasing in scale although those officially recognized by the UNHCR show a downturn in the late 1990s.

See also: *Ethnic Cleansing; Forced Migration; Internal Migration; Refugees, Demography of.*

BIBLIOGRAPHY

Cernea, Michael M., and Christopher McDowell. 2000. *Risks and Reconstruction: Experiences of Resettlers and Refugees.* Washington, D.C.: World Bank.

Heming, Li, and Phillip Rees. 2000. "Population Displacement in the Three Gorges Reservoir Area of the Yangtze River, Central China: Relocation Policies and Migrant Views." *International Journal of Population Geography* 6: 439–462.

FIGURE 1

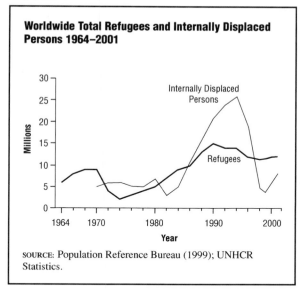

Worldwide Total Refugees and Internally Displaced Persons 1964–2001

SOURCE: Population Reference Bureau (1999); UNHCR Statistics.

Hessler, Peter. 1999. "Tibet through Chinese Eyes." *Atlantic Monthly* 283(2): 56–66.

Hugo, Graeme. 1996. "Environmental Concerns and International Migration." *International Migration Review* 30(1): 105–131.

Jacobson, Jodi L. 1988. *Environmental Refugees: A Yardstick of Habitability.* Washington, D.C.: Worldwatch Institute.

Oberai, Andrei S. 1986. "Land Settlement Policies and Population Redistribution in Developing Countries: Performance, Problems, and Prospects." *International Labour Review* 125 (2): 141–161.

United Nations. 1981. *Population Distribution Policies in Development Planning.* New York: United Nations.

GRAEME HUGO

RESIDENTIAL SEGREGATION

Residential segregation refers to the geographic differentiation of two or more population groups within a city or metropolitan area. When segregation is extreme (such as when an ethnic minority is confined to a ghetto), members of each group may live almost completely apart. Normally, however, segregation is a matter of degree. Even casual observation confirms that most urban neighborhoods exhibit some amount of internal diversity in socioeconomic status, ethnicity, life cycle stage, and other attributes of their inhabitants.

Measures of Segregation

To capture the variable nature of segregation, researchers have relied heavily on the index of dissimilarity (symbolized by D). This index measures the *evenness* dimension of segregation by comparing the proportional distributions of two groups, X and Y, across spatial units such as census tracts or blocks in a given region, typically a city or metropolitan area. The popularity of D lies in its intuitive appeal: It can be interpreted as the percentage of members of group X who would have to move to a different tract or block in order for the regional distribution of X to be the same as Y. Another segregation dimension of interest is *exposure*, which indicates the likelihood that a member of X shares the same neighborhood either with someone from Y (reflecting the potential for intergroup interaction) or with other members of X (reflecting intragroup isolation). Because exposure measures take group size into account, Stanley Lieberson concluded in 1980 that they are better than D for representing how segregation is experienced by average members of X and Y.

Segregation and Inequality

This concern with experience underscores the importance of residential segregation as a sociological as well as a spatial phenomenon. During the first half of the twentieth century, human ecologists tended to view the locational circumstances of a group as a natural expression of its position or standing in society. In the United States, these ecologists noted the benefits of segregation, especially to European immigrants for whom living side by side with compatriots offered familiarity, comfort, and support. Later scholars have adopted a less benign perspective, emphasizing the profound connection between segregation and inequality. While some see segregation as an outcome of economic disparities, others argue that segregation plays a causal role, shaping the life chances of group members. In 1993, Douglas S. Massey and Nancy A. Denton contended that the development of the urban underclass could be traced to the manner in which segregation concentrates disadvantage in particular neighborhoods.

Such neighborhoods are marked by physical deterioration, inadequate services, health hazards, and high rates of poverty and crime. They also limit a resident's access to the kinds of educational and employment opportunities that promote social and geographic mobility.

Segregation in U.S. Cities

The fateful nature of residential segregation in the United States has been documented most thoroughly for African Americans. In the early 1900s, members of this group were less segregated from native-born whites than were newcomers from Southern and Eastern Europe. Segregation then increased dramatically through mid-century as black migrants from the Southern states flooded into the northern industrial cities and encountered constraints on housing choices. By the latter part of the century, the most intense phase of segregation had passed. Nevertheless, data from the 2000 census revealed an average black-white dissimilarity (D) score for metropolitan areas that still exceeded 60—a level greater than that for segregation between whites and other minorities. In terms of exposure, the typical black urbanite today lives in a neighborhood containing a majority of black occupants.

The fact that even affluent African Americans are underrepresented in desirable residential settings demonstrates the inability of socioeconomic differences to explain fully black-white segregation. An alternative explanation stresses the institutional barriers that blacks continue to face in the housing market despite legislative efforts to curb discrimination (e.g., the Fair Housing Act of 1968 [amended in 1988], the Equal Credit Opportunity Act of 1974, the Community Reinvestment Act of 1977). Several audit studies, in which purported minority and white homeseekers (actually research confederates) approach real estate agents about advertised properties, document the unfavorable treatment received not only by African Americans but also by Latinos. In 1995 John Yinger reported that, compared to whites, these groups receive less information about homes for sale or rent, are shown fewer units, and are more often steered toward lower-income areas. Audit studies of mortgage lenders and insurers provide similar evidence of discrimination.

The residential preferences of individuals help to sustain segregation. There is ongoing debate in the United States over whether African Americans prefer to live in integrated neighborhoods or whether—perhaps in response to the anticipated negative reactions of whites—they would rather live in settings where they are numerically dominant. The influence of white preferences is less ambiguous. Some white residents of an area may move out when its racial mix exceeds their tolerance for integration. More importantly, other white homeseekers elect not to move in, prompting further compositional shifts and, ultimately, avoidance of the area by a greater number of whites. Whatever the motivation, the mobility decisions of whites and blacks drive the process of neighborhood racial transition. Such decisions are thus a key micro-level mechanism through which the aggregate pattern of segregation is perpetuated.

Though that pattern remains largely intact in U.S. cities, the period since 1970 has witnessed several noteworthy changes, including at least small declines in black-white segregation across most metropolitan areas, increasing black suburbanization, and a rising number of racially integrated neighborhoods. These changes may result from the strengthening of fair housing legislation or the expansion of the black middle class, but the evidence is not definitive. Decreases in black-white segregation coincide with increases in the racial and ethnic diversity of the United States as a whole. African Americans in cities with large Asian and Latino populations tend to be less segregated, suggesting that other minority groups serve as a buffer between whites and blacks. Intergroup contact in diverse communities may also reduce ethnic antagonisms.

Asian and Latino residential experiences in the United States differ from those of blacks in several ways. Although substantial variation exists within the two broad categories (Laotian vs. Japanese, Cuban vs. Salvadoran, etc.), Asians and Latinos are generally less segregated from whites than blacks are. Moreover, their segregation appears less permanent, with clustering in enclaves—a voluntary response of immigrants to language and cultural obstacles—diminishing as higher-status households move to suburban neighborhoods or settle in them directly. Spatial assimilation of households, however, does not always reduce the level of segregation. In fact, 1990–2000 census results show approximate stability for both Asians and Latinos on the evenness dimension of segregation and increases on the isolation dimension. In the cities that serve as major immigrant gateways, such as Los Angeles, new arrivals sometimes pile up at a faster pace than their predecessors are able to disperse. The resulting concentration of immigrants and minorities in relatively few destinations could produce a balkanized landscape in which segregation is apparent farther up the geographic scale, with groups sorted by municipality or metropolitan area instead of by neighborhood.

The Future

Should racial and ethnic discrimination weaken significantly, the major constraint on locational choice would be the ability to pay, potentially leading to heightened segregation by income. Such a trend may already have begun in the United States, although Paul Jargowsky's 1996 research found that levels of income segregation remain modest when compared to black-white levels. Life cycle segregation might also intensify as young singles, families with children, and the elderly of all ethnic groups are freer to pursue housing and neighborhood packages suited to their needs. One principle governing the future is clear: As long as societies are stratified, cities will be residentially segregated on some dimension, given the different resources and preferences represented among their populations.

See also: *Poverty and Income Distribution; Racial and Ethnic Composition; Suburbanization.*

BIBLIOGRAPHY

Alba, Richard D., John R. Logan, Brian J. Stults, Gilbert Marzan, and Wenquan Zhang. 1999. "Immigrant Groups in the Suburbs: A Reexamination of Suburbanization and Spatial Assimilation." *American Sociological Review* 64: 446–460.

Ellen, Ingrid Gould. 2000. *Sharing America's Neighborhoods: The Prospects for Stable Integration.* Cambridge, MA: Harvard University Press.

Farley, Reynolds, and William H. Frey. 1994. "Changes in the Segregation of Whites from Blacks during the 1980s: Small Steps toward a More Integrated Society." *American Sociological Review* 59: 23–45.

Farley, Reynolds, Charlotte Steeh, Maria Krysan, Tara Jackson, and Keith Reeves. 1994. "Stereotypes and Segregation: Neighborhoods in the Detroit Area." *American Journal of Sociology* 100: 750–780.

Frey, William H. 1996. "Immigration, Domestic Migration, and Demographic Balkanization in

America: New Evidence for the 1990s." *Population and DevelopmentReview* 22: 741–763.

Iceland, John, Daniel H. Weinberg, and Erika Steinmetz. 2002. *Racial and Ethnic Segregation in the United States: 1980–2000.* Washington, D.C.: U.S. Government Printing Office.

Jargowsky, Paul A. 1996. "Take the Money and Run: Economic Segregation in U.S. Metropolitan Areas." *American Sociological Review* 61:984–998.

Lieberson, Stanley. 1980. *A Piece of the Pie: Blacks and White Immigrants since 1880.* Berkeley: University of California Press.

Massey, Douglas S., and Nancy A. Denton. 1988. "The Dimensions of Residential Segregation." *Social Forces* 67: 281–315.

———. 1993. *American Apartheid: Segregation and the Making of the Underclass.* Cambridge, MA: Harvard University Press.

Yinger, John. 1995. *Closed Doors, Opportunities Lost: The Continuing Costs of Housing Discrimination.* New York: Russell Sage Foundation.

INTERNET RESOURCE.

Lewis Mumford Center for Comparative Urban and Regional Research, State University of New York at Albany. 2001. "The New Ethnic Enclaves in America's Suburbs." <http://www.albany.edu/mumford/census>.

BARRETT A. LEE

RESOURCES AND POPULATION

See *Energy and Population; Natural Resources and Population*

RISK

For demographers, the *risk* of a demographically significant event—such as birth, death, the onset of illness, marriage, migration, or labor force entry or exit—is the probability that the event will occur. Demographically significant events define entry or exit from demographically significant conditions, such as life, death, residence in a politically defined region, various marital statuses, employment, and school enrollment.

The demographic definition of risk ignores the desirability and impact of risked events. For example, sexually-active women of childbearing age are "at risk" of pregnancy, but the demographer's calculation of that risk does not consider if women regard pregnancy with delight or dread. Nor does the demographer's risk evaluation consider differences between pregnancy that is unwanted due to minor timing inconveniences and pregnancy that is unwanted because it would precipitate the mother's death. In common language, negative consequences of events are losses and positive consequences are benefits. The demographic approach is technical. The technical analysis is sometimes simplified by calling the consequence of a risked event a loss; a benefit then is a negative loss.

Demographic Rates

Individuals are *at risk* of an event if and only if their risk exceeds zero. A demographic rate is a time-related measure of exposure to risk. The rate is measured by the number of occurrences of an event per at-risk person per unit time. If events are nonrecurring (e.g., death), and the time interval for the measurement is one unit (e.g., a year), then the rate is the proportion of at-risk persons who experience the event per time period. In demography, rates at which an event occurs are distinguished from proportions of population segments who experience the event. The denominator of the proportion, but not the denominator of the rate, may include persons who are not at risk (e.g., men are not at risk of giving birth).

Rates are used to calculate or estimate important time-related measures, including the extent to which members of a population who enter a demographically significant state remain in it over time, the probabilities that an individual who enters that state will remain in it for various numbers of consecutive time periods, and the expected or mean future time remaining in a state for persons who already have been in the state a particular length of time. These measures include the so-called life-table quantities: age-specific death rates, age-specific expected length of remaining life, and proportion of the population surviving at each specific age.

Age-specific rates for a population are often applied to hypothetical or *standard* age distributions to compute standardized or adjusted rates, life expectancies, and other quantities for the entire population. Alternatively, hypothetical or standard rates are applied to the observed age distribution of a population to produce adjusted rates and expectancies for population aggregates.

Methods of Analysis

Risks can be simple or competing. For example, employed persons are at risk of job loss from mortality, retirement, layoff, mandatory military service, incarceration, and voluntary job termination; employed persons who leave their jobs by dying cannot also leave by retirement, layoff, or any other means. Competing risks are used to produce multiple decrement life tables in which members of a population can exit a demographic condition via several specified, mutually exclusive routes (e.g., one can exit the civilian non-institutionalized population by mortality, emigration, or institutionalization). Demographic risk analysis often focuses on socioeconomic differentials in exposure to risk of death and other demographically significant events, implicitly examining the effects on mortality of socioeconomic factors such as schooling, occupation, and race.

Because of practical limitations on the size of available datasets, empirical analysis of many socioeconomic differentials in risk requires multivariate statistical methods. Methods such as logit and probit analysis can be applied in some situations involving a risked event that can occur only once. Poisson regression methods are useful in those situations when the event can occur more than once. Multinomial logit and multinomial probit methods are useful in those situations when there are competing risks, only one of which can occur, and only once. For data that gives the duration of *spells* (uninterrupted periods spent in a demographic state of interest) various types of survival analysis methods are useful, including those based on exponential, Weibull, lognormal, and loglogistic distributions. Cox's proportional hazard method is frequently useful. Appropriate methods also appear in the literature on event history analysis.

Risk and Loss

Effective design of government policy and business strategy often requires prognostications of (a) future demographic risks, rates and proportions, and (b) the exposure to losses (i.e., costs and benefits) that would be associated with these risks, rates, and proportions, if they occurred as projected. The future or past size and age distribution of a population in a demographically significant condition can be projected or estimated by application of a set of age-specific survival rates to the current age-distribution of that population. In practice, all estimates and projections necessarily are based on a combination of information and conjecture about past, current, and sometimes future risks and other factors. Data limitations and methodological disputes add uncertainty. A common but incomplete response to this uncertainty is to make demographic projections in sets, each element of which is based on different assumptions about unknown information. But demography offers no standard procedures for choosing among the members of a set of projections, and the choice is inescapably subject to dispute. Production of a set of projections saves the demographer from the need to defend intrinsically-subjective speculation about the unknown, and it pushes disputes about demographic projections outside of demography.

The loss distribution. If it is possible to evaluate the losses associated with demographic events, then it is possible and often useful to evaluate the general level of exposure to loss from a set of risks, or from different subsets of those risks. Common descriptive statistics in addition to the mean and variance are informative but not routinely used. The expected loss is the first moment of the loss distribution, otherwise known as its mean or expectation. If outcomes x are continuously differentiable and occur with probability $\Pr(x)$ and loss $L(x)$, then the expected loss, $E(L)$, is given by $E(L) = \int L(x) \Pr(x) dx$. If outcomes are discrete, then $E(L) = \Sigma_i L(x_i) \Pr(x_i)$. The variance of $L(x)$ describes the accuracy with which loss can be anticipated without additional predictive information. The higher the variance, the less informative is the mean about the loss that one is likely to experience. The worst case loss is the maximum of the loss distribution.

In the absence of concrete knowledge about the future, insurance provides a defense against disruptively large losses and, more generally, a hedge against variance in the distribution of losses. Insurance permits individuals to experience some present loss with certainty (in the form of payment of premiums) in exchange for protection against uncertain future losses that exceed a threshold (the insurance deductible). Insurance commonly is available for only some risked events; for those that cannot be insured, the analysis of risk and loss exposure, and planning on the basis of that analysis, is particularly useful.

Valuing losses. Demography itself is seldom, if ever, informative about how to compare different types of losses. Comparison of dissimilar losses requires a theory of value, or at least some principles about how to compare dissimilar demographic states and the events, such as birth, death, employment, and migration that cause them to change. For example, how is one to compare the losses associated with 100 deaths from workplace injuries to job loss by 60,000 employed persons? Numerous and conflicting economic, legal, aesthetic, emotional, political, religious, and other analyses of value exist. Thus, disputes are endemic to considerations of the losses associated with demographic projections. Policies are often evaluated on their actual or projected effects on mortality and other demographically significant events. These disputes are especially severe when they concern social policies that involve trade-offs between risks of different types, such as increased unemployment risk and increased mortality risk.

Conflicts also often focus on risk (probability) estimation and worst case analysis. The *worst imaginable* event in any situation is likely to be the demographic tragedy of massive loss of human life. Imaginable events are not necessarily possible. Because the demographic framework examines risk only for those who are at risk, the first question is whether or not the risk of the worst imaginable event is zero or so close to zero that it should be treated as such. If this risk is distinguishable from zero, then this loss is the worst case loss. But if this risk is not distinguishable from zero, then this loss passes out of consideration. Heated debate over the risk of the worst imaginable event has been a prominent feature of public policy discussion concerning nuclear power, genetically modified plants and animals, environmental pollution, workplace safety, and other matters.

Expert Versus Popular Views of Risk

Much of the disagreement between experts and the lay public appears to stem from, or to be exacerbated by, the following:

Differences in probability estimation. Lacking technical training and often distrustful of expert pronouncements, substantial proportions of the lay public seem to prefer their own subjective estimates of risk probabilities to the data-based estimates of technical experts. A substantial segment of the population appears to lack intuitive understanding of very small decimal fractions, with consequent difficulty understanding the frequency of occurrence of low-probability events.

Differences in valuation of risked events. Experts tend to focus on quantitative loss measures and tend to use generally accepted estimation methods. In contrast, large segments of the general public rely on subjective evaluations that are quite dissimilar to expert evaluations.

Differences in attention. There are differences in attention given to the worst imaginable loss versus the average, expected, or most-likely loss. Attentive to the accuracy of their predictions over the long run, technical experts tend to give the greatest weight to scenarios that are most likely, and no weight to scenarios that have no probability of occurrence. Substantial segments of the general public focus on the worst imaginable case, perhaps because it inspires the greatest emotional response.

Differences in the conceptualization of losses. At their best, risk experts apply methods that let them make finely-graded comparisons of the losses associated with the occurrence of a risked event to the losses associated with its nonoccurrence. For example, technologies periodically fail disastrously, and disasters take lives (e.g., airplanes crash, bridges collapse, and physician errors kill patients). A simple and popular measure of the impact of technology failure is the number of lives lost from it. But technologies that fail periodically also can prolong and improve the quality of lives. At a minimum, one should compare the number of lives lost from a technology failure to the number of lives that would have been lost if the technology had not been deployed at all. And since everyone dies eventually, regardless of what technology is or is not deployed, the relevant measure is even better approximated by the number of person-years of life lost by the failure of a technology, compared to the number of person-years of life that would be lost by not deploying that same technology. Technical experts can apply life tables or analogous methods to calculate the loss of person-years of remaining life. Analysis and comparison of age-specific death rates (rather than numbers of deaths) is yet more complicated and directs attention to the societal rather than the individual consequences of deadly events. Quality-of-life issues are important too.

Differences in considerations of "spillover" effects. Experts tend to confine their analyses to variables that they can measure; substantial segments of the general public appear to consider the consequences of a risked event on their entire way of life. Losing a job can be seen as a simple loss of income, or it can be seen as the unraveling of everything supported by that income in the family of the employed person.

Differences in treatment of losses associated with unfamiliar risks. Substantial portions of the general public appear to respond to danger from an unfamiliar event (e.g., anthrax infection by contaminated mail, real or imagined illness from radiation-sterilized food) by increasing their estimate of the risk (probability) of experiencing the event, increasing their estimate of the loss that would result from the experience, or both, sometimes with anxiety, hostility, and the growth of social movements and collective action added.

Differences between technical and lay approaches to risk and loss exposure lead to questions about when it is useful to apply the technical analysis to public policy debates, and how to present it to those who combine high emotional interest in the subject with low exposure to the technical issues. Answers to these questions are external to demography, and they rest on judgments and strategic decisions about what is worth studying in detail, and what social choice inferences should be emphasized, stated, or left implicit. Widely-felt emotions and subjective impressions are social facts that cannot be ignored, but they are poor tools for analysis of risk and loss exposure. Those who claim that risk and loss exposure are equivalent to the general public's perception of them risk seriously flawed results.

Equally unstable analyses may result from the so-called *rival rationalities* view that conceives of experts as focused narrowly on statistical analysis of that which can be quantified, and an equally rational general public focused on a wide range of qualitative aspects of risk, including voluntariness and fairness of risk and loss exposure, and the dread with which a possible loss is perceived. The rival rationality view of risk assessment is not subject to any requirement for empirical evidence on risk magnitudes. This method is likely to be particularly troublesome when

the risks of advanced technologies are considered. When science is misunderstood, as it often is, then popular misconceptions can and do lead to perceptions of imagined risks involving horrible but imaginary future losses. Finally, there appears to be confusion regarding the perceptions that are the basis for lay assessments of risk and loss exposure: It has been argued that anxiety about a risked event makes exposure to that event seem less voluntary, thereby raising the perceived risk of the event and exposure to loss from it, regardless of any actual difference in risk or exposure.

Conclusion

In summary, demography offers a particular conceptual and methodological framework for the measurement and analysis of risk; for predicting, forecasting, and comparing risks in different times and places; and for understanding how a given risk structure affects a population. The demographic approach to risk emphasizes the explicit connection between the structure of risk experienced by a population and the structure of age—the time spent in a demographically significant condition—that the population develops over time.

Demographic techniques emphasize the proper technical calculation of demographic risk measures. Demographic methods permit and even encourage analysis based on hypothetical values of demographic risks. These calculations are an important step in the analysis of exposure to loss. But demography offers no guidance about how to value the losses (and benefits) associated with the occurrence of risked events. Thus, demographic analysis of loss exposure requires combining demographic risk calculation with loss evaluations provided by other disciplines, engendering all the difficulties described above.

See also: *Accidents; Disasters; Life Tables; Event History Analysis; Value of Life, Economic.*

BIBLIOGRAPHY

Margolis, Howard. 1996. *Dealing with Risk.* Chicago: University of Chicago Press.

Preston, Samuel, Patrick Heuveline, and Michel Guillot. 2001. *Demography: Measuring and Modeling Population Processes.* Oxford, Eng. and Malden, MA: Blackwell Publishers.

Slovic, Paul. 2000. *The Perception of Risk.* Earthscan Publications.

Timmreck, Thomas. 1994. *An Introduction to Epidemiology*. Boston, MA, and London: Jones and Bartlett.

ROSS M. STOLZENBERG
HOWARD MARGOLIS

RURAL-URBAN BALANCE

Large-scale shifts of population from the countryside to the city have been a feature of the demographic and geographic landscape for more than a century. Urbanization has accompanied the demographic transition in virtually all middle- and high-income countries. Urbanization, by definition, results in declining share of the population in rural areas. For instance, the Japanese rural population share dropped from 50 percent to 21 percent between 1950 and 2000, while in Canada the corresponding drop was from 39 percent to 21 percent. When urbanization is well advanced, it is accompanied by a decline also in the absolute size of the rural population, as is illustrated for the period from 1950 through 2000 by data for several major European nations: France (−21%), Germany (−47%), Italy (−12%), and the United Kingdom (−22%). (In the United States, the rural population was slowly increasing over that period—a rise of 14%—but is projected to gradually decline over the first half of the twenty-first century.) These shifts in population distribution are due to the combined effects of rural outmigration, the changing relative size of the rural and urban populations, rural-urban differences in natural increase, and the reclassification of territory from rural to urban.

Phases of Rural-Urban Population Balance

In the contemporary industrialized countries, shifts in the internal distribution of the population have moved well beyond simple urbanization. One can identify four broad phases of rural-urban population balance that characterize the trajectory of these societies.

A first phase could be termed classic urbanization. In Europe and North America this phase commenced with the Industrial Revolution and continued into the twentieth century. The growth of cities and urban territory outpaced that of the countryside, fed by net rural-urban internal migration. The second phase, commencing in the beginning of the twentieth century but accelerating by mid-century, might be characterized as suburbanization, or perhaps more accurately, as metropolitan expansion. Throughout this second phase the share of the population in the countryside continued to decline, and did so eventually also in terms of absolute size. With declining fertility, the rate of natural increase could no longer counterbalance the effect of net migration loss, initiating a process of outright rural depopulation. Rural depopulation was most notable in agricultural areas. In the United States the rural population of the heavily agricultural West North Central (northern Midwest) census division declined steadily in each decade from 1920 to 1970.

The third phase we might label "counterurbanization." The phenomenon was first noticed for the United States in the 1970s, but counterurbanization trends were soon also noticed in Europe, Japan, and Australia. This demographic surprise was alternately described as the "nonmetropolitan turnaround" or a "rural renaissance," and it generated a considerable amount of debate about its determinants and likely persistence. Observers variously attributed it to changes in industrial structure, technical issues in geographic classification, growth of retirement communities, and cultural shifts affecting locational preferences.

The fourth phase, about which there is less consensus, may be called "population diffusion." It describes a pattern of population redistribution discernible in most industrialized, high-income countries at the start of the twenty-first century. It can be characterized by (a) the location of a very large majority of the population in urban regions; (b) population deconcentration within urban regions; and (c) the absence of consistent, geographically pervasive, large-scale, unidirectional flows of population. For instance, the 5.2 percent U.S. nonmetropolitan gain in the 1970s was followed by only 2.7 percent in the 1980s, and then 10.3 percent in the 1990s. In Australia, selected outlying local government areas (LGAs) recorded losses between 1996 and 2001, while capital regions and some smaller coastal settlement areas grew. France, in particular, has shown appreciable variation in growth and decline across rural territory in recent decades. Contributing to these trends in population geography are shifts in underlying demographic dynamics. As fertility declines and natural increase diminishes to near-zero, much of the urban-rural population change is determined by net migration. The relative size of the urban and rural populations and their age structures also likely to come into play in determining population change over time. For example, labor migration may redistribute rural-origin persons away from the rural hinterland toward other metropolitan (and selected nonmetropolitan) employment sites, while retirement migration may relocate individuals away from these sites to lower density communities.

The declining share of the rural population, and also its decline in absolute terms, was accompanied by a significant shift in the character of rural economic activity and social life during the latter half of the twentieth century. Rurality has been associated with occupations such as farming, animal husbandry, fishing, and mining. At one time "rural" was also synonymous with limited education, high fertility, "traditional" values, and disengagement from urban-industrial life. This is no longer necessarily the case. At the dawn of the twenty-first century, urban and rural occupy locations along a geographic settlement spectrum. Residents of territory classified as rural or nonmetropolitan in high-income societies have access to many of the same products and services of contemporary society that city-dwellers enjoy. Their geographic distance from some employment and cultural opportunities tends to be offset by better access to modern transportation and communication technology. It remains true, however, that within this broad scale most urbanized societies retain pockets of rural areas for which social exclusion is an enduring reality.

As to middle-income countries, many of them have already experienced much of the demographic transition and are in the midst of the rural-urban transition. Major Latin American countries (Mexico, Colombia, Brazil) have experienced a substantial decline in the share of the rural population, generally from about one-half around 1950 to about one-quarter by the end of the twentieth century. Malaysia and the Philippines record less than half of their population in rural areas. With declining fertility and continued urbanization, those rural areas out of reach of metropolitan spillover and having little destination attractiveness for internal migrants, are likely to experience absolute declines in population before long.

Changing Concepts and Definitions

Concepts and definitions are intrinsically bound up with the description and analysis of trends in population concentration. In the first phase of population shift, the period of significant declines in the rural share, notions of "urban" and "rural" may have been relatively obvious and readily captured by a dichotomy. As urban populations became dominant in many countries—and with the prospect of a world half-urban early in the twenty-first century—definitions have shifted along with population. Most national population statistics still recognize "urban" and "rural." Conventionally, settlements exceeding a certain threshold—often from about 2,000 to 5,000 persons—are classified as urban. This definition worked well enough in a predominantly dispersed agrarian society. But as the share of the rural population declined, the classification of "urban" territory in industrialized societies needed elaboration, adding terms such as "metropolis," "megalopolis," and the like. The reclassification of territory and of persons by place of residence has implications for the "rural" population. Some metropolitan areas, as defined, extended far into their hinterland, even to include agrarian and very low-density settlements. (China and the United States both offer examples of this.) The resulting reclassification of persons from rural to urban would further reduce the rural population. These issues of classification and their evolution over the historical span of demographic data collection are at once an illustration of the difficulty of capturing the event, and more importantly, a recognition that re-definition often follows changes in behavior of people at the individual and societal level.

See also: *Suburbanization; Urbanization.*

BIBLIOGRAPHY

Bogue, Donald J. 1985. *The Population of the United States.* New York: Free Press.

Champion, Anthony G. 1992. "Urban and Regional Demographic Trends in the Developed World." *Urban Studies* 29: 461–482.

Lichter, Daniel, and Glenn V. Fuguitt. 1982. "The Transition to Nonmetropolitan Population Deconcentration." *Demography* 19: 211–221.

Long, Larry, and Diana DeAre. 1988. "US Population Distribution: A Perspective on the Nonmetropolitan Turnaround." *Population and Development Review* 14: 433–450.

White, Michael J., and Peter R. Mueser. 1989. "Explaining the Association Between Rates of Inmigration and Outmigration." *Papers of the Regional Science Association* 67: 121–134.

INTERNET RESOURCES.

Australia Bureau of Statistics. 2002. <http://www.abs.gov.au/ausstats>.

Bessy-Pietri, Pascale, et al. 2000. "Evolutions contrastées du rural." (Recensement de la population 1999, report #726.) Institut National de la Statistique et des Etudes Economiques (INSEE, France). <http://www.insee.fr.>.

Johnson, Kenneth M., and Calvin Beale. 2002. "The Rural Rebound." <http://www.luc.edu/dept/sociology/johnson/p99webn.html>.

United Nations, Population Division. 2002. *World Urbanization Prospects: The 2001 Revision.* New York. <http://esa.un.org/unpp>.

MICHAEL J. WHITE

RURAL-URBAN MIGRATION

See *Internal Migration; Urbanization*

RYDER, NORMAN B.

(1923–)

Canadian-American demographer and sociologist, Norman B. Ryder studied political economy at the University of Toronto and obtained his Ph.D. in sociology from Princeton University in 1951. In the first years of his career, he worked at the University of Toronto and the Dominion Bureau of Statistics—now Statistics Canada—in Ottawa. He joined the Department of Sociology at the University of Wisconsin in 1956, where he founded the Center for Demography and Ecology and was appointed Thorstein Veblen Professor of Sociology. He moved to Princeton University in 1971 as professor of sociology but was based primarily at Princeton's Office of Population Research. He was president of the Population Association of America (1972–1973) and of the Sociological Research Association (1974–1975).

Three articles published in 1964 and 1965 stemming from his doctoral thesis—on the concept of a population, on "demographic translation" (between period and cohort measures), and on the cohort as a concept in the study of social change—were early major contributions to theory and methodology in demography. (The thesis itself, *The Cohort Approach*, was published in 1980.) Independently of French demographer Louis Henry (1911–1991), he devised parity-progression measures of fertility change and he brought birth history and parity analysis to the center of fertility forecasting.

Ryder was co-director, with American demographer Charles F. Westoff (b. 1927), of the U.S. National Fertility Study, the three rounds of which (1965, 1970, and 1975) produced evidence of the widespread diffusion of modern contraception and recorded the distinctive patterns of reproductive behavior of American families in the middle decades of the twentieth century.

Ryder was an important interpreter of the post-World War II baby boom, emphasizing its elements of continuity with the past—for example, noting that the birth-rate increase did not entail a reversal of the long-run decline in higher-parity births. He took the Princeton side in asserting a determinative role of the pill in the renewed American fertility decline, as against the view from Berkeley, espoused principally by Judith Blake, of demand-driven change. In the 1970s he was a key player in the design of the World Fertility Survey, although later (in a 1986 review of a volume summarizing its findings) quite critical of WFS achievements. He also made significant contributions to family demography.

See also: *Cohort Analysis; Demography, History of; Henry, Louis.*

BIBLIOGRAPHY

SELECTED WORKS BY NORMAN B. RYDER.

Ryder, Norman B. 1964. "Notes on the Concept of a Population." *American Journal of Sociology* 69(5): 447–463

———. 1964. "The Process of Demographic Translation." *Demography* 1: 74–82.

———. 1965. "The Cohort as a Concept in the Study of Social Change." *American Sociological Review* 30(6) 843–861.

————. 1975. "Reproductive Behavior and the Family Life Cycle." In *The Population Debate: Dimensions and Perspectives. Papers of the World Population Conference, Bucharest, 1974.* New York: United Nations. Volume 2, pp. 278–288.

————. 1980. *The Cohort Approach: Essays in the Measurement of Temporal Variations in Demographic Behavior.* New York: Arno Press.

————. 1982. *Progressive Fertility Analysis.* (World Fertility Survey, Technical Bulletin no. 8) The Hague, Netherlands: International Statistical Institute.

————. 1983. "Fertility and Family Structure." *Population Bulletin of the United Nations* 15: 15–34.

————. 1986. "Observations on the History of Cohort Fertility in the United States." *Population and Development Review* 12: 617–643.

————. 1990. "What is Going to Happen to American Fertility?" *Population and Development Review* 16: 433–454.

Ryder, Norman B., and Charles F. Westoff. 1971. *Reproduction in the United States 1965.* Princeton: Princeton University Press.

Westoff, Charles F., and Norman B. Ryder. 1977. *The Contraceptive Revolution.* Princeton: Princeton University Press.

JACQUES LÉGARÉ

S

SANGER, MARGARET

(1879–1966)

Pioneer of the birth control movement in America, and internationally, Margaret Sanger arguably achieved more for reproductive choice than any other person in the twentieth century. The sixth of eleven children, Sanger was strongly influenced by her Freethinker, Irish father, Michael Higgins. Working as a nurse in New York, she saw what she called "the turbid ebb and flow of misery," and became convinced of women's need for birth control information. The 1873 Comstock Law prohibited distribution of such information through the U.S. mail. In 1914, Sanger was prosecuted under this law for the content of her magazine *The Woman Rebel,* although the case was eventually dropped. In 1916, she founded the American Birth Control League and was imprisoned briefly for opening a birth control clinic, the first in America, in Brooklyn. By curtailing her socialist views, she garnered substantial middle-class support for her cause. Partial victory was achieved in the Crane decision of 1918, in which the law was amended to permit contraceptive advice as a medical therapy.

Sanger had fled to England in 1914 to avoid prosecution and during that time she associated with members of the Malthusian League and with English psychologist and writer Havelock Ellis (1859–1939). In the 1920s, her interest in world population issues grew. Like many in her generation, she espoused eugenics. She was instrumental in setting up the first World Population Conference, in Geneva in 1927, which brought together the leading demographers of the time. Birth control, however, was deemed too sensitive to be discussed, and her own role in the meeting was kept at a low profile, although she did edit the published proceedings. An outgrowth of this conference was the establishment of the International Union for the Scientific Study of Population Problems.

Sanger was a timid but effective speaker and a master of publicity. Her 1938 autobiography, a number of laudatory biographies, and a tract from a Catholic publisher (entitled *Killer Angel*), focus on her early turbulent years. However, two of Sanger's greatest achievements came when she was over 70. In 1951, she challenged Gregory Pincus, the reproductive physiologist, to develop the "perfect contraceptive." With financial help from Sanger's friend, the philanthropist Katherine McCormick, Pincus and his colleagues went on to develop the first birth control pill in 1960. In 1952, in Bombay, Sanger played a key role in founding the International Planned Parenthood Federation, and became its first president.

Powered by an unshakeable belief in her cause, Sanger's protest against an unjust law grew into a crusade that changed the way women in America—and in a growing number of other countries—live.

See also: *Birth Control, History of; Eugenics; Family Planning Programs.*

BIBLIOGRAPHY

SELECTED WORKS BY MARGARET SANGER.

Sanger, Margaret. 1970 [1938]. *An Autobiography.* New York: Maxwell.

SELECTED WORKS ABOUT MARGARET SANGER.

Asbell, Bernard. 1995. *The Pill: A Biography of the Drug that Changed the World.* New York: Random House.

Gray, Madeline. 1979. *Margaret Sanger: A Biography of the Champion of Birth Control.* New York: Richard Marek Publishers.

Moore, Gloria, and Ronald Moore. 1986. *Margaret Sanger and the Birth Control Movement: A Bibliography, 1911–1984.* Metuchen, NJ: Scarecrow Press.

DAVID MALCOLM POTTS

SAUVY, ALFRED

(1898–1990)

Alfred Sauvy, French demographer, statistician, economist, and man of letters, was founding director of Institut national d'études démographiques and founding editor of the journal *Population.* After graduating from the Ecole polytechnique, Sauvy joined Statistique Générale de France, the country's central statistical office, predecessor of today's INSEE (Institut National de la Statistique et des Etudes Economiques). His work there involved him in demographic studies, such as an examination of the effect of immigration on France's population, and the preparation, in 1928, of the first modern-type population projections in France, distinguishing age and sex. These projections, repeated in the 1930s, shed light on the longer-term consequences of maintaining below-replacement levels of fertility. (His projections for France, published in 1932, predicted a 1975 population between 31 and 39 million. The actual population, reflecting a sharp turnaround in French fertility, falling mortality, and substantial immigration, turned out to be 53 million.) Sauvy, and his intellectual mentor, Adolphe Landry (1874–1956, Minister of Social Affairs and author of *La révolution démographique,* [1934]) were concerned about the effects of demographic trends on France's national strength and specifically with the fiscal problems inherent in the observed and anticipated shifting ratio between the old and the young. Both saw the solution to this in the rejuvenation of the population through higher birth rates. Sauvy, with Landry, was active in the late 1930s in the preparation of policy reforms aimed at stimulating fertility. He was also pro-immigration, favoring a selective policy, followed by assimilation. His first book, *Richesse et Population,* which appeared during World War II, was a recapitulation of his analysis of economic-demographic interactions in France.

After the war, Sauvy became an influential and highly visible figure in France—a demographer who was also an intellectual with a strong and distinctive voice in contemporary debates on issues of social and economic policy. More than any other demographer in France, or elsewhere, Sauvy reached a broad readership through his many books (more than 40 in all, over four decades) on population and economics, written in an appealing style and accessible to the intelligent reader. That influence was extended by his numerous articles in newspapers and periodicals, such as *Le Monde* and *L'Observateur.* He wrote on many themes but his principal and recurrent interests were the need for strengthening pro-family policies aimed at sustaining the postwar resurgence of birth rates, encouraging immigration in ways that serve well-conceived domestic interests, and fighting the spirit of Malthusianism (the great disease, manifest in psychological dispositions as much as demographic behavior, that he saw as the mortal enemy of France's greatness) by pursuing a pro-growth economic and social agenda. Sauvy's positions on these matters did not fit well, if at all, into the conventional political categories of the French left and right. Although a socialist at heart, his economic prescriptions, even though permeated with a spirit of dirigisme, were typically pro-market and pro-competition, and his demographic policies were easily classified as conservative or, on matters of birth control, even reactionary.

Sauvy's platform for his role as an advocate for specific policies was his directorship of the Institut national d'études démographiques (INED), founded in 1945, a post he held for 17 years; INED's scientific journal *Population,* which he launched in 1946 and which he edited until 1974; and Sauvy's own professional work, recognized in 1959 with his appointment as professor at the Collège de France. INED and *Population* were his lasting creations, with few, if any, peers among population research organizations and scientific population journals. Among his books two stand out as his most important contributions: the two-volume *Théorie générale de la popula-*

tion (1952–1954 and, in a revised edition, 1963–1966) and the four volume *Histoire économique de la France entre les deux guerres* (1965–1975). *Théorie générale de la population* was a bold synthesis of contemporary knowledge on population and its relationships with socioeconomic phenomena, discussing such issues as population optimums, technological progress and employment, social classes and social structure, ideas on overpopulation, and international migration. In addressing these and many other issues, Sauvy largely avoided use of the tool kit of modern social science. He did not hold those research instruments in very high esteem; his primary interests were in lucidity, directness, and social relevance. An English translation of *Théorie Générale de la population* appeared in 1969. *Histoire économique de la France entre les deux guerres* was a magisterial treatment of the subject, with strong emphasis on the role of demographic factors, that drew on Sauvy's personal observations about and active involvement in the events of the interwar period.

Sauvy's professional interests were firmly focused on France and its population problems—exclusively so in the first two decades of his professional career and largely so during the remainder of it. He played an international role, however, as France's representative on the United Nations Population Commission (from its inception in 1947 to 1974) and by serving as president of the International Union for the Scientific Study of Population (IUSSP) (1961–1963). The great acceleration of world population growth in the postwar decades and the consequent efforts toward development of international population policies did, from time to time, draw his attention, and some of his writings addressed global issues. As a case in point, he is the father of the term, now obsolete but once popular, "third world," that first appeared in his 1952 article in *L'Observateur* entitled "Three Worlds, One Planet." The term he actually used, *tiers monde*, reminiscent of associations with French revolutionary history, is, however, richer in meaning than the English equivalent. However, Sauvy was not a globalist. In a 1949 article, "The 'False Problem' of World Population" (an English translation appeared in 1990), he argued that the concept of "world population" was artificial, hence largely meaningless, and that using it could only lead to confused thinking and erroneous policy conclusions. He saw the international system as one built on the jealously guarded principle of national sovereignty. "Terrestrial compartmental-

izations," he observed, "are sufficiently well established to render any global calculus that ignores them quite pointless" (Sauvy 1990, p. 760). Problems of population, he contended, differed from country to country and required different, and preferably home-made, medicines.

Sauvy was utterly devoid of pretense—perhaps a reflection of his Catalan origin. He often rode his bicycle to his Paris office, wearing his inevitable beret. He was a devotee of rugby, and he played until he was well into his 50s. He assembled a unique collection of rare books, mostly from eighteenth-century French economic and demographic literature, and was the force behind INED's annotated re-editions of some of those works. He died on the eve of his 92nd birthday.

See also: *Demography, History of; Landry, Adolphe; Optimum Population; Population Thought, Contemporary.*

BIBLIOGRAPHY

SELECTED WORKS BY ALFRED SAUVY.

Sauvy, Alfred. 1943. *Richesse et population.* Paris: Payot.

———. 1945. *Bien-être et population.* Paris: Editions sociales françaises.

———. 1949. "Le 'faux problème' de la population mondiale." *Population* 4(3): 447–462. Transl. "The 'False Problem' of World Population." *Population and Development Review* 16(4), 1990: 759–774.

———. 1952–1954. *Théorie générale de la population,* Vol. I: *Economie et croissance,* Vol. II: *La vie des populations.* Paris: Presses universitaires de France. Transl.: General Theory of Population, trans. by Christophe Campos. New York: Basic Books, 1969.

———. 1953. *L'Europe et sa population.* Paris: Les éditions internationales.

———. 1958. *De Malthus à Mao Tse-Toung: le problème de la population dans le monde.* Paris: Denoël. Transl.: *Fertility and Survival: Population Problems from Malthus to Mao Tse-Tung.* New York: Criterion Books, 1961.

———. 1959. *La montée des jeunes.* Paris: Calmann-Lévy.

———. 1963. *Malthus et les deux Marx: le problème de la faim et de la guerre dans le monde.* Paris: Denoël.

———. 1965–1975. *Histoire économique de la France entre les deux guerres,* 4 Vols. Paris: Arthème Fayard.

———. 1973. *Croissance zéro?* Paris: Calmann-Lévy. Transl. *Zero Growth?* New York: Praeger, 1975.

———. 1973. *La Population: sa mesure, ses mouvements, ses lois.* Paris: Presses universitaires de France.

———. 1976. *Eléments de démographie.* Paris: Presses universitaires de France.

———. 1980. *La Machine et le chômage: le progrès technique et l'emploi.* Paris: Dunod.

———. 1987. *L' Europe submergée. Sud-Nord dans trente ans.* Paris: Dunod.

———. 2001. *La vieillesse des nations.* Anthology: selected and annotated texts by Jean-Claude Chesnais. Paris, Gallimard.

SELECTED WORKS ABOUT ALFRED SAUVY.

Institut National d'Etudes Démographiques. 1992. "Hommage à Alfred Sauvy." *Population* Special Issue (November–December) 47(6).

Keyfitz, Nathan. 1990. "Alfred Sauvy." *Population and Development Review* 16(4): 727–733.

Lévy, Michel. 1990. *Alfred Sauvy compagnon du siècle.* Paris: La manufacture.

Tabah, Léon. 1991. "Alfred Sauvy: Statistician, Economist, Demographer and Iconoclast (1898–1990)." *Population Studies* 45(2): 353–357.

JEAN-CLAUDE CHESNAIS

SECOND DEMOGRAPHIC TRANSITION

The French characterization of the onset of the decline in marital fertility late in the eighteenth century as a *révolution démographique,* found no international favor. Instead, the process became known as the "demographic transition." The implication was that populations were passing through a period of change from one demographic regime to another. More particularly, a regime marked by a combination of high mortality and compensatory high fertility would be replaced by a regime in which the combination of low levels of both mortality and fertility would ensure a new and stable equilibrium. Rapid population growth would be a transitional phenomenon. Thus, if fertility had indeed declined to replacement level, there would then have been little interest in post-transitional fertility trends. These trends would have been in line with the underlying concept.

Negative Population Growth

But things did not turn out that way. Advanced industrial societies face a new imbalance between the components of natural population growth. Fertility has declined well below replacement level. Life expectancies at advanced ages have risen substantially. The combination of the two leads to a rapidly aging population. Negative rates of natural population growth are already observed in numerous countries. National projections show that this phenomenon will spread. There are no indications this state of affairs is temporary; hence the conclusion that a second demographic transition is in progress.

The justification for that term lies in the crucial difference between the situation in the early twenty-first century and that of the late-eighteenth century. Then, the decline in mortality upset the balance and led to an adjustment in fertility behavior. Now it is the second natural population growth factor—fertility—that apparently makes reaching and maintaining a long-term population balance an unattainable objective. The fundamental changes in fertility and family formation in industrialized societies after the mid-1960s were revolutionary—completely unexpected and occurring with astonishing simultaneity. Continuation of unprecedented low levels of fertility is bound to generate a further adjustment in demographic regime.

The third determinant of population growth, international migration, is the obvious variable to provide compensation. Indeed, the term "replacement migration" has been coined to draw attention to that role. More importantly, positive rates of net migration already characterize advanced industrial societies.

FIGURE 1

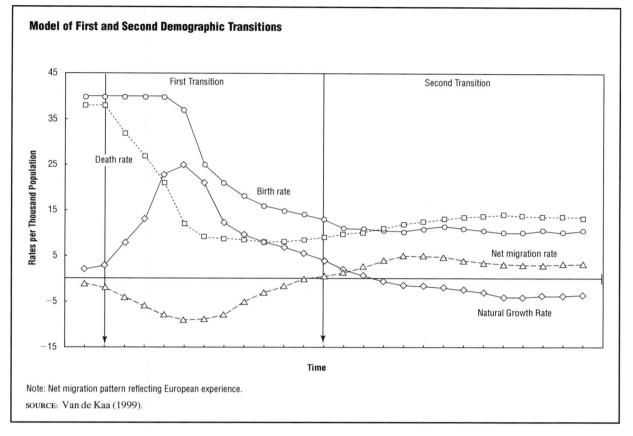

Model of First and Second Demographic Transitions

Note: Net migration pattern reflecting European experience.

SOURCE: Van de Kaa (1999).

Demographic Transition and Migration

Figure 1 illustrates graphically how the first transition may have evolved to become the second. The graph has some novel features. While most demographers are aware that in many industrializing countries emigration helped to reduce the pressure on resources during the period of rapid population growth, the classical picture of the demographic transition usually only displays the changes in the birth rate, death rate, and rate of natural population growth. The model of the first transition presented here rectifies that omission; net migration is included. The model of the second transition is, of course, largely prospective. The underlying assumptions are, however, straightforward and well founded in empirical data.

Aging will cause the death rate to rise; it will exceed the birth rate due both to the comparatively small number of women in the reproductive age groups and a completed family size that, owing to competing aspirations, typically will not reach replacement level. Immigrants, first attracted as guest workers well before population growth rates turned negative, are bound to find their way to more developed regions for many years to come. The assumption is that the inflow remains under some sort of control. Nevertheless, the influx of migrants, whether arriving as refugees, tourists overstaying their visas, asylum seekers, undocumented migrants brought in through trafficking, seasonal laborers, or economic migrants allowed entry under an official scheme, will be a crucial factor in the future growth and population structure of advanced industrial societies.

Changes in Values and the Second Demographic Transition

The suggestion that after the mid-1960s the industrialized countries of Western Europe had entered a new stage in their demographic history was first made by Ron Lesthaeghe and Dirk J. van de Kaa in a Dutch sociological journal in 1986. In selecting the term *second demographic transition* for it, they were clearly influenced by Philippe Ariès's 1980 conference paper entitled "Two Successive Motivations for the Declining of the Birth Rate in the West." In that paper Ariès argued that the decline in the birth rate that began at the end of the eighteenth century "was unleashed by an enormous sentimental and financial investment in the child." The current decrease was "on the contrary, provoked by exactly the opposite attitude. The days of the child-king are over. The under-forty generation is leading us into a new epoch, one in which *the child, to say the least, occupies a smaller place*" [emphasis added]. In their paper Lesthaeghe and van de Kaa extended the change to one from a "bourgeois family model" to an "individualistic family model" affecting not only childbirth but the whole process of family formation and dissolution. There the discussion rested for a while. van de Kaa attemped to broaden the concept to include mortality and migration in papers published in 1988 and 1999.

There can be no doubt that just as occurred during the first transition, the new shifts in demographic patterns result from the interplay of structural, cultural, and technological factors during a complex process of social change. The welfare state ensures citizens an income and protects them from the vagaries of life. New, highly efficient contraception has been introduced; frequently restrictions on abortion and sterilization have been lifted. Significant changes in value systems have been documented. These ideational transformations accentuate individual autonomy, involve the rejection of all forms of institutional controls and authority, and show a rise of expressive values connected with self-fulfillment, according to Lesthaeghe and Johan Surkyn. Thus, they strongly emphasize so-called "postmaterialist" values.

For a while it appeared as if the new transition process would remain limited to Northern and Western Europe. Data for the 1990s show, however, that Southern and Eastern Europe are increasingly affected. Lesthaeghe and Surkyn feel that even "economic recovery in Eastern Europe is not likely to alter the demographic trend in a fundamental way."

Understanding the Second Demographic Transition

Proving the existence of sequences and generalizations in the first transition has not been very easy. John Cleland concluded after surveying half a century of research: "Too many mediating factors obscure

any mechanical dose-response relationship between the probabilities of survival and fertility trends." Researching the second transition will be equally difficult. The increase in life expectancy at advanced ages may, perhaps, be interpreted as the lagged response to greater individual efforts to prevent disease, presumably fueled by the same value changes that generated the shifts in fertility behavior and family formation. The relationship with international migration is, no doubt, much more indirect. A number of theoretical postulates and considerations may apply. However, changes in population growth rates, in age structure, and in the composition of the labor force of advanced industrial societies, are of crucial importance in explaining the onset and continuation of inflows.

See also: *Aging of Population; Ariès, Philippe; Demographic Transition; Fertility, Below-Replacement.*

BIBLIOGRAPHY

Ariès, Philippe. 1980. "Two Successive Motivations for the Declining Birth Rate in the West." *Population and Development Review* 6(4): 645–650.

Cleland, John. 2001. "The Effects of Improved Survival on Fertility: A Reassessment." In *Global Fertility Transition*, Suppl. to Vol. 27: *Population and Development Review*, ed. Rodolfo A. Bulatao and John. B. Casterline. New York: The Population Council.

Lesthaeghe, Ron, and Dominique Meekers. 1986. "Value Changes and the Dimensions of Familism in the European Community." *European Journal of Population* 2: 225–268.

Lesthaeghe, Ron, and Johan Surkyn. 2002. "New Forms of Household Formation in Central and Eastern Europe: Are They Related to Newly Emerging Value Orientations?" IPD-WP 2002-2, Brussels.

Lesthaeghe, Ron, and Dirk J. van de Kaa. 1986. "Twee demografische transities?" In *Bevolking: Groei en Krimp*, eds. Dirk J. van de Kaa and Ron Lesthaeghe. Deventer, Netherlands: Van Loghum Slaterus.

———. 1994. "The Second Demographic Transition Revisited: Theories and Expectations." In *Population and Family in the Low Countries 1993* Amsterdam: Lisse, Zwets and Zeitlinger.

———. 1999. "Europe and Its Population: The Long View." In *European Populations: Unity in Diversity,* ed. Dirk J. van de Kaa, Henri Leridon, Guiseppe Gesano and Marek Okòlski. Dordrecht, Netherlands: Kluwer Academic Publishers.

van de Kaa, Dirk J. 1987. "Europe's Second Demographic Transition." *Population Bulletin* (42) 1.

DIRK J. VAN DE KAA

SEGREGATION

See *Residential Segregation*

SEX RATIO

In most human populations, male and female sub-populations are territorially integrated, but the sex ratio—the ratio of males to females—varies from place to place, especially among small localized populations. When reference is made to the short-lived ratios of men and women in workplaces, institutions, and organizations, the term *gender balance* is more appropriate and is increasingly preferred.

Measures, Accuracy, and Sub-Population Ratios

The sex ratio is usually expressed as a *masculinity ratio*—the number of males per 100 females. It may also be given as a *masculinity proportion* (i.e., percentage of males) or as a percentage excess or deficit of males. Sometimes the ratio is given in transposed form, as the number of females per 100 males (e.g., in India), and sometimes per 1,000 rather than per 100. The United Nations has unsuccessfully attempted to standardize the usage.

Published international data on sex ratios are neither very common nor very accurate, as census enumerations of the two sexes can vary in their reliability. One sex is often less completely enumerated than the other, particularly males in the West (especially among illegal immigrants and those opposed to authority) and females in numerous less developed countries (e.g., Afghanistan, Bangladesh, India, and Pakistan, where son and male preference predominates and females are habitually disadvantaged in numerous ways).

Sex ratios are calculated for many sub-populations (e.g., age, ethnic, and educational groups) as well as for different events, such as conceptions (known as primary sex ratios), births (secondary sex ratios) and deaths, and migration. Population sex ratios, sometimes termed tertiary sex ratios, are determined by sex-differentials in fertility, manifested in the preponderance of male births; sex-differentials in mortality, especially the normally greater longevity of females; and sex-differentials in mobility. The numerical significance of these three factors upon sex ratios of populations varies over time and space.

Sex Ratios at Birth

Sex ratios at birth have been, historically, the least important numerical influence on sex ratios of large populations in the past, being remarkably consistent within the range of 104–108 male births per 100 females. This biological disparity seems to be related particularly to hormonal levels at conception. The male surplus at conception is believed to be high but it is reduced by excess male mortality before birth, especially when health conditions are poor; sex ratios at birth rise somewhat when health conditions improve. First-order births tend to have slightly higher sex ratios than later-order ones, as seen in the sex balance of births in post-war baby booms. However, in many Asian cultures, the persistence of son preference in combination with access to techniques of fetal sex determination has resulted in a surge of female abortions in the late-twentieth century, substantially raising sex ratios at birth (recorded sex-ratios are also raised by under-enumeration). In a number of Asian countries, these ratios have risen to levels that are highly anomalous: 110 in South Korea, 111 in India, and 117 in China. In these countries, levels for later-order births are much higher. Beyond the practice of sex-selective abortion, the possible spread into large Asian and Muslim populations of the latest techniques of pre-implantation sex selection, sometimes known as gender choice, may further distort sex ratios at birth with major social and psychological implications. A growing excess of males is already affecting the marriage market in parts of China in the early twenty-first century.

Sex Ratios at Death

As all humans are mortal, the preponderance of male births implies higher numbers of deaths among males than among females. In age-specific terms, the differences between the sexes are, however, also pronounced: typically, male death rates are higher at every age. Thus the male numerical advantage at birth is eroded as a cohort ages, as can be observed in age-specific population sex ratios. When mortality is high, this effect is strong; hence females achieve a numerical equality with males at a relatively low age, such as around age 20. With low mortality, despite the female advantage in death rates, most males and females survive to middle age. Thus it takes longer in a cohort before the number of females equals the number of males, and, in a population, numerical equality of females with males occurs at a relatively high age. For example, in the United Kingdom in 2000, the number of males exceeded the number of females at every age up to roughly age 50. In the age group from 45 to 49, the sex ratio was 100.2; in the age group 50 to 54, it was 99.1. Since the sex ratio at birth is about 105—not greatly different from equality—the figures just cited indicate that in low mortality populations male and female numbers are broadly balanced in a large lower segment of the age pyramid. With mortality further lowered, the upper limit of that age segment is expected to rise further. Projections suggest, for example, that in the United Kingdom by the middle of the twenty-first century, the population sex ratio even at the age range from 60 to 64 will still exceed 100, reflecting the enduring influence of the sex ratio at birth on the sex ratio of the population up to the threshold of old age. But sex-differential mortality has a major effect on population sex ratios once survival rates start falling rapidly, as they do beyond age 60. Survival rates fall for both sexes but do so more steeply for males. In the United Kingdom, for example, expectation of life at birth in 2000 was approximately 80 years for females and 75 years for males. But the population sex ratios among the elderly (reflecting in part past differences in survivorship) show large male deficits: the sex ratio is 70.1 at ages 75 to 79 and 45.2 among those 80 years and older.

Several exceptions to this broad depiction of the pattern of population sex ratios and the mortality factors influencing them should be noted. One was signaled above, with reference to the anomalous sex ratios at birth owing to higher mortality among female fetuses found in some countries in Asia. Should such elevated sex ratios at birth persist, they would have a major effect on the balance of the sexes over time in a broadening segment of the age pyramid, spreading from lower to higher ages.

A second qualification has to do with anomalous female mortality relative to male mortality. Cultural factors operating to the disadvantage of females in a number of countries, notably in Pakistan, India, and Bangladesh, have tended to counteract the biological female advantage in survivorship, causing either excess female over male mortality or greatly reducing the natural female mortality advantage over broad age groups, especially among children and in younger adult ages. In such circumstances, population sex ratios can exceed the sex ratio at birth well up to the upper ranges of the age pyramid. But even in such populations, among the oldest of the old the number of females typically exceeds the number of males. As in recent decades, female mortality improvement has been faster than male mortality improvement even in these countries. This anomalous pattern of population sex ratios is expected to be gradually attenuating in future years.

Thirdly, in some populations, especially in Eastern Europe, while overall mortality is relatively moderate, the female mortality advantage over males is found to be exceptionally high. For example, in the Russian Federation in 2000, the expectation of life at birth for the entire population was 66 years but the gap between female and male life expectancy was 12 years: 60 years for males and 72 years for females. Such wide disparity in mortality strongly affects population sex ratios. In most East European countries, the sex ratios for those aged 60 and over were below 60, and overall population sex ratios were below 90. In Russia, for example, in 2000, the corresponding ratios were 53 and 88. However, exceptional war-time mortality, even after 55 years of peace, has contributed to this sharp imbalance.

Sex Ratios of Migrants

Sex ratios of migrants tend to vary much more than ratios at either birth or death. Some migrations have been male-dominated, as for example in the early colonization streams from Europe to the New World and in the major gold rushes; some have been female-dominated, including the widespread migrations of domestic servants to Latin American cities and much rural-urban migration in the West; and other migrations have been more or less balanced, especially when they have been forced by political or environmental conditions. Transient and temporary circulatory movements tend to be even more gender-selective. Gender selectivity tends to vary with the evolution of migration streams, men being more preponderant at earlier stages, with the proportion of women increasing over time. In the last quarter of the twentieth century, sex ratios of migrants changed rapidly in many countries, as women's greater autonomy and opportunities were reflected in their increased mobility. However, migration has less consistent effects on the overall sex ratios of populations than either births or deaths, as it tends to be spasmodic, linear, and localized in impact. In addition, its effects on the sex ratios of populations tend to decrease with increasing size of a real unit—at its limits, the sex ratio of the total world population is unaffected by migration.

Patterns of Sex Ratios

Toward the end of the twentieth century, the estimated sex ratio of the total world population was 102, having risen from 100 in 1950, reflecting improvements in mortality. The overall sex ratio in more developed countries was 94, well below that of the less developed countries, which was 103—the difference being mainly a result of the older age distribution in the former region. Sub-continental variations in sex ratio are greater than global variations over time, and range from 90 in Eastern Europe to 106 in South Central Asia, largely for the cultural and health reasons already cited.

Variations are much greater at the country level, mostly because migration plays a larger role in the population change of smaller countries. While the majority of countries have sex ratios of 96 to 103, a number of East European countries, including Russia, have ratios below 90 and several very populous Asian countries (e.g., Bangladesh, China, India, and Pakistan) have ratios of 105 or more. The main causes of low sex ratios of countries are recent conflicts and wars and high levels of male mortality (e.g., Belarus, Russia, Ukraine), as well as the emigration of men (e.g., Barbados, Lesotho, and Portugal). The main causes of high sex ratios are the immigration of men (e.g., oil-rich states of the Gulf, Libya, Brunei), the emigration of women (e.g., Ireland in the past, the Philippines, and many Pacific islands), and unusually high female mortality (e.g., Bangladesh, India, Nepal, and Pakistan).

Large countries like India, China, and the United States exhibit marked regional variations in sex ratios reflecting cultural and social differences. Owing largely to the influence of migration, there are also considerable rural-urban and local variations in sex ratios whose range generally increases inversely with population size. Thus, small mining towns have high sex ratios while retirement towns have low ones. Since populations are constantly changing and redistributing themselves, the patterns of sex ratios within countries are never stable.

See also: *Gender Preference for Children; Induced Abortion; One-Child Policy; Partner Choice; Sex Selection; Spontaneous Abortion; Women's Status and Demographic Behavior.*

BIBLIOGRAPHY

Boyle, Paul, and Keith Halfacree, eds. 1999. *Migration and Gender in the Developed World.* London and New York: Routledge.

Chahnazarian, Anouch. 1988. "Determinants of the Sex Ratio at Birth: Review of Recent Literature." *Social Biology* 35: 214–235.

Chant, Susan, ed. 1992. *Gender and Migration in Developing Countries.* London: Belhaven.

Clarke, John I. 2000. *The Human Dichotomy: The Changing Numbers of Males and Females.* Amsterdam: Pergamon.

Coale, Ansley J. 1991. "Excess Female Mortality and the Balance of the Sexes." *Population and Development Review* 17: 517–523.

Croll, Elisabeth J. 2000. *Endangered Daughters.* London: Routledge.

James, William H. 1987. "The Human Sex Ratio. Part 1: A Review of the Literature." *Human Biology* 59: 721–752; 873–900.

———. 1987. "The Human Sex Ratio. Part II: A Hypothesis and a Program of Research." *Human Biology* 59: 873–900.

Lopez, Alan D., and Lado T. Ruzicka, eds. 1983. *Sex Differentials in Mortality.* Canberra, Australia: Australian National University.

Mayer, Peter. 1999. "India's Falling Sex Ratios." *Population and Development Review* 25: 323–343.

Pollard, Tessa M., and Susan B. Hyatt. 1999. *Sex, Gender and Health.* Cambridge, Eng.: CUP.

Teitelbaum, Michael S. 1972. "Factors Associated with the Sex Ratio in Human Populations." In

The Structure of Human Populations, ed. G. A. Harrison and A. J. Boyce. Oxford: Clarendon Press.

JOHN I. CLARKE

SEX SELECTION

In many cultures, and especially in certain social classes and subpopulations distinguished by religion, there have long existed strong preferences concerning the sex composition of offspring. Sometimes the preference may have been for achieving gender balance; more often the preference was for offspring of a particular sex. While parental preferences regarding the sex of children are not particularly evident in many industrialized and developing countries currently, a strong preference for sons exists in much of South Asia, East Asia, the Middle East, and North Africa.

The ability of parents to act on such preferences by deliberately influencing the sex composition of their children has increased markedly over recent decades, and further changes are likely. In the countries where son preference is most pronounced, this influence has created situations in which there are millions of "missing females." As the methods of sex selection evolve, so do the ethical questions involved.

Fertility Methods of Sex Selection

Without recourse to manipulating the biology of reproduction, parents can influence the sex composition of their offspring through fertility strategies, infanticide, adoption, and differential neglect. In a fertility strategy, parents may stop having children after the desired number of a certain sex has been reached. In China in the 1980s, partly under pressure from the government's one-child policy, parents often stopped having children after the first boy had been born. However, this strategy does not affect the societal sex ratio at birth (or, by extension, the population sex ratio). Under a male-biased stopping rule, the male-dominated families with one son are offset by female-dominated families where parents first had several daughters before the desired son was born.

Post-Birth Methods of Sex Selection

After birth, parents can influence the sex composition of their children by adoption, infanticide, or differential neglect. They can adopt out children of the undesired sex and adopt in children of the desired sex. This strategy has a long history, particularly in aristocratic families where succession depended on having a child of a particular sex (usually male). According to a study by Sten Johannsson and Ola Nygren in 1991, in modern China it is another way for parents to get a son while complying with the one-child policy. This practice too would not affect the overall sex composition of births.

As discussed by Glenn Hausfater and Sarah Bluffer Hrdy in 1994, sex-specific infanticide has been practiced in many societies past and present. In modern times, outright infanticide is a relatively rare phenomenon and is not responsible for generating the fairly sizable imbalances in population sex ratios found in many parts of the developing world.

Sex-specific neglect, resulting in higher than expected mortality of young females as compared to males, is another practice affecting the sex composition of offspring. It occurs particularly in the form of differential access to health care in countries with strong son preference. Preferential access to health care for male children, coupled in some instances with a somewhat smaller sex differential in access to nutrition and health care among adults, is responsible for much of the large imbalance in population sex ratios observed in the 1980s in South Asia, China, the Middle East, and North Africa. The girls and women who have died as a result of this differential access have been called "missing women" by Amartya Sen (1990). Their number, around 1990, was estimated in a study by Stephan Klasen and Claudia Wink to be nearly 88 million, or 7.7 percent of all females in the countries affected. Ten years later the corresponding estimated figures were 94 million and 6.8 percent (see Table 1). Sex-specific neglect appears to have declined slightly during the intervening decade in most regions. On the other hand, other forms of sex selection particularly relating to manipulations of the sex ratio at birth have gained ground, most notably in China.

Manipulating the Sex Ratio at Birth

Ordinarily, for biological reasons, there are between 3 and 7 percent more male births than female births, the variation being dependent on the population

TABLE 1

Population Sex Ratios (Males per Female) and Estimates of "Missing Women," for Selected Countries, 1980s and Early 1990s and around 2000

| | 1980s and early 1990s | | | | Around 2000 | | | |
| | | | Missing Women | | | | Missing Women | |
	Year	Sex ratio	Number (millions)	Percent	Year	Sex ratio	Number (millions)	Percent
China	1990	1.060	34.6	6.3	2000	1.067	40.9	6.7
Taiwan	1990	1.071	0.7	7.3	1999	1.049	0.5	4.7
India	1991	1.079	38.4	9.4	2001	1.072	39.1	7.9
Pakistan	1981	1.105	4.3	10.8	1998	1.081	4.9	7.8
Bangladesh	1981	1.064	4.6	8.9	2001	1.038	3.7	6.9
Nepal	1981	1.050	0.6	7.7	2001	0.997	0.1	0.5
West Asia	1985	1.073	3.9	7.1	2000	1.043	3.8	4.2
Afghanistan	1979	1.059	0.6	9.7	2000	1.054	1.0	9.3
Egypt	1986	1.049	1.2	5.1	1996	1.048	1.3	4.5
Total			88.9	7.7			95.2	6.9

SOURCE: Klasen and Wink (2002).

group in question and on the prevailing fertility and health patterns. The sex ratio at birth can be manipulated, however, through sex-selective abortion following detection of the sex of the fetus. The latter can be achieved using amniocentesis, chorionic villi sampling (CVS), or ultrasound screening. The first two of these methods have a 100 percent reliability, but are invasive and thus risky (with around 1% risk of pregnancy loss). They can only be conducted between 12 and 20 weeks of gestation, and are fairly costly. Ultrasound screening is less expensive and virtually without risk; it is routinely performed during prenatal check-ups. Sex detection is simply based on visual inspection of the fetus on the screen. This method of detection is never fully reliable and is particularly error-prone in the first 20 weeks of pregnancy. When the tests are performed with the intent of subsequent sex-selective abortions, all three methods allow only late-term abortions (15–25th week) with significant health risks to the mother and serious ethical questions, as discussed below.

Ultrasound screening spread rapidly in China in the 1980s as ultrasound machines became available even in remote areas of the country. As shown by Judith Banister and Ansley J. Coale in 1994, sex-specific abortion based on ultrasound results has since become the method of choice in China for parents complying with the government's one-child policy to ensure that their child is of the desired sex, usually a boy. The practice is believed to be the major factor in China's very high recorded sex ratio

at birth, which exceeded 1.16 in the 2000 Census, and in the large and growing "missing" female population (see Table 1). In India, recent data on the sex ratio at birth and among children very likely also reflect an increasing prevalence of sex-selective abortions as parents shift from post-birth to pre-birth sex selection strategies, particularly based on ultrasound detection. The governments of both China and India have prohibited prenatal sex determination in order to prevent sex-selective abortion, although the measures are readily circumvented as shown by Ashish Bose in 2001.

New Developments and Technologies

Technological advances allow even earlier selection of the sex of offspring than through ultrasound screening and sex-selective abortion. In one method in use in some industrialized countries, sex selection takes place in the context of in-vitro fertilization (IVF). Multiple fetuses are created in vitro, their sex is determined, and those of the desired sex are implanted. This method is complex and expensive and might reduce the success rate of the IVF procedure, but it is highly reliable. Thus far it is chiefly used by parents who are at high risk of transmitting a sex-linked genetic disease to their children. A second method, less costly and invasive, involves separation of sperm into those carrying X and Y chromosomes and intrauterine injection of the selected sperm to produce offspring (X for female, Y for male). Clinical trials reported by E. F. Fugger and his colleagues in 1998 suggest a 70 to 90 percent success rate. While sex-specific implantation in the context of IVF is unlikely to spread to poor countries, sperm-sorting methods such as the ones currently being used might, if the costs can be lowered and success enhanced, eventually replace or at least accompany sex-selective abortions as the method of choice for parents, particularly those with high son preference.

Ethical Issues

Sex selection raises a number of ethical issues concerned with motivation, methods, and outcomes. The competing rights of parents and children (or fetuses) are central in an evaluation of various sex selection techniques.

While the goal of "balancing" the gender composition of a family might not be objectionable, deciding to only have children of a particular sex (often male) implies that parents value human beings differently depending on their sex. This motivation violates the precept of equal rights to life for all, which is common to most conceptions of human rights. This in itself might justify corrective action on the part of the state, even if there were not a societal interest in maintaining a rough gender balance in the population at large. In addition, the various methods of sex selection also have different ethical implications, depending on the likely outcome for the disfavored sex. In the case of adopting away daughters, considerable harm is likely to occur for those girls, but the harm done to the disfavored sex is less clear in the case of fertility strategies, although it is probable that families that first had several girls before the desired boy was born will treat their daughters worse than the favored boy. Post-birth methods of infanticide and differential neglect are ethically most objectionable as they ultimately lead to the death of a child purely because of its sex. Thus there are strong grounds for state action to combat the problem of "missing women" as it ultimately kills girls and women, whose rights surely trump the rights of parents for sex selection of their off-spring.

The ethical status of the various methods of pre-birth sex selection is more complicated. It overlaps with the broader ethical debate surrounding abortion in general. Some would argue that the reproductive rights of parents (in particular, of women) are as important or even more important than the right to life of the fetus so that any abortion, even one done for sex selection, should be permissible. As discussed by John A. Robertson in 2001, others argue that the motivation of sex selection is objectionable and thus find sex-selective abortions unethical, even if they would find abortions for other reasons acceptable. Whatever ethical stance is taken on early-term abortion, many would see the recourse to late-term abortion for sex-selection purposes, which is the current practice, as deeply objectionable. However, the rights of a fetus would generally be deemed to exceed those of a fertilized egg before implantation, and sperm sorting would, according to Robertson, be therefore considered the least ethically problematic method of pre-birth sex selection.

Where strong gender preferences exist, there may be a case for tolerating use of a pre-birth sex selection method such as sperm sorting while at same time seeking to change the underlying social influences that result in different valuation of offspring by sex.

See also: *Feminist Perspectives on Population Issues; Gender Preferences for Children; Reproductive Rights; Reproductive Technologies: Modern Methods, Ethical Issues; Women's Status and Demographic Behavior.*

BIBLIOGRAPHY

Banister, Judith, and Ansley J. Coale. 1994. "Five Decades of Missing Females in China." *Demography* 31: 459–479.

Bose, Ashish. 2001. "Fighting Female Foeticide." *Economic and Political Weekly* 36: 3,427–3,429.

Fugger, E. F., S. H. Black, K. Keyvanfar, and J. D. Schulman. 1998. "Births of Normal Daughters after MicroSort Sperm Separation and Intra-uterine Insemination, In-vitro Fertilization, or Intracytoplasmic Sperm Injection." *Human Reproduction* 13: 2,367–2,370.

Hausfater, Glenn, and Sarah Bluffer Hrdy, eds. 1984. *Infanticide: Comparative and Evolutionary Perspectives.* New York: Aladine.

Johansson, Sten, and Ola Nygren. 1991. "The Missing Girls of China: A New Demographic Account." *Population and Development Review* 17: 35–51.

Klasen, Stephan, and Claudia Wink. 2002. "A Turning Point in Gender Bias in Mortality? An Update on the Number of Missing Women." *Population and Development Review* 28: 285–312.

———. 2003. "Missing Women: Revisiting the Debate." *Feminist Economics* (March).

Registrar General. 2001. "Provisionary Population Totals." *Census of India Series 1*, Paper 1 of 2001. New Delhi: Ministry of Home Affairs.

Robertson, John A. 2001. "Preconception Gender Selection." *American Journal of Bioethics* 1(1): 2–19.

Sen, Amartya. 1990. "More than 100 Million Women Are Missing." *New York Review of Books,* 20 December.

STEPHAN KLASEN

SEXUALITY, HUMAN

Population-based studies of human sexuality investigate the sexual expression of women and men at different stages of the life course and across groups and societies. Sexual expression is composed of sexual functions, or capacities, of males and females; sexual behaviors, both partnered and alone; and sexual attitudes—interests, preferences, and beliefs about sexuality. Identifying and investigating biological, psychocognitive, demographic, and sociocultural determinants of sexual expression as well as the interrelationships among sexual attitudes, behavior, and function are a central concern. This research also assesses the consequences of sexual expression, which include but are not limited to effects on well-being, health, relationship quality, sexual satisfaction, fertility, the stability of sexual partnerships, and the transmission of sexually transmitted infections (STIs), especially HIV and AIDS.

In the 1990s the increasing availability of large-scale probability samples on sexual behavior, a result of international concern about HIV/AIDS, facilitated advances in the study of human sexuality. Studies employing nationally representative data on adult sexual behavior were published for several developed countries, including Great Britain, Finland, France, and the United States, along with cross-national comparisons of European, African, and Asian countries. The United States in particular has conducted additional large-scale, representative-sample surveys featuring modules on sexual behavior—the National AIDS Behavioral Survey, the National Survey of Adolescent Males, the National Survey of Men, the National Survey of Women, the General Social Survey, and the National Longitudinal Study of Adolescent Health—which represent vast improvements over research derived from convenience, local community, or self-selected samples.

These studies also marked the emergence of human sexuality as a distinct topic in population studies. Previously, many researchers had focused only on the limited set of sexual behaviors that are consequential for fertility outcomes (e.g., frequency of coitus, out-of-wedlock fertility, contraceptive practices). Lacking basic information about sexual attitudes and behavior, researchers were spurred by the threat of HIV/AIDS in the 1990s to develop a comprehensive approach focused on sexual expression. Many of these studies collected information on partnered sex, an approach that captured variation in status (e.g., married versus nonmarried), gender, and patterns of multiple partners or sexual networks.

Basic Concepts

Sexual expression has sociocultural, psychocognitive, emotional, physiological, and behavioral dimensions. It encompasses the content of sexual action: how people think about sex, what they do sexually, and the concomitant psychophysiological states. Sexual attitudes are the beliefs, preferences, and interests individuals express about sexual issues, conduct, and partners. Sexual behaviors specify the sexual practices individuals engage in alone, with another person, or with multiple others. Sexual functioning refers to how individuals experience sexual desire, pleasure, and other psychophysiological states associated with the sexual response cycle.

Although researchers recognize the significance of biological factors, particularly physiology, maturation, and aging, on sexuality, those working from a population perspective tend to emphasize the social control, or social organization, of sexuality. Of particular importance are institutional controls—religion, kinship, law, and medicine—and traditional demographic attributes, such as ethnicity, which imbue cultural meanings into sexual behavior, thus defining the proximate costs and benefits of sexual choices. Population-based research increasingly focuses on sexual partnerships as well as partnership networks as a key feature of sexual expression.

TABLE 1A

Prevalence of Same-Gender and Opposite Gender Partners (percentages)

	Partners in Last Year		Partners since Age 18		Partners since Puberty	
	Men	Women	Men	Women	Men	Women
No partners	10.5	13.3	3.8	3.4	3.3	2.2
Opposite gender only	86.8	85.4	91.3	92.5	90.3	94.3
Both men and women	0.7	0.3	4.0	3.7	5.8	3.3
Same gender only	2.0	1.0	0.9	0.4	0.6	0.2
Total	100.0	100.0	100.0	100.0	100.0	100.0
Any same-gender sex (%):						
Both men and women	25.3	25.0	81.6	89.9	90.7	94.9
Same gender only	74.7	75.0	18.4	10.1	9.3	5.1
Total	100.0	100.0	100.0	100.0	100.0	100.0
Total *N*	3,494	4,376	3,073	3,853	1,334	1,678

Note: Partner variables (last year, since eighteen and since puberty). "Partners since puberty" is based on age of first vaginal intercourse and age of first same-gender partner from NHSLS.

SOURCE: Laumann et al. 1994:311.

Sexual Expression

Reflecting the social and institutional bases of sexuality, a central research area in human sexuality is the comparative analysis of sexual expression. Key sources of variation include cross-national, intrasocietal, historical, and life-course stage differences. Because the United States currently has the most comprehensive data on sexual expression, including national probability samples of adolescents, adults, and high-risk groups, the following sections rely heavily on illustrative U.S. results. Reflecting the dominant research strategies in the literature, this section reviews each facet of sexual expression separately, although it should be kept in mind that sexual functioning, behavior, and attitudes are interrelated phenomena.

For example, homosexuality, which has attracted heated debate about its meaning, prevalence, and etiology, can be decomposed into three dimensions: desire, behavior, and identity. Tables 1a and 1b provide an overview of the prevalences of these dimensions. However, it should be stressed that asking people about homosexuality is fraught with difficulties because its stigmatization in popular opinion is likely to produce systematic biases towards underreporting in responses to survey questions.

Sexual attitudes. Sexual attitudes refer to the beliefs, preferences, and interests individuals hold about sexual conduct. Although sexual attitudes are culturally contingent, scholars have focused primarily on a limited set of attitudes: premarital sex, teenage sex, extramarital sex, and homosexuality. Research concentrates on two topics: (1) sexual permissiveness and (2) normative orientations. The first approach, pioneered by Ira Reiss, assesses levels of permissiveness for various sexual issues, including premarital sex and extramarital sex. In contrast, the normative orientations approach does not assume a one-dimensional scale of permissiveness; instead, it focuses on identifying different types of sexual regimes. Edward O. Laumann and colleagues (1994), for example, found three major classes in the United States: traditional, relational, and recreational orientations. Cross-national variation is even more dramatic. Eric D. Widmer et al. (1998) grouped countries into one of three major sexual regimes with reference to attitudes toward nonmarital sex—teen permissives (Germany, Austria, Sweden, Slovenia), sexual conservatives (United States, Ireland, Poland), and homosexual permissives (Netherlands, Norway, Czech Republic, Canada, Spain)—along with a heterogeneous residual category composed of countries with moderate sexual attitudes (Australia, Great Britain, Hungary, Italy, Bulgaria, Russia, New Zealand, Israel) and two isolates (Japan, Philippines).

Sexual behaviors. Sexual behavior covers autoeroticism, partnered sex, and the relationship between these two dimensions of sexual life. The central finding on autoerotic activity is the much greater incidence of such activity in men than in women.

FIGURE 1

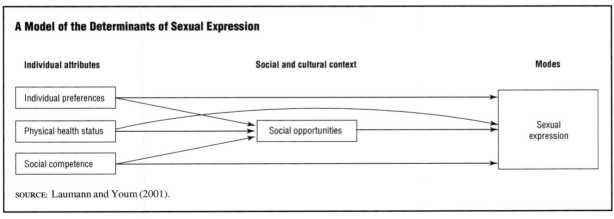

A Model of the Determinants of Sexual Expression

Individual attributes   Social and cultural context   Modes

Individual preferences

Physical health status   Social opportunities   Sexual expression

Social competence

SOURCE: Laumann and Youm (2001).

Major aspects of partnered sex include the number of sexual partners, the frequency of sex, sexual practices, the relational dimensions of sexual behavior, homosexuality, formative sexual experiences, and risk-related behaviors. Table 2 shows that partnered sex among Americans is remarkably conventional. The vast majority of Americans have only one sex partner over a one-year period, have few sexual partners in adulthood, have sex only occasionally, and engage in a limited set of sexual practices. Despite what appears to be a modest amount of sex, Americans are generally happy with their sex lives and their partners. Laumann et al. (1994) also focus on the prevalence of sexual practices relevant for the transmission of disease, such as vaginal, oral, and anal sex, as well as how certain sexual behaviors are correlated with types of sexual partnerships (e.g., marriages and monogamy). Findings about the prevalence of homosexuality and the impact of formative sexual experiences, such as sexual debut, forced sex, and adult and adolescent sexual contacts with children, have been published as well. Finally, a central topic in the demography of sexual behavior is the study of other risk-related behaviors of HIV/AIDS transmission, such as condom use, having paid sex, multiple partnering, and prior experience with STIs.

Sexual functioning. Sexual functioning covers individuals' experiences with sexual desire, sexual pleasure, and psychophysiological changes associated with the sexual response cycle. Demographic research focuses on three topics: sexual maturation, sexual problems, and the use of contraceptives, drugs, and sterilization procedures. Because the transition to sexual maturity has extensive implica-tions for sexual behavior and fertility, researchers are interested in trends, variation, and determinants of the pubertal development of males and females. Also associated with aging, but in a surprisingly more limited way than was expected, an emerging area of research focuses on sexual dysfunctions—disturbances in sexual desire and in the psychophysiological changes associated with the sexual response cycle. Laumann, Anthony Paik, and Raymond C. Rosen (1999) concluded that sexual problems are quite common among the U.S. adult population 18 to 59: More than 40 percent of adult women and 30 percent of adult men reported sexual problems of several months' duration during a 12-month period. Research on the cross-national and historical patterning of sexual problems is scanty, but new studies under way in 2003 will begin to remedy this situation.

A central development regarding sexual functioning is the availability of new technologies—contraceptives, drugs, and sterilization procedures—that directly affect the sexual response or reproductive cycles. Contraceptive and sterilization practices are traditionally covered in the study of fertility control, yet these technologies are significant for human sexuality, since their adoption severs the link between sex and fertility in many countries and directly affects sexual function. Another technological development is the introduction of drugs designed to enhance sexual performance, but little is known about this trend.

Determinants of Sexual Expression

When investigating determinants, most researchers have focused on one aspect or a few aspects of sexual expression. Alternatively, sexual expression can be approached as an integrated entity in which sexual attitudes and functioning act as proximate determinants for partnered and autoerotic sexual behaviors. Laumann and Yoosik Youm (2001) identify four broad classes of determinants, displayed in Figure 1: (1) individual preferences for particular sexual experiences, (2) state of physical health and capacity to engage in particular sexual activities, (3) competence to initiate and maintain social relationships of various sorts, and (4) social opportunities to secure appropriate sex partners. Subjective preferences refer to interests and beliefs about sexual conduct and derive from normative orientations. People with impaired physical or mental health (e.g., erectile or other sexual dysfunctions) may not be able to engage in certain patterns of sexual expression regardless of their preferences. Social competence refers to individuals' skills at and resources for initiating and maintaining ongoing sexual partnerships. These skills include communication and people-handling skills, time, money and goods, and reputation. Finally, these individual-level attributes are theorized to jointly affect the social contexts, or opportunities, in which sexual behavior is embedded. These contexts include the type of partnerships individuals are able to form, mode of meeting, participation in certain social scenes, and social membership factors.

Outcomes of Sexual Expression

There are substantial literatures linking specific aspects of sexual expression to health-related outcomes, such as the transmission of STIs, behavioral responses to HIV/AIDs, well-being, and family-related outcomes, including marital and nonmarital fertility, fertility control (e.g., abortion), and the dissolution of sexual partnerships. This section focuses on two of these outcomes: STIs/HIV and abortion.

STIs/HIV. An emerging paradigm in the study of the transmission of STIs and HIV is the integration of network approaches with survey data on partnered sex. Utilizing Martina Morris's (1993) epidemiological models, Laumann and Youm (1999) not only analyzed individual-level risk factors related to sexual expression, such as the number of partners, but also accounted for the potential infection status of partners as well as transmission dynamics related to the spread of STIs across socially distinct populations. A second area in the demography of human sexuality is the study of responses to the HIV/AIDs epidemic.

TABLE 1B

Prevalence of Sexual Identity and Sexual Attraction, by Gender (percentages)

	Men	Women
Sexual Identity		
Heterosexual	96.9	98.6
Bisexual	0.8	0.5
Homosexual	2.0	0.0
Other	0.3	0.1
Total	100.0	100.0
Total *N*	*1,401*	*1,732*
Sexual Attraction		
Only Opposite gender	93.8	95.6
Mostly opposite gender	2.6	2.7
Both genders	0.6	0.8
Mostly same gender	0.7	0.6
Only same gender	2.4	0.3
Total	100.0	100.0

SOURCE: Laumann et al. 1994, p. 311.

Abortion. The demography of human sexuality has led to better information linking sexual expression to fertility control. Before the emergence of national data sets on sexual behavior, little was known about this link, since few data sets collected comprehensive data on sexual attitudes and behavior. In one of the few national studies of abortion in the United States, Robert T. Michael (2001) found that economic and social incentives for having children, as well as having sexual attitudes against the legalization of abortion, had strong negative effects on the likelihood of this practice. Comparing several high-quality surveys with data reported by abortion providers and compiled by the Alan Guttmacher Institute (AGI), Elise F. Jones and Jacqueline Darroch Forrest (1992) found that survey-reported abortions were systematically and substantially underestimated. Indeed, underreporting of socially stigmatized, sex-related behaviors is a general methodological problem for research on the demography of human sexuality.

Future Issues for the Demography of Human Sexuality

Professional and public interest in human sexuality was sparked most recently by the threat of HIV/AIDS. In addition to the growing prevalence of HIV/AIDS, several trends highlight the continuing need for population-based data on sexual behavior. As an example, the United States underwent dramatic changes in sexual attitudes, sexual practices, and

TABLE 2A

Summary Finding that the Sexual Behavior of Most Adults in the United States is Remarkably Conventional

A. THE VAST MAJORITY OF THE US POPULATION AGED 18 TO 59 HAS ONLY ONE SEX PARTNER WITHIN A YEAR

	Number of Sex Partners in the Past 12 Months (Percent)			
	0	1	2-4	5+
All	11.9	71.1	13.7	3.2
Men	9.9	66.7	18.3	5.1
Women	13.6	74.7	10.0	1.7

B. THE MEDIAN NUMBER OF SEX PARTNERS SINCE AGE 18 IS 2 FOR WOMEN AND 6 FOR MEN

	Number of Sex Partners since Age 18 (Percent)						
	0	1	2-4	5-10	11-20	21+	Median
All	2.9	26.1	29.5	21.7	10.6	9.2	3
Men	3.4	19.5	20.9	23.3	16.3	16.6	6
Women	2.5	31.5	36.4	20.4	6.0	3.2	2

C. AMERICANS HAVE SEX NOT ALL THAT FREQUENTLY - FEWER THAN 2 TIMES A WEEK, ON AVERAGE

	Frequency of Sex in the Past Year (Percent)				
	Not at All	A Few Times a Year	A Few Times a Month	2-3 Times a Week	4+ Times a Week
Men	9.8	17.6	35.5	29.5	7.7
Women	13.6	16.1	37.2	26.3	6.7

D. A LARGE MAJORITY OF AMERICANS DO NOT FIND MANY SEX PRACTICES VERY APPEALING, SO THEY ENGAGE IN A RATHER LIMITED REPERTOIRE OF SEXUAL ACTIVITIES

	Percentage Saying Practice is Very Appealing		Percentage Engaged in Practice			
			Last Event		Ever in Lifetime	
	Men	Women	Men	Women	Men	Women
Vaginal intercourse	83.8	76.8	94.6	95.6	95.0	97.0
Watching partner undress	47.8	26.8				
Receiving oral sex	45.0	28.8	27.5	19.9	78.7	73.1
Giving oral sex	33.5	16.5	26.8	18.8	76.6	67.7
Group sex	13.3	1.1				
Using a dildo or vibrator	4.4	2.9				
Watching others have sex	5.3	1.5				
Same-gender sex	3.2	2.9	2.7*	1.3*	4.9*	4.1*
Having sex with a stranger	4.1	0.9				
Anal intercourse	2.8	1.0	2.3	1.2	25.6	20.4
Forcing someone to have sex	0.3	0.2			2.8	1.5
Being forced to have sex	0.1	0.1			3.9	22.8

*For same-gender sex the columns reflect "last 12 months" not last event, and lifetime since age 18.

[continued in Table 2B]

marital behavior in the last decades of the twentieth century. U.S. sexual attitudes continue to be liberalized, the median number of lifetime partners continues to increase, and individuals spend as much as one-quarter of their pre-age-60 adult lives as sexually active singles. Taken together, these trends suggest that sexual expression in the United States is still changing, perhaps making sexual markets more important than marriage markets. Indeed, HIV/AIDS and the changing nature of sexual expression will continue to make the demography of human sexuality an important research concern.

See also: *AIDS; Birth Control, History of; Contraceptive Prevalence; Culture and Population.*

TABLE 2B

Summary Finding that the Sexual Behavior of Most Adults in the United States is Remarkably Conventional

E. YET DESPITE THE MODEST AMOUNT OF SEX, THESE SAME MEN AND WOMEN REPORT THEMSELVES TO BE QUITE HAPPY WITH THEIR SEX LIVES AND WITH THEIR PARTNERS

	Satisfaction with Sex Life (%)		
	Extremely or Very Happy	Generally Satisfied	Unhappy
All	57.7	29.2	13.1
No. of Sexual Partners in Past 12 Months			
Zero	40.7	35.4	23.9
One	63.4	27.2	9.4
Two-Four	44.9	32.7	22.4
Five +	47.2	37.1	15.7
Frequency of Sex in Past 12 Months			
None	39.5	36.7	23.8
1-12 time/year	45.6	32.8	21.6
2 -3 times/month or once/wk	59.2	29.3	11.5
2-3 times/week	69.0	25.1	5.9
4+ times/week	64.5	22.0	13.6

			Satisfaction with Partner (%)				
			Partner Made Respondent Feel				
	Physically Pleased*	Emotionally Pleased*	Satisfied	Loved	Thrilled	Wanted	Taken Care of
Had Only One Partner							
Spouse	87.4	84.8	97.1	97.5	90.9	92.2	89.9
Cohabitant	84.4	75.6	95.5	95.2	89.6	88.2	84.0
Neither	78.2	71.0	92.9	87.6	90.8	87.1	76.0
Had More than One Partner							
Primary Spouse	61.2	56.7	88.1	86.4	77.6	77.6	68.7
Cohabitant	74.5	57.9	90.5	86.2	91.6	85.1	78.7
Neither	77.9	61.7	92.8	83.9	86.6	84.8	72.8
Secondary Partner	54.3	33.0	81.6	48.4	75.6	66.7	53.1

*Percentage "extremely" or "very" pleased or satisfied

SOURCE: Laumann and Michael (2001), pp.16–18.

BIBLIOGRAPHY

Bancroft, John. 1994. "Sexual Motivation and Behavior." In *Companion Encyclopedia of Psychology*, ed. Andrew M. Colman. London: Routledge.

———. 1995. "Sexuality and Family Planning." In *Handbook of Family Planning and Reproductive Health Care*, eds. N. B. Loudon, A. F. Glasier and A. Gebbie. Edinburgh: Churchill Livingston.

Bearman, Peter S., and Hannah Bruckner. 2001. "Promising the Future: Virginity Pledges and First Intercourse." *American Journal of Sociology* 106: 859–912.

Billy, John O. G., Koray Tanfer, William R. Grady, and Daniel H. Klepinger. 1993. "The Sexual Behavior of Men in the United States." *Family Planning Perspectives* 25: 52–60.

Browning, Christopher, and Edward O. Laumann. 1997. "Sexual Contact between Children and Adults: A Lifecourse Perspective." *American Sociological Review* 62: 540–560.

Catania, Joseph A., Thomas J. Coates, Ron Stall, Heather A. Turner, and J. Peterson. 1992. "Prevalence of AIDS-Related Risk Factors and Condom Use in the United States." *Science* 248: 1,101–1,106.

Catania, Joseph A., David R. Gibson, Dale D. Chitwood, and Thomas J. Coates. 1990. "Methodological Problems in AIDS Behavioral Research: Influences on Measurement Error and Participation Bias in Studies of Sexual Behavior." *Psychological Bulletin* 108: 339–362.

Cleland, John, and Benoît Ferry, eds. 1995. *Sexual Behaviour and AIDS in the Developing World.* London: Taylor and Francis.

DeLamater, John. 1981. "The Social Control of Sexuality." *Annual Review of Sociology* 7: 263–290.

Feinleib, Joel A., and Robert T. Michael. 1998. "Reported Changes in Sexual Behavior in Response to AIDS in the United States." *Preventive Medicine* 24: 400–411.

Halpern, Carolyn T., Kara Joyner, J. Richard Udry, and Chirayath Suchindran. 2000. "Smart Teens Don't Have Sex (or Kiss Much Either)." *Journal of Adolescent Health* 26: 213–225.

Hubert, Michel, Nathalie Bajos, and Theo Sandfort. 1998. *Sexual Behaviour and HIV/AIDS in Europe: Comparison of National Surveys.* London: UCL Press.

Johnson, Anne M., Jane Wadsworth, Kaye Wellings, and Julia Field. 1994. *Sexual Attitudes and Lifestyles.* Oxford: Blackwell Scientific Publications.

Jones, Elise F., and Jacqueline Darroch Forrest. 1992. "Underreporting of Abortion in Surveys of U.S. Women: 1976 to 1988." *Demography* 29: 113–126.

Kontula, Toimittaneet Osmo, and Elina Haavio-Mannila. 1993. *Suomalainen Seksi.* Helsinki: Werner Soderstrom Osakeyhtio.

Laumann, Edward O. 2001. "Sexual Expression in America." In *Sex, Love, and Health: Private Choices and Public Policy,* ed. E. O. Laumann and R. T. Michael. Chicago: University of Chicago Press.

Laumann, Edward O., John H. Gagnon, Robert T. Michaels, and Stuart Michael. 1994. *The Social Organization of Sexuality: Sexual Practices in the United States.* Chicago: University of Chicago Press.

Laumann, Edward O., and Robert T. Michael. 2001. *Sex, Love, and Health: Private Choices and Public Policy.* Chicago: University of Chicago Press.

Laumann, Edward O., Anthony Paik, and Raymond C. Rosen. 1999. "Sexual Dysfunction in the United States: Prevalence and Predictors." *Journal of the American Medical Association* 281: 537–544.

Laumann, Edward O., and Yoosik Youm. 1999. "Race/Ethnic Group Differences in the Prevalence of Sexually Transmitted Diseases in the United States." *Sexually Transmitted Diseases* 26: 250–261.

Michael, Robert T. 2001. "Abortion Decisions in the United States." In *Sex, Love, and Health: Private Choices and Public Policy,* ed. E. O. Laumann and R. T. Michael. Chicago: University of Chicago Press.

Michael, Robert T., Jane Wadsworth, Joel A. Feinleib, Anne M. Johnson, Edward O. Laumann, and Kaye Wellings. 1998. "Private Sexual Behavior, Public Opinion, and Public Health Policy Related to Sexually Transmitted Diseases." *American Journal of Public Health* 88: 749–754.

Michaels, Stuart, and Alain Giami. 1999. "Sexual Acts and Sexual Relationships: Asking about Sex in Surveys." *Public Opinion Quarterly* 63: 401–420.

Morris, Martina. 1993. "Epidemiology and Social Networks: Modeling Structured Diffusion." *Sociological Methods and Research* 22: 99–126.

Reiss, Ira L. 1967. *The Social Context of Premarital Sexual Permissiveness.* New York: Holt, Rinehart, and Winston.

Reiss, Ira L., Ronald E. Anderson, and G. C. Sponaugle. 1980. "A Multivariate Model of Determinants of Extramarital Permissiveness." *Journal of Marriage and the Family* 42: 395–411.

Resnick, Michael D., Peter S. Bearman, Robert W. Blum, Karl E. Bauman, et al. 1997. "Protecting Adolescents from Harm: Findings from the National Longitudinal Study on Adolescent Health." *Journal of the American Medical Association* 278: 823–832.

Smith, Tom W. 1991. "Adult Sexual Behavior in 1989: Number of Partners, Frequency of Intercourse and Risk of AIDS." *Family Planning Perspectives* 23: 102–107.

Sonenstein, Freya L., Joseph H. Pleck, and Leighton C. Ku. 1989. "Sexual Activity, Condom Use and AIDs Awareness among Adolescent Males." *Family Planning Perspectives* 21: 152–158.

———. 1991. "Levels of Sexual Activity among Adolescent Males in the United States." *Family Planning Perspectives* 23: 162–167.

Spira, Alfred, Nathalie Bajos, and the ASCF Group. 1994. *Sexual Behavior and AIDS.* Aldershot, Eng.: Avebury.

Tanfer, Koray, and Jeannette J. Schoorl. 1992. "Premarital Sexual Careers and Partner Change." *Archives of Sexual Behavior* 21: 45–68.

Udry, J. Richard, and R. L. Cliquet. 1982. "A Cross-Cultural Examination of the Relationship between Ages at Menarche, Marriage, and First Birth." *Demography* 19: 53–63.

Westoff, Charles F., and Norman B. Ryder. 1977. *The Contraceptive Revolution.* Princeton, NJ: Princeton University Press.

Widmer, Eric D., Judith Treas, and Robert Newcomb. 1998. "Attitudes toward Nonmarital Sex in 24 Countries." *Journal of Sex Research* 35: 349–358.

EDWARD O. LAUMANN
ANTHONY PAIK

SIMON, JULIAN L.

(1932–1998)

During most of the last quarter of the twentieth century Julian Simon was the best-known population economist in the world. Simon graduated from Harvard in 1953 with a degree in experimental psychology. His career began in the U.S. Navy, where, as he would later recount, he learned to distrust authority and the conventional wisdom it represented. Switching to business, he completed a master's of business administration degree at the University of Chicago in 1959 and a doctorate in business economics at the same institution in 1961. For the last 15 years of his life he was a professor of business administration at the University of Maryland.

Simon's intellectual output was enormous and diverse. His early work was in the economics of advertising and included a best-selling trade paperback, *How to Start and Operate a Mail Order Business* (1965). In a single year (1993) he proposed both a radical new approach to the teaching of statistics and a method for overcoming psychological depression. His research regularly appeared in major economics journals. (Some 80 articles published from 1965 to 1995 are collected in *Economics against the Grain* [1999].)

Simon's early work in population dealt mostly with the economics of fertility and was not controversial. He was a co-editor of the first four volumes (1978–1982) of the series *Research in Population Economics.* However, Simon primarily is known not for his output of original scientific research but for his polemical attacks on Malthusians and environmentalists, those who argue that population growth stifles economic development and harm the environment.

Simon's critique, best captured in *The Ultimate Resource* (1981, 1996), had several thrusts. First, he was a committed utilitarian who argued that individuals might rationally prefer having many children to having a high level of material wealth or a clean environment. "It All Depends on Your Values" was the title of one section of *The Ultimate Resource.* In the controversial introduction to that book Simon recounted how his conversion from a pessimistic to an optimistic view of population arose from a highly subjective emotional midlife experience.

Second, Simon argued that Malthusians systematically underplayed the importance of economies of scale and of agglomeration and the positive contribution of population pressure to technological innovation. Third, Simon had a passion for extremely long-term time-series data (for a range of welfare measures such as life expectancy and the real prices of natural resources), which in his view delivered the clear message that things were getting better, not worse. Fourth, he was an advocate of looking at all the data at the same time. Although some data series might show adverse trends, taken as a whole, the data delivered an optimistic message. This was the main theme of his second best-selling book, an edited volume (with Herman Kahn) entitled *The Resourceful Earth* (1984), a rejoinder to the pessimistic report of President Carter's *Global 2000* commission.

Simon became the favorite professional authority as well as fiery ideologue of the *laissez-faire* Reagan right as in dozens of articles in the popular press, television appearances, and lectures across the country he castigated what he called "the population establishment." In the later 1980s Simon added the economics of immigration to his interests. He became an advocate of the free movement of labor and argued in *The Economic Consequences of Immigration to the U.S.* (1989) that anti-immigration advocates systematically overestimated the costs and underestimated the benefits of immigration to the United States.

Like most polemicists, Simon thrived on exaggeration. He endorsed often wildly speculative arguments (for example, that a larger population meant more geniuses and thus more technological innovation). He engaged in publicity stunts such as a $1,000 bet with the environmentalist Paul Ehrlich about whether the price of copper and some other raw materials would be higher or lower in five years (Simon won). When in 1986 the U.S. National Academy of Sciences published a report refuting the conventional pessimism about the impact of rapid population growth on economic development, Simon accused the authors of having pulled their punches.

Will Simon's work stand the test of time? He was an excellent economist, and in his emphasis on scale effects and other nonlinearities, he anticipated much subsequent work in economic growth theory. However, nonlinearities can be used to argue against population growth as well as in favor of it. Perhaps Simon will be remembered primarily as an antidote to the gloom-and-doom excesses of the "Population Bomb" school of thought that flourished in the 1970s.

See also: *Economic-Demographic Models; Immigration, Benefits and Costs of; Natural Resources and Population; Population Thought, Contemporary; Technological Change and Population Growth.*

BIBLIOGRAPHY

SELECTED WORKS BY JULIAN L. SIMON.

Simon, Julian L. 1975. "The Population Establishment." In *Comparative Policy Analysis*, ed. R. Kenneth Godwin. Lexington, MA: Lexington Books.

———. 1977. *The Economics of Population Growth.* Princeton, NJ: Princeton University Press.

———. 1981. *The Ultimate Resource.* Princeton, NJ: Princeton University Press.

———. 1986. *Theory of Population and Economic Growth.* New York: Blackwell.

———. 1989. *The Economic Consequences of Immigration to the U.S.* New York: Blackwell.

———. 1990. *Population Matters: People, Resources, Environment, and Immigration.* New Brunswick, NJ: Transaction.

———. 1999. *Economics against the Grain,* 2 vols. Cheltenham, Eng.: Edward Elgar.

———. 1996. *The Ultimate Resource 2.* Princeton, NJ: Princeton University Press.

———. 2002. *A Life against the Grain: The Autobiography of an Unconventional Economist,* ed. Rita J. Simon. New Brunswick, NJ: Transaction.

Simon, Julian L., ed. 1995. *The State of Humanity.* Oxford: Blackwell.

Simon, Julian L., and Herman Kahn, eds. 1984. *The Resourceful Earth: A Response to Global 2000.* New York: Blackwell.

F. LANDIS MACKELLAR

SIMULATION MODELS

The term "simulation" is used to refer to a wide range of quantitative analytic strategies in the population sciences. Defining the term is thus a necessary task, but it also turns out to be a conceptually useful exercise. In a broad sense, demographers are nearly always engaged in simulating something. From aggregate population projections and forecasts to behavioral models for family and household formation, demographers use mathematical models to represent (i.e., *simulate*) the population processes and outcomes found in the real world. Using this general definition, simulation rapidly becomes indistinguishable from quantitative analysis, and ultimately applied mathematics. At the other end of the scale, the definition could be restricted to an explicit representation of the population dynamics of a stochastic process (e.g., a birth, or a job loss) that operates at the level of the individual, is not analytically tractable, and thus requires numerical methods for cumulating up to population-level outcomes over time. This definition would limit the term to the kinds of models that have become known as "stochastic microsimulation" and "agent-based modeling," and it would exclude all but a handful of current demographic methods and applications.

In the middle lies a definition that borrows slightly from each: the basic concept of projection from the most general version, and the absence of analytical tractability from the more restricted version. Under this definition, simulation is distinguished by a focus on dynamic modeling, and the need to explicitly calculate each step in the entire path of events to get from a starting to an ending state of the population. It is a projection of the path, rather than a solution for an end state. This definition excludes the standard life table methods for stationary and stable population projection that form the core of most formal demography, as these can be solved analytically for their equilibrium outcomes. It also excludes the statistical analysis of survey data that forms the core of most social demography, as this is focused on estimating the underlying rates and parameters of these processes rather than projecting their population-level outcomes over time. In effect, this definition of simulation excludes both the traditional macro methods of demographic analysis as well as the traditional micro methods.

That does not sound very promising at first glance, but what is left over is actually quite important: the middle ground that links the micro to the macro. Simulation techniques enable the analyst to specify interesting models of individual behavior and to investigate how these patterns interact and aggregate into population-level outcomes over time. Simulation is the social scientist's equivalent of a laboratory. It borrows from the micro level both the attention to individual level processes and the parameters estimated for these processes, without losing sight of the aggregate dynamic outcomes. And it borrows from the macro level the focus on population dynamics, without the constraint that the underlying model be analytically solvable. As a result, simulation allows a much more nuanced, theory-driven approach to investigating some of the most intriguing questions in the population sciences.

States and Rates

All forms of simulation have two basic components in the model: states—a set of classes that define the individuals in the population, and rates—a set of rules that define the dynamics of moving from one state to the next. The states can be indexed by attributes that divide the population into homogeneous classes, like race, years of experience with an employer, or vaccination status. But they can also be indexed at the level of the individual if maximal heterogeneity is desired. In that case, each individual has a unique index. The states can be based on attributes that do not change (sex), that change deterministically (age), or that change probabilistically (first birth) and allow return (marital status).

The rates are dynamic rules that describe the conditions under which events occur, and the states at risk of these events. In the simplest form, these rules can be specified as homogeneous fixed rates, such as a single aggregate fertility, mortality, or unemployment rate. But because most fixed rate systems are analytically tractable, they are typically not analyzed using simulation. Simulation is used instead to analyze settings in which the rates vary in more or less complex ways. They can vary over time, using any parametric or non-parametric specification. They can vary by the state indices described above, much like component projection life tables. And they can vary endogenously as a function of the state of the system, as in models for population growth that build in the carrying capacity of the environment. Rates can be specified in either deterministic or stochastic form.

Macro- and Micro-simulation

The range of models that emerge from these possible variations in states and rates can be grouped into two broad categories: macro-simulation models and micro-simulation models. (Evert van Imhoff and Wendy Post (1998) provide a good discussion of the similarities and differences.) Macro-simulation models divide the population into a limited number of states, with deterministic transition rates between states. Such models typically translate into a set of ordinary differential equations (often nonlinear) that can be solved numerically through iterative updating. Micro-simulation models operate with the states indexed at the individual level, and events specified as a stochastic process. These translate into an algorithm that can be implemented as a computer-generated Monte Carlo simulation.

A macrosimulation model. To get a feel for the difference, consider a model for the spread of an infectious sexually transmitted disease. A macro-simulation model might look something like Figure 1.

In Figure 1, three population states are S, the number of susceptible individuals; I, the number of infected individuals; and D, the cumulative number of deaths from infection. The two rates that govern transition from the states are R_i, the rate of infection (morbidity), and R_d, the death rate due to infection (mortality). The infection rate is a function of the number of susceptible and infected individuals, and the "force of infection" denoted by β. A simple specification for the force of infection is given by the following:

$$\beta = \frac{c\tau}{(S + I)}$$

which represents the average contact rate c, and the probability of transmission given contact τ, per person $(S + I)$. The death rate is a function of the number of persons infected and the death rate μ. The system of differential equations that describes this process is:

$$\frac{\partial S}{\partial t} = -R_i S = -\beta S I$$

$$\frac{\partial I}{\partial t} = R_i S - R_d I = \beta S I - \mu I$$

$$\frac{\partial D}{\partial t} = R_d I = \mu I$$

If the force of infection, β, is fixed, this system is analytically tractable, and one can solve for the usual quantities such as the reproduction rate, doubling time, and equilibrium prevalence. Norman Bailey's classic text (1957) and Roy Anderson's more recent volume (1982) are good references for these methods. But a slightly more realistic model would also include vital dynamics, at which point obtaining solutions for $S(t)$, $I(t)$, and $D(t)$ will require numerical methods.

To implement this model, one needs to specify a set of input parameters for the rates, and initial conditions, such as the starting number in each state. The equations can then be iteratively solved. For each iteration, the value of the state variables will be updated sequentially by the amounts defined by the system of equations above. Because the rates are deterministically specified, the values predicted for $S(t)$, $I(t)$, and $D(t)$ have no stochastic variability. If the simulation is run repeatedly with the same set of inputs, the results will be identical. Variation is only

FIGURE 1

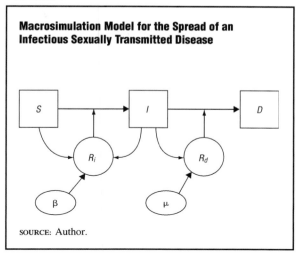

Macrosimulation Model for the Spread of an Infectious Sexually Transmitted Disease

SOURCE: Author.

obtained by varying the inputs (e.g., the components of the rates), and typically a researcher will vary some of the input parameters in order to conduct sensitivity analyses. With complex models that have many inputs, the dependence of the outcomes on the direct and interactive effects of the inputs is often of interest, and becomes an analytic task in its own right. One approach is to use a systematic scheme such as Latin hypercube sampling to generate data on both inputs and outputs; analyzing these data can in turn use more traditional statistical methods to provide numerical summaries of the sensitivity.

It is a relatively straightforward matter to modify models like this to obtain more realistic representations of the process, as there is no constraint that the system of equations remains analytically tractable. In the example above, one could add to the number of states—either breaking out additional states to represent stages of infection (e.g., the primary, latent, and secondary stages of syphilis; the variably infectious periods of HIV; or the acquired immunity of measles), or to represent population subgroups that may partner preferentially (e.g., age groups). The rates can also be modified, adding policy-relevant components like treatment or prophylaxis. Using sensitivity analyses on these rates, one can estimate the potential impact of alternative intervention strategies.

A microsimulation model. A micro-simulation model of this process, by contrast, consists of a repeated set of computer-generated experiments for the partnership and disease processes in which each person, partnership, and disease transmission is explicitly represented.

The procedure consists of the following steps:

1. Create a sample of (for example) 1,000 susceptible persons.

2. Randomly infect one person.

3. Randomly choose C pairs of persons without replacement to be the starting couples (which implies serial monogamy).

4. Randomly choose one pair of persons.

5. If these persons are both single: toss a coin with probability ρ, to form a partnership. If they are a couple: toss a coin with probability δ that the partnership is dissolved; if it is a discordant couple (one S, one I), toss a coin with probability τ that transmission occurs.

6. For each infected person, toss a coin with probability μ, that that person dies.

7. Return to step 3.

Given the probabilistic nature of the events, repeated runs of this micro-simulation model will result in different outcomes. In this particular case, the micro-simulation will lead, on average, to the same solutions for $S(t)$, $I(t)$, and $D(t)$ as the macro-simulation above, as long as the partnership dynamics are set to be consistent with the dynamics implied by the contact rate c in the macro model.

Differences between Micro- and Macro-simulation

For equivalent models of the underlying process, then, the difference between the micro- and macro-simulation is not in the outcomes they project, but in the flexibility they allow to represent the details of the process, and the different kinds of information they provide.

One of these differences is in the treatment of uncertainty. The variation in outcomes produced by repeated runs of the micro-simulation model provides an estimate of the uncertainty inherent in the dynamic process. In some settings this variation can be substantial, and the ability to quantify it very important. While principled methods for estimating the uncertainty associated with deterministic macro-simulation projections have been developed by Adrian Raftery and his colleagues (1995), they require additional effort to implement. For stochastic micro-simulation, the variability is part of the output, and can be analyzed using standard techniques. Another difference is the size of the population that can be modeled—a difference that is reflected in the labels macro and micro.

Macro models, dealing with aggregate subgroups, can be used to simulate arbitrarily large populations. Their limitations are driven by the number of subgroups rather than the number of persons within each subgroup. Micro models, because they represent each individual, are limited in the size of population that can be simulated. But this limitation is also the source of their flexibility. Micro-simulation models make it possible to investigate more complicated and detailed dynamics. In the disease transmission example used above, it is possible simply to relax the monogamy constraint in the micro-simulation to allow for much more complicated partnership network patterns. This requires a small change in the dynamic rule, removing the restriction against partnership formation for persons already in a partnership. The result will be not just the emergence of "two-stars" (a person with two partners), but larger configurations like three-stars, triangles, 4-cycles, and long paths. All of this will come from the relaxation of the constraint, not from explicit parameterization of each form. By contrast, the macro-simulation model would require that each network configuration (that is, each infection composition category) be explicitly broken out and represented as a state, and all of the transitions between the states would need to be specified. Both the model, and the data requirements, quickly become overwhelming.

Computational and Documentation Issues

Advances in computing power and software development have put the simulation toolkit within the reach of most researchers. For those interested in macro-simulation, there are a number of useful packages, like STELLA and Madonna, that allow the programming for macro-simulations to be done using a flexible, intuitive graphical interface, and require only a standard desktop computer. These packages can easily be self-taught, and, like popular statistical packages, they make it possible (for better or worse) to ignore almost all of the mathematical subtleties needed for the solution of the equation system. They allow the researcher to focus on modeling the states and rate functions, where demographic expertise is most important. This also makes them well suited for teaching basic introductory courses on modeling population dynamics. (An example is the text by Hannon and Ruth, included in the Bibliography.)

For those interested in micro-simulation, it is still typically necessary to be able to program in a language like Fortran, C+, or Java. But there are several packages that are useful for demographers, including the following:

- Socsim
  <http://www.demog.berkeley.edu/~wachter/socstory.html>;
- Lipro
  <http://www.nidi.nl/research/prj70101.html>;
- UrbanSim
  <http://www.urbansim.org/papers/Urbansim_Reference_Guide-09.pdf>;
- Swarm <http://www.swarm.org/index.html>; and
- Sugarscape <http://www.brook.edu/dybdocroot/sugarscape/>.

These programs require considerably more sophistication to use than their macro-simulation counterparts, and often use more computing power, but the payoff is much more control over the process being modeled. With the growing interest in these kinds of models in all of the sciences, it is likely that the software technology for micro-simulation modeling will evolve rapidly in coming years. For now, the choice of which model to use should be guided by the nature of the process being modeled, the level of detail needed, and the technical resources available.

One of the challenges posed by simulation models is how to describe them in published analyses. In contrast to standard statistical methods, the programs built to run both macro- and micro-simulations are purpose built, and every analysis is different—both in terms of the state space, and in the specification of the transition probabilities. There is no generally accepted standard for documenting these programs, and there is typically not enough space in published articles to describe the complete set of assumptions and algorithms. One proposed solution is to set up websites associated with journals to publish the programs behind the articles. This approach has been explored by journals like *Nature,* but in general, the question of how to validate and replicate simulation-based research through the standard publication mechanism remains an unsettled issue.

Role of Simulation in Demography

Simulation has been used in many areas of demography, for nearly as long as the computer has been available as a research tool. Examples include population projection, from the classic text by Mindel Sheps and Jane Menken (1973) to more recent volumes (for example, by Wolfgang Lutz, James Vaupel et al, 1999) and the projection of kinship resources under changing fertility (or mortality) regimes by Jane Menken (1985) and Ken Wachter (1997).

To take one instance, this kind of work is likely to play an increasingly important role in understanding the demographic impact of AIDS in populations experiencing a generalized epidemic. The study of the population dynamics of HIV transmission and the demographic consequences of AIDS has stimulated a substantial simulation-based literature, especially in the analysis of transmission networks. Examples include the work of Roy Anderson and Robert May (1988), John Bongaarts (1989), Alberto Palloni (1996), and Martina Morris (1997).

The concept of evolution is rooted in dynamic models, so simulation methods are also found in all areas of the population sciences that deal with evolution, from the population genetics of Hartl and Clark (1989) and the evolutionary biology of Simon Levin (1994) to the models of cultural evolution developed by Eugene Hammel and his colleagues (1979) and Luigi Cavalli-Sforza and Marcus Feldman (1981), and Herb Gintis's (2000) work on evolutionary game theory.

Simulation models have also played a major role in the study of the population-environment system. Examples include the work by Jay Forrester (1969) and Paul Waddell (2002) in urban ecology, and Elinor Ostrom's (1990) work on "governing the commons." In many of these areas, the models of evolutionary social dynamics, freed from the constraints of mathematical convenience, are providing insights into social systems that challenge the findings of general equilibrium models, and hold great promise for theory development in the social sciences. For the first time, the models enable researchers to represent the full range of dynamics induced by social interaction at the individual, institutional, and environmental levels. The research agenda opened by these methods is both daunting and exhilarating.

It would therefore be a mistake to file simulation methods under "advanced mathematical demography" and assume they are the province of a few select wizards and marginal to the field. Demography has always been fundamentally tied to its methods. Formal demography was for many years what distinguished a demographer from other social scientists. But, constrained by the requirements of mathematically tractable solutions, the development of formal demography became increasingly technical and difficult after the 1970s. As a result, the field grew rapidly where the data and the methods were more accessible, and the theory less constrained by the math—in the micro-level analyses that are the hallmark of contemporary social demography. Micro-level research has deepened the roots of demography in its constituent social science disciplines, and given it a stronger base in theories of human behavior. Without the macro-level connection, however, the population is missing from population science. That connection is what simulation has to offer. If there is going to be a vital demography in the future, the simulation methods described here will likely be at its core, linking the micro to the macro. With these new tools, demographers will again be able to explore the frontiers of research on population dynamics, with a set of tools that facilitates theoretically richer models.

See also: *Artificial Social Life; Family Demography; Projections and Forecasts, Population; Stochastic Population Theory.*

BIBLIOGRAPHY

Anderson, Roy M. 1982. *The Population Dynamics of Infectious Diseases.* London: Chapman Hall.

Anderson, Roy M., Robert M. May, et al. 1988. "Possible Demographic Consequences of AIDS in Developing Countries." *Nature* 332: 228–234.

Bailey, Norman T. J. 1975. *The Mathematical Theory of Infectious Diseases.* New York: Hafner Press.

Bongaarts, John. 1989. "A Model of the Spread of HIV Infection and the Demographic Impact of AIDS." *Statistics in Medicine* 8: 103–120.

Cavalli-Sforza, Luigi L., and Marcus W. Feldman. 1981. *Cultural Transmission and Evolution: A Quantitative Approach.* Princeton, NJ: Princeton University Press.

Forrester, Jay Wright. 1969. *Urban Dynamics.* Cambridge, MA: M.I.T. Press.

Gintis, Herbert. 2000. *Game Theory Evolving: A Problem-Centered Introduction to Modeling Strategic Behavior.* Princeton, NJ: Princeton University Press.

Hammel, Eugene A., Chad K. McDaniel, et al. 1979. "Demographic Consequences of Incest Tabus: A Microsimulation Analysis." *Science* 205: 972–977.

Hannon, Bruce, and Matthias Ruth. 1997. *Modeling Dynamic Biological Systems.* New York: Springer.

Hartl, Daniel L., and Andrew G. Clark. 1989. *Principles of Population Genetics.* Sunderland, MA: Sinauer.

Levin, Simon A., ed. 1994. *Frontiers in Mathematical Biology.* New York: Springer-Verlag.

Lutz, Wolfgang, James W. Vaupel and Dennis A. Ahlburg, eds. 1999. *Frontiers of Population Forecasting,* Supplement to Vol. 24 of *Population and Development Review.* New York: Population Council.

Menken, Jane A. 1985. "Age and Fertility: How Late Can You Wait?" *Demography* 22: 469–483.

Morris, Martina. 1997. "Sexual Networks and HIV." *AIDS* 11: S209–S216.

Ostrom, Elinor. 1990. *Governing the Commons: The Evolution of Institutions for Collective Action.* Cambridge, Eng.: Cambridge University Press.

Palloni, Alberto. 1996. "Demography of HIV/AIDS." *Population Index* 62: 601–652.

Raftery, Adrian E., Geof H. Givens, et al. 1995. "Inference from a Deterministic Population Dynamics Model for Bowhead Whales (with Discussion)." *Journal of the American Statistical Association* 90: 402–430.

Sheps, Mindel C., and Jane A. Menken. 1973. *Mathematical Models of Conception and Birth.* Chicago: University of Chicago Press.

van Imhoff, Evert, and Wendy Post. 1998. "Microsimulation Methods for Population Projection." *Population: An English Selection* 10: 97–138.

Wachter, Kenneth W. 1997. "Kinship Resources for the Elderly." *Philosophical Transactions of the Royal Society of London Series B-Biological Sciences* 352: 1,811–1,817.

Waddell, Paul. 2002. "UrbanSim: Modeling Urban Development for Land Use, Transportation and

Environmental Planning." *Journal of the American Planning Association.* 68(3): 297–314.

MARTINA MORRIS

SLAVERY, DEMOGRAPHY OF

The demography of slavery centers significantly on migration—physical migration of the newly enslaved to their place of captivity, and social migration from the status of free person to that of slave or from slavery to freedom. For a long time slavery did not fit easily into studies of demography, because these migrations and changes in status complicated the basic variables of fertility and mortality. Recent advances in demographic techniques, however, have made slavery a feasible and rewarding topic for analysis. Demographic analysis, linked to new research in social history and global history, has resulted in important advances in the analysis of slavery.

This article discusses the methodological development of demographic and historical studies of slavery, recent findings on the historical patterns in slavery since 1500, and current issues in demographic analysis of slavery. The article concludes with notes on slavery before 1500 and the heritage of slavery for society in the early twenty-first century.

Developments in the Study of Slavery

Studies of slavery conducted in the early and mid-twentieth century focused on analyses of slavery in several well-documented settings: the U.S. South, Brazil, the West Indies, and ancient Greece and Rome. More recent work focused on the slave trade and its volume and direction, especially the Atlantic trade, but also that of the Mediterranean and the Indian Ocean. Studies of the slave trade emphasized links among regions (e.g., between Angola and Brazil) and changes in the trade over time.

In the late-twentieth century, the expansion of social-historical analysis allowed the comparative study of legal definitions and social practices of slavery in Africa, the Americas, the Middle East, the Indian Ocean, and Russia. Advances in migration theory and in quantitative demographic techniques (spreadsheets, databases, and simulations) have enabled the new information to be explored more systematically. Slavery can be seen as a global system of labor with significant regional variants.

The Historical System of Slavery in the Modern World

Slavery expanded with the creation of the Atlantic commercial system, and Atlantic slavery brought expansion of slavery in other regions, especially in Africa and the Indian Ocean region. The global system of slave labor reached its peak in the period from 1700 to 1850 and declined thereafter, although slavery remained significant in some regions for another century. The following are brief descriptions of the major regional variants within the global system of slave labor in the modern era.

The Atlantic. Captives were taken from West and Central Africa mainly to Brazil and the Caribbean. In the course of four hundred years, some ten million enslaved persons were landed, creating a population that totaled, around 1850, some six million slaves and many more free people of African descent. North America received just over five percent of all enslaved immigrants, but its slave population in 1850 exceeded three million.

The Mediterranean and the Red Sea. In a trade that began well before 1500 but expanded around 1800, captives were taken from the fringe of the southern Sahara to the Mediterranean coast, and from the upper Nile Valley to Egypt and Arabia. Many but not all of these slaves lived within the territories of the Ottoman Empire. Some four million migrants over four centuries created a population that, in 1850, included perhaps two million slaves, plus many more descendants of slaves.

The Black Sea. Captives were taken from the Caucasus to the Black Sea territories under Ottoman rule. In addition, Slavic-speaking captives were brought to the Ottoman Empire, and in the sixteenth and seventeenth centuries there was a sizeable population of locally-enslaved Russians. Reliable estimates for the size of this slave trade are not available.

The Indian Ocean. Some 2 million captives were taken from East Africa to insular and mainland shores of the Indian Ocean. The trade was especially heavy in the nineteenth century. By 1850 the resulting slave population numbered about one million; there were smaller numbers of ex-slaves and descendants of slaves.

Sub-Saharan Africa. In around 1500 slavery existed in many parts of Africa, but slave populations were quite small. The growing export of captives to the west, north, and east expanded the population of slaves within Africa. Africans in slavery in 1850 numbered perhaps seven million; this number continued to grow until 1900, and declined steadily thereafter.

Viewed as a global system of labor, slavery exhibited broad and interactive patterns, so that change in one region brought about similar or contrasting change in other regions. Some examples illustrate this interaction. First, since an estimated two-thirds of persons sold to the Americas were male, the sending regions of West and Central Africa developed servile systems relying mainly on female slaves. Second, when abolition movements of the nineteenth century began to reduce the slave trade to the Americas, prices of slaves fell in Africa; in response, purchases of slaves in Africa, the Middle East, and the Indian Ocean region expanded. Third, for regions that abolished slave trade but not slavery, there ensued periods of 30 to 50 years of large-scale slavery without any further influx of captives. During these periods the prices of female and infant slaves increased and all slaves received better treatment, since they could not be replaced as easily as before. These regions included the United States and the British West Indies in the early nineteenth century, Brazil and Cuba in the late nineteenth century, the Ottoman Empire in the late nineteenth and early twentieth century, and several regions of East, Central, and West Africa in the twentieth century. Fourth, regional slave systems ended in two sharply different patterns: either a sudden state-decreed emancipation of slaves or a gradual end of slavery through private agency. For the United States and for British and French colonies of the Caribbean, governments passed acts of slave emancipation. For most other areas of the Old World and New World, slavery came to an end slowly, and more often at the individual and familial level than through governmental action.

Demographic Analysis of Slave Experience

To account for the demographic details of slavery, a three-leveled terminology is required. First, one may distinguish four types of status: free, captive (those taken from their homes but not yet settled as slaves), slave, and ex-slave. The captive status, lasting perhaps a year for each person, was a time of high mortality and low fertility. Second, one may distinguish five progressive stages in the slave experience: recruitment (typically by capture), transportation (by land and sea), "seasoning" (social initiation into slavery plus acclimation to a new disease environment), exploitation (the labor of the slave), and termination (departure from slave status by death, manumission, or escape). Third, in calculating demographic rates, one may distinguish between life-course analysis (mortality and fertility) and the analysis of physical and social migration.

The mortality of slaves was elevated in several ways. Death rates rose to high levels during capture and transportation, and were especially severe for the young and the old. Rates of infant mortality were so high for the Middle Passage—the ocean voyage between West Africa and the Americas on slave ships—as to make survival most unlikely. Mortality for slaves under regular exploitation rose because of heavy work loads, and also because slave plantations were commonly in high-mortality, lowland areas. A life table constructed for slaves in eighteenth-century Grenada yields an expectation of life at birth of 25 years.

The fertility of slaves was reduced in various ways, to a modest degree for women and to a substantial degree for men. For women, live births were low in the course of capture and transportation, and first-generation slave women had apparently small completed families, as they had some of their children before enslavement. For locally-born slave women, fertility was higher in the United States than in the Caribbean or Brazil. For male slaves, fertility was low in the many cases where women were scarce; this factor was reinforced because slave owners fathered children of slave women. Marriage and family among slaves was commonly distorted by law and practice: marriage was allowed and recorded in some areas, but in many areas it was not. Overall, the mortality of slaves usually exceeded their fertility, and manumission of some slaves (especially females) made for declining numbers in the enslaved populations. A self-reproducing or even growing population of slaves, which was the situation in the United States from 1810 to 1860, was most unusual.

Social reproduction of slave populations thus required steady importation of new captives. For the African regions from which slaves were taken, rates of slave export averaging perhaps two per thousand per year were probably sufficient to cause population decline for more than a century. Captures targeted young adults and caused significant mortality, so that population losses exceeded births. In addition to shipment of captives, there were at least two major migrations of those already enslaved: in the early nineteenth century roughly one million slaves were moved from the Old South to the New South in the United States, and about the same number were moved from the sugar fields in northeast Brazil to the coffee fields in southern Brazil.

Physical and social migration of captives and slaves created populations with many significant subgroups: immigrant vs. native-born slaves, and groups defined by language, ethnicity, or occupation. Variations in skin color became important in the Americas, while other markers of social difference distinguished slave populations in Africa. Prices of slaves took account of differences in age, sex, ethnicity, and skills. Children of a slave woman by her owner generally remained slaves in the Americas, but were mostly born free in Africa and the Middle East. In the Americas, slave women had most of their children with slave men, so a distinctive population of African descent grew up. In the Middle East and Africa, slave women had most of their children with free men, so that the enslaved assimilated into the general population. Prices were higher for male than for female slaves in the Americas, but the reverse was commonly true in Africa. On both sides of the Atlantic, female slaves were more likely to be manumitted than males.

Slavery Before the Atlantic World

Slavery has been documented for many regions of the world at many times. For times before 1500 C.E., however, there is a remarkable continuity in the existence of slavery as a labor system in lands adjoining the Eastern Mediterranean, the Black Sea, and the Persian Gulf. From Biblical times to Roman and Byzantine eras through the period of the Islamic Caliphates, this region maintained regimes of slavery, sometimes expanding and sometimes contracting, but always with a system of law enabling slavery. This system later spread to lands bordering the Atlantic and Indian Oceans.

Heritage of Slavery

The heritage of slavery affects each region differently. Patterns set by slavery for marriage and family life, and for racial discrimination or assimilation, may persist into later times. The emancipation of slaves brought creation of new restrictions on the formerly enslaved populations, including the formalization of racial segregation and other limits on access to public services or legal equality. In more recent times, calls have emerged for reparations to be paid to the descendants of slaves. While such reparations would be difficult to assess and administer, the concept does address the unmistakable social and racial discrimination borne by the descendants of slaves. Reparations would also address the unpaid contribution of slave labor to construction, agriculture, and industry in the modern Atlantic world.

See also: *African-American Population History; Ancient World, Demography of; Peopling the Continents; Trans-Atlantic Migration.*

BIBLIOGRAPHY

Eltis, David, Stephen D. Behrendt, David Richardson, and Herbert S. Klein, eds. 1999. *The Trans-Atlantic Slave Trade: A Database on CD-ROM.* New York: Cambridge University Press.

Fogel, Robert W., and Stanley L. Engerman. 1974. *Time on the Cross: The Economics of American Negro Slavery.* Boston: Little, Brown and Co.

Higman, Barry W. 1984. *Slave Populations of the British Caribbean, 1807–1834.* Baltimore: Johns Hopkins University Press.

Lovejoy, Paul E., and Jan S. Hogendorn. 1993. *Slow Death for Slavery: The Course of Abolition in Northern Nigeria, 1897–1936.* Cambridge, Eng.: Cambridge University Press.

Manning, Patrick. 1990. *Slavery and African Life: Occidental, Oriental, and African Slave Trades.* Cambridge, Eng.: Cambridge University Press.

———. 1990. "Slave Trade: The Formal Demography of a Global System." *Social Science History* 14: 255–279.

Mattoso, Katia M. de Queiros. 1986. *To Be a Slave in Brazil, 1550–1888.* trans. Arthur Goldhammer. New Brunswick, NJ: Rutgers University Press.

Meillassoux, Claude. 1991. *The Anthropology of Slavery: The Womb of Iron and Gold.* Trans. Alide Dasnois. Chicago: University of Chicago Press.

Miller, Joseph C., ed. 1993. *Slavery and Slaving in World History: A Bibliography, 1900–1991.* Millwood, NY: Kraus International Publications.

PATRICK MANNING

SMALL-AREA ANALYSIS

Demand for demographic data and analysis referring to localities and similar small areas has grown rapidly in recent decades, spurred by new business applications and government programs. To meet that demand, analysts have drawn on an expanding set of data sources, statistical techniques, and computer applications. The result has been improved data quality across a broad spectrum of variables and geographic areas, enhancing both the usefulness and the importance of small-area analyses. Analysts using small-area data include demographers, sociologists, geographers, economists, marketers, epidemiologists, planners, and others.

Analysts define small areas in several different ways. Under one definition, they are states and other subnational areas for which samples from national surveys are too small to provide meaningful estimates. More typically, small areas refer to counties and subcounty areas like cities, census tracts, postal code areas, and individual blocks. Small areas may range from less than an acre to thousands of square miles, and from no inhabitants to many millions.

This article reviews commonly-used data sources and application techniques and discusses several distinctive features of small-area demographic analysis. Although reference is primarily to the United States, many of the issues discussed transcend national boundaries.

Data Sources

Censuses, administrative records, and sample surveys are the major sources of data for small-area demographic analyses. In most countries, censuses constitute the most comprehensive source of small-area data, typically at five or ten year intervals. They cover a variety of population characteristics (such as age, sex, marital status, and education) and housing information (such as number of dwelling units, occupancy rates, household size, and housing value or monthly rent).

Administrative records kept by national, state, and local governments often provide small-area data for years between censuses. These records contain information on variables such as births, deaths, school enrollments, social insurance, building permits, drivers' licenses, and voter registration—each reflecting a facet of population structure and change that may be useful for constructing estimates and projections or for tracking demographic trends. Most industrialized countries maintain relatively accurate records of this kind; some European countries even produce census-type statistics based solely on administrative records. In many developing countries, however, administrative records are seriously incomplete.

Sample surveys are another potential source of demographic and socioeconomic data, provided that the samples are large enough to yield reliable estimates for small areas. A notable example is the American Community Survey, which is expected to cover some three million U.S. households annually by 2003. This survey will eventually generate estimates down to the block group level for the entire nation.

Estimates and Projections

Small-area estimates of total population generally rely on housing unit, component, or regression methods. The *housing unit* method derives population estimates from calculations of occupied housing units (i.e., households) and average household size, plus the number of persons living in group quarters facilities such as college dormitories, military barracks, and prisons. *Component methods* derive population estimates from birth, death, and migration data (births and deaths from vital statistics records, migration from changes in school enrollments or other indicators of population mobility). *Regression methods* derive population estimates from symptomatic indicators of population change—such as births, school enrollments, electric utility customers, registered voters, drivers licenses, and tax returns—in a multivariate model. All three methods produce useful estimates, but the housing unit method is the most commonly used for small-area estimates because it is relatively easy to apply and the requisite data are widely available.

Estimates of demographic characteristics such as age, sex, and ethnicity are typically based on the cohort-component method. Here, birth, death, and migration rates are applied separately to each age, sex, and ethnic subgroup in the population. Estimates of socioeconomic characteristics such as income, employment, and education are often based on imputation techniques, whereby known proportions of the population exhibiting a characteristic in a larger area (e.g., a state) are applied to population estimates for smaller areas (e.g., cities, counties). Typically, these proportions are calculated separately for different subgroups of the population. Estimates of demographic and socioeconomic characteristics can also be based on administrative records (e.g., Medicare data).

Population projection methods used for small areas are mainly of three kinds. *Trend extrapolation* methods extend observed historical trends. These methods may be simple, such as projecting past growth rates to remain unchanged, or complex, as in ARIMA time series models. These methods are frequently used for small-area projections because the data requirements are small, they are easy to apply, and their forecasts have often proven to be reasonably accurate.

The *cohort-component* method accounts separately for the three components of population change—births, deaths, and migration. Projections of each component can be based on the extrapolation of past trends, projected trends in other areas, structural models, or professional judgment. Simplified versions of the method such as those described by Hamilton and Perry (1962) can also be applied. The cohort-component method is the most frequently-used projection method because it can accommodate a broad range of data sources, assumptions, and application techniques, and can provide projections of demographic characteristics as well as total population.

Structural models are based on an entirely different logic from the other projection methods. They relate the projected population to variables known to drive population change, like comparative wages, employment, and land use. Some structural models involve only a single equation and a few variables; others contain many equations, variables, and parameters. They are often used in combination with the cohort-component method. Although they require highly-detailed data and substantial investments of effort and modeling skill, structural models provide a broader range of projections than the other methods.

Uses of Small-Area Analysis

To increase knowledge. Small-area data shed light on socioeconomic and demographic variations across states, counties, cities, census tracts, and other geographic areas, enlarging the knowledge available to scholars, policy makers, and other analysts. Empirical researchers have applied small-area analysis to many areas of inquiry. For example, Kathleen M. Day (1992) investigated how differences in government tax and expenditure policies affected interprovincial migration in Canada; Rene J. Borroto and Ramon Martinez-Piedra (2000) studied how poverty, urbanization, and geographic location affected the incidence of cholera among regions in Mexico; and Patricia E. Beeson, David N. DeJong, and Werner Troesken (2001) studied how differences in industrial, educational, geographic, and demographic characteristics affected county population growth rates in the United States.

To inform public policy. Small-area analysis supports decision-making by national, state, and local government agencies. Small-area data are indispensable for drawing administrative and electoral boundaries, allocating government funds, siting public facilities, developing program budgets, determining eligibility for public programs, and monitoring program effectiveness. For example, Tayman, Parrott, and Carnevale (1997) used block-level population and household projections to choose sites for fire stations; Gould and colleagues (1998) used birth data by postal code area to identify areas in need of adolescent pregnancy prevention programs; and Hashimoto, Murakami, Taniguchi, and Hagai (2000) developed techniques for monitoring infectious diseases by health district.

To support business decision making. Small-area data figure prominently in many types of business decisions—including site selection, sales forecasting, consumer profiles, litigation support, target marketing, and labor force analysis—analogous to their use in public policy. For example, small-area data were used by Morrison and Abrahamse (1996) to select locations for supermarkets; by Thomas (1997) to project the demand for a hospital's obstetrical services; and by Murdock and Hamm (1997) to produce population estimates and projections to support a company's bank loan application.

Problems of Small-Area Analysis

Several distinctive problems of small-area analysis require attention. First, unlike most larger administrative units, the geographic boundaries of many small areas change over time. Cities annex adjoining areas, census tracts get subdivided, postal code areas are reconfigured, service areas are redefined, and new statistical areas are established. Such changes undermine the consistency of historical data series.

Second, many types of data are not tabulated for some small areas of interest, such as census tracts, school districts, market sales territories, and traffic analysis zones. Consequently, analyses routinely performed for larger areas may be impossible for small areas or feasible only using proxy variables.

Third, even the best censuses and administrative record systems contain errors. The effects of data errors are typically greater for small areas than large areas, where errors are often mutually offsetting. In addition, survey data are generally less reliable for small areas than large areas because sample sizes are smaller and survey responses more variable.

Finally, trends at the small-area level are more likely to be disrupted by idiosyncratic factors—such as the opening or closing of a prison or military base, the construction of a large housing development, the opening of a new road or railway, and the addition or loss of a major employer—than trends at the larger-area level. The effect of growth constraints like zoning restrictions and seasonal populations such as migrant workers is also likely to be greater for small areas than large areas. Factors like these often distort small-area trends.

Developments

Several developments have broadened the scope and improved the quality of small-area analyses around the turn of the twenty-first century. A wider variety of small-area data has become available in many countries, primarily through administrative records and sample surveys. The Internet has greatly enhanced access to these data, and the rapid growth of computing power, data storage capacity, and software applications has expanded their potential usefulness. Geographic information systems (GIS) technology has facilitated the collection, organization, manipulation, analysis, and presentation of geographically-referenced data. These developments have prompted many new uses of small-area data, at ever finer levels of detail.

Concerns about privacy and confidentiality, however, pose a formidable barrier to the continued advancement of small-area analysis. To many citizens, the collection of personal information, whether by businesses or government, is an invasion of privacy. Confidentiality is potentially at risk when personal data are shared among public and private agencies. Such concerns have caused many government statistical offices to curtail the release of demographic data, and the use of administrative records has been restricted in the United States, Germany, the United Kingdom, and elsewhere. Devising acceptable ways to utilize information while preserving privacy and confidentiality is a major challenge for small-area analysts.

See also: *Business Demography; Census; Geographic Information Systems; Projections and Forecasts, Population; State and Local Government Demography.*

BIBLIOGRAPHY

Beeson, Patricia E., David N. DeJong, and Werner Troesken. 2001. "Population Growth in U.S. Counties, 1840–1990." *Regional Science and Urban Economics* 31: 669–699.

Borroto, Rene J., and Ramon Martinez-Piedra. 2000. "Geographical Patterns of Cholera in Mexico, 1991–1996." *International Journal of Epidemiology* 29: 764–772.

Cleland, John. 1996. "Demographic Data Collection in Less Developed Countries 1946–1996." *Population Studies* 50: 433–450.

Day, Kathleen M. 1992. "Interprovincial Migration and Local Public Goods." *Canadian Journal of Economics* 25: 123–144.

Gould, Jeffrey B., Beate Herrchen, Tanya Pham, Stephan Bera, and Claire Brindis. 1998. "Small-Area Analysis: Targeting High-Risk Areas for Adolescent Pregnancy Prevention Programs." *Family Planning Perspectives* 30: 173–176.

Hamilton, C. Horace, and Josef Perry. 1962. "A Short Method for Projecting Population by Age from One Decennial Census to Another." *Social Forces* 41: 163–170.

Hashimoto, Shuji, Yoshataka Murakami, Kiyosu Taniguchi, and Masaki Nagai. 2000. "Detection of Epidemics in their Early Stage through Infectious Disease Surveillance." *International Journal of Epidemiology* 29: 905–910.

Morrison, Peter A., and Allan F. Abrahamse. 1996. "Applying Demographic Analysis to Store Site

Selection." *Population Research and Policy Review* 15: 479–489.

Murdock, Steven H., and Rita R. Hamm. 1997. "A Demographic Analysis of the Market for a Long-Term Care Facility: A Case Study in Applied Demography." In *Demographics: A Casebook for Business and Government*, ed. Hallie J. Kintner, Thomas W. Merrick, Peter A. Morrison, and Paul R. Voss. Santa Monica, CA: Rand.

Siegel, Jacob S. 2002. *Applied Demography: Applications to Business, Government, Law and Public Policy.* San Diego, CA: Academic Press.

Smith, Stanley K., Jeff Tayman, and David A Swanson. 2001. *State and Local Population Projections: Methodology and Analysis.* New York: Kluwer Academic/Plenum Publishers.

Tayman, Jeff, Bob Parrott, and Sue Carnevale. 1997. "Locating Fire Station Sites: The Response Time Component." In *Demographics: A Casebook for Business and Government*, ed. Hallie J. Kintner, Thomas W. Merrick, Peter A. Morrison, and Paul R. Voss. Santa Monica, CA: Rand.

Thomas, Richard K. 1997. "Using Demographic Analysis in Health Services Planning: A Case Study in Obstetrical Services." In *Demographics: A Casebook for Business and Government*, ed. Hallie J. Kintner, Thomas W. Merrick, Peter A. Morrison, and Paul R. Voss. Santa Monica, CA: Rand.

STANLEY K. SMITH

SOCIAL CAPITAL

Social capital has been defined as "the resources that emerge from one's social ties" (Portes and Landolt 1996, p. 26). One of the first scholars to use the term was George Homans in *Social Behavior: Its Elementary Forms* (1961). Homans was interested in understanding how people in some small groups but not others are able to expand a group and transform it into a complex organization. This is accomplished, he argued, by group members engaging in social exchange to such a large extent that a "surplus" of interaction, activity, and sentiment (the building blocks of social exchange) accumulates (Homans 1950). That surplus can be directed toward the creation and maintenance of elaborate social structures, which facilitate more interaction and activity among group members in an iterative and self-reinforcing process. An input to production (in this case the production of a social form) that has been produced by a prior process (in this case a prior process of social exchange) is referred to by economists as a capital resource and, in this instance, as *social capital.*

Explorations of Social Capital

In the late 1970s the sociologist Pierre Bourdieu and the economist Glen Loury independently began to use the term. Bourdieu (1986) incorporated into his definition of social capital the Marxist idea that the raw material that produces a capital resource is always, at its ultimate origin, human labor. Loury's (1977) work examined the effect of differential access to social capital by ethnic group. His analysis found that in a society that is ethnically stratified, differential levels of resources by ethnicity at the group level are an important determinant of individual earnings.

Building on the work of Bourdieu and Loury as well as that of Mark Granovetter (1973, 1974, 1985) and Nan Lin (Lin 1982, 1988; Lin, Ensel, and Vaughn 1981), the sociologist James S. Coleman brought the concept of social capital into widespread use in the social sciences (Coleman 1988, 1990). Notable examples of its use are found in the work of the political scientist Robert D. Putnam. Putnam has been concerned mainly with the effects of social capital on political forms and levels of participation, such as the contrasting political outcomes in northern and southern Italy and the apparent fall in the level of associational activity in the United States. Other researchers have examined how social capital promotes child development and affects health outcomes for individuals.

Group Resource versus Individual Resource

There are two distinct views of social capital in this research. In one view social capital is considered a group-level resource to which all the members of a group have access; in the other it is considered an individual resource that is inherent in social structures. Coleman took the former position, in which it is thought that an individual's level of social capital can be measured by that individual's membership in a particular group.

Critics argue that construing social capital as a group resource leads to measurement ambiguities, for example, making it impossible to distinguish between social capital and its putative benefits, such as trust and norms. This position tends to downplay the effects of stratification within a group, making social capital merely a public good that is equally accessible to all. Moreover, this approach leads to the view that social capital by necessity confers benefits on individuals, which need not be the case.

The alternative view—social capital as a resource specific to individuals—ties the concept to the literature on social networks. Network analysis provides conceptual and analytic tools that can be applied to the study of social capital, investigating, for example, how a person's location in a social network affects that person's access to social capital or how the embedded resources in a particular social network affect network members' levels of social capital.

Applications in Population Research

For population scientists the concept of social capital has potential value in illuminating both the motivations of individuals to form social relationships and the consequences of social relationships for individual well-being. Many of the individual behaviors that in the aggregate produce demographic outcomes can be seen as investments (or disinvestments) in social capital. Such behaviors include forming sexual partnerships, rearing children, moving, coresidence, intergenerational exchange, and caring for the frail, the disabled, and the ill. Trends and differentials in these behaviors can be interpreted in part as resulting from shifts in the value of the social capital available to those who engage in them (Astone et al. 1999). Fertility transition, for example, could be seen as the outcome of a shift in investment from social capital to other kinds of capital, particularly human capital, perceived as offering higher returns.

See also: *Culture and Population; Diffusion in Population Theory; Social Networks.*

BIBLIOGRAPHY

Astone, Nan Marie, Constance A. Nathanson, Robert Schoen, and Young J. Kim. 1999. "Family Demography, Social Theory and Investment in Social Capital." *Population and Development Review* 25(1):1–32.

Bourdieu, Pierre. 1986. "The Forms of Capital." In *Handbook of Theory and Research for the Sociology of Education,* ed. John G. Richardson. New York: Greenwood.

Coleman, James S. 1988. "Social Capital in the Creation of Human Capital." *American Journal of Sociology* 94: S95–S120.

———. 1990. *Foundations of Social Theory.* Cambridge, MA: Harvard University Press.

Granovetter, Mark. 1973. "The Strength of Weak Ties." *American Journal of Sociology* 78(6): 1,360–1,380.

———. 1974. *Getting a Job: A Study of Contacts and Careers.* Cambridge, MA: Harvard University Press.

———. 1985. "Economic Action and Social Structure: The Problem of Embeddedness." *American Journal of Sociology* 91(3): 481–510.

Homans, George C. 1950. *The Human Group.* New York: Harcourt, Brace and World.

———. 1961. *Social Behavior: Its Elementary Forms.* New York: Harcourt, Brace and World.

Lin, Nan. 1982. "Social Resources and Instrumental Action." In *Social Structure and Network Analysis,* ed. Peter Marsden and Nan Lin. Beverly Hills, CA: Sage.

———. 1988. "Social Resources and Social Mobility: A Structural Theory of Status Attainment." In *Social Mobility and Social Structure,* ed. R. L. Breiger. Cambridge, Eng.: Cambridge University Press.

Lin, Nan, Walter M. Ensel, and John C. Vaughn. 1981. "Social Resources and Strength of Ties: Structural Factors in Occupational Attainment." *American Sociological Review* 46: 393–405.

Loury, Glenn C. 1977. "A Dynamic Theory of Racial Income Differences." In *Women, Minorities, and Employment Discrimination,* ed. Phyllis A. Wallace and Annette M. LaMond. Lexington, MA: Lexington Books.

Portes, Alejandro, and Patricia Landolt. 1996. "The Downside of Social Capital." *The American Prospect* 26: 18ff.

Putnam, Robert D. 1993a. *Making Democracy Work.* Princeton, NJ: Princeton University Press.

———. 1993b. "The Prosperous Community: Social Capital and Economic Growth." *The American Prospect* 13: 35–42.

———. 1995. "Bowling Alone: America's Declining Social Capital." *Journal of Democracy* 6: 65–78.

NAN MARIE ASTONE

SOCIAL INSTITUTIONS

Social institutions are the significant social structures and practices that organize societies in regular, patterned ways. Social norms and sanctions guide and maintain these institutions. Individuals' demographic decisions and behaviors are channeled by social institutions, which create constrained opportunities and choices. Social institutions help to define demographically relevant statuses, such as student, spouse, parent, and worker. Normative prescriptions associated with institutions further delineate the appropriate age for adopting one of these statuses, and the appropriate sequencing of associated "roles." Changes in social institutions may give rise to alternative life pathways for individuals, as with changes in marital roles in the United States when the labor market presented new work opportunities for married women.

The term "institution" is widely used within the discipline of sociology, but is not uniformly defined. Precise understandings vary with theoretical orientation. For example, functionalists are more inclined to conceive of institutions as structures that perform particular functions or roles in society. By contrast, social interactionists emphasize the fluid set of practices and behaviors which define institutions. Recent theoretical work on the life course points to the key role of institutions in connecting individual life histories to community influences and the forces of social history. This is a view of institutions as structures that channel behaviors. But social institutions also provide the way in which social historical changes are made real through their connection to individual persons. In economics the market system of capitalist states is a key institution, with effects on nearly every aspect of family life. Shifts from socialist to more market-oriented economies, as occurred in China and Vietnam at the end of the twentieth cen-

tury, have had pervasive effects on demographic behavior.

Beyond structures and practices, more general terms have been used to define social institutions, including "ideas" about how to accomplish societal goals and "focuses" of social organization. Despite diversity in precise definition, most social scientists agree that universality is a characteristic of significant social institutions. Social institutions are recognized for their place in organizing social life within and across societies. As such, they are significant in any given society, and provide a useful prism for organizing comparative analyses of population across societies.

Population events influence and are influenced by social institutions. These relationships are dynamic and subject to feedback. They are central to any understanding of the determinants and consequences of population change. The social institutions that are most widely recognized as relevant to population change include family and kinship systems, religious institutions, the education system, the health system, political organization, and the economy. These institutions are the social structures through which changes in fertility outcomes, infant and adult mortality, immigration and emigration, and the age structure of the population come about. Conversely, population processes are key to the shape and form of social institutions, creating a constant interplay between the two. The complexities of this interrelationship may be illustrated by drawing attention to three important features:

1. The multiple dimensions of interdependence of social institutions and population;

2. The multilevel and across-level aspects of the interdependence within and between social institutions and population processes; and

3. The embeddedness of the relationships between social institutions and population processes in social, economic, historical, and political contexts.

Institutions and Population Change

Educational and economic institutions structure individual demographic behaviors with resultant effects on population processes. Government decisions concerning universal education, the structure of the schools (local or national control, performance standards, single or mixed sex), and the location of schools are the basis for family calculations about the costs and benefits of education for sons and daughters. The educational system—through enrollment differentials by place of residence, class, and gender, as well as by the form and content of lessons taught in schools—shapes population-relevant knowledge, attitudes, and behavior. Educational content can make schooling a strong or a weak tool for obtaining human capital. Educational systems that train children from rural areas in basic intellectual and work skills help determine whether an individual will work locally or will migrate elsewhere in search of further schooling or other employment opportunities. Schools can increase knowledge about contraceptive use, and alter couple dynamics in ways that promote or hinder adoption of contraception.

Families recognize the value of education, and see education as one way to produce "higher quality" children. This growth in the demand for education, in turn, may overwhelm educational systems, which often lack the resources, school facilities, and teachers needed to meet the new demand. In cases where the public education system is not able to satisfy the demand for accessible and high quality education, parents may enroll their children in private schools, recasting the institutional structure of education.

The rapid decline in the infant and childhood mortality rates in much of Asia and parts of Africa over the second half of the twentieth century came about largely through improved public health systems and better transportation and communication systems, fostered by the development plans of national governments. These improved survival rates had unforeseen consequences, including rapid population growth, a younger age structure, and greatly increased successive cohort sizes. Such changes are particularly problematic for social institutions that are highly age-structured.

Typically, increased demand for skilled labor during economic development is met by improvements in the education of urban populations, by migration from rural to urban places, and by immigration. The result is the urbanization of society. As cities grow in size, national and local governments increasingly are faced with the need to provide expensive urban infrastructures and to address the interests of large cohorts of young persons whose aspirations are unmet.

Improvement in earnings opportunities for women leads to their higher labor force participation rates and, depending on the form of labor, more autonomy in determining the use of resources (such as the purchase of contraceptives and medical care for young children). The rising opportunity costs of withdrawing from the labor force lead to later marriage and smaller family size, and make it increasingly likely that more mothers of young children will work. Changes in the market demand for labor (a demand that is sensitive to internal migration, immigration, fertility, and mortality) can transform the family by redefining appropriate gendered activities, including expectations of mothers and fathers concerning their appropriate roles in the family.

Population and Institutional Change

Social institutions are enduring entities but they are not static. Changes in social institutions can be shaped by demographic change. Take fertility decline: fertility declines can have pervasive effects on the family. A primary activity of that institution is the nurturance of children. As the number of children in a family decreases, the activity of caring for children changes. Family members may spend less time in the activity of caregiving because there are fewer children. Traditional tasks of motherhood often become concentrated in a shorter time-span within women's lifetimes, freeing women to pursue alternative activities. Alternatively, children's needs may be redefined in a way that does not reduce family members' time in caring for young children, but instead qualitatively changes the nature of caregiving.

Fertility change also has implications for family and other social institutions through its effects on the age structure of a population. In Asia, where fertility decline has been rapid and pension schemes are limited, concern is emerging over the increasing burden of providing care to aging elders, a responsibility expected to fall to a generation of children that grows smaller with each successive cohort. Similarly, at the aggregate level, declines in fertility through the birth of smaller cohorts are linked to cohort size. Instability in successive birth cohorts has implications for the economy, as workers retire and are not easily replaced by the generations that follow.

Population change, especially that involving delays in marriage and limitation in family size (to levels below replacement) have produced an economically less favorable (older) population age structure in many countries. States are responding to this changed population age structure. Change in the population age structure affects the structure and composition of the labor force, and the schools that train workers. As schools become increasingly willing to admit girls and young women, women's educational attainment and labor force participation grows, creating new potential for increases in labor force size and productivity. In some countries where fertility rates have been below replacement for two or more decades, immigration has been encouraged as a way to facilitate adjustments to a declining indigenous labor force size. With such immigration new groups appear in the population that may espouse different religious beliefs, family roles and practices, and gender roles, challenging existing social institutions.

The connections between social institutions and demographic change depend on context. While particular relationships—such as that between education and union formation—exist across time and place, their form and content depend on social, economic, historical, and political context. Population policies, with their demographic consequences, are inherently political. States may set population goals and implement policies and programs to promote the achievement of those goals, usually with specific related aims in view. States can encourage population growth, perhaps of selected groups, to win or maintain political power, or to enhance their military strength. Or, as was more common in recent decades, states can discourage rapid population growth, hoping thereby to promote economic development.

In 1979 China adopted a one-child policy to spur modernization and development. In the implementation of this policy, which enforces fertility reduction, numerous social institutions were enlisted. Schools taught a curriculum that emphasized the importance of smaller families and the citizen's duty to the nation to abide by the policy. A family planning system, separate from the health system, was developed to promote birth control and ensure availability of related services even in the most remote places. Local governance and relationships between individuals and local leaders were shaped by the state's promotion of this policy. Local leaders were given birth quotas and could lose their jobs for failure to meet these targets. The resulting pressures were felt in daily interaction at the village or neigh-borhood level, as families were rewarded for adopting the prescribed behavior or sanctioned for violating state policy. In short, social institutions were used by the state to promote desired population change. These institutions (family, health care, education, and government), in turn, were substantially altered not only by the policy's demographic results, but also by the means adopted to implement it.

Conclusion

The study of social institutions, their structures and processes, is a first step toward understanding population processes and the causes of population change. Anthropological demographers and social historians have been among the leaders in emphasizing this approach, seeking to delineate the "opportunity structure" or "choice set" bounding individual demographic behaviors. Quantitative analyses of population survey data can benefit from understanding the impact of institutions on personal lives, although they often fail to do so. Changes over time in individual demographic behavior need to be interpreted in terms of the broad shape of social history, as filtered by institutional structure and change, linking individual lives to historical time. Gender, religion, and ethnicity are personal factors especially central to understanding whether and how these linkages are handled by families and individuals. Thus, attention to social institutions is critical to understanding nearly all aspects of demographic behavior and population change.

See also: *Action Theory in Population Research; Culture and Population; Social Mobility; Social Networks.*

BIBLIOGRAPHY

Davis, Kingsley. 1963. "The Theory of Change and Response in Modern Demographic History." *Population Index* 29: 345–366.

Easterlin, Richard A. 1980. *Birth and Fortune: The Impact of Numbers on Personal Welfare.* New York: Basic Books, Inc.

Elder, Glen H. 1974. *Children of the Great Depression: Social Change in Life Experience.* Chicago: University of Chicago Press.

Greenhalgh, Susan, ed. 1995. *Situating Fertility: Anthropological and Demographic Inquiry.* New York: Cambridge University Press.

Kertzer, David I., and Dennis P. Hogan. 1989. *Family, Political Economy, and Demographic Change:*

The Transformation of Life in Casalecchio, Italy, 1861–1921. Madison: University of Wisconsin Press.

McNicoll, Geoffrey. 1994. "Institutional Analysis of Fertility." In *Population, Economic Development, and the Environment,* ed. Kerstin Lindahl-Kiessling and Hans Landberg. Oxford: Oxford University Press.

Pampel, Fred C. 2001. *Institutional Context of Population Change.* Chicago: University of Chicago Press.

DENNIS HOGAN
SUSAN SHORT

SOCIAL MOBILITY

Social mobility is the movement of individuals or other social units between social statuses and positions. This mobility can be between the status of individuals and that of their forbears or their offspring ("intergenerational" mobility), or between different statuses of individuals within their own lifetimes ("intragenerational" mobility). The study of social mobility focuses on movement between occupations or, to a lesser extent, on changes in status signaled by income, wealth, poverty, or educational attainment. In principle, however, social mobility encompasses a wider set of social and cultural traits, such as family structure, religious affiliation, language, and political party identification.

Most modern research on social mobility focuses on the conceptualization, measurement, and description of mobility patterns at the national level for a variety of countries and periods. Motivated by an effort to examine the "openness" or "rigidity" of systems of social stratification and inequality, the study of mobility is part of the analysis of population composition. Social mobility, however, is also linked to dynamic aspects of demography because of its interdependence with basic demographic processes at both the individual and population levels.

Measurement and Analysis of Social Mobility

Research on social mobility focuses on either bivariate or multivariate relationships between dimensions of social position. Bivariate analyses of occupational mobility typically compare individuals by their occupational categories at their places of social origin and destination. The classification of occupations may be highly aggregated, focusing on only a small number of analytically important categories, or disaggregated to detailed occupations. Analytical categories may emphasize a general socioeconomic hierarchy or follow more relational, nonhierarchical class schemes. Regardless of the type of occupational classification, mobility analyses focus on the patterns of association between origins and destinations.

In the context of intergenerational occupational mobility, patterns include the degree to which offspring occupy the same social positions as their parents and, for those who are in different locations from those of their parents, whether flows between particular combinations of discrepant origins and destinations are unusually large or small. Using modern methods of categorical data analysis applied to mobility tables, researchers investigate the complex patterns of associations between origins and destinations. A cross tabulation of individuals by their origins and destinations is affected by the relative numbers of persons in the various categories of origins and destinations considered separately—the "marginal distributions" of the mobility table—and the associations between origins and destinations. Some degree of mobility may occur simply because the relative numbers of persons in origin positions differ from the relative numbers in destination positions. This mobility is often termed "structural mobility" because it is interpreted as resulting from changes in the occupational structure. Even in the absence of change in the occupational structure, however, substantial mobility typically occurs because of a certain degree of openness in a society. This mobility is termed "exchange," "circulation," or "relative" mobility.

A common focus of mobility analyses is to compare mobility patterns across populations and to discern the degree to which differences result from variation in the changes between the origin and destination marginal distributions, and which result from variation in the associations between origin and destination once the marginal distributions have been statistically controlled. In most Western societies during the twentieth century, secular changes in occupational mobility were mainly the result of changes in the distribution of occupations. These changes resulted from the shrinkage of agriculture, the shift from a manual to a largely non-manual workforce, and the shift from an industrial to a service economy. In comparison to these large changes in structural mobility, fluctuations in exchange or circulation mobility have been modest. Similarly, occupational mobility variations among industrial societies are mainly attributable to variations in occupational structure per se rather than cross-national variations in the net association between social origins and destinations.

The theoretical distinction between structural and circulation mobility, however, corresponds only roughly to the empirical distinction between marginal and associational variations in intergenerational mobility tables. The two marginal distributions of a social mobility table cannot both correspond directly to occupational structures at two points in time. For example, in mobility data derived from a cross-section survey of adult offspring, the destination marginal of the table does represent the occupational structure at the time of survey. The origin marginal of the table, however, does not represent the occupational structure at any single point in time because of variations in the timing of fertility among parents. Moreover, the relative numbers of parents in different occupation categories are affected by differentials in the level of fertility by parents' occupation, as well as by the occupational structures that prevailed during the periods when they raised their offspring.

Multivariate analyses of social mobility follow two general strategies. One is to examine the processes through which the statuses of social origins affect the statuses of destinations by identifying variables and statistical relationships that intervene between characteristics of parents and those of their adult offspring. These analyses typically focus on scalar measures, such as occupational status, years of school completed, earnings, and number of siblings, and attempt to isolate the direct and indirect effects of antecedent statuses on adult outcomes. For example, the gross effect of parent's occupational status on offspring's occupational status is attributable in part to the smaller average number of children born to higher status parents, the higher level of education acquired by offspring in such families, and the advantages that higher levels of education and fewer siblings bring to adult achievement. In most industrial and postindustrial societies, educational attainment plays a pivotal role in social mobility and achievement. Much of the association between par-

ent's and offspring's adult socioeconomic statuses is accounted for by the dependence of offspring's educational attainment on parents' socioeconomic position and by the strong effect of offspring's educational attainment on the offspring's own socioeconomic attainment. Across cohorts born during the twentieth century, moreover, the indirect effect of social origins on destinations via educational attainment has increased, while the direct effect of social origins net of educational attainment has decreased. A second multivariate approach to the investigation of social mobility is the direct investigation of movement between education levels, jobs, occupations, or wage levels. This approach relies on variants of event history and multivariate life table analysis and uses data on the detailed temporal sequences of statuses or positions that individuals hold. Such analyses are well suited for the description of careers and the interdependence of socioeconomic mobility and other demographic transitions, such as movement between marital and childbearing statuses.

Social Mobility and Population Renewal

Social mobility is linked to population renewal in a variety of ways at the individual, family, and aggregate population levels. A longstanding concern of demographers is the potential impact of intergenerational social mobility on the fertility of women. The social mobility hypothesis suggests that upwardly mobile individuals may have unusually low fertility because low fertility may facilitate career success and wealth accumulation. Rigorous efforts to substantiate this hypothesis, however, have been largely negative, showing that apparent mobility effects are largely reducible to the effects of fertility norms specific to a woman's socioeconomic origin and to her destination rather than to social mobility per se. In contrast, a much better established relationship is a negative effect of fertility in the family of *orientation*—that is, number of siblings—on adult socioeconomic success. This relationship occurs because number of siblings indexes the degree of dilution of the economic, social, and psychological resources that parents provide their children. It holds for most Western societies, even when multiple indicators of parental socioeconomic background and family structure are controlled. Exceptions to the generally negative effect of number of siblings, however, occur in populations in which larger kin networks provide a socioeconomic advantage.

At the aggregate level, social mobility is a key mechanism through which fertility, marriage, and immigration may affect population composition. The classic model of population renewal assumes an age-differentiated but otherwise homogeneous one-sex closed population subject to age-specific rates of fertility and mortality. This model can be extended to two-sex populations, to geographically heterogeneous populations, and to populations open to immigration and emigration. When considering how population renewal affects changes in the makeup of socially differentiated populations, however, it is usually necessary to also incorporate social mobility into the models. Differential fertility of social groups defined by, for example, language, religious affiliation, educational attainment, measured intelligence, or income strata, may affect the subsequent makeup of the population in these groups. The effect of fertility differentials on population composition, however, depends on the degree to which membership in these groups is open or closed across generations. In populations in which intergenerational social mobility is low—that is, in which the correlation between parental and offspring characteristics is high—differential fertility may strongly affect the differential growth rates of social groups. Conversely, when social mobility is high, the effects of differential fertility are offset by the tendency for offspring to belong to different social groups from their parents'. Similarly, high correlations between the socioeconomic characteristics of marriage partners may create higher levels of inequality in subsequent generations because of the reinforcing effects of both variation and covariation in parents' characteristics on inequality among their children. The inequality-producing effects of assortative marriage, however, may be nullified if high rates of intergenerational social mobility cause large proportions of offspring to belong to different social groups from their parents'. The few studies of the interdependence of social mobility, differential fertility, and assortative mating that have been carried out indicate that intergenerational social mobility rates in Western industrial societies are high enough to offset almost all of the potential effects of differential fertility and assortative mating on differential rates of population growth.

See also: *Caste; Dumont, Arsène; Intergenerational Transfers; Partner Choice; Social Institutions; Social Reproduction.*

BIBLIOGRAPHY

Blake, Judith. 1989. *Family Size and Achievement.* Berkeley: University of California Press.

Blau, Peter M., and Otis Dudley Duncan. 1967. *The American Occupational Structure.* New York: Wiley.

Duncan, Otis Dudley. 1966. "Methodological Issues in the Analysis of Social Mobility." In *Social Structure and Mobility in Economic Development,* ed. N. J. Smelser and S. M. Lipset. Chicago: Aldine.

Erikson, Robert, and John H. Goldthorpe. 1992. *The Constant Flux: A Study of Class Mobility in Industrial Societies.* Oxford: Clarendon Press.

Featherman, David L., and Robert M. Hauser. 1978. *Opportunity and Change.* New York: Academic Press.

Ganzeboom, Harry B. G., Donald J. Treiman, and Wout C. Ultee. 1991. "Comparative Intergenerational Stratification Research: Three Generations and Beyond." *Annual Review of Sociology* 17: 277–302.

Hauser, Robert M., and John Robert Warren. 1997. "Socioeconomic Indexes for Occupations: A Review, Update, and Critique." In *Sociological Methodology 1997,* ed. Adrian E. Raftery. Washington, D.C.: The American Sociological Association.

Hout, Michael. 1988. "More Universalism, Less Structural Mobility: The American Occupational Structure in the 1980s." *American Journal of Sociology* 93: 1,358–1,400.

Mare, Robert D. 1997. "Differential Fertility, Intergenerational Educational Mobility, and Racial Inequality." *Social Science Research* 26: 263–291.

Rosenfeld, Rachel. 1992. "Job Mobility and Career Processes." *Annual Review of Sociology* 18: 39–61.

Sørensen, Jesper B., and David B. Grusky. 1996. "The Structure of Career Mobility in Microscopic Perspective." In *Social Differentiation and Social Inequality: Essays in Honor of John C. Pock,* ed. J. N. Baron, D. B. Grusky, and D. J. Treiman. Boulder, CO: Westview Press.

ROBERT D. MARE

SOCIAL NETWORKS

Social network theory assumes that social interactions have the potential to influence attitudes and behavior. In the sphere of population this assumption has begun to be confirmed by demographers. Network models bear some similarity to diffusion models, but they offer a more structured approach to social interaction by focusing on the specific links that connect individuals and groups. In the 1980s interest in social networks by sociologists led to the collection of network data, the elaboration of theory, and the development of new analytic methods. Demographers have borrowed heavily from this theoretical and methodological work to guide their empirical analyses. Most have concentrated on fertility, investigating the fertility transitions of individuals in local communities, but network approaches have also been used in the study of migration and mortality, clusters of villages, population elites, and organizations.

Evidence that people do indeed talk with friends, relatives, and neighbors about fertility control can be found in historical sources, interviews with elderly people, and surveys conducted in developing countries in the 1960s and 1970s. In these surveys, the content and context of the conversations are missing. When researchers have collected qualitative data, they have found that talk about subjects such as family planning may be open, casual, and quite specific rather than private, formal, and vague. Qualitative data also provide insight into how network partners are selected, an issue relevant for determining appropriate statistical techniques. Both theory and data suggest that social interactions concerning fertility control are especially likely in situations of uncertainty.

Network theory postulates a variety of effects of networks, but in the study of fertility transitions the focus has been on new information transmitted and evaluated in networks and on the influence that networks exert on its members to adopt or resist innovations. Links among network partners are characterized in a variety of ways. An important distinction is that between strong and weak links: strong links are hypothesized to constrain the flow of new information and to exert more social influence than weak links. A variety of indicators of the strength of ties has been proposed, such as whether the network partner is a confidant, a friend, or an acquaintance and the duration of the relationship. Networks have also been characterized by the degree of homogeneity of members with respect to characteristics such as age, education, gender, and ethnicity. Heterogeneous networks may facilitate the spread of new information, whereas homogeneous networks may be more effective in exerting social influence.

Studies using cross-sectional data provide convincing evidence of an association between the attitudes and behavior of individuals and the characteristics of their networks. For example, the probability that a woman is using contraception is typically higher if her network partners are also using contraception, and the method she uses is likely to be the same as the methods used by those with whom she interacts. This probability has been found to depend also on the characteristics of the individual and her networks, as well as on the particular context; networks may also impede contraceptive use. Because of the dearth of network data, some analysts have used aggregate data to represent local or transnational networks, again finding associations that suggest the importance of networks.

While there is a clear empirical association between network characteristics and attitudes and behaviors, establishing a causal effect of networks on attitudes and behaviors has been difficult. Because actors may select those with whom they discuss topics such as family size and family planning or whether and when to migrate, determining the direction of causality requires longitudinal data or analytic techniques that take the selectivity of networks into account.

In summary, empirical work by demographers has established the potential significance of network approaches for examining processes of demographic change. By implication, analyses that treat individual actors in isolation are not sufficient. Fully realizing this potential may require further theoretical development; it will certainly require new efforts at data collection, including qualitative and survey data on the links among network partners, as well as further development of analytic techniques.

See also: *Diffusion in Population Theory; Fertility Transition, Socioeconomic Determinants of; Social Capital.*

BIBLIOGRAPHY

Bongaarts, John, and Susan C. Watkins. 1996. "Social Interactions and Contemporary Fertility

Transitions." *Population and Development Review* 22: 639–682.

Casterline, John B. 2001. "Diffusion Processes and Fertility Transition: Introduction." In *Diffusion Processes and Fertility Transition*, ed. John B. Casterline. Washington, D.C.: National Academy Press.

Entwisle, Barbara., Ronald R. Rindfuss, David K. Guilkey, Apichat Chamratrithirong, Sara R. Curran, and Yothin Sawangdee. 1997. "Community and Contraceptive Choice in Thailand: A Case Study of Nan Rong." *Demography* 33: 1–11.

Kohler, Hans-Peter. 2001. *Fertility and Social Interaction*. Oxford: Oxford University Press.

Kohler, Hans-Peter, Jere R. Behrman, and Susan C. Watkins. 2001. "The Density of Social Networks and Fertility Decisions: Evidence from South Nyanza District, Kenya." *Demography* 38: 43–58.

Montgomery, Mark R. and John B. Casterline. 1996. "Social Influence, Social Learning, and New Models of Fertility." In *Fertility in the United States: New Patterns, New Theories*, ed. John B. Casterline, R. D. Lee, and K. A. Foote. Supplement to *Population and Development Review*. New York: Population Council.

Valente, Thomas W. 1995. *Network Models in the Diffusion of Innovations*. Cresskill, NJ: Hampton Press.

Susan Cotts Watkins

SOCIAL REPRODUCTION

Social reproduction refers to the processes that ensure the self-perpetuation of a social structure over time, in rough analogy to biological reproduction for a population.

The idea of social reproduction has its origins in Karl Marx's analysis of capitalist society in Volume 1 of *Capital*. One of Marx's key sociological insights is that "every social process of production is at the same time a process of reproduction" (p. 71). Although his work is concerned specifically with economic processes, Marx discusses the subject in a broad social context, specifically the application of these processes to reproduction of social relations of capitalism. This idea was generalized by later Marxists to an argument that any mode of production also reproduces the conditions of its own existence. Further generalization extended use of the term beyond the ranks of Marxist writers. Although much of sociology might be said to be concerned with the ways in which social practices and institutions are self-perpetuating, the concept has tended to be used largely in relation to social inequalities. The fact that disadvantaged members of society engage in practices that contribute to the maintenance of a situation in which they are disadvantaged has often been seen as particularly problematic. For example, the revisionist socialists of the late nineteenth century, especially in Germany, argued that the high fertility of the proletariat—the producers of children—perpetuated their low-wage conditions; they advocated birth control (even a "birth strike") as a means of undermining capitalist exploitation.

The most extensive modern development of the concept of social reproduction has been by the sociologist Pierre Bourdieu (1930–2002). Bourdieu associates social reproduction with his concept of *habitus* which he defines in *The Logic of Practice* (1990) as something that "ensures the active presence of past experiences, which, deposited in each organism in the form of schemes of perception, thought and action, tend to guarantee the *correctness* of practices and their constancy over time" (p. 54). His work on different forms of style of life and of "taste" suggests how this process might operate. Bourdieu was also particularly concerned with the way in which the educational system functions, contrary to much conventional thought, to inhibit, rather than encourage, individual social mobility.

Despite the qualifying term "tend to," the use of "guarantee" in the above quotation does leave Bourdieu open to the charge, by Richard Jenkins, for example, of offering a structuralist account in which individual motivation and actions are ignored. The latter debate points to the general problem with theories of social reproduction: that they appear to be deterministic in character and do not allow for the possibility of social change. In that respect such theories are clearly deficient. However, the idea of social reproduction is valuable in suggesting areas of empirical investigation and theoretical development. In particular, it offers a useful corrective to the approach typically adopted in studies of social mobility. The very term social mobility carries with it the idea of intergenerational movement and so necessarily seems to require a theory of such movement. Lack of movement tends to remain untheorized. Conversely, the term social reproduction carries with it the idea of stability and calls for a theory that explains lack of movement; its difficulty, however, lies in the development of a theory of change. Empirical investigation requires an integration of both approaches.

See also: Marx, Karl; Social Mobility.

BIBLIOGRAPHY

Bourdieu, Pierre. 1984 [1979]. *Distinction: A Social Critique of the Judgement of Taste.* London: Routledge and Kegan Paul.

———. [1980] 1990. *The Logic of Practice.* Cambridge, Eng.: Polity Press.

Bourdieu, Pierre, and Jean-Claude Passeron. 1977 [1970]. *Reproduction in Education, Society and Culture.* London: Sage.

Jenkins, Richard. 1992. *Pierre Bourdieu.* London: Routledge.

Marx, Karl. 1976 [1886]. *Capital: A Critique of Political Economy,* Vol. 1. Harmondsworth, England: Penguin Books.

KENNETH PRANDY

SOCIOBIOLOGY

Sociobiology is the study of social behavior from a Darwinian evolutionary perspective. Edward O. Wilson named the field in 1975, when he published *Sociobiology, The New Synthesis.* Although the book stimulated controversy initially because some mistakenly believed that Wilson's ideas gave aid and comfort to political reactionaries, in the early twenty-first century sociobiology is a well-established field within evolutionary biology.

Sociobiologists (or behavioral ecologists or evolutionary psychologists, as they are also known) analyze the evolutionary foundations of social behavior

for all animal species. These researchers treat a social ability as if it were the historical product of natural selection. The process of selection occurs whenever individuals differ genetically in ways that affect their capacity to leave copies of their genes to the next generation, which is usually achieved by having surviving offspring. Selection theory enables the sociobiologist to identify puzzling social traits—namely, those that appear to reduce an individual's reproductive, and thus genetic, success.

Because of their interest in the genetic consequences of social behavior, sociobiologists have focused on those aspects of group formation, cooperation, reciprocity, parental care, and sexual interaction that carry disadvantages, as well as benefits, in terms of individual genetic success. For example, how can one explain the evolution of altruism, in which some individuals forego reproduction in order to help others survive and reproduce? Although altruism would seem to reduce genetic success, the trait is widespread—as, for example, in the self-sacrificing sterile worker and soldier castes of the social ants, bees, wasps, and termites. Moreover, in many social birds and mammals, helpers at the nest also give up a chance to reproduce in order to help rear the offspring of other adults.

In 1964 the biologist William D. Hamilton (1936–2000) offered a novel evolutionary explanation for altruism. He showed mathematically that altruists could increase their genetic success if their personal sacrifices resulted in an increase in the reproductive success of close relatives. Because relatives inherit some of the same genes from their recent common ancestors, discriminating altruism can enable the altruist to pass on his or her genes indirectly via helped kin. Hamilton's theory has been tested and supported by the discovery that altruists of most species generally only assist close relatives, thereby propagating the genes they share with these individuals, which helps maintain the potential for carefully targeted altruism within their species.

The Sociobiology of Human Behavior

Sociobiologists have used the logic of evolutionary theory to examine the social behavior of humans as well as that of ants and antelopes. This approach is based on the grounds that humans have certainly differed genetically in the past (just as they do currently). Some hereditary differences have had small but real effects on the development of the brain, thus influencing sensory and motor abilities with corresponding effects on one or another social behavior. If natural selection on hominids occurred in the past, people living in the twenty-first century can be assumed to carry the hereditary social predispositions exhibited by their reproductively successful predecessors.

The logic of the argument means that people, as well as other animals, are expected to act in ways that maximize their genetic success. Thus, if evolutionary theory is correct, altruism in humans should tend to be directed toward close relatives rather than toward genetic strangers, and there is considerable evidence that persons are predisposed to help their kin. Likewise, if past selection has shaped the human sexual psyche, then men in cultures around the world are predicted to find youthfulness, and therefore high fertility, attractive in potential partners whereas women are predicted to find strength, high social status, and thus, wealth to be sexually attractive attributes in men. In the past, men and women with these adaptively different mate preferences surely left more descendants than those people who chose mates at random. Cross-cultural data generally confirm these predictions. Men are endowed with evolved psychological systems that "encouraged" their male ancestors to seek out mates most likely to produce children. Women evidently possess quite different systems that "encouraged" their female ancestors to select protective, wealthy men able to offer above-average parental care to their children, a critical factor in determining the survival of offspring in the past.

The significance of sociobiological analyses for human population issues is obvious. The traits of humans (and all other organisms) that have been shaped by natural selection are expected to have promoted the genetic success of individuals in the past—and in the present as well, to the extent that modern environments resemble those of the past. Because present-day humans are the descendants of individuals who reproduced most successfully, human populations have the capacity to grow exponentially, just as do the populations of all other organisms. The evolutionarily-adaptive drive to reproduce leads the great majority of married couples to have at least one child rather than none at all, with infertile couples often divorcing or adopting or undergoing fertility treatments, despite the onerousness and expense of these options.

Not all aspects of human behavior, however, can be easily explained in evolutionary terms. Currently, the paramount problem in human social behavior for sociobiologists is the demographic transition, the decline in fertility that has occurred as countries have moved toward becoming modern industrial states. Among the several still incompletely-tested evolutionary hypotheses on the demographic transition is one that begins with the assumption that people have an evolved drive for high social status (because in the past this striving was correlated with better-than-average reproductive success). If so, wealthy persons in modern nations with an economically advantaged class may consider themselves in social competition with others of similar status. If this is true, then major investments are required for each offspring in order to provide him or her with the wherewithal for social success. These investments are possible only through a reduction in fertility. Thus, according to this hypothesis, humans' evolved psychological mechanisms might lead individuals in novel modern environments to act in ways that reduce, rather than increase, the absolute number of surviving offspring they produce. Additional research is required to evaluate this and other sociobiological hypotheses, but the discipline has already demonstrated the productivity of evolutionary theory as a tool for investigating human behavior.

See also: *Animal Ecology; Biodemography; Darwin, Charles; Evolutionary Demography; Primate Demography.*

BIBLIOGRAPHY

Alcock, John. 2001. *The Triumph of Sociobiology.* New York: Oxford University Press.

———. 2001. *Animal Behavior, An Evolutionary Approach.* Sunderland, MA: Sinauer Associates.

Dawkins, R. 1989. *The Selfish Gene,* 2nd edition. New York: Oxford University Press.

Gaulin, Steven J. H., and Donald H. McBurney. 2001. *Psychology, An Evolutionary Approach.* Upper Saddle River, NJ: Prentice Hall.

Trivers, Robert. 1985. *Social Evolution.* Menlo Park, CA: Benjamin Cummings.

Williams, George C. 1966. *Adaptation and Natural Selection.* Princeton, NJ: Princeton University Press.

Wilson, Edward O. 1975. *Sociobiology, The New Synthesis.* Cambridge, MA: Belknap Press.

JOHN ALCOCK

SOMBART, WERNER

(1863–1941)

Werner Friedrich Wilhelm Carl Sombart was a German economist and sociologist. He was born in the Harz mountains and studied law and economics from 1882 to 1888 in Pisa, Rome, and Berlin, together with Adolph Wagner and Gustav Schmoller. In his dissertation on *The Roman Campagna* (1888), he discussed the relationship between landowners and agrarian labor in Italy. He became an expert on Italian economics; his studies were rich in statistical and historical detail. At the age of 27 he was appointed professor at Breslau University in Silesia. His studies of Fredrick Engels and Karl Marx, together with a widely-read collection of his lectures, *Socialism and Social Movements during the Nineteenth Century* (1896), were seen as endorsements of Marxism and delayed further advancement in his academic career until 1916, when he became a full professor at Berlin University. His later work became more nationalist and, in a 1934 tract, *A New Social Philosophy,* even sympathetic to the then new Nazi regime. Sombart was a colleague of Max Weber and participated with him in the *Verein für Socialpolitik* as well as in founding the German Society for Sociology in 1909. Sombart's major work, the three-volume treatise, *Modern Capitalism* (1902–1927), traced capitalism's origins to Enlightenment ideas rather than, as Weber did, to Protestantism.

Sombart's historical and economic studies on population are contained in the third (1927) volume of *Modern Capitalism* and in a later book, *Humanistic Anthropology* (*Vom Menschen* [1938]). In the former work, the main population-related question he tackled, like Marx, was how early capitalist development recruited the masses of workers that were needed, and how this population surplus developed in agrarian societies. Marx had famously asserted that there cannot be a general theory of population but only a theory specific to each period of economic development and structure; Sombart's sociological theory of population applied to the conditions of early and high capitalism. *Humanistic Anthropology* proposed another theory of population. There his main argument was that all action, including all demographically relevant action, was founded in mental concepts and motives, and thus cannot be explained in biological terms. In 1938 such a stance was in explicit opposition to the racial, eugenic, and Volk-theories of the Nazi regime. The book was banned during the Third Reich and was almost forgotten afterwards, but it deserves a secure place in the history of population thought.

See also: *Population Thought, Contemporary.*

BIBLIOGRAPHY

SELECTED WORKS BY WERNER SOMBART.

Sombart, Werner. 1896. *Sozialismus und Soziale Bewegung.* Jena: Fischer. (Translated as: *Socialism and the Social Movement.* New York: Putnam, 1898.)

———. 1915. *The Quintessence of Capitalism.* London: Unwin.

———. 1927: *Der Moderne Kapitalismus.* Vol. 3: Das Wirtschaftsleben im Zeitalter des Hochkapitalismus. München u. Leipzig: Duncker u. Humblot.

———. 1933. *History of the Economic Institutions of Modern Europe: An Introduction to Der Moderne Kapitalismus of Werner Sombart,* ed. Frederick L. Nussbaum. New York: Crofts.

———. 1938. *Vom Menschen. Versuch einer geistwissenschaftlichen Anthropologie.* Berlin: Buchholz & Weisswange.

———. 2001. *Economic Life in the Modern Age.* New Brunswick, NJ: Transaction Publishers.

RAINER MACKENSEN

SPONTANEOUS ABORTION

Spontaneous abortion is defined as the involuntary loss of the fetus before the 20th week of pregnancy. Later involuntary loss of pregnancy is considered preterm birth. The definition is less clear on the starting point: at what stage after conception should the loss of the products of fertilization be counted as a spontaneous abortion. Many of these losses occur to women who never recognized that they were "pregnant," and there are no chemical or laboratory tests to establish the presence of a fertilized egg until about seven to ten days after fertilization takes place. The general term "abortion" refers to the interruption of a pregnancy after nidation has begun (the nesting of the developing zygote in the wall of the uterus, which generally occurs around the sixth day after fertilization). According to the definition accepted by the American College of Obstetrics and Gynecology and the World Health Organization, it is reasonable to use this starting point for calculating rates of spontaneous abortion. On this basis, the incidence of spontaneous abortion is approximately 20 percent of recognized pregnancies between the 4th and 20th weeks of gestation (counting from the last menstrual period). Approximately 80 percent of these losses occur in the first 12 weeks and the rate declines steadily thereafter, so that in week 20 the incidence of spontaneous abortion is less than 4 percent. Extrapolating back to immediately after fertilization, the rate of loss of all fertilized eggs may be as high as 50 percent, according to published accounts. Most of these very early losses occur between fertilization at mid-cycle and the onset of the next expected menses. In these cases the woman is unlikely to be aware of the prospective pregnancy.

Early spontaneous abortion is usually due to chromosomal abnormalities or fetal malformations. One study has reported that 60 percent of spontaneous abortions have polyploidy, trisomy, or aberrations of the sex chromosomes. Both maternal and paternal factors have been causally linked to spontaneous abortion. Caffeine or alcohol consumption by the mother increases the frequency of pregnancy loss on a dose-related basis. Maternal smoking results in lower birth weight of newborns, and several constituents of tobacco smoke have been associated with fetal death. While active smoking increases the rate of spontaneous abortion by a statistically significant amount, the epidemiological data available on the effect of passive smoking (exposure to environmental tobacco smoke) are too limited to reach a definitive conclusion. Similarly, paternal exposure to toxins may increase the risk of spontaneous abortion, but there is conflicting evidence on this subject.

An accurate determination of the primary sex ratio at fertilization in humans is impractical, for it would require recovery and assignment of sex to zygotes that fail to cleave, blastocysts that fail to implant, and early pregnancy losses. The secondary sex ratio, the ratio at delivery, is usually quoted as approximately 106 males to 100 females. Hence there are either more XY zygotes than XX zygotes at the time of fertilization or there is a greater loss of female than male embryos. The primary sex ratio may be even higher than 106:100 if there is a greater loss of males than females during gestation. The limited epidemiological evidence on the sex distribution of spontaneous abortions in humans supports this possibility: male conceptuses appear to be spontaneously aborted more frequently than females. Thus, the normally higher age-specific mortality rate of males for every age group may prevail even in pre-natal life.

See also: *Fertility, Proximate Determinants of; Sex Ratio; Tobacco-Related Mortality.*

BIBLIOGRAPHY

American College of Obstetricians and Gynecologists. "Methods of Mid-trimester Abortion." October 1987. *Technical Bulletin* No. 109.

Armstrong, B. G., A. D. McDonald, and M. Sloan. 1992. "Cigarette, Alcohol, and Coffee Consumption and Spontaneous Abortion." *American Journal of Public Health* 82: 85.

Cunningham, F. Gary, et al. 2001. *Williams Obstetrics.* 21st edition. New York: McGraw Hill.

Simpson, J. L. 1980. "Genes, Chromosomes, and Reproductive Failure." *Fertility and Sterility* 33: 107.

Snijders, R. J. M., N. J. Sebire, and K. H. Nocholaides. 1995. "Maternal Age and Gestational Age-specific Risk for Chromosomal Defects." *Fetal Diagnosis and Therapy* 10: 356.

SHELDON J. SEGAL

STATE AND LOCAL GOVERNMENT DEMOGRAPHY

State and local government demography involves the application of demographic concepts, data, and techniques to public-sector problems at the sub-national level.

The field is considered part of applied demography, in which demographic data and methods are used to solve real-world problems. (Another closely-related field is business demography: the application of demography to private-sector issues and decisions.) As Hallie J. Kintner and colleagues (1994) and Jacob S. Siegel (2002) explain, applied demographers' work products are used by government agencies, schools, businesses, legal practitioners, and policy makers. State and local government demography, along with the rest of applied demography, tends to be practical rather than theoretical.

This article describes contemporary state and local demographic practice in the United States, where demographic data (mainly from the national census and birth and death records) are fairly current and reasonably accurate. In a few other countries, universal population registers and frequent censuses simplify the work of demographers on sub-national geographic units because it is much easier to quantify migration. In many other countries, there are fewer sources of reliable and current data on such sub-national units.

The scope of the field continues to broaden, however, as additional data sources, analytical tools, and data processing technology are developed. The lag time associated with data collection has shortened markedly—suggesting the eventual possibility of almost "real time" population estimates. Increasingly, the results of state and local demographers' work are available to potential users through the Internet.

Fundamentals of State and Local Demography

The core activity in this field is small-area population estimation. State and local agencies often engage individuals with demographic training to do this work, some contract with academic consultants, and some purchase estimates for small geographic areas from commercial data vendors. Regardless of the source, these estimates are the foundation of state and local demographic work. In addition to population estimates, state and local demographers also provide population forecasts for states and smaller geographic areas.

Data used for state and local population estimates include national and sub-national censuses, administrative records, and other surveys. Periodic census results provide a check of the quality of the procedures used in deriving those estimates. Recent U.S. censuses have included extensive data on population characteristics and information (much of it on a sample basis) on housing and various socioeconomic measures. Census data releases reflect imposition of stringent restrictions protecting individuals's privacy, but allow detailed cross-tabulations and provide some data for areas as small as a single city block.

Administrative records consist of federal, state, and local governmental data gathered for purposes of registration, licensing, regulation, and program administration (e.g., Stanley K. Smith, et al. 2001). They include vital statistics (births, deaths, marriages, divorces); measures of income and poverty; some information on health, employment, and housing; school enrollment data; and records of other activities that are registered or known to the government.

Sample survey data are also sometimes used in state and local demography. In the United States, the Current Population Survey (for larger geographic entities) and the American Community Survey are important sources of such data. State and local government agencies (such as public health departments, housing agencies, and school systems) sometimes conduct special-purpose sample surveys.

Several methods are commonly used to make small-area population estimates. Stanley K. Smith and colleagues describe these methods in detail. The simplest involves multiplying the number of housing units in the area of interest by the average number of persons per household, and adding the estimated numbers in group quarters and the homeless population. The number of housing units can be derived from administrative records like building permits, utility customers, and property tax records. Persons per household can be estimated in a variety of ways, but is typically calculated from census data. This is called the housing unit method.

The component method of population estimation starts with the area's base population (often the latest census count) and adjusts it for the subsequent numbers of births, deaths, in-migrants, and out-migrants. Vital statistics provide birth and death data. Migration is estimated using a combination of administrative records, which may include data from income tax returns, public health insurance membership (in the United States, Medicare), school enrollments, driver's license applications and address changes, and international immigration records. The method can be used to provide separate estimates by age, sex, race or ethnicity, and other characteristics.

Demographers also use regression methods to adjust base populations for current small-area estimates. Regression models may incorporate data on vital events (births and deaths), school enrollment, utility customers, building permits, voter registration, driver's license applications and address changes, tax returns, and other data from administrative records as independent variables. A variety of such models have been developed and applied by the U.S. Census Bureau and similar organizations.

State and local demographers use small units of geographic analysis. These include individual real estate parcels or street addresses, neighborhoods, census divisions (city blocks, block groups, tracts, places, counties, groups of counties), postal codes, special administrative districts (school, water, hospital, sanitation, etc.), public health regions, traffic zones, and political entities like city council and state legislative districts. Population estimates tend to be more accurate for larger geographical areas and those that have relatively stable populations; greater uncertainty attaches to population estimates for smaller geographical units and those that have unstable demographic processes.

State and local demographers increasingly make use of geographic information systems (GIS) software in addition to statistical and database software. GIS can link all types of data to relevant geographical features and thus facilitate the spatial analysis and mapping that are essential to understanding regional variation in many variables of interest. GIS software uses an electronic base map of a region (such as the U.S. Census Bureau's TIGER) identifying roads, political boundaries, census geography, and other manmade and natural geographical features. Each type of feature may be depicted as a separate region, line, or point layer that can be turned on or off as needed. Databases can be linked to each layer. Individual data records with street addresses can be geocoded (assigned latitude and longitude coordinates, or electronically pin-mapped) and aggregated by the enclosing regions. Satellite and aerial photographic images can also be incorporated into a GIS database. The software allows data associated with any type of feature to be aggregated, disaggregated, transferred to other layers, and analyzed.

Many U.S. states have official state demographers, as well as web sites with extensive offerings of data and reports that can be viewed online and downloaded. For example, the California Department of Finance's Demographic Research Unit has posted population estimates (historical and current), projections, and research papers on its web site. Many states' web sites offer census data for the state and its political subdivisions.

Some cities and regional government councils or associations also have web sites containing census and other specialized demographic data (see, for example, the site of the San Diego Association of Governments). Data sometimes include estimates and forecasts of employment, economic conditions, household numbers, and housing, as well as other demographic information. Universities sometimes perform these services for states and smaller jurisdictions (for example, the Bureau of Economic and Business Research (BEBR) at the University of Florida web site).

Applications of State and Local Government Demographic Analysis

The work of state and local government demographers is used by urban, rural, and regional planners, as well as by public organizations and businesses. Fields of application include housing, public health, education, law enforcement, traffic control, environmental impact analysis, disaster planning, and electoral redistricting.

Housing. Demographers can track housing stock at the local and regional levels using permit data on building construction and demolition, utility hookups, and property tax records. Data on housing numbers and characteristics are used to target areas for redevelopment and for the location of public housing, subsidized housing, and housing for the elderly. Housing data by age and race or ethnicity are used to identify possible housing discrimination. Database software makes it simple to connect housing data from administrative records (such as property tax rolls) with population characteristics. GIS software permits mapping and visualization of geographical variation.

Public health. Public health agencies use state and local demographic data to develop community health indicators, analyze population health in terms of outcomes as well as social and environmental determinants, locate clinics and health services, and for disease surveillance. Epidemiologists need population estimates for calculation of fertility, morbidity, mortality, and other rates, which are often calculated by age, sex, race or ethnicity, and other demographic variables. Health maintenance organizations, hospitals, and health insurers also use demographic data. Su-Lin Wilkinson and colleagues (1999), and Jeanne G. Gobalet and Richard K. Thomas (1996) give examples of demographic techniques used in the public health field. The work of Louis G. Pol and Richard K. Thomas (2001) provides an extensive discussion of health and health care demography.

School enrollment. State and local government demographers help public schools forecast enrollments. They make projections of future student body size by grade using past data on grade progression rates and information on births five years earlier (to forecast kindergarten enrollments). Alternatively, or additionally, future enrollments can be gauged from housing data.

Demographic data are an important input to educational planning: in siting schools, deciding on school closure, realignment of internal attendance area boundaries, and design of desegregation strategies. GIS software is particularly useful in these activities.

Law enforcement. Law enforcement agencies use demographic data to compute crime rates and plan enforcement and prevention measures. Demographic data are used to select trial jury members when laws require that juries be representative cross-sections of the community. State and local demographic data are also used for drawing political boundaries that conform to legal requirements. For example, in the United States, most political subdivision boundaries must be evaluated after each national census and redrawn, if necessary, to achieve population equality across the subdivisions. Civil rights laws also require that political subdivision boundaries permit protected minority group members the opportunity to elect representatives of their choice. State and local government demographers sometimes provide technical support for political redistricting.

Accident patterns and disaster response. State and local government agencies use demographic data to understand traffic accident patterns, to assess environmental impacts, and in planning for major natural disasters. For example, Stanley K. Smith (1996) and the California Department of Finance (1995) have analyzed the effects of hurricanes, earthquakes, and other natural disasters. Programs are developed to assist particular at-risk populations, such as the elderly, poor children, substance abusers, and school dropouts on the basis of local-area demographic characteristics.

Sharing Demographic Data

The Population Association of America's Committee on Applied Demography facilitates interaction among state and local government demographers. The Census Bureau's Federal State Cooperative for Population Estimates and Federal State Cooperative for Population Projections, and the State Data Centers provide a forum for sharing census data with state and local agencies. A significant share of state and local demographers' work entails making national census and other types of demographic, social, and economic data accessible to the public. This sub-area of demographic practice is likely to grow rapidly for the foreseeable future.

See also: *Business Demography; Census; Geographic Information Systems; Population Registers; Small-Area Analysis.*

BIBLIOGRAPHY

Gobalet, Jeanne G., and R. K. Thomas. 1996. "Demographic Data and Geographic Information Systems for Decision Making: The Case of Public Health." *Population Research and Policy Review* 15: 537–548.

Kintner, Hallie J., Thomas W. Merrick, Peter A. Morrison, and Paul R. Voss, eds. 1994. *Demographics: A Casebook for Business and Government.* Boulder, CO: Westview Press.

Myers, Dowell. 1992. *Analysis with Local Census Data: Portraits of Change.* New York: Academic Press.

Pol, Louis G., and Richard K. Thomas. 2001. *The Demography of Health and Health Care,* 2nd edition. New York: Kluwer Academic/Plenum Publishers.

Siegel, Jacob S. 2001. *Applied Demography: Applications to Business, Government, Law and Public Policy.* San Diego: Academic Press.

Smith, S. K. 1996. "Demography of Disaster: Population Estimates after Hurricane Andrew." *Population Research and Policy Review* 15: 459–477.

Smith, Stanley K., Jeff Tayman, and David A. Swanson. 2001. *State and Local Population Projections: Methodology and Analysis.* New York: Kluwer Academic/Plenum Publishers.

Wilkinson, S. L., Jeanne G. Gobalet, M. Majoros, B. Zebrowski, and G. S. Olivas. 1999. "Lead Hot Zones and Childhood Lead Poisoning Cases, Santa Clara County, California, 1995." *Journal of Public Health Management and Practice* 5(2): 11–12.

INTERNET RESOURCES.

Bureau of Economic and Business Research (BEBR) at the University of Florida Website. <http://www.bebr.ufl.edu>.

California Department of Finance's Demographic Research Unit. <http://www.dof.ca.gov>.

Hoag, Elizabeth, and California Department of Finance. 1995. "The Effect of the Loma Prieta Earthquake on California Migration." <http://www.dof.ca.gov/HTML/DEMOGRAP/Disaster.pdf>.

San Diego Association of Governments. <http://www.sandag.org>.

JEANNE GOBALET

STATES SYSTEM, DEMOGRAPHIC HISTORY OF

It is commonplace in the early twenty-first century, as it has been for the past two centuries, to speak of nation states as the primary unit of territory, identity, and citizenship for the world's population. Indeed, it is difficult to conceive of a world without nation states. The nation state system however has a specific history of geographic, social, political, and economic organization and is a comparatively recent phenomenon. There is also an emerging body of work on globalization that questions the longevity of the nation state system and proposes scenarios for a post-national world. Intriguing as the "end of the nation state" thesis may be, the nation state system appears to be firmly intact without any outward signs of collapse or major reconfiguration—although still characterized by the rise and fall of nations. How natural is this system? What historical shifts have taken place to shape the present geography of nation states? What, if any, are the indications that this "natural order of things" is undergoing a transformation?

The nation state system developed in Europe between the sixteenth and nineteenth centuries after the collapse of the Holy Roman Empire and the emergence of the centralized state upholding the right of exclusive authority within the defined territorial state. The concept of *we the people, we the nation* became the new geography of association and citizenship. Hence, the people constituting the nation became the ultimate source of the state's legitimacy and the idea of the nation itself became the natural repository of political loyalty. This emergence, however, is the product of complex circumstances and historical contexts that warrant careful scrutiny.

Many commentators refer to the Treaty of Westphalia (1648) as representing the beginning of the modern system of states. The Treaty, really a series of treaties that collectively ended the hostilities of the Thirty Years War, marked the culmination of the anti-hegemonic struggle against the Hapsburg ambitions for a supranational empire while also signifying the collapse of Spanish power outside the Iberian Peninsula, the fragmentation of Germany, and the rise of France as a major power in Europe. The principles that were established at Westphalia are of critical importance. It was now to be an accepted organizational pattern that the independence of a state invariably meant that it had jural rights, which all other states were bound to respect. This was the beginning of the modern framework of interstate relations. The Treaty established a secular concept of international relations, permanently replacing the medieval idea of a universal religious authority acting as the final arbiter of Christendom. Thus, any notion of an authority above the sovereign state was now rendered redundant.

An Old World Geography

The treaty of Westphalia may have set the stage for a new global geography of independent nation states and its associated claims over sovereignty and citizenship. However, this took place on an already networked globe. Some of the newly salient borders seemed natural, others completely arbitrary. Well before the European imperial expansion there were wide-ranging linkages among populations that were the result of identifiable material processes. One such linkage derived from the development of contending hegemonic political and military systems, which sought to extract surpluses from distant populations through conquest and empire building. Another linkage was the growth of long-distance trade, which connected zones of specialization along the routes of commerce. These developments in turn produced extensive grids of communication, which bound together different populations under the aegis of dominant religious or political ideologies.

The extension of this system beyond the European heartland has been a contradictory and profoundly disturbing process. In the nineteenth century the system of states each claiming sovereign rule was far from complete. Through various colonial and imperial arrangements, the "comity of nations" spread into lands distant from its origin; but it was not yet coterminous with the globe. The system was economically, culturally, and ideologically less heterogeneous than it was to become in the twentieth century.

The expansion of European powers and the secular transformations of culture, science, political and administrative organization, and technology provided the framework for the modern system. The demographic shifts associated with the crisis of feudalism, involving changing relationships between town and country, and between city and city, were also significant factors.

For some scholars the obvious context within which to analyze and understand the origins of nation states is the historical emergence of the capitalist world economy. Most of Europe in the late Middle Ages was feudal—consisting of relatively small, self-sufficient economic units based on the direct appropriation of the small agricultural surplus produced within a manorial economy by a small class of nobility. Areas of economic activity and trade were well defined. Expansion and contraction occurred at three levels—geography, commerce, and demography—each of which played a part in the establishment of new forms of surplus extraction based on more efficient and expanding production and the development of core states within this world system.

State formation is also inextricably linked to various attributes of civilizations quite apart from commercial activity. The historian Fernand Braudel points out that an expanding Europe should also be juxtaposed with biological and demographic circumstances of equal historical significance. Famines, overpopulation, falls in real earnings, popular uprisings, and grim periods of slump were characteristic of early European civilization. Epidemics and biological disasters such as the Black Death and the epidemics that followed, which occurred in the second half of the fourteenth century, produced major contractions in populations.

The concept of nation states became a natural part of Western political thinking as commerce, industry, and trade intensified around the globe. The expansion in the mid-eighteenth-century, from about 1733 onward, was also a period of setbacks such as those experienced on the eve of the French Revolution, but overall economic growth continued throughout this transformative period. Material gain and growing and more concentrated populations provided the context for the intellectual development of the Enlightenment.

European Romanticism coincided with a long economic downturn between 1817 and 1852. But apart from the effects of economic change, the development of nation states and their demographic history are inextricably linked to the cultural, political, and intellectual canvas involving real and perceived notions of collective identity and unity. The medieval image was one of reasonably stable feudal states ruled by monarchs who held authority over populations divided into classes or estates, from nobility to peasant. As Europe expanded this image gradually disappeared. As the civilizing forces of modern state formation progressed, a new consciousness about borders and new conceptions of national differences emerged. But this was not a simple transition from medieval geography into neatly divided territories replete with nationalist fervor. In what resembles the ebb and flow of sentiment in the world at the start of the twenty-first century, early forms of national identity involved a struggle between nationalism and universalism.

The Italian patriot and revolutionist Giuseppe Mazzini proclaimed the nineteenth century as the age of the arrival of the nations. The nation was a confraternity, a sharing of the same destiny. Its appearance signified the arrival of the masses, the decline of privilege, the emergence of political and religious freedom, and equality before the law, while providing a meaningful counter to excessive self-indulgence and rabid individualism. For Mazzini, the nation was the essence of morality although not a law unto itself. Germany stood in contrast to this model: For a long time it celebrated disunity with the claim that the destiny of the Germans was that of the Greeks of the modern world—a nation composed of many states, but a single flourishing civilization. Indeed in the late eighteenth and early nineteenth centuries, Germans took pride in being free of any feelings of nationalism. Later, of course, forms of German nationalism were to take on a pathological dimension concerned with domination and racial purity, though this development can be linked to the concept of universal empire building that transcended territorial Germany.

The history of states is thus inescapably bound to the political and cultural aspirations of people—often encapsulated in heroic myths about the past. Demography was an essential ingredient of such mythmaking. Natural shifts in population size and density became the basis of contested claims over territory and tradition. Some nationalist movements seek to regain "authenticity"—reacquiring what was taken from them through colonization or conquest by neighboring states. Viewed from this perspective the geographical borders of nation states are quite arbitrary; they can be altered or indeed created where none existed previously, as was the case for much of the African continent, in Europe, through the Treaties that followed the two World Wars, and, more recently, in the break-up of the USSR and Yugoslavia into component nations.

States, Nations, and Globalization

Some commentators claim that the forces of globalization are reshaping the world of nation states, possibly creating a postnationalist order. The combined influence of transnational trade, economic relations, and the virtual fields of telecommunications and finance are said to be creating a world without borders. A new system of global politics, one that is not nation-state-centered, is supposedly emerging. Other observers take the opposite view, suggesting

a new era of balkanization and instability, wherein nations will become even more important.

Demographic change is an important consideration in any debate over the salience and permanence of state borders. Population shifts, brought about particularly by migration and refugee flows, are altering the demographic composition of nations. Optimistic visions of transnational democracy and, more generally, of the end of the nation state, need to be balanced against the rise of aggressive nationalism based on xenophobic sentiment concerning the protection of borders. Globalization does not necessarily produce a stable world polity and reduction in nation state conflict. The new worlds of communications and economics may be globalized but all indications suggest that the politics of this transformation is thoroughly grounded in an old-world territorial geography. Concepts and terms like sovereignty and citizenship that have previously been taken for granted by scholars of international politics are being placed under scrutiny by shifts in migration patterns.

The demographic history of nation states is associated with a dynamic geography. The global system of states at the beginning of the nineteenth century does not resemble the mosaic of nation states at the beginning of the twenty-first century. New states have emerged; old states have disappeared. The nation state system has evolved through the ravages of war, the demise of colonialism, and the creation of new states as communities gained or regained collective identities and sought to establish territorial homes. Regional groupings of nations explore arrangements that relinquish some elements of sovereignty to a supranational entity—most notably, as in the European Union. And international organizations with global reach, if little sway, proliferate under the United Nations system. Contemporary problems of border surveillance and migration control, the growing movement of refugees, and the increasing demands by populations for national autonomy suggest that the system of states will remain a dominant feature of the global political system for some considerable time. That notwithstanding, emerging global issues such as how to deal with ominous environmental trends, and the transnational impact of anti-globalization social movements, indicate that the charmed life of state sovereignty may be entering unsettling times.

See also: *Geopolitics.*

BIBLIOGRAPHY

Braudel, Fernand. 1993. *A History of Civilizations.* New York: Penguin.

Held, David, Anthony McGrew, David Goldblatt, and Jonathan Perraton. 2000. *Global Transformations.* Oxford: Polity.

Huizinga, Johan. 1966. *The Autumn of the Middle Ages.* trans. Rodney Payton and Ulrich Mammitzsch. Chicago: University of Chicago Press.

Poggi, Gianfranco. 1978. *The Development of the Modern State.* Stanford CA: Stanford University Press.

Talmon, Jacob L. 1979. *Romanticism and Revolt: Europe 1815–1848.* New York: W. W. Norton and Company.

Wallerstein, Immanuel. 1974. *The Modern World System.* New York: Academic Press.

PETER MARDEN

STATISTICAL METHODS

See *Data Assessment; Estimation Methods, Demographic; Event-History Analysis; Life Tables; Simulation Models*

STERILIZATION

See *Birth Control, History of; Contraception, Modern Methods of; Family Planning Programs*

STOCHASTIC POPULATION THEORY

Stochastic theory deals with random influences on populations and on the vital events experienced by their members. It builds on the deterministic mathematical theory of renewal processes and stable populations. Concentrating on structural and predictive models, it is distinct from statistical demography, which also deals with randomness but in the context of data analysis and inference under uncertainty. This entry treats macrodemographic processes of population growth and structure first, and microdemographic processes of individual experience second. Basic background for all these subjects is found in the classic textbooks by the demographer Nathan Keyfitz published in 1968 and 1985.

Random Rates and Random Draws

The population theorist Joel Cohen, in a 1987 encyclopedia article, has drawn a useful distinction between two sources of randomness, which he called *environmental* and *demographic* and that are also denoted with the terms *random rates* and *random draws*. Random rate models assume that the schedules of fertility, mortality, and migration that govern population change are not fixed but themselves fluctuate in response to partly haphazard exogenous influences from climate, economic and political factors, resources, or disease. Models with random draws take the population-level schedules as fixed and concentrate on the chance outcomes for individuals, like drawing cards from a shuffled deck. The lifetable is a model for random draws. Its l_x column tells the probability that a randomly selected member of the population will "draw" an age at death older than x from the lottery of fate.

Random rate models for population growth and age structure have been proved to share some of the best properties of deterministic models. In particular, population age pyramids tend to forget their past, in the sense that the distribution of the population by age tends over time to become independent of the initial age distribution. This property is called *ergodicity*. Following the work of Z. M. Sykes, which was expanded upon by Young Kim, powerful theorems were proved by Hervé LeBras in 1971 and 1974 and by Cohen in 1976 and 1977. For example, under certain reasonable conditions, means, variances, and other moments of the proportions in age groups become independent of the initial age distribution and the number of births per year comes to fit a lognormal distribution. Much of the general theory of population dynamics in variable environments can be brought to bear; Shripad Tuljapurkar's 1990 book *Population Dynamics in Variable Environments* is a good source.

Time series models from economic demography, like ARIMA (Autoregressive Integrated Moving Average) models, are examples of random rate models. The economic demographer Ronald Lee and his colleagues, from the 1970s onward, studied short-term fluctuations in births and deaths in European preindustrial populations. They discovered systematic patterns of lagged responses to prices and previous vital rates, shedding light on historical population regulation.

In the 1990s random rate models were applied to the practical problem of putting measures of uncertainty analogous to confidence intervals around population projections. In 1992 Lee and Larry Carter introduced a stochastic model for forecasting mortality from historical trends and fluctuations in the logarithms of age-specific death rates. For many developing countries, the index of the level of overall mortality turns out to be well-modeled by a random walk with a constant country-specific drift. However, variability from age to age around the overall level remains poorly understood. Harking back to work of Keyfitz and Michael Stoto, Nico Keilman, Wolfgang Lutz and other demographers and statisticians have modeled historical patterns of errors in earlier forecasts and used them to generate uncertainty bounds for new forecasts, an approach surveyed in the National Research Council's 2000 volume "Beyond Six Billion," edited by John Bongaarts and Randy Bulatao.

Models for random draws, given fixed vital schedules, underlie much of demography. Branching processes were invented by I. J. Bienyamé in 1845 and rediscovered by Francis Galton and H. W. Watson around 1873. The number of progeny (males or females but not both) in each family in a population is assumed to be drawn independently from a given family-size distribution, and lines of descent form a random tree through succeeding generations. If the mean number of progeny is less than or equal to one, the probability of extinction is one. The randomness rules out eternally stationary populations.

The general model for random population dynamics in use by demographers, with age-dependent branching structure, was given its full mathematical specification by the statistician David Kendall in 1949. With random draws, the assumed statistical independence from unit to unit makes the standard deviations in demographic observables (like the sizes of age groups or counts of births and deaths) tend to vary like the square root of population size, but with a constant of proportionality that can be predicted from the models. With random rates (random from time to time but uniform across members of a population), the standard deviations tend to

vary like the population size itself, and the constant of proportionality is a free parameter. Kenneth Wachter has studied the relative strengths of the two kinds of randomness in historical populations. Mixed models with partial independence from place to place and group to group are now on the horizon, drawing on measurements of geographical heterogeneity and covariation featured, for instance, by LeBras.

The rise of genomics has created new interest in stochastic models like branching processes which generate genealogical trees for individuals or genes in populations. With branching processes, total population size varies endogenously from generation to generation. Geneticists tend to prefer the models of Sewell Wright and R. A. Fisher in which total population size is constrained to be constant or to vary in an exogenously specified fashion. Samuel Karlin and Howard Taylor give full accounts in their 1981 textbook. In 1982 John Kingman developed a general theory of coalescence. Coalescent processes work backwards in time, starting, for instance, with living women and tracing their mothers, their mothers' mothers, and their maternal ancestors in each prior generation until all the lines coalesce in a single most recent common ancestress. A central result of this subject is a formula equating the mean number of generations back to coalescence with twice the (constant) "effective" population size. Data on differences in DNA sequences in present-day populations can be combined with these stochastic models to yield estimates, still controversial, of population sizes over hundreds of thousands of years or more. This work promises new opportunities for understanding the balance between random fluctuations and the dynamics of long-term population control.

Microdemographic Processes

At the microdemographic level, elements of chance impinge on most life-course transitions for individuals, on social determinants and motivations, and on the basic biology of conception, childbirth, survival, and death. The attention of demographers has focused particularly on the sources and consequences of heterogeneity from person to person in probabilities of vital events.

Drawing on statistical renewal theory, the demographers Mindel Sheps and Jane Menken, in their classic 1973 study *Mathematical Models of Conception and Birth,* modeled a woman's interval between births as a sum of independent random waiting times with their own parametric probability distributions. An important feature is heterogeneity from woman to woman in fecundability—that is, in probability of conception given full exposure to the risk of conception. James Wood and Maxine Weinstein applied refined models to the analysis of reproductive life history data. Inferring the strength of components of heterogeneity from observational data is difficult, and birth intervals provide one of the prime examples for non-parametric methods for estimating unobserved heterogeneity developed by James Heckman and Burton Singer in 1984.

In microdemography, stochastic models are required when variances are important along with mean values. For instance, the proportion of older people without living children may be more important than the mean number of living children per older person across the population. For such purposes, estimates of mean numbers of kin from stable population theory developed in 1974 by sociologists Leo Goodman, Keyfitz, and Thomas Pullum, need to be extended, generally through the use of demographic microsimulation. In microsimulation, a list of imaginary individuals is kept in the computer, and, time interval after time interval, the individuals are assigned events of marriage, childbirth, migration, death, and other transitions by comparing computer-generated pseudo-random numbers with user-specified schedules of demographic rates. An example is the SOCSIM program (short for "Social Structure Simulation") of Eugene Hammel and Kenneth Wachter. SOCSIM was first applied to estimate demographic constraints on preindustrial English households in collaboration with Peter Laslett, and later applied, as in Wachter's 1997 study, to forecasts of the kin of future seniors in the United States, England, and elsewhere.

Longevity and Frailty

Given that the life table is, in a sense, the oldest stochastic model in demography, it is not surprising that stochastic models for mortality by age, and specifically for heterogeneity in mortality, are prominent. From the 1980s onward, the Duke demographer Kenneth Manton and his colleagues developed multivariate stochastic models for health and survival transitions. These models are macrodemographic models inasmuch as they are driven by transition rates for population aggregates, but they are designed to make efficient use of individual-level data from longitudinal studies. They have become a prime tool for disentangling the roles of interacting covariates, including behaviors like smoking or physical conditions like blood pressure, in risks of death. Singer has pressed stochastic modeling into service for studies of effects of whole sequences of life-course experiences on health.

James Vaupel, Anatoli Yashin, Manton, Eric Stallard, and their colleagues developed, between 1979 and 1985, a model for hazard curves based on a concept of heterogeneous frailty. The hazard curve is a mathematically convenient representation of age-specific rates of mortality in terms of the downward slope of the logarithm of the proportion of a cohort surviving to a given age. In the frailty model, the shape of the hazard curve as a function of age is the same for everyone, but the level varies from person to person by a factor, fixed throughout each person's life, called the person's frailty. Frailties are often assumed to follow a Gamma probability distribution, while the common shape of the hazard curves at older ages is often taken to be an exponential function in line with the model of Benjamin Gompertz introduced in 1825. As a cohort ages, people with higher frailties die more quickly, leaving a set of survivors selected for lower frailties. The 2000 article "Mortality Modeling: A Review" by Yashin, Ivan Iachine and A. Begun is a good introduction.

The frailty model of Vaupel and his colleagues figures prominently in the biodemography of longevity, where human hazard curves are compared with hazard curves in other species including fruit flies, nematode worms, and yeast. Such heterogeneity may be a significant contributor to observed tapering in hazard curves at extreme ages found across species. Alternative stochastic models include models based on statistical reliability theory for complex engineered systems proposed by Leonid Gavrilov and Natalia Gavrilova, and Markov models for the evolution of hazard curves through step-by-step transitions suggested by genetic theory.

The study of fertility transitions, in the aspect in which it emphasizes social interaction and the diffusion of attitudes, information and innovations, relies extensively on a broader class of stochastic models. In 2001 Hans-Peter Kohler drew on random path-dependent models advanced in the 1980s by Brian Arthur and other economists, to explain patterns of contraceptive choice. The amplifying effects of peer-group influences is a significant theme in accounts of very low fertility in developed societies.

Stochastic theory provides a unifying framework which ties together the many substantive areas of demography as a whole and links them with active research fronts in the other biological and social sciences.

See also: *Archaeogenetics; Artificial Social Life; Biodemography; Event-History Analysis; Life Tables; Projections and Forecasts, Population; Renewal Theory and the Stable Population Model; Simulation Models.*

BIBLIOGRAPHY

Bongaarts, John, and R. Bulatao, eds. 2000. *Beyond Six Billion.* Washington, D.C.: National Academy Press.

Cohen, Joel. 1981. "Stochastic Demography." In *Encyclopedia of Statistical Science,* ed. Samuel Kotz and Norman Johnson. New York: John Wiley.

Karlin, Samuel, and Howard Taylor. 1981. *A Second Course in Stochastic Processes.* New York: Academic Press.

Keyfitz, Nathan. 1968. *Introduction to the Mathematics of Population.* Reading, MA: Addison-Wesley.

———. 1985. *Applied Mathematical Demography.* Berlin: Springer.

Kohler, Hans-Peter. 2001. *Fertility and Social Interaction.* Oxford: Oxford University Press.

Sheps, Mindel C., and Jane Menken. 1973. *Mathematical Models of Conception and Birth.* Chicago: University of Chicago Press.

Tuljapurkar, Shripad. 1990. *Population Dynamics in Variable Environments.* Berlin: Springer.

Wachter, Kenneth. 1997. "Kinship Resources for the Elderly." *Philosophical Transactions of the Royal Society of London* B352: 1,811–1,817.

Yashin, Anatoli, Ivan Iachine, and A. Begun. 2000. "Mortality Modeling: A Review." *Mathematical Population Studies* 8: 305–332.

KENNETH W. WACHTER

TABLE 1

Distribution of the Population of the United States by Central City, Suburb, and Nonmetropolitan Status, 1960–1990 (percent)

Status	1960	1970	1980	1990
Central city	32.3	31.4	30.0	31.3
Suburb	30.9	37.6	44.8	46.2
Nonmetropolitan	36.7	31.0	25.2	22.5
Total	100.0	100.0	100.0	100.0

SOURCE: U.S. Population Censuses.

SUBURBANIZATION

Suburbanization became a significant dynamic in urban development during the latter part of the nineteenth century, as professional people and better-paid artisans followed the example of successful entrepreneurs in taking up residence in new homes on the outskirts of the growing factory towns and commercial centers. This process was aided by the emergence of inexpensive forms of mass transit that loosened the ties between home and workplace for those with secure jobs and relatively "social" hours of work. With the growth of private car usage beginning in the 1920s, the process surged ahead; by the second half of the twentieth century, suburban living had become the modal pattern in many countries including the United States (see Table 1).

Over time, however, the nature of suburbanization has changed considerably. The most significant change has been in terms of the geographical scale of the process. Once experienced chiefly in the form of the lateral extension of the urban core, suburbanization has come to involve residential decentralization over a much broader commuting field. As in the case of Great Britain (see Table 2), the main commuting "ring" was already the zone of most rapid population growth by the 1950s, but the growth of outer areas accelerated in the 1960s and overtook that of the rings in the 1970s. Also very notable in the British case is the population turnaround of the rural areas since the 1950s, with a growth rate exceeding that of the suburban rings in the 1980s.

This more extensive outward movement of population has been interpreted by many commentators as a distinctive phenomenon going beyond suburbanization. To the extent that it has involved the

TABLE 2

Change in Population Size per Decade in Great Britain by Functional Region Zone Type, 1951–1991 (percent)				
Zone Type	1951–1961	1961–1971	1971–1981	1981–1991
Core	4.0	0.7	−4.2	−0.1
Ring	10.5	17.8	9.1	5.9
Outer area	1.7	11.3	10.1	8.9
Rural area	−0.6	5.4	8.8	7.8
All zones	5.0	5.3	0.6	2.5

SOURCE: Great Britain Population Censuses.

growth of relatively self-contained, medium-sized and smaller settlements lying beyond the main commuting reach of the major metropolitan centers, it has been seen as a process of "urban deconcentration" rather than of "urban decentralization." Given that this is not simply overspill from a too-full urban core but is commonly associated with absolute population loss from the latter, urban deconcentration has been interpreted as evidence of the loss of appeal of urban life and of the quest for a rural idyll, hence dubbed "counterurbanization" by Brian Berry (1976). Though most of those involved in this centrifugal movement are destined for small towns rather than the deep countryside, and very few are seeking out an alternative lifestyle without modern urban facilities, the majority see themselves as escaping the hectic pace of metropolitan life, with most sooner or later switching to nearby jobs rather than commuting back to the city.

This notion of an escape from metropolitan life in general is supported by a second major change that has affected the suburbs in recent decades: the urbanization of the suburbs or, in the words of David Birch, a transformation "from suburb to urban place" (1975, p. 25). Traditionally, the term suburb carries connotations of being something less than *urbs,* the city. Suburban areas were once largely residential in character, acting as dormitories and being dependent on the city center for work, recreation, and all but the most basic of shopping needs. Notably since the 1950s, however, outward residential movement has been followed by the decentralization of industrial, commercial, and high-level retail activities, and more recently by the growth of office and high-tech sectors, the latter being seen as the "third wave" of suburbanization in the United States. While commentators seem reluctant to aban-

don the epithet "suburban"—using terms like "the new suburbanization" with its "suburban downtowns"—it would seem that the once-clear distinction between city and suburb is fading fast. Joel Garreau's (1991) "edge city" concept better captures the nature of recent changes, as these threaten to turn the traditional metropolitan area inside out—or at least replace the monocentric city with an essentially polynuclear form of urban region.

Not surprisingly, the demographic character of the suburbs is also changing. As portrayed most effectively by the Chicago School of urban sociology in the 1920s, the suburbs in the United States were the domain of the white family where the wife was engaged full-time in raising children while the bread-winner husband commuted to work in the city. Partly through the process of *in situ* aging, over time these areas have seen a steady increase in the proportion of older couples whose children have left home and—despite some exodus of retirees—of the elderly. Along with the decentralization of nondormitory urban functions, these areas have also witnessed a suburban apartment boom, drawing in younger single adults and childless couples.

The ethnic complexion of the suburbs has also been changing. While in aggregate there remains a considerable contrast between city and suburb in the proportion of non-whites, the suburb is now far from being a preserve of white families. According to the 2000 U.S. census, as many as 41 percent of the United States' non-whites lived in suburbs, not far short of the 47 percent accounted for by central cities. In 1990, minorities in the United States already accounted for one in six suburban residents, following a decade when their number grew by 53 percent compared to an increase in the minority population of the city by only 25 percent. In the United Kingdom, too, the suburbanization of ethnic minorities was already well advanced by 1991, with non-whites comprising 17 percent of the residents of Outer London, compared to 26 percent for Inner London. According to William Frey (2002), this process is linked to a "new white flight" that in America is helping to push people further away from suburbia towards the metropolitan periphery and into communities that have a rural ambiance.

See also: *Cities, Systems of; Internal Migration; Residential Segregation; Rural-Urban Balance; Urbanization.*

BIBLIOGRAPHY

Berry, Brian. 1976. *Urbanization and Counterurbanization.* Beverly Hills, CA: Sage.

Birch, David. 1975. "From Suburb to Urban Place." *Annals of the American Academy of Political and Social Science* 422: 25–35.

Cervero, Robert. 1989. *America's Suburban Centers: The Land Use–Transportation Link.* Boston: Unwin Hyman.

Champion, Tony. 2001. "A Changing Demographic Regime: Consequences for the Composition and Distribution of Population in Polycentric Urban Regions." *Urban Studies* 38(3/4): 657–677.

Frey, William. 2002. "The New White Flight." *American Demographics* June: 20–23.

Garreau, Joel. 1991. *Edge City: Life on the New Frontier.* New York: Doubleday.

Robert, Stephen, and William Randolph. 1983. "Beyond Decentralization: The Evolution of Population Distribution in England and Wales, 1961–81." *Geoforum* 14: 175–192.

Tony Champion

SÜSSMILCH, JOHANN

(1707–1767)

Known as the father of German demography, Johann Peter Süssmilch was the eldest child of a Berlin brewer and corn merchant. When he was 17, he began medical studies, but, under parental pressure, changed to law at Halle. Believing that he had a religious vocation, he registered at the Faculty of Divinity. There he was advised to read Canon William Derham's *Physico-Theology* (1713, 1726), which aroused his interest in population matters, albeit viewed from a theological perspective. In 1728, he moved to Jena to study philosophy, oriental languages, mathematics, and physics, and to complete his thesis. He was ordained in 1736. The following year he married, eventually having 10 children, among whom 9 survived. After a short stay in a Brandenburg parish, Süssmilch was called to the Court of Prussia by Frederick the Great. He served as a chaplain during the Silesian war in 1740 and in 1742 was named *pastor primarius* in the Petrikirche of Berlin. The first edition of his massive treatise *Die Göttliche Ordnung* (full title translation, The Divine Order in the Transformations of the Human Race as Demonstrated through Birth, Death, and the Multiplication of the Same) in 1741 gained him entry to the Royal Academy of Sciences. Süssmilch, who was financially independent, spent the following years supplementing his statistical documentation and presenting several historical, linguistic, and demographic papers to the Academy. He was also in an economic position to publish two additional, greatly enlarged, editions of his *magnum opus* (1761–1762, 1765). He died as a result of a stroke in 1767.

This "God-intoxicated man," influenced by German philosopher and mathematician Gottfried Wilhelm Leibniz (1646–1716) and English mathematician and physicist Isaac Newton (1642–1727), who wanted to reconcile Calculation and Revelation, asserted that beyond the chaotic appearance of vital events, humankind obeys a constant, general, beautiful, and harmonious order. This divine order is rendered visible only for large numbers of individuals observed over wide regions and long periods, with the help of the theory of probabilities. Süssmilch did not wish to give a precise numerical account of this order, but, rather, to show that the arithmetic of Life and Death was ruled by the hidden or invisible hand of the Supreme Political Arithmetician. By articulating Political Arithmetic (like English political economist William Petty [1623–1687]) and Physico-Theology, demography, as a faithful *ancilla theologiae*, gave birth to a kind of demographic theology.

From a scientific point of view, Süssmilch was not an innovator, but rather a compiler. He did not make any major technical discovery, nor did he make the most of the methodological possibilities of his time. But his aim was different. He was prepared to set aside "all those algebraic calculations," for, in Süssmilch's opinion, Faith did not need any data. Drawing on his encyclopedic knowledge, he wrote the first general treatise of quantitative and qualitative demography in any language, contributing to the triumph of Anglo-Dutch political arithmetic over the German *Staatenkunde*, or descriptive statistics. At the end of the eighteenth century, Süssmilch's theory of divine order gave way to that of the natural order, and positivist thought displaced theological argument. After a period of relative oblivion, Süssmilch's work experienced an unexpected revival in the second half of the twentieth century. The religious and philosophical origins of demography were again of interest to the scientific community; Süssmilch's contribution was reappraised, and sometimes exaggerated. If it cannot be compared with the mathematical contributions to demographic thinking of figures such as Condorcet Pierre-Simon Laplace, or Antoine Cournot, Süssmilch certainly is the indispensable intermediary linking the political arithmetic of John Graunt to the population theorizing of T. R. Malthus (1766–1834) and Adolphe Quetelet (1796–1874). As such, Süssmilch's work represents a major step forward in the history of demography.

See also: *Demography, History of; Population Thought, History of.*

BIBLIOGRAPHY

SELECTED WORKS BY JOHANN SÜSSMILCH.

Süssmilch, Johann Peter. 1983. English Translation of Sections of the 4th Edition of *Die göttliche Ordnung Population and Development Review* 9: 521–529.

————. 1998 [1741]. *Ordre divin dans les changements de l'espèce humaine, démontré par la naissance, la mort et la propagation de celle-ci,* trans. and ann. Jean-Marc Rohrbasser. (Die göttliche Ordnung in den Veränderungen des menschlichen Geschlechts, aus der Geburt, dem Tode und der Fortpflanzung desselben erwiesen) Paris: Institut National d'Études Démographiques.

SELECTED WORKS ABOUT JOHANN SÜSSMILCH.

Birg, Herwig, ed. 1986. *Ursprünge der Demographie in Deutschland, Leben und Werk Johann Peter Süssmilch (1707–1767).* Institut für Bevölkerungsforschung und Sozialpolitik. Bielefeld/Frankfurt/New York: Campus Verlag.

Hax, Herbert, ed. 2001. *Über Johann Peter Süssmilchs "Göttliche Ordnung." Vademecum zu dem Deutschen Klassiker der Bevölkerungswissenschaft,* annotated reprint of the 1st edition. Düsseldorf, Germany: Verlag Wirtschaft und Finanzen.

Hecht, Jacqueline, ed. 1979–1984. *Johann Peter Süssmilch 1707–1767: L'"Ordre divin" aux origines de la démographie. . . ,* partial annotated translation of the 2nd edition, 3 vols. Paris: Institut national d'études démographiques.

JACQUELINE HECHT

SUSTAINABLE DEVELOPMENT

Sustainable development is the process of enhancing all people's well-being while maintaining the integrity of the Earth's ecological systems. The concept brings together two interdependent imperatives: on the one hand, the traditional goal of "development," that is, to provide satisfying lives for all people; and on the other, a concern for "ecological sustainability," to live within the ecological capacity of the planet.

The term sustainable development emerged in the 1980s as a result of a critique of traditional development projects. Conventional economic development efforts were recognized as often contributing to ecological degradation and social injustice, thereby undermining the ecological, social, and even economic capital of communities. The qualifier "sustainable" was intended to remedy this limited idea of development.

The most frequently cited definition of sustainable development is from the Brundtland Commission, established by the UN Secretary-General in 1993 to formulate a global agenda for change that would protect the environment and strengthen development. In their widely read report *Our Common Future* (1987), they proposed sustainable development as "development that meets the needs of the present without compromising the ability of future generations to meet their own needs" (World Commission on Environment and Development 1987, p. 43). The Report helped establish sustainable development as a legitimate goal globally and at all levels of government. However, the inability to operationalize the Brundtland Commission's definition stimulated a wide array of interpretations. As originally proposed by David Pearce and his colleagues in 1989, two particularly relevant interpretations have been identified, called *weak* and *strong* sustainability.

Weak and Strong Sustainability

Weak sustainability is said to be achieved if the per capita monetary value of the combined physical, social, and natural assets is maintained. The underlying assumption is that declining overall asset value ("wealth") likely leads to a decline in future social well-being.

This conceptualization links sustainability to economic thinking. However, its practical application is limited by the difficulty of determining many of the relevant asset values. Monetary values can be assigned for assets traded in a market, such as timber or cereals; it is much more difficult to determine a proper value for social and natural assets. More importantly, even if values can be determined, they may not accurately signal that ecological limits are being breached, with serious consequences for human welfare. Also, measures of overall wealth say little about social justice or equitable access to resources and institutions. In spite of such limitations, monetary accounts extended in this fashion can provide valuable information about the future viability of a nation's economy. The "genuine savings" measure is among the most advanced of these measures.

Strong sustainability addresses the difficulty of monetizing assets and combining social and ecological assets by recognizing that some natural assets do not have substitutes. An example is the ozone layer, the loss of which would entail serious harm to human beings and nature. Strong sustainability requires that some critical amount of the non-substitutable natural capital be preserved, independent of any increases in value of other social or physical assets. This criterion is best captured by biophysical measures of the human enterprise.

Essentially, strong sustainability postulates the need for living within the planet's biological capacity or limits; it emphasizes the ecological bottom-line condition for sustainable development. This can serve as a specific, measurable criterion with direct relevance to ecological health as well as to equitable resource access, since limited ecological capacity links directly to questions of distributional justice. Strong sustainability, therefore, becomes the effort to secure quality of life for all, within the means of nature.

Science-based definitions largely agree with the strong view of sustainability. For example, a joint strategy document of the World Conservation Union, the United Nations Environment Programme, and the World Wide Fund for Nature defines sustainable development as "improving the quality of human life while living within the carrying capacity of supporting ecosystems" (*Caring for the Earth* 1991, p. 10). This is spelled out in more specific terms in the four system conditions for sustainability developed by The Natural Step. Through a consensus process among scientists this organization has developed core conditions for sustainability, which can guide planning decisions at all levels towards sustainability. In essence, these conditions maintain that sustainability requires providing satisfying lives for all without turning the Earth's resources into waste any faster than nature can reconstitute waste back into resources.

Limits, Overshoot, and Accounting

When humanity's demands in terms of resource consumption and waste generation exceed the capacity of nature's sources and sinks, human populations move into what is termed ecological overshoot. Ecological limits are not like a rigid wall that brings a speeding car to a halt. Rather, ecological limits are more like financial budgets—they can be transgressed easily. More timber can be harvested than regrows, more fish can be caught than are spawned, more CO_2 can be emitted than nature can reabsorb, and topsoil can be eroded while crops grow.

Initially, most of these transgressions go unnoticed. The signs that humanity has exceeded the biological limits of the planet are separated from consumption decisions by space and time. This separation is compounded by the fact that, at the country level, governments do not keep track of the use of nature in relation to how much is available. As a result, they are unaware of the degree to which development is being achieved through the running down of natural capital rather than through use of nature's regenerative capacity.

A common misperception is that because there are no apparent shortages of raw materials, the concern over ecological limits has been overstated. This confusion comes from the illusion that ecological limits are elastic. This misperception is created by new technologies that enable more rapid resource extraction and easier access to remote locations. As a simple analogy, if a car is low on gas, the fact that it is still possible to accelerate does not disprove the gas gauge's indication of the decreasing total amount of gas remaining in the tank. Similarly, the ability to pump water out of an aquifer more quickly does not change its ultimate capacity or its recharge rate. For this reason, systematic resource accounting—

documenting the cumulative effect of humanity's consumption of natural capital and generation of waste—is a core necessity for achieving ecological sustainability as well as secure access to resources for all. To detect overshoot in advance and avoid it, decision-makers must know whether human demands on nature exceed nature's rate of renewal.

Measuring the Biophysical Dimension

Overshoot is measured by determining how much nature or, more specifically, biological capacity is available and then comparing this supply with human demand. As a simple indicator of the "supply" of nature available, one can measure all of the Earth's biologically productive land and sea spaces: a total of 11.4 billion hectares. Divided by the human population (6.2 billion in 2002), this means that there is an average of 1.8 hectares of space available per person. Adding more people reduces the amount of space, or the supply of nature, available per person.

Humans coexist on Earth with over 10 million other species, most of which are excluded from the spaces occupied intensively for human purposes. This means some of the 1.8 hectares per person need to be set aside and left relatively untouched if a significant number of those other species will be present also in the future.

Conservation biologists suggest setting aside at least one quarter of the Earth's biologically productive space for biopreservation, and in some areas up to 75 percent. The Brundtland Commission proposed protecting 12 percent, which was politically courageous if perhaps ecologically insufficient. Still, this proposal would lower the available bioproductive space per person to just 1.6 hectares—a figure that will diminish as the size of the world's population grows.

This available capacity can be compared to how much biologically productive space people already appropriate to produce their resources and absorb their wastes. One measurement to capture this demand on nature is the "ecological footprint." Ecological footprint accounts are based on two assumptions: first, that it is possible to keep track of most of the resources people consume and the wastes they generate; second, that it is possible to translate many of these demands into a corresponding land or sea area needed to produce those resources. These areas can then be added up and expressed in "global hect-ares"—standardized hectares with global average productivity. Because they leave out those human impacts on nature that cannot be associated with ecological area, ecological footprints provide a conservative estimate of the human use of nature.

Calculations for 1999, based on Food and Agriculture Organization and other United Nations statistics and documented in the *Living Planet Report 2002,* show that the average ecological footprint for the United States population amounts to 9.6 global hectares per person, more than five times the average that is available per person worldwide. Over half of this footprint is attributed to fossil fuel use, calculated as the area needed to absorb the CO_2 from fossil fuel burning or to replace the fossil fuel energy consumed with biomass energy.

In contrast, the footprint for the average resident of India is 0.8 global hectares, and for the average Italian, 3.8. Worldwide, the average footprint is 2.3 global hectares per person, exceeding the total ecological supply of 1.8 global hectares per person by one quarter. One interpretation of this calculation is that it would take one year and three months to regenerate the resources that are used in one year by the human population.

See also: *Carrying Capacity; Ecological Perspectives on Population; Land Use; Limits to Growth.*

BIBLIOGRAPHY

Caring for the Earth: A Strategy for Living Sustainable Living. 1991. Gland, Switzerland: The World Conservation Union, United Nations Environment Programme, and World Wide Fund for Nature.

Dasgupta, Partha, and Karl-Goran Mäler. 2000. "Net National Product, Wealth and Social Well-Being." *Environment and Development Economics* 5(1 & 2): 69–93.

Hamilton, Kirk. 2000. *Genuine Savings as a Sustainability Indicator.* Washington, D.C.: World Bank.

———. 2002. *Sustaining Per Capita Welfare with Growing Population: Theory and Measurement.* Presented to the 2nd World Congress on Environmental and Resource Economics, Monterey CA, June 24–27, 2002.

Lélé, Sharachchandra M. 1991. "Sustainable Development: A Critical Review." *World Development* 19(6): 607–621.

Living Planet Report 2002. 2002. Gland, Switzerland: World-Wide Fund for Nature, Redefining Progress, and the United Nations Environment Programme's World Conservation Monitoring Centre.

Meyer, Aubrey. 2001. *Contraction and Convergence: The Global Solution to Climate Change.* Schumacher Briefings No. 5 and Global Commons Institute. Totnes, Eng.: Green Books.

Pearce, David, Anil Markandya, and Edward Barbier. 1989. *Blueprint for a Green Economy.* London: Earthscan Publications.

Robért, Karl-Henrik, Herman Daly, Paul Hawken, and John Holmberg. 1997. "A Compass for Sustainable Development." *International Journal of Sustainable Development and World Ecology* 4: 79–92.

Wackernagel, Mathis, Niels B. Schulz, Diana Deumling, Alejandro Callejas Linares, Martin Jenkins, Valerie Kapos, Chad Monfreda, Jonathan Loh, Norman Myers, Richard Norgaard, and Jørgen Randers. "Tracking the Ecological Overshoot of the Human Economy." *Proceedings of the National Academy of Science USA* 99 (14): 9266–9271.

World Commission on Environment and Development [Brundtland Commission]. 1987. *Our Common Future.* Oxford: Oxford University Press.

INTERNET RESOURCES.

Food and Agriculture Organization. 2002. <http://apps.fao.org>.

Redefining Progress. 2002. <http://www.redefiningprogress.org>.

The Natural Step. 2002. <http://www.naturalstep.org>.

MATHIS WACKERNAGEL
KARL STEYAERT
KIM RODGERS

T

TAEUBER, IRENE B.

(1906–1974)

One of the most distinguished demographers of her generation, Irene Taeuber was born in Missouri and graduated from the University of Missouri in 1927. Her graduate training was at Northwestern University and the University of Minnesota from which she received a doctorate in sociology in 1931. Married to Conrad Taeuber, a noted demographer employed for many years at the U.S. Bureau of the Census, she had two children, Richard and Karl, both of whom have pursued careers in demography.

Apart from three years of teaching at Mt. Holyoke College and a brief stint in Washington where, with the eminent demographer Frank Lorimer she edited *Population Literature* for the Population Association of America, most of Irene Taeuber's career was spent at the Office of Population Research at Princeton University which she joined shortly after its founding. There, from 1937 when the first volume appeared, for the rest of her life she co-edited *Population Index,* an annotated bibliography of the world's population research literature, carrying the main responsibilities for the journal during its first 17 years and writing most of the journal's opening "Current Items." Her reputation as a demographer, however, is based primarily on her research contributions, contained in some 200 published items— books, monographs, articles, book chapters, and reviews. The geography of her demographic interests was wide-ranging, covering all continents. Her best-known book, a 462 page volume entitled *The Population of Japan,* appeared in 1958 and was later trans-lated and published in Japan. In the same year she also co-authored with her husband the massive volume *The Changing Population of the United States.* Although primarily a specialist on the populations of Asia—China, Pakistan, India, and the Philippines as well as Japan —Taeuber also wrote on Europe and the United States and on different parts of sub-Saharan Africa. Measurement issues in demography captured her attention too, as did the science of demography itself. Her contributions to the population field can be characterized as demographic description and analysis at its best, with a truly international purview. A full bibliography of her writings appears as an appendix to a 1975 memorial note in *Population Index* by Frank Notestein.

Professional appreciation of Taeuber's research contributions was signaled by the many academic honors she received during her lifetime. She was president of the Population Association of America from 1953 to 1954 (the first woman to serve in that capacity) and vice-president of the International Union for the Scientific Study of Population from 1961 to 1965. In Princeton, her formal rank was initially Research Associate at the Office of Population Research and, from 1961 until her retirement in 1973, Senior Research Demographer. At that time, Princeton employed very few women as faculty; under later circumstances she would probably have had a "regular" professorial career. After her death the Population Association of America established the biennial Irene B. Taeuber Award to honor her memory.

See also: *Demography, History of.*

BIBLIOGRAPHY

SELECTED WORKS BY IRENE B. TAEUBER.

Taeuber, Conrad, and Irene B. Taeuber. 1958. *The Changing Population of the United States.* U. S. Bureau of the Census and the Social Science Research Council, Census Monograph Series. New York: John Wiley.

Taeuber, Irene B. 1958. *The Population of Japan.* Princeton: Princeton University Press. Published in Japanese as *Nihyon Jinko* (Tokyo: Mainichi Press, 1965).

———. 1962. "Japan's Population: Miracle, Model, or Case Study?" *Foreign Affairs* 40 (July): 595–604.

———. 1964. "Population and Society." In *Handbook of Modern Sociology,* ed. Robert E. L. Faris. Chicago: Rand McNally.

———. 1969. "Population Growth in Less Developed Countries." In *The Population Dilemma,* 2nd edition, ed. Philip M. Hauser. Englewood Cliffs, NJ: Prentice-Hall.

———. 1972. "Chinese Population in Transition: The City-States." *Population Index* 38 (January–March): 3–34.

———. 1972. "Growth of the Population of the United States in the Twentieth Century." In *U.S. Commission on Population Growth and the American Future, Research Reports,* Vol. 1: *Demographic and Social Aspects of Population Growth,* ed. Charles F. Westoff and Robert Parke, Jr. Washington, D.C.: Government Printing Office.

———. 1973. "The Data and the Dynamics of the Chinese Populations" *Population Index* 39 (April): 137–170.

Taeuber, Irene B., and Conrad Taeuber. 1971. *People of the United States in the Twentieth Century.* U.S. Bureau of the Census and the Social Science Research Council, Census Monograph Series. Washington, D.C.: Government Printing Office.

CHARLES F. WESTOFF

TECHNOLOGICAL CHANGE AND POPULATION GROWTH

The relationship between population growth and technological change has been debated since the end of the eighteenth century—a debate whose main configuration has proved remarkably persistent. During the ensuing 200 years, historically unprecedented rates of change have been observed in both variables: in industrial, commercial, and communications revolutions spreading out from Europe, North America, and Japan; in parallel (though spatially and temporally uneven) revolutions in the technological base of agricultural production; and in a demographic transition—in which mortality decreased and fertility first increased, then decreased —that is still underway in many developing countries. Interconnections there must be, yet the attribution of primacy and direction of causation among these variables, not to mention the nature of the mechanisms involved and means of influencing outcomes in the interest of meeting social goals, remain controversial. Meanwhile, a new awareness of the emergence of complex social-environmental systems, whether at local or global levels, has extended the debate beyond the discipline of economics, and broadened its emphasis from the welfare of the human race to that of the planet.

Malthus: Limits and Closed Systems

Two grand theories dominate the macro-demographic debate, differing on whether technological change is regarded as originating from within (endogenous) or outside (exogenous) the system in question. Proponents of "neo-Malthusian" views, following T. R. Malthus's *Second Essay* of 1803 and its subsequent revisions, emphasize the biophysical limits to resources (whether renewable or nonrenewable), in a system that is essentially closed. Technological advances, which are introduced to the system by autonomous invention, can increase productivity, thus buying time for growing populations, but they serve to stimulate further growth. Continued growth entails eventual diminishing returns to labor or capital and scarcities in food or other commodities. As the prevailing technology determines the "carrying capacity" of natural resources, in Malthus's own time it seemed natural to point to the famous "checks" which, by increasing mortality, brought the population back into equilibrium. In the world of the early twenty-first century, the environmental agenda interposes scenarios of the destruction or degradation of natural resources between predicted population growth and an eventual Malthusian outcome. Indeed, the threat of mass mortality has receded in a post-Cold War world in which boundless confidence in the potential of induced technological change, and a capacity to ship food and other necessities in large quantities from surplus to deficit regions, have shifted the geographical reference from local or national to global.

Technological change holds out the promise of rising global income levels, following the example of the developed world. Yet it also brings potential threats—two in particular. On the one hand, it is seen as having facilitated population growth in poor societies to ultimately insupportable levels (as in Ireland in the mid-nineteenth century), and on the other, it has generated demands, especially in richer societies, for an unsustainable exploitation of nature, with effects that may be global (e.g., atmospheric warming). It is far from obvious that the economic benefits of urban-industrialism can eventually be extended to the world's poor. Led by writers such as Paul and Anne Ehrlich and Lester Brown, a powerful constituency emerged in support of population limitation in countries with high fertility. To reflect the multivariate nature of the environmental threat, Ehrlich and Holdren in 1974 invented the $I=PAT$ formulation (Impact of an economic system on the environment = Population × Affluence × Technology). However, although its simplicity has recommended it to many researchers and policy makers, the complex interdependencies and dynamics among P, A, and T render it unsuitable as a model of complex systems.

Boserup: Technological Change and Agricultural Growth

A view of technological change as endogenous is often associated with the economist Ester Boserup (1910–1999), who explored the implications of this assumption for agricultural growth. Such views see necessity as the mother of invention and the uptake of technology as a process driven by changing factor proportions, in particular (in the agricultural case) those between labor and land. As scarcity drives up the value of land, and of agricultural and other outputs, investments in higher productivity become possible, first as additional labor per hectare (by increasing the frequency of cultivation or the intensity of weeding and fertilizing) and then, as increasing

population densities generate markets and urban concentration, in the form of investments in land improvements. At low population densities, labor-saving investments best respond to poor farmers' factor ratios; but as densities increase, land-saving investments become necessary. Adoption of known technologies (whether indigenous or imported) is the key process, though Boserup acknowledged that demographically-driven demand can also play a role in spurring new inventions. An analysis of the technological history of agriculture and its relations with the growth of dense and secure populations, cities, and commerce, suggests "a quantitative relationship between an area's population density and its predominating food supply system" (Boserup 1981, p. 15). However, a growing density is a necessary, but not a sufficient, condition for labor-intensive agricultural growth. This is reflected in the technological diversity among contemporary farming systems in developing countries.

The economist Julian Simon (1932–1998) took this argument further. National data from many countries—rich and poor, North and South—suggested a correlation between indicators of population size and growth on the one hand and technical innovation and cultural creativity on the other. Inventive potential is considered to be randomly distributed in a population (equity, education, interaction, and other variables being equal). "Hence the net result of an additional person is an increase in the total number of new ideas" (Simon 1986, p. 377). Taking a strong stance on the potential of technology to extend the effective size of resource inventories, to enable recycling, and if necessary to substitute for scarce resources, Simon argued against the advocates of population limitation. "Population growth spurs the adoption of existing technology as well as the invention of new technology" (Simon 1996, p. 376).

There is indeed an accumulation of knowledge about historical achievements in food and agriculture that calls into question models and scenarios predicting imminent scarcity or ecological collapse such as those found in *The Limits to Growth* (Meadows et al., 1972). FAO data show that in the 1990s, developing countries were increasing cereal output by 1.5 to 2.2 percent yearly on a cultivated area-per-person that had declined from 0.18 ha in 1960 to 0.10 ha in 1995. However, investing in technology requires economic incentives, as shown by the history of the green revolution in Asia or improved corn yields in Africa. An urban-industrial sector may be essential to motivate surplus production and offer a stream of new technologies, which in turn provide a route to high-productivity agriculture and promote the structural transformation needed in countries having abundant rural labor.

African Case Studies

A case study from Kenya illuminates these relationships. In the Machakos and Makueni Districts of Kenya, decades of rapid population growth, massive losses of natural capital through soil erosion and deforestation, and high food insecurity appeared to justify a Malthusian perspective—which was in fact embraced by the government and its advisers. However, closer investigation reveals a revolution in land conservation and economic productivity since the 1930s, favoring instead a broadly Boserupian process of change. In the 1930s wealth was channeled into livestock as the most readily marketable commodity the farming families in these districts could produce. Between 1930 and 1990, against a background of a sixfold increase in population and a massive transfer of land from common grazing land and woodland to permanent, privately owned farmland, the value of agricultural output per head increased nearly fourfold and its value per hectare more than elevenfold. Keys to this achievement were changes in the profitability, sources, and technological priorities of private investment. Aggressive (even coercive) promotion of soil conservation measures by the government during the 1940s and 1950s produced a minor "Machakos miracle" of landscape transformation, which did not survive for long after independence (1962). The real "miracle" occurred later, beginning in the 1970s, when farmers in the long-settled and very densely populated hills recognized that conservation terraces improved crop yields (through their beneficial effects on soil moisture) and embarked energetically on private investment in terracing.

Further incentives for investment derived from improved access to markets (especially the coffee market, previously restricted to European producers), a loosening of restrictions on selling corn outside the district, and above all the rapid growth of urban demand for fruit and horticultural crops, which progressively opened up new agricultural options. Farmers could draw on a growing bank of technological knowledge from both government and private sources. The agrarian transformation extended even to the driest areas, although the inhabitants of those areas were acutely aware of their constrained farming opportunities (due to drought, risks to animal health, and high cost of access to markets) and were more dependent on diversifying their incomes through education and migration. The social distribution of the benefits of this transformation were far from equitable and farmers continued to face significant economic and ecological risks. However, in broad terms a Boserupian framework appears to offer a valid explanation of the outcomes of long-term interaction between the growth of population and of technology.

The Boserupian model originally reflected Asian rather than African experience. The vigor of debate on the African cases (of which there are many; see Turner et al., 1993) reflects both the rapidity of economic and ecological change under rapid rates of population growth (fertility has only recently begun to decline in Africa) and the severity of environmental degradation as perceived by some international agencies. As the African drylands have a low agroecological potential, high risk of drought, and high rates of population growth, they pose the sharpest challenges to adaptive technology. Yet the possibility of a transition from more extensive (land-using) technologies, which are unsustainable under conditions of population growth, to more intensive (labor-using)—and sustainable—ones, even where the supply of capital is severely constrained by poverty, is suggested by a variety of African evidence. In Kano in Nigeria, on-farm population densities of over $220/km^2$ have evolved on a time-scale of centuries, supported by a system of fertilized annual cultivation, and in symbiosis with major urban product and labor markets. In Maradi in Niger a build-up of population through rapid in-migration, with extensive deforestation for farming, collided with the drought cycles of the 1970s and 1980s to threaten a collapse in productivity in a classic Malthusian crisis. But subsequently, there is evidence that a mix of market forces, project interventions, and indigenous investments have halted and in places begun to reverse this trajectory. Grain production per head has been maintained, in part through additional labor and investment.

A Synthesis

An opposition between a view of population (Malthus) or technology (Boserup) as the dependent variable has not discouraged some analysts—including Pryor and Maurer (1982), Lee (1986), and

Simon (1992)—from suggesting that a theoretical synthesis is possible. Simon proposed a single integrative model of technological change in which Malthusian "innovation-pull" and Boserupian "population-push" hypotheses coexist. The real world has also moved on: just as no closed Malthusian systems exist at the local or national level in the early twenty-first century, so Boserup's open system is finally closed at the global scale.

At its core, Malthusian theory posits an equilibrium between population and resources. Many environmentalists seek to control or reverse what they see as maladaptive departures from that equilibrium. However, some ecologists challenge this view of nature, seeing in many ecosystems evidence of variability, irreversibility, crisis, and surprise. A Boserupian frame of reference appears better suited to a dynamic and nonlinear view of social-environmental systems as it contains implicit provision for such concepts as thresholds, transitions, creative changes between states, and resilience under stress. Analysis of the complex interactions among populations, technologies, and environments should not be constrained in advance by modeling assumptions.

See also: *Boserup, Ester; Carrying Capacity; Energy and Population; Limits to Growth; Natural Resources and Population; Simon, Julian L.; Sustainable Development.*

BIBLIOGRAPHY

Boserup, Ester. 1965. *The Conditions of Agricultural Growth.* London: Allen and Unwin.

———. 1981. *Population and Technology.* Chicago: University of Chicago Press.

Ehrlich, Paul R., and Anne H. Ehrlich. 1970. *Population, Resources and Environment: Issues in Human Ecology.* New York: W. H. Freeman.

Ehrlich, Paul R., and J. Holdren. 1974. "The Impact of Population Growth." *Science* 171: 1212–1217.

Gunderson, L. H., C. S. Holling, and S. S. Light. 1995. *Barriers and Bridges to the Renewal of Ecosystems and Institutions.* New York: Columbia University Press.

Kasperson, J. X., R. E. Kasperson, and B. L. Turner II, eds. 1995. *Regions at Risk: Comparison of Threatened Environments.* Tokyo: United Nations University Press.

Lee, Ronald D. 1986. "Malthus and Boserup: A Dynamic Synthesis." In *The State of Population Theory: Forward from Malthus,* eds. D. Coleman, and R. Schofield. Oxford: Basil Blackwell.

Meadows, Donella et al. 1972. *The Limits to Growth: A Report for the Club of Rome.* New York: Picador.

Mortimore, Michael. 1998. *Roots in the African Dust: Sustaining the Sub-Saharan Drylands.* Cambridge, Eng.: Cambridge University Press.

Rosenberg, Nathan, and L. E. Birdzell Jr. 1987. *How the West Grew Rich: The Economic Transformation of the Industrial World.* New York: Perseus Books.

Simon, Julian L. 1986. *Theory of Population and Economic Growth.* New York: Blackwell.

———. 1992. *Population and Development in Poor Countries.* New Haven, CT: Princeton University Press.

———. 1996. *The Ultimate Resource 2.* Princeton, NJ: Princeton University Press.

Tiffen, M., and Michael Mortimore. 1994. "Malthus Controverted." *World Development* 22: 997–1,010.

Tiffen, M., Michael Mortimore, and F. Gichuki. 1994. *More People, Less Erosion: Environmental Recovery in Kenya.* Chichester, Eng.: John Wiley.

Tomich, T. P., P. Kilby, and B. F. Johnson. 1995. *Transforming Agrarian Economies: Opportunties Seized, Opportunities Missed.* Ithaca, NY: Cornell University Press.

Turner, B. L. II, G. Hyden, and R. W. Kates. 1993. *Population Growth and Agricultural Change in Africa.* Gainesville: University Press of Florida.

MICHAEL MORTIMORE

TEMPORARY MIGRATION

A temporary worker generally enters a country for a fixed-time period for a particular occupation or employer, must leave when the period expires, and in most cases is not entitled to family reunification or adjustment to permanent residence. Temporary worker programs cover both unskilled and highly skilled labor. A typical program range was categorized by Heinz Werner (1996) as follows:

1. One-year work permits for experts and executives;

2. Border crossing permits allowing residents of neighboring countries or territories to enter the host country daily or weekly to work;

3. Seasonal work permits;

4. Project-tied contract labor authorizing entry for completion of a specific project; and

5. Trainee permits allowing individuals to work in the country for a defined period of time to gain certain occupational or language skills.

Many countries simultaneously operate multiple programs.

The majority of temporary work is defined as contract labor, which includes both project-tied labor and seasonal labor. Often an employer or recruiter organizes workers for a specific project or for an agricultural season. Project-tied labor involves giving a contract to a foreign company, which can then bring in its own labor for the duration of the project. The International Labor Organization (ILO) has attempted to create standards applying to temporary workers that cover their employment conditions (e.g., hours worked, paid holidays, ability to unionize, access to social security, written contract), provision of equal opportunity, rights to family visitation, and the right to have their grievances investigated fairly.

Contract labor frequently is part of a bilateral agreement between two countries as one component of an economic development plan. Countries also use temporary worker programs to regularize the flow of labor, reduce undocumented migration, and improve bilateral relations more generally. Contracts under bilateral agreements, particularly for seasonal workers, often specify duration of stay, wages, employer, workers' rights (if any), and employer coverage of travel and housing.

Seasonal programs generally require certification of the unavailability of domestic labor prior to employers being allowed to recruit foreign workers. The duration of stay varies in length: three months in Germany, six months in France, nine months in Switzerland, and up to one year in the United States. The size of the programs varies from country to country as well: Germany admitted between 125,000 and 225,000 workers annually in the 1990s (and allowed for up to 20,000 information technology pro-

fessionals); Canada admitted approximately 17,000 under its seasonal agricultural programs; and the United States permitted entry to approximately 75,000 unskilled temporary workers annually during that same time frame, as well as another 100,000 or so high-skilled workers.

Frontier programs have been used primarily in Germany (with Polish and Czech workers) and in Switzerland (with French, Italian, German, and Austrian workers). While there is no quota or required labor market test, employers must pay prevailing wages. Trainee program participants generally range from a few hundred to a few thousand per country, are not normally subject to a labor market test, and have limited opportunities for adjustment to a permanent status.

Certain nationalities tend to comprise the majority of the world's temporary workers; the Philippines, for example, is the world's largest exporter of labor. Filipino and Sri Lankan workers go to the Gulf States; Bangladeshi workers go to Singapore; Mexicans (in the lower-skilled tier) and Indians (in the higher-skilled tier) are prominent in the U.S. programs; Thai and Romanian workers can be found in Israel; Ukrainian and Turkish workers drift to Russia; Moroccan workers predominate in Spain; and Polish workers fill many of Germany's programs.

Similarly, only particular sectors and occupations have turned to foreign labor, historically and currently, to remedy micro-level shortages. Temporary workers played a vital role in driving twentieth century economic growth, including during European industrialization, during the United States's wartime labor shortages, during the Gulf States's oil boom, and during Asia's rapid economic growth in the 1980s. Specific occupations include physically demanding or dangerous jobs such as construction, agriculture, mining, domestic services, and tourism, as well as newer occupations such as computer programming and other highly skilled information technology jobs.

Common Issues

Regardless of country, all entities designing or managing temporary worker programs face similar challenges. Among the issues they must consider are: (1) the extent of government involvement; (2) the impact on the domestic labor force; (3) unintended, but predictable consequences; and (4) internal program consistency. The first issue was discussed above in terms of whether sending and receiving governments choose to engage in bilateral agreements, but it also includes considerations such as whether the program is administered by a government agency or the private sector, and whether the sending country is actively engaged in worker screening and in protecting the rights of its workers abroad.

The second issue is the challenge to design a program that avoids any adverse impact on the existing native-born work force or any financial advantage to employers in hiring foreign workers. Countries address this through a variety of means, including highly regulated recruitment requirements, worker quotas, required certification of labor shortages, provision of rights and benefits to foreign workers equal to those of domestic workers, access to social security credits, and taxes on employers who import foreign labor. Imposition of a tax for each worker aims to prevent employer dependence on foreign labor; often it is earmarked for a fund to train and recruit domestic workers.

Third, a review of previous temporary worker programs indicates that, in many cases, the creation of such programs stimulates additional migration by creating new migration chains that continue long after the program's termination. Governments, then, must be careful in designing new programs and in considering the potential consequences of existing initiatives that attract new pools of migrants. Research also has demonstrated that a small percentage of workers will likely remain in the receiving country after expiration of the program. Some receiving governments discourage this by allowing only short stays, providing workers with few protections, engaging in repatriation programs, placing responsibility on employers for workers' departures, and even seizing workers' travel documents. Some sending governments encourage workers to return by withholding a percentage of their pay until their return or by offering higher interest rates for the foreign currency brought home. Broader efforts include joint development programs with receiving governments that provide housing and job training for the workers upon their return home, as well as the ability of workers to earn social security credits for their work abroad.

Finally, many countries face the challenge of developing and maintaining internal consistency in their programs. Mixed policy messages, such as de-

vising strict admissions regulations but allowing adjustment after a certain period of time, or issuing long-duration but still "temporary" visas, tend to undermine program success. Moreover, programs that have process-intensive, but ineffective, labor market tests and programs that have stringent but poorly enforced rules pose great challenges to the effectiveness of temporary worker programs.

See also: *Internal Migration; Labor Migration, International.*

BIBLIOGRAPHY

Böhning, W. R. 1984. *Studies in International Labor Migration.* New York: Macmillan.

Cohen, Robin, ed. 1995. *The Cambridge Survey of World Migration.* Cambridge, Eng.: Cambridge University Press.

Congressional Research Service (CRS). 1989. *Temporary Worker Programs: Background and Issues* (1980). Washington, D.C.: U.S. Government Printing Office.

International Organization for Migration (IOM). 2000. *World Migration Report 2000.* New York: International Organization for Migration and United Nations.

Martin, Philip L. 1998. "Germany: Reluctant Land of Immigration." *German Issues,* Vol. 21. Washington, D.C.: American Institute for Contemporary German Studies, Johns Hopkins University.

Miller, Mark J., and Philip L. Martin. 1982. *Administering Foreign-Worker Programs.* Lexington, MA: D.C. Heath.

Organisation for Economic Co-operation and Development. 2001. *Trends in International Migration. Annual Report.* Paris: OECD.

Stalker, Peter. 1994. *The Work of Strangers: A Survey of International Labour Migration.* Geneva, Switzerland: International Labor Organization.

Werner, Heinz. 1996. "Temporary Migration of Foreign Workers." In *Temporary Migration for Employment and Training Purposes.* Strasbourg: Council of Europe.

DEBORAH WALLER MEYERS

THOMAS, DOROTHY SWAINE

(1899–1977)

Dorothy Swaine Thomas was born in Baltimore, Maryland, and educated at Barnard College (B.A. 1922) and the London School of Economics (Ph.D. 1924). Her principal mentors were the sociologist William F. Ogburn, the economist Wesley C. Mitchell, the statistician Arthur L. Bowley, and one of the founders of American sociology, W. I. [William Isaac] Thomas, whom she married in 1936.

Between 1924 and 1948 Thomas received research or academic appointments at the Federal Reserve Bank of New York, the Social Science Research Council, Columbia University Teachers College, Yale University, the Social Science Institute at the University of Stockholm, and the University of California at Berkeley. In 1948 she became the first woman professor in the Wharton School of the University of Pennsylvania, where she was a research professor of sociology. At the Wharton School she initiated an interdisciplinary doctoral training program in demography and helped found and direct the Population Studies Center.

After her retirement from the Wharton School in 1970, Thomas taught at Georgetown University for four years. She served on numerous occasions as a technical consultant to the United Nations and to U.S. government agencies. She was the first woman elected president of the American Sociological Association (1952), was president of the Population Association of America (1958–1959), and received an honorary doctorate from the University of Pennsylvania in 1970 for her work in demography.

In her demographic career two features are evident in Thomas's work: the importance of careful measurement and sensitivity to the interplay between demographic change and economic change. In Thomas's demographic work her concern with measurement centered primarily on internal migration, the subject that eventually became the focus of her research. As chair of the Social Science Research Council's Committee on Migration Differentials, she authored a 1938 study that set the research agenda of the field for the next several decades. Subsequently she codirected with the economist Simon Kuznets the University of Pennsylvania project on population redistribution and economic growth (Thomas, 1957, 1960, 1964). Among its other findings, this project produced definitive estimates of internal migration in the United States by sex, age, race, nativity, and state of origin and destination by decade, covering the period 1870–1950; the study was authored by Everett S. Lee. As chair of the Committee on Internal Migration of the International Union for the Scientific Study of Population Thomas collaborated in producing United Nations Manual VI, *Methods of Measuring Internal Migration*, in 1970.

Thomas's attention to economic–demographic relationships dates from her 1925 doctoral dissertation, *Social Aspects of the Business Cycle*, which documented statistically the relationship of vital rates and other social phenomena to short-term business cycles. In her 1941 study *Social and Economic Aspects of Swedish Population Movements*, the focus shifted to economic–demographic relationships over the long term, again with statistical time series as the basis of analysis. Her 1964 collaborative project on U.S. population redistribution and economic growth demonstrated that decade-to-decade swings in internal migration were linked to the level of economic activity.

Thomas's most famous work, which is not cited frequently by demographers, is her coauthored two-volume 1946 and 1952 study of the forced evacuation, detention, and resettlement of West Coast Japanese Americans during World War II. This work was pieced together under difficult circumstances with the aid of graduate student assistants, and—according to Thomas's 1977 obituary in the American Sociological Association's *Footnotes*—its scientific objectivity "was vindicated when the Supreme Court accepted her books as unbiased evidence of our crimes against our fellow Americans" (quoted in Roscoe 1991, p. 406).

Thomas was a gifted scholar capable of making fundamental contributions to many areas in demography and sociology. At a time when professional academic careers were virtually closed to women, she made a lasting mark and can be considered one of the founders of American demography.

See also: *Demography, History of; Kuznets, Simon.*

BIBLIOGRAPHY

SELECTED WORKS BY DOROTHY SWAINE THOMAS.

Thomas, Dorothy S. 1925. *Social Aspects of the Business Cycle*. London: Routledge and Kegan Paul.

(New York: Knopf, 1928.) Reprinted, New York: Gordon and Breach, 1968.

———. 1938. *Research Memorandum on Migration Differentials.* New York: Social Science Research Council.

———. 1941. *Social and Economic Aspects of Swedish Population Movements, 1750–1933.* New York: Macmillan.

———. 1952. "Experiences in Interdisciplinary Research." *American Sociological Review* 17: 663–669.

———. 1964. "Temporal and Spatial Interrelations between Migration and Economic Opportunities." In *Population Redistribution and Economic Growth, United States 1870–1950,* Vol. III: *Demographic Analyses and Interrelations,* ed. Hope T. Eldridge and Dorothy Swaine Thomas. Philadelphia: American Philosophical Society.

Thomas, Dorothy S., Charles Kikuchi, and James Sakoda. 1952. *Japanese American Evacuation and Resettlement: The Salvage.* Berkeley: University of California Press.

Thomas, Dorothy S., ed., with Simon Kuznets. 1957, 1960, 1964. *Population Redistribution and Economic Growth, United States, 1870–1950.* Philadelphia: American Philosophical Society. Vol. I: *Methodological Considerations and Reference Tables,* 1957; Vol. II: *Analysis of Economic Change,* 1960; Vol. III: *Demographic Analyses and Interrelations,* 1964. Memoirs of the American Philosophical Society, 45, 51, 61.

Thomas, Dorothy S., and Richard S. Nishimoto. 1946. *Japanese American Evacuation and Resettlement: The Spoilage.* Berkeley: University of California Press.

SELECTED WORKS ABOUT DOROTHY SWAINE THOMAS.

Bannister, Robert C. 1998. "Dorothy Swaine Thomas: The Hard Way in the Profession." Originally published as "Dorothy Swaine Thomas: Soziologischer Objectivismus: Der harte Weg in die Profession." In *Frauen in der Soziologie,* ed. Claudia Honeggerund and Teresa Wobbe. Munich: Oscar Beck.

Goldenstein, Sidney. 1977. "Dorothy Swaine Thomas, 1899–1977." *Population Index* 43: 447–450.

Lee, Everett S. 1979. "Thomas, Dorothy Swaine." In *International Encyclopedia of the Social Sciences,* Vol. 18: *Biographical Supplement,* ed. David L. Sills. New York: Free Press.

Roscoe, Janice. 1991. "Dorothy Swaine Thomas (1899–1977)." In *Women in Sociology: A Bio-Bibliographical Sourcebook,* ed. Mary Jo Deegan. New York: Greenwood Press.

United Nations. 1970. *Methods of Measuring Internal Migration,* Manual VI, Department of International Economic and Social Affairs. New York: United Nations.

INTERNET RESOURCE.

University Archives and Records Center, University of Pennsylvania. "Guide to Dorothy Swaine Thomas Papers, 1929–1977." <http://www.archives.upenn.edu/faids/upt/upt50/thomasdot.html>.

RICHARD A. EASTERLIN

THOMPSON, WARREN S.

(1887–1973)

Warren Simpson Thompson received his Ph.D. in sociology from Columbia University in 1915. As a student of the sociologists Alvan A. Tenney and Franklin Giddings, and the statistician Robert E. Chaddock, he developed an early interest in international population trends and in problems associated with rapid population growth. In his dissertation, *Population: A Study in Malthusianism* (1915), he argued that U.S. population growth rates directly responded to changes in the food supply. In the early 1920s, Edward W. Scripps, the newspaper publisher, grew concerned about population and sought out Thompson on the basis of his dissertation. After a tour of Asia aboard Scripps's yacht, Thompson agreed to head the first foundation exclusively focused on the study of population. The Scripps Foundation for Research in Population Problems, located at Miami University in Oxford, Ohio, in Scripps's home county of Butler, was established in 1922. Pascal Kidder Whelpton (1893–1964), an agricultural economist from Cornell University, joined Thompson as assistant director in 1924. After Scripps's death in 1926, finances for the foundation were fixed at a modest level, preventing its further expansion. As director of this foundation, Thompson engaged in studies of both international and domestic demographic trends for 30 years.

In 1929, Thompson published two notable works on international population dynamics: a book, *Danger Spots in World Population* and an article "Population" in the *American Journal of Sociology.* In the latter, Thompson elaborated an early version of demographic transition theory. He placed all countries into three groups based on trends in their rates of natural increase. He assumed that countries would progress from Group C (high birth and death rates) to Group B (high birthrates but declining death rates) to Group A (low birth and death rates) as they became increasingly industrialized. In *Danger Spots in World Population,* Thompson used this framework to identify regions experiencing population problems and to derive policy recommendations. In a controversial analysis, he concluded that Japan, then in a period of rapid population expansion, had only one policy alternative: "to expand by the acquisition of more territory" (Thompson, p. 43). This theory that seemed to support Japanese imperialism generated little interest among Western policymakers during the interwar period.

Thompson's *Population Problems,* first published in 1930, was the major textbook in population studies until the 1960s. *Population Trends in the United States* (1933), written with Whelpton, established him as a leading forecaster of U.S. population trends. (His and Whelpton's set of projections for the United States, published in 1943, gave 2000 totals under variant assumptions ranging from 129 million to 198 million.) In 1944, Thompson again turned his attention to international population trends in *Plenty of People,* which contained an updated version of his 1929 transition framework. In the period from 1944 to 1946, Thompson, sociologist Dudley Kirk (1913–2000), economist Frank Notestein (1902–1983), and sociologist Kingsley Davis (1908–1997) all generalized the Western demographic experience in similar ways. Together, their work constitutes the classic theory of the demographic transition.

In *Population and Peace in the Pacific* (1946), Thompson outlined the major population problem of the post-World War II period: rapid population growth in colonial areas. Internal order, improved transportation systems, and public health innova-

tions were lowering mortality, yet mother countries were not fostering the industrialization and urbanization that would work to lower fertility. Thompson predicted that this "Malthusian dilemma" would bring about the end of colonialism. In the immediate post-World War II period, Thompson went to Japan as an advisor to General Douglas MacArthur leader of the Occupation forces. Japan's birth rate experienced a sharp increase from 1946 through 1949, and Thompson predicted severe overpopulation. He called on the Japanese government to take "positive measures" to reduce the birth rate. Japan did, in fact, make abortion and contraception readily available and its total fertility rate fell by 50 percent over the next decade, a decline that Thompson had thought impossible. In 1953, Thompson stepped down as director of the Scripps Foundation and was succeeded by Whelpton.

See also: *Demography, History of; Demographic Transition; Population Thought, Contemporary; Whelpton, P. K.*

BIBLIOGRAPHY

SELECTED WORKS BY WARREN S. THOMPSON.

Thompson, Warren S. 1929. *Danger Spots in World Population.* New York: Alfred A. Knopf.

———. 1929. "Population." *American Journal of Sociology* 34(6): 959–975.

———. 1930. *Population Problems* (5th edition, 1965) New York: McGraw Hill.

———. 1946. *Population and Peace in the Pacific.* Chicago: University of Chicago Press.

———. 1948. *Plenty of People: The World's Population Pressures, Problems and Policies and How They Concern Us,* Rev. edition. New York: Ronald Press.

———. 1959. *Population and Progress in the Far East.* Chicago: University of Chicago Press.

Thompson, Warren S., and P. K. Whelpton. 1943. *Estimates of Future Population of the United States, 1940–2000.* Washington, D.C.: National Resources Planning Board.

———. [1933] 1969. *Population Trends in the United States.* New York: Gordon and Breach Science Publishers.

DENNIS HODGSON

TOBACCO-RELATED MORTALITY

Of all the risks to human health, perhaps none has been studied as extensively as tobacco use. Claims about the hazards of smoking tobacco had been voiced for centuries prior to the first scientific studies on the extent of the risk in the early 1950s. Beginning with the pioneering work carried out in the United Kingdom by epidemiologists Richard Doll and Austin Bradford-Hill, cigarette smoking was first identified as a cause of lung cancer and, later, as a cause of numerous other cancers, as well as major respiratory and vascular diseases.

The evidence on causality for tobacco use as a cause of disease and death has become irrefutable. It has been firmly established in numerous case-control, as well as cohort, studies in several developed countries including the United Kingdom, the United States, Sweden, and Japan. Studies in China and India confirm that tobacco use in parts of the developing world is becoming an increasing health hazard in these populations.

In populations where smoking has been prevalent for decades, tobacco causes about 90 percent to 95 percent of lung cancer deaths, about two-thirds of upper aero-digestive tract cancers (and 40% to 50% of all cancer deaths), three-quarters of chronic bronchitis and emphysema deaths, and about one-fifth of all deaths from ischemic heart disease and stroke. Smokers typically have a 20- to 25-fold higher risk of lung cancer than non-smokers, and about a 3-fold higher risk of suffering a heart attack or stroke, compared with lifelong non-smokers. In younger smokers (less than 50 years of age), the risk of coronary heart disease or stroke is typically five to six times higher than in non-smokers. Overall, death rates for smokers are about 2.5 to three times higher than for non-smokers at all ages above 35 years.

The epidemiology of tobacco often leads to a serious misunderstanding of the full health effects of tobacco use. Most of the excess risk of diseases caused by tobacco only occurs several decades after persistent smoking has become widespread. This long delay between the uptake of tobacco use in a population and its full health effects can be misinterpreted to mean that tobacco is not a major cause of death. In developed countries, males began smoking in large numbers in the early decades of the twentieth century (a 60–70% prevalence of smokers among male adults was not uncommon), and by the early

1960s, cigarette consumption had peaked among men in these countries. However, mortality from tobacco use only began to rise beginning in the 1950s, increasing from an estimated annual death toll of about 300,000 in 1950 (20% of all deaths) to 1.45 million (28%) in 1995.

Women in developed countries began smoking much later than men, the practice being adopted first by women in Britain, the United States, Australia, Canada, and New Zealand in the 1930s and thereafter, and, since 1950, increasingly by women in Europe. Prevalence among women has become similar to that of men in these countries, but because they have been smoking for much shorter periods the full health effects are not yet evident. From causing virtually no deaths in 1950, tobacco in the early twenty-first century causes around 500,000 deaths annually among women in developed countries, half of these in the United States alone. This toll is expected to increase dramatically over the first and second decades of the twenty-first century as the impact of past consumption among women becomes apparent.

Overall, cigarette consumption in developed countries peaked in the 1980s and has been steadily declining at the rate of about 1.0 percent per year since then. Much of this decline can be attributed to the success of tobacco control measures taken by these countries, including bans or restrictions on advertising, restricting smoking in public places, increased taxation on cigarettes, banning vending machines for cigarettes, the inclusion of warning labels on cigarette packets, and public information campaigns. As a result, the annual toll of about 2 million deaths from tobacco use in these countries may not rise much higher. The effect of declining mortality among men will progressively outweigh the expected increases in female tobacco-caused deaths over the first two or three decades of the twenty-first century.

In developing countries, cigarette consumption has been relatively low, especially among women. However, smoking of either manufactured or home-made cigarettes has now become increasingly common in most developing countries: about half of all men are regular smokers, and about 10 percent of women. Hence, tobacco-related mortality, still comparatively low, can be expected to increase steeply. In China, where cigarette consumption has quadrupled since 1975, tobacco already causes about 1 million deaths annually. A comparable number (1 to 1.5

million) of deaths occur in the remainder of the developing world. If current trends continue, and cigarette consumption proves as hazardous in developing countries as elsewhere, tobacco use is projected to cause 10 million deaths per year by 2030, 7–8 million of which will be in developing countries. This would make tobacco use by far the greatest contributor to the burden of disease world-wide.

The reduction of cigarette smoking and other forms of tobacco use, particularly in developing countries, has become a global priority for public health action. The dramatic reductions in prevalence and consumption observed over several decades in many industrialized countries, most notably the United Kingdom, demonstrate that success is possible. Specific measures to curtail tobacco use such as advertising bans and price increases are likely to be much more effective in the context of strong political commitment to reducing consumption.

See also: *Alcohol, Health Effects of; Cancer; Cardiovascular Disease; Disease, Burden of; Diseases, Chronic and Degenerative; Mortality Differentials, by Sex.*

BIBLIOGRAPHY

Doll Richard, and Austin Bradford Hill. 1950. "Smoking and Carcinoma of the Lung: Preliminary Report." *British Medical Journal* ii: 739–748.

Liu, B. Q., R. Peto, Z. M. Chen, et al. 1998. "Emerging Tobacco Hazards in China: 1. Retrospective Proportional Mortality Study of One Million Deaths." *British Medical Journal* 317: 1411–1422.

Pampel, Fred C. 2002. "Cigarette Use and the Narrowing Sex Differential in Mortality." *Population and Development Review* 28: 77–104.

Peto, Richard, et al. 1994. *Mortality from Smoking in Developed Countries, 1950–2000.* Oxford: Oxford University Press.

Peto, Richard, and Alan D. Lopez. 2001. "Future World-wide Health Effects of Current Smoking Patterns." In *Critical Issues in Global Health,* ed. C. Everett Koop, C. E. Pearson, and M. Roy Schwarz. San Francisco: Wiley.

ALAN D. LOPEZ

TRANS-ATLANTIC MIGRATION

Numerically the greatest and probably the most consequential population movement in modern history has been the transatlantic migration from Europe to the Western Hemisphere. It is estimated that more than 60 million Europeans emigrated to the Americas from the beginning of the period of colonization (approximately 1500) to 1940. Subsequent to 1940, about 5.8 million persons left Europe for the United States as immigrants, much of this before 1960. Canada received over 2 million migrants from Europe between 1945 and 1981. Latin America was the destination of about 600,000–700,000 Europeans between 1945 and 1960.

Most of this migration was to North America (the United States and Canada), but significant numbers of migrants went to Argentina, Brazil, Chile, Cuba, Mexico, Uruguay, and other areas of Latin America and the Caribbean. In addition, there was a large coerced migration of black Africans as slaves, almost entirely before 1820, when Britain began to use its naval power to suppress the slave trade. It is estimated that about 9.4 million slaves were taken to the Western Hemisphere, but only about 400,000 to British North America. The largest single recipient was Brazil (3.6 million). The mortality rate of slaves outside North America was very high, so that by about 1825 North America had 36 percent of the slaves in the Western Hemisphere even though it had received only 4.2 percent of the imported slaves.

Early Migration

Information on migration for the colonial and early national periods in British North America and the United States is scarce because regular collection of immigration statistics began only in 1819 at major ports in the United States. Estimates of European emigration to British North America and the United States for the period 1700–1820 range between 765,000 and 1.3 million. Most of the migrants originated in Britain (England, Scotland, and Wales) and Ireland, but some came from the Rhineland area of Germany and the Netherlands, and a number of Huguenots (French Protestants) sought refuge in British North America. Although there was a gross flow of about 25,000 migrants from France to the Saint Lawrence Valley and other areas of New France in the seventeenth and eighteenth centuries, most of

TABLE 1

Intercontinental Emigration (all Western Hemisphere destinations), Europe, 1851–1924

Country	1851–1860	1861–1870	1871–1880	1881–1890	1891–1900	1901–1910	1913	1921–1924
	Average Annual Emigration Rates per 100,000 Population							
Austria-Hungary	—	—	29	106	161	476	611	105
Belgium	—	—	—	86	35	61	102	28
British Isles[1]	580	518	504	702	438	653	1,035	607
Denmark	—	—	206	394	223	282	321	178
France	11	12	15	31	13	14	15	4
Germany	—	—	147	287	101	45	40	97
Ireland[2]	—	—	661	1,417	885	698	679	298
Netherlands	50	59	46	123	50	51	40	52
Norway	242	576	473	952	449	833	419	357
Sweden	46	305	235	701	412	420	312	211
Switzerland	—	—	130	320	141	139	165	161
Finland	—	—	—	132	232	545	644	210
Italy	—	—	105	336	502	1,077	1,630	433
Portugal	—	190	289	380	508	569	1,296	321
Spain[1]	—	—	—	362	438	566	1,051	461
	Average Annual Number of Emigrants in Thousands							
Austria-Hungary	—	—	11.1	43.6	72.4	234,218	313.6	57.2
Belgium	—	—	—	5.0	2.2	4,321	7.6	2.1
British Isles:								
Passengers	164.1	157.1	167.9	255.9	174.3	284.1	469.6	287.5
Emigrants Proper							389.4	204.4
Denmark	—	—	3.9	8.2	5.2	7.3	8.8	5.8
France	3.9	4.6	5.7	12.0	5.1	5.3	5.7	1.6
Germany	—	—	62.6	134.2	52.7	27.4	25.8	58.1
Ireland[2]	—	—	35.0	70.0	40.6	30.9	29.8	13.2
Netherlands	1.6	2.0	1.7	5.2	2.4	2.8	2.3	3.6
Norway	3.6	9.8	8.5	18.7	9.5	19.1	9.9	9.5
Sweden	1.7	12.2	10.3	32.8	20.5	22.4	17.2	12.5
Switzerland	—	—	3.6	9.2	4.4	4.9	6.2	6.3
Finland	—	—	—	2.9	5.9	15.9	20.1	7.1
Italy	—	—	28.9	99.1	158.0	361.5	565.0	167.9
Portugal	—	7.8	13.1	18.5	26.6	32.4	77.3	19.4
Spain:								
Passengers	—	—	—	63.6	79.1	109.1	209.7	98.3
Emigrants Proper							151.0	76.7
Malta	—	—	—	—	—	—	1.6	1.7

Note:
[1] Passengers.
[2] For the period 1921–1924, Irish Free State for 1921–23.
—: Not available

SOURCE: Ferenczi and Willcox (1929).

the population growth in that region after about 1680 (from about 9,400 to about 70,000 in 1770) came from natural increase. Spain and Portugal did not encourage immigration into their Western Hemisphere colonies, and so the migration from Europe to those areas was relatively low. Most of the relatively small numbers of French, British, and Dutch persons who went to West Indian colonies migrated to work in the civil administration or military or to seek wealth from sugar cultivation. Many of them died there; some returned to Europe.

In the period after 1820 increasingly large numbers of migrants began to move from Europe to North America. Table 1 shows the overall flows and emigration rates from various European countries, and Table 2 gives the flows and immigration rates to Canada, the United States, Cuba, Argentina, and Brazil in the nineteenth and early twentieth centuries. Table 2 indicates that North America received about three-quarters of the migrants recorded for those five countries for the period 1821–1924. Even for the decade 1901–1910 North America was still

TABLE 2

Immigration to the Western Hemisphere, 1821–1924

Country	1821–1830	1831–1840	1841–1850	1851–1860	1861–1870	1871–1880	1881–1890	1891–1900	1901–1910	1913	1921–1924
	Average Annual Rates of Immigration per 100,000 Population										
Canada	—	—	—	992	832	548	784	488	1,676	3,840	941
United States	121	377	829	928	649	546	858	530	1,020	1,215	331
Cuba	—	—	—	—	—	—	—	—	1,184	1,541	1,358
Argentina	—	—	—	385	991	1,170	2,217	1,639	2,918	3,831	1,525
Brazil	—	—	—	—	—	204	411	723	338	771	197
	Average Annual Number of Immigrants (in Thousands)										
Canada	—	—	—	27.8	28.3	22.0	35.9	24.9	105.4	276.7	82.7
United States	13.6	56.5	166.8	253.6	227.2	242.4	485.2	368.4	856.7	1,117.7	349.6
Cuba	—	—	—	—	—	—	—	—	24.3	33.1	39.2
Argentina	—	—	—	5.0	16.0	26.1	84.1	64.8	176.4	302.0	145.6
Brazil	—	—	—	—	—	21.9	53.1	114.4	68.9	189.8	60.3

Note: — not available

SOURCE: Ferenczi and Willcox (1929).

the destination of over three-quarters (78%) of those migrants.

In the century 1820–1920, when the United States had relatively few restrictions on immigration, about 33.7 million persons were recorded as having entered the country, of whom 29.8 million (over 88%) were from Europe; this does not include some migrants who entered as first-class passengers, through minor ports, or across land borders (mostly from Canada earlier in the century). This is a gross flow because immigrant returns were not recorded until 1908. Even allowing for substantial return migration, these are huge numbers. In that period net immigration represented about a quarter of American population growth, up to a third in some decades (1850–1860 and 1900–1910).

During that century a dramatic shift took place in the composition of migrants by area of origin within Europe. In the first half (1820–1890) 82 percent of all migrants and 91 percent of European migrants came from Northern and Western Europe (Britain, Ireland, Scandinavia, France, the Low Countries, and Germany). However, a major change began in the 1880s. In the period 1891–1920 only 25 percent of all migrants (and 28% of European migrants) originated in northwestern Europe, whereas about 64 percent of all migrants (and some 72% of European migrants) were from regions in southern, central, and eastern Europe (Italy, Spain, Portugal, Austria-Hungary, and Russia and regions in the Bal-

kans). The course of these changes is shown in Table 3, which provides decade-by-decade numbers of migrants entering the United States by region of origin.

Migration in the Twentieth Century

This was the first great shift in migration to the United States, while the second was in and after the 1960s. Earlier in the twentieth century migration was restricted by the passage of the Literacy Test Act (1917), the Emergency Immigration Act (1921), and the Immigration and National Origins Act (1924), which established annual quotas of 2 percent of the share of a nationality group in the census of 1890. In 1929 the basis for the quotas was changed to the census of 1920, but the total number of immigrants was set not to exceed 150,000 per year, in contrast to the levels in excess of a million per year in the years just before World War I.

These quotas remained more or less the rule until 1965, when the passage of immigration reform legislation included liberal rules on family reunification and modified quotas for areas outside Europe. The Immigration Reform and Control Act of 1986 further modified the rules. Whereas total gross immigration to the United States was 8 million over the period from 1921 to 1960, of which 58 percent was from Europe, the inflow over the years 1961–1997 was 22 million, of which only 17 percent was from Europe. Flows from Asia, Africa, and especially Latin

TABLE 3

United States: Number of Immigrants by Region of Origin, 1821–1997; Canada: Total Number Immigrants, 1851–1990 (in Thousands)

Year	United States								Canada
	All Countries	Total Europe	North-western Europe	Central Europe	Eastern Europe	Southern Europe	Total Africa	All Other & Unknown	All Countries
1821–31	143.4	98.8	88.9	6.8	0.1	3.1	0.0	44.6	—
1831–40	599.1	495.7	337.3	152.8	0.3	5.3	0.0	103.4	—
1841–50	1,713.3	1,597.5	1,157.4	434.7	0.6	4.7	0.0	115.7	—
1851–60	2,598.2	2,452.7	1,479.7	952.8	0.5	19.6	0.2	145.3	243.7
1861–70	2,314.8	2,065.3	1,244.2	797.3	2.6	21.2	0.3	249.2	174.8
1871–80	2,812.2	2,272.3	1,352.2	804.1	39.6	76.3	0.4	539.6	343.1
1881–90	5,246.6	4,737.0	2,325.7	1,858.5	221.2	331.7	0.9	508.7	886.2
1891–19	3,687.6	3,559.0	1,138.3	1,194.6	521.8	704.2	0.4	128.2	339.1
1901–10	8,795.5	8,136.0	1,568.5	2,486.8	1,769.6	2,311.1	7.4	652.1	1,644.1
1911–20	5,735.8	4,376.6	853.5	1,050.4	1,012.5	1,460.2	8.4	1,350.8	1,712.3
1921–30	4,107.2	2,477.9	871.8	854.7	177.6	573.7	6.3	1,623.1	1,230.2
1931–40	528.4	348.3	83.9	162.7	14.5	87.1	1.8	178.4	158.6
1941–50	1,035.0	621.7	261.7	272.4	5.8	81.9	7.4	406.0	491.3
1951–60	2,515.5	1,328.3	445.4	600.6	10.1	272.2	14.2	1,172.9	1,574.8
1961–70	3,321.7	1,129.0	392.1	294.0	14.4	428.5	29.1	2,163.6	1,409.6
1971–80	4,493.3	800.4	214.2	164.2	56.3	365.6	80.8	3,612.2	1,440.0
1981–90	7,338.1	761.6	273.0	226.0	92.6	169.9	176.9	6,399.6	1,328.7
1991–97	6,944.6	1,039.1	239.7	269.6	355.2	112.0	242.7	5,725.4	—

Note: — not available

SOURCE: United States: U.S. Bureau of the Census, (1975). *Historical Statistics of the United States: Colonial Times to 1970.* Washington, DC: Government Printing Office, Series C89-119, and various INS reports. Canada: F. H. Leacy, ed., (1983). *Historical Statistics of Canada,* 2nd ed. Ottawa: Statistics Canada; and United Nations, (1991). *Demographic Yearbook 1989,* New York: United Nations.

America came to dominate migration into the United States.

Canada

The situation for Canada was somewhat different. Canada had experienced immigration rates comparable to or even higher than those for the United States from the middle of the nineteenth century to the 1920s (see Table 2). Regular and consistent data are not available before the 1850s. Although the gross flows were substantial, many of the migrants went on to the United States. For the four decades between 1861 and 1901 net immigration to Canada was actually negative as outflows to the United States outpaced gross inflows. Since that time the net inflow has been positive with the exception of the 1930s, which was also a decade of net outflow from the United States.

Since 1901 net migration has contributed between a quarter and a third of Canada's population growth. Regular statistics on migrants' countries of origin were not reported until 1956. Before that year, however, census data on population by country of birth reveal that most of the foreign born originated

in the British Isles: 60 percent in 1871, 55 percent in 1921, and 48 percent in 1951. The remainder came mostly from other European countries: 48 percent in 1871, 42 percent in 1921, and 49 percent in 1951. More recently, however, immigration in Canada shifted away from persons of European origin. In 1989, for example, only 31 percent of migrants were from Europe, the former Soviet Union, the United States, Australia, and New Zealand. Overall, about 13 million persons migrated into Canada between 1852 and 1990.

Among the sending countries, Table 1 indicates that the highest emigration rates out of Europe were in Ireland, Norway, Sweden, and Britain until about 1900, when Italy began to emerge as a major country of origin. In 1913 the highest emigration rates were from Italy, Portugal, Spain, Britain, and Ireland.

Motivation for and Composition of Migration

Most migrants were motivated by expectations of better wages and greater lifetime economic opportunities. Also, over the nineteenth century transportation costs fell with the advent of the railroad, better canal and river transportation, and iron- and steel-hulled propeller-driven steamships. In general cycles in migration over time to the United States were more closely attuned to economic conditions in the United States (a "pull") rather than to poor conditions in Europe (a "push"). Exceptions were the late 1840s with the potato famines and serious political unrest and the two world wars of the twentieth century.

In the nineteenth and early twentieth centuries migration tended to be selective for young single men. For example, the sex ratio of the foreign-born population in the United States was 124 males per 100 females in 1850 in contrast to 103 for the native white population; the corresponding sex ratios in 1910 were 129 and 103. Migration from Europe between 1820 and 1920 also tended to be weighted more toward unskilled and semiskilled workers.

There has been a substantial return migration back to Europe, especially after trans-atlantic travel became less costly. For example, in the 1908–1912 period it is estimated that the return rate was about 50 percent. Nonetheless, the effect of transatlantic migration on the population growth and ethnic composition of the United States and Canada has remained strong. In answering the ancestry question in the 1990 U.S. census, 73.1 percent of the population responding claimed European ancestry and another 8.2 percent claimed African-American ancestry.

See also: *African-American Population History; Famine in Ireland; Immigration Trends; Peopling of the Continents; Slavery, Demography of.*

BIBLIOGRAPHY

Ferenczi, Imre, and Walter F. Willcox. 1929. *International Migrations.* Vol. 1: *Statistics.* New York: National Bureau of Economic Research.

———. 1931. *International Migrations.* Vol. 2: *Interpretations.* New York: National Bureau of Economic Research.

Gemery, Henry A. 1984. "European Emigration to North America, 1700–1820: Numbers and Quasi-Numbers." *Perspectives in American History* (New Series) 1: 283–342.

Haines, Michael R., and Richard H. Steckel, eds. 2000. *A Population History of North America.* New York: Cambridge University Press.

Hatton, Timothy J., and Jeffrey G. Williamson. 1998. *The Age of Mass Migration: Causes and Economic Impact.* New York: Oxford University Press.

Jones, Maldwyn Allen. 1992. *American Immigration.* Chicago: University of Chicago Press.

Nugent, Walter. 1992. *The Great Transatlantic Migrations, 1870–1914.* Bloomington: Indiana University Press.

MICHAEL R. HAINES

TUBERCULOSIS

Tuberculosis (TB) is a disease that played a major role in mortality decline in developed countries, and it remains a major cause of morbidity (illness) and mortality in developing countries. Tuberculosis is caused by infection with the bacterium *Mycobacterium tuberculosis,* discovered in 1882 by the German scientist Robert Koch (1843–1910). The related germ *Mycobacterium africanum* also causes TB in sub-Saharan Africa, but even in this region *Mycobacterium tuberculosis* predominates. The bovine form of TB, caused by *Mycobacterium bovis,* can also be transmitted to humans, but pasteurization of milk has reduced the chances of this. In historical texts, TB is sometimes referred to as consumption or pthisis. A notable aspect of TB is that it is an infectious disease of adults, not primarily of youth or the elderly.

Both historically and at present, tuberculosis of the lungs, called pulmonary tuberculosis, accounts for the major portion of TB morbidity and mortality. But tuberculosis can assume many forms, including tuberculosis meningitis, Pott's disease (TB of the vertebral column), and infection of any internal organ. Tuberculosis is a notable example of the difference between infection and disease. Those infected with TB (i.e., harboring the bacilli in their bodies) may develop clinical signs of the disease either immediately or sometimes many years after the first infection. Person-to-person spread occurs when someone with active tuberculosis coughs, producing droplets containing bacilli, which can infect someone nearby. Not all active cases are contagious (i.e., produce bacilli when coughing), however.

A tuberculosis vaccine, BCG (bacille Calmette-Guerin), exists, but its protective efficacy against TB in adults is variable; it is more effective in protecting children. In some populations, vaccination with BCG also protects against leprosy, which is caused by *Mycobacterium leprae*, a cousin of the TB-causing bacterium. The first antibiotic against TB was streptomycin, first used widely in 1947. Before the introduction of antibiotics, TB patients were treated in specialized sanatoriums, reflecting the belief that fresh air was curative. While this is not true, the sanatoriums did diminish the chances of TB transmission by removing the infected from the general population.

Figure 1 shows age-specific death rates, by sex, for TB (all forms), for the United States. Death rates are shown for 1900, when TB as a cause of death was of overwhelming importance; for 1939, by which time TB mortality had declined markedly but was still fairly high; and for 1998, after a half-century of antibiotic use. The figure depicts four key facets of the demography of TB. First, the data highlight the radical decline of tuberculosis mortality during the twentieth century, with most of the drop occurring before the introduction of antibiotics. Second, they show that TB is as much a disease of middle age as it is of the young and the elderly. This is in contrast to most other infectious diseases of similar importance: Diseases such as measles or pertussis are concentrated in childhood; other diseases such as influenza cause morbidity at all ages, but mortality is typically concentrated at the youngest and oldest ages. Third, death rates for males and females exhibit distinctly different patterns, with males having on average significantly higher TB mortality rates, yet at some ages female mortality is higher. Finally, when TB death rates decline, they do not fall evenly at all ages; both the shape and the level of the age-mortality curves change. The figure is broadly representative of the decline of TB in other developed countries.

Worldwide, there is great variability across nations in TB death rates. In 2002, the following nations had the highest TB death rates in their respective world regions (deaths per 100,000 population): Zambia, 290; Djibouti, 164; Haiti, 137; Cambodia, 90; Indonesia, 68; Russia, 17. Estimates for other nations include: South Africa, 166; India, 46; China, 21; Mexico, 6; Portugal, 5; United Kingdom, 2; United States, 1. These are crude death rates, not adjusted for population age composition, but they do correct-

FIGURE 1

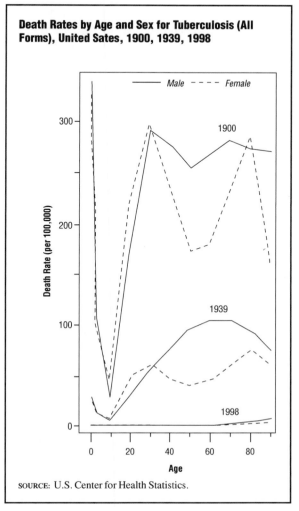

Death Rates by Age and Sex for Tuberculosis (All Forms), United Sates, 1900, 1939, 1998

SOURCE: U.S. Center for Health Statistics.

ly reflect overall tuberculosis disease burden in terms of deaths per capita. Compare these data to the following sample of historical estimates of pulmonary TB death rates (listed by country, year, and death rate per 100,000 population), in chronological order: England and Wales in 1861, 258; Japan in 1899, 127; United States in 1900, 168; Chile in 1904, 270; Australia in 1911, 67; Portugal in 1920, 125; England and Wales in 1921, 89; France in 1926, 143; and South Africa (nonwhite population) in 1951, 300.

Tuberculosis is central to the story of what was one of the great debates in population studies. The British epidemiologist Thomas McKeown (1911–1988) maintained that the standard of living in general, and improved nutrition in particular, played a more important role than did medicine and public-health measures in the historical decline of mortality. He used the case of TB in support of the thesis, noting, among other things, that much of the decline in TB mortality occurred before the introduction of antibiotics. While improved nutrition was certainly a factor in the decline of TB, a number of objections have been raised against McKeown's general argument. His analysis rested mainly on data from England and Wales, in which the decline of TB in the nineteenth century played an idiosyncratically large role in the decline of mortality overall, thus exaggerating the importance of the decline of TB. And the use of sanitariums to reduce TB transmission is best viewed as a public-health measure, not a factor reflecting improved living standards.

In the 1990s TB strains resistant to multiple antibiotics became a significant problem in several countries, most notably in the former Soviet Union—a worrisome development. In any region where such strains become prevalent, reversal of progress against TB cannot be ruled out. This is of particular concern in developing countries, where TB prevalence, transmission, and mortality are still relatively high and where historical declines have been much less rapid than in the advanced industrialized countries. Infection with human immunodeficiency virus (HIV) is a major risk factor for developing active TB disease, with initial HIV-positive status followed by TB exposure being more severe in most cases than the reverse order of infection. In regions where prevalence of TB and HIV/AIDS are both high, most notably in sub-Saharan Africa, HIV-TB coinfection is a strong contributing factor to the lack of progress in reducing tuberculosis morbidity and mortality.

See also: *AIDS; Diseases: Infectious; Health Transition; Mortality Decline; Mortality Reversals.*

BIBLIOGRAPHY

Dormandy, Thomas. 1999. *The White Death: A History of Tuberculosis.* London: Hambledon Press; New York: New York University Press.

Dye, Christopher, Suzanne Scheele, Paul Dolin, Vikram Pathania, and Mario C. Raviglione. 1999. "Global Burden of Tuberculosis: Estimated Incidence, Prevalence, and Mortality by Country." *Journal of the American Medical Association* 282: 677–686.

Espinal, Marcos A., Adalbert Laszlo, Lone Simonsen, Fadila Boulahbal, Sang Jae Kim, Ana Reniero, Sven Hoffner, Hans L. Rieder, Nancy Binkin, Christopher Dye, Rosamund Williams, and Mario C. Raviglione. 2001. "Global Trends in Resistance to Antituberculosis Drugs." *New England Journal of Medicine* 344: 1,294–1,303.

McKeown, Thomas. 1976. *The Modern Rise of Population.* London: Edward Arnold; New York: Academic Press.

Preston, Samuel H. 1990. "Sources of Variation in Vital Rates: An Overview." In *Convergent Issues in Genetics and Demography,* ed. Julian Adams, David A. Lam, Albert I. Hermalin, and Peter E. Smouse. New York: Oxford University Press.

ANDREW NOYMER

U

UNITED NATIONS, POPULATION ACTIVITIES OF

See *Population Organizations: United Nations System*

UNWANTED FERTILITY

The concept of unwanted births that is now so familiar in population studies has been in use for more than half a century. It plays an important role in the design and analysis of population policy. Early criticism of the concept—on both methodological and measurement grounds—has abated but not disappeared.

The origin of the concept is unclear, but its first systematic quantifiable use seems to have been by Pascal K. Whelpton and Clyde V. Kiser in the 1940s in the Indianapolis Study, formally known as *Social and Psychological Factors Affecting Fertility*. A classification of fertility planning status was developed in which the category termed "excess fertility" became the prototype for the later designation of unwanted fertility. This measure was further refined and applied in two subsequent U.S. fertility surveys.

Definition and Measurement

The basic idea is deceptively simple: Some births are wanted and some are not. The current professional usage of the concept is more complicated. The term *unwanted* means that no additional birth as recalled at the time of conception was wanted. In theory, this means that if preferences had prevailed, the birth

would never had occurred, a "non-event" of considerable importance for rates of fertility and population growth as well as for the individuals involved. A distinction is drawn between an unwanted and a mistimed birth—the latter being a birth that occurred earlier than preferred but that was nonetheless wanted, although at a later time. Both mistimed and unwanted births are frequently designated collectively as *unintended births* in contrast to births that were wanted and that occurred approximately at the desired time.

Reports on the planning status of births are based typically on interviews with women in sample surveys and involve memories about events in the past and about feelings that may be complex and highly ambivalent—and affected too by the typically uninvestigated preferences and power of the male partner. Hence there are inevitable questions about the meaning of responses and about the reliability of recall. In recent practice, the question is usually focused on births in the preceding five years but it is still subject to recall problems, especially the understandable tendency to rationalize an unwanted event as wanted. The typical question in the surveys is: "At the time you became pregnant with [name] did you want to become pregnant then, did you want to wait until later, or did you want no more children at all?" Recent evidence, based on reinterviews with women who were asked the same questions about the same births some time later indicates considerable inconsistency in responses—increasing with the duration of recall and biased in the (expected) direction of rationalizing unwanted as wanted births. Thus, it seems reasonable to assume that the level of unwanted fertility in a population based on this approach is underestimated. The magnitude of this underesti-

TABLE 1

Total Fertility Rate (TFR), Wanted Total Fertility Rate (WTFR), and Percent Unwanted: Selected Developing Countries, Late 1990s

	TFR	WTFR	Percent Unwanted
Bangladesh	2.3	2.2	4
India	2.8	2.1	25
Indonesia	2.8	2.4	14
Vietnam	2.3	1.9	17
Egypt	3.5	2.9	17
Turkey	2.6	1.9	27
Bolivia	4.2	2.5	40
Brazil	2.5	1.8	28
Haiti	4.7	2.7	42
Peru	2.8	1.8	36
Ghana	4.4	3.6	18
Nigeria	5.2	4.8	8
Ethiopia	5.9	4.9	17
Kenya	4.7	3.5	25
South Africa	2.9	2.3	21
Uganda	6.8	5.3	22
Zimbabwe	4.0	3.4	15

Note: Rates are based on the three years prior to each survey.

SOURCE: Demographic and Health Surveys conducted between 1997 and 2000.

trated. The estimates of unwanted fertility based on this procedure tend to be somewhat higher than those based on the first approach of asking about the wanted status directly but the ranking of countries is very similar for the two measures.

The estimates in the table show an average of about 20 percent of births to be unwanted. This provides some sense of the possible future fertility levels as birth control becomes more common and more effective.

Unwanted fertility presumably begins at a very low level in traditional societies, then increases as the small family norm develops, frequently outpacing the availability of contraception, and eventually diminishes as effective means to control fertility become widespread.

See also: *Contraceptive Prevalence; Family Planning Programs; Family Size Intentions.*

BIBLIOGRAPHY

Bankole, Akinrinola, and Charles F. Westoff. 1988. "The Consistency and Validity of Reproductive Attitudes: Evidence from Morocco." *Journal of Biosocial Science* 30: 439–455.

Bongaarts, John. 1997. "Trends in Unwanted Childbearing in the Developing World." *Studies in Family Planning* 28(4): 267–277.

Freedman, Ronald, Pascal K. Whelpton, and Arthur A. Campbell. 1959. *Family Planning, Sterility and Population Growth.* New York: McGraw-Hill.

Lightbourne, Robert E. 1985. "Individual Preferences and Fertility Behavior." In *Reproductive Change in Developing Countries: Insights from the World Fertility Survey,* eds. John Cleland and John Hobcraft. London: Oxford University Press.

Lightbourne, Robert E., and Alphonse MacDonald. 1982. "Family Size Preferences." In *WFS Comparative Studies.* Voorburg, The Netherlands: International Statistical Institute.

Osborn, Frederick. 1963. "Excess and Unwanted Fertility." *Eugenics Quarterly* 10(2): 59–72.

Westoff, Charles F., Robert G. Potter, Philip C. Sagi, and Elliot G. Mishler. 1961. *Family Growth in Metropolitan America.* Princeton, NJ: Princeton University Press.

mate is unknown but is certainly greater when the births are further back in time.

Wanted Fertility Rate

Another approach to the assessment of unwanted fertility is based on comparing the number of children desired with the number actually born. The now standard question to determine the desired number is: "If you could go back to the time you did not have any children and choose exactly the number of children to have in your whole life, how many would that be?" In order to preserve the current status of the measure, this approach estimates a synthetic Total Wanted Fertility Rate (TWFR) analogous to the familiar standard Total Fertility Rate (TFR) by subtracting from each age-specific component those births occurring in the recent past (usually three or five years) that exceed the total number wanted by the woman. The resulting TWFR is interpreted as the number of births women would have by the end of their childbearing years if at each age they experienced only the number of births wanted in the recent time period. The difference between the TWFR and the TFR is the component representing unwanted births. In Table 1 the results of such calculations for a sample of developing countries are illus-

Westoff, Charles F., and Norman B. Ryder. 1977. "Wanted and Unwanted Fertility in the United States." In *The Contraceptive Revolution*. Princeton, NJ: Princeton University Press.

Whelpton, Pascal K., and Clyde V. Kiser. 1950. "The Planning of Fertility." In *Social and Psychological Factors Affecting Fertility*. New York: Milbank Memorial Fund.

CHARLES F. WESTOFF

URBANIZATION

Urbanization is the process by which an increasing proportion of the population lives in urban areas. The level of urbanization is the proportion of population living in urban areas. Urbanization must be distinguished from urbanism, a term referring to the style of life usually found in large urban centers. A prior issue in studies of urbanization is to determine what constitutes an urban area. In medieval Europe or China, it may have been easy to distinguish between towns—generally tight-knit settlements, often fortified by walls to enable them to be protected from attack—and rural areas. This is no longer the case, either in the developed or the developing world, largely because transportation improvements have made it possible for people to reside a considerable distance from their place of work.

Defining Urbanization

Studies of urbanization are mostly forced to rely on the definitions of urban areas adopted in each country. These vary considerably, thus complicating inter-country comparisons. For example, some countries count all localities with 2,000 inhabitants or more as urban; others designate certain categories of administrative area as urban; still others use criteria such as population density and presence of certain urban facilities. Moreover, many areas, particularly those on the outskirts of large cities, are no longer easy to classify in terms of a rural-urban dichotomy. There is great diversity among areas defined as urban, and likewise among those defined as rural. It has been argued that a more complex breakdown of localities according to degree of urbanness or ruralness is needed.

Historical Trends

In 1950 only 30 percent of the world's population was living in urban areas. By 2000 nearly half the population—some 47 percent—was urban. The second half of the twentieth century was therefore a highly significant period in the history of world urbanization.

Some Western countries had already reached a 50 percent level of urbanization in the second half of the nineteenth century. The United Kingdom led the way, reaching this level in 1851. Australia reached it shortly after 1901, Germany in about 1910, and the United States in about 1918. Such countries therefore have a long history of predominantly urban populations. Japan, some Gulf states, and some Latin American countries have been predominantly urban since the middle of the twentieth century, but most of the Asian and African countries that are predominantly urban at the beginning of the twenty-first century reached that status only in the last two or three decades of the twentieth century.

This does not mean that there is no tradition of urbanization in Asia and Africa. In Egypt and China, for example, urban traditions go back to antiquity. In Southeast Asia, cities were substantial in pre-colonial times and at least one fifth of the population of the Malay Peninsula was urban in the sixteenth century. Even in sub-Saharan Africa, generally thought of as lacking in urbanization before colonization by Europeans, the Yoruba towns in Nigeria were already substantial in the nineteenth century.

Nevertheless, by the middle of the twentieth century, there were sharp differences in levels of urbanization between, on the one hand, the entire continents of Europe and North America and countries of European settlement such as Argentina, Chile, Uruguay, Australia, and New Zealand, and, on the other hand, Asia, Africa, and the rest of Latin America. In Asia, only Japan and a few city-states and oil producers had reached 50 percent urbanization; in Africa, only some countries of the western Sahara. The general situation by continent is shown in Table 1.

Over the second half of the twentieth century, Latin America experienced an exceptionally rapid pace of urbanization, reaching European and North American levels by 2000. Eastern Europe, which had lagged behind the rest of Europe at mid-century, similarly caught up. In both of these regions, the

TABLE 1

Proportion of the Population Living in Urban Areas and Rate of Urbanization by Major Area, Estimates and Projections, 1950–2030

	Proportion Urban (percent)				Annual Rate of Urbanization (percent)		
	1950	1975	2000	2030	1950-75	1975–2000	2000–30
Africa	14.7	25.2	37.9	54.5	2.18	1.65	1.21
Asia	17.4	24.7	36.7	53.4	1.41	1.60	1.25
Europe	52.4	67.3	74.8	82.6	1.01	0.42	0.33
Latin America*	41.4	61.2	75.3	83.2	1.58	0.83	0.33
North America	63.9	73.8	77.2	84.4	0.58	0.18	0.30
Oceania	61.6	71.8	70.2	74.4	0.61	-0.09	0.19
World	29.7	37.9	47.0	60.3	0.98	0.87	0.83

*Including the Caribbean
Note: The rate of urbanization is calculated as the rate of growth in the urban proportion of the population. Figures for 2030 are UN projections.

SOURCE: United Nations (2001).

level of urbanization increased by more than 30 percent over this period. The pool of rural population from which rural-urban migrants can be drawn has been declining since 1950 in Europe and North America; in Latin America the rural population leveled off around 1985. Many urban centers in countries such as the United Kingdom, Ukraine, Spain, and Italy are actually declining in population. Japan and the Republic of Korea are also reaching this point.

But urbanization was a universal phenomenon in the late twentieth century. Throughout Africa and Asia there was a marked increase in urban proportions, and an even larger increase in the growth of the urban population, since urbanization was occurring in a period of historically unprecedented rates of overall population growth. So far, Africa and Asia have only reached the levels of urbanization attained in Latin America in the 1940s. Whether they will follow the very rapid urbanization that Latin America experienced over the 1950s and 1960s will depend on many factors, particularly the pace and style of economic development.

Percentage of Population Living in Urban Agglomerations

The proportion of the total population residing in truly large cities differs greatly across countries, but in general has been rising over time. Table 2 presents information for selected countries on trends in proportions residing in urban agglomerations of 750,000 or more in 1995. Differing definitions of the term urban raise problems of comparability for per-

centages of populations in urban areas, but this is less of a problem with data on urban agglomerations.

Over the period from 1950 to 1975, the proportion of population living in large cities increased in all the countries shown except the United Kingdom. However, in the period from 1975 to 2000, Italy, Australia, and Argentina also registered a fall in the proportion of the population living in large cities. This appears to reflect the phenomenon of counter-urbanization—the tendency in recent decades for population to be redistributed down the urban hierarchy, either through the absolute decline of the largest cities or through the faster growth of smaller urban places. Many Asian and African countries have much lower proportions of their population living in urban agglomerations (many of them below 20%), but this proportion has almost everywhere been rising over time.

In some countries, the largest city dominates the urban hierarchy, in many cases containing more than half of the total urban population. Many medium size and small countries demonstrate such "urban primacy." In the most populous countries such as China, India, the United States, or Brazil, however, one city is never dominant.

What Causes Urbanization?

The underlying explanation for urbanization involves changing employment opportunities as structural change takes place in the economy. The industrial and service sectors greatly increase their share of output during the course of economic development. Changes in employment structure also reflect increasing productivity in agriculture, which releases agricultural labor. Primary industry's share of employment thus can fall from as high as 70 percent to well below 10 percent. Since employment in secondary and tertiary industries is more heavily concentrated in urban than in rural areas, these structural changes are associated with urbanization.

Factors Contributing to City Growth and Overall Urban Growth

In accounting terms, there are three sources of population growth in urban areas: natural increase of the population living in urban areas, net migration from rural to urban areas, and reclassification of areas formerly defined as rural to urban. Though these three sources are neatly differentiated if calculated over short periods of time (perhaps up to one year), there is in fact considerable interaction between them over the medium to long term. Migrants increase the stock of urban dwellers whose balance of births and deaths makes up the natural increase of the urban population. The natural increase of the rural population increases the "pool" from which rural-urban migrants are drawn. Finally, reclassification is normally based on changes in the characteristics of localities, and increase in population density resulting from natural increase and net migration is frequently a major factor in modifying the characteristics of particular localities toward a more "urban" nature.

Studies by Samuel H. Preston (1979) and Martin Brockerhoff (1999) have examined the factors contributing to city growth over the period from 1960 to 1970, and in developing countries between 1970 and 1990, respectively. In the earlier period, there was an almost perfect association between national population growth rates and city growth rates, suggesting that the same forces fuel population growth in cities and in the countries where they are located. In the more recent period, however, a 1 percent increase in total population growth raises the size of the city population by a lesser percentage, suggesting (in light of continuing increases in urbanization) that smaller urban centers not included in the analysis have been growing more rapidly. In both periods, faster growth of national GDP per capita raised city growth rates, presumably through stimulation of demand for labor in urban industries.

TABLE 2

Proportion of Total Population Living in Urban Agglomerations with 1995 Populations of 750,000 or More, Selected Countries, 1950, 1975, and 2000 (percent)

	1950	1975	2000
United States	33.6	40.0	42.0
United Kingdom	33.4	28.8	26.3
Italy	22.1	28.5	22.5
Germany	38.4	42.2	44.6
Australia	51.2	58.3	57.3
Argentina	36.4	43.9	43.8
Brazil	15.3	29.8	34.9
Peru	12.8	24.1	29.0
Japan	17.7	33.6	39.3
China	11.9	14.2	16.3
Philippines	7.9	12.8	15.9
India	6.0	8.2	11.7
Nigeria	2.3	7.3	13.6
Kenya	1.4	4.9	7.7
Egypt	16.0	22.3	22.9
Senegal	8.9	16.0	21.9

SOURCE: United Nations (2001), Table A.16.

Future Prospects

Virtually all of the world's population growth between 2000 and 2030 is expected to take place in urban areas. During that period the urban population is expected to increase by 2 billion (from 2.9 billion to 4.9 billion), the same number that will be added to the population of the world. The growth rate of the urban population will average 1.8 percent per annum, a rate sufficient to cause a doubling in 38 years. Globally, the population of rural areas will remain roughly constant, reflecting a decline in rural populations of the developed countries offset by a continuing (though slowing) rural growth in developing countries. From 2020 to 2025, the rural population of developing countries will begin a steady decline, repeating the experience of the developed countries since 1950.

The level of urbanization is expected to continue increasing, even in the highly urbanized developed countries, where the urban population is expected to reach 84 percent in 2030. But the rise is likely to be much more rapid in Africa and Asia, which will both pass the 50 percent urban mark before 2025. Between 2000 and 2030, the urban population in Africa is expected to increase from 38 percent to 55 percent, and in Asia from 37 percent to 53 percent. Given that population growth rates are higher in Africa than in any other continent, the substantial rise in urbanization expected over the period implies very rapid increases in Africa's urban population over this period—over 3.5 percent per annum from 2000 to 2010, 2.6 percent from 2025 to 2030.

Very large cities—those with populations over 10 million—will continue to increase their share of the world's population, but only to a level of about 5 percent by 2015. United Nations demographers in the past have tended to overestimate the growth of large cities, and in recent years have made substantial downward adjustments to the population projections for many of them. On the other hand, the populations living in the "mega-urban regions" surrounding these cities are both larger and growing more rapidly than the populations in the official urban agglomerations, because the most rapid growth tends to be in areas outside the agglomeration limits.

See also: *Cities, Demographic History of; Cities, Systems of; Internal Migration; Rural-Urban Balance; Suburbanization; World Population Growth.*

BIBLIOGRAPHY

Brockerhoff, Martin. 1999. "Urban Growth in Developing Countries: A Review of Projections and Predictions." *Population and Development Review* 25(4): 757–778.

Champion, Anthony. 2001. "Urbanization, Suburbanization, Counterurbanization and Reurbanization." In *Handbook of Urban Studies,* ed. Ronan Paddison. London: Sage.

Jones, Gavin W., and Pravin Visaria, eds. 1997. *Urbanization in Large Developing Countries.* Oxford: Clarendon Press.

Kelley, Allen C., and Jeffrey G. Williamson. 1984. *What Drives Third World City Growth? A Dynamic General Equilibrium Approach.* Princeton, NJ: Princeton University Press.

Preston, Samuel H. 1979. "Urban Growth in Developing Countries: A Demographic Reappraisal." *Population and Development Review* 5(2): 195–215.

Reid, Anthony. 1993. *Southeast Asia in the Age of Commerce 1450–1680. Volume Two: Expansion and Crisis.* New Haven: Yale University Press.

Skinner, G. William, ed. 1977. *The City in Late Imperial China.* Stanford, CA: Stanford University Press.

Tarver, James D. 1994. *Urbanization of Africa: A Handbook.* Westport, CT: Greenwood Press.

United Nations. 1980. *Patterns of Urban and Rural Population Growth.* New York: United Nations.

United Nations, Department of Economic and Social Affairs, Population Division. 2001. *World Urbanization Prospects: The 1999 Revision.* New York: United Nations.

Weber, Adna. 1963 [1899]. *The Growth of Cities in the Nineteenth Century.* Ithaca, NY: Cornell University Press.

GAVIN W. JONES

V

VALUE OF LIFE, ECONOMIC

Many public sector investment and regulatory decisions have significant effects—typically, but not invariably, beneficial—on the safety of human life. It therefore follows that if a society's scarce resources are to be allocated efficiently and to greatest advantage, then that society requires some means of associating explicit monetary values with safety, and costs with risk. This allows safety effects to be weighed against the other costs and benefits of the investment or regulation, or against other expenditures affecting public welfare.

Plainly, if such explicit monetary values of safety and costs of risk are not applied, it is virtually inevitable that there will be a degree of randomness in the way in which scarce resources are utilized. A measured, strategic approach to safety and risk is optimal.

Defining Monetary Values of Safety

Over the years a number of different approaches have been proposed for defining and estimating values of safety and costs of risk. Two of these deserve serious consideration: the so-called *gross output* (or *human capital*) approach and the *willingness-to-pay* approach.

Under the gross output approach, the cost of the premature death of an individual is treated as the sum total of the monetary value of the individual's future output that is extinguished as the result of his or her premature demise. In some cases advocates of the gross output approach recommend the addition of a more or less arbitrary allowance for the pain, grief, and suffering of the victim and his or her surviving dependents and relatives. In turn, the value of preventing premature death is treated as the cost avoided. As an example of the sort of figures that emerge under the gross output approach, the British Department of Transport's most recent gross output-based cost of an average fatality was £180,330 in 1985 prices (roughly $270,000), of which about 28 percent was an allowance for pain, grief, and suffering.

To the extent that it effectively treats human beings as little more than pieces of productive capital equipment, it is not surprising that the gross output approach has been the subject of fairly vigorous criticism. (It was, in fact, abandoned by the Department of Transport in 1988 in favor of the willingness-to-pay approach discussed below.)

It has been argued that most people value safety *not* because of a desire to preserve current and future productive potential, as the gross output approach implies, but rather because of an aversion to the prospect of premature death per se. This suggests that values of safety and costs of risk should be defined in such a way as to reflect people's pure preferences for safety. But to do so requires some means of measuring the extent of a person's preference—and more particularly the strength of that preference—for safety.

A natural measure of a person's strength of preference for a good or service is the maximum amount that he or she would be willing to pay for it. This sum is a clear indication of what the good or service is worth to the person, relative to other potential objects of expenditure. Moreover, since willingness to pay is conditioned by ability to pay (i.e., income), the sum concerned takes account of the resource constraints that society inevitably faces.

Under what has come to be known as the willingness-to-pay (WTP) approach to the valuation of safety, the monetary value of a safety improvement is defined as the aggregate amount that the group of people affected by the improvement would be willing to pay for the (typically very small) reductions in individual risk that result from the improvement. For example, suppose that a group of 100,000 individuals are each afforded a 1 in 100,000 reduction in the risk of premature death during the forthcoming year, thereby preventing one premature death, on average. (This is referred to as the prevention of one "statistical death" during the period concerned.) Suppose, furthermore, that individuals in the affected group would, on average, each be willing to pay a maximum of $10 for the safety improvement. Aggregated over the group of 100,000 individuals, total willingness to pay would be $1 million; this sum is referred to as the *value of preventing one statistical fatality* (VPF) or the *value of statistical life* (VOSL). Correspondingly, costs of risk are defined in terms of the aggregate amount that affected individuals would be willing to accept as compensation for (typically small) increases in the risk.

It is important to appreciate that, defined in this way, the VPF is not the price of life in the sense of a sum that any one individual would accept as compensation for the certainty of his or her immediate death: For most people, no finite sum would suffice for that purpose.

Estimating Monetary Values of Safety

How are willingness-to-pay-based values of safety to be estimated in practice? Since the early 1970s, an extensive literature has developed on this subject. For a detailed survey see Michael Jones-Lee (1989), Chapter 2, or W. Kip Viscusi (1993). The body of literature broadly divides into two approaches, which can be viewed as complementary rather than competing.

In the first approach, researchers seek to identify situations in which people actually do trade off wealth or income against risk, as in labor markets where riskier occupations can be expected to command clearly identifiable wage premiums, and safer ones carry corresponding discounts. The two main difficulties with this approach are that wage rates depend on many other factors besides job risk, so that it is necessary to control for the effects of these other factors in identifying the pure wealth-risk tradeoff.

A second and arguably more fundamental problem is that workers may have only a limited knowledge of the job risks that they actually face.

By contrast the second approach, known as *contingent valuation,* aims to ask a representative sample of the population more or less directly about their willingness to pay for improved safety or willingness to accept compensation for increased risk. While this approach has the advantage of getting directly to the wealth-risk tradeoff, it does rely upon the somewhat debatable assumption that people are able to think rationally about hypothetical situations, and respond in an unbiased manner to relatively unfamiliar questions.

Under the contingent valuation approach, willingness-to-pay-based values for the prevention of a statistical fatality in the British case are in the region of £1–2 million ($1.5–3.0 million). (The Department of Transport's figure as of 2002 is £1.14 million at 2000 prices.) The labor market wage premium-for-risk approach yields values that are not grossly dissimilar but typically larger.

Conclusion

Any attempt to place an explicit monetary value on human life raises a variety of difficult ethical and empirical questions. Some of these are discussed in detail in the works of John Adams (1995) and John Broome (2002). Nonetheless, it is a fact of life that safety improvements resulting in the avoidance of statistical death are rarely costless; careful public sector decisions in this area must confront these issues.

See also: *Disease, Burden of; Risk.*

BIBLIOGRAPHY

Adams, John. 1995. *Risk.* London: UCL Press.

Broome, John. 2002. *Weighing Lives.* Oxford: Oxford University Press.

Jones-Lee, Michael. 1989. *The Economics of Safety and Physical Risk.* Oxford: Blackwell.

Viscusi, W. Kip. 1993. "The Value of Risks to Life and Health." *Journal of Economic Literature* 31: 1,912–1,946.

M.W. JONES-LEE

VALUES AND DEMOGRAPHIC BEHAVIOR

The use of values to explain demographic behavior, or change in behavior, has been controversial among demographers. Some argue that individual behavior is driven by values. This position considers values to be an essential part of the micro-level processes that connect macro forces with individual action. Thus behavior cannot adequately be explained without knowledge of the underlying values that motivate individuals to make particular decisions. Others argue that values are really part of the behavior that needs explanation, so invoking values as an explanation is not useful. For example, it is circular to say that fertility is high in a population because individuals value large families. The underlying disagreement revolves around the question of whether values arise out of economic, political, and social institutions, or whether values, at least to some extent, are autonomous from institutional contexts and thus have an independent effect on behavior.

Defining Values

What are values? A useful discussion of values must begin with a clear understanding of what this term means. There is some confusion, however, because the term is used in various ways by different authors. Sometimes the term is used simply as a synonym for preferences or attitudes. For example, preferences for sons over daughters or negative attitudes toward women working in the labor force are sometimes referred to as values that influence fertility behavior. Sometimes a norm (e.g., women should not choose to be childless) is equated to a value. A more restrictive definition of values states that they are "evaluative concepts that are internal, durable, and general" (Casterline, 1999, p. 358). This approach emphasizes that values are strongly-held general principles that are applicable to a wide range of situations, and that particular values may be linked to form value systems. When values are conceptualized as unobservable, internal principles, researchers face the challenge of how to measure them.

Fertility

There is little agreement among demographers about the role that values play in fertility behavior. This is evident in the essays on the topic assembled in the edited volume, *Dynamics of Values in Fertility Change* (Leete 1999). In the general literature on theories of fertility change, three different positions can be identified.

One argument emphasizes the importance of changes in social and economic institutions as the catalyst for changes in fertility. For example, John Caldwell argues that the rise of compulsory education in the nineteenth century increased the cost of children. More recently, when educational and work organizations instituted policies allowing women to participate on an equal footing with men, opportunity costs of bearing children increased and existing gender roles in the family were challenged. In both the historical and recent contexts, individuals responded to the social changes by having fewer children *and* by shifting values related to children. In other words, the same forces that affect fertility affect values, and so it is more reasonable to view values as a rationalization of behavior than a cause of that behavior.

A second position argues that underlying values are important because they influence how fertility behavior responds to changes in social and economic institutions. Indeed, values may not need to change in order to influence fertility patterns. For example, in some situations it appears that an effort to maintain existing values in the face of social change produces declining fertility. Also, cultural differences in values could explain why similar social changes do not have the same impact on fertility behavior in all societies. In a 2000 study, Peter McDonald suggests that social changes providing women opportunities approximately equal to those of men has led to greater fertility reduction in southern Europe than in northern Europe because of regional differences in preference for traditional, male-dominated family systems. Surprisingly, fertility is lower in countries preserving traditional family values because of the incompatibility this creates between families and other modern institutions.

The third position argues that value changes play a direct and critical role in changing fertility behavior. The way that this is seen to occur is through cultural diffusion. As secular individualism, liberalism, and freedom from religious authority are imported to a society that does not traditionally hold these values, individuals begin to alter their fertility behavior. High fertility cannot be maintained in a society when individuals adopt values that fail to support this behavior.

Mortality

The clearest example of a value that may affect mortality patterns is the cultural value of preferring sons over daughters. In most populations, age-specific mortality rates are higher for males than females at every age. However, in South Asia death rates are higher for girls than for boys. In their 1998 article, for example, Fred Arnold, Minja Kim Choe, and T. K. Roy note that in India in the 1980s and early 1990s, child mortality (ages one to four) was 43 percent higher for girls than boys. The most plausible explanation for this exceptional mortality pattern in South Asia is the strong preference for (or value attributed to) sons over daughters. Studies suggest that under these conditions daughters experience higher death rates than sons because they receive less effort in disease and accident prevention and less medical attention when sick. In addition to mortality, a strong preference for male offspring sometimes leads to sex-selective abortion and/or female infanticide. When this occurs, the sex ratio at birth (normally about 105 males to 100 females) can be greatly distorted. (Rates well exceeding 110 males to 100 females have been reported recently in China and South Korea, and in some states in India).

Migration

As in fertility theories, values enter the migration literature primarily when the focus is on micro-level models of decision-making. The most explicit formulation of a theoretical model of migration focusing on values is the *value-expectancy model,* presented by Gordon F. De Jong and James T. Fawcett in 1981. The underlying assumption of this model is that individuals are motivated by personal goals and values, and that they rationally calculate how best to achieve them. Multiple values may be involved, each requiring a subjective assessment of wellbeing attained through migration or nonmigration. In deciding whether or not to undertake a particular move, an individual will make a "cognitive calculus" involving the expectancy that the move would produce a net gain in valued outcomes. Little empirical migration research has utilized the value-expectancy model, perhaps because of the complexity of operationalizing and measuring all of the relevant values and collecting data on subjective expectations. However, aspects of this approach are included in studies of migration that investigate place preferences of individuals.

Conclusion

Individuals in modern society tend to believe that they have significant freedom to choose their own life course path, and they have no difficulty in invoking values to explain their choices. Social scientists generally have been skeptical of these explanations, arguing that powerful, unrecognized social forces constrain and direct the behavior of individuals. But many social scientists also want to provide a place for human agency in their theories of behavior. Do individuals choose values that that then independently influence their demographic behavior? Or, are values byproducts of the social conditions that shape the behavior? A lively debate regarding the place of values in explaining demographic behavior persists among population researchers.

See also: *Culture and Population; Diffusion in Population Theory; Fertility Transition, Socioeconomic Determinants of; Gender Preferences for Children; Quetelet, Adolphe; Second Demographic Transition.*

BIBLIOGRAPHY

Arnold, Fred, Minja Kim Choe, and T. K. Roy. 1998. "Son Preference, the Family-Building Process and Child Mortality in India." *Population Studies* 52: 301–315.

Caldwell, John C. 1980. "Mass Education as a Determinant of the Timing of Fertility Decline." *Population and Development Review* 6: 225–255.

Casterline, John B. 1999. "Conclusions." In *Dynamics of Values in Fertility Change,* ed. Richard Leete. New York: Oxford University Press.

De Jong, Gordon F., and James T. Fawcett. 1981. "Motivations for Migration: An Assessment and a Value-Expectancy Research Model." In *Migration Decision Making: Multidisciplinary Approaches to Microlevel Studies in Developed and Developing Countries,* ed. Gordon F. De Jong and Robert W. Gardner. New York: Pergamon Press.

Leete, Richard, ed. 1999. *Dynamics of Values in Fertility Change.* New York: Oxford University Press.

Lesthaeghe, Ron. 1995. "The Second Demographic Transition in Western Countries: An Interpretation." In *Gender and Family in Industrialized Countries,* ed. Karen Oppenheim Mason and An-Magritt Jensen. Oxford: Clarendon Press.

McDonald, Peter. 2000. "Gender Equity in Theories of Fertility." *Population and Development Review* 26: 427–439.

PETER UHLENBERG

VERHULST, PIERRE-FRANÇOIS

(1804–1849)

Belgian mathematician and demographer Pierre-François Verhulst, best known for the conceptualization and specification of the logistic curve, was born in Brussels to wealthy parents. Adolphe Quetelet (1796–1874), the Belgian mathematician and demographer, was first Verhulst's mathematics teacher at the Royal Atheneum, then his professor at the University of Ghent, where Verhulst also earned a doctoral degree in mathematics after just three years of study. Verhulst was a highly versatile man who wrote Latin poetry and even drafted a constitution for the Papal States when he was in Italy, a country that eventually expelled him for that reason. Back in Brussels, Verhulst was invited to join the Academie Royale, of which Quetelet was also a member. Verhulst occupied his chair at the academy in 1848, only one year before his death at age 45.

Verhulst's work in demography was essentially completed by 1833. Through Quetelet, he had been invited to present a mathematical formulation of T. R. Malthus's theories. However, Verhulst was convinced that the geometric or exponential growth of population would be curtailed by constraining factors before Malthus's "positive checks" (emigration, excess mortality due to famine or declining living standards) could limit them. That, in itself, was a departure from Malthus's work. Verhulst also believed that the strength of the curtailing factors would increase in a proportional way to the population expansion itself. To elucidate this, Verhulst needed to introduce a hitherto unknown negative function into the overall formula. The result of the work was a demonstration that any population growth rate would essentially follow a bell-shaped curve, starting from zero, steadily increasing to a maximum, and declining once again to zero in a fashion symmetrical to the positive growth phase. The population stock then evolves according to the elongated S-curve, which has a point of inflection at the maximal value of the growth rate, and then levels off at a new but higher plateau, at which point the growth rate declines to zero. Verhulst checked his theory empirically against population data for France, Belgium, Essex, England, and Russia. Quetelet, however, was not convinced by his student since he knew of no counterpart in physics. After the publication of Verhulst's theory, the logistic curve was forgotten until its rediscovery by the American biometrician Raymond Pearl and demographer Lowell J. Reed in 1921, and British statistician G. Udny Yule's 1925 acknowledgment of the significance of Verhulst's finding of almost a century earlier.

From the 1920s onward, many applications for the theory were found in a wide variety of fields. The logistic curve became one of the essential cornerstones of world systems modeling. It also proved to provide good descriptions of certain diffusion processes, especially of those based on the principles of contagion. Diseases, technical novelties, new ideas and rumors would all grow within a virgin population and reach a maximum, but each would eventually encounter resistance and burn out, or be challenged by a better invention or concept. In the field of mathematics, Verhulst's logistic curve was rediscovered in 1975 by two German physicists who determined that it was one of the essential formulas in the mathematics of fractals.

In the early twenty-first century, Quetelet's contributions to demography have largely faded, while those of Verhulst have steadily increased in importance. However, he is still rarely cited by demographers as the inventor of the logistic curve or the contagion model of diffusion.

See also: *Demography, History of; Pearl, Raymond; Quetelet, Adolphe; Diffusion in Population Theory; Projections and Forecasts, Population.*

BIBLIOGRAPHY

SELECTED WORKS BY PIERRE-FRANÇOIS VERHULST.

Verhulst, Pierre-François. 1838. "Notice sur la loi que la population suit dans son accroissement." *Correspondances mathématiques et physiques* 10: 113.

———. 1845. "Recherches mathématique sur la loi d'accroissement de la population." *Mémoires de l'Académie Royale des Sciences et des Lettres de Bruxelles* 18: 1–38.

————. 1847. "Deuxième mémoire sur la loi d'accroissement de la population." *Mémoire de l'Académie Royale des Sciences, des Lettres et des Beaux Arts de Belgique.* 20: 1–38.

SELECTED WORKS ABOUT PIERRE-FRANÇOIS VERHULST.

Kint, Jos. 1990. "Verhulst, Pierre-François: wiskundige en demograaf." *Nationaal Biografisch Woordenboek* 13: 822–827.

Yule, G. Udny. 1925. "Verhulst." *Journal of the Royal Statistical Society* 88: 1.

R. LESTHAEGHE

VITAL STATISTICS

In population studies the term *vital events* generally includes births, deaths, marriages, divorces, fetal deaths (stillbirths), and induced terminations of pregnancy (abortions). In a majority of countries most, if not all, of these events are recorded through the government's civil registration system, which creates a permanent record of each event.

Vital records have two primary uses. First, they are personal legal documents that are needed by citizens to prove the facts surrounding the event (e.g., age, identity). Second, vital statistics—the data derived from these administrative records—constitute one of the most widely used statistical data systems in the world. Vital statistics form the basis of fundamental demographic and epidemiologic measures and are used in planning and operating health programs, commercial enterprises ranging from life insurance to the marketing of products for infants, and a wide range of government activities.

Early Registration of Vital Events

An early form of the registration of vital events in Western countries were baptisms, burials, and weddings typically recorded in church registers. The first systematic parish register system was established in Sweden in 1608, and similar systems were soon established in Quebec (1610), Finland (1628), and Denmark (1646). However, consolidation of records for entire countries was not attempted until the eighteenth century in France and the early nineteenth century in the United Kingdom.

The Massachusetts Bay Colony was the first government derived from the European tradition to establish a secular vital registration system, requiring that the actual events rather than the ceremonies be recorded and that registration be done by government officials rather than by the clergy. In 1804 France, as part of the Napoleonic Code, made the state responsible for recording births, deaths, and marriages and prescribed who should record each event and what the record should include.

The registration of births, marriages, and deaths in the United States began with registration laws enacted by the Grand Assembly of Virginia in 1632 and the General Court of the Massachusetts Bay Colony in 1639. Connecticut, Plymouth, and eventually the other colonies followed suit. Little or no statistical use was made of these records. They were regarded as statements of fact essential to the protection of individual rights, especially rights relating to the ownership and distribution of property.

Modern Use of Vital Records

The impetus for using vital records as the basis of a statistical data system came from the realization that records of births and deaths constituted a source of information about the condition of the human population. The modern origin of vital statistics can be traced to the analysis of the English Bills of Mortality published by the pioneer demographer John Graunt (1620–1674), in 1662. Graunt's work was followed by that of Edmund Halley (1656–1742), mathematician and astronomer, who in 1693 constructed the first scientific life expectancy table. Over time the analysis of mortality data by cause of death became an important source of information that was used in the control of epidemics and to support sanitary reform.

The United States Constitution, adopted in 1787, provided for a decennial census but not a national vital registration system. Thus, legal authority for the registration of vital events was left to the states. The geographic scope of the U.S. registration areas expanded rapidly, but it was not until the 1930s that it included all the states and the District of Columbia. When the U.S. Census Bureau became a permanent agency of the federal government in 1902, the enabling legislation authorized the bureau to obtain annually copies of records filed in the vital statistics offices of states and cities that had adequate death registration systems and to publish data from those records. This marked the beginning of the National Vital Statistics System. Ten states and cities provided death records to the Census Bureau in 1902. In 1915 birth registration was added to the system, and by 1933 all states were registering live births and deaths with acceptable event coverage and providing the required data.

In 1946 responsibility for collecting and publishing national vital statistics in the United States was transferred from the Census Bureau to the Public Health Service, first in the National Office of Vital Statistics and later (1960) in the National Center for Health Statistics (NCHS), which is now part of the Centers for Disease Control and Prevention, Department of Health and Human Services.

International Statistics

Vital statistics are one of the few data systems that are generally available throughout the world. The United Nations and the World Health Organization have led efforts to standardize registration practices, definitions, and statistical measurement. Most industrialized nations have vital statistics systems that in scope and accuracy equal or exceed that of the United States. In addition, most developing countries have at least a rudimentary vital statistics system. Although there are intercountry variations, in general countries adhere to similar registration principles and statistical measures. These data, ideally in combination with census statistics, are widely used to make international comparisons of life expectancy, cause-specific mortality, infant deaths, and the like. Vital statistics also are used to monitor population growth through measures such as total fertility rates. The United Nations publishes many international vital statistics comparisons in its *Demographic Yearbook,* which has been issued annually since 1948.

Sources of Vital Statistics

The best source of vital statistics is a complete civil registration system. In countries in which data from civil registration do not exist or are deficient, other demographic data collection methods may be used to gather information on the incidence of vital events and to estimate vital statistics. These methods include population censuses, demographic sample surveys, and sample registration areas.

A *population census* is a complete enumeration of the population of a defined area with reference to a specified date. If the census includes appropriate questions (e.g., births and deaths in each household during the past year), the data can be used to estimate vital rates in the recent past.

A *sample survey* collects more detailed information than does a census, but from only a portion of the population. Thus, although it provides added depth, rare events may be missed and reliability may be diminished because of sampling errors.

In general population censuses and sample surveys are less desirable sources of vital statistics because they typically do not provide the detail available from a civil registration system. In addition, the methods used to estimate vital statistics rates from these data sources are based on assumptions about and approximations of the relationships between various characteristics of the population. Thus, they may be less useful for the analysis of trends and detailed statistics. Furthermore, data from these sources cannot serve the important legal purposes of administrative records from a civil registration system.

In countries where civil registration is not fully developed *sample registration* may be used to register vital events and estimate vital rates. Events are registered in a specific area of the country on a continuous basis. If it is gradually expanded, a sample registration system can evolve into national civil registration. The main drawback of a sample registration system is that it does not provide vital rates for local areas outside the sample area.

See also: *Census; Demographic Surveillance Systems; Demographic Surveys, History and Methodology of; Farr, William; Graunt, John; Population Registers.*

BIBLIOGRAPHY

Hetzel, Alice M. 1997. *U.S. Vital Statistics System.* Hyattsville, MD: National Center for Health Statistics.

United Nations, Department of Economic and Social Affairs. 2000. *Demographic Yearbook 1998: Fiftieth Issue.* New York: United Nations.

United Nations, Department of Economic and Social Affairs. 2001. *Principles and Recommendations for a Vital Statistics System, Revision 2.* New York: United Nations.

INTERNET RESOURCE.

National Vital Statistics System and Vital Statistics of the United States. 2002. <http://www.cdc.gov/nchs/nvss.htm>.

MARY ANNE FREEDMAN
JAMES A. WEED

W

WAR, DEMOGRAPHIC CONSEQUENCES OF

War ranks last on the political economist T. R. Malthus's list of the chief checks to population growth, following "vicious customs with respect to women, great cities, unwholesome manufactures, luxury" and "pestilence" (Malthus 1970, p. 103). Two centuries later, war appears as problematic as the other items on the list. Its demographic effects are hardly susceptible to scientific analysis.

Definition of War

There are obvious problems with definitions. What is war? When military historians and some archaeologists hypothesize that warfare is as old as the human race, they lump together all forms of conflict involving more than a single pair of combatants. Most scholars have abandoned the search for a definition based on social or technological organization, preferring instead to define wars in terms of casualties suffered. Thus political scientist David Wilkinson's 1980 reworking of Lewis Richardson's register of wars since 1820 lists 315 conflicts in which the overall death toll exceeded 300. The mortality cutoff line is 1,000 in successive editions of Peace Studies specialist Ruth Sivard's *World Military and Social Expenditures* that deal with wars since 1900. Using an alternative methodology the historical anthropologist Lawrence Keeley searched cross-cultural indices for evidence of conflict between *bands and tribes.*

A related problem is that ideas about war and records of war before the nineteenth century derive almost entirely from Europe and the Near East. Gilbert and Sullivan's "Modern Major General" was very much the model in his ability to "quote the fights historical, from Marathon to Waterloo in order categorical" (*Pirates of Penzance,* Act I). Wars elsewhere barely figured in scholarly studies. Evidence about warfare and its effects on population in the pre-Columbian Americas, Asia, and Africa is scant and unreliable. A typical example is the claim that a million people perished as the result of wars unleashed by the Zulu king Shaka in the 1820s—a figure cited in the political theorist Hannah Arendt's influential *Origins of Totalitarianism* (1951). The origin of that statistic was a casual remark made by an English hunter-trader in the late 1830s who was hardly in a position to judge. His unsubstantiated estimate probably exceeded the total population of Southeast Africa at that time. Widespread warfare was undoubtedly associated with the growth of the Atlantic slave trade from Africa, but as no statistically-inclined observers were present to document them, the conduct, extent, and effects of the wars waged in the African interior can only be guessed.

It is difficult to generalize even about wars in Europe because their nature changed so much from era to era. The migrations of the Huns, Wends, and Vikings led to wars that were very different from the campaigns of the Roman legions. Apart from the Crusades, medieval warfare involved small numbers of irregular cavalry and ragtag assemblages of archers. The wars of religion that raged for long periods on the European continent during the sixteenth and seventeenth centuries were destructive largely because the armies lived off the land, commanding food from and imposing other levies on hapless civilian populations. Eighteenth and nineteenth century European wars weighed much less heavily on noncombatants. Twentieth-century strategists rediscovered the merits of deliberately targeting large populations with conventional and nuclear bombs.

The demographic effects of war naturally vary with the organization, conduct, and objectives of the conflict. In feudal Europe the objective of most wars was the acquisition of fertile land that was populated by a settled workforce. Any campaign that killed agricultural laborers or frightened them into fleeing the district was counterproductive. Precolonial wars in southern Africa, before the advent of the slave trade, mainly aimed at the capture of cattle, resulting in relatively low levels of human mortality. Naval warfare rarely killed anyone apart from sailors and officers. In wars waged by well-equipped professional armies, deaths in battle are concentrated among young single men. The effects of their removal from the population on the birth rate seem not to have been very significant before the twentieth century. Prior to the nineteenth century in Europe rises in general prosperity were associated with increased fertility. Thus Malthus was not surprised that "the fertile province of Flanders, which has been so often the seat of the most destructive wars, after a respite of a few years, has appeared always as fruitful and as populous as ever. Even the Palatinate lifted up its head again after the execrable ravages of Louis the Fourteenth" (Malthus 1970, p. 107). The huge losses suffered in the major battles of World War I led European élites to speak of a "lost generation" of young men whose sweethearts remained unmarried, but it is difficult to document the assertion. At a time when fertility was declining due to increased use of birth control, the spread of education, and shifts from country to city-living, the effect of the loss of World War I soldiers on overall population is a matter for surmise.

The demographic effects of war are better documented for the twentieth century than for any previous era. Body counts before the nineteenth century cannot be relied on. In the twentieth century deaths among serving military and naval personnel in Europe and North America were painstakingly recorded in archives. So many of the dead were remembered by name on monuments that the *unknown soldier* for the first time became an object of public solicitude. Unquestionably, the high water mark of state-sponsored killing was reached in the first half of the twentieth century. While estimates range widely, plausible sizes of the military and civilian death toll would be around 8.5 million in World War I and 40 million in World War II.

Collateral Effects of War on Demographics

A difficulty facing the analyst seeking to quantify the demographic effects of war is calculating mortality associated with war but not directly caused by losses on the field of battle. War has often created conditions conducive to famine and epidemic disease. Sivard follows the common practice of including all war-related deaths associated with twentieth-century conflicts in the mortality rate. Since war itself is defined as a conflict generating more than a thousand deaths, this statistical practice increases the number of wars. Famines and epidemics associated with the failed Biafran secession from Nigeria, the Sudanese civil war, and India's intervention in Bangladesh are estimated to have cost in total 4.5 million lives. Some scholars class the 1919 influenza pandemic as a consequence of World War I. World War II made it possible for the Nazi regime to target Jews, gypsies, and other populations beyond German borders in a wholesale fashion that would have been impossible in peacetime. Another problem in calculating mortality statistics for the twentieth century is raised by factors such as the holocaust deaths in Germany during World War II. Should losses in campaigns conducted against internal forces be counted as death in war? Civil wars involving organized armies (for example, the United States, Russian, and Spanish civil wars) figure on all lists.

But more problematic are deaths arising from state-sponsored violence against internal enemies, such Stalin's campaigns against the kulaks and Crimean Tartars, Mao's Cultural Revolution, and the killings in Cambodia under Pol Pot. R. J. Rummel (2000) calls such campaigns *democide*. By excluding interstate wars, and adding up the deaths caused principally by totalitarian regimes, he concludes that "nearly 170 million people probably have been murdered by governments in this [twentieth] century; over four-times those killed in combat in all international and domestic wars during the same years." A related issue concerns conflicts that pit unorganized ethnic groups against each other as was the case during the communal violence at the time of British India's partition in 1947 and what is usually called Rwandan genocide of 1994 in which as many as 1 million people are estimated to have died. Typically, statistics for such conflicts are given in suspiciously round numbers.

Peace groups that lament the increasing numbers of civilians who have died in the wars of the late twentieth and early twenty-first centuries arrive at that conclusion by including deaths associated with any conflict even when the numbers of formal combatants were relatively small. The net effect is to annex statistics of mortality which, in previous centuries, would have been counted as losses from famine and pestilence. This practice obscures the most striking aspect of wars since 1945: the sharp decline in military personnel dying in battle. Sivard's estimates of numbers of military persons killed in wars in the twentieth century show a total of some 35 million deaths in the period 1900–1945, but less than one-quarter as many in the period 1946–1995.

War from the Mid-Twentieth Century

Battlefield deaths declined sharply after the end of the Vietnam War in 1975. Since there have been no important naval battles since World War II, deaths at sea have declined to a demographically insignificant figure.

Apart from losses of combatants, the most important impact of war on population in the twentieth century arose from advances in military technology and the practice of deliberately targeting civilians. Whereas previous wars had mainly killed young single men, twentieth century warfare was indiscriminately directed at men, women, and children. This was particularly true after the advent of airborne bombing and deliberate campaigns of extermination (for example, the firebombing of Dresden, the atomic bombs dropped on Japan, the Holocaust, the Pol Pot regime, and the Rwandan genocide). The removal of large numbers of women of childbearing age undoubtedly reduced fertility in certain regions. While the civilian populations of the Americas and Africa escaped such devastating attacks in World War II, some countries were very hard hit. Deaths from all war-related causes in the Soviet Union have been estimated to be as high as 29 million, a figure many times greater than the number of military personnel involved.

If all things were equal, fertility might have been expected to decline drastically. But, as Malthus noted when marveling at the rapid recovery of population in late-eighteenth-century Flanders, all things are never equal. Postwar prosperity was associated with a *baby boom* not just in the United States. Many parts of the world, including war-ravaged East and Central Europe, experienced a relative jump in prosperity compared with the Depression of the 1930s.

The rise in optimism about the future and high levels of employment generated by postwar reconstruction led to increased fertility. Where war coincides with large movements of refugees, famine, and disease—as it did in Rwanda, Ethiopia, Sudan, and Somalia in the 1980s and 1990s—it becomes very hard to specify the effects of war on population. Those African countries have also felt the impact of relatively late demographic transitions in fertility and the AIDS pandemic. Despite all its problems Rwanda's population appears to have grown from 7,165,000 in 1991 to nearly 9 million in 2002.

The impact of improved killing technology on population losses due to war is debatable. During the Cold War the United States and the Soviet Union acquired the capability to obliterate each other's cities with nuclear weapons. The number of nations possessing such weapons has grown steadily. But by the end of the twentieth century not one of the nuclear states had dared to employ them against an enemy, or even to openly threaten their use. The standoff between the United States and the USSR was often attributed to a "balance of terror" generated by the knowledge of the probability of "mutually assured destruction." The same could not be said of other nuclear powers. Whether this restraint is due to respect for the opinions of humankind or is attributable to some other reason is not clear.

Paradoxically, the highest rate of killing in late-twentieth-century wars occurred in the worst equipped states. About half the war deaths between 1945 and 2000 occurred in three countries—Sudan, Nigeria, and Bangladesh—which rate near the bottom of any list of military powers. Armies and modern weapons played very minor roles in these contests. In Rwanda, as in Pol Pot's Cambodia, people used agricultural implements to slaughter their neighbors.

In the early twenty-first century it is no easier to generalize about the effects of war on population than it was in Malthus's time. Battlefield losses in the wars of the only remaining superpower, the United States, have been minuscule. On the other hand, both military campaigns and threats to use force have frequently generated tides of refugees. The permeability of borders in an age of globalization has spread those refugees across the globe, with demographic consequences that are as yet impossible to calculate.

See also: *Ethnic Cleansing; Forced Migration; Genocide; Holocaust; National Security and Population; States System, Demographic History of.*

BIBLIOGRAPHY

Addington, Larry H. 1994. *The Patterns of War since the Eighteenth Century,* 2nd edition. Bloomington: Indiana University Press.

Arendt, Hannah. 1951. *Origins of Totalitarianism.* New York: Harcourt, Brace.

Eckhardt, William. 1992. *Civilizations, Empires and Wars: A Quantitative History of War.* London: McFarland & Co.

Elliot, Gil. 1972. *Twentieth Century Book of the Dead.* London: Penguin.

Hayes, Brian. 2002. "Statistics of Deadly Quarrels." *American Scientist* 90: 10–15.

Keeley, Lawrence. 1996. *War Before Civilization: The Myth of the Peaceful Savage.* New York: Oxford University Press.

Malthus, T. R. [1830] 1970. *A Summary View of the Principle of Population.* Harmondsworth: Penguin.

———. [1789] 1970. *An Essay on the Principle of Population.* Harmondsworth: Penguin.

Richardson, Lewis. 1960. *Statistics of Deadly Quarrels,* ed. Quincy Wright and C. C. Lienau. Pittsburgh: Boxwood Press.

Rummel, R. J. 1994. *Death by Government.* New Brunswick, NJ: Transactions Publishers.

Sivard, Ruth L., ed. 1978–1996. *World Military and Social Expenditures.* Leesburg, VA: WSME Publications.

Small, Melvin, and J. David Singer. 1982. *Resort to Arms: International and Civil Wars, 1816–1980* London: Sage.

———. 1972. *The Wages of War, 1816–1965.* New York: John Wiley.

Wilkinson, David O. 1980. *Deadly Quarrels: Lewis F. Richardson and the Statistical Study of War.* Berkeley: University of California Press.

Wright, Quincy. 1965. *A Study of War.* rev. edition. Chicago: University of Chicago Press.

INTERNET RESOURCE.

Rummel, R. J. 2000. *20th Century Democide.* <http://www2.hawaii.edu/~rummel/20TH.HTM>

NORMAN ETHERINGTON

WATER AND POPULATION

Fresh water is essential for human survival and for most human activities. The human body depends on a daily throughflow of drinking water. Unless that water is safe, people get ill; this is a problem of enormous dimensions because an estimated 1.1 billion persons are still without safe water supply and over 2.4 billion do not have safe sanitation. Water also is fundamental for productive activities in society, especially to produce the food people eat. Water precipitating over land is partitioned at the ground: Some evaporates directly; some infiltrates into the soil, is picked up by plant roots, and vaporizes; and the rest recharges rivers and aquifers. In the early twenty-first century an average of some 1,200 cubic meters of water is consumed (evaporated) annually per person, about 50 times the amount an average person uses in the household.

Predicament of Countries with Rapidly Growing Populations

Food production problems tend to be significant in regions that have monsoon climates with a short rainy season and a long dry season, an atmosphere in which rainwater evaporates rapidly, large variability in rainwater both interannually (recurrent drought years) and in the rainy season (large risk of dry spells hurting growing plants), and vulnerable soils that easily degrade into crushed and eroded lands. The difficulties of coping with these complex problems, most of which are unknown in the temperate zone, have left large regions of the world in poverty and with undernutrition. The problems are particularly significant in southern Asia and sub-Saharan Africa. However, it was in regions with such climatic challenges that agrarian civilization emerged.

Using human ingenuity, riverine populations developed intricate irrigation systems to protect growing crops from deficiencies in rainfall. In the contemporary world agricultural development presents the greatest difficulties in regions where rivers are absent, carry water only during heavy rains, or are shared with other countries so that the water supply is contingent on international agreements.

Irrigated areas should be able to produce much more food than most currently do by turning to less wasteful methods of irrigation. However, food production in most countries is heavily dependent on rain-fed agriculture. Large-scale upgrading of rainfed agriculture is needed to forestall recurrent crop failures and food shortages in those regions as their populations rise. Fortunately, there is enough rainfall for much better yields: Rainfall now wasted through flood flows and evaporation could be caught and put to productive use. The problem thus is not so much lack of rainfall as lack of soil infiltrability and inadequate plant uptake capacity caused by dry spell damage. Better soil conservation methods can raise the level of soil infiltration, and better harvesting of local water runoff can improve the ability of plants to absorb soil water.

Policy Implications

Figure 1 shows current similarities and differences in the water resources predicaments of different clusters of regions. Moving up the vertical scale is equivalent to mobilizing more of the streamflow to make it accessible for withdrawal for household use, productive activities, and irrigation. Because a certain amount has to remain in rivers to protect aquatic ecosystems and fisheries, there is a ceiling beyond which no more water can be put to use except through the reuse of upstream wastewater. Countries and regions find themselves in different situations. As long as it is still possible to mobilize more, increased water demands can be met through supply management, provided expertise, labor power, and financial resources will allow the necessary infrastructures to be built. Countries that are already close to their "water ceilings" have to change their water management policies and promote water-saving approaches (demand management).

The effect of larger population size, and thus indirectly of population growth, can be traced in the figure by moving out along the horizontal scale, which shows the level of "water crowding": the number of persons per flow unit. Higher values of this measure indicate more people polluting every unit of water flow and imply increasing proneness

FIGURE 1

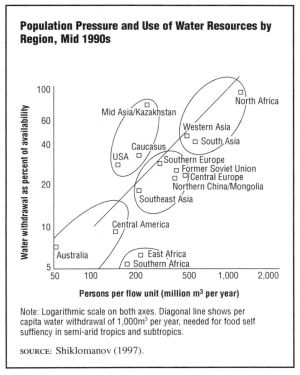

Population Pressure and Use of Water Resources by Region, Mid 1990s

Note: Logarithmic scale on both axes. Diagonal line shows per capita water withdrawal of 1,000m³ per year, needed for food self suffiency in semi-arid tropics and subtropics.

SOURCE: Shiklomanov (1997).

to disputes. In such situations water pollution abatement becomes essential, as does dispute mitigation, supported by legislation, mediation, flexible institutions, and public participation in order to secure social acceptance of the remedial action that is decided on. It is evident that with high levels of water crowding, efforts to curtail population growth are called for because the population-supporting capacity of the existing water resources is being exhausted. Solutions that could support an even larger population include reliance on imported food and nonconventional means of expanding water availability, such as desalination, water importation in tankers (or in towed plastic megabags), and water transfers through pipelines and canals from countries with better water resources.

Shift in Thinking

In the increasingly precarious conditions created by continued population growth in water-short regions political leaders are expected to guide their countries safely toward water security, food security, and environmental security. The task of constructing safe water supply and sanitation systems remains fundamental. In addition, the situation calls for a broadening of perspectives to encompass pollution abatement so that the available water stays usable, food imports to compensate for shortfalls in food self-reliance, income-generating activities to pay for that food, dispute risk minimization in a climate of increasing water crowding, and preparedness for recurrent droughts and floods linked to variability in rainfall.

Among experts on water resources, attention is moving away from seeing current streamflow as a stable resource and toward seeing rainfall as the original resource. This resource is partitioned between evaporation, linked especially to biomass production in forests, grasslands, wetlands, and croplands, and the surplus that is feeding the rivers and aquifers and is used for societal purposes. In tropical regions changes in land use may alter the streamflow considerably. Large-scale deforestation may increase the streamflow and/or raise the water table (causing damage from salination, as it did in Australia); large-scale forest plantations may reduce the streamflow (as in South Africa, where such plantations are considered a streamflow-reducing activity and require special permits). These linkages make land use decisions water management decisions. As a consequence, the currently recommended long-term route is integration of land and water management as part of a catchment-based ecological approach.

See also: *Carrying Capacity; Ecological Perspectives on Population; Food Supply and Population; Limits to Growth; Natural Resources and Population.*

BIBLIOGRAPHY

Chaplin, M. F. 2001. "Water: Its Importance to Life." *Biochemistry and Molecular Biology Education.* 29: 54–59.

Falkenmark, Malin. 1994. "Landscape as Life Support Provider: Water-Related Limitations." In *Population—The Complex Reality,* ed. Sir F. Graham-Smith. London: Royal Society.

———. 1997. "Meeting Water Requirements of an Expanding World Population." *Philosophical Transactions of the Royal Society, Biological Sciences* 352: 929–936.

———. 2001. "The Greatest Water Problem: The Inability to Link Environmental Security, Water Security and Food Security." *Water Resources Development* 17(4): 539–554.

Falkenmark, Malin, and Gun Nar Lindh. 1976. *Water for a Starving World.* Boulder, CO: Westview Press.

Haraddin, M. J. 2001. "Water Scarcity Impacts and Potential Conflicts in the MENA Region." *Water International* 26(4): 460–470.

Lundqvist, Jan, ed. 2000. *New Dimensions in Water Security.* Rome: FAO, AGL/MISC/25/2000.

Shiklomanov, Igor. 1997. *Assessment of Water Resources and Water Availability of the World.* Background report to the Comprehensive Assessment of Freshwater Resources of the World. Stockholm: Stockholm Environment Institute and World Meteorological Organization.

INTERNET RESOURCE.

Rockström, Johan et al. 1999. "Linkages among Water Vapour Flows, Food Production, and Terrestrial Ecosystem Services." *Conservation Ecology* 3(2). <http://www.consecol.org/vol3/iss2/art5/index.html>.

MALIN FALKENMARK

WELFARE STATE

A welfare state has been defined as a "state which has a policy of collective responsibility for individual well-being" (Clegg 1980, p. 7). For some commentators the term refers to the services produced, provided, and delivered by public agencies; however, for others it also includes benefits and services that are purchased by public resources but may be provided by commercial or voluntary bodies. Others even include welfare services produced and provided by employers (occupational welfare) and the family.

Welfare is difficult to define in light of the fact that both its source and its delivery vary widely. Welfare can be derived from a range of activities, including paid work, private activity such as savings and insurance, and voluntary activity as well as through the state. Benefits can be in cash or in kind; benefits in kind include both free services such as public education and health care and subsidized services such as low-rent housing provided along with employment, community care services, and dental care. A service may be publicly funded, publicly produced, both, or neither.

The objectives of welfare also are varied, ranging from poverty relief or the reduction of inequality to strengthening social inclusion and increasing social cohesion (Barr 2001). Most welfare states act both as a lifetime "piggy bank"—using social insurance to redistribute funds from one point in an individual's life to another—and as a "Robin Hood"—redistributing income and wealth from the rich to the poor to alleviate poverty and reduce social exclusion. The balance between these two roles varies from country to country, depending on the priority assigned to different objectives.

Types of Welfare Regimes

Gøsta Esping-Andersen, in *The Three Worlds of Welfare Capitalism* (1990), constructed "decommodification" indexes to measure the coverage, accessibility, and performance of social security schemes in eighteen Organization for Economic Cooperation and Development (OECD) countries. Using these indexes, he distinguished three ideal-type welfare regimes:

1. Liberal welfare regimes, in which the government provides only a minimum or "residual" level of welfare services and the family or religious and charitable institutions play the major role in providing health and social welfare services. Such regimes assign priority to promoting economic growth and aim to reduce poverty in a way that impinges minimally on that goal. Examples are southern European countries such as Greece, Portugal, and Spain, as well as the United States.

2. Conservative/corporatist regimes, in which the government plays a leading role in both organizing and providing welfare services. Services are highly developed, are of good quality, and are funded by a mixture of private and social insurance schemes. In addition to the state, nongovernment institutions such as churches, employers, and trade unions are important. Corporatist welfare states assign priority to social stability and tend to be conservative in their approach to welfare issues such as the family and the role of women in the labor market.

Examples are Germany, Austria, Belgium, and France.

3. Social democratic regimes, in which the government emphasizes social equality as well as the alleviation of poverty. Services tend to be comprehensive and universal. Public spending is usually very high, and welfare benefits tend to be generous. However, there is also an emphasis on the work ethic and supporting people to remain in the labor force, for example, through extensive child-care services. The classic examples are the Scandinavian countries, especially Sweden.

Although they are theoretically useful, these classifications are highly stylized and have been subject to debate and criticism. In particular Robert Goodin and his associates (1999) claim that it is not sufficient to measure the performance of social security systems by using data from only one point in time. They argue that the assessment of welfare regimes needs to take account of their impact on people's lives *over* time. With the increasing availability of longitudinal panel data, this type of assessment is becoming possible.

Scale of Public Transfers

The scale of public transfers varies considerably among OECD countries, ranging in 1998 from around 5 percent of gross domestic product (GDP) in Korea to 31 percent in Sweden (Figure 1). It is notable that expenditures on public transfers increased considerably in most countries between 1980 and 1998, doubling from 11 percent in 1980 to 23 percent in 1998 in Greece and rising in that period from 15 percent to 28 percent in Switzerland.

Much of this rise in welfare spending is attributed to changes in the structure of the beneficiary population as a result of population aging. Public spending on old-age cash benefits (pensions and social assistance) has increased steeply, amounting to nearly 13 percent of GDP in Italy in 1998. Older people are also major consumers of health services, and public spending on health care, which by the late 1990s typically was over 5 percent of GDP, generally has risen over time (although some countries have experienced a fall, such as Denmark, Ireland, and Sweden).

FIGURE 1

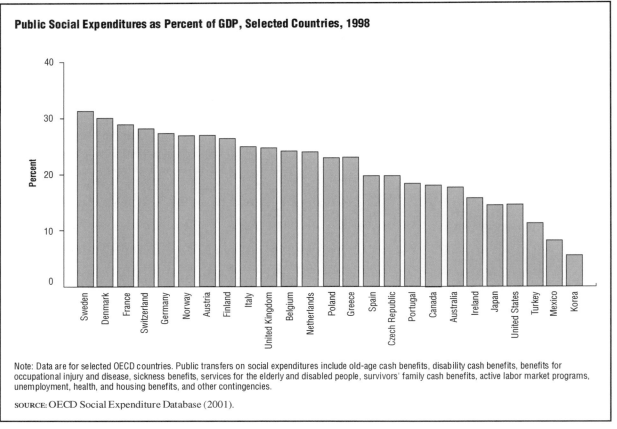

Public Social Expenditures as Percent of GDP, Selected Countries, 1998

Note: Data are for selected OECD countries. Public transfers on social expenditures include old-age cash benefits, disability cash benefits, benefits for occupational injury and disease, sickness benefits, services for the elderly and disabled people, survivors' family cash benefits, active labor market programs, unemployment, health, and housing benefits, and other contingencies.

SOURCE: OECD Social Expenditure Database (2001).

Responding to an Aging Population

Recent growth in levels of public expenditure and changes in the relative size of different age groups have given rise to the notion of a "demographic time-bomb": It is argued that severe fiscal problems will arise as a result of the relative fall in the number of workers making pension contributions and the relative growth of those drawing pension benefits.

Demographers typically have examined the pressures of population aging by examining the size of the "dependent" population in relation to the size of the population of working age:

$$\frac{(0\text{--}15 \text{ years}) + (65 \text{ and over})}{(16\text{--}64 \text{ years})}$$

This is taken to be a rough index of the number of dependent people per nondependent person.

A dependency ratio defined only by age has, however, come under significant criticism for being simplistic. Economic dependency is complex and multifaceted, and many things in addition to age determine whether a person is dependent. A more sophisticated dependency ratio that is suited to an examination of pressures on public finances:

$$\frac{\text{non-economically active population}}{\text{economically active population}}$$

This ratio takes into account people of working age who are out of the labor market because they are studying, are unemployed (but not seeking work), or have caring responsibilities as well as people of postretirement age who are still working. However, this more refined ratio also can be criticized. Many social gerontologists argue that older people are contributors as well as recipients, particularly if unpaid work outside the formal labor market is taken into account. In the United Kingdom, for example, one-third of the people who provide unpaid care to frail older people are elderly themselves. Many older people are taxpayers as well as beneficiaries.

The key advantage of the refined dependency ratio is that it draws attention to the fact that the fiscal burden is determined by a range of factors beyond purely demographic ones. In particular, the effects of population aging in developed countries have been exacerbated by changes in the length of working life. Since the mid-1970s there has been a sharp fall in the number of years of life men spend in employment and a corresponding increase in the number of years spent in other activities or states, such as school, unemployment, and especially retirement. In a typical OECD country at the start of the twenty-first century a man might spend only half his life in employment (OECD 2000). Women, in contrast, are spending more of their lives in paid employment than was the case in earlier times.

It is increasingly recognized that "the burden of supporting an older population over the coming decades will depend crucially on the extent to which the population of working age in general, and older workers in particular, will participate in the labour market" (OECD 1996, p. 65). Many countries are adopting policies to slow and reverse trends toward early retirement. For example, work incentives in pension schemes are being strengthened. In addition, several countries are considering or implementing an increase in the retirement age (or, more accurately, the age at which state pensions are payable).

Moves toward later retirement may be politically unpopular. When pensions were first introduced, however, the period of expected life after the age of retirement was relatively short. For example, the first old-age pension, introduced in New Zealand in 1898, was payable at age 65; the pension introduced in the United Kingdom in 1908 was payable at age 70. In 1901 expectation of life at birth in the United Kingdom was 56 years for men and 63 years for women; in 2001 it was around 75 years for men and 80 years for women.

Because health-care costs are known to rise with age, it is feared that an aging population will lead to higher health-care expenditures. However, recent studies show that unlike the case with pensions, increased longevity in the population need not translate into increased health costs. Evidence suggests that the greatest proportion of health-care spending among older people is incurred in the final year of an individual's life regardless of the length of that life. In the United Kingdom it is estimated that people consume about a quarter their lifetime consumption of health care during the last year of life. If greater longevity means only that the cost of dying is postponed, the implications for future health spending are limited. If, however, there are additional costs to greater longevity, the implications will be very different. A critical factor will be whether the additional years of life are spent in good or poor health. So far the evidence regarding the compression of morbidity is mixed.

It is important to bear in mind that trends in health-care expenditures are largely determined by factors other than demographic change. For example, three-quarters of the rise in medical spending in the United States between 1960 and 1993 was attributable to technological change in contrast to only 3 percent that was due to demographic change. Thus, there are upward pressures on welfare spending for a whole range of reasons, including aging of the population. The future performance of the economy, and the levels of unemployment and early retirement in particular, will have as great an effect as will demographic change. The question of whether societies can continue to afford the welfare state will be answered as much by ideology as by fiscal concerns.

See also: *Aging of Population; Cost of Children; Family Allowances; Family Policy; Intergenerational Transfers.*

BIBLIOGRAPHY

Barr, Nicholas. 2001. *The Welfare State as Piggy Bank: Information, Risk, Uncertainty and the Role of the State.* Oxford: Oxford University Press.

Clegg, Joan. 1980. *Dictionary of Social Services: Policy and Practice,* 3rd edition. London: Bedford Square Press.

Cutler, David, and Ellen Meara. 1999. "The Concentration of Medical Spending: An Update." Cambridge, MA: National Bureau of Economic Research, Working Paper 7279.

Esping-Andersen, Gøsta. 1990. *The Three Worlds of Welfare Capitalism.* Cambridge, Eng.: Polity Press.

Goodin, Robert et al. 1999. *The Real Worlds of Welfare Capitalism.* New York: Cambridge University Press.

Johnson, Paul, and Jane Falkingham. 1992. *Ageing and Economic Welfare.* London: Sage.

Organization for Economic Cooperation and Development. 1996. *Aging in OECD Countries: A Critical Policy Challenge.* Paris: Organization for Economic Cooperation and Development.

———. 2000. *Reforms for an Ageing Society.* Paris: Organization for Economic Cooperation Development.

Zweifel, Peter, Stefan Felder, and Markus Meier. 1999. "Ageing of the Population and Healthcare Expenditure: A Red Herring?" *Health Economics* 8: 485–496.

JANE FALKINGHAM

WHELPTON, P. K.

(1893–1964)

Pioneer American demograher. Pascal Kidder Whelpton did his undergraduate studies at Cornell University and obtained a graduate degree from the University of Nebraska. His career started with extension work for the Department of Agriculture in agricultural economics and then in a faculty position at Texas A & M University. In 1924 he joined Warren S. Thompson at the Scripps Foundation for Research in Population Problems at Miami University in Oxford, Ohio. His relationship with the Scripps Foundation—he became Associate Director in 1940, Director in 1953—continued until his retirement in 1963. He was president of the Population Association of America in 1941-42 and director of the United Nations Population Division (1950–1953).

Thompson and Whelpton together won national prominence with their 1928 article "Population of the United States 1925–1975," published in the *American Journal of Sociology* and with a series of subsequent publications on U.S. future population trends. They presented population projections using the cohort component method, which had been introduced by English economist Edwin Cannan at the end of the nineteenth century and then used by the statistician Arthur Bowley in the 1920s. The method used a life table to calculate survivors of the initial populations classified by age and sex and added al-lowances for births and immigration. All three projection inputs—life table, birth rate, and rate of net immigration—required arbitrary assumptions about future demographic conditions; however, the resulting population trajectories seemed to accord with a wholly independent projection method, the logistic curve fitted to observed past population totals in studies by Raymond Pearl and Lowell Reed of Johns Hopkins University. (Both kinds of projection, as it turned out, were large underestimates: U.S. population surged in the baby boom years and with high rates of immigration.).

Whelpton's main contribution to demography lies in his studies of fertility. Notable among these was *Social and Psychological Factors Affecting Fertility,* known as the Indianapolis Study, published in five volumes over 1946–1958. This innovative research project, of which he was a principal investigator (together with Clyde V. Kiser), was based on field interviews and began the rich tradition of survey research on fertility. Whelpton was also closely involved with the Growth of American Families studies carried out in the 1950s and 1960s. He contributed to cohort methods of analyzing fertility, work that culminated in his book *Cohort Fertility* (1954). A selected bibliography of his writings is given in Durand (1964).

Demography has become more sophisticated since Whelpton's time, and some of the methods he used are obsolete, but his role as one of the founders will remain a permanent part of the history of the discipline.

BIBLIOGRAPHY

SELECTED WORKS BY P. K. WHELPTON.

Freedman, Ronald, Pascal K. Whelpton, and Arthur A. Campbell. 1959. *Family Planning, Sterility, and Population Growth.* New York: McGraw-Hill.

Grabill, Wilson H., Clyde V. Kiser, and Pascal K. Whelpton. 1958. *The Fertility of American Women.* New York: Wiley. (Census Monograph Series).

Thompson, Warren S., and P. K. Whelpton. 1933. *Population Trends in the United States.* New York: McGraw-Hill. Reprinted by Gordon and Breach Science Publishers, New York, 1969.

Thompson, Warren S., and P. K. Whelpton. 1943. *Estimates of Future Population of the United*

States, 1940–2000. Washington: National Resources Planning Board.

Whelpton, P. K. 1954. *Cohort Fertility: Native White Women in the United States.* Princeton, NJ: Princeton University Press.

Whelpton, Pascal K., Arthur A. Campbell, and John E. Patterson. 1966. *Fertility and Family Planning in the United States.* Princeton, NJ: Princeton University Press.

Whelpton, P. K., and Clyde V. Kiser. 1953. "Résumé of the Indianapolis Study of Social and Psychological Factors Affecting Fertility." *Population Studies* 7: 95–110.

Whelpton, P. K., and Clyde V. Kiser, eds. 1946–1958. *Social and Psychological Factors Affecting Fertility.* 5 vols. New York: Milbank Memorial Fund.

SELECTED WORKS ABOUT P. K. WHELPTON.

Durand, John D. 1964. "Pascal Kidder Whelpton (1893–1964)." *Population Index* 30: 323–328.

Kiser, Clyde V. 1973. "Contributions of P. K. Whelpton to Demography." *Social Biology* 20: 438–447.

NATHAN KEYFITZ

WICKSELL, KNUT

(1851–1926)

Swedish economist and prominent exponent of neo-Malthusian ideas, Johan Gustav Knut Wicksell was born in Stockholm and graduated from Uppsala University in mathematics in 1871. After a period living, in Paul Samuelson's words, "a bohemian existence of preoccupation with anti-religion, anti-sexual puritanism, anti-alcoholism, anti-monarchism and anti-militarism" (1987, p. 908). Wicksell turned to the social sciences, studying economics and eventually obtaining a doctorate at Uppsala. In 1904, at age 53, he became professor of economics at Lund University where he remained until his retirement in 1916.

Wicksell's most important scholarly contributions were to price theory and monetary policy (where he was an influence on Keynes), and to the creation of neoclassical theory. He was also one of the first economists to study decision-making within political assemblies, particularly with regard to taxation; this work was a forerunner of public choice theory. Wicksell's prestige as an economist lent intellectual weight to his vigorous propagation of neo-Malthusianism in Sweden. Inspired by the British neo-Malthusian George Drysdale (1825–1904), Wicksell argued in a widely distributed 1880 speech that Sweden was overpopulated and needed to decrease its birth rate. He called for early marriages and the use of contraceptives within marriage as an alternative to celibacy and prostitution. Concerned about resource scarcity and pessimistic about the speed of technological development, in a number of lectures and articles he not only pleaded for reduced natality but for a reduction of the population. He placed Sweden's optimum population at three million, at a time when its actual population was five million.

Wicksell retained his interest in "the population question" and neo-Malthusianism until his death. He was active at European congresses on birth control, and in 1906 he became one of the vice presidents of the English Malthusian League. His views made him a rebel in Sweden's conservative society. Wicksell was an atheist (he was imprisoned for two months in 1910 for blasphemy), a republican, and a strong advocate of women's suffrage. His wife, Anna Wicksell Bugge (1862–1928), was a pioneer in the women's movement in Scandinavia.

See also: *Demography, History of.*

BIBLIOGRAPHY

SELECTED WORKS BY KNUT WICKSELL.

Wicksell, Knut. 1910. *The Theory of Population, Its Composition, and Models of Change.* Stockholm: Bonniers.

———. 1954. *Value, Capital and Rent* (1893). London: Allen & Unwin.

———. 1958. *Selected Papers on Economic Theory,* ed. Erik Lindahl. London: Allen & Unwin.

———. 1977–1978. *Lectures on Political Economy,* 2 vols, trans. E. Classen, ed. Lionel Robbins. Fairfield, NJ: Augustus M. Kelly.

———. 1997–1999. *Selected Essays in Economics,* 2 vols, ed. Bo Sandelin. London and New York: Routledge.

SELECTED WORKS ABOUT KNUT WICKSELL.

Samuelson, Paul A. 1987. "Wicksell and Neoclassical Economics." In *The New Palgrave: A Dictionary of Economics* Vol. 4. London: Macmillan.

Uhr, C. G. 1951. "Knut Wicksell—A Centennial Evaluation." *American Economic Review* 41(5): 829–860.

LARS-GÖRAN TEDEBRAND

WOMEN'S STATUS AND DEMOGRAPHIC BEHAVIOR

Research on many aspects of population change in the contemporary world has highlighted the significance of relationships between women's status and demographic behavior. In particular, knowledge of these relationships has been important in understanding demographic transition, increasing the complexity of the classical depiction in which fertility decline is seen as a natural outcome of mortality decline and economic development. Especially in conditions where economic growth is slow or stagnant, considerations of women's status and autonomy have yielded key insights into trends in health and fertility.

Conceptual and Methodological Issues

Kingsley Davis, an influential theorist of social and demographic change, has argued that in contemporary high-fertility societies the status of women is an important factor influencing demographic change, whereas in Western societies that have experienced demographic transition gender equality might well have been a consequence (although incidental) of low fertility. The principal cultural anchor for persistently high levels of fertility, according to Davis, is a complex of institutional factors with their accompanying attitudes and norms that determine women's status. The most important of these factors are patriarchal, patrilineal, and patrilocal marriage and kinship systems in which the filial bond dominates the marital bond in family organization and kinship and family are the principal bases of social organization; a young age at marriage and higher proportions married, and thus early exposure to intercourse; and taboos on the free mixing of the sexes

and consequent poor interspousal communication, particularly with regard to sexual behavior, resulting in relatively little use of contraception.

The most important effect of such institutional patterns is the subordination of women: their seclusion; lack of autonomy in making decisions, including decisions pertaining to their fertility; and the denial to them of opportunities for formal education and economic independence, opportunities that can enhance their ability to interact with the world outside the home, with attendant gains in knowledge and self-confidence.

By and large demographers agree that strongly patriarchal systems in which women have a high degree of economic dependence on men and experience social subordination through patrilocal exogamy are associated with high fertility. They are less agreed on the direction of the underlying cause-effect relationships, if any exist, and how such relationships might vary in different cultural contexts.

Women's status can be seen as being embedded in a gender system—the complex of roles, rights, and statuses that surround being male and female in a particular society or culture. Gender systems embody institutionalized inequality in power, autonomy, and well-being between male and female members, typically to the disadvantage of females. They are reinforced by state, community, family, and kin and perpetuated by socializing new generations into behaving in accordance with the dominant gender norms. In this manner, gender systems affect individual behavior, including behavior bearing on fertility.

Women's Status and Demographic Outcomes

Empirical investigations of the relationship between women's status and demographic outcomes, however, have mostly taken a narrower approach, focusing on a few variables that plausibly are linked to women's status. The most significant of these variables are:

- *the perceived advantages of high fertility* resulting from the denial to women of other sources of cultural and economic worth;
- *son preference*, both as a security measure, reflecting women's concern to protect themselves against the risks inherent in their low status and economic dependence on

husband, and as a religious or social duty toward the husband's lineage;

- *female education*, which confers self-esteem and self-confidence, access to new information, and a greater propensity to adopt innovative behavior;

- *women's autonomy*, indicated by mobility outside the home and participation in decision making in the household;

- *women's economic worth*, indicated by ownership of property and participation in the labor force;

- *women's health-care-seeking behavior* for themselves and their children; and

- *marriage and kinship systems* (age at marriage, social support systems, etc.).

The fertility-related variables generally considered in these studies are age at marriage, use of modern contraception, age at termination of childbearing, attitudes toward birth control, and number of children (and number of sons and daughters separately) desired; an indicator of child health and mortality is female disadvantage in survival.

Social demographic analysis has found strong links between women's status and their demographic behavior. Discrimination against women appears to be the root cause of much of the high fertility and female disadvantage in survival, with regional variations reflecting differences in cultural systems. (Disadvantage in survival is sometimes manifest in higher female than male age-specific mortality rates; more commonly, it is seen in female survival rates that are higher than male survival rates but by less than would be expected in the absence of gender discrimination.)

Conventional demographic survey research on this topic often produces ambiguous results, perhaps because of weaknesses in the proxy variables typically used in the analysis or because gender inequality cannot be adequately captured by a single quantitative indicator. Broad generalizations on cause-effect relationships have also been confounded by the different levels at which influences work: On the one hand, the sphere of individual actions affecting fertility and child mortality, and on the other, the macro level at which cultural configurations of women's status are generally conceptualized. More recent studies have attempted to work with direct indicators of women's autonomy (freedom of move-

ment, participation in household decision-making), their empowerment (sense of self, ability to negotiate with agents outside the domestic sphere), and their control over material resources (economic security, property rights, inheritance rights).

Illustrative Findings

Illustrative findings on this topic frequently come from studies in South Asia, a region characterized by women's low status and moderate or high fertility. The findings point to women's economic activity, education, and mobility/autonomy as factors affecting fertility, although these variables may well behave differently in different circumstances.

The link between female labor force participation and child survival is well established. Women who engage in economic activity tend to provide better chances for the survival of their female offspring than do women with no wage income. The precise reason working women seek as prompt health care for daughters as for sons remains unclear. Possible explanations may lie in the effect of particular agricultural regimes, such as southern Indian and Southeast Asian rice cultivation, in enhancing women's economic worth; women's culturally sanctioned greater economic independence, as in Africa; or their greater mobility and sense of self-worth. Very likely, there is a combination of several factors.

There is no conclusive evidence that gender bias in child survival is lower among poor households. Nevertheless, landless households are believed to show less discrimination against girls.

The relative female disadvantage in infant survival appears to be greater in cultures that value female seclusion, accentuate women's economic and social dependence on men, or place a higher comparative value on sons than on daughters. The disadvantage increases with socioeconomic status as defined by caste, income, and maternal education. Gender discrimination works both through less attention given to health care for girls and, more recently, through resort to sex-selective abortion (practiced in China, South Korea, and Vietnam as well as in South Asia). Improved educational levels help women gain the independence and autonomy needed to ensure better nutrition and medical care for their children, enhancing overall child survival, but do not necessarily narrow the relative female disadvantage in regard to infant survival.

Paradoxically, education (a covariable with class and therefore improved status) may contribute to the intensification of patriarchal norms such as women's seclusion and reduced autonomy in fertility decisions in these cultures. In the long run education is probably the most potent engine of both demographic change and women's overall well-being. In this respect it would be superior to labor force participation, which among poor women entails the double burden of work outside and inside the home to the detriment of their own health. In the short run, however, education may not always be an unmixed blessing. To yield its effects in reducing fertility and lessening gender discrimination education means more than just literacy; it calls for formal schooling up to the secondary level, and for women as well as men.

Other Modernizing Influences

Demographic behavior does not respond only to broad trends in economic development and social stratification: There are other modernizing influences at work. These influences are, most notably, access to newer contraceptive technologies; diffusion of modern ideas through the mass media, especially the electronic media, and the health and educational systems; the wider availability of health services and their public information component; and the forces that lead to family nucleation among urban dwellers. Such factors have the potential to alter aspirations for self and family, in turn affecting both women's status and demographic outcomes.

The alacrity with which contraception is often resorted to, even—sometimes especially—by illiterate women when high-quality family planning services are sensitively offered, suggests that these services might have equivalent effects to female education on fertility and child survival.

The field of women's health, by bringing in other disciplinary perspectives, has contributed new insights into how gender inequalities actually affect women's fertility decisions. Research has highlighted the value of smaller-scale, qualitative methods of investigation in understanding the layers of meaning that fertility and its regulation have for women and the complex strategies that women devise to achieve some measure of control over their own bodies even when constrained by the unequal power structures that operate in both the domestic and public domains.

See also: *Education; Feminist Perspectives on Population Issues; Fertility Transition, Socioeconomic Determinants of; Gender Preferences for Children.*

BIBLIOGRAPHY

Balk, Deborah. 1997. "Defying Gender Norms in Rural Bangladesh: A Social Demographic Analysis." *Population Studies* 51: 153–172.

Basu, Alaka M. 1992. *Culture, the Status of Women and Demographic Behaviour.* Oxford: Clarendon Press.

Caldwell, John C. 1976. "Toward a Restatement of Demographic Transition Theory." *Population and Development Review* 2: 321–366.

———. 1998. "Mass Education and Fertility Decline." In *The Earthscan Reader in Population and Development,* ed. Paul Demeny and Geoffrey McNicoll. London: Earthscan Publications.

Das Gupta, Monica, and P. N. Mari Bhat. 1995. "Intensified Gender Bias in India: A Consequence of Fertility Decline." Working paper No. 95.02. Cambridge, MA: Harvard Center for Population and Development Studies.

Davis, Kingsley. 1984. "Wives and Work: The Sex Role Revolution and Its Consequences." *Population and Development Review* 10(3): 397–417.

Davis, Kingsley, and Judith Blake. 1956. "Social Structure and Fertility: An Analytic Framework." *Economic Development and Cultural Change* 14(2): 211–235.

Dyson, Tim, and Mick Moore. 1983. "On Kinship Structure, Female Autonomy and Demographic Behaviour in India." *Population and Development Review* 9(1): 35–60.

Freedman, Ronald. 1979. "Theories of Fertility Decline: A Reappraisal." *Social Forces* 58: 1–17.

Jejeebhoy, Shireen J. 1996. *Women's Education, Autonomy and Reproductive Behaviour: Assessing What We Have Learnt.* Honolulu: East-West Center.

Malhotra, Anju, Reeve Vanneman, and Sunita Kishor. 1995. "Fertility, Dimensions of Patriarchy, and Development in India." *Population and Development Review* 21(2): 281–305.

Mason, Karen O. 1997. "Gender and Demographic Change: What Do We Know?" In *The Continu-*

ing *Demographic Transition,* ed. G. W. Jones, R. M. Douglas, J. C. Caldwell, and R. M. D'Sousa Oxford: Clarendon Press.

Murthi, Mamta, Anne-Catherine Guio, and Jean Dreze. 1995. "Mortality, Fertility and Gender Bias in India: A District-Level Analysis." *Population and Development Review* 21(4): 745–782.

Petchesky, Rosalind P. 2000. "Re-Theorising Reproductive Health and Rights in the Light of Feminist Cross-Cultural Research." In *Cultural Perspectives in Reproductive Health,* ed. C. M. Obermeyer. Oxford: Oxford University Press.

RADHIKA RAMASUBBAN

WORLD FERTILITY SURVEY

The World Fertility Survey (WFS) was one of the most important international undertakings in demographic data collection and analysis of the twentieth century. Between 1973 and 1984, 66 countries carried out comparable surveys of human fertility. Forty four of these were developing countries that received substantial financial and technical assistance channeled through WFS's headquarters. Thus, an impressive geographical coverage was achieved, though some of the largest countries (China, India, Brazil, and the Soviet Union) declined to participate.

The idea for this international program probably originated with Reimert Ravenholt, the forceful head of the Office of Population at the U.S. Agency for International Development, as a means to resolve conflicting assessments of the fertility impact of family planning programs. The United Nations Fund for Population Activities gave its support for the project and these two organizations became the dominant financial sponsors of the WFS.

Coordination of the enterprise was entrusted to the International Statistical Institute, based in the Netherlands, which brought the necessary scientific respectability and political independence. The institute appointed the eminent British statistician Maurice Kendall (1907–1983) to head the program, which, at his insistence, was based in London. Thus this unique program was funded by two U.S.-based organizations, managed in the Netherlands, and executed in the United Kingdom.

Because of its mandate to yield internationally comparable data, the WFS developed core instruments to be used in all developing countries. These consisted of a household schedule or roster, and a more detailed questionnaire to be administered to ever-married women of reproductive age. Single women were also included in some surveys. Only 3 of the 44 surveys also canvassed husbands.

The core questionnaire for women included complete marriage and pregnancy histories, and sections on socioeconomic background, contraception, breastfeeding, and fertility preferences. This content was not linked to any theory of fertility, but proved ideal for demographic description. The survey allowed a degree of flexibility in the form of optional sets of questions that permitted more in-depth analysis of specific topics. Only two such "modules" were commonly used: one on family planning and one that enquired into biological determinants of childbearing other than contraception.

The imperative to maximize quality of information drove the data collection strategy. Questionnaires were carefully translated into all major languages. Female interviewers were specially recruited and intensively trained. They worked in teams under close supervision. Major efforts were put into producing clean, well-documented, standardized data sets, a pioneering emphasis that WFS's successor, the Demographic and Health Surveys project, has maintained.

The WFS developed a formidable analytic capacity to complement its data collection expertise. The survey made significant contributions to analytic methods such as the adaptation of linear models to individual-level measures of fertility and the application of hazard models to event histories. Its contribution to a greater understanding of the determinants of fertility change was less impressive, nor did it provide a conclusive answer to key policy questions concerning the impact of state-sponsored family planning programs. The name of the enterprise notwithstanding, the World Fertility Survey's contribution to an understanding of childhood mortality probably exceeded its contribution to studies of fertility.

See also: *Demographic and Health Surveys; Demographic Surveys, History and Methodology of.*

BIBLIOGRAPHY

Cleland, John, and John Hobcraft. 1985. *Reproductive Change in Developing Countries: Insights from the World Fertility Survey.* Oxford: Oxford University Press.

Cleland, John, and Christopher Scott. 1987. *The World Fertility Survey: An Assessment.* Oxford: Oxford University Press.

Kendall, Sir Maurice. 1979. "The World Fertility Survey: Current Status and Findings." *Johns Hopkins University Population Reports,* Series M(3).

Population Information Program. 1985. "Fertility and Family Planning Surveys: An Update." *Johns Hopkins University Population Reports,* Series M(8).

JOHN CLELAND

WORLD POPULATION GROWTH

The human race, even if its destiny appears unique, is part of the general evolution of the animal kingdom. But it is in the vanguard of that evolution since it is able to gain increasing mastery over its environment. Humanity's dominance of the planet and its exploitation of the Earth's resources have been accompanied by major increases in the size of human populations.

Prehistoric Beginnings

Possibly as long as 3 million years ago, *Homo habilis* emerged in East Africa. Its distinguishing characteristics were that it made, and more or less systematically used, tools of wood or flint stone, and that it exhibited a novel, more advanced type of social behavior: It consumed food not where it was obtained but at the group's campsites. The territory occupied by these early humans covered some 4 million square kilometers (about 1.5 millon square miles) of wooded savanna-land between today's Ethiopia and Zimbabwe. According to an estimate by János Nemeskéri, there may have been a population as great as 100,000, already exhibiting subgroups with distinct physical features.

From then onward, human genetic change has been very rapid: Most notably brain size, which at the start was less than 500 grams, increased by more than 1 kilogram in less than 3 million years. In successive stages of evolution, the great selective advantage that resulted gave humans the ability to eliminate their nearest competitors. *Homo habilis* thus yielded its place to *Homo ergaster,* which, having quadrupled the territory it occupied in Africa, spread to Europe and to southern Asia, taking on the closely similar form of *Homo erectus.*

In the twenty-first century, numerous methods are available for making estimates about prehistoric populations. The most commonly used method assigns to a given territory the population density among peoples with similar culture and who are living under similar climatic conditions, observed in some recent period. The resulting estimates indicate small populations, despite technical advances such as the domestication of fire. The extent of the territory occupied and variations in climate thus appear more influential than technical progress. The population size of *Homo erectus* over the entire earth may have varied between 500,000 and 700,000.

Later, three branches of humanity emerged: *Homo sapiens* in Africa and south Asia, *Homo neanderthalensis* (Neanderthal man) in Europe, and Java man in Indonesia. Hypothetically, the maximum population of *Homo sapiens* was about 800,000 in the Afro-Asian territory, while the corresponding numbers for Neanderthal man and Java man may have been 250,000 and 100,000.

From around the onset of the last Ice Age, some 70,000 years ago, *Homo sapiens* were ascendant and in the subsequent millennia spread over continental territories theretofore unoccupied by man: Australia, Siberia, and eventually the Americas. (Up to about 15,000 years ago, large parts of North America and Europe were under ice cover.) The world population may have reached 1.5 million during this period, most of it in Africa and Asia. Technical progress became the main driving force of demographic expansion.

Settlement of North Africa came relatively late. Taking advantage of the narrowness of the straights between Sicily and Tunisia, Europeans crossed over to Africa in two waves—around 20000 B.C.E., and around 12000 B.C.E.—thus peopling the whole of North Africa from the Canary Islands to Egypt.

In Europe, population size may have attained 200,000 persons in the period from 10000 to 8700

B.C.E. Then there was a sudden warming of the climate, coinciding with a brutal end to the flourishing Paleolithic cultures. At the beginning of the Mesolithic period that followed, population size diminished, but subsequently the peopling of Northern Europe, earlier under ice cover, renewed demographic growth. Toward 7000 B.C.E., population size in Europe as a whole may have approached 400,000.

Late Prehistoric Populations

About that time, a small sedentary population, engaged in agriculture and animal husbandry, established the first known Neolithic village, near twenty-first-century Saloniki in Greece. From this region two streams originated, together forming the population of Neolithic Europe: one, a maritime group, occupying the coastal regions all the way to Britain; the other a terrestrial group, occupying the inland. By 4000 B.C.E., almost all Europe was Neolithic, with a population of some 2 million, and growing. That population peaked around 2000 B.C.E. at some 23 million, followed by a sharp drop early in the Bronze Age, which was then beginning.

This Neolithic culture was born in the Near East. Its main constituting elements—the hoe, animal husbandry, pottery, and maritime navigation—make their appearance in the period from 10000 to 8000 B.C.E. The region's population increased over this period from about 200,000 to around 5 million, and reached some 10 million by 2000 B.C.E. From its core, the culture spread to Mesopotamia, Egypt, the Caucasus, the Persian Highland, the Punjab, Nubia, Ethiopia, and Yemen.

The Asian subcontinent—present-day Pakistan, India, Bangladesh, and Sri Lanka—had a larger population: perhaps about 600,000 people by 4000 B.C.E., 3 million by 3000 B.C.E., and a peak of some 20 to 25 million by 2000 B.C.E.

In East Asia, beginning around 8000 B.C.E., a Neolithic culture arose in the lowlands of the Hoang-Ho (Yellow River), covering a region of some 600,000 square kilometers, and spread rapidly to the East and later to the South. The population may have reached 800,000 by 4000 B.C.E., 3 or 4 million by 3000 B.C.E., and 20 million by 2000 B.C.E.

Other Neolithic populations appeared somewhat later in Mexico and the Andean Highlands. Based on the examination of pottery evidence, Neolithic-type cultures also arose in Japan from around

12000 B.C.E. and in the African Sahel from around 8500 B.C.E.

From 6000 B.C.E. to 4000 B.C.E., the world's population may have risen from 6 or 7 million to near 30 million; 2,000 years later, as the plough was replacing the hoe, it may have reached 100 million.

Population Growth Since Antiquity

If chronologically widely-spaced estimates are made, a curve connecting the plotted points of these estimates gives the impression of smooth exponential growth from the distant past to the present. Colin McEvedy and Richard Jones, starting from 400 B.C.E., presented this type of curve with some light fluctuations; but the dominant impression conveyed is virtually uninterrupted exponential growth.

Yet the best known populations since Antiquity—the populations of Europe, China, the Near East, and Japan, which together comprise more than half of all humanity—exhibited marked fluctuations. Compartmentalization of the overall total into broad cultural subgroups reveals these fluctuations (see Table 1). The estimates shown in the table are not precise; even data from twentieth-century census counts from developed countries cannot be claimed to be such. But various checks on the estimates for early dates tend to support the numbers, and as to recent census data, the typical error in census counts has been demonstrated to be about 1 to 2 percent in developed countries and 5 to 30 or even 40 percent in certain developing countries up to the middle of the twentieth century.

Recent studies provide population estimates since Antiquity for various Near Eastern populations—notably for Egypt and Palestine—but interpretation of the underlying data from the ancient, medieval, and Ottoman periods is problematic.

China has a remarkable series of population counts starting at the beginning of the era shown in the table. Use of that data requires great care, but the broad lines of population growth have been established.

For Japan, even if the early estimates are uncertain, the population numbers are well known starting with the early seventeenth century, thanks to the use of temple-registers in which all persons residing in a given village or town district were required to be recorded.

For Europe, documents from Antiquity relating to population are rare. For the medieval period, fis-

TABLE 1

World Population Estimates, by Region, Selected Dates, 400 BC–AD 2000 (millions)

Region	400BC	0	500	1000	1300	1400	1500	1700	1800	1900	2000
China	19	70	32	56	83	70	84	150	330	415	1273
India	30	46	33	40	100	74	95	175	190	290	1320
South-West Asia	42	47	45	33	21	19	23	30	28	38	259
Japan	0.1	0.3	2	7	7	8	8	28	30	44	126
Rest of Asia	3	5	8	19	29	29	33	53	68	115	653
Europe	32	43	41	43	86	65	84	125	195	422	782
North Africa	10	13	12	10	9	8	8	9	9	23	143
Rest of Africa	7	12	20	30	60	60	78	97	92	95	657
North America	1	2	2	2	3	3	3	2	5	90	307
Latin America	7	10	13	16	29	36	39	10	19	75	512
Oceania	1	1	1	1	2	2	3	3	2	6	30
World total	152	250	205	257	429	374	458	682	968	1613	6062

Note: China includes the Korean Peninsula. India includes Pakistan, Bangladesh, and Sri Lanka. Europe includes the former Soviet Union. Latin America includes the Caribbean.

SOURCE: Biraben (1979) and United Nations (2001).

cal records provide an important basis for estimates. The main difficulty is to correctly interpret the concept of the hearth: The term originally corresponded to the household, but its meaning shifted starting with the late fourteenth century. Later, for the sixteenth and seventeenth centuries (and for the eighteenth century in Eastern Orthodox countries), the use of parish registers allow accurate estimates of population characteristics and population change.

For the Indian subcontinent, the estimates shown follow those by Ajit Das Gupta, starting with the estimate of 150 million for the year 1600. That number is broadly confirmed by Shireen Moosvi who gives an estimate of 145 million for the year 1595. For earlier periods, the interval estimates provided by John Durand are used; these show peaks of 50 to 60 million persons for the three most prosperous periods: those of the Mauryan Empire (321–185 B.C.E.), the Gupta Empire (320–470 C.E.), and during the rule of Harsha (612–627 C.E.).

For the Americas and for Australia, despite occasional claims on the matter, there is no plausible evidence to support any substantial population densities for the early periods.

For Africa, existing records yield population estimates for the northern part of the continent, but very little is known prior to 1800 for Africa south of the Sahara. The slave trade (involving some 10 million persons taken to the Americas and some 4 million or more to Muslim lands) very likely removed the larger part of natural increase over the period it

existed, causing long-term stagnation of population size. Censuses from the nineteenth century and for the early part of the twentieth century almost certainly substantially underreported population sizes. The figures in Table 1 take this into account.

Estimates for the world population as a whole can be taken as accurate within plus or minus 5 percent since 1900, within 7 to 8 percent between 1700 and 1900, within about 10 percent between 1500 and 1700, and perhaps within 15 percent before 1500.

Population Surges and Fallbacks

Three major technological revolutions resulted in three great population surges in the course of human history:

- acquisition of clothing and hunting and fishing tools in the Upper Paleolithic period (c. 30000–10000 B.C.E.);
- sedentarization and the introduction of agriculture, animal husbandry, and maritime navigation in the Neolithic period (c. 8000–5000 B.C.E.);
- the industrial revolution, which began in the eighteenth century and will conclude in the twenty-first century, as the post-industrial era takes over.

The amplitude of recurrent falls in population due to climate change in prehistoric times, and due to disease, war, and famines starting with the Neolithic period, may be put at between 10 and 20 percent.

Extrapolations of population size based on historical estimates spanning only a few centuries have been demonstrated to be worthless. Based on the population growth rate of the fourth and third centuries B.C.E., an extrapolation would yield a year 2000 population of more than 20 billion. Extrapolation of the growth rate for the third and fourth centuries C.E. would yield a population in 2000 of only 35 million.

Changing Behaviors

By and large, in prehistoric populations the level of mortality allowed a modest measure of natural growth for several years on end. Typically, a bad year removed that gain in numbers. Starting with the Neolithic era, the level of mortality decreased slightly and the expectation of life at birth reached about 25 years. In Europe, these underlying health conditions persisted until the sixteenth century when a fall in mortality commenced, gathering speed up to and into the twentieth century. In Western Europe, in around 1800, the expectation of life at birth was about 35 years; by 1900 it was about 50 years; and by 2000, 75 years (with a six to eight year difference favoring the female population), while in Eastern Europe it was about 40 years in 1900 and 65 years in 2000. Outside Europe, only the countries of European settlement (North America, Australia, and New Zealand) and Japan had a similar mortality record. Finally, at the middle of the twentieth century, the achievements of modern medicine caused a spectacular rise in life expectancy globally.

It seems that up to the Mesolithic era, the causes of death due to climatic factors (the scarcity of edible plants and wild game) played an important role in the regulation of population. In the Mesolithic era, production and, to a certain degree, storage of harvests and of domestic animals greatly lowered vulnerability to climatic risk, and the population increased rapidly. But above a certain population density, epidemic illnesses, previously rare, multiplied and played an increasingly important role in population regulation. From sixteenth-century Europe, there begins to be some success in the struggle against these epidemics. The plague was almost eliminated in the course of the seventeenth century; smallpox was under attack in the eighteenth century (and nearly eliminated in the nineteenth century); and in the twentieth century, all infectious diseases, which formed the second-most common cause of death up to the middle of the nineteenth century,

were attacked and in most cases brought under control.

Fertility, with an average number of children per woman of around 6 or 7, showed little evidence of being voluntarily limited until well into the seventeenth century. Contraceptive practice was largely nonexistent. Voluntary limitation of births among the general populace can be traced back to the early eighteenth century in three French regions—Champagne, Normandy, and Aquitania—commencing even before any decline of mortality began. In France at large, from an average level of 6 children per woman at the beginning of the eighteenth century, fertility fell to 3 children per woman by 1800. From then on, the absolute number of births in France stagnated, while it doubled in all the other countries of Europe. Only Japan had a similar fertility experience. Elsewhere in Western Europe, fertility began falling only in the last quarter of the nineteenth century, and in Eastern Europe in the first decade of the twentieth century, long after mortality had shown a decrease. Among European colonists in America, fertility was very high in the eighteenth century, with an average of about 7 children per woman. In the United States, however, a decline of fertility started in the late eighteenth century and continued up to the second third of the twentieth century. A similar process began in the second half of the twentieth century in much of Latin America, then in East Asia and, more slowly, in India, and finally in most Muslim countries (with the exception of Palestine) in the 1980s and, more hesitantly, also in Africa south of the Sahara.

Structural Changes

The age distribution of the world population remained very young for a long period, reflecting both high fertility and high mortality. Thus, the effects of dramatic demographic shocks were rapidly erased from the age pyramid. Starting around 1800, however, both France and Japan showed an increase in the proportion of older persons. In effect, the decrease of fertility shrinks the proportion of persons who are young and increases the share of the elderly. The decline of mortality, especially when it improves infant survival, also contributes to a rejuvenation of the population age structure.

Once voluntary limitation of fertility appears, changes in the age distribution also become irregular. Twentieth-century age pyramids in Europe show marked perturbations resulting from fluctuations in the annual number of births—with differences between peaks and troughs that may amount to as much as 50 percent.

Populations of European origin in America and Oceania show more regular changes in the number of births, and substantial immigration also contributes to smoothing the jaggedness of the age pyramids.

In the developing world, from about the middle of the twentieth century, medical advances lowered mortality and increased fertility by improving health and extending the number of years spent in the married state. This resulted in exceptionally rapid population growth, further amplified by a rejuvenated age distribution. Coping with such growth without impoverishment requires heavy economic investment, which many of the countries affected were unable to afford and that consequently experienced serious economic difficulties. Economic outcomes also varied with ownership of resources and other assets and with political conditions—with some countries losing their elite class and their wealth through wars and other calamities.

The decline of fertility that began in almost all developing countries between 1970 and 1990 halted the trend toward younger age distributions. But, by 2000, the phenomenon of population aging was still in a very early phase.

Over the first half of the twenty-first century the global population is projected to increase from 6 billion to around 9 billion. But by the end of this period the growth rate is likely to be much diminished. The very youthfulness of the twenty-first century developing world favors rapid generational change, including change of ideas and attitudes. If so, the future pace of decline in fertility may turn out to be more rapid than is now anticipated.

See also: *Archaeogenetics; Climate Change and Population: History; Epidemics; Health Transition; Mortality Decline; Peopling of the Continents; Prehistoric Populations; Projections and Forecasts, Population.*

BIBLIOGRAPHY

Biraben, Jean-Noël. 1979. "Essai sur l'évolution du nombre des hommes." *Population* 34(1): 13–25.

———. 1988. "Préhistoire." In *Histoire de la population française*, Vol. 1, ed. Jacques Dupâquier. Paris: Presses Universitaires de France.

———. 1999. "Le peuplement de l'Europe préhistorique." In *Histoire des populations de l'Europe*, Vol. 1, ed. Jean-Pierre Bardet and Jacques Dupâquier. Paris: Arthème Fayard.

Caldwell, John. C., and Thomas Schindlmayr. 2002. "Historical Population Estimates: Unraveling the Consensus." *Population and Development Review* 28(2): 183–204.

Cartier, Michel. 1973. "Nouvelles données sur la démographie chinoise a l'époque des Ming (1368–1644)." *Annales Economies, Sociétés, Civilisations* 1341–1359.

Cartier, Michel, and Pierre-Etienne Will. 1971. "Démographie et institutions en Chine: contribution à l'analyse des recensements de l'époque impériale (2 ap. J.C.–1750)." *Annales de démographie historiques* pp. 161–245.

Das Gupta, Ajit. 1972. "Study of the Historical Demography of India." In *Population and Social Change*, ed. D. V. Glass and Roger Revelle. London: Arnold.

Durand, John D. 1977. "Historical Estimates of the World Population: An Evaluation," *Population and Development Review* 3(3): 253–296.

McEvedy, Colin, and Richard Jones. 1978. *Atlas of World Population History.* London: Penguin.

Nemeskéri, János. 1974. *Esquisse d'histoire de peuplement humain.* Budapest: Akadémiai Kiadó.

United Nations. 1972-2001. *Demographic Yearbook.* Special Topic (in selected years): Population Census Statistics. New York: United Nations.

United Nations. 1973. *The Determinants and Consequences of Population Trends: New Summary of the Findings on Interaction of Demographic, Economic and Social Factors.* New York: United Nations.

———. 2001. *World Population Prospects: The 2000 Revision,* Vol. 1, *Comprehensive Tables.* New York: United Nations.

JEAN-NOËL BIRABEN

POPULATION TABLES

Selected Demographic Indicators and Rankings for Countries with a Population of 10 Million or More in 2000

Table 1. Selected Demographic Indicators for Countries with a Population of 10 Million or More in 2000

Table 2. Countries with a Population of 10 Million or More in 2000 Ranked by Population Size in 1950, 2000, and 2050

Table 3. Countries with a Population of 10 Million or More in 2000 Ranked by Total Fertility Rate, Expectation of Life at Birth, and Population Growth Rate

Table 4. Countries with a Population of 10 Million or More in 2000 Ranked by Area and Population Density

TABLE 1

Selected Demographic Indicators for Countries with a Population of 10 Million or More in 2000

Country	Population 2000 (millions)	Area (1000 km²)	Population Density 2000 (per km²)	Total Fertility Rate 2000	Expectation of Life at Birth, 2000 (years)	Population Growth Rate 2000 (% per year)	Population 1950 (millions)	Population 2050 (millions)
Afghanistan	21.8	652	33	6.9	42.5	2.64	8.2	72
Algeria	30.3	2,382	13	3.3	68.9	1.82	8.8	51
Angola	13.1	1,247	11	7.2	44.6	2.94	4.1	53
Argentina	37.0	2,780	13	2.6	72.9	1.26	17.2	55
Australia	19.1	7,741	2	1.8	78.7	1.15	8.2	27
Bangladesh	137.4	144	954	3.8	58.1	2.12	41.8	265
Belarus	10.2	208	49	1.3	68.5	−0.28	7.7	8
Belgium	10.2	33	311	1.5	77.9	0.22	8.6	10
Brazil	170.4	8,547	20	2.3	67.2	1.33	54.0	247
Burkina Faso	11.5	274	42	6.9	45.3	2.32	4.0	46
Cambodia	13.1	181	72	5.3	56.5	2.80	4.3	30
Cameroon	14.9	475	31	5.1	50.0	2.28	4.5	32
Canada	30.8	9,971	3	1.6	78.5	0.93	13.7	40
Chile	15.2	757	20	2.4	74.9	1.36	6.1	22
China	1,252.8	9,561	131	1.8	69.7	0.90	547.3	1,437
Colombia	42.1	1,139	37	2.8	70.4	1.77	12.6	71
Congo (Zaire)	50.9	2,345	22	6.7	50.5	2.56	12.2	204
Cuba	11.2	111	101	1.6	75.7	0.42	5.9	11
Czech Republic	10.3	79	130	1.2	74.3	−0.11	8.9	8
Ecuador	12.6	284	45	3.1	69.5	1.97	3.4	21
Egypt	67.9	1,001	68	3.4	66.3	1.82	21.8	114
Ethiopia	62.9	1,104	57	6.8	44.5	2.55	18.4	186
France	59.2	552	107	1.7	78.1	0.37	41.8	62
Germany	82.0	357	230	1.3	77.3	0.09	68.4	71
Ghana	19.3	239	81	4.6	56.3	2.20	4.9	40
Greece	10.6	132	80	1.3	78.0	0.30	7.6	9
Guatemala	11.4	109	104	4.9	64.0	2.64	3.0	27
Hungary	10.0	93	107	1.4	70.7	−0.49	9.3	7
India	1,008.9	3,288	307	3.3	62.3	1.69	357.6	1,572
Indonesia	212.1	1,905	111	2.6	65.1	1.41	79.5	311
Iran	70.3	1,633	43	3.2	68.0	1.69	16.9	121
Iraq	22.9	438	52	5.3	58.7	2.70	5.2	54
Italy	57.5	301	191	1.2	78.2	0.08	47.1	43
Ivory Coast	16.0	322	50	5.1	47.7	2.14	2.8	32
Japan	127.1	378	336	1.4	80.5	0.26	83.6	109
Kazakhstan	16.2	2,717	6	2.1	64.1	−0.54	6.7	15
Kenya	30.7	580	53	4.6	52.2	2.32	6.3	55
Korea, North	22.3	99	225	2.1	63.1	0.82	10.8	28
Korea, South	46.7	99	472	1.5	74.3	0.78	20.4	52
Madagascar	16.0	587	27	6.1	51.6	2.94	4.2	47
Malawi	11.3	118	96	6.8	40.7	2.42	2.9	31
Malaysia	22.2	330	67	3.3	71.9	2.09	6.1	38
Mali	11.4	1,240	9	7.0	50.9	2.68	3.5	42
Mexico	98.9	1,958	50	2.8	72.2	1.63	27.7	147
Morocco	29.9	447	67	3.4	66.6	1.87	9.0	50

[continued]

TABLE 1 [CONTINUED]

Selected Demographic Indicators for Countries with a Population of 10 Million or More in 2000

Country	Population 2000 (millions)	Area (1000 km²)	Population Density 2000 (per km²)	Total Fertility Rate 2000	Expectation of Life at Birth, 2000 (years)	Population Growth Rate 2000 (% per year)	Population 1950 (millions)	Population 2050 (millions)
Mozambique	18.3	802	23	6.3	40.6	2.31	6.2	39
Myanmar (Burma)	47.7	677	71	3.3	55.8	1.48	17.8	69
Nepal	23.0	147	157	4.8	57.3	2.40	8.5	52
Netherlands	15.9	41	387	1.5	77.9	0.52	10.1	16
Niger	10.8	1,267	9	8.0	44.2	3.46	2.5	52
Nigeria	113.9	924	123	5.9	51.3	2.74	29.8	279
Pakistan	141.3	796	177	5.5	59.0	2.66	39.7	344
Peru	25.7	1,285	20	3.0	68.0	1.73	7.6	42
Philippines	75.7	300	252	3.6	68.6	2.03	20.0	128
Poland	38.6	323	120	1.5	72.8	0.01	24.8	33
Portugal	10.0	92	109	1.5	75.2	0.20	8.4	9
Romania	22.4	238	94	1.3	69.8	−0.22	16.3	18
Russian Federation	145.5	17,075	9	1.2	66.1	−0.36	102.7	104
Saudi Arabia	20.3	2,150	9	6.2	70.9	3.49	3.2	60
Serbia and Montenegro	10.6	102	103	1.8	72.2	0.01	7.1	9
South Africa	43.3	1,221	35	3.1	56.7	1.57	13.7	47
Spain	39.9	506	79	1.2	78.1	0.09	28.0	31
Sri Lanka	18.9	66	287	2.1	71.6	0.96	7.5	23
Sudan	31.1	2,506	12	4.9	55.0	2.13	9.2	64
Syria	16.2	185	88	4.0	70.5	2.59	3.5	36
Taiwan	22.3	36	617	1.6	76.5	0.87	7.5	25
Tanzania	35.1	945	37	5.5	51.1	2.58	7.9	83
Thailand	62.8	513	122	2.1	69.6	1.34	19.6	82
Turkey	66.7	775	86	2.7	69.0	1.62	20.8	99
Uganda	23.3	241	97	7.1	41.9	2.95	5.2	102
Ukraine	49.6	604	82	1.3	68.1	−0.78	37.3	30
United Kingdom	59.4	245	243	1.7	77.2	0.27	50.6	59
United States of America	283.2	9,364	30	2.0	76.5	1.05	157.8	397
Uzbekistan	24.9	447	56	2.9	68.3	1.76	6.3	41
Venezuela	24.2	912	27	3.0	72.4	2.02	5.1	42
Vietnam	78.1	332	235	2.5	67.2	1.40	27.4	124
Yemen	18.3	528	35	7.6	59.4	4.17	4.3	102
Zambia	10.4	753	14	6.1	40.5	2.46	2.4	29
Zimbabwe	12.6	391	32	5.0	42.9	1.91	2.7	24
Other countries and territories	357.8	17,845	20				151.0	653
World	**6,056.7**	**133,572**	**46**	**2.8**	**65.0**	**1.35**	**2,519.5**	**9,322**

Notes: Countries with a population of 10 million or more made up 94.1 percent of the total world population in 2000. Estimates shown of fertility, life expectancy, and population growth refer to the 5-year period 1995-2000. Expectations of life are for both sexes combined. Estimates for China exclude Hong Kong, Macao, and Taiwan. Population figures for 2050 are the UN's "medium" projection.

SOURCES: Estimated and projected population characteristics are from United Nations, *World Population Prospects: The 2000 Revision, Volume I: Comprehensive Tables*. New York, 2001. Area statistics are from World Bank, *World Development Report 2000/2001*. New York: Oxford University Press, 2001. Estimates for Taiwan compiled from various sources.

TABLE 2

Countries with a Population of 10 Million or More in 2000 Ranked by Population Size in 1950, 2000, and 2050

Rank	Country	Population 1950 (millions)	Country	Population 2000 (millions)	Country	Population 2050 (millions)
1	China	547.3	China	1,252.8	India	1,572
2	India	357.6	India	1,008.9	China	1,437
3	United States of America	157.8	United States of America	283.2	United States of America	397
4	Russian Federation	102.7	Indonesia	212.1	Pakistan	344
5	Japan	83.6	Brazil	170.4	Indonesia	311
6	Indonesia	79.5	Russian Federation	145.5	Nigeria	279
7	Germany	68.4	Pakistan	141.3	Bangladesh	265
8	Brazil	54.0	Bangladesh	137.4	Brazil	247
9	United Kingdom	50.6	Japan	127.1	Congo (Zaire)	204
10	Italy	47.1	Nigeria	113.9	Ethiopia	186
11	France	41.8	Mexico	98.9	Mexico	147
12	Bangladesh	41.8	Germany	82.0	Philippines	128
13	Pakistan	39.7	Vietnam	78.1	Vietnam	124
14	Ukraine	37.3	Philippines	75.7	Iran	121
15	Nigeria	29.8	Iran	70.3	Egypt	114
16	Spain	28.0	Egypt	67.9	Japan	109
17	Mexico	27.7	Turkey	66.7	Russian Federation	104
18	Vietnam	27.4	Ethiopia	62.9	Yemen	102
19	Poland	24.8	Thailand	62.8	Uganda	102
20	Egypt	21.8	United Kingdom	59.4	Turkey	99
21	Turkey	20.8	France	59.2	Tanzania	83
22	Korea, South	20.4	Italy	57.5	Thailand	82
23	Philippines	20.0	Congo (Zaire)	50.9	Afghanistan	72
24	Thailand	19.6	Ukraine	49.6	Colombia	71
25	Ethiopia	18.4	Myanmar (Burma)	47.7	Germany	71
26	Myanmar (Burma)	17.8	Korea, South	46.7	Myanmar (Burma)	69
27	Argentina	17.2	South Africa	43.3	Sudan	64
28	Iran	16.9	Colombia	42.1	France	62
29	Romania	16.3	Spain	39.9	Saudi Arabia	60
30	Canada	13.7	Poland	38.6	United Kingdom	59
31	South Africa	13.7	Argentina	37.0	Kenya	55
32	Colombia	12.6	Tanzania	35.1	Argentina	55
33	Congo (Zaire)	12.2	Sudan	31.1	Iraq	54
34	Korea, North	10.8	Canada	30.8	Angola	53
35	Netherlands	10.1	Kenya	30.7	Nepal	52
36	Hungary	9.3	Algeria	30.3	Niger	52
37	Sudan	9.2	Morocco	29.9	Korea, South	52
38	Morocco	9.0	Peru	25.7	Algeria	51
39	Czech Republic	8.9	Uzbekistan	24.9	Morocco	50
40	Algeria	8.8	Venezuela	24.2	South Africa	47
41	Belgium	8.6	Uganda	23.3	Madagascar	47
42	Nepal	8.5	Nepal	23.0	Burkina Faso	46
43	Portugal	8.4	Iraq	22.9	Italy	43
44	Australia	8.2	Romania	22.4	Venezuela	42
45	Afghanistan	8.2	Taiwan	22.3	Peru	42

[continued]

TABLE 2 [CONTINUED]

Countries with a Population of 10 Million or More in 2000 Ranked by Population Size in 1950, 2000, and 2050

Rank	Country	Population 1950 (millions)	Country	Population 2000 (millions)	Country	Population 2050 (millions)
46	Tanzania	7.9	Korea, North	22.3	Mali	42
47	Belarus	7.7	Malaysia	22.2	Uzbekistan	41
48	Peru	7.6	Afghanistan	21.8	Canada	40
49	Greece	7.6	Saudi Arabia	20.3	Ghana	40
50	Taiwan	7.5	Ghana	19.3	Mozambique	39
51	Sri Lanka	7.5	Australia	19.1	Malaysia	38
52	Serbia and Montenegro	7.1	Sri Lanka	18.9	Syria	36
53	Kazakhstan	6.7	Yemen	18.3	Poland	33
54	Uzbekistan	6.3	Mozambique	18.3	Cameroon	32
55	Kenya	6.3	Syria	16.2	Ivory Coast	32
56	Mozambique	6.2	Kazakhstan	16.2	Spain	31
57	Malaysia	6.1	Ivory Coast	16.0	Malawi	31
58	Chile	6.1	Madagascar	16.0	Ukraine	30
59	Cuba	5.9	Netherlands	15.9	Cambodia	30
60	Uganda	5.2	Chile	15.2	Zambia	29
61	Iraq	5.2	Cameroon	14.9	Korea, North	28
62	Venezuela	5.1	Angola	13.1	Guatemala	27
63	Ghana	4.9	Cambodia	13.1	Australia	27
64	Cameroon	4.5	Ecuador	12.6	Taiwan	25
65	Cambodia	4.3	Zimbabwe	12.6	Zimbabwe	24
66	Yemen	4.3	Burkina Faso	11.5	Sri Lanka	23
67	Madagascar	4.2	Guatemala	11.4	Chile	22
68	Angola	4.1	Mali	11.4	Ecuador	21
69	Burkina Faso	4.0	Malawi	11.3	Romania	18
70	Mali	3.5	Cuba	11.2	Netherlands	16
71	Syria	3.5	Niger	10.8	Kazakhstan	15
72	Ecuador	3.4	Greece	10.6	Cuba	11
73	Saudi Arabia	3.2	Serbia and Montenegro	10.6	Belgium	10
74	Guatemala	3.0	Zambia	10.4	Serbia and Montenegro	9
75	Malawi	2.9	Czech Republic	10.3	Portugal	9
76	Ivory Coast	2.8	Belgium	10.2	Greece	9
77	Zimbabwe	2.7	Belarus	10.2	Czech Republic	8
78	Niger	2.5	Portugal	10.0	Belarus	8
79	Zambia	2.4	Hungary	10.0	Hungary	7
	Other countries and territories	151.0	Other countries and territories	357.8	Other countries and territories	653
	World	**2,519.5**	**World**	**6,056.7**	**World**	**9,322**

Note: Countries are listed in descending order according to population size in the respective year. Population figures for 2050 are the "medium" projections from the UN's 2000 projection series. Estimates for China exclude Hong Kong, Macao, and Taiwan.

SOURCES: Estimated and projected population totals are from United Nations, *World Population Prospects: The 2000 Revision, Volume I: Comprehensive Tables*. New York, 2001. Estimates for Taiwan compiled from various sources.

TABLE 3

Countries with a Population of 10 Million or More in 2000 Ranked by Total Fertility Rate, Expectation of Life at Birth, and Population Growth Rate

Rank	Country	Total Fertility Rate 2000	Country	Expectation of Life at Birth (years) 2000	Country	Population Growth Rate (% per year) 2000
1	Spain	1.2	Japan	80.5	Ukraine	−0.78
2	Czech Republic	1.2	Australia	78.7	Kazakhstan	−0.54
3	Italy	1.2	Canada	78.5	Hungary	−0.49
4	Russian Federation	1.2	Italy	78.2	Russian Federation	−0.36
5	Ukraine	1.3	Spain	78.1	Belarus	−0.28
6	Belarus	1.3	France	78.1	Romania	−0.22
7	Greece	1.3	Greece	78.0	Czech Republic	−0.11
8	Romania	1.3	Belgium	77.9	Poland	0.01
9	Germany	1.3	Netherlands	77.9	Serbia and Montenegro	0.01
10	Hungary	1.4	Germany	77.3	Italy	0.08
11	Japan	1.4	United Kingdom	77.2	Germany	0.09
12	Poland	1.5	United States of America	76.5	Spain	0.09
13	Portugal	1.5	Taiwan	76.5	Portugal	0.20
14	Korea, South	1.5	Cuba	75.7	Belgium	0.22
15	Netherlands	1.5	Portugal	75.2	Japan	0.26
16	Belgium	1.5	Chile	74.9	United Kingdom	0.27
17	Cuba	1.6	Korea, South	74.3	Greece	0.30
18	Canada	1.6	Czech Republic	74.3	France	0.37
19	Taiwan	1.6	Argentina	72.9	Cuba	0.42
20	United Kingdom	1.7	Poland	72.8	Netherlands	0.52
21	France	1.7	Venezuela	72.4	Korea, South	0.78
22	Serbia and Montenegro	1.8	Serbia and Montenegro	72.2	Korea, North	0.82
23	Australia	1.8	Mexico	72.2	Taiwan	0.87
24	China	1.8	Malaysia	71.9	China	0.90
25	United States of America	2.0	Sri Lanka	71.6	Canada	0.93
26	Korea, North	2.1	Saudi Arabia	70.9	Sri Lanka	0.96
27	Kazakhstan	2.1	Hungary	70.7	United States of America	1.05
28	Sri Lanka	2.1	Syria	70.5	Australia	1.15
29	Thailand	2.1	Colombia	70.4	Argentina	1.26
30	Brazil	2.3	Romania	69.8	Brazil	1.33
31	Chile	2.4	China	69.7	Thailand	1.34
32	Vietnam	2.5	Thailand	69.6	Chile	1.36
33	Indonesia	2.6	Ecuador	69.5	Vietnam	1.40
34	Argentina	2.6	Turkey	69.0	Indonesia	1.41
35	Turkey	2.7	Algeria	68.9	Myanmar (Burma)	1.48
36	Mexico	2.8	Philippines	68.6	South Africa	1.57
37	Colombia	2.8	Belarus	68.5	Turkey	1.62
38	Uzbekistan	2.9	Uzbekistan	68.3	Mexico	1.63
39	Peru	3.0	Ukraine	68.1	Iran	1.69
40	Venezuela	3.0	Peru	68.0	India	1.69

[continued]

TABLE 3 [CONTINUED]

Countries with a Population of 10 Million or More in 2000 Ranked by Total Fertility Rate, Expectation of Life at Birth, and Population Growth Rate

Rank	Country	Total Fertility Rate 2000	Country	Expectation of Life at Birth (years) 2000	Country	Population Growth Rate (% per year) 2000
41	Ecuador	3.1	Iran	68.0	Peru	1.73
42	South Africa	3.1	Vietnam	67.2	Uzbekistan	1.76
43	Iran	3.2	Brazil	67.2	Colombia	1.77
44	Algeria	3.3	Morocco	66.6	Egypt	1.82
45	Malaysia	3.3	Egypt	66.3	Algeria	1.82
46	Myanmar (Burma)	3.3	Russian Federation	66.1	Morocco	1.87
47	India	3.3	Indonesia	65.1	Zimbabwe	1.91
48	Egypt	3.4	Kazakhstan	64.1	Ecuador	1.97
49	Morocco	3.4	Guatemala	64.0	Venezuela	2.02
50	Philippines	3.6	Korea, North	63.1	Philippines	2.03
51	Bangladesh	3.8	India	62.3	Malaysia	2.09
52	Syria	4.0	Yemen	59.4	Bangladesh	2.12
53	Ghana	4.6	Pakistan	59.0	Sudan	2.13
54	Kenya	4.6	Iraq	58.7	Ivory Coast	2.14
55	Nepal	4.8	Bangladesh	58.1	Ghana	2.20
56	Sudan	4.9	Nepal	57.3	Cameroon	2.28
57	Guatemala	4.9	South Africa	56.7	Mozambique	2.31
58	Zimbabwe	5.0	Cambodia	56.5	Kenya	2.32
59	Cameroon	5.1	Ghana	56.3	Burkina Faso	2.32
60	Ivory Coast	5.1	Myanmar (Burma)	55.8	Nepal	2.40
61	Cambodia	5.3	Sudan	55.0	Malawi	2.42
62	Iraq	5.3	Kenya	52.2	Zambia	2.46
63	Pakistan	5.5	Madagascar	51.6	Ethiopia	2.55
64	Tanzania	5.5	Nigeria	51.3	Congo (Zaire)	2.56
65	Nigeria	5.9	Tanzania	51.1	Tanzania	2.58
66	Zambia	6.1	Mali	50.9	Syria	2.59
67	Madagascar	6.1	Congo (Zaire)	50.5	Afghanistan	2.64
68	Saudi Arabia	6.2	Cameroon	50.0	Guatemala	2.64
69	Mozambique	6.3	Ivory Coast	47.7	Pakistan	2.66
70	Congo (Zaire)	6.7	Burkina Faso	45.3	Mali	2.68
71	Ethiopia	6.8	Angola	44.6	Iraq	2.70
72	Malawi	6.8	Ethiopia	44.5	Nigeria	2.74
73	Burkina Faso	6.9	Niger	44.2	Cambodia	2.80
74	Afghanistan	6.9	Zimbabwe	42.9	Madagascar	2.94
75	Mali	7.0	Afghanistan	42.5	Angola	2.94
76	Uganda	7.1	Uganda	41.9	Uganda	2.95
77	Angola	7.2	Malawi	40.7	Niger	3.46
78	Yemen	7.6	Mozambique	40.6	Saudi Arabia	3.49
79	Niger	8.0	Zambia	40.5	Yemen	4.17
	World	**2.8**	**World**	**65.0**	**World**	**1.35**

Note: Countries are listed in ascending order by fertility and population growth rate and in descending order by expectation of life. Estimates refer to the 5-year period 1995-2000. The total fertility rate can be interpreted as the average lifetime births per woman at the prevailing rate of childbearing. Expectations of life are for both sexes combined.

SOURCES: United Nations, *World Population Prospects: The 2000 Revision, Volume I: Comprehensive Tables*. New York, 2001. Estimates for Taiwan compiled from various sources.

TABLE 4

Countries with a Population of 10 Million or More in 2000 Ranked by Area and Population Density

Rank	Country	Area (1000 km²)	Country	Population Density (per km²)
1	Russian Federation	17,075	Bangladesh	954
2	Canada	9,971	Taiwan	617
3	China	9,561	Korea, South	472
4	United States of America	9,364	Netherlands	387
5	Brazil	8,547	Japan	336
6	Australia	7,741	Belgium	311
7	India	3,288	India	307
8	Argentina	2,780	Sri Lanka	287
9	Kazakhstan	2,717	Philippines	252
10	Sudan	2,506	United Kingdom	243
11	Algeria	2,382	Vietnam	235
12	Congo (Zaire)	2,345	Germany	230
13	Saudi Arabia	2,150	Korea, North	225
14	Mexico	1,958	Italy	191
15	Indonesia	1,905	Pakistan	177
16	Iran	1,633	Nepal	157
17	Peru	1,285	China	131
18	Niger	1,267	Czech Republic	130
19	Angola	1,247	Nigeria	123
20	Mali	1,240	Thailand	122
21	South Africa	1,221	Poland	120
22	Colombia	1,139	Indonesia	111
23	Ethiopia	1,104	Portugal	109
24	Egypt	1,001	France	107
25	Tanzania	945	Hungary	107
26	Nigeria	924	Guatemala	104
27	Venezuela	912	Serbia and Montenegro	103
28	Mozambique	802	Cuba	101
29	Pakistan	796	Uganda	97
30	Turkey	775	Malawi	96
31	Chile	757	Romania	94
32	Zambia	753	Syria	88
33	Myanmar (Burma)	677	Turkey	86
34	Afghanistan	652	Ukraine	82
35	Ukraine	604	Ghana	81
36	Madagascar	587	Greece	80
37	Kenya	580	Spain	79
38	France	552	Cambodia	72
39	Yemen	528	Myanmar (Burma)	71
40	Thailand	513	Egypt	68
41	Spain	506	Malaysia	67
42	Cameroon	475	Morocco	67
43	Uzbekistan	447	Ethiopia	57
44	Morocco	447	Uzbekistan	56
45	Iraq	438	Kenya	53

[continued]

TABLE 4 [CONTINUED]

Countries with a Population of 10 Million or More in 2000 Ranked by Area and Population Density

Rank	Country	Area (1000 km²)	Country	Population Density (per km²)
46	Zimbabwe	391	Iraq	52
47	Japan	378	Mexico	50
48	Germany	357	Ivory Coast	50
49	Vietnam	332	Belarus	49
50	Malaysia	330	Ecuador	45
51	Poland	323	Iran	43
52	Ivory Coast	322	Burkina Faso	42
53	Italy	301	Tanzania	37
54	Philippines	300	Colombia	37
55	Ecuador	284	South Africa	35
56	Burkina Faso	274	Yemen	35
57	United Kingdom	245	Afghanistan	33
58	Uganda	241	Zimbabwe	32
59	Ghana	239	Cameroon	31
60	Romania	238	United States of America	30
61	Belarus	208	Madagascar	27
62	Syria	185	Venezuela	27
63	Cambodia	181	Mozambique	23
64	Nepal	147	Congo (Zaire)	22
65	Bangladesh	144	Chile	20
66	Greece	132	Peru	20
67	Malawi	118	Brazil	20
68	Cuba	111	Zambia	14
69	Guatemala	109	Argentina	13
70	Serbia and Montenegro	102	Algeria	13
71	Korea, South	99	Sudan	12
72	Korea, North	99	Angola	11
73	Hungary	93	Saudi Arabia	9
74	Portugal	92	Mali	9
75	Czech Republic	79	Niger	9
76	Sri Lanka	66	Russian Federation	9
77	Netherlands	41	Kazakhstan	6
78	Taiwan	36	Canada	3
79	Belgium	33	Australia	2
	Other countries and territories	17,845	Other countries and territories	20
	World	**133,572**	**World**	**46**

Note: Population density is for 2000.

SOURCES: World Bank, *World Development Report 2000/2001.* New York: Oxford University Press, 2001. Estimates for Tawain compiled for various sources.

ACKNOWLEDGMENTS

Business Demography. The authors thank Linda Jacobsen and Jeff Tayman for numerous helpful suggestions.

Diseases, Infectious. The authors would like to thank Drs. Heidi Davidson and Robert Pinner for allowing the reprint of their graph on infectious disease mortality rates during the twentieth century.

Population Journals. The author gratefully acknowledges the comments on the draft text received from NIDI librarian Jolande Siebenga.

Public Opinion. Most of the questions cited in this article were obtained via the Roper Poll Database at the Roper Center for Public Opinion Research at the University of Connecticut. All other results are taken from the RAND Corporation study. Further analysis of public attitudes about population issues is available on the "Americans and the World" web site (<http://www.americans-world.org>), which is maintained by the Program on International Policy Attitudes.

Reproductive Health. Thanks are due to Jane Cottingham and John Maurice of the World Health Organization for updated data and references. Adrienne Germain of the International Women's Health Coalition and Ms. Cottingham gave valuable comments on earlier versions.

Small Area Analysis. The author thanks Peter Morrison, Linda Jacobsen, and Jeff Tayman for numerous helpful suggestions.

INDEX

Page references to entire articles are in **boldface.** *References to figures and tables are denoted by italics.*

Cambodia
  genocide, 456
  political prisoners, 165
  refugees, 437
  state-sponsored violence, 164
Cambridge Group for the History
    of Population and Social
    Structure, 343, 345, 346, 486
Campbell, Arthur, 73, 207
The Camp of the Saints (Raspail),
    608–609
Canada
  censuses, 123
  cigarette smoking, 941
  Citizenship and Immigration
    Canada, 740
  immigration, 515–516, *521,* 521–
    523, 945, *945*
  indigenous peoples, 525–526
  industry classification, 702
  international labor migration, 572
  unintentional injury death rates
    by cause, *3*
Cancer, **110–112,** *111*
  breast cancer, 44
  mortality decline, 660
  sex differences in mortality, 663
  tobacco use, 941
Cannan, Edwin, **112–113,** 219, 710,
    808, 972
Cantillon, Richard, **113–114,** 776
Capitalism
  ecological degradation, 301–302
  globalization, 141–143, *142*
  Marxist population theory, 626,
    781
  sociological theory of population,
    913
Capital (Marx), 910
Capoid race, 792
Caraël, M., 39
Card, David, 282
Cardiovascular disease, **114–115**
  alcohol consumption, 44
  epidemiological transition, 309,
    659–660
  sex differences in mortality, 664
Caregiving, 401–402
Carey, James R., 85
Caribbean African population, 727
Carnes, Bruce, 30
Carolina Population Center,
    University of North Carolina,
    82–83
Carroll, Glenn R., 712, 713
Carr-Saunders, Alexander, 753
Carrying capacity, **115–117**
  North American prehistoric
    populations, 802
  technology, 932
Cartagena Declaration on Refugees,
    827
Carter, Larry, 922
Caste, **117–119**

Catholicism, 93–94, 831–832, 835,
    852
CATI (Computer Assisted
    Telephone Interviewing) system,
    209
Cat's Cradle (Vonnegut), 607
Cattell, Raymond, 818
Cause-deleted life tables, 601
*Cause della grandezza e magnificenza
    delle città* (Botero), 104
Causes of death, **119–122**
  age patterns, *653,* 653–654
  classification, 80, 119–120
  early cities, 135
  early Massachusetts records, *249*
  epidemiological transition, **307–**
    310
  France, *653*
  identifying, 120
  infant and child mortality, 533–
    534
  leading, *261*
  limitations, 254–255
  low-mortality countries, 659–660
  maternal mortality, 628–631
  multiple causes, 120
  reporting, 244, 249
  sex differentials, 662–663
  socioeconomic mortality
    differentials, 666
  United States, 254–255, *256, 261*
Cavalli-Sforza, Luigi, 893
Cavendish, W., 159
Censoring data, 326
Census, **122–126**
  British Census of 1911, 319
  childlessness data, 129
  data errors, 900
  definition, 961
  England, 467, 731, 778
  ethnic and national groups
    classification, 314–315
  France, 778
  georeferencing census data, 459
  history, 123, 216–217, 776, 778
  internal migration data, 545–546
  national, 776
  Quetelet's contribution, 819
  race/ethnicity, 314–315, 821–822
  religious affiliation, 835
  as small-area demographic
    sources, 898, 915
  socioeconomic classes, 319
  surveys as alternative to, 206
  United States, 123, 124–126, 206–
    207, 778, 960–961
Census Bureau, U.S. *See* U.S.
    Bureau of the Census
Census Occupational Classification,
    702
Census 2000 Occupational Index,
    702
Centenarians, 706
Central American refugees, 827

Central place theory, **126–128,** *127*
Centro Latinoamericano y Caribeño
    de Demografia, 747
Centuries of Childhood (Ariès), 343
Cereal yield and world population
    size, *434*
Cernea, Michael, 856
CFCs (chlorofluorocarbons), 272
Chad, 176, 790
Chadwick, Edwin, 248
Chalk, Frank, 455
Chang, M. C., 97, 849
Chang, Yuan, 285
*The Changing Population of the
    United States* (Taeuber and
    Taeuber), 931
Charity and famine relief, 383–384
Cherlin, Andrew, 75–76
Chiappori, Pierre-Andre, 632
Chicago Council on Foreign
    Relations (CCFR) poll, 814
Child abandonment, 537
Child allowances. *See* Family
    allowances
Childbearing
  insurance hypothesis, 670
  nonmarried, 154, 359, 537, 583,
    624, 636, 847
  rates, *413,* 414–416
Child benefits. *See* Family
    allowances
Child care, 373–374, 721
Childe, V. Gordon, 55
Childhood's End (Clarke), 607
Child labor, 569–570, 703
Childlessness, **128–130,** 720
Child mortality. *See* Infant and
    child mortality
Children
  child labor, 569–570, 703
  child support and divorce, 635–
    636
  cost of, 159–160, **177–180,** 338,
    636, 670–671
  dependency, 28, 229
  in developed countries/less
    developed countries, *25*
  economic benefits and costs, 231
  elder-child ratio, 33
  family and household
    composition, 360
  family policy, **371–374**
  as function of marriage, 622
  gender preferences for children,
    446–448, 709, 875, 878–880,
    958, 975
  infant and child health programs,
    535–536
  intergenerational transfers, 544–
    545
  longitudinal demographic
    surveys, 613
  replacement of dead children,
    669–670

reproductive technologies, 854
same-sex couples, 624
socialization, 721
treatment, 448
undernutrition indicators in
African countries, *387*, 388
well-being, 360
Children Act (England), 17, 18–19
The Children of Men (James), 606
China
adoption, 878
birth rates, 389–390
collectivization of agriculture, 163
Cultural Revolution, 163–164
as demographic model, 113
family planning programs, 758
famine, 163, 383, **388–390**
fertility control programs, 770
food supply, 432
forced internal resettlement, 856
gender preference, 709
homeostasis, 493–495
mortality, 162–163, 389
oldest old, *706*, 707
one child policy, 164–166, **707–
710**, 711, 905
political prisoners, 165
population estimates, 979
population growth, 390, 493–494,
709
population quality, 818
prehistoric populations, 793–795
rapid population growth, 388,
708
refugees, 165
sex ratio, 166, 875
social institutions, 905
state-sponsored violence, 163–164
total fertility rate, 708, 709
ultrasound screening for sex
detection, 879
urbanization, 136, 708
Chinese, overseas, **130–133**
Chlorofluorocarbons (CFCs), 272
Choe, Minja Kim, 958
Choice, reproductive, 848, 869
Cholera, 260
Christaller, Walter, 127, 616
Christensen, Kaare, 86
Christianity
birth control, 93–94
doctrine, 831–832
induced abortion, 527–528
population thought, 772–773
vital records, 217
Chronic and degenerative diseases,
253–258, 285
Chu, C. T. Cyrus, 188, 494
Church registration, 217
Cigarette smoking, 115, 664, 941–
942
Circulation mobility, 906, 907

Cities
agglomerations, 136–137, *138*,
952–953
central place theory, **126–128**,
127
city/state relationships, 141
city systems, **140–144**
connectedness, 142–143
cooperation, 142–143
demographic history, **133–136**
ecology, 502–503
estimations of size, 729
future directions, **136–140**
global, 141–143, *142*
governance, 139–140
growth of, 953
history, 141
industrial, 138
land use, 576–578
Lebensraum, 584
mortality, 133, 667–668
population estimates, 731
preindustrial, 138
quality of life, 139
residential segregation, 858–859
suburb/urban area distinction,
925
United States, *924*
urban graveyard effect, 133–135
See also Urbanization
Citizenship and Immigration
Canada, 740
*Citizenship and Nationhood in
France and Germany* (Brubaker),
517
City-states, 141, 730
Civilian casualties of war, 965
Civil registration, 217
Clarke, John, 461
Classical eugenics, 817
Classical Greece and Rome. *See*
Ancient world
Classification
causes of death, 80, 119–120
disease, **247–250**, 252, 258–259
ethnic and national groups, 314–
315
family, 356
industry, 701–702, *703*
international migration, 549–550
life span, 592
occupation, 702
socioeconomic class, 319
urban/rural, 865
welfare regimes, 969
Cleaver, Kevin, 160
Cleland, John, 428, 429, 671, 874
Climate
mortality, 981
population density, 222
prehistoric Asia, 794
Climate change, **144–152**
ecological dangers, 271
energy use projections, 290

as environmental security threat,
687
foraging societies, 505
future directions, 149–152
history, 144–149
measures of 20,000 years of
climate change, *147*
natural resources, 691
population policy, 150–151
population size and distribution,
799
Cloning, 852, 854
Clovis tradition, 802
Clustering, fertility pattern, 238
Cluster sampling, 208
Coale, Ansley J., **152–153**
demographic transition, 215,
427–428
developing economies, 275
European Fertility Project, 488
family planning, 229
fertility control programs, 766
geographical dimension of
demographic change, 461
high fertility and economic
growth, 277
history of demography, 219
indirect measurement of fertility
control, 418, 419
model life tables, 600
sex-specific abortion, 879
unstable populations estimation,
842
Coale-Demeny model life tables,
652
Coalescent theory, 63–65, 922
The Coal Question (Jevons), 690
Coal resources, 690
Coase, Ronald, 337
Coastal areas and population
density, 222
Cobb, John, 294
Cohabitation, **153–155**
declines in marriage, 625
as determinant of fertility, 414
dissolution, 624
matching patterns, 635
nonmarital fertility, 410
nonmarried childbearing, 624
partner choice, 724
sexual activity, 622
United States, 357–358, 625
Cohen, Joel E., 493, 842, 921
Cohen, Mark N., 55, 802
Cohort analysis, **155–157**
age structure, 738
baby boom, 73, 74–75
balance equation, 737–738
cohort-parity analysis (CPA) of
fertility control, 418–419
demographic surveys, 205
high school, 613–614
homocide, 498
labor market, 187

life tables, 594–596
small cohort size and fertility, 409
synthetic, 595
total fertility rates, 423–424
Cohort component method of population projection, 112, 725, 768, 808–809, 841–842, 899, 972
Cohort Fertility (Whelpton), 972
Coitus interruptus, 93, 94, 171
Cold War, 71, 436–437, 520, 826–827
Coleman, James S., 901
Collective beliefs, 504
Collectivization, 163, 394
Colonial Africa, 385, 694
Colonial America, 20–21, 123
Colonialism, European, 919
Colonization
  animal ecology, 50
  outer space, **714–716**
  prehistoric populations, 796–797
Commission on Population Geography of the International Geographical Union, 461
Commission on Population Growth and the American Future, 735, 769
Committee on Applied Demography, Population Association of America, 917
Common property resources, **157–161**
Commons, 158–160, 229, 297, 475
Communism, **161–167**
Communist Manifesto (Marx), 625
Communitarian support systems, 338
Competing risks, 12–13, 328, 861
Competitive interaction, 91
Complications, pregnancy, 630–631
Component method of population estimates, 898, 915–916
Computer Assisted Telephone Interviewing (CATI) systems, 209
Computer technology
  artificial social life, 68–70
  business demography, 107
  data processing and demographic surveys, 208–209
  See also Software
Comstock laws, 94–96
Comte, Auguste, 819
Conception, *397*, 397–398, 415
Condoms, 96
Condorect, Marquis de, **167–168**
Conference on Environment and Development, Rio de Janeiro, 1992, 771
Conferences, international population. *See* International population conferences
Confidentiality and research subjects, 195–196

Conformity and fertility, 338
Congdon, Peter, 461
Connecticut, Griswold v., 96
Connell, John, 462
Consanguineous marriage, 46
Conservative/corporatist welfare regimes, 969
Consistency checks in demographic estimation, 311–312
Constitution, United States, 960
Consumer markets, 107–108
Contingent valuation of safety, 956
Contraception
  abstinence, 1–2, 171, 175
  Buddhism, 833
  Christianity, 831, 832
  Contraceptive Prevalence Surveys (USAID), 207
  demographic behavior, 976
  effectiveness, 415
  fertility intention, 380
  Hinduism, 833
  impact on family planning programs, 364–365
  infertility, 539–540
  intrauterine devices (IUDs), 96, 173–174, 365–366
  Islam, 832
  Judaism, 831
  liberal states, 755
  methods, **170–174**
  pregnancy rates associated with various methods, *174*
  prevalence, **174–177**, *365, 368*
  as proximate determinant of fertility, 415
  sexuality, 883
  voluntary parenthood, 720
  See also Birth control; Family planning
Contract labor, 574, 936
Controlled Fertility (Notestein and Stix), 696
Control of Communicable Diseases Manual (American Public Health Association), 259
Convention Governing the Specific Aspects of Refugee Problems in Africa, 826–827
Convention on the Elimination of All Forms of Discrimination Against Women, 847
Convention on the Prevention and Punishment of the Crime of Genocide, 455
Convention on the Rights of the Child, 750
Convention Relating to the Status of Refugees, 70–71, 436–437, 825–826
Conversion, religious, 836
Cook, Sherburne, 726
Cooperative bargaining models, 353
Copán, Honduras, 803

Copper-releasing IUDs, 173–174
Cornelius, Wayne, 517
Coronary heart disease. *See* Cardiovascular disease
Costa, Dora, 482
Cost/benefit analysis
  fertility, 231
  immigration, 509–511
  internal migration, 546–547
Cost of children, 159–160, **177–180,** 338, 636, 670–671, 721, 957
Cost of time, 634
Cost-sharing, 337–338
Costs of risk, 955–956
Council of Europe
  European Population Committee, 739
  Parliamentary Assembly, 739
Counterurbanization, 137, 864, 925
Cours d'économie politique (Pareto), 722
Court cases
  Griswold v. Connecticut, 96
  Roe v. Wade, 96, 770
  United States v. One Package of Japanese Pessaries, 96
Coutinho, Elsimar, 97, 172
Covariates, time-varying, 326
Cox regression models. *See* Proportional hazard models
CPA (cohort parity analysis) of fertility control, 418–419
Crews-Meyer, Kelly, 838
Crime, demographic aspects of, **180–183,** *181*
Crimmins, Eileen M., 269, 666
Crisis mortality, 304–305
Critical minimum effort thesis, 585
Critical Perspectives on Schooling and Fertility in the Developing World (U.S. National Research Council), 279–280
Critical theory, 7–8
Critique of the Gotha Program (Marx), 626
Cromwell, Thomas, 217
Cropland, 200, 578, 579
Crowding, 337
Crude birth rates, 420–421, 768
Crude death rates, *260,* 637, 672–673
Crude divorce rate, 266, 267
Cruelty to animals, 292–293
Cryptosporidium, 262
Cuban refugees, 165
Culture
  Ariès, Philippe, **67–68**
  carrying capacity, 116
  contemporary analysis, 183–184
  cultural evolution, 333–334
  defining, 57
  fertility transition, 427–428
  homeostasis, 495
  ideational theory, 428

as models *of* and *for* reality, 183–
184
motivation, 185
population and, **183–186**
Current Population Survey (U.S.
Bureau of the Census)
employment and income, 612–
613
family demography, 356
history of demographic surveys,
207
as interim source of data, 122
internal migration data, 546
small-area population data, 915
Customs and fertility, 752–753
Cycles, population, **186–188**
Cytogenetic tests, 453
Czochralski, Jan, 689

D

Dagum, Camilo, 466
DALE (disability-adjusted life
expectancy), 256
Dalkon Shield, 96
DALYs (disability-adjusted life
years), 244–246, *246*, 256, 297
Dam construction, 856
Danger Spots in World Population
(Thompson), 940
Darwin, Charles, **189–190**
health transition, 480
influence on Galton, 443
life cycles, 89
mental life of animals, 53
natural selection, 782
variability and natural selection,
56
Das Gupta, Ajit, 980
Das Gupta, Monica, 447
Dasgupta, Partha, 158, 710
Data
assessment, **190–193**
comparison, 191–192, *192*, 563
standardization, 782
Databases
bibliographic and statistical, 82
census, 125
demographic, 106, **193–195**
Demographic and Health Surveys
project, 203–204
LandScan Global Population 1998
Database, 838
for measuring poverty and
income inequality, 786
Utah Population Database, 450
Data collection
age measurement, **22–24**
censuses, 123–125
contraceptive prevalence, 176
diseases, 252–253
ethical issues, **195–197**, *196*
ethnography, 56–57
genocide, 456

international migration, 549
life course data, 588–589
literacy, 604
longitudinal, 326
maternal mortality, 629
occupation and industry, 701
pastoral nomads, 695–696
research institutes, 748
time depth, 57
World Fertility Survey, 977
See also Demographic surveillance
systems; Studies, surveys and
reports
Data errors, 23, 900
Data processing
census, 124–125
demographic surveys, 208–209
Data sources
bibliographic resources, **81–84**,
556
for burden of disease
measurement, 245
business demography, 107
content, 191
coverage, 191
crime, 180–181
defined, 190–191
genealogical records, **448–451**
georeferencing, 458–459
internal migration, 545–546
mortality decline, 655
national governmental
organizations, 740
population registers, 763–765
religious affiliation, 836–837
small-area demography, 898, 915
urban historical demography, 134
vital statistics, 961
See also Internet; Studies, surveys
and reports
Davenant, Charles, 729, 776
Davenport, Charles B., 320
David, Paul A., 418, 419
David and Lucile Packard
Foundation, 746
Davis, Hugh, 96
Davis, Kingsley, **197–199**
cause of mortality and fertility
decline, 669
demographic transition, 213–214,
215, 427
fertility and social systems, 766
mortality/fertility relationship,
671
proximate determinants of
fertility, 412
status of women, 974
Deadbeat dads, 635–636
Death, sex ratios at, 875–876
Death rates
age specific, 85, *651*, 673
annual death rates for females,
652
crisis mortality, 304–305

crude death rates, 637, 672–673
Egypt and United States
compared, *674*
France, *653*
influenza pandemic of 1918, 305,
540–542, *541*
plague, 303–304
slaves, 896
standardized, 674–675
tuberculosis, United States, 947,
947
See also Causes of death;
Mortality
Debert archaeological site, 802
De-carbonization, 288
Decision-making
business demography, 106
family bargaining, **352–355**
fertility, 632–634
small-area analysis, 899
structuralist/diffusionist theories,
238–240
"X-efficiency," 586
Declaration of Independence,
United States, 730
The Decline of Fertility in Europe
(Coale and Watkins), 152
Decompositional demographic
analysis, 74, *76*
Decomposition of greenhouse gas
emission rates, 149–150
Decrement rates, 12–13
Defection, religious, 836
Definitions
accidents, 2
African American, 21
age, 22–23
asylum seekers, 826
baby booms and echoes, 73
birth order, 129
carrying capacity, 115–116
childlessness, 128
contraceptive prevalence, 174–175
culture, 57
data, 190–191
demographic history, 484
demographic surveys, 206
demography, 216, 744
disability, 241
ecosystem, 270
epidemics, 303
ethnic cleansing, 317
ethnic group, 314
ethnicity, 821
famine, 382
fecundity, 397
fertility, 397
gender, 444
genocide, 455
geopolitics, 462
grandparenthood, 471
health systems, 477
historical demography, 484
household, 499

eradication, 260–261
etiological classification, 120
explaining, 251–252
famine, 383, 387–388
genetic testing, 453–454
germ theory, 247–248, 252
history, **251–253**
infectious, **258–264**
International Classification of
    Diseases (ICD), 2–3, 254, *254*
susceptibility, 272
tobacco-related, 941–942
war as cause of, 964
See also Specific diseases
Disincentives, fertility control, 708
DISMOD software, 245
Disposable income, 785–786
Dissipative structures, 602
Dissolution, family, 362–363
Dissolution of cohabiting unions,
    154
Distance Advancement of
    Population Research, 83
Distance learning, 83
Distribution of income, **785–789**
Distribution of population. *See*
    Population distribution
*The Divine Order with regard to the
    Human species, as demonstrated
    by birth, death and reproduction*
    (Süssmilch), 218
Division for Social Policy and
    Development, United Nations,
    749
Division for the Advancement of
    Women, United Nations, 749
Division of labor
    marriage, 635
    United States, 703
Divorce, **265–267**
    ancient world, 46
    child support, 635–636
    Christianity, 831, 832
    demography, 358
    as determinant of fertility, 414
    family life cycle, 362–363
    Islam, 832
    Judaism, 831
    laws, 372, 621
    United States, 265, *358, 359,* 621,
        623–624
Divorce bounds, 354
Divorce-threat model, 353
DNA, 64–65, 719
DNA testing, 196
Dobson, James, 10
Dobyns, Henry F., 726
Dobzhansky, Theodosius, 84, 92
Doctrine, religious, **830–835**
Domestication of plants and
    animals, 791
Domestic worker protection, 572–
    574
Dommenges, D., 683

Donnay, Jean-Paul, 838
Donor eggs, 851
Donor insemination, 849
Doomsday argument, 341
Dorset culture, 802
Doubling time, 737
Drake, Daniel, 248
Drèze, Jean, 387
DRI economic model, 275
Drought, 147–148
Drugs, sexual performance
    enhancing, 883
Drysdale, George, 973
DSS. *See* Demographic surveillance
    systems
Dublin, Louis, 768
Dubois, Eugene, 793
Dumont, Arsène, **267–268,** 766
Duncan, Otis Dudley, 502
Duncan, Ronald, 431
Du Pont de Nemours, Pierre
    Samuel, 775
Durand, John, 980
Durkheim, Émile, 497, 819, 833
*Dynamics of Values in Fertility
    Change* (Leete), 957
Dysgenics (Lynn), 818
Dyson, Tim, 185, 431
Dyson-Hudson, Paul Rada, 695

E

EAP (EurAsian Project on
    Population and Family History),
    476
EAPS (European Association for
    Population Studies), 743
Early Childhood Longitudinal
    Study, 614
Earth Abides (Stewart), 607
Earth Observing-1, 837
Earthquakes. *See* Disasters
East Asia
    food supply, 432
    Neolithic populations, 979
    Notestein's study of, 697
    See also Asia; Specific countries
Easterlin, Richard A., **269–270**
    baby boom, 74–75
    birth control and fertility decline,
        215
    cohort size, 498
    feedback relationship, 843
    fertility trends, 766
    Growth Triumphant, 233
    mortality decline and standard of
        living, 671–672
    population cycles, 187
    small cohort size and fertility,
        409
Easterlin-Crimmins model, 269
Easterlin cycles, 26, 187–188
Easterlin hypothesis, 269

Eastern Europe
    abortion rates, 530
    age at marriage, 625
    family structure, 344–345
    forced migration, 437–438
    mortality reversals, *676,* 676–677
    See also Europe; Specific
        countries
Eastern marriage patterns, 344
Eastern Orthodox Church, 831
Eastern religions, 830
East German refugees, 165
ECA (Economic Commission for
    Africa), 749
ECE (Economic Commission for
    Europe), 749
Echoes, 73, 738
ECLAC (Economic Commission for
    Latin America and the
    Caribbean), 749
Ecological issues, **270–274**
    anthropocentrism, 293
    biodiversity, 88
    cities, 502–503
    climate change, 271
    ecodemography, 85
    ecological change, 503–504
    ecological degradation, 271–272,
        296–298
    ecological footprint analysis, 117,
        929
    habitat destruction, 88–89
    historical perspective, 298–302
    Lotka-Volterra equation, 85, 618
    metapopulation studies, 731
    overshoot, 928–929
    simulation models, 893
    sustainable development, **927–930**
    See also Environmental issues
Ecology, evolutionary, 55–56, 91
Economic and Social Commission
    for Asia and the Pacific (ESCAP),
    749
Economic and Social Commission
    for Western Asia (ESCWA), 749–
    750
Economic Commission for Africa
    (ECA), 749
Economic Commission for Europe
    (ECE), 749
Economic Commission for Latin
    America and the Caribbean
    (ECLAC), 749
Economic Covenant, 847, 848
Economic development, **226–234**
    Asia, 229
    energy use, 287–289, *288, 290*
    epidemics, 305
    female labor force patterns, 568–
        569
    fertility decline, 237–238, 761
    fertility transition, 230–232
    future directions, 603
    growth models, 276–277

alternative family structures, 624
assisted-reproduction services, 853
partnership registration, 154, 624
prevalence, 882, *882*
Hoover, Edgar M., 229, 275, 277
Hormonal contraception, 171–173
Horney, Mary J., 353
Hornik, Robert, 627
Horowitz, Irving Lewis, 455
Hospital admissions, 5
Host countries
governmental immigration organizations, 740
impact of immigration on, **509–512**, 551–552
major refugee populations, *828*
See also Immigration; International migration; Migration; Refugees
Host-parasite interactions, 91
Hotz, V. Joseph, 634
House, James S., 667
Household demography, 682–683
Household production, 633–634, 635
Households
composition, **499–501**
family demography, 343–344, 360
formation, 337–338, 487, 500, 582–583
mean size, 377
structure in the ancient world, 46
Housing, 916–917
Housing unit method of population estimates, 898, 915
How to Start and Operate a Mail Order Business (Simon), 888
Hrdy, Sarah Bluffer, 878
Hu, Yuanreng, 667
Human adaptation, 501–502
Humanae Vitae, 94, 831
Human capital migration models, 643
Human-centered thinking, 292–293
Human Development Report (United Nations), 788
Human ecology, 146–148, **501–504**
Human embryos, 850–851, 852–853
Human extinction, **340–342**
Human Immunodeficiency Virus. *See* HIV/AIDS
Human impact on the environment, 271–272, **298–302**
Humanistic Anthropology (Sombart), 913
Human life history, 330–331
Human life span, 592–593, *594*
Human Poverty Index, 788
Human prehistory. *See* Prehistoric populations
Human research subjects, 195–196
Human resource planning, 107–108

Human rights, **70–72**
fetal rights, 880
religious freedom, 835
reproductive rights as, 847
Hungary, 437, 563, *677*
Hunter-gatherers, 234–235, 330–333, **504–507**, 791–792
Hunting, 300, 301–302, 332–333
Hurricanes. *See* Disasters
Hutterites, 418
Huygens, Christiaan, 473, 601
Hygiene, 259–260

I

Ice ages, 145–146, 799, 978
ICIDH (International Classification of Impairment, Disability, and Handicap), 241
ICSI (intracytoplasmic sperm injection), 850
Ideal family size, 378
Ideational theory, 428
Identical twins, 679, 680
IDPs (internally displaced persons), 829, 856–857, *857*
IEC (information, education, and communication) campaigns, 627
IFRC (International Federation of Red Cross and Red Crescent Societies), 740
IIASA (International Institute for Applied Systems Analysis), 747, 808–813
IIPS (International Institute for Population Sciences), 747
IKONOS, 837
Iliffe, John, 385
Illegal immigrants. *See* Unauthorized immigration
Illiteracy, *604*
ILO (International Labour Organization), 702, 751, 936
Immigration
aging population, 26, 34
benefits and costs of, **509–512**
economics of, 888–889
generational accounting, 452–453
globalization theory, 517
history, 519–522
national organizations, 740
policy, **515–519**, 552, 643–644, 736, 753, 767
population replacement, 736, 759, 771
quotas, 944
racial/ethnic composition, 821–823
sex ratios of immigrants, 876–877
skills, immigrant, 509–510
social institutions, 905
trends, **519–523**
unauthorized, **512–515**, *514*, 515–516, 521

western hemisphere, *944*
See also International migration; Labor migration; Migration; Refugees
Immigration and National Origins Act, 944
Immigration and Naturalization Service, 740
Immigration Reform and Control Act (United States), 514, 944
Impairment, 241
Imperialism, European, 919
Incan empire, 803
Incentives
fertility control, 708, 754
pronatalist, 756, 760, 771
Income
comparison, *787*
demographic transition, 621
distribution, 781, **785–789**
fertility, 232, *232*, 632–633
health/income correlation, 593
income-pooling hypothesis, 353–354
income transfer and family bargaining, 354
inequality, 785
life expectancy, 230, *231*
longitudinal surveys, 612–613
national income studies, 776
segregation, 859
See also Economic issues; Poverty; Socioeconomic status; Wages
Increasing returns, 710
Increment-decrement life tables, 601
Independent living, 356
India
age structure, 738
caste, 117–119
family planning, 97
famine, 392–393
fertility control programs, 770
food supply, 432–433
International Institute of Population Sciences (IIPS), 747
models of developing economies, 275
morbidity, *481*
oldest old, *706*
population estimates, 980
prehistoric agricultural societies, 793
sex differences in death rates, *663*
sex ratios, 876
sex-selective abortion, 879
Indian Act (Canada), 526
Indianapolis Study, 949, 972
Indian Ocean slave trade, 895
Indian Remote Sensing, 837
Indigenous peoples, **523–527**
commodity-linked ecological degradation, 301–302
environmental impact, 298–302

Reparations for slavery, 897
Repeatable events in event-history analysis, 329
Repeat polymorphisms, 65–66
Replacement, population, 647–648, 736, 759, 771, 872–874
Replacement-level fertility, *405*, 405–406, 840
Reproduction
  demographic transition, 334
  gross reproduction rate, *423*, 424
  natural fertility regimes, 331–333
  parental investment, 592
  reproductive life span, *413*, 413–414
  sociobiology, 912
  techniques, 349
  See also Fertility; Net reproduction rate
Reproductive health, 369, 758, 771, **843–846**, *845*
Reproductive Health Gateway, Johns Hopkins University, 82
"Reproductive Institutions and the Pressure for Population" (Davis), 197–198
Reproductive rights, **846–848**
  choice, 869
  critical theory, 8
  feminist perspective, 399–400
  reproductive health movement, 369–370
Reproductive technologies, **849–854**
  ethics, 851, **852–854**
  modern methods, **849–852**
  population quality, 818
  sex selection, 879–880
Reproductive value, 841
The Republic (Plato), 584
Repugnant Conclusion, 440–441
Research in Population Economics, 888
Research institutions, 204, 220, **744–748**
Resettlement, 72, **854–857**
  See also Internal migration
Residential mobility, 545, *548*
Residential segregation, **857–860**
Resolution, remote sensing, 837
Resource allocation, 78, 89–90
Resource base, 689
The Resourceful Earth (Simon and Kahn), 888
Resource-partitioning theory, 713
Resources
  agriculture, 150, 690, 776
  animal ecology, 48
  common property, **157–161**
  open access, 158
  population/resources interactions, 55, 56, 227–229
  sustainability, 116–117
  use, 602
  See also Natural resources

Restoration, ecological, 271
Retail use of business demography, 107
Retirement
  age, 32, 971
  dependency, 27–28
  Health and Retirement Study, 614
  male labor force patterns, 569
  oldest old, 705
Retrospective intent in fertility research, 380
Return migration, 946
Reurbanization, 137–138
Revoredo, Cesar, 431
Revue des Revues Démographiques (journal), 557
Revue Européenne des Migration Internationales (journal), 556
Rhythm method of birth control, 171, 175
Ricardo, David
  agricultural resources, 690
  East India Company, influence on, 392
  economic-demographic models, 274
  Malthus, correspondence with, 620
Riccioli, Giovanni, 217
Richardson, Lewis, 963
Rich/poor geopolitical conflict, 464–465
Right censoring, 326
Right of asylum, **70–72**
Riley, James, 480
Risk, 12–13, 328, 341, **860–864**, 955–956
Rival rationalities view of risk assessment, 863
Roan, Carol, 470
Robertson, John A., 880
Robine, Jean-Marie, 309
Rock, John, 97
Rockefeller, John D., 3rd, 697, 745, 769
Rockefeller Foundation, 770
Roe v. Wade, 96, 770
Rogers, Andrei, 547, 681
Rogers, Richard G., 667
Rohwer, Götz, 589
Romania, 164
Romano, C., 160
Romanticism, 919
Rome, ancient. *See* Ancient world
Roosevelt, Theodore, 766
Rose, Harold, 461
Rosenblat, Angel, 726
Ross, John A., 79
Ross, Ronald, 91
Rostock protocol, 718
Rotten Kid Theorem, 78, 353
Rousseau, Jean-Jacques, 775
Roussel, Louis, 356

Rowe, John, 706
Roy, T. K., 958
Royal Commission on Population (England), 735
Royal Commission on the Care and Control of the Feeble Minded of 1909, 320
Royal Society of London, 218, 742
RU-486, 97
Rüdin, Ernst, 321
Ruhlen, Merritt, 801
Rummel, R. J., 964
Rural areas, 503, 667–668
Rural-urban balance, **864–866**
Russell, John, 391
Russia
  life expectancy, 1927-1939, *395*
  population estimates and projections, *735*
  refugees, 435–436
  sex differences in death rates, *663*
Ryder, Norman B., **866–867**
  baby boom and baby bust, 74, 76
  cohort analysis, 155–156
  fertility decline, 380
  National Fertility Surveys, 207
Ryder, Richard, 294

S

Sabean, David, 346
Safeguards in demographic data collection, 196–197
"Safe third country" concept, 71
Safety, monetary values of, 955–956
Sagan, Carl, 715
Sahel region of Africa, 385–386
Saito, Yasuhito, 666
Salmonella, 262
Same People Choice, 440
Sample registration, 961
Sample surveys, 898, 915, 961
Sampling, demographic, 208
Samuelson, Paul A., 187–188, 543, 711
Sanders, Seth, 624
Sanderson, Warren C., 418, 419
Sanger, Margaret, **869–870**
  birth control movement, 767
  establishment of World Population Conference, 743
  eugenics, 321
  family planning programs, 363
  role in history of birth control, 96, 399
  World Population Conference of 1927, 168
Sanitation, 259–260, 781
San people, 792
Sanskritization, 118
Sassen, Saskia, 142–143
Sauvy, Alfred, **870–872**
  economic effects of population decline, 735

Wang, Gungwu, 131
Wanted fertility rates, 380, 950
The Wanting Seed (Burgess), 608
War, demographic consequences of, **963–966**
Wargentin, Pehr, 218, 601
Waterborne diseases, 260
Water management policies, 967
Water quality, 271
Water resources, 686, 691–692, 714–715, **966–968**, *967*
Watkins, Susan Cotts, 279, 428, 461
Watson, Alfred, 12
Watson, H. W., 922
Watts, Michael, 385
Weak sustainability, 927–929
Wealth distribution, 464–465
Webb, Patrick, 386
Webber, Melvin, 138
Weber, Max, 833
Weight and height studies, 699
Weinberg, Wilhelm, 321
Weinstein, Maxine, 86, 923
Weiss, Yoram, 354, 635, 636
Welfare expenditures, selected countries, *970*
Welfare state, **968–972**
Welfare systems
    costs of children, 177–180
    family allowances, 177–180, **350–352**, *351*
    fertility, 760
    immigrants, 510–511
Well-being, 360, 788, 976
Wellcome Trust, 746, 748
Werner, Heinz, 935
West Africa, 386
Westergaard, Harald, 666
Western countries
    centenarians, 706
    family, 348–350
    fertility decline, 756–757
    marriage patterns, 344
    partner choice, 723–724
    social mobility, 906–908
    urbanization, 951
    vital events registration, 960
    See also Specific countries
Western Europe
    abortion rates, 530
    demographic transition, 768
    fertility, 981
    immigration, 519–523, *522*
    life expectancy, 981
    mortality, 981
    population decline, 732
    projected proportion of population above age 80, *811*
    pronatalism, 736
    second demographic transition, 873–874
    unauthorized immigration, 513–514, 521

See also Europe; European Union; Specific countries
Western religions, 830
West Indies, 20–22
West model life tables, 652
West Nile virus, 263
Westoff, Charles F., 76, 207, 380, 866
WFS. *See* World Fertility Survey (WFS)
Wharton economic model, 275
Wharton School, Population Studies Center, 938
Wheat, Joe, 802
Whelpton, Pascal K., **972–973**
    Indianapolis study, 207
    population projection, 219, 768, 808, 841
    unwanted fertility, 949
White, Paul, 462
White collar occupations, 703
White Eye (d'Alpuget), 609
WHO. *See* World Health Organization (WHO)
Wicksell, Knut, **973–974**
Widmer, Eric D., 882
Widowhood, 35, 414
Wilkinson, David, 963
Wilkinson, Su-Lin, 917
Willcox, Walter, 766
Willekens, Frans, 682
Willems, Michel, 448
William and Flora Hewlett Foundation, 746
Williamson, Jeffrey G., 277
Willingness-to-pay approach to value of life, 955, 956
Willis, Robert J., 354, 633–636
Wilson, Alan, 461
Wilson, Chris, 428
Wilson, Edward O., 293, 911
Wink, Claudia, 878
Winterhalder, Bruce, 506
Wittwer-Backofen, Ursula, 86
Wolf, Aaron, 686
Wollstonecraft, Mary, 118
Wolpin, Kenneth I., 635
Wolpoff, Mulford, 793
Women
    abstinence, 1–2
    annual death rates for females, *652*
    cigarette smoking, 941–942
    cohabitation, 625
    death rates, *650, 651, 652*
    fecundity, 397–398
    fertility, 332
    health issues, 976
    labor force, 568–569, 633–634
    life tables, Austria, *597*
    life tables, Sweden, *598*
    maternal mortality, **628–631**, *629*
    missing women, 878, *879*, 880
    occupational trends, 703–704

oldest old, 707
proximate determinants of fertility, **412–417**, *416*
rights of, 169–170
status of, **974–977**
undernutrition indicators in African countries, *387, 388*
See also Gender
Women's Convention, 847
Wood, Bernard, 792
Wood, James W., 495, 923
Woods, Robert, 461
Worker protection, domestic, 572–574
Working mothers, 371–372, 569, 721
Working women, 703–704, 760–761
World Bank
    establishment, 751
    global population projection, 809–810
    maternal mortality, 628
    World Development Indicators Data Query, 82
World Christian Encyclopedia (Barrett, Kurian, and Johnson), 837
World Christian Trends, AD 30-AD 2200 (Barrett and Johnson), 837
World cities, 141–143, *142*
World Conservation Union, 928
World Development Indicators Data Query, World Bank, 82
World Development Report (World Bank), 788
World Education Report (United Nations Educational, Scientific, and Cultural Organization), 605
World Fertility Survey (WFS), 207, 217, 367–368, 428, 746, 866, **977–978**
World Health Organization (WHO)
    establishment, 750–751
    Expanded Program on Immunization, 260
    identifying causes of death, 120
    infertility definition, 538
    Integrated Management of Childhood Illnesses, 536
    International Agency for Research on Cancer, 111
    International Classification of Diseases (ICD), 2–3, 254, *254*
    International Classification of Impairment, Disability, and Handicap, 241
    International Lists of Diseases and Causes of Death, 249
    International Statistical Classification of Diseases and Related Health Problems, 259
    maternal mortality, 628, 629
    reproductive health, 844–845

ISBN 0-02-865679-2

DISCARD